Women in Shakespeare
A Dictionary

ARDEN SHAKESPEARE DICTIONARY SERIES

Women in Shakespeare

A Dictionary

ALISON FINDLAY

BLOOMSBURY

LONDON · NEW DELHI · NEW YORK · SYDNEY

Bloomsbury Arden Shakespeare
An imprint of Bloomsbury Publishing Plc

50 Bedford Square	1385 Broadway
London	New York
WC1B 3DP	NY 10018
UK	USA

www.bloomsbury.com

Bloomsbury is a registered trade mark of Bloomsbury Publishing Plc

This edition of *Women in Shakespeare* by Alison Findlay, first published 2010 by
the Continuum International Publishing Group

© Alison Findlay, 2010
This paperback edition © Alison Findlay, 2014

Alison Findlay has asserted her right under the Copyright, Designs and
Patents Act, 1988, to be identified as Author of this work.

British Library Cataloguing-in-Publication Data
A catalogue record for this book is available from the British Library.

ISBN: PB: 978-1-4725-2047-0

Library of Congress Cataloging-in-Publication Data
A catalog record for this book is available from the Library of Congress.

Typeset by Pindar NZ, Auckland, New Zealand
Printed and bound in Great Britain

Contents

Acknowledgements

Women in Shakespeare has been ongoing through a period in which I was completing another project, then acting as Head of Department followed by two terms sabbatical leave in 2007–8, and finally a year's teaching in 2008–9. These different environments of management, teaching and personal research have all contributed to my appreciation of Shakespeare's work while writing the dictionary. My first thanks must be to Sandra Clark, General Editor of the Shakespeare Dictionary Series and to Colleen Coalter and the staff at Continuum for allowing me freedom to mould the project, and for their patience in waiting for its completion. I received excellent editorial advice in response to my draft entries and queries, a crucial element of the success of the Series. Colleen and Kim Pillay at Pindar Press prepared the text for publication for which I am extremely grateful. I owe thanks to a large number of colleagues and students who have helped me by offering comments. Juliet Dusinberre, Stanley Wells, Katherine Duncan-Jones and Peter Holland all read entries at remarkably short notice, encouraging me with the more unusual ideas I proposed and providing corrections. I am also grateful to the Shakespeare students at Lancaster University who responded to draft versions of the entries posted on our course website. Vassiliki Markidou at the University of Athens kindly read and commented on a larger section of the manuscript and I offer her my warm thanks. My colleagues in the English Department at Lancaster have been supportive in intellectual and practical ways especially during the final period of writing over the exam term in Summer 2009. In the academic context, my deepest debt goes to Liz Oakley-Brown who has read through numerous individual draft entries and shared ideas more informally. I thank her very warmly for her continued interest in the book's progress; it has made all the difference. The book has been a massive undertaking that would not have been possible without the support of my immediate family. I thank my son Robert who compiled individual entries into letter files and my daughter Eleanor who took the pink highlights away from entries like 'girl'. I thank my mum who helped us in very practical ways on her visits to Lancaster in the run-up to submission of the manuscript. My husband David undertook the daunting task of supplying missing line references to the plays. Although this was exhausting, immersion in Shakespeare proved once again to be what William Gouge calls 'an indissoluble glue' binding us together. Without the glue, there would be no book. I thank David for engaging in the sticky process of completing the book with love.

Alison Findlay

Abbreviations

SD	stage direction
Ind.	Induction

Texts by Shakespeare

A&C	*Antony and Cleopatra*
AWW	*All's Well That Ends Well*
AYLI	*As You Like It*
Cor.	*Coriolanus*
Cym.	*Cymbeline*
EIII	*Edward III*
Err.	*The Comedy of Errors*
Ham.	*Hamlet*
1HIV	*The First Part of King Henry the Fourth*
2HIV	*The Second Part of King Henry the Fourth*
HV	*King Henry the Fifth*
1HVI	*The First Part of King Henry the Sixth*
2HVI	*The Second Part of King Henry the Sixth*
3HVI	*The Third Part of King Henry the Sixth*
HVIII	*King Henry the Eighth*
JC	*Julius Caesar*
KJ	*King John*
KL	*King Lear*
LC	*A Lover's Complaint*
LLL	*Love's Labour's Lost*
Luc.	*The Rape of Lucrece*
MAdo	*Much Ado About Nothing*
Mac.	*Macbeth*
MM	*Measure for Measure*
MND	*A Midsummer Night's Dream*
Mer.	*The Merchant of Venice*
MWW	*The Merry Wives of Windsor*
Oth.	*Othello*
Per.	*Pericles*
PP	*The Passionate Pilgrim*
PT	*The Phoenix and Turtle*
RII	*Kind Richard the Second*

RIII	*King Richard the Third*
R&J	*Romeo and Juliet*
Shrew	*The Taming of the Shrew*
Son.	*Sonnets*
STM	*Sir Thomas More*
T&C	*Troilus and Cressida*
Temp.	*The Tempest*
TGV	*The Two Gentlemen of Verona*
Tim.	*Timon of Athens*
Tit.	*Titus Andronicus*
TN	*Twelfth Night*
TNK	*The Two Noble Kinsmen*
V&A	*Venus and Adonis*
WT	*The Winter's Tale*

Journal titles

ANQ	*American Notes and Queries*
CE	*College English*
CLS	*Comparative Literature Studies*
ELH	*English Literary History*
ELN	*English Language Notes*
ELR	*English Literary Renaissance*
MLN	*Modern Language Notes*
MLQ	*Modern Language Quarterly*
MP	*Modern Philology*
NQ	*Notes and Queries*
PMLA	*Publications of Modern Language Association*
RES	*Review of English Studies*
RMRLL	*Rocky Mountain Review of Language and Literature*
RQ	*Renaissance Quarterly*
SEL	*Studies in English Literature 1500–1900*
SP	*Studies in Philology*
SQ	*Shakespeare Quarterly*
ShSt	*Shakespeare Studies*
ShS	*Shakespeare Survey*

Reference titles

OED	*Oxford English Dictionary*
ODN	*Oxford Concise Dictionary of First Names*

Series Editor's preface

The Arden Shakespeare Dictionaries aim to provide the student of Shakespeare with a series of authoritative guides to the principle subject-areas covered by the plays and poems. They are produced by scholars who are experts both on Shakespeare and on the topic of the individual dictionary, based on the most recent scholarship, succinctly written and accessibly present. They offer readers a self-contained body of information on the topic under discussion, its occurrence and significance in Shakespeare's works, and its contemporary meanings.

The topics are all vital ones for understanding the plays and poems; they have been selected for their importance in illuminating aspects of Shakespeare's writings where an informed understanding of the range of Shakespeare's usage, and of the contemporary literary, historical and cultural issues involved, will add to the reader's appreciation of his work. Because of the diversity of the topics covered in the series, individual dictionaries may vary in emphasis and approach, but the aim and basic format of the entries remain the same from volume to volume.

Sandra Clark
Birkbeck College
University of London

Introduction

'Who is't can read a woman? Is there more?' asks Cymbeline (5.6.49–50). Women in Shakespeare is a vast and fascinating topic: from roles as complex as Rosalind to words as emotive as *mother*, as multi-layered as *moon*, or as secret as *maidenhead*. To answer Cymbeline, there is always more: more than can be conveyed in a single word entry or a series of entries jostling for space and attention. *Women in Shakespeare* is selective in its choice of headwords in an attempt to do justice to the depth and richness of Shakespeare's writing while simultaneously giving some sense of the breadth of the canon's engagement with the topic.

At the level of roles and names, Shakespeare's texts offer a rich range of starting points for investigation. Female roles in the plays and the poems are examined under name entries of varying length. These bring together figures from different texts. Hippolyta covers a part from an early comedy and a very late, joint-authored play, for example. Entries on Katherine or Helen group together several figures by given name with the aim of exploring what kinds of common attribute Shakespeare associated with that name or how he deliberately played off expectations about a given name. 'Emilia' is used for characters from across the canon renowned for their loyalty, steadfastness and self-determination (*Comedy of Errors, Winter's Tale, Othello, The Two Noble Kinsmen*). The Biancas in *Taming of the Shrew* and *Othello* and the Margarets in history plays and comedies do not match up to the purity implied by their names. Names taken from classical or biblical sources carry their own histories and reference to Shakespeare's sources forms part of these entries, as with Virgilia in *Coriolanus*, for example. Some, like Helen and Cleopatra, carry histories from popular culture.

Character names in the speech headings in the early texts can be misleading, however. Viola is not named as such until the end of *Twelfth Night*; the widow Lady Grey becomes Queen Elizabeth in *3 Henry VI*. Spellings and forms of name also vary to fit the metre of the verse as with Helen and Helena, Katherine and Katherina, Cressid and Cressida. Character names do, nevertheless, provide a useful organizing principle by which parts can be recognized so *The Riverside Shakespeare*'s name forms have been adopted to discuss these roles and are used consistently. The female lead in *Taming of the Shrew* who is called Katherine, Katherina and Kate, is referred to as Katherina, following *The Riverside Shakespeare*, but is discussed alongside the other roles named Katherine. Where family names are used more frequently, or perhaps exclusively, these are used for headwords, as in the case of Mistresses Ford, Page, Quickly or Elbow.

As should already be evident, the proper name entries are not character studies; instead, the name and its meanings are a starting point from which to cast a particular light on the role. The dictionary has the effect of fragmenting a part (for example Paulina) across a range of different subject positions (wife, good lady, mother, midwife, widow, callet, witch, crone and hag that will not stay her tongue), reminding us that no role or identity functions as a coherent whole but is built up from a range of different, often contradictory elements. This is, arguably, especially pertinent when considering the identities of women. Early modern women who informed, watched or read Shakespeare's texts, and the women who appeared on stage as the creations of boy actors were all the constructs of a variety of different ideologies, cultural practices and material traces. Cross-referencing in heavy type and use of the index will allow readers to reconstruct the identity of a Juliet, Volumnia or Imogen from these fragments.

Female icons often shadow or inform characterization in Shakespeare's plays and separate entries on these figures – historical, mythical, supernatural and allegorical – address their representation in the Shakespearian canon, directly as characters or indirectly through allusion. The dictionary entries for Venus and Diana consider their characterization in *Venus and Adonis* and *Pericles* alongside references or invocations to them elsewhere in the canon. The entry on Diana, for instance, considers the defiantly chaste character in *All's Well That Ends Well*, and the goddess, alongside textual allusions to her as an icon of chastity in *As You Like It* and *The Merchant of Venice*, and the physical representation of the French Princess as huntswoman in *Love's Labour's Lost*. The entry on Isis examines how Cleopatra strategically blends her identity as empress of Egypt with that of the goddess. Classical and mythological figures such as Hecuba, Iris, Ceres and Philomel haunt the canon. Entries offer guidelines to the significance of such classical and biblical icons as models for early modern concepts of womanhood. Entries on feminized personifications like Fortune, Patience and Peace are also included. A third category of name entries covers significant 'living' icons of the early modern period (e.g. Anna of Denmark) and the women in Shakespeare's own life (e.g. Anne Hathaway, Mary Arden, Susanna and Judith Shakespeare, Mary Mountjoy). The most pervasive of these is Queen Elizabeth I who figures in entries on Elizabeth and Queen and then in diverse others linked to her royal iconography, such as Diana, Phoebe, vestal, moon. Cross-referencing via heavy type allows readers to follow a thread of allusions.

Titles of rank are another important way of defining female figures on stage or in a narrative poem, so name entries include empress, queen, duchess, countess, marchioness, hostess, lady, waiting-gentlewoman. Some roles such as the Countess of Salisbury in *Edward III* have no proper name entry and some smaller roles, such as the Duchess of Auvergne in *1 Henry VI* or the Duchess of Gloucester in *Richard II* are analysed under these broader generic headwords.

Key female roles in family and political arenas, as they appear in Shakespeare's texts, receive separate entries, listing all the characters who fall into the type and discussing the differences / similarities between them. In addition to looking at a role or character under a proper name, references to that role will also appear in entries on, for example, 'queen'; 'princess'; 'mother'; 'daughter'; 'maid'; 'wife';

'nurse'; 'widow'; 'whore'; 'mistress' (often indicating self-possession); 'nun'; 'gossip'; 'witch'; 'prophetess'; 'hostess'. The ambiguity of such labels is often demonstrated by bringing them together. As Launce points out in *Two Gentlemen of Verona*, his mistress is 'a maid, yet it is not a maid, yet 'tis a maid for she is her master's maid' (3.1.268). Shakespeare's critical treatment of misogynistic defamation in names becomes clear in the study of terms like 'drab', 'whore', 'callet', 'strumpet' across the canon. Interesting variations on woman's traditional duty appear in Shakespeare's use of the word 'hostess' as applied to Mistresses Quickly and Overdone, Perdita at the sheepshearing and Lady Macbeth. The dictionary examines Shakespeare's presentations by discussing the cultural construction of women and their social framings in early modern England. Brief descriptions of the current, often conflicting, opinions on the mother's role, for example, provide a context for understanding the relationship between Lady Capulet, Juliet and the nurse in *Romeo and Juliet*.

It is hoped that entries on key issues surrounding female experiences and early modern expectations about female behaviour will enrich readers' experiences of Shakespeare's work. Many of Shakespeare's female characters are represented in ways that provoke debates on such issues. They also provide a form of dramatic commentary on the constraints within which women in early modern England were obliged to operate and the amazingly inventive ways in which women could negotiate pathways to achieve their desires and ambitions. Entries cover a range of physical, emotional and social aspects of female experience. Although women's bodies were literally absent from the stage, their presence is invoked by references to body parts such as 'breast', 'dug', 'belly' / 'womb', 'lap'. Ways in which female bodies are categorized and labelled in Shakespeare's texts are examined in entries like 'blazon', 'beauty'. Olivia's ironic description of herself 'inventoried and every particle and utensil labelled to my will' (*Twelfth Night* 1.5.234), indicates one way in which the texts often take an ironic perspective on the blazoning of the female body in dramatizations of elevated courtly praise. Entries on 'betrothal', 'dower' / 'dowry' 'gift' draw attention to the ways in which woman is often constructed as a gift and how, in Shakespeare's texts (most obviously in *Merchant of Venice*), she can work within such a definition and still achieve a degree of self-determination.

Pivotal moments that shaped or changed women's subject positions receive entries drawing together examples from the canon to discuss Shakespeare's representation of topics like 'youth', 'betrothal', 'wedding', 'birth'. Beatrice's description of marriage as 'mannerly, modest, as a measure, full of state and ancientry' (*Much Ado About Nothing* 2.1.68), increases the reader's sense of violation in the maimed rites which follow, or in the fantastical ceremony in *The Taming of the Shrew*, or the rushed communion of Romeo and Juliet, for example. In the case of very closely linked entries like wedding and marriage, readers are explicitly directed to the parallel term. Pivotal events include crises, with entries on 'rape' (*Titus Andronicus, Rape of Lucrece, Cymbeline*), 'divorce' and 'adultery', for example.

An important set of entries focuses on the material representation of women on Shakespeare's stage. The entry on 'boy actors' is accompanied by entries on aspects of women's costume (e.g. 'chopine', 'handkerchief', 'glove', 'smock', 'fan' – and the important 'codpiece' for cross-dressers). How women use props is also important, especially with props with sexual or symbolic connotations like 'ring' so entries on these material objects are included.

The entries are laid out in three sections: the first giving a simple definition of the word, particularly as understood in early modern England, without any referencing. At this level, *Women in Shakespeare* relies on the magnificent resource of the *Oxford English Dictionary* and, rather than acknowledge it under each individual entry, I here record my profound debt to the work that has gone into this amazing book, which I have delighted in consulting. In addition, I have used the electronic, public-access *Oxford Dictionary of Names* as a starting point for proper names. Additional information from the *Oxford Classical Dictionary* edited by N. G. L. Hammond and H. H. Scullard and the highly useful *Shakespeare Name Dictionary*, by J. Madison Davis and A. Daniel Frankforter has been acknowledged in individual entries.

The second, usually lengthier, section of each entry is an account of how the word is used in Shakespeare's plays and poems, including the joint-authored texts *Henry VIII* and *The Two Noble Kinsmen* and those which it is now accepted Shakespeare authored at least some of, such as *Pericles* and *Edward III*. In entries where a role occurs in only one text, Act, Scene and Line references are given. For other entries abbreviated forms of each text's name are included before the Act, Scene and Line references so that the quotation can be found easily. All quotations and references are taken from *The Riverside Shakespeare*. Short quotations from other early modern texts by men and women are included in some of the discussions to provide a fuller picture of how the Shakespearean examples work. The entries are designed to work at a level of conveying information but also, often, as mini-essays making an argument about how a word or name is used or might have functioned in performance, as in the entries on 'Hippolyta', 'Phoebe' or 'Youth', for example. I thus hope they will serve as a useful reference tool for readers and that they will also provide new ideas for editors and researchers.

In composing each entry I have become aware of the wealth of critical writing that helps us to interpret the words that have come down to us. It is impossible to do justice to this properly or to include more than a small selection in the final section of each entry, which suggests further reading on the topic. What will become apparent when consulting *Women in Shakespeare* is that critical writing on individual female roles is a feature of Victorian literary culture and second-wave feminism that has been in decline more recently. Essays on Shakespeare's heroines by pioneering figures like Anna Murphy Jameson, Elizabeth Griffith and M. Leigh Noel have been reprinted in valuable editions by Cheri Larsen Hoeckley, Ann Thompson and Sasha Roberts, and so have been referred to frequently as setting out important ideas, often controversial for their time, about how the roles worked. The flourishing of feminist criticism in groundbreaking books like Juliet Dusinberre's *Shakespeare and the Nature of Women*, Lisa Jardine's *Still Harping on Daughters* and the inspiring collection of essays *The Woman's Part*, edited by Carolyn Ruth Swift Lenz, Gayle Greene and Carol Thomas Neely, is also recorded in the further reading recommendations. Post-structuralist criticism and its particular focus on the illusory nature of early modern subjectivity has inevitably fought shy of 'character-based' studies. Theatre history has, however, become aware of the woman's voice. My recommendations for secondary reading have endeavoured to draw attention to the views of actors who have lived with and performed the roles. Essays and interviews in the *Players of Shakespeare* volumes, in Carol Rutter's *Clamorous Voices* and in accounts by earlier performers like Sarah Siddons and the anonymous actress who recorded her very strong opinions on Lady Capulet have been recommended as a vital, dynamic part of the theatre history of Shakespeare's women. Although it has not been possible to survey each role's theatre history, references to Judith Cook's *Women in Shakespeare*, Liz Schaefer's *Ms Directing Shakespeare*, and Penny Gay's *As She Likes It*, offer starting points for those interested in pursuing further work on theatre history. The fascinating questions raised by boy actors as performers of the roles has also received recent attention in the work of Stephen Orgel, David Kathman, Scott McMillin, Stanley Wells and David Mann.

Bonnie Lander's view that 'the Shakespearean character is the site at which external forces acting on and shaping the interior life collide with internal forces acting on and shaping the external world' (Lander 2008: 157) gives a strong lead for a politically sensitive and theoretically informed return to character-based criticism. Simon Palfrey and Tiffany Stern's *Shakespeare in Parts* likewise focuses on the actor's response to an individual 'part' as something that must be pieced together from fragments and made to live theatrically. Although there were no women on Shakespeare's stage, his canon suggests, following Cymbeline's 'Who is't can read a woman? Is there more?' (5.6.49–50), that there is always more than meets the eye.

abbess, (a) the name given to a **Mother** Superior or commander of an Abbey.
(b) Shakespeare's one dramatic portrait of an Abbess is A**emilia** in *Comedy of Errors*.
Before she is named, she is referred to as 'Abbess' and 'Lady Abbess', a position
of considerable authority. She holds Antipholus and Dromio (of Syracuse) within
the Abbey with a stern determination, insisting – as a Mother Superior – on her
right to give them sanctuary and **nurse** Antipholus with professional care, in spite
of Adriana's **wif**ely protests:

> Abbess: It is a branch and parcel of my oath
> A charitable duty of my order,
> Therefore depart, and leave him here with me.
> Adriana: I will not hence, and leave my husband here;
> And ill it doth beseem your holiness
> To separate the husband and the wife.
> Abbess: Be quiet and depart thou shalt not have him.
> (*Err.* 5.1.106–12)

The Abbess's potentially scandalous determination to possess her man is rendered
more comic in the light of **Adriana**'s aggressive wish to 'take perforce my husband
from the Abbess' (*Err.* 5.1.117), and the Duke's belief that the Abbess is 'a virtuous
and a reverend **lady** / It cannot be that she has done thee wrong' (*Err.* 5.1.134–5).
Further details of the character's more subversive qualities are found in the entry
on **Emilia**. In *Measure for Measure*, the **Mother** Superior of the Franciscan convent
is referred to but does not appear on stage (*MM* 1.4.84).
(c) Claire Walker (2003) gives detailed analysis of the typical abbess's role in
religious communities on the continent after the Reformation. Dorothea Kehler
(1991: 157–80) compares the Emilias in Shakespeare's work, regarding celibacy
and connections with widowhood as the most striking common characteristics.

Daryl Gless (1979) discusses the importance of the convent as an all-female community.

Adriana, (a) a character in *The Comedy of Errors*, married to Antipholus of Ephesus. Her name may allude to the Adriatic Sea. As the feminine form of Adrian, it perhaps functions more obliquely as part of the network of the religious language with which the play is riddled. Adrian IV was name taken by the only English pope, Nicholas Brakespear (d. 1159).

(b) Adriana enters the play forcefully criticizing the double standard which allows men to be masters of their will and liberty out of doors while women are limited to domestic servitude (2.1.10–25). She does not fit into the role of *femme covert* easily, a problem exemplified by the exchange of the chain in the play. Her 'headstrong liberty' (2.1.15) rejects docile subjection to husbandly authority as foolish: 'There's none but asses will be bridled so' (2.1.15), and she bears similarities with **Katherina**, though, importantly, she is never called 'shrew'. Instead, like **Emilia** in *Othello*, she is a powerful spokeswoman against sexual double standards, asking how her husband would react to news of her **adultery** (2.2.130–33). She confesses to the Abbess that she has reprimanded him incessantly for desiring other women (5.1.63–6). The Abbess chastises her, claiming that the 'venemous clamors of a jealous woman' (5.1.69) have driven Antipholus mad. Nevertheless, the play encourages sympathy for Adriana by clearly endorsing her fears about her husband, and letting her express poignantly the position of the deserted **wife** (2.1.87–101), confined to passive suffering since 'he's master of my state' (2.1.95). Adriana contributes a wifely dimension to the play's extended trope of mirroring and twinning, claiming that she is Antipholus's 'better part', indivisible from him as a drop of water from the sea (2.2.123–9). Her intelligence allows her to use the image of man and wife as one flesh as a counter-argument to his infidelity. She deftly accuses Antipholus of corrupting her honour by being unfaithful 'I do digest the poison of thy flesh, / Being **strumpet**ed by thy contagion' (2.2.143–4).

(c) Ruth Nevo discusses how the play forces Adriana to confront her identity as a possessive wife (1980: 24–34). Thomas P. Hennings (1986) shows how she is a spokeswoman for affectionate marriage. Dusinberre reads this as a source of her authority (1996: 77–82, 102–5). Jardine argues that her wifely appeals to the wrong man would have had a comic effect (1983: 44–7). Adriana's confinement to the household is the subject of Ann Christensen's (1996) article which argues that Antipholus of Ephesus fails to see the connections between the domestic world of his wife and the wider economy.

adulteress, adultery (a) a woman who commits adultery or sexual intercourse outside marriage.

(b) In addition to the emotional, psychological and spiritual damage caused by the betrayal of marriage vows, adultery represented a significant and often invisible threat to patriarchy in early modern England so the adulteress is a dangerous character type, liable to destroy the family from within. William Gouge referred to it as 'one of the most capitall vices' in the estate of **marriage**, 'whereby way is made for *Diuorce*' (1622: 118). King Lear tells **Regan** that, should she not be pleased to see him, he would suspect her legitimacy: 'I would divorce me from thy mother's tomb, / Sepulchring an adult'ress' (*KL* 2.4.131–2). Gouge pointed out that although men and women were equally culpable before God, 'more inconueniences may follow vpon the womans default then vpon the mans: as, greater infamy before men, worse disturbance of the family, more mistaking of legitimate, or illegitimate children, with the like' (Gouge 1622: 118). In Shakespeare's texts, it is therefore unsurprising that the majority of uses of adultery and adulterate (as adjective and verb), are in relation to female figures. In spite of the numerous accusations made against female characters' sexual fidelity (see, for example, **Desdemona**, **Hero**, **Imogen**), only **Hermione** is openly slandered with the term 'adultress', although **Tamora** claims she has been

> call'd foul adulteress,
> Lascivious Goth, and all the bitterest terms
> That ever ear did hear to such effect.
> (*Tit.* 2.3.109–11)

Tamora's adulterous relationship with Aaron the Moor is exposed by the birth of their blackamoor child in Act 4 Scene 2.

The verb adulterate, to commit adultery, is used of **Fortune**, who, according to **Constance**, 'adulterates hourly' with Arthur's uncle King John (*KJ* 3.1.56). Constance reconstructs the political situation in marital terms, asserting that the proper marriage between Fortune and Prince Arthur has been corrupted, with John usurping Arthur's proper position on the throne. As an adjective, adulterate usually connotes corruption. **Adriana** sees herself corrupted by her husband's infidelity, carrying the stain of his sin like an 'adulterate blot' (*Err.* 2.2.140). The **Dowager** Queen **Margaret** uses the word to insult 'th' adulterate' Hastings, Rivers, Vaughan, Grey' (*RIII* 4.3.69), although adultery is a sin she was guilty of. In *Henry VI Part II*, her relationship with Suffolk is charged with passion and tenderness (3.2), but Margaret's ruthless plotting implicitly suggests that adultery is one sin among many. *Titus Andronicus* fully endorses the view of **Tamora** as a 'foul adulteress' (*Tit.* 2.3.109), capable of murder, infanticide and revenge. Female characters suspected of adultery such as **Desdemona**, **Hermione**, or **Imogen**, are treated far more harshly than their male equivalents (such as Antipholus of Syracuse or even Gloucester in *King Lear* and Claudius in *Hamlet*, whose adultery is associated with sin). Hermione in *The Winter's Tale* is brought to trial by the paranoid Leontes and 'arraigned of high treason in committing adultery with Polixenes, King of Bohemia' (*WT* 3.2.14–15). The ease with which adultery is associated with other crimes is clear in Leontes's view that Hermione is 'an adult'ress' and 'a traitor' (*WT* 2.1.88) plotting his death. In a patriarchal culture, the crime of adultery was an abuse of husband's immediate property, in the form of the wife's body. In *Cymbeline* it is no accident that Iachimo cheats Posthumus Leonatus of his **ring** in the lie of 'hers and mine adultery' (*Cym.* 5.5.185–6).

Adultery had much wider implications. Since there was no way of determining paternity, the offspring of adultery were legally legitimate according to English law, unless the husband was beyond the distance of the four seas for the whole time of the pregnancy (see *King John* 1.1.116–27). The fear of female adultery informs Leontes's rejection of the baby **Perdita** as 'the issue of Polixenes' (*WT* 2.3.94). **Lucrece** commits suicide partly to prevent the birth of a 'bastard graff' or fruit which would shame her husband (*Luc.* 1062–4). In *Henry VI Part II*, the idea of noble stock polluted lies behind Suffolk and Warwick's slanders of bastardy (*2HVI* 3.2.223). For sons as much as husbands, female adultery is a fundamental threat to identity. The most concise expression is Posthumus's view that Imogen's adultery casts doubt on his mother's chastity and his own legitimacy

> We are all bastards
> And that most venerable man which I
> Did call my father was I know not where
> When I was stamped.
>
> (*Cym.* 2.5.2–5)

The possibility of female adultery creates anxieties for male characters who sense the pressure to prove their paternity and identity. In *Hamlet,* Laertes fears that any calm drop of blood in his veins that does not stir to avenge his father's death raises doubts about his paternity and brands his **mother** as an adulterate **harlot** (*Ham.* 4.5.118–121).

King Lear's mocking threat that his subjects should 'Die for adultery' is carried out in the case of female characters (*KL* 4.6.111). **Desdemona** is killed so that she will not corrupt more men; **Lucrece** kills herself after being raped by Tarquin so as not to bring disgrace to her husband. The slandered **Hermione** disappears into a kind of death after the trial until **Perdita** is acknowledged as legitimate. The only case in Shakespeare where female adultery is celebrated is in *King John,* where **Lady Faulconbridge** yielded to King Richard's *droit de seigneur,* and bore a son who is legally legitimate, but embraces royal bastardy instead. The bastard tells his mother

> Your fault was not your folly;
> Needs must you lay your heart at his dispose
> Subjected tribute to commanding love
>
> (*KJ* 1.1.262)

and goes on to reverse conventional morality, claiming that it would have been sin to refuse the King rather than to commit adultery (*KJ* 1.1.175–6). The power of the King's right, or *droit de seigneur* in *Edward III* gives remarkable dramatic charge to the **Countess** of Salisbury's refusal of Edward III's suit. Adultery even in these circumstances is 'bed-blotting shame' (*EIII* 2.1.457), her father reminds her. She invokes the trope of man and wife as one flesh to outwit Edward (*EIII* 2.2.172–7), proposing a suicide pact which eventually makes him ashamed of his adulterous desires (*EIII* 2.2.178–192).

Only occasionally is the word 'adultery' a source of comedy and even here, it betrays male anxiety. In *Measure for Measure*, it is one of the few words Elbow does not distort with malapropism in his solemn report that his wife might have fallen into 'fornication, adultery and all uncleanliness' in **Mistress Overdone**'s tavern (*MM* 2.1.81). When Nym draws his sword, Mistress **Quickly** exclaims 'If he be not hewn now, we shall see willful adultery and murther committed' (*HV* 2.1.37–8), in a line rich with innuendo.

(c) William Gouge discussed the difference between male and female adultery (1622: 218–33). Women's legal position is summarized by Anne Laurence (1994: 47–50). Ronald B. Bond, '"Dark Deeds Darkly Answered": Thomas Becon's *Homily against Whoredome and Adultery*, Its Contexts and Its Affiliations with Three Shakespeare Plays' (1985) argues that Shakespeare's references to adultery engaged with current concerns about the lack of rigorous punishment of the crime in early modern England. Alison Findlay (1994b) considers the dramatization of adultery and bastard offspring.

ale-wife, (a) a woman that keeps an ale-house. The brewing of ale, unlike beer, was a domestic activity rather than an industry and frequently managed by women on a small scale, especially in rural locations, although it was in decline during the time Shakespeare was writing. An ability to manage supplies, finances, customers and credit meant that ale-wives were often characterized as sharp-witted. Ale-houses and the consumption of ale (as opposed to beer or wine) were associated with those at the bottom of the social scale. The ale-wife was thus often seen, especially by Puritans, as helping to promote subversion and disorder.

(b) In *The Taming of the Shrew*, it is not surprising that '**Marian** Hacket, the fat ale-wife of Wincot' (Induction. 2.21–2) is the figure Christopher Sly calls on to verify his identity as a pedlar by birth and now a tinker. This ale-wife, like the **Hostess**, Mistress **Quickly**, is apparently indulgent and has given Sly 14 pence worth of ale on credit. In *Henry IV Part II*, the Page's joke about Bardolph's red face: 'methought he had made two holes in the ale-wife's **petticoat** and so peep'd through' (2.2.82–3), suggests liberality of a sexual kind. The term 'ale-wife' may be a disparaging remark about Mistress Quickly, from the socially superior perspective of the court page.

(c) Francis Lenton, 'A Countrey Alewife' in *Characterisms: Or Lentons Leasures* (1631: sigs D3v–D4v), gives a contemporary cameo of the type. Judith M. Bennett (1996), discusses women's contributions to the brewing industry.

Alice, (a) name of the gentlewoman of **Katherine**, **Princess** of France. It is, appropriately, a Norman name, associated with nobility and often with the countryside.

(b) With these associations, there is perhaps humour when Christopher Sly suggests he should call his lady 'Al'ce madam, or **Joan** madam', the latter being a lower-class name (*Shrew* Induction 2.110), but is told that 'Madam' is the proper form of address. In *Henry V*, the stage direction indicates that Alice is 'old' (*HV* 1.4.SD). She has been in England, speaks a little of the language, and teaches Katherine a selection of words in English, in a scene written otherwise in French. While Alice is duly deferential, her flattery of Katherine is probably also born of a delight in seeing her young charge learn so quickly. She tells the Princess 'vous prononcez les mots aussi droit que les natifs d'Angleterre' (*HV* 3.4.37–8). Lines like this would have been a source of comedy to those who could understand French in the light of its currency at the English court, the fact that Elizabeth I spoke excellent French, and it was the native and preferred language of the Queen of Scots. In the play's final scene, Alice is a chaperone when Henry V is left on stage to woo Katherine. At the start of their exchange, Alice mediates briefly as an interpreter, telling Katherine that Henry thinks she is like an **angel** and confirming Henry's translation of her response, 'dat de tongues of de mans if be full of deceits' (*HV* 5.2.119). Although it is apparent that Alice's mediation is not always necessary for them to communicate, the role allows her to support Katherine's protection of her modesty when Henry offers to kiss her. As a perfect demonstration of Katherine's claim that French maids do not kiss before they are married, Alice claims that she doesn't know the English word 'to kiss'. There is at least a suspicion that Henry sees through this pretence, suggesting that Alice did not lead such a sheltered existence when she was in England. Simple refers to 'Alice Shortcake' as one of his master's acquaintances in *Merry Wives of Windsor*, the name here suggesting the infantile desires of the foolish Abraham Slender (*HV* 1.1.204).

(c) Mason (2002), esp. p. 190 considers Alice as a buffer between Henry V and Princess Katherine while Loehlin (1996) p. 164–7 describes the Company of Women 1994–95 feminist production in which the wooing scene was played as political rape in which both Alice and Katherine were victims.

Althaea, (a) in Greek mythology was the vengeful **mother** of Meleager, Prince of Calydon. When he was born, the **Fates** told her that her son's life would last only as long as it took for a log burning in the hearth to be extinguished by fire and so she hid the brand carefully. Later, when Meleager killed her two brothers for their refusal to honour the goddess **Diana**, Althaea took revenge by throwing the brand onto the fire. As its flames consumed the log, Meleager burned from the inside and died what he felt was a dishonourable death for a soldier.

(b) Shakespeare would have known the story from Ovid. He uses Althaea as a frightening image of destructive, castrating maternal power. In *Henry VI Part II*, the Duke of York refers to Althaea's betrayal of her son to illustrate his own sense of dishonour and betrayal when the French provinces of Anjou and Maine are given in exchange for the hand of Queen Margaret, who is implicitly aligned with Althaea. Believing the crown is rightfully his, he claims that its realms 'Bear that proportion to my flesh and blood / As did the fatal brand Althaea burnt / Unto the Prince's heart of Calydon' (*2HVI* 1.1.234–5). The same associations appear in *Henry IV Part II*, where Falstaff's page confuses the figures of Althaea and **Hecuba** (who imagined she would give birth to a firebrand that would burn Troy, cf. *T&C* 2.2.110), by jokingly referring to the red-faced Bardolph as 'Althaea's dream' (*2HIV* 2.2.87). Prince Hal appears not to notice the mistake and pays the Page for his good instruction.

(c) Ovid's *Metamorphoses* translated by Arthur Golding (1567), Book VIII, Lines 586–705 (Ovidius, 2000: 208–11) tells Althaea's story with much emphasis on the struggle between her love for her brothers and her son. Thomas Heywood's *General History of Women* (1657) cites her as an example 'Of Women Contentious and Bloody' (p. 495) and as a witch who sets her son on fire (p. 579).

Amazon, (a) A member of a race of female warriors, who were supposed to have lived in Scythia. Their mythical reputation as an all-female community who associated with males only to reproduce before expelling them and any male children from the **sister**hood, was accompanied by one of military prowess. Amazons supposedly cut off the right **breast** so they would be able to shoot the bow more effectively. As hunters dedicated to chastity, they are closely associated with the goddess **Diana**. Achilles defeats their leader **Penthesilea** in the Trojan War and Theseus defeats and captures and marries their Queen **Hippolyta**. In the early modern period, the term is frequently used figuratively as shorthand for a very strong or belligerent woman, often one with masculine qualities.

(b) **Hippolyta**'s Amazonian background is referred to in *A Midsummer Nights Dream* and Shakespeare and Fletcher's *Two Noble Kinsmen*. In the former, Theseus admits 'I woo'd thee with my sword, / And won thy love doing thee injuries' (*MND* 1.1.16–17) and **Titania** describes her as a 'bouncing Amazon', Oberon's 'buskin'd mistress' and 'warrior love' (*MND* 2.1.70–1). The buskin, a half-boot, carries associations with masculine hunting and with tragedy, since this was the footwear worn by the actors in ancient Athenian tragedy; perhaps implying **Titania** has a degree of sympathy with **Hippolyta**'s subjection by Theseus. Oberon then points out that another Amazonian Queen, Antiope, was also abandoned by the faithless Theseus (*TNK* 2.1.80). A short history of Theseus' conquest over **Hippolyta** and her reputation as an Amazon huntress and warrior is given in the opening scene of *Two Noble Kinsmen*, which presents the couple on their way to be married. The second of three weeping **Queen**s of Thebes appeals to **Hippolyta** as a 'Most dreaded Amazonian' who as well as being an excellent huntress, 'wast near to make the male / To thy sex captive', before she was defeated by Theseus (*TNK* 1.1.77–85). Hippolyta's Amazonian attempt to make the male sex 'captive' to her own is corrected by Theseus who shrinks her power within so-called proper boundaries. Nevertheless, the Queen believes that Hippolyta is still the dominant partner; that in love 'thou hast much more power on him / That ever he had on thee' (*TNK* 1.1.87–8). This proves to be the case when Hippolyta kneels alongside the **Queen**s, followed by **Emilia** her sister, and Theseus is obliged to interrupt the wedding celebrations in order to send succour to Thebes. The Amazons' strong, but disturbing influence in love is shown again in *Timon of Athens* when they appear with Cupid in a masque held at Timon of Athens' house. Apemantus distrusts their 'sweep of vanity', fearing 'those that dance before me now / Would one day stamp upon me' (*Tim.* 1.2.143–4). In this case the Amazons are associated with the fickleness of court favouritism, perhaps with reference to the Amazonian figures who appeared in Jonson's *Masque of Queens* in 1608, the conjectured date for *Timon*.

The word 'Amazon' is used as a shorthand to signal unexpected, masculine behaviour from women in the early history plays and *Coriolanus*. When a battle of the sexes is set up in *Henry VI Part I*, **Joan** La **Pucelle**'s victory with her sword over Charles the Dauphin makes him exclaim 'Thou art an Amazon' and give her control of the French army (*1HVI* 1.2.104). In *King John*, the unnaturalness of John's rule forces women to take on the abnormal behaviour of the Amazons. The bastard reports that 'Pale visaged **maid**s / Like Amazons come tripping after drums' (*KJ* 5.2.155), changing thimbles and needles, the common tools of women's work (**sewing**), for gauntlets and lances, and their gentle hearts 'To fierce and bloody inclination' (*KJ* 5.2.158). Queen **Margaret** in the *Henry VI* plays best exemplifies the Amazonian qualities that transgressed expected gender norms in early modern England. Indeed, in *Henry VI Part III* her reaction to the news that King Edward IV has jilted the Lady **Bona** is to put on armour, which prompts Edward to say 'Belike she minds to play the Amazon' (*3HVI* 4.2.106). In the Wars of the Roses, she leads the Lancastrian forces in the place of her husband and, like the Amazons who cut off one breast to fight better, seems to reject any sense of maternal sensitivity or pity until Prince Edward's death. She triumphs in giving the Duke of York a handkerchief stained with the blood of his son, Rutland, and inviting York to use it to wipe his tears at being defeated and captured. In upbraiding her with the words 'how ill-beseeming is it in thy sex / To triumph like an Amazonian trull / Upon their woes whom fortune captivates' (*3HVI* 1.4.115), he articulates the feelings of the other men on stage, who weep. The Amazon here is all that is unnatural for a **woman**: 'Women are soft, mild, pitiful and flexible / Thou stern, obdurate, flinty, rough, remorseless' (*3HVI* 1.4.141–2). Even unexpected military valour from young men is labelled 'Amazonian'. In *Coriolanus*, Cominius refers to the sixteen-year-old, beardless Coriolanus who goes 'beyond the mark of others' as 'Amazonian' for his courage in driving away the apparently more masculine soldiers before him (*Cor.* 2.2.91). The Amazon in Shakespeare is thus something extraordinary, disruptive of gender norms and usually unnerving but also dramatically exciting.

(c) C. H. Oldfather, in his translation of Diodorus, discusses the origins of the race (Oldfather, 1935: 245–61). Thomas Heywood's *Gyneikon* (London, 1624) gives an early modern account. Kathryn Schwartz (2000) offers a wide survey of representations of the type while Sue Blundell (1995), pp. 58–62 considers Amazons in the wider context of women in ancient Greece. Simon Shepherd (1981) analyses how the type inspired varieties of feminism in seventeenth-century drama. Robert C. Fulton III (1976) discusses the significance of Amazons with special reference to *Timon*.

Andromache, (a) the wife of Hector and daughter of the King of Thebes, who appears as a character in *Troilus and Cressida*. Classical texts define her as a woman who suffers tragic family losses with dignity. Her father and seven brothers are killed by Achilles after the capture of Thebes and her mother slain by Artemis. During the Trojan war, her husband Hector was then slain by Achilles. After Troy was captured her son, Astyanax, was hurled from the city walls. Andromache was taken by Pyrrhus, Achilles's son, in marriage, and bore him three sons in Epirus.

(b) Shakespeare's character follows the pattern of tragic dignity, appearing only in Act 5 Scene 3 of *Troilus and Cressida* where she pleads with Hector to unarm and stay away from the battle because she has had an ominous dream of 'shapes and forms of slaughter' (5.3.12). The relationship between husband and **wife** has previously been one of reasonable negotiation. We learn that she has admonished him in the past (5.3.3) and that he is normally even-tempered and patient (1.2.3–4). However, fighting the Greeks, and Ajax in particular, has caused him to chide her (1.2.6), and in this scene he warns her he will lose his temper, and orders her inside. The arrival of **Cassandra** gives Andromache renewed strength to argue against the war, which she does eloquently, as if inspired by her dream:

> . . . do not count it holy
> To hurt by being just; it is as lawful,
> For we would give much, to use violent thefts,
> And rob in the behalf of charity.
>
> (5.3.19–22)

Andromache focuses on the simple truth of inflicting hurt and its injustice. To claim that war is holy is just as perverse as saying that violent theft for the sake of charity is virtuous. Her plain viewpoint powerfully qualifies Hector's belief that honour is 'more precious-dear than life' (5.3.28) or Cassandra's grander vision of the gods' indifference to his vows. In spite of Andromache's strength in challenging Hector's values, as a virtuous wife her love for him entails obedience, most poignantly when she exits on his words 'I am offended with you, / Upon the love you bear me, get you in' (5.3.77–8).

(c) Hammond and Scullard (1970: 63) outline Andromache's profile in Greek mythology. Aerol Arnold (1953) discusses how Andromache's dream draws on Lydgate's poem and compares Shakespeare's representation of the dialogue with Thomas Heywood's more sentimental one, featuring the child Astyanax. Boitani (1989: 252–5) comments on how Andromache's character was adapted by Dryden.

angel, (a) a spiritual being, superior to humans in power and intelligence and usually imagined with wings. In Christian, Jewish and Islamic tradition, a messenger from the Deity. Although angels are incorporeal and thus without sex, in the Bible they are masculine, as are the fallen angels who follow Satan. However, the word is used in figurative terms to signify women or men who are bright, gracious, lovely or innocent, or whose behaviour in ministering to others or protecting others is like that of a guardian angel. Angel, or angel-noble, is also the name of an old English gold coin worth ten shillings depicting the arch-angel Michael.

(b) In Shakespeare's texts, the figurative description of women as angels usually creates an ironic effect. Romeo speaks what is probably the best-known example of the Petrarchan cliché that elevates the beloved to semi-divine status:

> She speaks!
> O speak again, bright angel, for thou art
> As glorious to this night, being o'er my head,
> As is a winged messenger from heaven
> Unto the white-upturnèd wond'ring eyes
> Of mortals that fall back to gaze on him
> When he bestrides the lazy puffing clouds,
> And sails upon the bosom of the air.
>
> (*R&J* 2.2.25–32)

Perhaps it is simply the youthful candour of Romeo that makes the audience adopt his wondering look and accept the cliché, but the description of a male angel also adds surprise and complexity. Emerging from the security of an intimate all-male group, Romeo gives voice to an awakening passion whose orientation is still not firmly defined. Edward III, who is entranced by the **Countess** of Salisbury, believes she speaks with 'an angel's note from heaven' (*EIII* 2.1.34).

Male characters' use of 'angel' as a form of flattery is frequently undermined in the texts. Henry V's crass attempt to woo **Katherine** by telling her 'An angel is like you Kate, and you are like an angel' causes immediate suspicion; only proving to her that the tongues of men are full of deceit (*HV* 5.2.110). **Cressida** shares this view, shrewdly recognizing that 'women are angels' only for as long as they are being wooed (*T&C* 1.2.286). Male characters, too, know that it is a fiction. Valentine lists it in a catalogue of wooing devices: 'Though ne'er so black, say they have angels' faces' (*TGV* 2.1.103). The term carries additional ironic resonance in the voice of the immoral Richard of Gloucester who describes **Anne**, the 'divine perfection of a **woman**' as an angry angel (*RIII* 1.2.74–5). The **blazon** tradition where the angelic beloved is fragmented into parts like commodities is satirized through the behaviour of Autolycus. He extravagantly praises the haberdashery he is trying to sell, worshipping the wrist band and the embroidered yoke of the neckline: 'you would think a **smock** were a she-angel, he so chaunts to the sleeve-hand and the work about the square on't' (*WT* 4.4.208–10). The King of Navarre's extravagant praise for the **Princess** of France as an angel who might dumbfound the Page, is ridiculed (*LLL* 5.2.103). Boyet uses the same comparison coquettishly when warning the ladies not to remove their **masks** in front of the suitors. To do so would be to lose their mystery like 'angels vailing clouds', that is, letting the clouds drop to reveal their brightness (*LLL* 5.2.297).

Shakespeare's texts advertise the commodification of woman that often lies behind comparisons of a desired mistress to an angel in worldly rather than heavenly terms. In *Merchant of Venice*, for example, the Prince of Morocco crudely but aptly conflates the figurative and monetary senses of angel in his anticipation of winning the hand of the rich heiress, **Portia**, by choosing the golden casket:

> They have in England
> A coin that bears the figure of an angel
> Stamp'd in gold, but that's insculp'd upon;

> But here an angel in a golden bed
> Lies all within.
>
> (*Mer.* 2.7.55–9)

Benedick makes a wittier pun on the full name of the coin, angel-noble, and the qualities of a woman, in joking that any potential wife must be 'noble, or not I for an angel' (*MAdo* 2.3.33). Whatever her angelic qualities, she must also be of noble birth and, implicitly, with a dowry of more than ten shillings. A similar implicit conflation occurs in *Merry Wives of Windsor*, where Falstaff imagines seducing Mistress Ford and Mistress Page and, through the golden beam of her favouring smile, gaining control of her husband's purse (*MWW* 1.3.52–3).

In the context of such ironic uses, the Second Gentleman's description of **Anne** Bullen as 'an angel' (*HVIII* 4.1.44) rings hollow, particularly in comparison with the appearance of angels to Katherine in the following scene (*HVIII* 4.2.82). The 'six personages' who wear golden vizards and white robes are ungendered (although they were presumably played by male actors) and may be Christian martyrs (from Rev. 7.9) rather than angels. The word carries additional resonance in a play dominated by religious allusion, such as *All's Well That Ends Well*. **Helena** idealizes the domestic married life by imagining the **Countess** of Rossillion's house as a 'paradise' where 'angels offic'd all' (*AWW* 3.2.125–6). It is perhaps only because she is excluded from the routine of female domestic ministry, since Bertram has rejected her as a wife, that she can think of it in such utopian terms. The Countess of Rossillion regards Helena as an angel, far superior to the unworthy Bertram. 'What angel shall / Bless this unworthy husband!' she exclaims (*AWW* 3.4.25). Only Helena's prayers will offer him the chance of forgiveness and salvation, she believes, and the abundance of religious allusion in this play does much to foster Helena's self-made image as Bertram's guardian angel. The conflation of female care and angelic guardianship lies behind Laertes's claim that **Ophelia** will be 'a minist'ring angel' (*Ham.* 5.1.241). Angelic associations in *Cymbeline* serve to distinguish **Imogen** from the flawed characters around her. Iachimo calls her a 'heavenly angel' (*Cym.* 2.1.50) and when she is cross-dressed as **Fidele**, Belarius sees her as 'an angel! or, if not / An earthly paragon', her boyish 'divineness' perhaps reminding him of images of cherubim (*Cym.* 3.6.42–3).

Complexity haunts Shakespeare's other sincere use of the term in *Othello*. **Emilia**'s description of **Desdemona** as an angel makes explicit the play's indebtedness to morality play tradition: 'O the more angel she; And you the blacker devil!' (*Oth.* 5.2.130) but unwittingly repeats the racism that was partly responsible for the tragedy. Iago's misogyny that can turn virtue into pitch, making a demonic false angel out of the divine Desdemona, also haunts Sonnet 144, where the woman as bad angel or 'worser spirit' tempts the 'better angel' or fair young man away from the poet (*Son.* 144.3–4). In *Comedy of Errors* too, **wench**es such as the **Courtezan** are compared to fallen angels by Dromio, who argues that, like the devil, they will 'appear to men like angels of light' to tempt them (*Err.* 4.3.55–7). The name Angelica, meaning angelic, found in *Romeo and Juliet* as an appellation, may be referring to Lady **Capulet** or the **Nurse** (*R&J* 4.4.5).

11

(c) A work edited by Peter Marshall and Alexandra Walsham (2006) gives an overview of the subject. David N. Beauregard (1999), discusses the angelic quality of Helena in *All's Well* while Bettie Ann Doebler (1967) offers a reading of angels in *Othello*. The romantic idealization of a mistress in *Love's Labour's Lost* is studied by Neal L. Goldstein (1974). Broader studies of angel iconography include Harry Morris's useful overview (1958).

Anna of Denmark (1574–1619), (a) Queen consort to James VI of Scotland (and, from 1603, James I of Britain), whom she married in 1589.
(b) Anna's journey to Scotland was fraught with difficulties, which James believed were due to witchcraft, and which may be alluded to in *Macbeth*. From 1593 Anna's religious inclinations turned from her Lutheran upbringing to Catholicism, which she continued to practise privately while maintaining and appearance of conformity in attending Anglican services and keeping Protestant chaplains in her household. Anna gave birth to seven children (Henry, Elizabeth, Margaret, Charles, Robert, Mary and Sophia), so intimacy between her and the allegedly homosexual King obviously continued until at least 1605. Anna established a very distinctive and separate royal household, however. In cultural terms, she brought continental artistic tastes and performance traditions to Britain from her upbringing in the Danish and Norwegian court and her family ties to the courts of Denmark, Dresden, Wolfenbüttel and Saxony. In particular, she developed the form of the court masque, featuring female as well as male aristocratic perform-ers. The masque of **Amazon**s in *Timon of Athens* may draw on the Amazonian figures performed by Anna and her ladies in Jonson's *Masque of Queens* in 1608. Shakespeare only uses 'Anna' (the Queen's preferred form of her name) once in *Taming of the Shrew* (1.1.154–5), to refer to the sister of **Dido** in whom Dido confides her love for Aeneas. Nevertheless, the powerful figure of **Paulina**, who keeps her own house and is unafraid to challenge King Leontes's authority in *The Winter's Tale*, may owe something to Queen Anna's independence. As Leeds Barroll astutely observes, she was 'temperamentally unsuited to a purely symbolic role' (Barroll 2001: 34) as Queen consort and in many ways she perpetuated the iconography of Queen **Elizabeth I**.
(c) Leeds Barroll (2001) gives a wonderfully detailed and nuanced discussion of Anna's changing fortunes and cultural significance. Clare McManus (2002) discusses Anna's theatrical influence. Essays by Clare McManus (2003), James Knowles (2003) and Mara Wade (2003) discuss, respectively, Anna's influence on theatre, her adaptation of Elizabeth I's royal iconography, and her important continental connections.

Anne, (a) derived from the Hebrew Hannah, meaning 'grace', is the name given to the mother of **Mary** in apocryphal literature, and of two historical characters: **Queen** Anne, wife of Richard of Gloucester, and Anne Bullen in *Henry VIII*. In addition, Anne Page is the name of the fictional young lover in *Merry Wives of Windsor*. Anne was also the name of Shakespeare's wife (*see* **Hathaway**).
(b) Saint Anne, the patroness of women in labour, is used as a vow in the first

scene of *The Taming of the Shrew* and in *Twelfth Night.* Christopher Sly insists 'by Saint Anne' he is paying attention to the play (*Shrew* 1.1.250) and Feste vows 'by Saint Anne' that, in addition to cakes and ale, 'ginger will be hot in the mouth too' (*TN* 2.3.117–18). Neither case makes any connection to childbirth but in the latter example, the saint's name may be used deliberately to challenge and provoke Malvolio, the puritan Steward, in the staged battle between saturnalian revelry and puritan Lent. Saint Anne is part of a wider Catholic discourse used in Olivia's household.

Anne Mortimer, mother of Richard Plantagenet, Duke of York does not appear on stage in *Henry VI Part II* but is alluded to by Richard as the source of his claim to the throne (*2HVI* 2.2.34–52). She is **daughter** to Mortimer, Earl of March and granddaughter to Lionel, Duke of Clarence, third son of King Edward III. Richard makes his claim through the maternal line more confused by pointing out that she is also wife to Richard, Earl of Cambridge, son to Edward III's fifth son, Edmund Langley, Duke of York. Warwick's dry comment 'What plain proceedings is more plain than this?' (*2HVI* 2.2.54) casts further doubt on the maternal line as the basis of the Yorkist claim.

In *Richard III*, Anne Neville, daughter of Warwick the kingmaker, appears first as the **widow** of Prince Edward, son to Henry VI, both of whom have been slaughtered by Richard of Gloucester. In contrast to the pall-bearers, she is unafraid of Richard and offers a spirited verbal attack on him as a devil who has made the earth hell. She also spits at him. The opposition set up when he praises her as an **angel**ic 'divine perfection of a woman', while she sees only his deformity in addressing him as 'defus'd infection of a man' (*RIII* 1.2.75 and 78), makes the success of Richard's wooing all the more unnerving. It may be that she is susceptible to his perversely erotic flattery that her **beauty** made him commit the murders. Ultimately, though, Anne's goodness is what makes her incapable of murder (unlike him), and doomed to accept his love when he offers her his sword and bears his breast. Anne's goodness means that she must also rejoice in the possibility of his repentance, even though she suspects he is dissembling. Just as Richard is 'determinèd' to prove a villain; Anne is predestined to become a victim to his evil. The curse of misery she places on Richard's wife (*RIII* 1.2.26–8) returns to haunt her (*RIII* 4.1.71–80).

Anne's marital misery is set off by a bond of **sister**ly comradeship with Queen **Elizabeth** and the **Duchess** of York in Act 4 Scene 1 where they meet near the Tower. Anne's 'pure heart's love' (*RIII* 4.1.4) allows her to share the other women's maternal concern for the princes within. She claims she is 'in love their **mother**' (*RIII* 4.1.27), telling Brakenbury that she will take the blame if he lets them inside the Tower. Anne takes no joy in the news that she is to be crowned Richard's queen. Her response to Stanley's proclamation: 'Dispiteful tidings, O displeasing news!' (*RIII* 4.1.36) has the potential for comic effect in performance. She wishes the crown would burn her brows and the women's mutual sympathy stands in strong contrast to the earlier rivalry over **queen**ship. The Duchess of York prays that 'good angels' will attend her (*RIII* 4.1.92) but Anne is grimly aware of the future that awaits her as queen; that Richard 'will, no doubt, shortly be rid of me' (*RIII* 4.1.86). Her prediction is fulfilled less than seventy lines later when Richard orders Catesby to give out 'That Anne, my wife, is very grievous sick' (*RIII* 4.2.51) and plots her death. She is not seen alive again on stage but her ghost appears to exact retribution on Richard, disturbing his sleep as he had made hers wretched (*RIII* 5.3.100–1). By encouraging Richmond that even his enemy's **wife** is praying for him, Anne vocalizes the way in which Richard has destroyed family bonds.

In contrast to the character in *Richard III*, Lady Anne Bullen (later **Queen** Anne and mother to **Elizabeth I**), in Shakespeare and Fletcher's *Henry VIII* is characterized by her appearance rather than her voice. The text diplomatically avoids polarizing the characters of **Katherine** and Anne as wronged wife and whore, delicately balancing favourable characterizations of both instead. Anne is attractive because of her physical beauty and coquettish, though not immodest manner. King Henry's personification of her: 'O **Beauty** / Till now I never knew thee!' (*HVIII* 1.4.75–6) is supported by the opinions of other characters. The Second Gentleman exclaims

> Heaven bless thee!
> Thou hast the sweetest face I ever looked on.
> Sir, as I have a soul, she is an **angel**.
> Our King has all the Indes in his arms,
> And more, and richer, when he strains that **lady**.
> (*HVIII* 4.1.42–6)

The text celebrates Anne's sensual fertility. The Third Gentleman describes the crowd at the coronation, men and pregnant women, driven to a frenzy by her beauty. Such comments serve to legitimize the King's actions. The text relies heavily on the beauty of the **boy actor**, and the lavish use of spectacle to construct a regal identity for Anne. She never speaks as queen, but is presented under a canopy of state in her coronation robe, '*her hair richly adorned with pearl*' (*HVIII* 4.1.36SD), a possible retrospective compliment to the late **Elizabeth** I, whose costumes were frequently decorated with pearls, signifying purity.

Anne Bullen is not quite as pure as the pearls suggest. At the masked ball at Wolsey's house, she readily understands the sexual innuendo in Lord Sands' dinner-table conversation (*HVIII* 1.4.45–8). She expresses pity at Queen Katherine having fallen from the King's favour, but the Old **Lady** perceptively chastises Anne for 'all this spice of your hypocrisy' (*HVIII* 2.3.26) in claiming that she does not have ambitions to be **queen** herself. In that, she is typical of womankind, the Old Lady states:

> You, that have so fair parts of **woman** on you,
> Have too, a woman's heart, which ever yet
> Affected eminence, wealth, sovereignty;
> Which, to say sooth, are blessings; and which gifts
> (Saving your mincing) the capacity

> Of your soft cheveril conscience would receive
> If you might please to stretch it.
>
> > (*HVIII* 2.3.27–33)

Even Anne's conscience is metaphorically linked to her body here since the word cheveril, the very softest, pliable leather, is used to signify the vagina. Anne disappears from the stage and from the other characters' discourse. Certainly in this scene, Anne protests too much when it comes to the question of being queen. Whether affectation, what the Old Lady calls 'mincing', characterizes her behaviour throughout is difficult to say. Given that she has such a weak non-corporeal stage presence, it is difficult to think of her as potentially nurturing an ambition for the crown, like Bolingbroke in *Richard II*. Shakespeare seems to create this character primarily as a creature of the present: to create a powerful effect on others in her physical appearance, but without a future existence. Having become queen, Anne disappears from the stage and from the other characters' speech, as her **daughter**, the baby **Elizabeth**, becomes the new focus of attention.

Anne Page is an attractive prospect to the bachelors of the small Windsor community in *The Merry Wives of Windsor*, in that she is heiress to £700 of her grandfather's wealth on her seventeenth birthday, is pretty and 'speaks small like a woman', so is not **shrew**ish. This, as Parson Hugh Evans points out is 'pretty **virgin**ity' (*MWW* 1.1.45–54), although Anne turns out to be more intelligent and more assertive than this initial picture suggests. She is the focus of three men's attentions: Master Abraham Slender, whose tedious repetition of the phrase 'O sweet Anne Page' (*MWW* 3.1.40ff) declares his immaturity; the irascible French Doctor, Caius; and the gentleman Master Fenton. The audience and Master Fenton know from the end of the first act that Anne has confided in **Mistress Quickly**, and has, comically, spent an hour discussing a wart on Master Fenton's face (*MWW* 1.4.145–52). Anne firmly rejects the matches favoured by her parents, appealing against the 'fool' Slender, her father's choice, and against Dr Caius, her mother's choice: 'I had rather be set quick i' th' earth, / And bowl'd to death with turnips' (*MWW* 3.4.86–7). Mistress Quickly claims Anne does not love Fenton (*MWW* 1.4.163) and when we see them on stage together, she reveals her suspicions (based on her father's opinion) that Fenton only loves her 'as a property' (*MWW* 3.4.10) whose **dowry** will sustain his gentlemanly title. She urges Fenton to win her father's approval but also plots a means to escape from her parents' ludicrously inappropriate matchmaking, thus mirroring the clever plotting of her mother, **Mistress Page** and **Mistress Ford**. Using the masked nocturnal entertainment-within-the-play of Herne the Hunter, Anne plays off one parent against the other, promising her **mother** that she will appear as a fairy dressed in green to be carried off by Dr Caius; telling her father she will appear in white, so be secretly snatched and married by Slender; and writing to Fenton of her intention to subvert both these plots by planting boys as substitutes so that she can abscond and marry him (*MWW* 4.3.8–47). Her device to escape the prospect of loveless and thus shameful **marriage** (*MWW* 5.5.221–2) is excused and a strong argument presented for young people's choice of their marriage partners.

(c) Anne Page is discussed in Nancy Cotton, 'Castrating Witches: Impotence and Magic in *The Merry Wives of Windsor*' (1987). Analyses of Anne Bullen are found in articles by Linda Micheli (1987), Kim H. Noling (1988) and Paul Dean (1988).

Antiochus's daughter – *see* **daughter** and **mother**

apron, (a) a protective piece of clothing worn at the front of the body with ties round the waist. Worn by both sexes at work, men's aprons usually being made of leather and women's of linen or wool. There were worn by the working classes and country **housewives**. Towards the end of the sixteenth century, finer aprons of gauze and embroidery were sometimes worn by upper-class fashionable women.

(b) On the Shakespearean stage, the apron is an immediate indicator of class. The commoner John Holland points out in *Henry VI Part II*, 'the nobility think scorn to go in leather aprons' (4.2.12). It would be a shorthand means to establish characters such as the **Hostess** in the Induction to *Taming of the Shrew* or Mistress **Quickly** as hostess (*Henry IV Parts I and II*) and housekeeper (*Merry Wives*) or Mistress **Overdone**, keeper of the brothel in *Measure for Measure*. When aprons are named in the text it is with bawdy implications. In the brothel at Myteline, Boult counsels **Marina** to entertain the Lord Lysimachus well so that 'he will line your apron with gold' (*Per.* 4.4.58–9) and Timon of Athens tells the **whores Timandra** and **Phrynia** to 'Hold up, you sluts / Your aprons mountant' (*Tim.* 4.3.135–6) to accept his gold. The association with pollution may derive ultimately from Genesis 3.7 where Adam and Eve make 'aprons' out of fig leaves to cover their shame.

(c) Jane Ashelford (1983: 142); illustrations (ibid.: 75, 77, 143 and 144) show aprons. Gordon Williams (1994: 32–3) outlines how the garment is particularly associated with whores and as a cover for pregnancy.

Arden, Mary, (a) maiden name of the mother of Shakespeare.

(b) **Mary** Arden was the youngest daughter of Robert Arden, a husbandman (with about 70 acres of land in Wilmcote and property to rent in Snitterfield) and his first **wife**, whose name we do not know. Mary's **mother** gave **birth** to eight children, all **girls**, and must have died before 1550 when Robert married again, to Agnes Webb, who had four children by a previous marriage. Mary's birth is estimated as c. 1539–43. She grew up at Glebe Farm in Wilmcote, a three-roomed dwelling with a kitchen, a communal hall and a chamber. Here she would have been involved in the running of the farm with household activities such as milking, cooking and brewing of ale, work related to the kitchen garden, farmyard animals and possibly work in the fields at harvest time. Robert Arden died in November 1556 leaving an estate valued at £77 11s and 10d, including land and animals. Mary Arden was named one of the two executors and supervised the inventory of his goods and moveables in December 1556. Her four eldest sisters (Agnes (m. Stringer), **Joan** (m. Lambert), **Katherine** and **Margaret** (m. Webbe) were all married by the time Robert Arden died in November 1556. Of the four younger sisters, **Elizabeth** married a man called Skarlett, Joyce and **Alice** Arden probably died unmarried because their inheritances in Robert's estate in Snitterfield eventually passed to their sisters, and Mary Arden married John Shakespeare (some time between November 1556 and 1558) at the comparatively young age of between 18 and 22. Mary had inherited between 86 and 120 acres at Wilmcote, including the land named 'Asbyes' and 'the crop upon the ground sown and tilled as it is', and a marriage portion of £6.13s and 4d., which would have given her considerable freedom in arranging a match. She probably met John Shakespeare through family contacts since his father Richard Shakespeare had been one of Robert Arden's tenants at Snitterfield. For Mary, the move to Henley Street would have been from farm-based activities to running a town household centred on her husband's business as a glover, whittawer (a dresser of leather) and wool merchant. In addition, she bore and reared children. The parish register records the baptisms of a **Joan** Shakespeare on 15 September 1558, Margaret Shakespeare on 2 December 1562, William Shakespeare on 26 April 1564, Gilbert in October 1566, Joan in April 1569, Ann in September 1571, Richard in March 1574 and Edmund in 1580. During the 1560s John Shakespeare's affairs prospered, and Mary's social status rose as her husband became a bailiff and justice of the peace in 1568. After 1572, however, the family experienced increasing financial difficulties and in 1578 one part of Mary's inheritance – the Asbyes – was mortgaged to her brother-in-law, Edmund Lambert, and at the same time property in Snitterfield was conveyed to her nephew, Robert Webbe, an inevitable source of ill-feeling between the Shakespeares and Mary's siblings. John and his son William's applications for the title and arms of a gentleman, incorporating the Arden and Shakespeare coats of arms must have seemed bitterly ironic in the circumstances. Mary also experienced loss in the deaths of her children. Margaret Shakespeare died at five months old and Ann Shakespeare just before her eighth birthday. Edmund, her youngest son, was buried in London on 31 December 1607. It is assumed that after John Shakespeare's death, Mary continued to live in Henley Street until her death in September 1608. She was buried on 9 September as 'Mary Shakespeare, widow' with no mention of her husband's earlier public prominence and nothing about her more famous son.

(c) The fullest information can be found in Germaine Greer (2007: 17–18, 29–41, 202–6) and Christopher Dyer (2003).

Atalanta, (a) a woman from Greek mythology famed for her athletic excellence, especially in running, and her ability to equal or excel men in traditionally masculine activities such as hunting. Atalanta took part in the hunt for the Calydonian boar. She challenged any man who wanted to marry her to beat her in a race. With the help of Venus, Hippomenes was able to do so by dropping three golden apples on the track which distracted Atalanta as she stooped to pick them up. For omitting to honour **Venus** and defiling the Temple of Zeus, the couple were changed into lions.

(b) Shakespeare would have known Atalanta's stories from Ovid's *Metamorphoses* but only refers to her in relation to running. Orlando's verse compiles 'Atalanta's better part' (*AYLI* 3.2.142) as one of the qualities combined in **Rosalind**, perhaps referring to her height. Jaques admiringly compares Orlando's nimble wit to 'Atalanta's heels' (*AYLI* 3.2.275–6).

(c) The story of Atalanta racing is in Ovid, *Metamorphoses* Book 10, Lines 648–830 (Ovidius, 2000: 266–70).

Ate, (a) a Greek goddess, who, according to Book 19 of Homer's *Iliad*, was thrown from Mount Olympus down to earth, and is associated with mischief, rash impulse, destruction, infatuation and **revenge**.

(b) Ate does not appear as a character in Shakespeare's texts, although she does open Peele's *The Arraignment of Paris* (1584) and *The Lamentable Tragedy of Locrine*, attributed to W.S. on the title page of the 1595 Quarto, and entering the Shakespeare apocrypha when it was reprinted in the 1685 third Folio. There are four allusions to Ate in the canon, however, which may have derived from Shakespeare's knowledge of the anonymous *The Tragedy of Caesar and Pompey, or Caesar's Revenge* (c. 1592), produced by students at Trinity College, Oxford. In Shakespeare's *Julius Caesar*, Antony imagines Ate come hot from hell after Caesar's assassination to accompany his spirit in 'ranging for revenge' and unleashing havoc on Rome (*JC* 3.1.270–3). More humorously, in the pageant of the nine worthies in *Love's Labour's Lost*, Berowne encourages a fight between Armado (playing Hector) and Costard (playing Pompey) over the pregnant **Jaquenetta** by calling on 'More Ates, more Ates!' to stir them on (*LLL* 5.1.598–9). When female characters are compared to Ate, military associations of discord again predominate, although in each case the characters have reasons to want revenge. **Queen Eleanor** accompanies her son King John to France defend his right to the crown as 'An Ate stirring him to blood and strife', at the head of an army of rash, inconsiderate unruly volunteer soldiers (*KJ* 2.1.63). Benedick, whose pride has been wounded by **Beatrice**'s sharp tongue, which 'speaks poinards' (*MAdo* 2.1.247) calls her 'the infernal Ate in good apparel' since 'all disquiet, horror and perturbation follows her' (*MAdo* 2.1.255–6 and 260–1). The sense of Ate as a mischief maker comes across here although Beatrice's behaviour may include an element of revenge, since in the past Benedick won her heart 'with false dice' as she goes on to reveal a few lines later (*MAdo* 2.1.280–1).

(c) Braginton (1926) and Pearson (1981) both give brief analyses of Ate.

Audrey, (a) a character in *As You Like It*, whose name derives from St Audrey, a corruption of St Ethelreda, a saint from Ely. Because her altar was highly decorated by votaries, the name became associated with garish or cheap goods and mismatched colours, sold at the Audrey Fair (tawdry).

(b) Touchstone picks upon this sense of the name in calling Audrey 'a toy in hand' (3.3.76) when he is about to be married by the hedge-priest Sir Oliver Martext, and when he introduces her to the Duke:

a poor **virgin**, sir, an ill-favour'd thing, sir, but mine own; a poor humor of
    mine, sir to take that no man else will'

                                               (5.4.57–9)

Audrey is self-confessedly 'foul' (3.3.30) but, as Touchstone well knows, she has another suitor in the person of William, who appears in a single cameo scene and was possibly played by Shakespeare. Touchstone is therefore wrong in referring to Audrey as remaindered goods. His admonishment 'bear your body more seeming, Audrey' (5.4.68–9) suggests that her posture is not sufficiently ladylike for the courtly context in the presence of Duke Senior. The earliest list of roles for the play in a manuscript copy from the Catholic college at Douai describes her as 'a country girl' and the text immediately establishes her as a goatherd. When Touchstone says that a husband's plentiful supply of 'good horns' are 'the **dowry** of his wife, 'tis none of his own getting' (3.3.54–6), his joke may include an allusion to the goats as the source of Audrey's financial independence. She certainly does not have to consult anyone about her intended **marriage**. In choosing to accept Touchstone's proposal, she follows her own honest desire to be a 'woman of the world' (5.3.4–5). The character of Audrey (and that of William), are Shakespeare's independent creations, not found in Thomas Lodge's *Rosalynde*, the source for the play.

(c) William M. Jones (1960) looks at the scene in which Touchstone apparently outwits Will, the rival suitor for Audrey, and argues that Shakespeare wrote the role of Will for himself, giving extra comic effect. Elisha Coles (1676) defines the connection between Audrey and tawdry.

aunt, (a) the sister of one's father or mother; in the early modern period also used more generally to mean an old woman and a **gossip**, or, in a bawdy sense, a procuress or **whore**.

(b) Shakespeare's texts use the term to draw attention to family bonds in the positive sense of affection, frequently linking it comparatively with the term **mother**, with the suggestion that the aunt takes over the maternal role. In *Richard III*, Lady **Anne** looks after the orphaned daughter of Clarence who enters the stage 'Led in the hand of her kind aunt' (*RIII* 4.1.2) and then proclaims her love to the Princes in the Tower with the words 'Their aunt I am in law, in love their **mother**' (*RIII* 4.1.24). In *Titus*, Young Lucius is assured that 'my noble aunt / Loves me as dear as e'er my mother did' (*Tit.* 4.1.22–3). Poignantly, the copy of Ovid's *Metamorphoses* that **Lavinia** chooses in order to tell of her rape, was given to Young Lucius by his mother. Marcus comments tellingly that Lavinia may have chosen it 'for love of her that's gone' (*Tit.* 4.1.42–4).

The aunt's kindness can also take a more powerful material form. Warwick assures Edward, Duke of York, that his 'kind aunt' is sending soldiers to assist the Yorkist forces (*3HVI*, 2.1.146). Lysander's confidence that he and **Hermia** will be helped by his 'widow aunt, a **dowager** / Of great revenue' (*MND* 1.1.157) who lives at the other side of the forest may have some autobiographical origin since Shakespeare's maternal aunts, the sisters of Mary **Arden** were considerably more wealthy than the Shakespeares when he married Anne **Hathaway**. Shakespeare's aunts kept their distance and did not intervene to help when John Shakespeare fell into financial difficulties. This may go some way toward explaining why aunts are pictured as dominant figures or comic butts in other parts the canon.

The aunt can be a threateningly dominant figure. Henry VI's lack of authority is clear when he vainly tries to intervene in the dispute between his **wife** and **Eleanor**, Duchess of Gloucester, with the words 'Sweet aunt, be quiet' (*2HVI* 1.3.143). In *Richard II*, the **Duchess** of York plays on the normal respect accorded to the aunt as a senior kinswoman by announcing herself to her nephew Henry IV as 'thine aunt' and then appealing, on her knees, for the life of her son. Henry IV's appeals 'Rise up, good aunt' and twice 'Good aunt, stand up' (*RII* 5.3.93, 111 and 129) show how embarrassed he is by her determination to 'walk upon my knees' (*RII* 5.3.93) until Aumerle is pardoned. In performance, the scene should have a sense of the ridiculous as the aged aunt kneels to the usurping monarch, a physical manifestation of how normal hierarchies have been inverted. The Duchess's ostentatious deference effectively subverts the spirit of Bolingbroke's kingly power in spite of her words 'a god on earth thou art' (*RII* 5.3.136).

Associations of the aunt with the comfortable world of **gossips** and storytelling are evoked in Puck's image of the 'wisest aunt telling the saddest tale' who slips from her stool to the ground. Here the aunt's authority is comically undermined in an imagined scene of rural community. The Young Lucius makes a futile attempt to create a normal family scene in *Titus Andronicus* by asking his grandfather to 'make my aunt merry with some pleasing tale' (*Tit.* 3.2.48). The bitter irony that **Lavinia** cannot play the normal role of aunt as gossip because she has lost her tongue continues into the following scene where she pursues Lucius while he is reading, frightening him with her urgency and making him believe she is mad.

Autolycus's song uses aunt in the bawdy sense celebrating the summer bird songs 'for me and my aunts / While we lie tumbling in the hay' (*WT* 4.3.11–12). In *Merry Wives of Windsor* Ford's distrust of his wife is projected onto the figure of the lecherous Falstaff disguised as the 'aunt of **Brainford**', someone Ford is convinced is an 'old cozening quean' and a **witch** (*MWW* 4.2.171–2). Aunt appears again alongside the pun on **queen** / **quean** in *Troilus and Cressida* and betrays Troilus's vulgar commodification of women when he explains that Paris's theft of **Helen** is only an exchange for Hesione, sister of Priam: 'for an old aunt, whom the Greeks held captive / He brought a Grecian queen' (*T&C* 2.2.77–8). The implied slander to Priam's sister does not overcome the power of consanguinity in the battle against the Greeks, however. The honourable Hector refuses to wound his cousin Ajax (son of Hesione) because the gods forbid him to shed the blood 'thou borrow'dst from thy mother / My sacred aunt' (*T&C* 4.5.133–4). No such compunction restrains Hamlet's tongue. He artfully combines the senses of consanguinity and sexual innuendo in his scornful reference to **Gertrude** as his 'aunt-mother' (*Ham.* 2.2.394). By marrying her husband's brother, she has literally become his aunt, but the word also betrays his disgust at her sexuality. Part of his revulsion may be attributed to the belief that such a match was incestuous, although it probably also betrays his own repressed desire.

(c) Gordon Williams (1994: 48–9) outlines uses of aunt to mean prostitute in Shakespeare and seventeenth-century literature.

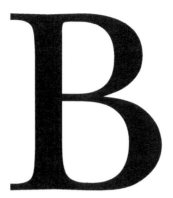

bake, (a) an activity undertaken commercially by men in early modern England but, as a domestic activity, a task undertaken by the **housewife** or a woman employed in service to a household. In smaller households that did not have an oven, women took their loaves to the bakehouse to be cooked.

(b) Women are only mentioned as subsidiary contributors to the commercial bakery in Shakespeare's texts, and often with bawdy implications since bakers' **daughter**s and wives were associated with prostitution in early modern England. Falstaff refers to bakers' wives sewing bolters, or cloths for sifting flour (*2HIV* 3.3.70) while **Ophelia**'s wandering mind refers to an apocryphal folk tale of the baker's daughter who refused Christ bread and was turned into an owl (*Ham.* 4.5.43). There are more references to domestic baking, however.

Mistress **Quickly** describes it as part of her daily routine as Dr Caius's housekeeper: 'I wash, wring, brew, bake, scour, dress meat and drink, make the beds and do all myself' (*MWW* 1.4.95–7). **Juliet**'s **nurse** is responsible for looking to the 'bak'd meats' for the impromptu Capulet wedding feast (*R&J* 4.4.5). **Cressida** picks up on the culinary metaphors of spice and salt that Pandarus introduces to tempt her appetite for the well-seasoned Troilus, but responds with a superior knowledge of baking saying that with such a mixture of good qualities he is 'a minc'd man, and then to be bak'd with no date in the pie, for then the man's date is out' (*T&C* 1.2.256–7). In an early modern version of the 'real men don't eat quiche' joke, she puns on 'date' as an essential ingredient for a proper pie, to imply that Troilus is out of date, not a proper man.

Perversion of the housewifely duty of baking is a sign of female monstrosity. Titus Andronicus models himself on **Progne**, who avenged her **sister**'s **rape** by her husband Tereus by baking his sons in a pie and serving it to him. Titus, who has been denied any lawful means to redress his wrongs vows to 'play the cook' (*Tit.* 5.2.204) and take revenge by baking Chiron and Demetrius in a pie to be consumed by their **mother Tamora**. The **weird sisters** with **beards** in *Macbeth* collect ingredients and 'in the cauldron boil and bake' a 'hell-broth' (*Mac.* 4.1.13 and 19) while Queen **Mab** 'bakes the elf-locks' or matted hair of slovenly people (*R&J* 1.4.90).

(c) Laurence (1994: 135–6) and Mendelson and Crawford (1998: 209, 265, 303–5) outline women's involvement in baking. Tracy (1966) explains the tradition of associating bakers' daughters with prostitutes, which lies behind Ophelia's lines in *Hamlet*.

Barbary, (a) the **maid** of Desdemona's mother, remembered by Desdemona in *Othello*. Her name is a version of Barbara, from the Latin for 'foreign woman' or stranger and may derive from the name for the northern coast of Africa, the Barbary States.

(b) **Desdemona** reports that Barbary was forsaken in love and died singing a song of willow, the willow garland being a characteristic accessory of the unrequited lover. Desdemona is haunted by the song, repeating snatches of it. The image of the weeping young woman singing 'willow, willow, willow' by the 'fresh streams' (*Oth.* 4.3.40–57) prophesies Desdemona's own helpless sense of desertion by Othello as well as figuring the experiences of **Ophelia** and the **Jailer's daughter**. One of the maiden dancers in Shakespeare and Fletcher's *Two Noble Kinsmen* is called 'bouncing Barbary' (*TNK* 3.5.27).

(c) Davis and Frankforter (2004: 42) explain the geographical associations of the name.

bawd, (a) a person employed in pandering to sexual debauchery; in the early modern period either a man or a woman, but increasingly applied to women as procuresses or keepers of brothels.

(b) In *Measure for Measure* both Pompey and **Mistress Overdone** are referred to as bawds, the latter known as 'Madam Mitigation' (*MM* 1.1.45) because, as keeper of a 'hot-house' or 'bawd's house' (*MM* 2.1.66 and 76) she allays sexual desire. The madam of the brothel in *Pericles*, is simply known as 'Bawd'. She and her partner 'Pander' have bought **Marina** from the pirates and employ Boult, but the Bawd is obviously in charge of running the brothel. It is she who advertises Marina's virginity and tries in vain to teach her the appropriate behaviour for a prostitute before leaving her with Lord Lysmachus, warning him 'she's not pac'd yet' (*Per.* 4.6.63). The Bawd's outrage when she hears that Marina has spoken 'holy words' to him is comic but she is also a threatening figure. She commands Boult to **rape** Marina: 'crack the glass of her **virgin**ity and make the rest malleable' (*Per.* 4.4.142–3). The Bawd simply cannot understand Marina's **chastity** as anything other than a **commodity** to attract male appetite. In the light of the imminent rape, there is something sinister in her scornful words: 'Will you not go the way of womankind? Marry, come up, my dish of chastity with rosemary and bays' (*Per.* 4.4.149–51). Although Marina persuades Boult to help her to another means of earning money (by teaching singing, dancing and **needle**work), she still has to give her income to the 'the cursed bawd' (*Per.* Gower. 5.11).

In the history plays, Mistress **Quickly** presides over a tavern which provides board and lodging for 'a dozen or fourteen gentlewomen' and is thought of as a 'bawdy house' (*HV* 2.1.32–5). Quickly fits into the stereotypical role of the madam, offering the younger **whore** Doll to Falstaff and then preparing her to meet him (*2HIV* 2.4.22–9). This is an example of the fact that older women are more likely than younger ones to be referred to as 'bawds' in Shakespeare's work. Timon of Athens rages against the 'counterfeit **matron**' whose decent clothes are only a mask to disguise the truth: 'Herself's a bawd' (*Tim.* 4.3.113–15). Mercutio teases the aged **nurse** by answering her question about the time of day with the words the 'bawdy hand of the dial is now upon the prick of noon', and then insulting her as 'a bawd, a bawd, a bawd!' luring Romeo to supper (*R&J* 2.4.112–13, 130). Since the nurse is helping to arrange what both Capulets and Montagues would regard as a transgressive **marriage** between Romeo and **Juliet**, there is an undercurrent of truth behind the insult. Imagery in the poems draws on the assumption that bawds are older women. Adonis insults the older, passionate **Venus** for her attempts to seduce him with reason, claiming that she should know better and 'reason is the bawd to lust's abuse' (*V&A* 792). **Lucrece** refers to the female personification **Night** as a

> Blind muffled bawd, dark harbor for defame,
> Grim cave of death, whisp-ring conspirator
> With close-tongu'd treason and the ravisher!
>
> (*Luc.* 768–70)

In the eyes of jealous husbands, their wives' confidantes are transformed into bawds who conspire to promote and disguise sexual debauchery. Othello interrogates **Emilia** about **Desdemona**'s behaviour and then argues that any 'simple bawd' would be practised in proclaiming her friend's innocence (*Oth.* 4.2.20–1). Similarly, the closeness between **Paulina** and **Hermione** makes Leontes refer to Paulina as a 'most intelligencing bawd' when he mistakenly believes Hermione has committed **adultery**. Paulina stoutly rejects the name, asserting her **honesty** and Leontes' ignorance.

(c) Norberg (1993) discusses the role of the bawd, *marcheuse* or *macquerelle* in the context of the criminalization of prostitution in the early modern period in Europe.

bear, (a) to carry, hold up or tolerate and, for females, to give **birth** (although this seemingly fundamental process is only listed as meaning 41 in the *Oxford English Dictionary*).

(b) Shakespeare's texts play on the literal meanings of giving birth and carrying, often with the bawdy association of supporting a man during intercourse, and the metaphorical meaning of tolerance. To begin his process of taming a **shrew**, Petruchio confidently tells **Katherina** 'Women were made to bear and so are you', meaning support a man during intercourse, bear children and, thirdly, subject herself to her husband's authority. Petruchio's words invert the gender hierarchy of Katherina's taunt that 'Asses were made to bear and so are you', sharply reminding her that women occupy the subordinate position (*Shrew* 2.1.199–200). Similar vulgar comparisons between women and **mares** who bear their male riders are made by the Dauphin in *Henry V*, giving rise to a series of bawdy puns on horse / whores (*HV* 3.7.44–67), and by **Cleopatra** whose longing for Antony makes her jealous of his war steed: 'O happy horse to bear the weight of Antony' (*A&C* 1.5.21). Physical and abstract forms of bearing again come together in *Henry IV Part II*, where, trying to mediate in a dispute between Doll **Tearsheet** and Falstaff, Mistress Quickly tells the former she must submit:

> . . . one must bear, and that must be you, you are the **weaker vessel**, as they say, the emptier vessel.
> Doll: Can a weak, empty vessel bear such a huge full hogshead? There's a whole merchant's venture of Burdeaux stuff in him . . .
>
> (*2HIV* 2.4.58–64)

Doll's complaint that if women are so weak and empty, they would be unable to support anything like the extravagance of Falstaff neatly reminds spectators that Mistress **Quickly** is the economic source that sustains Falstaff's material needs in the play. Woman's categorization as the subordinate 'weaker vessel' who must support men and bear their children is brought under critical scrutiny through the comedy.

The origin of the associations between **birth**, **sex** and female subordination is in Scripture, where **Eve**'s punishment for yielding to the serpent and tasting the fruit of the tree in Genesis is twofold: 'in sorrow shalt thou bring forth children and thy desire shall be to thy husband, and he shall rule over thee' (Gen. 3.16). In the prayers for childbirth in Thomas Bentley's *The Fift Lampe of Virginitie*, women's pain in labour is explained as a result of Eve's sin: 'Ease, O Lord, the paines which thou most righteouslie hast put upon hir, and all women, for the sinne and disobedience of our grand-mother Eve' (Bentley 1582: 126). Egeus's memory of his wife **Aemilia**'s pregnancy 'almost fainting under / The pleasing punishment that women bear' (*Err.* 1.1.45–6) recalls the biblical judgement. **Juliet** in *Measure for Measure* is catechized in similar terms by the Duke, disguised as a friar, when she is pregnant by Claudio:

> Duke: Repent you, fair one, of the sin you carry?
> Juliet: I do; and bear the sin most patiently
>
> (*MM* 2.3.19–20)

Even though their sin was mutually committed, for Juliet, as for Eve, the wages of sin are 'of heavier kind', literally in that she is carrying the baby, and culturally in that she is apparently more guilty than the man (*MM* 2.3.28). In cases of **rape**, the injustice of woman's burden of suffering is felt even more acutely. Once Tarquin has raped **Lucrece**, 'She bears the load of lust he left behind' (*Luc.* 734), and, regardless of whether she is physically pregnant, the weight of this pollution drives her to suicide.

A notable, more positive exception to the general rule is the case of Lady

Faulconbridge in *King John*, who has committed **adultery** with Richard Cœur de Lion, the results of which are a cause of celebration rather than shame. 'Some sins do bear their privilege on earth / And so doth yours' explains their son (*KJ* 1.1.261–2). The play demonstrates that her dutiful submission to the King has indeed borne valuable fruit when the Bastard proves largely responsible for defeating a foreign invasion. The twin senses of 'to bear' as holding up and giving birth are used in a patriotic context by the banished Bolingbroke who, in order to construct himself as a loyal English subject, addresses the native soil of **England** as 'my **mother** and my **nurse** that bears me yet' (*RII* 1.3.307).

In the Sonnets, husbandry is a much more exclusively male activity. Regeneration of the young man's qualities is the priority while the women who might bear his children are reduced to anonymous vegetable matter in the lines: 'Many maiden gardens yet unset / With virtuous wish would bear your living **flowers**' (*Son.* 16.6–7). In Sonnet 59, literary production is celebrated by the poet as a substitute for bearing children but with strong reservations about the dangers of striving too hard to produce something original. The poet fears that men's brains can be beguiled by not paying attention to the older ideas of **beauty** and 'laboring for invention bear amiss / The second burthen of a former child' (*Son.* 59 2–4). Such rhetorical appropriations of the processes of labour or travail, and **birth** by male speakers are frequent in the canon.

For women, an introduction to intercourse and bearing the weight of a man invariably carries additional associations with childbirth. Mercutio conjures fantasies of Queen **Mab** the fairies' **midwife**, who sends dreams of lovers

> when **maid**s lie on their backs,
> That presses them and learns them how to bear,
> Making them women of good carriage.
>
> (*R&J* 1.4.92–4)

The Old **Lady** teases **Anne** Bullen with the thought of being King Henry's mistress and a duchess, if not a queen. 'Have you limbs / To bear that load of title? (*HVIII* 2.3.38–9), she asks, and quickly follows up the idea of limbs for childbearing with the taunt, 'If your back / Cannot vouchsafe this burthen, 'tis too weak / Ever to get a boy' (*HVIII* 2.3.42–4). When the androgynous figure of the **boy actor** addresses female spectators with the words, 'I charge you women, for the love you bear to men' (*AYLI* Epilogue. 13), the word is charged with multiple significations of sexual pleasure and the consequences of pregnancy and cultural submission into the bargain.

(c) Thomas Bentley's *The Fift Lampe of Virginitie* (1582) illustrates contemporary ideas about birth as the legacy of Eve. Bicks (2003), Krier (2001) and Laoutaris (2008) offer fine analyses of the ways pregnancy was represented in early modern England. *See* entries on **birth** and **womb** for further reading.

beard, (a) growth of hair upon the face, a feature marking the physical coming of age of a man or boy actor.

(b) As **Beatrice** jokes, 'he that hath no beard is less than a man' (*MAdo* 2.1.37). Growth of facial hair was equated with the production of semen and thus understood as a mark of male fertility in early modern England. The beardless face, along with a voice that had not broken, was shorthand for a **boy actor**'s suitability to play the woman's part. Flute complains 'Let me not play a woman; I have a beard coming' (*MND* 1.2.47–8). References to beards, or lack of them, in relation to cross-dressed heroines draw attention to both female character and boy actor, and the play on ambiguities of gender and sexual attraction set up by such figures. The androgynous boy actor who plays **Rosalind** in *As You Like It* tells the men in the audience 'If I were a woman I would kiss as many of you as had beards that pleased me' (*AYLI* Epilogue. 18–19). Lack of a beard is a cause of suspicion when Feste tells the disguised **Viola** 'Now Jove in his next commodity of hair, send thee a beard.' Cesario / Viola's aside, 'I tell thee I am almost sick for one but I would not have it grow on my chin' (*TN* 3.1.44–8) suggests both his/her desire for Orsino and, either that she does not wish to have facial hair like an old woman or more bawdily – if the actor emphasizes the word 'chin' – s/he refers to the growth of pubic hair. The brief mention of women's growth of facial hair in early modern texts is seen as a mark of monstrosity. In Shakespeare, it often marks the supposedly inappropriate assumption of authority. In *Macbeth*, Banquo tells the **weird sisters** 'You should be women, / And yet your beards forbid me to interpret / That you are so' (*Mac.* 1.3.45). **Goneril**'s inappropriate assumption of her father's authority is mocked by Lear in his madness when he calls Gloucester 'Goneril with a white beard' (*KL* 4.6.96) and Cornwall's servant tells **Regan**, 'If you did wear a beard upon your chin / I'ld shake it' (*KL* 3.7.76).

(c) Fisher (2001) analyses the beard as a sign of masculinity. *See also* entries on **boy actor** and **youth**.

Beatrice, (a) the witty heroine in *Much Ado About Nothing* whose name means the 'one who blesses'.

(b) Beatrice is a character not found in any of Shakespeare's possible sources for the play, apart from Luigi Pasqualigo's Italian play *Il Fedele* (1579), which has a witty maid called Beatrice (Bullough Vol. II 1958: 68). The name echoes the semi-divine heroine of Dante's *Divine Comedy*, and links Beatrice to Benedick, or '*benedictus*', he who is blessed, as Margaret teases (3.4.73–8). Beatrice is an orphan and, on the surface, a fiercely independent character who rejects marriage since it entails the subjection of **woman**:

> Would it not grieve a woman to be overmaster'd with a piece of valiant dust? to make an account of her life to a clod of wayward marl? . . . Adam's sons are my brethren, and truly I hold it a sin to match in my kinred.
>
> (2.1.60–5)

Such lines give an impression of Beatrice as a proto-feminist thinker who sees herself as men's equal. She is undoubtedly clever, observant and outspoken, gaining a reputation as 'curst' for her sharp, **shrew**ish **tongue** (2.1.19–20). Benedick refers to her as '**Lady** Disdain' (1.1.118) and 'Lady Tongue' (2.1.275) but her uncle Leonato recognizes her ability to 'apprehend passing shrewdly' or see things as they are (2.1.82). In describing her determination to remain unmarried and **lead apes in hell**, the proverbial fate of **spinster**s, she jokes that the devil rejects her saying, '"Get you to heaven, Beatrice, get you to heaven"' (2.1.45–6), a witty allusion to her namesake, the heroine of *The Divine Comedy*, who leads Dante to paradise. For all her joking, Shakespeare's Beatrice is no stranger to sadness, gently correcting Don Pedro's suggestion that she was 'born in a merry hour' by pointing out that 'my mother cried', a reference to the pain of **birth** and possibly a death that made Beatrice an orphan (2.1.334). There are hints in the play that, underneath the assertive exterior, she has suffered from a previous rejection of her love by Benedick who won her heart with false dice (2.2.281–2). When Don Pedro and her cousin **Hero** plot to trick her into believing that Benedick loves her and criticize her for being proud and scornful, her previous assertions of female equality collapse: 'maiden pride, adieu', and she looks forward to taming her wild heart to Benedick's loving hand, implicitly adopting a position of subjection in marriage (3.1.108–12). Beatrice is fiercely loyal to her younger cousin Hero who is rejected by Claudio on their wedding morning. This confirms Beatrice's earlier belief that men, even Benedick, are not to be trusted. She longs to be a man so that she can defend Hero herself. Her charged demand to Benedick to 'Kill Claudio' (4.1.289) is a test of the sincerity of Benedick's love for her this second time round. When he does take up the challenge, Beatrice's skill with language is modified from railing bitterly against Benedick to writing a sonnet declaring her affection, and jesting with him, though her tongue, a symbol of female assertiveness, is still a threat and is silenced with a kiss: 'Peace I will stop your mouth' (5.1.96).

(c) Bullough (Vol. II 1958: pp. 68–70), notes the name of the servant called Beatrice in *Il Fedele*, translated by Munday. Anna Jameson, the Victorian pioneer of studies of Shakespeare's women, measures the character quite unsympathetically from the point of view of Victorian feminine propriety in 1858, and without any acknowledgement of Beatrice's thinly disguised sense of injury at Benedick's earlier rejection (Jameson 2005: 100–17). Nevertheless, Jameson does acknowledge a reading '*against the grain*' (ibid.: 113), long before Eagleton (1975) or Kate Millet (1970) identified this strategy. Findlay (2004) discusses Beatrice as a role that invites spectators and readers to identify the circulation of proto-feminist ideas in early modern England. Page (1935a) analyses Beatrice's characterization as Lady Disdain while McGrady (1993) analyses Hero's reshaping of Beatrice in the description of her qualities in the overhearing scene.

beauty, (a) a quality or combination of qualities that give pleasure to the senses, especially the sense of sight. Beauty can also be understood in a non-material sense, as quality or qualities giving pleasure to the intellect or the spirit of the beholder. Both physical and inward beauty are a manifestation of the divine in the early modern period.

(b) Physical beauty is predominantly seen through the eyes of men in Shakespeare's texts, although **Venus**'s praise of Adonis's beauty which 'set / Gloss on the rose, smell to the violet' is a notable exception (*V&A* 935–6). Adonis emphasizes the gender inversion when he complains that love has been usurped by Lust, a predatory male personification (implicitly Venus) who 'hath fed / Upon fresh beauty, blotting it with blame' (*V&A* 794–6). Physical beauty invariably has considerable power in both dramatic and non-dramatic texts. The truth 'Beauty itself doth of itself persuade / The eyes of men without an orator' (*Luc.* 29–30) is borne out in scenes where male characters react extravagantly to a beautiful female character's appearance with little exchange of dialogue. The action of the battle against the French in *Henry VI Part I*, for example, takes an unexpected turn when Suffolk captures **Margaret** of Anjou as a prisoner:

> Suffolk: Be what thou wilt, thou art my prisoner.
> *Gazes on her*
> O fairest beauty, do not fear nor fly,
> For I will touch thee but with reverend hands.
> I kiss these fingers for eternal **peace**,
> And lay them gently on thy tender side.
> Who art thou? say, that I may honor thee.
> (*1HVI* 5.3.45–50)

Suffolk's infatuation with Margaret leads to his proposal that she should become **Queen** of England and marry Henry VI. 'She's beautiful and therefore to be woo'd' (*1HVI* 5.3.77) he determines, even though he is married. Far from bringing any **dowry**, the match proves disastrous to English interests: the surrender of the hard-won territories of Anjou and Maine. Henry, who claims he has found a 'world of blessings' in her 'beauteous face' (*2HVI* 1.1.21), learns to his cost this is far from the truth. The physical beauty of the on-stage figure of **Anne** Bullen transfixes Henry VIII with equally significant consequences. 'O Beauty, / Till now I never knew thee' he exclaims (*HVIII* 1.4.75–6), and the Lord Chamberlain quickly recognizes that her looks and honour 'have caught the King' (*HVIII* 2.3.77). Anne's beauty is corporeal in comparison to the spiritual beauty and goodness of Queen **Katherine**. At Anne's coronation she exhibits 'The beauty of her person to the people' provoking a frenzied reaction, charged with sexual energy, from the crowd of men and women (*HVIII* 4.1.67–79). In the wooing scenes of *Edward III* that have been ascribed to Shakespeare, the physical beauty of the **Countess** of Salisbury is announced as a positive power that can subdue tyrants as the 'pernicious winds / Hath sullied, wither'd, overcast and done' a May blossom (*EIII* 2.1.95–7). This proves to be the case. King Edward is instantly reduced to 'doting admiration' (*EIII* 2.1.96), referring to her as 'the queen of beauty's queen' (*EIII* 2.1.57). The Countess's behaviour demonstrates the early modern idea that female physical beauty is a reflection of inner, spiritual goodness (deriving from neo-platonic texts like Castiglione's *The Courtier*, and Dante's *Divine Comedy*). She responds by refusing his offers of love with wise and virtuous words:

> Whether is her beauty by her words divine,
> Or are her words sweet chaplains to her beauty?
> Like as a wind doth beautify a sail,
> And as a sail becomes the unseen wind,
> So do her words her beauties, beauty words.
>
> (*EIII* 2.1.277–81)

The plot traces the moral complexity facing Edward over whether to insist on his *droit de seigneur*, or sovereign right to enjoy her. She points out the perversity of her beauty becoming potentially destructive 'O, perjur'd beauty' (*EIII* 2.2.163), in proposing that only after the murder of her husband and Edward's Queen (and her own suicide), would she yield to him. This leads him to recognize that his desire is at fault, so her beauty and goodness ultimately prove to be a morally educative force.

The powerful on-stage presence of female beauty is satirized in *Troilus and Cressida* where the appearance of **Helen** of Troy, the face 'that launch'd above a thousand ships' (*T&C* 2.2.82) is exaggeratedly delayed and over-anticipated. A servant introduces her as 'the mortal **Venus**, the heart-blood of beauty, love's immortal soul' but Pandarus's question 'Who, my cousin **Cressida**?' comically deflates the grand idea that beauty resides in one woman (*T&C* 3.2.32–4). Venus, who tells Adonis that 'My beauty as the spring doth yearly grow' (*V&A* 141) is an unattractively dominant character in *Venus and Adonis*, so the comparison of Helen to 'the mortal Venus' would probably have had an additional satiric twist for those who knew the poem, reprinted 15 times after the first quarto of 1593. Sonnet 53 argues that Helen of Troy is a poor copy of the young man's beauty: 'On Helen's cheek all art of beauty set / And you in Grecian tires are painted new' (*Son.* 53.7–8). Such lines remind us of the confidence dramatists must have had in **boy actor**s to personate beautiful women convincingly in scenes like those from *Henry VI Part I*, *Henry VIII* and *Edward III*.

Although women's use of **masks** lends a fetishistic aspect to beauty's erotic attraction, physical beauty is always dependent on external value. As Achilles notes, 'The beauty that is borne here in the face / The bearer knows not, but commends itself / To others' eyes' (*T&C* 3.3.103–5). Female beauty frequently causes suspicion from those not immediately affected by it. Speed believes that **Silvia**'s beauty is constructed either from painting (make up), or from the biased viewpoint of Valentine that has 'deform'd' her image (*TGV* 2.1.55–6, 63). Claudio's praise of diminutive **Hero**'s beauty and Benedick's opinion that the taller Beatrice 'exceeds her as much in beauty as the first of May doth the last of December' (*MAdo* 1.1.194) comically advertise that beauty is in the eye of the beholder, as does Demetrius and Lysander's changing affections for the tall **Helena** and the smaller **Hermia** (*MND* 3.2). Theseus's belief that a lover 'sees Helen's beauty in a brow of Egypt' (*MND* 5.1.11) is amply demonstrated in *Love's Labour's Lost* where Berowne's love for the dark lady **Rosaline** dramatizes the unconventional redefinition of beauty:

> Where is a book
> That I may swear beauty doth beauty lack,
> If that she learn not of her eye to look:
> No face is fair that is not full so black.'
>
> (*LLL* 4.3.246–9)

Sonnets to the **Dark Lady** offer an extended non-dramatic rewriting of beauty, where 'Beauty herself is black' (*Son.* 132.13).

Beauty is the first in a list of attributes looked for in a wife, being an expression of goodness; and **Thaisa**'s father in *Pericles* introduces her to her suitors as 'beauty's child, whom nature gat / For men to see and, seeing, wonder at' (*Per.* 2.2.6–7). Beauty may not be sufficient to secure a match, however, as Silvia's angry father assumes when he declares 'Let her beauty be her **wedding**-dow'r' (*TGV* 2.1.78) and as Mæcenas in *Antony and Cleopatra* acknowledges. Only 'if beauty, wisdom, modesty can settle / The heart of Antony' will **Octavia** and her **dowry** be a 'blessed lottery' (*A&C* 2.2.240–1). In *King John*, the Dauphin's hunt for a **bride** is a knightly quest for beauty, virtue and noble birth equal to his own. He is encouraged to find all three in a political match with Lady **Blanch** (*KJ* 2.1.432) but the text satirizes the narcissistic quality of his wooing when he claims he looked at her face and 'beheld myself / Drawn in the flattering table of her eye' (*KJ* 2.1.496). Even more narcissistically, women's beauty becomes a source of male bonding and competition in *Cymbeline*, where it forms the basis of Iachimo's plot (*Cym.* 5.2.161–8).

Petruchio inverts the convention of beauty being the first item on the suitor's shopping list by provocatively telling the shrewish **Katherina**

> Hearing thy mildness prais'd in every town
> Thy virtues spoke of and thy beauty sounded,
> Yet not so deeply as to thee belongs . . .
> Myself am moved to woo thee for a wife
>
> (*Shrew* 2.1.191–4)

Katherina's physical beauty has a significant effect on the self-declared fortune hunter. At the end of the interview in which she has shown no mildness and none of the conventional womanly virtues, her beauty still remains:

> For by this light whereby I see thy beauty
> Thy beauty that doth make me like thee well,
> Thou must be married to no man but me.
>
> (*Shrew* 2.1.273–5)

Arguably, Petruchio now perceives beauty in Katherina's wit as well as in her appearance. If so, his viewpoint contrasts with the superficial judgement of **Bianca** by Lucentio whose stare identifies 'such beauty in her face' (*Shrew* 1.1.167) to make her an immediate prospect for **marriage**. The play's discussion of beauty extends to the ridiculous challenge that Petruchio makes to view the old man Vincentio as a fair young woman: 'What stars do spangle heaven with such beauty / As those two eyes become that heavenly face?' and to embrace her 'for her beauty's sake' (*Shrew* 4.5.31–2, 34). Katherina accepts his idiosyncratic definition of beauty and, by the end of the play, says that female beauty is an inner quality of wifely co-operation, telling Bianca and the widow that angry behaviour 'blots thy beauty as frosts do bite the meads' (*Shrew* 5.2.139).

Whether this is Katherina's own opinion or one dictated by an oppressive patriarchal regime and ventriloquized is not clear. A few female characters have space to comment on beauty, although, as the case of Viola shows, their gaze is male, in that it tends to value what is perceived according to male ideas of beauty. The play makes fun of this exclusive viewpoint. **Viola**, disguised as Cesario, ventriloquizes Orsino's perception of **Olivia** as a 'Most radiant, exquisite and unmatchable beauty –' (*TN* 1.5.170). Since Olivia and her gentlewoman have both **veil**ed their faces and Viola cannot tell which is Olivia the vagueness of the courtly praise causes humour. Viola's curiosity about her rival's appearance produces a more heartfelt but equally conventional definition of female beauty as a perfect mixture of red and white: ''Tis beauty truly blent whose red and white / Nature's own sweet and cunning hand laid on' (*TN* 1.5.239–40), and Olivia goes on to mock the **blazon** in which female body parts are itemised for praise of female beauty (*TN* 1.5.244–9). Even the young Florizel commodifies Perdita as 'a piece of beauty' (*TN* 4.3.32). Sonnet 127 argues that the courtly tradition has devalued what it seeks to praise: 'Sweet beauty hath no name, no holy bow'r / But is profan'd, if not lives in disgrace' (*Son.* 127.7–8).

The French **Princess** in *Love's Labour's Lost* summarizes female dislike of the flamboyant courtly tradition most succinctly in her words

> . . . my beauty, though but mean
> Needs not the painted flourish of your praise:
> Beauty is bought by judgment of the eye,
> Not utter'd by base sale of chapmen's tongues.
> (*LLL* 2.1.13–16)

The anti-blazon of Sonnet 130 is the most extreme example of its rejection. Not surprisingly female characters mistrust compliments to their beauty, often suspecting, quite rightly, that these have been applied to other mistresses. Proteus complains that when he commends Silvia's beauty, 'she bids me think how I have been foresworn', by shifting his praise from Julia (*TGV* 4.2.9–10). **Paulina** mocks a courtier who wonders at Perdita by quoting his original praise of Hermione's beauty '"She had not been, / Nor was to be equalled"' (*WT* 5.2.100–1). **Margaret** teases Benedick by promising to bring him to talk to Beatrice but only if he will 'then write a sonnet in praise of my beauty' (*MAdo* 5.2.4–5). Older women in Shakespeare are acutely aware that 'beauty's a flower' (*TN* 1.5.53), an image of transience that comes from Isiah 28.1. Mistress **Page** wonders 'have I scaped love-letters in the holiday-time of my beauty' only to receive them now (*MWW* 2.1.2) while **Adriana** is deeply sad that she can no longer attract her husband: 'Hath homely age th' alluring beauty took / From my poor cheek' (*Err.* 2.1.89–90). More positively, Portia looks back to her 'once commended beauty' as a step to the love and vows that made her and Brutus one, and have given her the right to assume he will confide in her (*JC* 2.1.271).

The platonic idea that physical beauty, most perfectly realized in a young man, is a reflection of the divine, had been adapted by the early modern period to elevate female beauty as a means to apprehend God. Shakespeare's sonnets and *Venus and Adonis* still idealize young male beauty in the tradition of Plato's *Symposium*, but do so nostalgically. The young man of the sonnets shows 'false Art when beauty was of yore' (*Son.* 68.13–14), while Adonis is lamented since 'true-sweet beauty liv'd and died with him' (*V&A* 1080). The 'pure and princely beauty' of Arthur (*KJ* 4.3.35) or the Princes in the Tower (*KJ* 4.3.13) is also short-lived. The argument (set out most fully in Castiglione's *The Courtier*), that apprehension of female beauty is the first step on a ladder to reach virtue and abstract, divine beauty, lies behind Berowne's opinion that women's faces are 'the ground of study's excellence' (*LLL* 4.3.295–7), and that no author in the world 'Teaches such beauty as a woman's eye?' (*LLL* 4.3.308–9). The correspondence between woman's external beauty and goodness informs the lyric to Silvia 'Is she kind as she is fair? / For beauty lives with kindness' (*TGV* 4.1.44–5) and gives a moral imperative to the lover's pleas to a mistress to preserve her beauty by procreation: 'For beauty starv'd with her severity / Cuts beauty off from all posterity' (*R&J* 1.1.219–20). This argument is, of course, adapted at much greater length to the young man of the Sonnets.

Desdemona and **Juliet**'s beauty is perceived as a reflection of the divine. Cassio implicitly compares the former to Christ calming the waters since the storms at sea have abated 'as having sense of beauty' in the 'divine Desdemona' on board ship (*Oth.* 2.1.71). Juliet is 'Beauty too rich for use, for earth too dear!' (*R&J* 1.5.47) and in the final scene her beauty takes on a transcendent quality. It is apparently unconquered by death, reigning still in her lips and cheeks and making 'This vault a feasting presence, full of light' (*R&J* 5.1.85–6).

A sense of slippage between the alliance of physical beauty and inner goodness in women is revealed in Posthumus's assertion that if Imogen is not the best in all ways, she would be like a **whore**:

> . . . let her beauty
> Look through a casement to allure false hearts
> And be false with them.
>
> (*Cym.* 2.4.34)

Female infidelity shatters the idea that physical beauty is a reflection of virtue. Troilus's hope that in Cressida's constancy he will see the perpetuation of a spiritual beauty 'Outliving beauties outward, with a mind / That doth renew swifter than blood decays' (*T&C* 3.1.162–3) is doomed in the play. Her betrayal splits apart his method for understanding the world around him. 'If beauty have a soul, this is not she' (*T&C* 5.2.138), he declares, meaning that he can't believe it is Cressida; that, if so, Cressida is no longer the epitomy of inner beauty; and, even more disturbingly, that outward beauty is not matched by a 'soul' of inner beauty. Claudio suffers the same disillusionment, declaring 'Beauty is a witch / Against whose charms faith melteth into blood' (*MAdo* 2.1.179–80), a proverb that he soon comes to fulfil himself in losing trust in Hero. He determines to make his eyes look differently in future to 'turn all beauty into thoughts of harm' and see the corruption beneath (*MAdo* 4.1.107).

The dangers female beauty presents to men lead to identifications with **witch**craft again in *The Winter's Tale* (4.1.425–6), where **Perdita** makes Florizel forget his duties as Polixenes's son and heir and in the figure of **Cleopatra** where 'witchcraft join[s] with beauty' (*A&C* 2.1.22). The beauty of Antiochus's **daughter** in Pericles is a temptation which lures many princes to their deaths (*Per.* Gower. 1.31). Beauty deforms men by changing their behaviour, Berowne apologizes (*LLL* 5.2.756–7), making them behave oddly. According to the angry Romeo, Juliet's beauty effeminizes him (*R&J* 3.1.110). Othello too fears that, if he speaks to her, Desdemona's 'body and her beauty' will distract him from his principle or 'cause' of killing a woman who will corrupt more men (*Oth.* 4.1.205–6 and 5.2.1–6).

It is an even more immediate danger to women since, as **Rosalind** says, 'Beauty provoketh thieves sooner than gold' (*AYLI* 1.3.110). Laertes believes that the most chaste young woman courts danger 'If she unmask her beauty to the **moon**' (*Ham.* 1.3.37) and Lucrece is witness to this. After she has been **rape**d, she can no longer see the virtuous **wife** she was in her mirror which has 'shiver'd all the beauty of my glass / That I can no more see what once I was' (*Luc.* 1763). Beauty is also a moral danger to women. The Duke in *Measure for Measure* believes 'the goodness that is cheap in beauty makes beauty brief in goodness' (*MM* 3.1.180–2), and York claims ''Tis beauty that doth oft make women proud (*3HVI* 1.4.128). Hamlet argues that, far from being an external sign of goodness, beauty corrupts woman's **honest**y or **chastity**:

> Hamlet: . . . if you be but **honest** and fair [your honesty] should admit no
> discourse to your beauty.
> Ophelia: Could beauty, my lord, have better commerce than with
> honesty?
> Hamlet: Ay, truly, for the power of beauty will sooner transform honesty
> from what it is to a **bawd** than the force of honesty can translate beauty
> into his likeness. This was sometime a paradox, but now the time gives
> it proof.
>
> (*Ham.* 3.1.106–14)

Honesty here is chastity and Touchstone, in licentious mood, relies on the home truth that unattractive women are more likely to be chaste since 'honesty coupled to beauty is to have honey a sauce to sugar' (*AYLI* 3.3.30–1). Bassanio shares the same idea: that beauty, like gold, is dangerously self-destructive, producing wantonness or 'Making them lightest that wear most of it' (*Mer.* 3.2.88–91) This is a long way from the lightness that Juliet's beauty brings into the Capulet tomb.

(c) Sara F. Matthews Grieco (1993) and Veronique Nahoum-Grappe (1993) both give generalized overviews of early modern European ideas of female beauty. Kelso (1956: 124–36) discusses the influence of *The Book of the Courtier*, N. H. Keeble (1994: 54–70) reprints a range of extracts from seventeenth-century texts in English about female beauty. Synnott (1989) concentrates on the face and gives an excellent, detailed account of the correlation between beauty and goodness from classical and early church writing through to the early modern period and beyond. Madeleine Doran (1976) discusses beauty as part of the courtly love tradition.

beldam, (a) grandmother, a father or mother's mother, or, more generally, a physically aged woman or **matron**. In the sixteenth century the term was often used to address nurses or, more depreciatively, to indicate a furious or disorderly woman, a **hag** or a **witch**.
(b) The sense of an aged matriarchal figure is present in *The Rape of Lucrece*, where time will 'show the beldame daughters of her daughter' (*Luc.* 953), and where **Lucrece** models her woe on that of 'Time's ruin' (*Luc.* 1451): the wrinkled, care-worn 'beldame' **Hecuba** (*Luc.* 1458). Physical decay and sinister connotations of prophecy and threat combine in Shakespeare's uses of the word. When five moons are seen in the sky following Prince Arthur's death in *King John*, the wrinkled 'old men and beldames in the streets / Do prophesy upon it dangerously' (*KJ* 4.2.185–6). **Margery**, or '**Mother** Jordan', the supposed witch in *Henry VI Part II*, is referred to as 'beldam' (*2HVI* 1.4.10 and 1.4.42). The word carries associations of subversion and disorderly behaviour when used by **Hecate**, who calls the **weird sisters** 'beldams' for being 'saucy and overbold' in engaging in prophecy with Macbeth (*Mac.* 3.5.2–3). The term's links with prophecy are mocked in *Henry IV Part I*, where the 'beldame **earth**' (*1HIV* 3.1.31) is a grotesquely corporeal figure. Hotspur mocks Glendower's extravagant claims of natural portents at his birth, saying that the 'strange eruptions' are a case of the old woman (earth) suffering from colic or wind trapped in her womb, causing earthquakes that topple 'Steeples and moss-grown towers' (*1HIV* 3.1.26–31).

Bellona, (a) the Roman goddess of war, a virgin.
(b) The appearance of a Roman goddess in the Greek setting of *Two Noble Kinsmen* is apparently not an issue for Shakespeare or Fletcher since Theseus suggests the widows pray to 'the helmeted Bellona' (*TNK* 1.1.75) and Emilia promises to make offerings to 'great Bellona' to assure success for Theseus (*TNK* 1.3.13). Hotspur's passion for fighting is reflected in his depiction of her as a 'fire-eyed maid of smoky war / All hot and bleeding' hungry for sacrifices (*1HIV* 4.1.114–15). Further erotic resonances are found in *Macbeth* where she is the metaphorical bride of Macbeth. The phrase 'Bellona's bridegroom' (*Mac.* 1.2.54) effectively captures the essence of Macbeth's expertise as a soldier rather than a politician.

belly, (a) normally the front part of the human body between the breast and the thighs but in relation to women, an alternative name for the **womb**.

34

(b) 'Belly' is only used of women in Shakespeare's texts with reference to pregnancy out of wedlock. **Jaquenetta** is 'quick; the child brags in her belly already' (*LLL* 5.2.676). **Celia** jokes bawdily with **Rosalind** that, by drinking her fill of Orlando 'you may put a man in your belly' (*AYLI* 3.2.115), meaning to conceive a male child. Leontes, mistakenly suspecting **Hermione** of adultery, concludes there is 'no barricado for a belly', or fortification to protect chastity on this 'bawdy planet' (*WT* 1.2.201–4). **Cressida** claims she will lie on her back 'to defend my belly' but fears that it will 'swell past hiding' (*T&C* 1.2.260 and 269). Lorenzo chastises Launcelot Gobbo for 'getting up the Negro's belly; the Moor is with child by you' (*Mer.* 3.5.38–9). Falstaff draws a parallel between womb and belly in using the term to mean a womb full of illegitimate voices, in a comic equivalent to Lear's 'hysterica passio' or rising sorrow (*KL* 1.4.56–8). He declares 'I have a whole school of tongues in this belly of mine, and not a tongue of them all speaks any word but my name . . . My womb, my womb, my womb undoes me' (*2HIV* 4.3.18–22).
(c) Keeble (1994: 26). *See also* **womb**.

betrothal, (a) an engagement or pledge to be married, also known as **hand**-fasting and affiance and contract. Betrothal in early modern England transformed successful courtship into a contract between the man and woman to marry. Social practices varied but it was usually a ritual performance that involved a spoken pledge expressing either immediate, indissoluble commitment to marry, a promise of future action, or a conditional promise using the words 'if' or 'when'. Exchanges of rings were a material token of the vows of commitment. In cases of a formal contract where the parties were not both present, a **jewel** or **ring** might be sent via a proxy. The sexual behaviour of contracted couples varied considerably although it was widely thought acceptable to risk chastity in anticipation of **marriage**.
(b) The gap of time between betrothal and marriage is imagined spatially in Sonnet 56 where 'two contracted new' meet daily on the shores of an ocean and look across in longing for their union (*Son.* 56.10). The gap is exploited for dramatic effect in Shakespeare's plots. *Much Ado About Nothing* stages a formal, public betrothal between Claudio and **Hero** and subsequently dramatizes what can go wrong in between that ceremony and marriage. The ritual aspect is emphasized by **Beatrice**'s prompt: 'Speak, Count, 'tis your cue' (*MAdo* 2.1.305); by his ritualized language: 'Lady, as you are mine, I am yours. I give away myself and dote upon the exchange', followed by another prompt from Beatrice to Hero: 'Speak, cousin, or (if you cannot), stop his mouth with a kiss.' (*MAdo* 2.1.308–11). The couple's need for prompting marks an emotional gap that Don John's plot builds on easily, throwing the **wedding** into disorder and the play into potential tragedy. The form of the second betrothal allows Claudio to prove that he has matured and repented for his lack of faith in Hero's chastity. He must take the **veil**ed figure by the **hand** (the ritual gesture of **hand**-fasting) on trust and swear to her before the Friar, 'I am your husband if you like of me' before she will answer him and reveal herself as his 'other **wife**' (*MAdo* 5.2.56–61).

Rosalind comments that time seems to travel painfully slowly 'with a young maid between the contract of her marriage and the day it is solemnized' (*AYLI* 3.2.313–7). **Helena** in *All's Well That Ends Well* certainly experiences the frustration of a long and difficult delay between the formal contract with Bertram in Act 2 Scene 3, their **wedding** ceremony that evening, and the final consummation of their marriage (*AWW* 3.2.173–8). Bertram's reluctance makes the betrothal an excruciatingly embarrassing event, not only for Helena but for the King too. The scene's effectiveness relies on disruption of the hand-fasting ritual: Bertram's protest 'I cannot love her, nor will strive to do't' (2.3.144) and his refusal to offer his hand. Helena asks the King to 'Let the rest go', but he insists:

> My **honour**'s at the stake, which, to defeat,
> I must produce my power. Here, take her **hand**
> Proud, scornful boy, unworthy this good **gift**
>
> (2.3.149–51)

Even by Act 5, all may not end well. The couple are re-matched in a ritual of **ring** giving initiated by **Helena** who returns Bertram's ring in fulfilment of the terms he set down in his letter. Whether he responds by offering her his hand is unclear, and it is notable that his vow of love is still conditional: 'If she, my liege, can make me know this clearly / I'll love her dearly, ever, ever dearly' (*AWW* 5.3.315–6).

The obligations of a betrothal are indicated in Falstaff's view that 'contracted bachelors, such as had been ask'd twice on the banes' or marriage banns in church, would not be willing to join the army (*1HIV* 4.1.16–17). Nevertheless, betrothal did not formally entitle couples to live together as man and wife, a fact that drives the plot of *Measure for Measure*. Claudio and **Juliet**'s sexual relationship follows a 'true contract' which is conditional: only the **dowry** and formal church ceremony wanting to complete the marriage (*MM* 1.2.145–53). Angelo's strict enforcement of the law against sex outside wedlock transforms what was often acceptable practice for betrothed couples into a crime. Clandestine betrothal can be a form of agency for Shakespeare's female characters, as with Juliet's declaration of her true love's vow to Romeo, in spite of the fact she thinks 'this contract to-night' is 'too rash, too unadvis'd, too sudden' (*R&J* 2.2.117). Her second betrothal to Paris is unconventional in that she is absent, supposedly grieving for her cousin's death. Perversely, the father whose 'care hath been / To have her matched' (*R&J* 3.5.177–8) drives the action towards its tragic ending, suggesting that the play took a more liberal position in the 1590s' debate over choice in marriage. **Olivia**'s sudden betrothal to Sebastian appears to produce a happier outcome to women's agency in *Twelfth Night*. Although private, this is witnessed by a priest and follows all the ritual practices as he reports:

> A contract of eternal bond of love,
> Confirm'd by mutual joinder of your hands,
> Attested by the holy close of lips,
> Strengthened by interchangement of your rings,

And all the ceremony of this compact
Seal'd in my function, by my testimony.

(TN 5.1.156–61)

Sebastian's teasing reminder that Olivia would have been 'contracted to a **maid**' and assurance that 'you are betroth'd both to a maid and man' (*TN* 5.1.261–4) exploit the gap between betrothal and marriage in a much more positive way than Shakespeare's other plays. He gives spectators an important reminder that the marriages are deferred beyond the end of the performance and that, meanwhile, the ambiguities about gender and sexual orientation, the 'what you will' of the title, can be kept alive and held in suspense to serve the desires of everyone on and off stage.

Secret betrothals could be a risk when it involved deceiving a parent or parents. In *The Winter's Tale* Florizel takes **Perdita**'s hand and pledges his love and she returns it. The request for witnesses to the betrothal meets with approval from the Old Shepherd who says 'Come, your hand / And, daughter, yours' (*WT* 4.4.390–1) but before he can join their hands, Polixenes rejects the invitation to 'Mark our contract' by removing his disguise with the words 'Mark your divorce, young sir' (*WT* 4.4.417). The couple are left in limbo; Perdita fears the heavens 'will not have / Our contract celebrated' (*WT* 5.1.203–4) until her identity is revealed and they are welcomed as 'contracted / Heirs of your kingdoms' (*WT* 5.3.5–6). **Anne** Page and Master Fenton are 'long since contracted' (*MWW* 5.2.223) and marry secretly to escape her mother and father's choice of suitors. Valentine and **Silvia**'s contract precedes an elopement to escape the attentions of a parentally-sponsored suitor, Thurio. Valentine claims

we . . . are betroth'd; nay more, our marriage hour,
With all the cunning manner of our flight
Determin'd of.

(TGV 2.4.179–81)

In this play, the danger comes not from Silvia's father but from Proteus. When he also offers his love to Silvia, she chastises him with the reminder that she has already betrothed herself to Valentine, with Proteus as witness (*TGV* 4.1.109–11). What is even more shocking to modern (and perhaps early modern, especially female) ears, is that when the two young men confront each other, Valentine gives up his vows to Silvia in favour of his friend's interests.

High birth raises additional problems in betrothal choices. **Imogen**'s relation to Posthumus is described as a hand-fast or betrothal rather than a marriage by the **Queen**, probably because she wants her son to marry Imogen. She dislikes Pisanio for reminding Imogen 'to hold / The hand-fast to her lord' (*Cym.* 1.5.77–8). Cloten raises doubts about the validity of the pledge between Imogen and the lower-born Posthumus: 'it is no contract none', claiming that while those of meaner birth may be allowed 'to knit their souls' in private bethrothals, her status as heir to the throne means she may not contract herself (*Cym.* 2.3.113–21).

The father's right to give his daughter in a betrothal is vigorously dramatized in *Pericles*, where Simonides pretends to be angry at **Thaisa**'s choice, merely to 'make you / Man and wife. Nay come, your hands, and lips must seal it too' (*Per.* 2.5.83–5). Probably the most elaborately orchestrated betrothal in Shakespeare is that between **Miranda** and Ferdinand. It is, at first, a private event, although conducted under the unseen, watchful eye of Prospero. It is Miranda who instigates the contract, declaring to Ferdinand 'I am your wife, if you will marry me' (*Temp.* 3.2.83), to which he responds with his heart and the typical gesture for hand-fasting:

> Ferdinand: Here's my hand
> Miranda: And mine, with my heart in't.
> *(Temp.* 3.2.89–90)

The contract is celebrated with a masque (*Temp.* 4.1.1–138) but not before Prospero has formalized the **gift** of his daughter and warned Ferdinand to keep chaste until 'all sanctimonious ceremonies may / With full and holy rite be minister'd' or their contract and future marriage will be cursed with 'barren hate' (4.1.15–22). The masque with appearances from **Ceres**, **Juno** and **Iris** celebrates a future of ever-renewing fertility for the couple: 'Spring come to you at the farthest / In the very end of harvest' (*Temp.* 4.1.114–15). **Venus** and Cupid's banishment from the masque reinforces Prospero's message about chastity within marriage. Nevertheless, reminders of the plot of the illegitimate 'beast Caliban and his confederates' (4.1.140) which disrupt the masque, make it clear that Prospero cannot totally exclude the possibilities of transgressive sexual behaviour.

Women are often vulnerable to false betrothal vows in Shakespeare's texts. Edmund boasts that he has contracted himself to both **Goneril** and **Regan** in *King Lear* (5.3.228). **Helena** in *A Midsummer Night's Dream*, **Mariana** in *Measure for Measure*, and the Lady **Bona** in the first tetralogy of English histories all fall victim to such vows. Demetrius pursues **Hermia** even though he admits he was 'betroth'd' to Helena first (*MND* 4.1.178). Mariana is Angelo's 'old betrothed (but despised)' (*MM* 3.2.279), in spite of their affiance by oath. After the bed-trick, designed to 'perform an old contracting' (*MM* 3.2.282), she appears veiled, like Hero in *Much Ado*, to tell Angelo 'This is the hand which, with a vow'd contract / Was fast belock'd in thine' (*MM* 5.1.209–10). Henry VI is swiftly persuaded to marry **Margaret** of Anjou, in spite of being betrothed to the Earl of Armagnac's **daughter**, to whom he sends 'in argument and proof of which contract', a jewel (*1HVI*, 5.1.46–7). There is no satisfactory answer to Gloucester's question 'How shall we then dispense with that contract? / And not deface your honor?' (*1HVI* 5.5.28–9). The Lady **Bona** has to suffer an indignity when Edward IV rejects her in favour of **Elizabeth** Woodville. Buckingham gives Richard of Gloucester a blunt account of Edward's untrustworthiness in pledges of marriage:

> . . . first was he contract to Lady Lucy –
> Your mother lives a witness to his vow –

And afterward by substitute betroth'd
To Bona, sister to the King of France.
These both put off . . .

(RIII 3.7.179–83)

Shakespeare creates a scene at the French court in *Henry VI Part III* dedicated to dramatizing the embarrassment of the rejected Bona as the contract is agreed on stage, with Queen **Margaret** as witness, and then broken less than 40 lines later. Although Bona seeks revenge for the slight, it is her hurt rather than her anger that dominates in the conventional trope of unrequited love: 'Tell him, in hope he'll prove a widower shortly, / I wear the willow garland for his sake' (*3HVI* 3.3.237–8). The betrothal between Antony and **Octavia** (*A&C* 2.2.116–52) is likewise loaded with foreknowledge about Octavia's inevitable suffering, since Antony will not leave **Cleopatra**.

(c) David Cressy (1997), pp. 267–81) offers a detailed account of the ritual practices surrounding betrothal and handfasting in early modern England. *See also* entries on **gift** and **hand**. Ann Jennalie Cook (1991) looks as betrothal as a major event in the lifestyles of young people and at the ways Shakespeare's texts dramatize this. Neely (1993) gives a sensitive account of the broken or disrupted contracts in Shakespeare's plays.

Bianca, (a) the name of two characters: the younger sister of Katherina in *Taming of the Shrew* and the **courtezan** who loves Cassio and to whom he gives the handkerchief in *Othello*. The name is the Italian word for 'white', and by association, implies purity, although neither character fulfils this quality.

(b) Bianca in *Taming of the Shrew* is, to all surface appearances and in comparison with her elder sister, **Katherina**, the model woman: beautiful, silent, modest and obedient, a blank sheet on which the male characters (apart from Petruchio) write their desires. At the end of the play, the 'fair Bianca' (*Shrew* 5.2.4) is compared to the white bull's eye on an archery target, reminding the audience that she has been the prize for which the suitors Lucentio, Gremio and Hortensio have been competing (5.2.186). She is praised as 'sweeter than perfume itself' with coral lips and 'modesty' proclaiming her **beauty** (*Shrew* 1.2.246–51). Lucentio sees in her silence '**Maid**'s mild behavior and sobriety' (*Shrew* 1.1.71). Bianca primly promises to subscribe to her father's pleasure in confining herself to the household until Katherina is betrothed: 'My books and instruments shall be my company' (*Shrew* 1.1.81–2). This leads the besotted Lucentio to compare her to **Minerva**, goddess of wisdom and Hortensio, disguised as a music master, praises her as 'the patroness of heavenly harmony' (*Shrew* 2.1.6). Her father automatically takes her side against Katherina, believing that Bianca can do no wrong. He bids her 'Go ply thy needle', **sew**ing being another mark of womanly virtue (*Shrew* 2.1.25). Katherina's complaint 'She is your treasure, she must have a husband; / I must dance barefoot on her **wedding** day' (*Shrew* 2.1.32–3) comes perilously close to the truth; Baptista swiftly invites Bianca to take her sister's place as bride at Katherina's wedding feast (*Shrew* 3.2.250).

Bianca's words and actions give a different impression of her character. Her first line 'Sister, content you in my discontent' (*Shrew* 1.1.80) suggests a long-standing rivalry between them. Although Katherina shows physical violence in tying Bianca's hands, the latter's apparently submissive attitude 'what you command me will I do / So well I know my duty to my elders' (*Shrew* 2.1.6–7) disguises a taunt, in boasting her primary position as the good daughter. Bianca's flirtatious behaviour with Lucentio, wishing he would become master of the art of love when he teaches her Ovid's *Ars Amatoria* (*Shrew* 4.2.8–9), and subsequently eloping with him, would not mark her out as a good daughter in the eyes of early modern spectators. There is some truth in the rejected Hortensio's complaint that Bianca is a 'foul, disdainful haggard' (*Shrew* 4.2.39); she shows no compassion towards her rejected suitors, being unnecessarily rude to Gremio at her wedding feast (*Shrew* 5.2.40–1). She leaves the feast to avoid being the target of any equivalent bitter jest from Petruchio (*Shrew* 5.2.45–7) and when her new husband asks her to return, sends the reply 'She is busy and she cannot come' (*Shrew* 5.2.81). This is not outright defiance but a material failure to conform. In many ways it typifies Bianca's style of paying ostentatious lip-service to the ideal model of womanly obedience while flouting it absolutely in the pursuit of her own selfish desires.

Bianca in *Othello* is appropriately, like her namesake in *Shrew*, 'most fair' (*Oth.* 3.4.170) – suggesting a boy actor with light hair and complexion. She is named in the *dramatis personae* as 'a **courtezan**', however, so her job immediately contradicts the name's associations with sexual purity. Iago describes her as 'a hussy that by selling her desires / Buys herself bread and cloth' (*Oth.* 4.1.92–3), so even his misogyny acknowledges Bianca's economic need. In addition to prostitution, she also **sews**, thereby contradicting the traditional associations between needlework and female virtue. As a paradox herself, Bianca is of a kind with the play's pattern of moral inversion where virtue is turned into pitch. As the real lover of Cassio, she is a doppelgänger for Desdemona and, in believing that Cassio is being unfaithful, for the deluded Othello. She is voluble and spirited in her appeals for Cassio's company (*Oth.* 3.4.172–87); her helpless wish to please him echoes Emilia's desperate attempts to win the approval of Iago. When Cassio is injured, her shocked pallor allows her to live up to her name: 'Look you pale, mistress? / Do you perceive the gastness of her eye?' (*Oth.* 5.1.105–6). She is not white though guiltiness, as Iago imputes, but through fear born of her love for Cassio. Her final declaration that she is 'of life as honest / As you that thus abuse me' (*Oth.* 5.1.122–3) raises uncomfortable questions about her treatment at the hands of Emilia, Cassio and Iago.

(c) Crocker (2003) analyses the contrast between Bianca's appearance of passivity and Katherina's strategies of playing the shrew or obedient wife. Dympna Callaghan (2001), discusses Bianca's needlework as part of the play's interest in the circulation of linens as part of its commodification of women. Jardine (1996: 19–34) argues that Bianca's identity as a Venetian courtezan makes her uncomfortably like Desdemona.

birth, (a) the bearing of offspring, an act of the **mother**, usually assisted by a

midwife, **nurse** or **gossips** but always in an exclusively female environment in early modern England. Social and economic differences between élite and humble women were often dissolved in the community of female fellowship that surrounded the primary activity of birth.

(b) Birth is a defining moment, most famously in the repeated, totemic phrase 'of woman born' in *Macbeth* (*Mac.* 5.8.13). The moment of birth is never presented on stage in Shakespeare, or, indeed, in any other early modern play, but is a significant off-stage event in *Titus Andronicus, The Winter's Tale, Pericles* and *Henry VIII*. In all cases, the audience is restricted, like the male characters, to wait for news from within the birthing chamber. While female spectators would know what went on in the imagined scene, for men in the audience the dramatic non-representation of the event effectively magnifies its mystery and danger, along with their sense of exclusion and impotence.

Tension animates the opening scene of Act 5 of Shakespeare and Fletcher's *Henry VIII or All Is True*, the subtitle of which is certainly apt in the sharply drawn portrayal of the court's agonized waiting during **Anne** Bullen's confinement. Lovell reports

> The Queen's in labor,
> They say in great extremity, and fear'd
> She'll with the labor end.
>
> (*HVIII* 5.1.18–20)

Birth was perceived as a dangerous process. Women probably had a 6 or 7 per cent chance of dying in childbirth as R. Schofield (1986) has argued, and new-borns much higher. Titania's votaress dies giving birth to the changeling child for example (*MND* 2.1.135) and it is assumed that **Thaisa** in *Pericles* has died giving birth to **Marina** (*Per.* 3.1.17–20). In *Henry VIII* Bishop Gardiner's extremely unchristian attitude is encapsulated in his hopes that the fruit of Anne's womb will live while she, the stock, will be 'grubb'd up now' (*HVIII* 5.1.20–3). Lovel gives voice to the feelings of anxious menfolk in his reproof that Anne 'does / Deserve our better wishes' (*HVIII* 5.1.25–6). Good wishes could be accompanied by prayer, although in post-Reformation England attendance at special forms of mass for childbearing women was no longer a legitimate part of established worship. Thomas Bentley's *Fift Lampe of Virginitie* (1582), for example, included 'praiers to be said for women with child, before or in *travell by the midwife, husband or anie other man or woman*' (p. 126) and prayers 'for a Queene being with child' (Bentley 1582: 127–30), the latter entreating for the baby's safe delivery and that the mother 'through thy speciall grace and mercie may in the time of her travell avoid all excessive dolorous paine, and abide perfect and sure from all perill and danger of death' (p. 129). Anne Bullen sends the character of Henry VIII a message asking him to 'most heartily pray for her' (*HVIII* 5.1.66) amidst her suffering. He breaks off from the game of cards, on which he is unable to concentrate, and sends the Duke of Suffolk off to pray before bed, while he discusses politics with Cranmer. Suffolk can be read as a figure for the British populace who were encouraged by

James I's government to participate in *Prayers appointed to be used in the Church at Morning and Evening Prayer by Every Minister for the Queenes Safe Deliverance* (1605). God's help for **Anna** of Denmark's 'deliverance from the paines and danger in childbirth' was sought to provide 'such an increase in the kings royall issue' to bring joy to King, church and people (*Prayers* 1605: sig. A2v).

Prayers for a safe delivery are the only active intervention that the Goths Demetrius and Chiron can make to help their mother **Tamora** 'in her pains' (*Tit.* 4.2.47). Both are horrified, like Tamora and the **nurse**, by the 'joyless, dismal, black and sorrowful issue', a baby whose black skin declares her **adultery** (*Tit.* 4.2.66). Secrecy over the birthing chamber allows room for deception. It gives rise to Aaron's plot to swap his son with a fair-skinned newborn (*Tit.* 4.2.153–4) and to Jack Cade's ridiculous conspiracy story that he was the twin of Edmund Mortimer, put out to nurse and stolen away by a beggar woman (*2HVI* 4.2.139–45).

The birth event was traditionally associated with pollution and original sin. Women were separated from everyday life in confinement until they were delivered, recovered and were then 'churched', a ritual of purification marking their return to the everyday community. The associations of pollution and separation inform the dramatic representation of **Hermione**'s confinement in *The Winter's Tale*. Leontes's jealous suspicions that her pregnancy is the result of an adulterous relationship with Polixenes magnify the idea of 'pollution' and transform her cultural confinement to a legal one, as she is separated from her son Mamillius and imprisoned (*WT* 2.1.). Here, as her woman attendant **Emilia** reports, she is 'something before her time, deliver'd' of a baby girl (*WT* 2.2.23). In her trial, she complains that she has been 'barr'd, like one infectious' from her son (*WT* 3.2.98), and, before she has regained physical strength from the birth, has been forced into the public forum:

> . . . with immodest hatred
> The child-bed privilege denied, which longs
> To women of all fashion
>
> (*WT* 3.2.102–4)

In early modern England the usual period of confinement for a woman after delivery was about a month, although traditional wisdom (derived from Hippocrates and Leviticus) prescribed thirty to thirty-three days after the birth of a boy and forty to forty-six days after the birth of a **girl**, whose bodily humours were thought to be more cold and moist. In *The Winter's Tale*, Leontes's disruption of the female management of childbirth heightens the physical and emotional crisis of parturition. Hermione loses both her children and collapses after her abrupt and premature exposure to 'th'open air' (*WT* 3.2.105). The sixteen years that intervene are a magnified version of the period of confinement needed for her recovery and eventual reunion with her daughter and husband. The ritualistic qualities of the scene in **Paulina**'s chapel can be read as a 'churching', the ceremony in which the woman was declared pure and formally reintroduced to society as a mother.

Thaisa, who gives birth on board ship during a storm is also denied the normal requisites for labour as Pericles acknowledges in his lament: 'A terrible child-bed hast thou had, my dear, / No light, no fire' (*Per.* 3.1.56–7). The fierce waves and wind are anthropomorphic reminders of the terrible 'pangs' of her 'travail' over which Pericles has no control. He can only pray to **Lucina**, goddess of childbirth and 'gentle midwife / To those that cry at night' to speed Thaisa's delivery (*Per.* 3.1.10–14), and has not even time to commit her body to the sea during the storm. The play's reminders of the closeness between birth and death register the fears of women about to experience labour. In Act 5, Thaisa faints and recovers a second time as though recreating the crisis of childbirth as a time of loss and renewal: 'did you not name a tempest, / A birth and death?' (*Per.* 5.3.33–4).

The vividness with which Thaisa feelingly recalls the moment of parturition is shared by other female characters. The mysteries of childbirth, held in women's memories, often have a determining power in the drama. In *Cymbeline*, they solve the question of Posthumus's identity. The second gentleman admits 'I cannot delve him to the root' (*Cym.* 1.1.27–8) and the question 'What's his name and birth?' is finally answered five acts later in an account by a ghostly **Matron**, his mother. His Roman father was absent, having 'died whilst in the **womb** he stay'd / Attending nature's law' (*Cym.* 5.1.37–8). She reveals:

> **Lucina** lent not me her aid,
> But took me in my throes,
> That from me was Posthumus ripp'd,
> Came crying 'mongst his foes
> A thing of pity!
>
> (*Cym.* 5.4.43–47)

Like Macduff, who 'was from his mother's **womb** / Untimely ripp'd' (*Mac.* 5.8.15–16) and can fight with England to free Scotland, so the alienated Posthumus fights against the Romans to restore Cymbeline's Britain. The mysteries of his birth serve to unite English and Roman blood in the comic resolution through his **marriage** to Imogen.

The moment of birth, however long ago, seems to stay with mothers and their female companions as a means against which to measure the present. Paulina recalls of the Princes Mamillius and Florizel, 'there was not a full month / Between their births' (*WT* 5.1.117–18). Likewise, **Constance** looks back to the time of Arthur's nativity, saying that if he had been born 'Full of unpleasing blots and sightless stains / Lame, foolish, crooked, swart, prodigious' (*KJ* 3.1.45–6) she would not have minded the loss of his rights to the crown because she would not have loved him, 'But thou art fair, and at thy birth, dear boy, / **Nature** and **Fortune** join'd to make thee great' (*KJ* 3.1.51–2). She can still see the 'native beauty of his cheek' (*KJ* 3.4.3). In contrast, the Duchess of York recalls the difficult breech birth of her son Richard of Gloucester as prodigious in all senses of the word:

> I have stay'd for thee
> God knows, in torment and in agony . . .
> A grevious burthen was thy birth to me
>
> (*RIII*, 4.4.163–5)

The physical details, which she has often recounted, have become apocryphal with the effect of explaining (and perhaps with the sinister power of determining) Richard's villainous behaviour. Her memory that 'The **midwife** wonder'd and the women cried, / "O Jesus bless us, he is born with teeth!"' (*3HVI* 5.6.74–5), for example, make both Henry VI and Richard himself believe that his destiny is 'to bite the world' (*3HVI* 5.6.54).

Male characters, who, unlike their female counterparts, have no immediate material experiences of birth to draw on, recall it in very different terms. Often it is an abstract concept linked to name and status, as when Richard Plantagenet begins to rouse his Yorkist faction with the words 'Let him that is a true-born gentleman / And stands upon the honor of his birth . . .' (*1HVI* 1.4.27–8). It is difficult to imagine a more striking contrast between the 'honour' of one's birth and the corporeal reality described by his wife as she was delivered of Richard of Gloucester. Women's sense of urgency and uncertainty in the birthroom is a long way from Ulysses's vision of 'the primogenity and due of birth' (*T&C* 1.3.106) as one of the structuring principles of order in the universe. When Laertes warns Ophelia that Prince Hamlet is 'subject to his birth' (*Ham.* 1.3.18), he does not mean the practical arrangements of the birthing chamber but his social position as Prince of Denmark.

Some male characters attempt to engage obliquely with the corporeal dimensions of parturition, but usually as part of a status-raising exercise. Glendower claims that

> At my nativity
> The front of heaven was full of fiery shapes
> Of burning cressets, and at my birth
> The frame and huge foundation of the earth
> Shak'd like a coward.
>
> (*1HIV* 3.1.13–17)

Unlike the sympathy between the sea storm and Thaisa's labour pains, these natural events are cited to show that Glendower is 'not in the roll of common men' (*1HIV* 3.1.42). Hotspur instinctively senses the perversity of Glendower's words (which deny the extraordinary miracle of birth itself); he dryly remarks that the natural world would have behaved just the same 'if your mother's cat had / But kittened' (*1HIV* 3.1.18–19). Burgundy's utopian image of fertile **France** giving birth to new prosperity and beauty, aided by the midwife **Peace** is an equally unrealistic account of childbirth (*HV* 5.2.34–67).

Given men's distance from the corporeal realities of childbirth it is not surprising that they often respond with mental calculations of nativity, like Bassanio in

Webster's *The Duchess of Malfi* or the cunning man who calculated the Duke of Suffolk's birth and told him 'that by water I should die' (*2HVI* 4.1.34–5). Iago's mental calculations against Othello and Desdemona are expressed as a demonic perversion of procreation: 'It is engend'red. Hell and night / Must bring this monstrous birth to the world's light' (*Oth.* 1.2.403–4). A more positive appropriation of the birth metaphor for plotting is made by the Friar in *Much Ado* who suggests they proclaim Hero dead, 'But on this travail, look for greater birth' (*MAdo* 4.1.213).

What dominates male and female characters' use of birth as a metaphor is a shared sense of its danger and uncertainty. Perdita's description of the changing weather at 'the birth / Of trembling winter' (*WT* 4.4.80–1) captures the fragility of new life. The fear that all labour would be lost in a still-birth lies behind the French **Princess**'s warning to the King of Navarre that 'great things laboring perish in their birth' (*LLL* 5.2.520) or in Hastings's sense that 'our hopes (yet likely of fair birth) / Should be still-born' (*2HIV* 1.3.63–4). The terror of deformity in the newborn baby runs through Gloucester's allusion to 'loathly births of nature' (*2HIV* 4.4.122) and to **Juliet**'s fears that her passion for the enemy Romeo is a 'prodigious birth of love' (*R&J* 1.4.141–1). Men, and women who are not yet mothers, share these doubts, but for the female characters they are more immediately prodigious: Shakespeare's women speak with foreboding about what the experience of childbirth may hold for them.

(c) David Cressy gives a magnificently detailed account of the different practices surrounding birth (1997: 15–31, 50–4, 55–73, 197–210). R. Schofield (1986) considers the mortality rate for women in childbirth. Fissell (2004) describes how images of the Virgin Mary and Elizabeth raised the status of childbearing. Rose (1991) opened discussion of Shakespearean representations of birth. Kathryn Moncrief and Kathryn R. McPherson's *Performing Maternity in Early Modern England* (2007), especially the essay by Janelle Jenstad (2007), gives an excellent introduction to the staging of labour. Bicks (2003) considers images of midwiving as a crucial part of the birth process. Laoutaris (2008) provides a fine discussion of how pregnancy, childbirth and its dangers are a preoccupation in Shakespearean texts, particularly in *Hamlet, Macbeth, The Tempest* and *Antony and Cleopatra*. Richard Wilson (1993) discusses *The Winter's Tale* with reference to the gynaecological practices of Shakespeare's son-in-law Dr John Hall.

Blanch, (a) The name of a character, Lady Blanch of Castile, in *King John* and of one of King Lear's dogs. The name is from French 'white' thus closely linked to **Bianca**.

(b) King Lear complains that his dogs 'Tray, Blanch and Sweetheart' now bark at him, just as his daughters now appear to reject him. The dogs' cruel behaviour does not match the innocence or sweetness suggested by their names but does effectively suggest the hypocrisy of Goneril and Regan (*KL* 3.6.63). Lady Blanch, niece to King John, is based on the historical character who was daughter to the King of Castile and Elinor, youngest daughter of the English King, Henry II. In the play, Hubert introduces her as 'that daughter there of Spain, the lady Blanch' who is 'near to England' in birth (*KJ* 2.1.423). As in history, she is married to the French Dauphin, Lewis, to create an alliance between King John and the French King Philip. In the wooing process, like in that of **Bianca** in *The Taming of the Shrew*, she is a blank page onto which the male characters can write: here they write their political strategy and Lewis can construct a fantasy of chivalric conquest in peace. Her name's associations of whiteness and purity construct her as virgin territory:

> If lusty love should go in quest of beauty,
> Where should he find it fairer than in Blanch?
> If zealous love should go in search of virtue,
> Where should he find it purer than in Blanch?
> If love ambitious sought a match of birth
> Whose veins bound richer blood than Lady Blanch?
> (*KJ* 2.1.423–31)

Tellingly, all that Lewis can see in Blanch is an image of himself. Blanch is well aware that she is a political pawn in an arranged marriage and her response makes no pretence of affection. She will not flatter him that 'all I see in you is worthy love', and can only tell him that she finds nothing 'should merit any hate' (*KJ* 2.1.516–20). Like the blank sheet of her name, she remains neutral and ready to follow her uncle's direction. Like a blank piece of paper, she is metaphorically ripped apart on her **wedding** day as the alliance breaks down. She embodies the divided loyalties so uneasily glued together in political marriage and so imagines herself dismembered through the war between England and France.

> Which is the side that I must go withal?
> I am with both, each army hath a hand,
> And in their rage, I having hold of both,
> They whirl asunder and dismember me.
> (*KJ* 3.1.326–30)

By focusing on Blanch's hopeless entrapment: 'whoever wins on that side shall I lose' (*KJ* 3.1.335), the text highlights the tragic consequences of political marriage for women caught in the middle (an experience shared by **Octavia**). Blanch becomes no more than a claim for the English crown when Prince Arthur, the rightful heir to the English throne, is murdered, and Cardinal Pandulph tells Lewis that he, 'in the right of Lady Blanch, your wife / May then make all the claim that Arthur did' (*KJ* 3.4.142–3).

(c) Dusinberre (1996: 296–7) and Howard and Rackin (1997: 122–4) focus on Blanch's role as a political pawn in a world where masculine authority is undercut by the stronger female voices of Eleanor and Constance. Rackin (1990: 180) calls Blanche 'an instrument of kinship arrangements, political alliance and patriarchal succession'. Virginia Mason Vaughan, '*King John*', in Dutton and Howard (2003: 379–94) discusses Blanch as a victim.

blazon, (a) a courtly literary trope, usually found in love poetry and particularly in sonnets, which involves listing and proclaiming the physical features of a person, usually a woman, as an idealized form of beauty. The blazon became popular in the French court in the sixteenth century, and fashionable in English literature in the later sixteenth and early seventeenth century. It is a word derived from heraldry, in which the blazon was an illustrative device on a shield. Applied to women's bodies, it has the effect of reducing the subject to a series of commodities.

Shakespeare's texts rewrite the blazon tradition in radical ways, most broadly by applying its conventional praise of female beauty to a male subject, the master-mistress of the Sonnets. Sonnet 106 takes up the romantic and heraldic elements of the tradition to argue that all previous descriptions have only served as a prologue to praising the present subject, who dominates a previously feminine realm in his mastery of beauty:

> When in the chronicle of wasted time
> I see descriptions of the fairest wights,
> And beauty making beautiful old rhyme
> In praise of ladies dead and lovely knights,
> Then in the blazon of sweet beauty's best,
> Of hand, foot, of lip, of eye, of brow,
> I see their antique pen would have express'd
> Even such a beauty as you master now.
> (*Son.* 106.1–8)

The blazon tradition is not just inadequate to describe the young man. Distrust of its conventional response is expressed most famously in the anti-blazon of Sonnet 130 where the female body is anatomized according to the usual form, but with much less idealized comparisons:

> My mistress' eyes are nothing like the sun
> Coral is far more red than her lips' red;
> If snow be white, why then her breasts are dun
> If hairs be wires, black wires grow on her head.
> (*Son.* 130.1–4)

The sonnet's potential for offence is brilliantly deflected in the final couplet where the poet discredits the whole blazon tradition and elevates his mistress above it in a single move: 'I think my love as rare / As any she belied with false compare' (*Son.* 130.13–14). The blazon is also inadequate in *Othello*, where Cassio, schooled in the court tradition of aestheticism in Florence, points out that Desdemona's beauty is such that it 'paragons description' and 'excels the quirks of blazoning pens' (*Oth.* 2.1.62–3). *Twelfth Night* dramatises women's rejection of the blazon tradition. Olivia refuses to listen to Cesario's speech of praise as part of Orsino's suit, claiming she has heard it already. She appropriates the form satirically to proclaim ownership of her own body and determination to dispose of it according to her own will.

> I will give out divers schedules of my beauty. It shall be inventoried and every particle and utensil labell'd to my will; as, *item*, two lips, indifferent red; *item*, two grey eyes with lids to them; *item*, one neck, one chin, and so forth.
>
> (*TN* 1.5.244–9)

(c) Sawday (1995: 197–212) analyses the blazon as a process akin to dissection in dismembering a woman as the object of male scrutiny. Doran (1976) discusses the blazon as part of the courtly love tradition.

Bona, Lady, (a) a character in *Henry VI Part III*, sister to the French King Lewis, based on the historical figure who was daughter of the Duke of Savoy and Louis' sister-in-law.

(b) Warwick goes to France to propose a marriage between Bona and the Yorkist King Edward IV to bind England and its former enemy together (*3HVI* 2.5.89–92). Bona is the compliant object of an on-stage **betrothal** by proxy and its subsequent collapse. In addition she is a sentimental figure. She says that reports of Edward have awakened her desire (*3HVI* 3.3.131–3) so the sudden news that he has secretly married **Elizabeth** Woodville is more than simply a blow to her pride. Bona uses the conventional trope of unrequited love to tell Edward 'in hope he'll prove a widower shortly, / I wear the willow garland for his sake' (*3HVI* 3.3.237–8). She follows Warwick's cue in asking Lewis to avenge her wrong and allies her cause with that of the Lancastrian Queen **Margaret** (3.3.216). Bona may perhaps feel doubly abandoned in this scene since Margaret and Warwick cement their alliance by matching the Lancastrian Prince Edward (3.3.242–50) to Warwick's daughter **Anne**, leaving Bona as a solitary, apparently unwanted figure.

(c) Howard and Rackin (1997: 93) discuss Bona as a compliant, dutiful woman who is manipulated. John D. Cox (2000) gives an account of how Shakespeare changes the sources in the French scene with Lady Bona. McNeir (1974) analyses the ludicrous changes in the French court scene, arguing that Bona is spiteful.

bona roba, (a) literally, beautiful dress, a name for a **courtezan**, deriving from the wealthy and richly dressed prostitutes of Venice. Like 'courtezan', this name implies higher social class than **whore** or **harlot**.

(b) Justice Shallow, unique user of the term in Shakespeare, is definitely boasting his social superiority as part of the fashionable world of gallants at the Inns of Court when he observes 'we knew where the bona robas were and had the best of them all at commandment' (*2HIV* 3.2.23–4). Since he goes on to refer to the aptly named **Jane** Nightwork as a 'bona roba' when he recalls a 'merry night' at the Windmill (a brothel in St George's Field) (*2HIV* 3.2.194–210), one suspects that his grandiose claims about his liaisons may be socially inflated as well as fantastically exaggerated. Falstaff simply calls them 'whores' (3.2.304 and 314–15). Cotgrave's 1611 dictionary definition 'A Bona Roba: good stuffe, sound lecherie;

a round, fat plumpe wench' suggests that the high quality signified by the term may refer to the sexual health of the woman rather than simply her social class.
(c) Randale Cotgrave, *A Dictionary of the French and English Tongues* (London, 1611).

bondmaid, (a) a slave girl, a term used in the Tindale and Coverdale Bibles.
(b) There is only one occurrence in Shakespeare, although in the 16 uses of 'bond slave' or 'bondman' for male figures, the term always carries negative connotations, usually of shame. This is also the case in *Taming of the Shrew*, where Katherina's behaviour, in tying her sister, Bianca's, hands makes the latter protest: 'Good sister, wrong me not, nor wrong yourself, / To make a bondmaid and a slave of me' (*Shrew* 2.1.1–2). The stage action and Bianca's words both give a strong impression of Katherina's dominance as unjust tyranny.

bosom, (a) the **breast** of a human being or, poetically, a bird; the surface of the earth or the ocean, which are often feminized. In early modern English the term does not, as in more recent usage, mean specifically a woman's breasts. It can, however, indicate the area of contact in an embrace with the arms and the physical covering of the heart and feelings. To be of someone's bosom is to be in their confidence. Secondarily, bosom is used to refer to the clothing to cover the breast and the space between the clothing and the breast in which small items could be kept (usually secretly).
(b) Bosom is a material hiding place used by characters of both genders as the examples of Aumerle (*RII* 5.2.56–71 SD) and Julia show. Reading Proteus's letter with his name, **Julia** promises that 'my bosom as a bed / Shall lodge thee' (*TGV* 1.2.11–12), probably a cue for her to hide the piece of paper down the front of her dress. One piece of advice offered by Edward Williams to keep silkworms safe and warm for hatching was 'the keeping them in a Boxe, in ones pocket, between a womans Breasts, &c.' (Williams 1650: 18).
As a location for the heart and feelings, the term is used of both genders and as a lodging for the heart of one's lover. Hymen proclaims that **Rosalind**'s heart is within Orlando's bosom (*AYLI* 5.1.115) and Lysander riddles about how his heart and **Hermia**'s are 'knit' through their vows and in each other's bosoms: 'Two bosoms interchained with an oath / So then two bosoms and a single troth' (*MND* 2.2.49–50). The heterosexual alliance pointedly supersedes Hermia's earlier bond of friendship and confidence with Helena in which the two emptied 'our bosoms of their counsel sweet' (*MND* 1.1.216). Egeus complains that Lysander has 'bewitched the bosom of my child' (*MND* 1.1.26) and, bewitched himself, Lysander tells Helena 'nature shows art / That through thy bosom makes me see thy heart' (*MND* 2.2.104–5). The bosom, although flesh and blood, is transparent to the eye perceiving love. **Olivia**'s open declaration of affection makes her tell Cesario that 'a cypress [the translucent mourning material], not a bosom / Hides my heart' (*TN* 3.1.121–2). Being within someone's embrace or bosom offers an opportunity to declare one's feelings, though this often carries erotic suggestions. Don Pedro promises that in dancing with **Hero** at the masked ball 'in her bosom

I'll unclasp my heart' (*MAdo* 1.1.323) to further Claudio's suit. Cardinal Wolsey, meanwhile, believes it is 'not wholesome' that the Lutheran **Anne** Bullen 'should lie i' the bosom of / Our hard-ruled king' (*HVIII* 3.2.100).

When used by and of female figures, bosom frequently carries erotic or maternal associations. In *Venus and Adonis* the two combine. **Venus** holds Adonis on her bosom to protect him with her heart panting (*V&A* 646–8); her tears course down it when he dies (*V&A* 957–8) and she lodges the purple flower there 'Comparing it to her Adonis' breath, / And says, within her bosom it shall dwell, / Since he himself is reft from her by death' (*V&A* 1172–4). In *King Lear* **Cordelia** commits Lear to the 'professed bosoms' of her **sisters**, knowing that their insincere professions of love mean that they will not provide the kind nursery that they should (*KL* 1.1.271). **Regan** uses the verb 'bosomed' meaning to share confidence, with erotic overtones to refer to Edmund's physical relationship with **Goneril**: 'I am doubtful you have been conjunc't / And bosom'd with her' (*KL* 5.1.12–13). Erotic and maternal resonances colour Leontes's view that the pregnant Hermione's bounteous entertainment of Polixenes at the beginning of the play derives from a 'fertile bosom' (*WT* 1.1.113), looking forward to lactation. The romance pattern of reuniting mothers and daughters is given added poignancy in the words of **Marina** who declares 'My heart / Leaps to be gone into my mother's bosom' (*Per.* 5.3.44–5). In *Macbeth*, 'bosom' reinvokes the maternity Lady **Macbeth** has tried to repress with her appeal to the spirits to 'take my milk for gall' (*Mac.* 1.5.48). The doctor must find a cure to 'cleanse the stuff'd bosom of that perilous stuff / Which weighs upon the heart' (*Mac.* 5.3.44–5).

Used of a female figure, the bosom is often imagined as a reward and home for male characters. Antony's use carries maternal associations when he says **Cleopatra**'s 'bosom was my crownet, my chief end' (*A&C* 4.12.27). Richard III tells Lady Anne he committed all the murders 'So I might live one hour in your sweet bosom' (*RIII* 1.2.124). The bosom of the earth is feminized as nurturing in several texts, most literally in *Romeo and Juliet* where Friar Lawrence gathers herbs from the earth where 'from her **womb** children of divers kind / We sucking on her natural bosom find' (*R&J* 2.3.11–12). Timon pleads with the 'common mother' earth to yield him 'From forth thy plenteous bosom, one poor root!' (*Tim.* 4.3.186). The bosom of the earth becomes a metaphor for the mother country for male characters in history plays, and is usually invoked with associations of guilt. Salisbury, who sees himself and his forces as 'children of this isle' feels guilty at joining the French to invade England 'after a stranger, march / Upon her gentle bosom' (*KJ* 5.2.25–9). As Governor of England, in whose 'bosom' the power of the king is lodged, the Duke of York chastises Bolingbroke for bringing forces to march 'So many miles upon her peaceful bosom, / Frighting her pale-fac'd villages with war' (*RII* 2.3.94–5). Even the common soldier Williams remarks on the sin of soldiers who 'have before gor'd the gentle bosom of peace with pillage and robbery' (*HV* 4.1.165–2). Rome, too, is a mother country; Lucius has defended her from invasion, 'And from her bosom took the enemy's point / Shielding the steel in my adventurous body' (*Tit.* 5.3.111–12), even though he was not able to protect his **sister Lavinia** from **rape**.

(c) *The Countesse of Lincolns Nurserie*, a much-reprinted early modern text, uses bosom to describe the nurturing breast in her exhortation to women to **nurse** their own children 'this nursing and nourishing of their own children in their owne bosomes is Gods ordinance' (1622: 4–5). Williams (1650), discusses the protection of silkworms as part of a broader account of the flora and fauna of Virginia.

boy actor, (a) performer of women's roles in the professional theatres of early modern England.

Boys were apprenticed to adult members of Shakespeare's company (notably Richard Burbage, Augustine Phillips, and John and later William Heminges), lived at their houses and were trained to act, probably specifically by those masters who may have inducted them into the profession in 'restricted' roles where the majority of their cue lines would be from one or two of the masters (McMillin 2004: 234–8). Boys who were part of the Chamberlain's Men (later the King's Men), and the first performers of the women's roles, included Christopher Beeston, apprenticed c. 1580, George Burge or Birch (4 July 1610), Alexander Cooke (27 January 1597), John Wilson, Richard Sharpe, Thomas Holcomb, John Rice, Robert Pallant, c. 1620 and William Trigg c. 1625 (all apprenticed to Heminges); Samuel Gilbourne and James Sands (apprenticed to Phillips); Nicholas Tooley or Wilkinson (apprenticed to Burbage). Other notable boy players who had been members of the Blackfriars' boys' company and later became sharers in the Globe were Richard Robinson (from 1611) and John Underwood (from 1608). In the testimonies made in a dispute over shares in the Globe in 1635, William Heminges claimed that he had 'of his owne purse supplyed the company for the service of his Majesty with boyes as Thomas Pollard, John Thompson deceased (for whom Hee payd £40) your supplicant having payd his part of £200 for other boyes since his coming to ye Company, John Honiman, Thomas Holcome and diverse others & at this time maintaines 3 more for the sayd service' (Gurr 2004: 277). Once apprenticed in this way to their master's guild (like the Grocers' Guild, in the case of the Heminges' apprentices), the boys were not paid wages for playing in the theatre company where they were trained to act. As McMillin (2004: 233) neatly summarizes, boys or **youths** were used to portray women's roles for economic reasons; because of their erotic appeal to their male masters and spectators; and for the practical reason that until their voices broke, they were able to convincingly look and sound like women. Henry Jackson's account of a performance of *Othello* in Oxford in 1610 shows that boy actors could become invisible behind the female characters since he describes **Desdemona** throughout using the feminine form:

> the celebrated Desdemona, slain in our presence by her husband, although she pleaded her case very effectively throughout, yet moved [us] more after she was dead, when, lying on her bed, she entreated the pity of the spectators by her very countenance.
>
> (*The Riverside Shakespeare*, p. 1978)

It is not only Shakespeare's words and the boy's voice that makes the performance effective; the boy is able to move spectators by his convincing physical presentation of the woman's part.

(b) Shakespearean roles in which the boy actor's identity appears to be completely subsumed by the female character are predominantly in the tragedies or in problem comedies (see, for example, **Helena**, **Cressida**, **Isabella**, **Margaret** of Anjou, **Volumnia**, Lady **Macbeth** and **Cleopatra**). Although women generally play a smaller part in the histories or the tragedies, such roles ask a great deal of the boy actors in terms of vocal strength, physical presentation and emotional progression. The boy playing **Rosalind** argues that the close similarity between 'boys and women' means that he can successfully ape all the aspects of women's behaviour (*AYLI* 3.3.409–15) but in addition to these demands, the texts contain numerous references to physical contact, such as kissing, and draw attention to the physical womanly features the boys lack. Romeo and **Juliet** kiss at least three times and in Suffolk's passionate farewell to Margaret he longs to die in her arms like a baby 'with mother's dug beneath its lips' and to 'have thee with thy lips to stop my mouth' (*2HVI* 3.2.391–9). Queen **Elizabeth** from *Richard III* commands 'cut my lace asunder' (4.1.33); **Desdemona** and Lady Macbeth appear in their nightgowns; Iachimo scrutinizes **Imogen**'s breast (*Cym* 2.3.37–9); and, most significantly, Cleopatra directs the audience's view to the asp with the words 'Dost thou not see my baby at my **breast** / That sucks the **nurse** asleep?' (*A&C* 5.2.309–10). In these cases, the text deliberately invokes the audience's 'imaginary forces' (*HV* Prologue. 18) along with an awareness of woman's absence from the scene (Adelman 1999). Shakespeare evidently had absolute confidence in the boys' acting skills to create and sustain an illusion of woman that would hold spectators' conviction at the same time as their double consciousness registered her absence from the stage. For testament, we need look no further than Cleopatra's remarkable, majestic lines rejecting a parodic performance of her identity in Rome: 'I shall see / Some squeaking Cleopatra boy my greatness / I' th' posture of a **whore**' (*A&C* 5.2.219–21). The boy actor is carefully distanced from and subsumed by the female character at such poised tragic moments.

In plays featuring cross-dressing the two rub against each other, frequently with the effect of eroticizing the actor as object of the viewers' gazes. The boy playing Rosalind, who has disguised herself as Ganymede, slips in and out of role in the Epilogue promising 'If I were a woman I would kiss as many of you as had **beards** that pleas'd me' and assumes that her offer will be accepted by 'as many as have good beards, or good faces, or sweet breaths', according to their own desires (*AYLI* Epilogue. 18–23). The dual registers of the lady epilogue and the boy actor recall the former scenes' appeal to heterosexual, homo-erotic and lesbian desires, signalled by the title *As You Like It*. In *Twelfth Night* the boy playing **Viola** cross-dressed as Cesario and finally, facing her brother Sebastian, similarly offers on-stage characters and spectators 'what you will'. Since Viola is unable to resume her 'woman's weeds', betrothal and heterosexual closure are deferred beyond the performance climax, and the possibility of alternative couplings, explored through Cesario's relationships with **Olivia** and with Orsino, and Antonio's with Sebastian, is left in suspense. **Julia**, dressed as Sebastian, puns on the word 'shadow' to indicate her uncertain, hermaphoditic status and her identity as an actor (*TGV* 4.2.127). Verbal markers help the boy actor who is dressed as a boy to sustain the female identity in such cases. Rosalind reminds **Celia** 'Do you not know I am a **woman**? when I think I must speak' (*AYLI* 3.2.249–50). Viola and Julia recreate themselves more subtly in extended invented anecdotes. Viola (as Cesario) tells of a sister who never told her love (*TN* 2.4.107–15) and Julia (as Sebastian) recounts how she borrowed Julia's gown at a Whitsun pageant to a play a tragic role recreating her own sense of betrayal:

> Our **youth** got me to play the woman's part,
> And I was trimm'd in Madam Julia's gown,
> Which served me as fit, by all men's judgments,
> As if the garment had been made for me;
> Therefore I know she is about my height.
> And at that time, I made her weep agood,
> For I did act a lamentable part.
> Madam, 'twas Ariadne passioning
> For Theseus' perjury and unjust flight;
> Which I so lively acted with my tears
> That my poor mistress, moved therewithal,
> Wept bitterly; and would I might be dead
> If I in thought felt not her very sorrow.
>
> (*TGV* 4.4.160–72)

Unlike Rosalind's reference to a female disposition under a male costume (*AYLI* 3.2.194–6), these lines ultimately refer back to the boy actor who has assumed Julia's costume and is playing the woman's part.

Boy actors appear as characters in *Taming of the Shrew*, *Hamlet* and *A Midsummer Night's Dream*. Bartholomew the Page is ordered to '**bear** himself with honourable action / Such as he hath observ'd in noble ladies' towards their husbands, speaking softly, embracing and kissing Sly (*Shrew* Ind. 1.110–21). Hamlet greets the boy with a reminder that his time for playing women's roles is limited because of his physical maturation: 'your ladyship is nearer to heaven than when I saw you last, by the altitude of a chopine. Pray God your voice, like a piece of uncurrent gold, be not crack'd within the **ring**' (*Ham.* 2.2.425–8). Although Flute protests he has 'a beard coming' (*MND* 1.2.47–8) he can play in a mask as long as he can still 'speak as small as you will' (*MND* 1.2.50). Boys playing women in a play-within-the-play such as 'The Mousetrap' or 'Pyramus and Thisbe' heighten the double consciousness effect noted in tragedy. At one level they draw attention to the absence of any women on stage; at the same time, they reinforce, by contrast, the female identities of the on-stage women characters watching them (**Gertrude** and **Ophelia** and **Hermia**, **Helena** and **Hippolyta**). Modern audiences are beginning to read female roles with an automatic acceptance of the female character and suspended awareness of the boy actor in all-male productions such as those by Propeller Theatre or at the Globe.

(c) Information about the boy actors in Shakespeare's company is detailed in Gurr (2004). See Kathman (2004) for more detailed research on the system of apprenticeship of boy actors in the Lord Chamberlain's Company and the rival Lord Admiral's Men, and Kathman (2005) for work on the ages of the actors. Wells (2009) applies this to the range of roles in each play, concluding that even the most complex parts were played by boys or youths rather than adult members of the company. McMillin (2004) gives a fascinating analysis of how the rehearsal process between master and apprentice boy actor might have worked. Stephen Orgel (1996) offers an account of apprenticeship and the cultural similarities between boys and women as the objects of male desire and discusses how Shakespeare's plays accommodate the desires of spectators and the bending of gender boundaries. Janet Adelman (1999) shows that, instead of relying on audience awareness of the one-sex model, Shakespeare's plays point up differences between the boy actor and the absent woman. James L. Hill (1986: 235–58) argues that women's roles in comedy make use of ensemble acting techniques while tragic female roles are deliberately constructed to accommodate the physical, emotional experience of the apprentice and to create the illusion of complexity to match that of the tragic heroes. Laura Levine (1994) discusses stage practices in relation to anxieties about cross-dressing and Jean Howard (1994: (esp.) 93–128) considers how Shakespeare's plays actively engage with such anxieties. Michael Shapiro (1996) focuses on the dynamic between boy heroines and female pages, while David Mann (2008) examines the practice of male actors performing female roles. Phyllis Rackin's chapter 'Boys will be Girls' (2005) considers the range of different dynamics between boy actor and female character with examples from across the canon and a focus on Cleopatra. *See also* **Thisbe** and **youth**.

bracelet, (a) an ornamental **ring** or band worn around the arm. Like the ring, it becomes a synecdoche for female genitalia in early modern discourse. It also has associations with ownership, restraint and slavery, linked to the use of hand cuffs on prisoners or slaves.

(b) As adornments, bracelets were courtly fashion statements and formed part of the fashionable gift-giving culture of the court since the exchange expressed the owner's special relationship with the recipient (Harris, 1990: 266). Shakespeare's texts show how the courtly fashion is popularized amongst gentlewomen and even rural peasants. Petruchio uses the promise of a bracelet as a bribe, telling Katherina he will take her back to her father's house decorated 'with amber bracelets, beads and all this knavery' (*Shrew* 4.3.58). Autolycus sells such knacks for ladies in *The Winter's Tale*, advertising his wares as 'Bugle-bracelet, necklace amber, / Perfume for a lady's chamber' (*WT* 4.2.222–3). The bugle-bracelet is one decorated with tube-shaped glass beads, usually black (Arnold 1988: 70). Autolycus triumphs in selling every 'brooch, table-book, ballad, knife, tape, **glove**, shoe-tie, bracelet, horn-ring' in his pack (*WT* 4.4.598–9).

Bracelets carry extra resonance as love tokens, their significance probably originating in the Song of Songs 'Put me as a token of remembrance vpon thy heart, & as a bracelet on thy arme' (Becon 1566: 44r). Francis Bacon explained, somewhat sceptically, the received opinion that 'it helpeth to *Continue Loue*, if one weare a *Ring*, or a *Bracelet*, of the *Haire* of the *Party Beloued*. But that may be by the *Exciting* of the *Imagination*' (Bacon, 1627: 264). Egeus complains that Lysander has taken his daughter's affections prisoner 'with bracelets of thy hair, rings, gawds' and other knacks' (*MND* 1.1.33). The bracelet is a symbol of ownership in *Cymbeline* when Posthumus gives it to Imogen in return for her gift of a ring as a token of his love and their marriage.

> For my sake wear this:
> It is a manacle of love, I'll place it
> Upon this fairest prisoner.
> [*Putting a bracelet upon her arm*]
>
> (*Cym.* 1.2.121–3)

The bracelet as love token carries great symbolic significance, as Iachimo recognizes. Removing it gives a physical dimension to his violent attempts to break their relationship, and his difficulty in doing so testifies to Imogen's faith.

> Come off, come off;
> [*Taking off her bracelet*]
> As slippery as the Gordian knot was hard!
> 'Tis mine, and this will witness outwardly,
> As strongly as the conscience does within,
> To th' madding of her lord.
>
> (*Cym.* 2.2.33–7)

Frederyk of Jennen, a recognized source for Shakespeare's play, does not include a bracelet but Iachimo's subsequent tale of how Imogen gave it to him follows the account in Ariosto's *Orlando Furioso* (1607) where Angelica gives Orlando's pledge to her host Orko. Here too it is a 'token' which she has worn through good and ill fortune 'since she was a gerle' (p. 148). When Iachimo returns Posthumus's ring followed by 'the bracelet of the truest **princess** / That ever swore her faith' (*Cym.* 5.5.415–17), the ritual formally enacts the return of her **chastity** and the restoration of their marriage.

(c) Thomas Becon's *A new postil conteinyng most godly and learned sermons vpon all the Sonday Gospelles* (1566), gives the commentary on Chapter 8 of the biblical Song of Songs. Francis Bacon (1627) discusses the bracelet of hair as a token between lovers. Donne's poem 'The Bracelet' (Donne 1990: 9) and Lodovico Ariosto's *Orlando Furioso*, translated by Sir John Harrington (1607) make reference to the tradition. Barbara J. Harris (1990: 259–81 (266)) describes the courtly fashion of bracelets as tokens in the early modern England. Barry Lording's play *Ram-Alley or Merry Tricks* (1611: sig. G2) and Fletcher's *Cupid's Revenge* (1615: sig. B4) show the popularization of the token tradition amongst the merchant and lower classes.

Y. Hackenbroch (1979) and Arnold (1988) include examples of early modern decorative bracelets. Lewis (1991) discusses the bracelet as a pledge and token of faith in *Cymbeline*, considering how characters come to move beyond a reliance on outward material signs as their faith increases.

Brainford, Old Woman of, (a) the name of Falstaff's disguised persona at the house of Mrs Ford. The name appears to be a corruption of Brentford, a village 15 miles from Windsor.

(b) The old woman is introduced as 'the **witch** of Brainford' and 'my maid's **aunt** of Brainford' (*MWW* 4.2.98 and 171) and referred to as 'a **quean**, an old cozening quean' by Ford. In the first two quarto texts of the play she is called Gillian of Brainford after an apocryphal tavern-**hostess** memorialized by Robert Copland's poem *Iyl of braintford's Testament* (1567). Copland's subject is a 'mery **widow**' (sig A3) and in her mock-testament, dictated to a curate, she bequeathes 25 farts to her neighbours, including a **widow** and a **maid**.

> A widdowe that once hath beene in the brake
> And careth not whome that she dooth take
> Shall have a fart though mine ars ake
>
> A maid that marrieth, not caring whome,
> And doth repent whan she commeth home
> Shal have a fart to by her a combe
> (Copland 1567: B1–B1v)

Memories of her bequest to one that 'suffereth his wife to do her lust / And seeth that to folly she is ful trust' probably inflame Ford's jealousy in Shakespeare's play. The testament's focus on 'Gyllyan' lifting 'up her buttok somewhat awry / And lyk a handgun she let a fart fly' (B2) may explain the name **Mother** Prat (meaning buttock) that Mrs Page invents for the Old Woman persona.

(c) Robert Copland, *Iyl of braintfords testament* (London, 1567); Madison Davis and Frankforter (2004), p. 62, note that John Lowin, one of Shakespeare's company, had a tavern in Brentford, a town which had a reputation for being dirty.

breast(s), (a) in females, soft protuberance(s) on the chest in which milk is secreted to **nurse** and feed their young. Thus, figuratively, it means the source of nourishment. The term also refers more generally to the whole of the area between the neck and the belly in humans and other animals. The breast, like the **bosom**, is conceived of as the physical lodging of feelings and emotions. Since it lodges the lungs and voice box it can be used figuratively to mean the voice.

(b) Shakespeare gives extensively detailed descriptions of Lucrece's breasts in *The Rape of Lucrece* using territorial metaphors to make them the site of male desire and conquest. They are 'like ivory globes circled with blue, / A pair of maiden worlds unconquered', except by her husband, and so Tarquin longs to usurp Collatine's position in 'this fair throne' (*Luc.* 407–13). Shakespeare seems to mock such elevated praise of a mistress in Sonnet 130, admitting that 'If snow be white, why then her breasts are dun' (*Son.* 130.3). The territorial metaphors for ravishment continue in *Lucrece*, however, where Tarquin 'march'd on to make his stand / On her bare breast, the heart of all her land'. The breast is a maiden castle or walled city and the gaze of the poem moves into close-up as his invading hand moves across it: 'Whose ranks of blue veins, as his hand did scale, / Left there round turrets destitute and pale' (*Luc.* 438–41 and 463–9). After the rape, Lucrece 'wakes her heart by beating on her breast' and the poem puns on 'chest' as body part and as box when she bids her heart leave to 'find / Some purer chest' (*Luc.* 759–61). Bodily pollution and hidden cruelty become entwined in images of corruption. Lucrece asks why should 'tyrant folly lurk in gentle breasts' (*Luc.* 851) and, enraged, directs her anger onto herself as '**patience** is quite beaten from her breast' (*Luc.* 1563). To clear herself from the stain of pollution she repeats Tarquin's invasive action and assails 'her harmless breast' with a knife (*Luc.* 1723–4), following the model of the ravished **Philomel**, who presses her nightingale's breast against a thorn. The final image focuses on Lucrece's breast as a spoiled territory, surrounded with blood:

> And bubbling from her breast, it doth divide
> In two slow rivers, that the crimson blood
> Circles her body in on every side,
> Who, like a late-sack'd island, vastly stood
> Bare and unpeopled in this fearful flood.
>
> (*Luc.* 1737–41)

Unlike the close up, detailed focus of the narrative poem, the breast on stage creates different effects. It can be a powerful sign of vulnerability for male characters, as in *The Merchant of Venice*, where Antonio must bear his breast to Shylock's knife in the trial scene. The appearance of the female breast on stage is much more problematic, however, given the embodiment of women's roles by **boy actor**s. In spite of the absence of a physical breast, Shakespeare does focus in on it in *Antony and Cleopatra* and *Cymbeline*. In the case of Imogen, it is possible that Iachimo could have made his observations by lifting the bedcoverings and thus obscuring the boy actor's chest where he observes 'On her left breast / A mole cinque-spotted, like the crimson drops / I' the bottom of a cowslip' (*Cym.* 2.2.37–9). He does refer to this as 'secret' (*Cym.* 2.2.40). In *Antony and Cleopatra*, however, the boy's breast and the asp prop must have been at least partly visible. Cleopatra applies the asp to her breast and asks Charmian, 'Dost thou not see my baby at my breast, / That sucks the nurse asleep?' (*A&C* 5.2.308–9). Dollabella subsequently notes 'Here, on her breast, / There is a vent of blood and something blown: / The like is on her arm (*A&C* 5.2.348–50). Shakespeare must have had complete confidence in the boy actor's skill in embodying a woman and the audience's willingness to suspend their disbelief. 'Breast' is used for voice in Shakespeare too. Feste 'the fool has an excellent breast' (*TN* 2.3.19) Sir Andrew declares, so perhaps, for boy actors like Richard Robinson (who came from the Blackfriars' boys' company) a good voice made an excellent breast in the minds of the audience.

A *Midsummer Night's Dream* appears to set up a deliberate contrast between the boy and the man actor when Bottom's performance ensures that the pap of Pyamus is pierced very ostentatiously by 'bloody blameful blade' (*MND* 5.1.146), and Flute as Thisbe, a boy character self-consciously playing a woman, delivers the lines 'Come, blade, my breast imbrue' (*MND* 5.1.344). Shakespeare's references to stabbing the breast in love plots, as in *Romeo and Juliet*, draw on the common belief in medical texts that the breast is 'the seate of the spiritual members, which are most noble, as the heart and lights', the physiological home of the highest emotions (*Problemes of Aristotle* 1595: D1v).

Breast, used of female characters, carries associations with desire, pleasure and sin. Hermia awakes from a nightmare bidding Lysander 'pluck this crawling serpent from my breast' (*MND* 2.2.146). Romeo uses it erotically and as source of comfort, bidding Juliet good night with the words 'Sleep dwell upon thine eyes, peace in thy breast / Would I were sleep and peace, so sweet to rest!' (*R&J* 2.2.186–7). In *Venus and Adonis*, Venus's desire makes her breast shake with passion in holding Adonis there (*V&A* 647–8) but he refuses to admit the sounds of love into 'quiet closure of my breast' (*V&A* 782). After his death, Venus's breast also takes on the gentler, maternal role as a 'hollow cradle' in which the **flower** will be kept safe. (*V&A* 1183–5). The same emotional pattern operates in *Henry VI Part II*, where **Margaret** grieves over the death of her lover, Suffolk, and commands 'Here may his head lie on my throbbing breast' (*2HVI* 4.4.5) even though it is decapitated. The cradle of passion to which it is consigned recalls Sufolk's own desire, at their parting, to die in her arms and be nursed at her bosom (*2HIV* 3.2.390–2).

The breast as a source of nourishment and security was a strong part of early modern consciousness. William Gouge's conduct book *Of Domesticall Duties* (London, 1622) made the point with admirable clarity:

> God hath giuen to women two breasts fit to containe and hold milke: and nipples vnto them fit to haue milke drawne from them. Why are these thus giuen? to lay them forth for ostentation? There is no warrant for that in all Gods word. They are directly giuen for the childs food that commeth out of the wombe.
>
> (Gouge 1622: 511)

Women writers such as Dorothy Leigh (1616) and the Countess of Lincoln (1622) appear to share this view. The latter notes 'God hath put milke in our breasts against the time of our childrens birth . . . this worke of his provision sheweth that hee tieth us likewise to nourish the children of our own wombe with our own breasts, even by the order of nature' (pp. 9–10). Given the strong cultural pressures on women to **nurse** their children, alongside the emotional need to do so, **Hermione**'s distress at having her newborn baby torn away 'from my breast / (The innocent milk in its most innocent mouth)' (*WT* 3.2.99–100), effectively demonstrates the brutality of Leontes.

Lady **Macbeth** perverts the maternal role as **hostess** turned killer, invoking the evil spirits to 'Come to my woman's breasts / And take my milk for gall, you murdering ministers' (*Mac* 1.5.47–8). The ungrateful or undutiful child perverts the course of natural justice in betraying the nurture given by the **mother**'s breast at **birth**. Thus the shepherd, father to **Joan** La **Pucelle**, is horrified when she denies his paternity. He tells her 'I would the milk / Thy mother gave thee when thou suck'dst her breast, / Had been a little ratsbane for thy sake!' (*1HVI* 5.4.28).

The natural elements are feminized with references to the breast in charged encounters between male characters and the sky, sea or earth or mother **nature**. There is a certain erotic frisson in Cassisus's proud boast that he has 'bar'd his bosom' to the storm when lightning 'seem'd to open / The bosom of heaven' (*JC* 1.2.50–1). Mother **earth** is more kindly in Nestor's image of the smooth sea where 'bauble boats dare sail / Upon her patient breast' (*T&C* 1.3.35–6) and Timon invokes her 'infinite breast' as a source of food for all (*Tim.* 4.3.177–9). The breast as a metaphor for the surface of the land carries nationalistic associations in *Henry VI Part I.* Joan makes Burgundy feel guilty for betraying his mother country, France, and fighting with the English. She bids him 'Behold the wounds, the most unnatural wounds, / Which thou thyself hast given her woeful breast' (*1HVI* 3.3.50–1). More abstract associations of the breast with peace, perhaps drawing on the idea of the dove, are found in *1HIV* where Blunt chastises the rebels for conjuring hostility 'from the breast of civil peace' (*1HIV* 4.3.43). Shakespeare certainly made the association between the breast, the security of peace and the dove in *The Phoenix and the Turtle* where 'the Turtle's loyal breast' (*PT* 57) carries the certainty of eternity.

(c) Influential early modern texts which advocate the use of breasts for nursing one's own children include William Gouge, *Of Domesticall Dueties* (1622), *The Countess of Lincolns Nurserie* (1622) in which the Countess encourages women of all classes to breastfeed, and Dorothy Leigh, 'A Mother's Legacie' (1616). The latter is republished in an annotated edition in Sylvia Brown (1999: 1–87) and argues 'that a mother will never forget her child: will shee not blesse it every time it suckes on her breasts, when shee feeleth the bloud come from her heart to nourish it?' (ibid.: 23). Richard Robinson's earlier translation *A Moral Method of Civil Policie* (1576: 44v) celebrates the pleasures and 'benefite of the mothers breaste' as a tradition dating back to the ancients. For the appearance of the boy's breast on stage see Peter Strallybrass's brilliant essay 'Transvestism and the "body beneath": speculating on the boy actor' (1992).

breath, (a) the air exhaled from the lungs, in early modern English, as made manifest by its smell or perfume. Breath is one of the physical features frequently included in the **blazon** or catalogue of features used to praise the **beauty** of the beloved in the courtly love tradition. A sweet breath indicated healthy teeth and gums, of course and, used metaphorically, breath also meant the voice.

(b) Lucentio makes a comment typical of the blazon tradition in praising **Bianca** as one whose coral lips did move 'And with her breath she did perfume the air; / Sacred and sweet was all I saw in her' (*Shrew* 1.1.174–6) For many male characters, the breath of female figures frequently carries an erotic attraction. Enobarbus recounts how **Cleopatra** breathed forth power over all who watched her, even when she lost her breath amd 'did make defect perfection' (*A&C* 2.2.231). Christopher Sly is promised erotic pictures of **Cytherea** (**Venus**) hidden in the reeds 'Which seem to move and wanton with her breath / Even as the waving sedges play wi' th' wind' (*Shrew* Ind. 1.52–3). Similarly, **Lucrece**'s golden hair, 'play'd with her breath' flirtatiously in her sleep as if 'showing life's triumph in the map of death' (*Luc.* 400–3). As in this example, the erotic power of breath is often linked to imminent death and its early modern associations with orgasm. Looking on the dead **Juliet**, Romeo laments that death 'hath suck'd the honey of thy breath' (*R&J* 5.3.92). Othello, determined to kill **Desdemona**, compares her to a rose on a tree and, having kissed her, describes her breath as a temptation to divert him from his purpose: 'Ah balmy breath that dost almost persuade / Justice to break her sword!' (*Oth.* 5.1.16–17). **Lavinia**'s **ravish**ment is signalled by the mingling of a fountain of blood at her 'rosed lips', stirred with wind and 'Coming and going with thy honey breath' (*Tit.* 2.3.23–5).

The sweetness of female breath is sometimes used as a sign of the fragility of innocent life and the possibility of resurrection. In *Cymbeline* at the apparent death of **Fidele** (the cross-dressed Imogen), Arviragus claims that the honeysuckle 'Out-sweet'ned not thy breath' (*Cym.* 4.2.223–4). More tragically, Lear searches for signs of **Cordelia**'s breath (*KL* 5.3.307–12) and Leontes, gazing on the statue of **Hermione**, is amazed to sense 'an air comes from her' inviting him to kiss her. The miraculous transformation of art into life is neatly encapsulated in his words 'What fine chisel / Could ever yet cut breath?' (*WT* 5.78–80). Arguably, Shakespeare's dramatic references to the fragility and miraculous preservation of female breath may refer to the voices of the **boy actors** who played these roles for a limited time. When used of the female voice, and implicitly that of the boy actor, 'breath' carries associations of enchantment. Juliet's breath will sweeten the 'neighbor air' with 'rich [music's] tongue' (*RJ* 2.5.26–7) while the **mermaid** described by Oberon utters 'such dulcet and harmonious breath / That the rude sea grew civil at her song' (*MND* 2.1.150–4).

Bassanio's comment on **Portia**'s breath registers the artificiality of the **blazon** tradition in which women's breath was compared to sweet foods.

> Here are sever'd lips,
> Parted with sugar breath; so sweet a bar
> Should sunder such sweet friends.
> (*Mer.* 3.2.118–20)

The artificiality is blatant since he is referring to her picture in the casket rather than her real lips and breath. The probability that women's breath was not likely to match up to this ideal is comically broadcast in Bottom's mispronunciation of Pyramus's lines praising Thisbe's breath:

> Bottom: Thisby, the flowers of odious savors sweet –
> Quince: [Odorous], odorous.

> Bottom: – odors savors sweet,
>   So hath thy breath, my dearest Thisby dear.
>   (*MND* 3.1.82–5)

Shakespeare as sonnet writer mocks the tradition in what is probably the best-known reference to a woman's breath: 'And in some perfumes is there more delight / Than in the breath that from my mistress reeks' (*Son.* 130.7–8). In another satiric blazon, Launce's mistress 'is not to be kiss'd fasting in respect of her breath' (*TGV* 3.1.325). Because of Beatrice's sharp tongue, Benedick says 'if her breath were as terrible as her terminations, there were no living near her; she would infect to the north star' (*MAdo* 2.1.248–50), although implicitly he has noticed that her breath is not foul.

breeches, (a) a pair of short trousers, usually worn by men but also by cross-dressing female characters.
(b) Julia's waiting-woman Lucetta jokes 'what fashion, madam, shall I make your breeches?' (*TGV* 2.7.49).
(c) *See also* **codpiece**.

breeder, (a) bearer of offspring, used mostly of animals and pejoratively of women as objects of male desire.
(b) In *Venus and Adonis*, 'fair breeder' is used to describe the 'breeding jennet' that tempts Adonis's horse (*V&A* 260 and 282). Richard, Duke of Gloucester uses the term pejoratively in joking that his brother Edward loves 'the breeder better than the male' (*3HVI* 2.1.42) while Hamlet, apparently revolted by female sexuality, sends Ophelia to a nunnery (meaning both a convent and a brothel) with the words 'why would'st be a breeder of sinners?' (*Ham.* 3.1.120). In *Titus*, the **Nurse** uses the word more generically in describing **Tamora**'s black baby as loathsome 'Amongst the fair-fac'd breeders of our clime' (*Tit.* 4.2.48).

brew, (a) to make beer or ale, a important job usually undertaken by women in early modern England for domestic purposes and sometimes for commercial purposes by the **ale-wife** who might also keep a tavern.
(b) Launce is pleased that second in the list of his mistress's virtues, after being able to milk, is that 'She brews good ale' (*TGV* 3.1.303). Mistress Quickly lists it as one of her duties as Caius's housekeeper: 'I wash, wring, brew, bake, scour, dress meat and drink, make the beds' (*MWW* 1.4.95–7).
(c) Judith M. Bennett (1996) gives a history of women's involvement in the brewing industry.

bride, (a) a woman to be married or very recently married, and invariably at the centre of attention on the **wedding** day. The bride occupies a liminal position between her father who, according to custom, gives her away at the wedding, and her husband, with whom she will create a new family unit. In relation to her own sex, the bride's role is also transitional: she is led to the church by her fellow bride's **maid**s, but will emerge as a wife, bound to her husband and ready to become a **housewife**.

(b) Characters who appear as brides in Shakespeare's work include **Katherina** and **Bianca** Minola, **Hero** in *Much Ado* and **Rosalind**, **Celia**, **Phoebe** and **Audrey** in *As You Like It*, **Hippolyta**, **Hermia** and **Helena** in *Midsummer Night's Dream*, and Helena in *All's Well*. In the tragedies, **Tamora** and **Juliet** are presented as brides and in the English history plays, **Blanch** in *King John*, **Margaret** of Anjou and **Elizabeth** Woodville appear as stage brides. The **wedding** is as a threshold in which the woman's identity changes. In Samuel Rowlands's poem *The Bride* the maid Susan tells the bride 'no longer than the wedding day / You hould with us, but turne to tother side' (Rowlands 1617: A4v). In *Pericles*, Gower tells of **Thaisa**'s off-stage transformation as 'Hymen hath brought the bride to bed / Where, by the loss of **maid**enhead, / A babe is moulded' (Chorus. 3.9–11). The bride's inappropriate sense of shame at losing her virginity is perversely appropriated later in the play by the keepers of the brothel, where **Marina** is expected to lose her virginity. 'Your bride goes to that with shame which is her way to go with warrant', observes the Bawd, but Boult remarks wryly 'Faith, some do and some do not', indicating that not all brides are **virgins** (*Per.* 4.2.127–8).

The age of the bride is an issue for fathers unwilling to lose their daughters. Timon of Athens intervenes in a case where a father refuses to let his **daughter** who is 'a' the youngest for a bride' (*Tim.* 1.1.123), marry the servant Lucilius. It is unclear whether class snobbishness or emotional reasons prompt the father's behaviour. Old Capulet argues that another two summers must pass, until **Juliet** is nearly 16, 'Ere we may think her ripe to be a bride' (*R&J* 1.3.10–11), although he later changes his mind. After Juliet has hastened secretly to Friar Lawrence's cell to marry Romeo in Act 2 Scene 6, she makes it clear that the role of bride is not one she can repeat in an arranged marriage to Paris:

> Lady Capulet: The County Paris, at Saint Peter's Church,
> Shall happily make thee there a joyful bride.
> Juliet: Now, by Saint Peter's Church, and Peter too,
> He shall not make me there a joyful bride.
> (*R&J* 3.5.114–17)

As in *Much Ado*, a sense of anticipation is created with Juliet's preparation of 'those attires are best' (*R&J* 4.3.48) for the wedding, but the **Nurse** fails to rouse her with the appellation 'why, bride!' (4.5.3) and Capulet laments that death has lain with Paris's **wife** (4.5.36). Juliet is carried to church in her best attire with her 'bridal flowers' of rosemary now serving to deck what appears to be her corpse. The association between death and the bride, played out so strongly and with sexual innuendo here, also informs the condemned Claudio's boast that if he must die 'I will encounter darkness like a bride / And hug it in mine arms' (*MM* 3.1.83–4). Somewhat unexpectedly, Iago describes the soldiers in the barracks 'in terms like bride and groom / Devesting them for bed' a significant same-sex alternative to the wedding night of Othello and Desdemona (*Oth.* 3.3.180–1).

The bride is a figure of temptation in *Pericles* and in *King John*. The incestuous Antiochus tempts suitors to their death by presenting his **daughter** 'clothed like a bride' with music to accompany her entrance (*Per.* 1.1.6–12). In Act 3 Scene 1 of *King John*, Lady **Blanch** appears as a newly-wed bride to the Dauphin Lewis, but **Constance** warns him 'the devil tempts thee here / In likeness of a new untrimmed bride' (*KJ* 3.1.208–9). Blanch is emotionally torn apart on her wedding day by her divided loyalties. The bride's liminal position is invariably one of vulnerability in Shakespeare. Katherina is utterly humiliated on her wedding day by the late arrival and outlandish behaviour of Petruchio. He exclaims 'where is Kate, where is my lovely bride' (*Shrew* 3.2.92), but, having paid lip service to her precedence as **mistress** of the feast, 'Obey the bride, you that attend on her' (*Shrew* 3.2.223), he then denies her the pleasure of the wedding breakfast leaving **Bianca** to 'bride it' in her place (*Shrew* 3.2.251). Bianca subsequently appears at her own wedding celebration where Hortensio refers to her as 'mistress bride' (*Shrew* 5.2.42). **Hero** and **Helena** are subjected to even more humiliating treatment. After a scene of anticipation in which Hero's wedding dress and favours are discussed and the wedding ceremony begun, Claudio rejects her as unchaste at the altar in *Much Ado About Nothing* (4.1), which makes her collapse and remain concealed until her name is cleared and she reappears veiled as a bride in the final scene. Bertram goes through with the marriage ceremony to Helena but then runs away to war on the wedding night 'when I should take possession of the bride' (*AWW* 2.5.26).

Brides in arranged or political marriages are exposed to the hostile attitudes of other characters. Richard, Duke of York bitterly refers to **Margaret** of Anjou as the King's 'new bride and England's dear-bought queen', (*2HVI* 1.2.252) since Anjou and Maine have been the price of her hand. Edward IV's impolitic choice of **Elizabeth** Woodville as his bride makes them both vulnerable to the criticism of the English nobles and the French King, whose sister **Bona** had been **betrothed** to Edward. King Lewis threatens to send soldiers as masquers 'To revel it with him and his new bride' (*3HVI* 3.3.224–5) and Warwick boasts that the King's 'new-made bride' will not be able to 'succor him' against a rebellion (*3HVI* 3.3.207). At Elizabeth's entrance with her bridegroom, Richard, Duke of Gloucester refers sarcastically to her as 'his well-chosen bride' (*3HVI* 4.1.7) and later complains 'in your bride you bury brotherhood' (*3HVI* 4.1.55) by giving the Queen's brother the richest heiress as a bride. The shamble of changed betrothals and instant **weddings** in the opening scene of *Titus Andronicus* prepares for the confusion to follow. **Lavinia** is seized from the Emperor Saturninus by his younger brother Bassianus to be married while **Tamora** is instantly transformed from Saturninus's prisoner of war to his 'lovely bride'. He insists that since priest and holy water 'In readiness for Hymenaeus stand' he will marry immediately and 'lead espous'd my bride along with me' (*Tit.* 1.1.319–37). The wedding breakfast offers a superficial appearance of reconciliation between all parties when Saturninus says 'the Emperor's court can feast two brides' (*Tit.* 1.1.489).

(c) Samuel Rowlands' *The Bride* (1617) presents a debate in verse dialogue between the bride and the bride's maids in which the superiority of marriage and the wife's duties are explained. Cressy outlines the cultural traditions of bridal flowers, processions, cakes and celebrations (1997: 335–76). Linda E. Boose (1982: 325–47) discusses the bride's liminal position in the betrothal ceremony, a ritual of transition designed to ease the emotional crisis of fathers losing their daughters. Neely (1993) offers chapters on *Much Ado* and *All's Well* in the context of a broader examination of Shakespeare's presentation of marriage. Dash (1981) looks at the emotional and dramatic dynamics of weddings. Page (1935b) examines the public repudiation of Hero while Ranald (1979) argues that a knowledge of English matrimonial law is important to understand the representations of Hero, Katherina and Helena (in *All's Well*) as brides. *See also* **wedding** and **marriage**.

callet, (a) a lewd or sexually profligate woman, or a **prostitute**, a **drab**, **trull** or a **strumpet**. In early modern English, the analogy between sexual looseness and women's volubility means the term also indicates an outspoken and unruly woman. The verb 'to callet' means to **scold** or rail.

(b) The word is used to mean **whore** in **Emilia**'s protest 'a beggar in his drink / Could not have laid such terms upon his callet' as Othello did in calling **Desdemona** whore (*Oth.* 4.2.120–1). Queen **Margaret** of Anjou, insecure about her own social status, slanders the Duchess of Gloucester as a 'contemptuous base-born callet' (*2HVI* 1.3.83) and is later subject to the same slander for daring to insult Richard of Gloucester's birth. The scold should be given a wisp of straw 'To make this shameless callet know herself' (*3HVI* 2.2.144–5), Edward declares. In all cases, the insults are exaggerated and say more about the insecurity of the speaker than the woman herself. The most ridiculous case is when **Paulina** criticizes Leontes and is condemned as

> A callat
> Of boundless tongue, who late hath beat her husband
> And now baits me!
>
> (*WT* 2.3.91–3)

Nothing in the play suggests that Paulina has been a strumpet, beaten her husband, or speaks anything but common sense to the deluded, tyrannical king.

Calphurnia, (a) **wife** to Caesar in *Julius Caesar* and daughter of the consul Lucius Calpurnius Piso.

(b) Attention is immediately drawn to Calphurnia and to her barrenness by Caesar on his first appearance in Act 1 Scene 2 at the Lupercalian ceremony. Having called her name, he gives directions to ensure Antony touches her during the course, or race 'for our elders say / The barren touched in this holy chase / Shake off their sterile curse' (1.2.7–9). In Act 2 Scene 2, she appears in a domestic setting, attempting to protect her husband by urging him to stay at home. Like the **prophetess Cassandra**, she has the ability to observe but not, finally, to influence events. She fears the import of her dream that Caesar's statue was spouting blood in which Romans bathed their hands, a prescient image of what is to follow at the Capitol and of Antony's interpretation of Caesar as a generous ruler of the city (2.1.76–9). She lists other portents and pleads on her knee that Caesar will stay at home. Caesar at first agrees, suggesting a degree of affection and perhaps a shared apprehension between them. However, when Decius Brutus reinterprets the dream as figuring Caesar as the nurturing **mother** of Rome, he upstages the barren Calphurnia. By suggesting the Senators will mock Caesar for placing his wife's private fears above the important public business of the State, Decius Brutus relocates fear as an exclusively womanly trait, and Caesar rejects her prescience as 'foolish' (2.2.105).

(c) Coppélia Kahn (1997: 103–4) interprets Calphurnia's meeting with Caesar as a feminizing encounter that adds to the ambiguity of images of him as both mighty ruler and sick **girl**.

Capulet, Lady, (a) wife of Capulet in *Romeo and Juliet* is not addressed as Lady Capulet in the play, though the name appears in the Douai manuscript and in the stage directions of the Second Quarto, where she is also referred to as Capulet's **Wife**, Wife, Old **Lady** and **Mother**. It is possible that she is the Angelica referred to by Capulet (4.4.5) although since the **Nurse** responds, it is more likely to be her name.

(b) Lady Capulet says that she became mother to **Juliet** when she was Juliet's age, nearly fourteen (1.3.71–3), relatively young in comparison with the average age of first motherhood for early modern Englishwomen. According to this evidence, she would therefore be 28, and much younger than her husband who says he was last in a masque 25 or 30 years ago (1.5.33–40). However, the stage directions in the Second Quarto refer to her as 'Old Lady'. Hosley (1967) explains the discrepancy by suggesting that compositorial error printed 'your mother' instead of 'a mother', and that Juliet is the only surviving child of the couple. In the excitement of preparations for the wedding, they joke about Capulet's past reputation for chasing women and her jealousy (4.4.11–13). She is referred to as 'the lady of the house' (1.5.113) and appears as a **housewife**, holding the keys to the stores where spices and preserved fruits are kept and concerned that the family will not be sufficiently prepared for a **wedding** feast (4.4.1–2). Lady Capulet has a more formal relationship with her **daughter** than does the Nurse who **suckle**d Juliet, as can be seen when the topic of **marriage** to Paris is first introduced (1.3) and when she is angered by Juliet's refusal of the match to Paris. She responds to Juliet's appeal 'O sweet my mother, cast me not away!' by refusing to speak a word: 'Do what thou wilt. I have done with thee' (3.5.198–203). Such indifference may be explained as a symptom of her grief at the death of Tybalt. She is certainly passionate in her wish for revenge; determined to find someone to poison Romeo (3.5.87–92).

(c) Richard Hosley (1967), puts the case for Lady Capulet as an older figure. An interesting performance choice is outlined in the anonymous *The True Ophelia: And Other studies of Shakespeare's Women by An Actress* (1913), where the author argues in an account of 'The Insignificant Mother of Juliet' (pp. 65–93), that Lady Capulet is the strongest character in the play, fired by jealousy of Lady Montague, who has a son (pp. 69–70).

Cassandra, (a) a **prophetess** from Greek mythology, **daughter** of Priam, King of Troy, and a character in *Troilus and Cressida*.

(b) Cassandra makes a dramatic entry into the Trojan Council chamber '*raving*' with prophetic tears for the suffering and grief to come with the downfall of Troy unless they return **Helen** (2.1.97–102). The stage directions '*raving*' in the Quarto and '*enter Cassandra with her* hair *about her eares*' in the Folio, both occur at line 97, giving her some time to make an impact on the audience before she is acknowledged by the Trojan Princes. She looks beyond the immediacy of the play's action to the wider, tragic picture and appeals to her fellow Trojans: infants, **virgins**, boys and the elderly to add their voices and tears to hers:

> Let us pay betimes
> A moi'ty of that mass of moan to come.
> Cry, Troyans, cry! practice your eyes with tears!
> Troy must not be, nor goodly Ilion stand.
> Our fire-brand brother Paris burns us all.
> Cry, Troyans, cry!
>
> (*T&C* 2.2.106–11)

The majority of spectators, who knew the fate of Troy, would have seen the truth and poignancy of Cassandra's prophecy. Although she speaks fewer than 30 lines in the play, her fatalistic vision acts as a focal point for the prophetic hints in other characters' language. Her presence in the prophecy scene undermines the high ideals of honour propounded by the princes, with reminders of the consequences. Although Hector seems to recognize their force as 'divination' (2.2.114), Troilus chooses to dismiss his sister as 'mad' and her words as 'brain-sick raptures' (2.2.122). Her loose hair and 'raving' could be symptoms either of madness or of grief. Earlier in the play Pandarus's comment 'I will not dispraise your sister Cassandra's wit–' (1.1.47) may include a snide reference to her reputation for mental instability. **Cressida**, however, believes that Cassandra has a 'temperate fire' under her eyes that would not make her weep at a silly joke (1.2.146–7).

Cassandra's words are taken more seriously in Act 5 Scene 3 when she confirms the truth of her sister-in-law **Andromache**'s ominous dream of slaughter, and pleads alongside her against Hector's wish to fight. With a chilling confidence in destiny, she tells Hector that the gods are deaf to his vows, then brings King Priam to join his voice with theirs. Priam states unequivocally 'Cassandra doth foresee', and commands 'thou shalt not go', making Hector's determination to fight to uphold his honour in battle appear all the more unnatural (5.3.64, 70). Troilus's peevish complaint that the omens are caused by nothing more than Cassandra's foolish dreaming and superstition (5.3.79–80) is quickly upstaged by the strength of her prophetic voice when she bids Hector farewell. She forsees in his dying eye and bloody wounds, the suffering and ruin of Troy itself: 'distraction, frenzy and amazement' (5.3.85). Assured and outspoken to the last, she tells him that he is deceiving himself and the whole of Troy (5.3.90).

(c) Richard D. Fly (1975) discusses Cassandra's authority as a **prophetess**.

cates, (a) literally, cakes but also used as a metaphor for the female body as a sexually pleasing dainty for men.

(b) Petruchio puns on Katherina's name 'my super-dainty Kate', to praise her desireability 'For dainties are all Kates' (*Shrew* 2.1.188–9), but warns her he will make her 'conformable as other household Kates' (2.1.278). In *Henry VI Part I*, Talbot claims victory in a battle of the sexes with the **Countess** of Auvergne by asking her to let the English soldiers 'Taste of your wine and see what cates you have / For soldiers' stomachs always serve them well' (*1HVI* 2.3.79–80). The request and acquiescence politely masks the potential for military rape and pillage.

caul, (a) a finely woven or netted covering for the hair, worn by women; often richly decorated, it is a specific type of **tire**, or head-dress; a piece of ornamental network or a net to wrap something in. Metaphorically, caul can be a spider's web. In addition, the term refers to the amnion covering a baby's head at birth. It was a sign of good luck and was believed to prevent drowning.

(b) As a hair covering, the caul would have been a useful tool for the boy actor playing female roles who needed to display the woman's hair, such as **Constance** in *King John*. The netting would have helped to secure any false hair worn by the actor. Roger Montague, who made cauls for Queen Elizabeth's household, made double cauls of hair-coloured stitched cloth, lined with hair colour and decorated with 'stringes of heare colour silk' (Arnold 1988: 205). **Julia** in *Two Gentlemen of Verona* may intend to use such a caul to tie up her long hair to be a page: 'I'll knit it up in silken strings, / With twenty odd-conceited true-love knots' (*TGV* 2.4.45–6). Sometimes cauls were made of knotted human hair. In 1603 Dorothy Speckard supplied 'two heare Cawles curiouslie made in workes of haire' (Arnold 1988: 226).

(c) Arnold (1988: 205, 225–6) gives details of cauls ordered and paid for from Queen Elizabeth's royal wardrobe.

Celia, (a) a character in *As You Like It*, daughter of the usurping Duke Frederick and cousin to **Rosalind**. The name, which suggests heaven and sky, is probably a shortening of Saint Cecilia, a second century Roman **virgin** who committed herself to **chastity**, telling her husband Valerianus that her body was guarded by an **angel**, who subsequently crowned them with roses and lilies. In 1595 her tomb was opened and her body declared incorruptible, as celebrated in the Chapel of St Cecilia of Trastevere in Rome. St Cecilia is patron of music and the blind.

(b) Shakespeare would have known the story from Chaucer's Second Nun's Tale. In Britain, the saint's name is often shortened to Celia. In Lyly's *Midas* (1592), for example, Midas boasts 'Chastity will grow cheap where gold is not thought dear. Celia, chaste Celia, shall yield' (1.2.128–9). The saint's reputation for chastity may have influenced Ben Jonson's choice of Celia for the romantic heroine in *Volpone*. 'Cicely' is another shortening used, perhaps with ironic reference back to the chaste saint, in the Induction to *Taming of the Shrew* where Christopher Sly calls out for Cicely Hacket 'a woman's **maid** of the house' (possibly the daughter of the **ale-wife**, Marion Hacket) and is told he knows 'no such maid' (*Shrew* Ind. 2.89–91). Cic'ly is named as a servant in Adriana and Antipholus's household in *Comedy of Errors* (3.1.31) and the historical figure of the **Duchess** of York, mother of the Yorkist kings Edward IV and Richard III was also called Cicely but is never named as such in Shakespeare's texts.

In *As You Like It*, Celia perhaps follows the chaste saint in asking her cousin to 'love no man in good earnest, nor no further in sport neither, than with safety of a pure blush come off again' (*AYLI* 1.2.27–9). She certainly clings to a sisterly bond with **Rosalind**, who has been her constant companion since childhood: 'like **Juno**'s swans / Still we went coupled and inseparable' (*AYLI* 1.3.75–6). When Rosalind is banished from court, Celia determines to go with her and proposes their flight to the Forest of Arden disguised in 'mean attire'. She changes her name Celia to 'Aliena' to indicate her own status as an outcast (*AYLI* 1.3.127–8). While the cross-dressed Rosalind woos the younger brother Orlando, Celia becomes more and more isolated and quickly falls in 'in the very wrath of love' (*AYLI* 5.2.40) with the elder brother Oliver, thus ensuring that each couple are matched with fortunes in the comic resolution blessed by Hymen.

(c) Clara Calvo (1992) analyses the dialogue between Celia and Rosalind in *As You Like It* as a guideline to their changing statuses. Montrose's 'The Place of a Brother in *As You Like It*' (1981) discusses how by shifting their primary affections to Orlando and Oliver, Rosalind and Celia provide the means to resolving the brotherly rivalries that operated in the past. Fiona Shaw and Juliet Stevenson (1988) give an illuminating account of how they approached the roles of Celia and Rosalind and how these worked in performance.

Ceres, (a) the ancient Italian goddess of corn and harvest, worshipped by the Romans who appears in Act 4 of *The Tempest*. She is closely associated with the seasonal cycle via the myth of **Proserpina**, her daughter, who is kidnapped by Dis and held in the underworld for six months of the year. During this time, Ceres is in mourning and the corn will not grow.

(b) Shakespeare, who would have known this narrative from Ovid's *Metamorphoses*, follows early modern tradition by figuring Ceres as a symbol of plenty and the fruitfulness to be exploited through agriculture. **Eleanor**, the **Duchess** of Gloucester refers to Ceres to criticize her husband's drooping gaze as an example of bad husbandry, metaphorically construing his lack of political ambition as unnatural. He is 'like over-ripen'd corn / Hanging the head at Ceres' plenteous load' (*2HVI* 1.2.1–2), unwilling to grasp the natural opportunities for power which his current position as Lord Protector offers. Thomas Rogers described Ceres as '**Goddess**e of Corne drawen in her chariot by dragons, crownde with sheaues of wheat' (Rogers 1598: sig. B6). The wedding procession in *Two Noble Kinsmen* features a **Nymph** with '*a wheaten garland*' (*TNK* 1.1.SD0). Arcite refers to 'teeming Ceres' foison' (*TNK* 5.1.53), conflating images of human and agricultural fertility in a phrase which recalls the elaborate betrothal masque of *The Tempest*. Here Ceres is 'presented' (possibly meaning performed by), Ariel (*Temp.* 4.1.167) alongside **Juno** and **Iris**, as 'most bounteous lady', an embodiment of productive harmony between humans and nature. She presides over fields of 'wheat, rye, barley, fetches [vetch, used for animal fodder], oats and pease', meadows providing hay for winter and carefully pruned vineyards (*Temp.* 4.1.60–3, 68). Her streams have banks of flowers 'to make cold nymphs chaste crowns' (*Temp.* 4.1.66) like **Ophelia**'s, while the groves of yellow broom shelter the love-lorn bachelor, and the rocky sea coast is 'sterile and rocky-hard' (*Temp.* 4.1.64–9). All these are examples of implicitly unnatural withdrawal from Ceres's bounteous model of carefully managed fertility. Ceres's blessing of prosperity to the couple prefigures the incessant agricultural cycle of sowing and harvest that **Miranda**'s body will be subjected to under the husbandry of Ferdinand, apparently without even a break for winter:

> **Earth**'s increase, foison plenty,
> Barns and garners never empty
> Vines with clust'ring bunches growing,
> Plants with goodly burthen bowing;
> Spring come to you at the farthest
> In the very end of harvest!
>
> (*Temp.* 4.1.110–15)

The '*graceful dance*' (*Temp.* 4.1.SD138) of **nymph**s and reapers represents kinetically Ceres's careful supervision and containment of fertility. It is, the masque implies, a result of her **daughter**'s kidnap. Ceres has rejected the extra-marital sexual activity promoted by **Venus** and Cupid, who plotted with Dis (*Temp.* 4.1.87–91), although the breakdown of dance and masque because of Caliban's conspiracy shows that a threat remains.

(c) Ceres' role as mother of agriculture and her search for her daughter Proserpina is found in Golding's 1567 translation of Ovid's *Metamorphoses*, Book 5 lines 434–712 (Ovidius 2000: pp. 125–35). Thomas Rogers' words are one of a series of explanatory notes on the mythography used in his *Celestiall Elegies of the Goddesses and the Muses* on the Countess of Hertford (1598: sig. B6). Ceres also appears in John Lyly's play *Loue's metamorphosis: A vvittie and courtly pastorall* (1601). For more details about Ceres, see Barbette Stanley Spaeth (1996). Stevie Davies reads the Ceres / Demeter myth in relation to *The Winter's Tale* (1986: 52–65). On Ceres and the representation of a court masque in *The Tempest*, see Glynne Wickham (1975), Kevin McNamara (1987) and David Lindley (1984: 47–59).

Charmian, (a) one of two companions or **waiting-gentlewomen** to **Cleopatra** in *Antony and Cleopatra*. The name is of Greek origin, meaning 'delight' or 'joy'.
(b) Shakespeare's expansion of the role from the brief mention in Plutarch's *Lives* creates a character who appears witty and fun-loving. In the second scene, Charmian and **Iras** tease Alexas and the Soothsayer who tells fortunes. Charmian asks that her 'excellent fortune' should be to 'marry three kings in a forenoon, and **widow** them all', or to have a child to whom Herod would pay homage, or to marry Octavius Caesar and reverse positions with her **mistress** who would become her companion (1.2.26–30). Although Charmian is joking, her fantasies betray a hidden desire for power like that enjoyed by her mistress. Nevertheless, she remains utterly loyal; the Soothsayer's warning 'you shall be more beloving than beloved' (1.2.23) prophesies her absolute devotion to **Cleopatra** in choosing to commit suicide with her. By showing the path not taken – Charmian's lively desires for social success and for children in the future (1.2.37–40) – the text makes her commitment to Cleopatra appear all the more poignant. 'You shall be yet far fairer than you are' (1.2.17) the Soothsayer predicts, as if elevating an idealized form of courtly loyalty.

Such loyalty does not prevent Charmian from teasing her mistress with reminders of her former affection for Julius Caesar (1.4.66–72) or recalling the tricks Cleopatra played on Antony (2.5.15–18). Charmian is, likewise, unafraid to counsel her mistress. She criticizes Cleopatra's 'method' of contrary behaviour for encouraging Antony's love, saying 'Tempt him not so far' (1.3.11) and in the face of Cleopatra's uncontrolled anger towards the messenger Charmian calmly advises 'keep yourself within yourself, / The man is innocent' (2.5.75–6). There may even be a wicked irony in her later comment that the messenger has 'seen majesty' in 'serving you so long' (3.3.43–4).

Charmian's primary role is always to support Cleopatra, literally so when she bids her women 'sustain me' (3.11.45) as she goes to comfort Antony after the defeat at Actium. It is Charmian who instigates the final tragedy by counselling Cleopatra to retreat 'to th' monument!' and send Antony word of her death. (4.13.3–4), later helping Cleopatra to draw his dying body up there to her (4.15.12). It is to Charmian that Cleopatra confides directions for her suicide plot (5.2.192). While Iras kills herself before Cleopatra, Charmian remains staunchly loyal to close the 'downy windows' of her mistress's 'royal' eyes, and to rearrange her crown before using the asp herself (5.2.316–19).
(c) In '"Companion Me with My Mistress": Cleopatra, Elizabeth I and their Waiting Women', Elizabeth A. Brown (1999: 131–45) gives a detailed analysis of the scenes featuring Charmian and Iras as part of Cleopatra's household in comparison with that of Elizabeth I and her waiting women.

Charybdis, (a) a whirlpool between Italy and Sicily, personified as a female monster eager to drown ships and devour the sailors. *See* **Scylla**.

chastity, (a) the quality of being chaste, or free from unlawful sexual intercourse (outside marriage), of being continent or celibate. As applied to early modern women the adjective 'chaste' carries huge significance, signifying not only the sexual purity which guarantees male ownership, identity and inheritance lines, but also carrying meanings of moral purity, innocence, virtue and worth. Along with silence and obedience, chastity was one of the three principal female virtues. It is frequently associated with **Diana**, goddess of chastity, and with the moon.

(b) Juan Luis Vives summarized the dominant view in early modern culture, that 'chastity is the principal virtue of a woman and counterpoiseth with all the rest; if she have that, no man will look for any other, and if she lack that, no man will regard other' (Aughterson 1995: 70). Shakespeare's texts follow this gender bias: chaste is used of men twice in *Merry Wives* (2.1.80 and 5.5.85), once of Florizel (*WT* 4.4.33–5), and once of the stars (*Oth.* 5.2.2), and Celia jokes to Rosalind that 'the very ice of chastity' is in Orlando's kisses (*AYLI* 3.4.17), but otherwise it is a term applied to women. Even Adonis, who rejects the love of Venus, is no match in iconic terms for '**Lucrece** the chaste' (*Luc.* 7). Petruchio boasts his wife will swap places with Diana and rival 'Roman Lucrece for her chastity' (*Shrew* 2.1.296).

Chaste is usually employed to mean physically celibate in allusions to the virgin goddess Diana, as in **Portia**'s fear she will live 'as chaste as Diana' or in Claudio's bitter regret that **Hero** seemed 'As chaste as is the bud ere it be blown' (*MAdo* 4.1.58). Edward III puns on Diana's identity as goddess of hunting to say of the **Countess** of Salisbury 'I had rather have her chas'd than chaste' (*EIII* 2.1.153). The most we learn about **Valeria** is from Coriolanus's hyperbolic greeting:

> The **moon** of Rome, chaste as the icicle
> That's curdied by the frost from purest snow
> And hangs on Dian's temple – dear Valeria!
> (*Cor.* 5.3.65–7)

Corporeal purity lies behind the command to **Ophelia** not to lose her heart or lay her 'chaste treasure' open to Hamlet's desire (*Ham.* 1.3.31). In comic contrast, the keepers of the brothel are disturbed to find that **Marina**'s virginity is not a 'dish of chastity with rosemary and bays' to be served up to customers, but a troublesome hindrance to trade (*Per.* 4.1.150–5). The young **woman** in *A Lover's Complaint*, which may possibly be by Shakespeare, describes the loss of her **virgin**ity as taking off 'my white stole of chastity' (*LC* 297). Physical celibacy is also meant in **Rosaline**'s vow to 'live chaste' from Romeo's love (*R&J* 1.1.217) and **Isabella**'s to protect her 'chaste body' (*MM* 5.1.97) from Angelo's lust. More frequently, chastity signifies the full resonance of female virtue, indeed a woman's whole identity, as in Isabella's remarkable declaration, 'More than our brother is our chastity' (*MM* 2.4.185). Orlando uses chaste as a tag for **Rosalind**'s goodness, publishing her as Diana's follower, 'the fair, the chaste, and unexpressive she' (*AYL* 3.2.10) as if this were quite sufficient to explain his love.

Chastity becomes even more important in the case of married females, as the necessary guarantee of paternity, inheritance, and identity. Diana in *All's Well* refers to her chastity as 'the **jewel** of our house / Bequeathed down from many ancestors' (*AWW* 4.2.46–7). William Gouge's popular conduct book *Of Domesticall*

Duties (1622) described chastity within wedlock as 'that virtue whereby parties married, observing the lawful and honest use of marriage, keep their bodies from being defiled with strange flesh' (Keeble 1994: 129). Shakespeare's description of the Phoenix and the Turtle outlines an extreme version of 'married chastity' based on platonic celibacy (*PT* 61). Suggestions of an unconsummated marriage also inform the dramatic depictions of Queen **Katherine**, wife of Henry VIII, and possibly **Desdemona**. Katherine refers to **Princess Mary** as 'the model of our chaste loves' (*HVIII* 4.2.132) and requests a **virgin** burial for herself:

> When I am dead, good **wench**,
> Let me be us'd with **honour**: strew me over
> With **maid**en flowers, that all the world may know
> I was a chaste wife to my grave.
>
> (*HVIII* 4.2.167–70)

References to Desdemona as chaste (*Oth.* 5.2.249) may also imply an unconsummated marriage with Othello, represented materially by the white **wedding** sheets (*Oth.* 4.2.105). Desdemona's innocence makes her a model of wifely purity; if she is not '**honest**, chaste and true' then the 'purest' of men's wives is 'foul as slander', as Emilia observes (*Oth.* 4.2.17–19). The problem is that no married woman's chastity can be absolutely guaranteed; Iago delights in the fact that 'many worthy and chaste **dames**' who are innocent meet reproach (*Oth.* 4.1.46–7). As Hamlet tells Ophelia, if she marries 'be thou as chaste as ice, as pure as snow, thou shalt not escape calumny' (*Ham.* 3.1.135–6) and this is precisely what drives the plots of *Othello*, *Cymbeline* and *Winter's Tale*, in which chaste wives are falsely accused. Hermione knows that stating 'my past life / Hath been as continent, as chaste, as true, / As I am now unhappy' will mean little in the light of Leontes' deluded nightmares about her adultery (*WT* 3.2.33–5). The oracle's first words 'Hermione is chaste' (*WT* 3.2.132) are declared as the foundation of order, in opposition to his tyranny.

The high stakes associated with a wife's chastity as a mark of male ownership are raised even further when such chastity is widely advertised and vaunted, often in a competitive context. Posthumus prompts Iachimo's plot by boasting that **Imogen** is more 'chaste, constant-qualified and less attemptable than any the rarest of our ladies in France' (*Cym.* 1.4.60–1). A similar competition precedes the action of *Lucrece*, where the Argument explicitly states that Collatine inflames Tarquin's desire to rape her by extolling 'the incomparable chastity of his wife' (*Luc.* Argument. 12–13). Chastity is elevated as a rich jewel, ready to be stolen:

> Happ'ly that name of 'chaste' unhapp'ly set
> This bateless edge on his keen appetite
> When Collatine unwisely did not let
> To praise the clear unmatched red and white
> Which triumph'd in that sky of his delight.
>
> (*Luc.* 8–12)

By association with Lucrece, **Lavinia** in *Titus* is set up as a prize for ravishment when Aaron tells Chiron and Demetrius 'Lucrece was not more chaste / Than this Lavinia, Bassianus' love' (*Tit.* 2.1.108–9). It is Lavinia's pride in her chastity and 'nuptial vow' (*Tit.* 2.3.124–5) that makes Chiron want to **rape** her on top of her husband's body. Marcus later swears to follow the pattern of Lucrece's father and husband, in taking revenge for the rape (*Tit.* 4.1.89–94). In Shakespeare's poem, it is Lucrece's suicide that metaphorically restores her chastity: stabbing herself to death in another violent penetration rewrites the rape as loss rather than pollution. Vives described chastity as 'the most goodly treasure that a woman can have' (Aughterson 1995: 169), a sentiment Lucrece echoes in her lament 'O that is gone for which I sought to live' (*Luc.* 1051). Shakespeare's poem points out that Tarquin has an empty victory: 'Poor Chastity is rifled of her store / And Lust, the thief, far poorer than before' (*Luc.* 692–3).

The fact that chastity sometimes depends more on reputation than corporeal purity is the cause of jokes as well. Lysimachus cynically remarks that the Bawd's modest speech can undeservedly give 'a good report to a number to be chaste' (*Per.* 4.6.40). The most blatant example of such a false report is in Joan La Pucelle's description of herself as

> A virgin from her tender infancy,
> Chaste, and immaculate in very thought,
> Whose maiden blood, thus rigorously effus'd,
> Will cry for vengeance at the gates of heaven.
> (*1HVI* 5.4.50–3)

Joan's implicit comparison of herself to the **Virgin** neatly summarizes the complex depiction of female chastity in Shakespeare's texts. It is simultaneously the distinguishing mark of a virgin and a virtuous **mother** (Joan is mocked as a holy maid with **child** when she claims pregnancy to escape execution 5.4.65); it is regarded by men as culturally sacred, desirable in the erotic sense, and, paradoxically, difficult to believe in.

(c) Aughterson reprints a good selection of popular early modern texts advocating chastity as a female virtue (1995: 22, 26–8, 67, 70–4, 112–13, 123–4, 166–9). Dusinberre (1996: 30–76) outlines the mystique of chastity, the valuation of married chastity after the Reformation, and the relationship between female chastity and property. Baines (1990) evaluates the positive value of **Isabella**'s chastity in *Measure for Measure*. Joan Gibson (2006) discusses how three different women writers (Sor Juana De La Cruz, Luisa Siega and Tullia D'Aragona) challenge the idea that chastity, as a primary female virtue, is incompatible with rational thought. Suzanne Hull (1982) considers the recommended reading for women which promoted the model of woman as chaste, silent and obedient.

child, (a) a human offspring, or, sometimes more specifically, a **girl**. The term is used of younger boys but is used more frequently and longer of, and to, females.
(b) Shakespeare certainly uses the word with this gender bias, most explicitly

when the Old Shepherd finds the abandoned baby **Perdita** and exclaims 'a very pretty barne! A boy or a child, I wonder?' (*WT* 3.3.70). 'Child' indicates dependence and closeness to the **mother** so it is unsurprising that female characters use 'child' or 'my child' more frequently than their male counterparts to refer to younger male characters, most notably **Constance** in *King John*. Nowhere does Shakespeare use 'my child' to or of an adult son. Even Cymbeline, who compares himself to 'a mother to the birth of three' (*Cym.* 5.5.369) in recovering his lost 'children', distinguishes Guiderius and Arviragus as 'a pair of worthier sons' (*Cym.* 5.5.354–6), from **Imogen** 'my flesh, my child' (*Cym.* 5.5.264). The term often marks a continued dependence by adult daughters, or an illusion of parental protection a father believes he can provide. For example, Leonato and Lord Capulet refer to the marriageable **Hero** and **Juliet**, respectively, as 'my child' (*MAdo* 5.1.274; *R&J* 4.5.62), and Lear regains consciousness and some self-possession in recognizing his daughter: 'I think this lady / To be my child Cordelia' (*KL* 4.7.68–9). The Earl of Warwick in *Edward III* realizes how viciously he is perverting the role of protector by asking his daughter to commit adultery with the King: 'I must not call her child, for where's the father / That will in such a suit seduce his child?' (*EIII* 2.1.374–5). *Love's Labour's Lost* offers another apparently gender-specific use of the word in describing the adult **Jaquenetta** as 'a child of our grandmother Eve, a female; or, for thy more sweet understanding, a woman' (*LLL* 1.1.263–5).

childbed, *see* **birth**

chopine, (a) a type of shoe or overshoe with high cork soles which lifted garments out of any dirt on the ground and made the wearer appear taller. Chopines, of Italian origin, were much higher than most English varieties of corked-sole shoes and the shoes were detachable from the cork platforms.
(b) A single reference, in *Hamlet*, is made to the **boy actor** in the company of visiting players, whom Hamlet addresses as 'my young **lady** and **mistress**!' He comments that 'your ladyship is nearer to heaven than when I saw you last, by the altitude of a chopine' (2.2.424–7), and hopes the boy's voice has not broken to prevent him playing female parts. It is possible that cork-soled shoes could have been worn by younger boy actors to make them look taller when they played adult female characters. If so, Hamlet may qualify his original surprise at the boy's growth on discovering his footwear. Ashelford (1983) points out that chopines ranged from 4 to 18 inches in height.
(c) Ashelford describes a 1592 illustration of a Venetian **courtezan** wearing chopines (1983: 123). Arnold gives an illustrated discussion of chopines and pantobles, the English cork-soled shoes worn on their own or as overshoes (1988: 214–15).

Circe, (a) a mythic enchantress famous for her magic potions, who charmed Odysseus's followers and changed them into pigs.
(b) Circe is a symbol of the loss of control experienced by the male characters in *Comedy of Errors*, an implicit contrast to the order restored by the Abbess. The

Duke says 'I think you all have drunk of Circe's cup' (*Err.* 5.1.270) after Antipholus is presumed possessed and in need of exorcism. Since Ephesus was a meeting point of Christian and pagan beliefs, the reference is especially appropriate. The Duke of York aligns Circe's shape-changing abilities with witchcraft when comparing Joan La **Pucelle**: 'See how the ugly witch doth bend her brows, / As if, with Circe, she would change my shape' (*1HVI* 5.3.34–5).

(c) Yarnall's transhistorical study (1994) considers how Circe herself has been transformed in Western literature from her appearance in Homer's *Odyssey*, arguing that the myth proved especially compelling to Spenser and other Renaissance writers (pp. 99–144).

circle, (a) like **ring**, a bawdy metaphor for the female vagina.

(b) Shakespeare uses the term twice in this bawdy sense, the first in *Romeo and Juliet* where Mercutio says that it would anger Romeo 'to raise a spirit in his **mistress**' circle / Of some strange nature, letting it there stand / Till she had laid it and conjured it down' (*R&J* 2.1.23–6). More surprisingly, Burgundy also uses it to tease Henry V when he has been wooing **Princess Katherine**, that if he would conjure love in her 'you must make a circle; if conjure up Love in her in his true likeness, he must appear naked and blind' which will inevitably shock her 'if she deny the appearance of a naked blind boy in her naked seeing self' (*HV* 5.2.292–8). It is no accident that Lucrece's suicide visually magnifies the violent penetration of her vagina where 'the crimson blood / Circles her body in on every side' (*Luc.* 1738–9).

city-wife, (a) and 'city woman' are both generic types based on the citizens' wives of early modern London. As members of an increasingly prosperous middle class, citizens' wives were popularly characterized as socially ambitious, imitating the fashions of gentle or noble classes, especially those at court. Citizens' wives often worked as part of their husband's businesses and so were a visible presence in the public arenas of the city. As dramatic types, they are often presented as desirable commodities and as confident and self-assertive.

(b) Jacques satirizes the type's obsession with fashion in lines that would have offered a powerful comic critique when addressed to members of an early modern audience:

> What woman in the city do I name,
> When that I say the city-woman bears
> The cost of princes on unworthy shoulders?
> Who can come in and say that I mean her,
> When such a one as she, such is her neighbor?
> (*AYLI* 2.7.74–8)

Buckingham slanders Edward IV's reputation by rumouring 'his enforcement of the city wives' (*RIII* 3.7.9), probably an allusion to his affair with Jane **Shore**.

(c) City comedies by Middleton, Dekker and Heywood, for example, offer numerous examples of the generic type in action. Gibbons (1980), McLuskie (1994), Dillon (2000) and Howard (2007) offer critical readings.

Claribel, (a) the **daughter** of Alonso, King of Naples in *The Tempest*. She does not appear in the play but the boat carrying Alonso, Ferdinand, Sebastian, Gonzalo and the other visitors to the island is wrecked on its way back from transporting Claribel to Tunis to marry its king.
(b) Claribel is 'a paragon' (*Temp.* 2.1.76), compared with **Dido**, Queen of the nearby city of Carthage (2.1.2.1.77–86). Her name means 'bright and beautiful', and Shakespeare may have derived it from the romance heroine in Spenser's *Faerie Queene*, whose father, the Lord of Many Islands, is renowned 'For his great riches and his greater might' and 'through the wealth, wherein he did abound / This daughter thought in wedlocke to have bound / Unto the Prince of *Pictland*' (Spenser 1970: 390).
(c) Claribell appears in *The Faerie Queene* Book VI, Canto 12, Stanzas 4–13 (Spenser 1970: 390–1).

Cleopatra, (a) the Queen of Egypt famous for her erotic attraction of the Roman leaders Julius Caesar, Pompey the Great, and Mark Antony; a character in *Antony and Cleopatra*. She was the daughter of Ptolemy XI Auletes and, after his death, married her brother Ptolemy XII, in line with Egyptian custom.
(b) Cleopatra's name conjures desire. In the opening scene of *Antony and Cleopatra* Antony admits he will be himself 'but stirr'd by Cleopatra' (*A&C* 1.1.43) and Pompey refers to her lasciviousness by calling her 'Salt Cleopatra' (*A&C* 2.1.21). Alongside this, deprecatory comments identify Cleopatra's erotic power with exotic difference. According to Mercutio, Romeo's racist view is that Cleopatra is nothing better than 'a gipsy' (*R&J* 2.4.41) compared with his love. The word 'gipsy', which derives from Egyptian, is also used disparagingly by Philo in the opening lines of *Antony and Cleopatra* (*A&C* 1.1.10). Cleopatra's name is thus something of a paradox. On the one hand, it conjures up images of immense power. Cleopatra reminds spectators of her history in conquering the hearts of Roman leaders:

> Broad-fronted Caesar,
> When thou wast here above the ground, I was
> A morsel for a monarch; and great Pompey
> Would stand and make his eyes grow in my brow;
> There would he anchor his aspect, and die
> With looking on his life.
>
> (*A&C* 1.5.29–34)

Such power is legendary. Orlando feels that **Rosalind** shares 'Cleopatra's majesty' (*AYLI* 3.2.146), among her other outstanding qualities. The hangings in **Imogen**'s bedchamber picture 'Proud Cleopatra' meeting Antony on the banks of Cydnus (*Cym.* 2.4.70–1), the scene narrated by Enobarbus (*A&C* 2.2.191–226).

In *Edward III*, the King, overpowered by his desire for the **Countess** of Salisbury, compares his subjection to that of Julius Caesar: 'What says the more than Cleopatra's match / To Caesar now?' (*EIII* 2.2.35–44).

At the same time, Cleopatra's name, linked indelibly with her identity as **Queen** of Egypt, is always overshadowed by the imperialist, masculine power of Rome. Her sovereignty is one that she is always in danger of losing. Antony refuses to name her when she allows Ceasar's servant to kiss her hand: 'should I find them / So saucy with the hand of she here – what's her name / Since she was Cleopatra?' (*A&C* 3.13.97–9). Cleopatra, too, sees her name as sovereign of Egypt. Only when they are reconciled later in the scene and determined to fight Octavius Caesar does she reclaim her identity and birthright as Egyptian Queen:

> It is my birthday,
> I had thought t' have held it poor; but since my lord
> Is Antony again, I will be Cleopatra.
>
> (*A&C* 3.13.184–6)

Because she identifies her name so completely with her nation, she cannot bear the prospect of subjecting herself to Octavius Caesar. To do so will be to be reduced to 'some squeaking Cleopatra' a diminished version of herself as a spoil of Octavius Caesar's victory, who will be displayed in Rome by an actor who will 'boy my greatness' (*A&C* 5.2.220–1). To be a colony of Rome rather than Queen of Egypt is equated with the boy actor's vain attempt to conjure the identity of a powerful, independent woman. Shakespeare's play thus seems to acknowledge the illusion of greatness presented in Cleopatra who is always under erasure from masculinist and imperial Roman domination.

(c) Hughes-Hallett (1990) gives a broad cultural history of the myth of Cleopatra while Kleiner (2005) analyses the myth's development from 1700 and offers a historical account of Cleopatra's influence on Rome. The pioneering critic Anna Jameson refuses to be 'an apologist' of Cleopatra's historical character 'nor of such women as resemble her', but considers the 'antithetical construction' of the dramatic character 'its *consistent inconsistency*' (2005: 260–88). Alfar (2003) persuasively reads the political strategies adopted by Shakespeare's character in the play's dynamics of gender and power, developing the approach in Kahn (1997). Peggy Munoz Simonds (1994) reads Cleopatra in relation to the iconographic tradition of the goddess **Fortune**. Catherine Belsey's 'Cleopatra's Seduction' (1996) examines the heterogeneous desires catered for by Cleopatra's seductive strategies. Singh (2003) analyses critical responses to Cleopatra. Adelman (1999) uses the representation of Cleopatra by a boy actor to interrogate assumptions about an early modern one-sex model. Judith Cook (1980) traces the shortcomings of representations of role in productions from the Restoration to the 1970s. Frances De La Tour (2005) discusses playing the role. The repeated failure of Anglo-European stage tradition to cast Cleopatra as black is taken up by Carol Rutter (2001). This follows a racist distrust of Cleopatra's exotic otherness going back at least to **Aemilia** Lanyer's poem *Salve Deus Rex Judaeorum* (1611) in which

Cleopatra's worldly love makes her appear as 'a blacke Egyptian' in comparison to the purity of heavenly love (Lanyer 1993: 112–13 ll. 1409–32). Helen Wilcox and Rina Walthaus (2008) offer an interesting comparison between Cleopatras in English and Spanish Golden Age Drama.

cod-piece, (a) a bag or case attached to the front of the hose that concealed the opening and protected the male genitals. As an external marker of male identity, cod-pieces were often flamboyantly decorated. They are assumed as a disguise by female characters who cross-dress.
(b) **Lucetta** identifies the cod-piece as a crucial part of **Julia**'s male disguise as Sebastian in *Two Gentleman of Verona*, protesting that Julia will need one on top of her hose to pass for a fashionable or 'well-reputed' page: 'A round hose, madam, now's not worth a pin / Unless you have a codpiece to stick pins on' (*TGV* 2.7.53–6). The cod-piece is an important finishing touch that distinguishes a man from a boy. Although the Host regards Sebastian as a 'pretty **youth**', he asks 'How do you, man?' (4.1.56) and not even Proteus suspects Julia. An early modern satire complains that in the present hermaphroditic climate, the 'codpis' is necessary for men 'thereby to disclose / What sexe they are, since strumpets breeches use' (Marston 1598: 46). In cases of cross-dressing, however, Garber (1992: 122) argues that a cod-piece becomes an unstable signifier; it is impossible to know whether it is full or empty.
(c) Marston, John, *The metamorphosis of pigmalion's image and other satires* (1598), discusses the codpiece. Margerie Garber's *Vested Interests* (1992) is a trans-historical study of cross-dressing and cultural anxiety. Its psychoanalytic approach and readings provide a rich resource for reading cross-dressed heroines in Shakespeare.

coif, (a) a close-fitting linen cap covering the top, sides and back of the head and tied under the chin. This was worn by women and by men (as nightcaps or as part of their official or professional attire) and as part of medical treatments. The coif could be tied close to the neck at the back to contain the hair.
(b) Tied under the chin, a coif or a **caul** (hair net) would help the boy actor to secure any false hair, just as many women did. (Boasting of his horse, the Dauphin says 'I'll tell thee Constable, my mistress wears his own hair' (*HV* 3.7.61).) Autolycus advertises 'Golden quoifs and stomachers / For my lads to give their dears' (*WT* 4.4.224–5) among the fashionable accessories he has for sale. Cross-dressing may have made a special feature of the coif. For example, when **Portia** cross-dresses as Bellario, the actor would have replaced Portia's woman's coif or caul with the professional white linen coif worn exclusively by lawyers as a mark of their profession.
(c) Ashelford gives illustrations of male and female examples (1983: 40, 72). Arnold presents more elaborately decorated examples including those made by Roger Montague for Queen Elizabeth and her household (1988: 48–9 202–8).

commodity, (a) generally, the quality of something in relation to the desires or needs of men, a mark of profit, and more specifically, an item produced for use or sale to be exchanged for profit, related to goods, or merchandise. More recently the term has been popular in feminist criticism to describe the traffic in women, or exchange of women between men.

(b) Shakespeare personifies 'tickling Commodity' as a 'smooth fac'd gentleman' and 'broker' or 'bawd' who cheats **maids** of their virginity (*KJ* 2.1.568–72), and Parolles warns **Helena** that **virginity** is 'a commodity will lose the gloss with lying: the longer kept, the less worth' and recommends 'off with 't while 'tis vendible; answer the time of request' (*AWW* 1.1.153–5). In both cases, commodity is related to male desire and to profit. Tranio uses it to refer to the traffic in women when Baptista claims that he has 'played a merchant's part' by matching Katherina to Petruchio. Tranio describes her as 'a commodity lay fretting by you', like remaindered or unused goods (*Shrew* 2.1.28). Used of a **woman** in early modern England, the term implies prostitution, as in Dekker's definition of 'the **Whore**, who is called the commoditie' (1608: sig. H2). Thersites refers to 'a commodious **drab**' or whore in *Troilus and Cressida* (5.2.94) and in plays with brothels, a commodity is implicitly a prostitute. In *Pericles* the Pander complains that 'our credit comes not in like the commodity nor the commodity wages not with the danger' (*Per.* 4.2.30–1). In *Measure for Measure* prostitution and financial dealings are paralleled when Master Rash, like many of the former customers of Mistress **Overdone**'s brothel, is imprisoned 'for a commodity of brown paper and old ginger' (*MM* 4.3.5).

(c) Thomas Dekker's *The Belman of London* (1608) lists 'commodity' as the cant term for a 'prostitute' amongst rogues and beggars. Gayle Rubin, 'The Traffic in Women: Notes on the "Political Economy" of Sex' (1975), and Luce Irigaray's 'Women in the Market' (1997) are two classic feminist essays on women as commodities. Singh (2000) gives a specific reading of how this operates in *Merchant of Venice*, while Cohen's essay (2001) on the mercantile geography of Shakespeare's plays gives an overview of the economic exchanges in which commodity features. *See also* **gift**.

conceive, (a) used of women, to receive seed in the womb and become pregnant with offspring; more generally, the verb means to take into the mind, or think of.

(b) Popular medical books such as Thomas Raynalde's *The Birth Of Mankind* (1565) or Helkiah Crooke's *Microcosmographia* (1618) explained that the woman 'affordeth the playce wherein the seed is conceived and sustained and the matter wherein the conception is nourished and sustained' (Aughterson 1995: 54). Benedick acknowledges this basic physiological truth about human origins: 'that a woman conceiv'd me, I thank her; that she brought me up, I likewise give her most humble thanks' (*MAdo* 1.1.238–40). **Titania** and her pregnant **votaress** celebrate the natural fertility of the female body in comparison with masculine endeavours to generate through commerce and trade on the seas:

> . . . we have laugh'd to see the sails conceive
> And grow big-bellied with the wanton wind;

Which she, with pretty and with swimming gait,
Following (her **womb** then rich with my young squire)
Would imitate, and sail upon the land
To fetch me trifles.

(*MND* 2.1.128–33)

Bawdier references to conception out of wedlock are made in *Hamlet* and *King Lear*. Hamlet warns Polonius, 'Conception is a blessing, but as your daughter may conceive, friend, look to 't' (*Ham.* 2.2.184) and Gloucester answers Kent's polite refusal to understand Edmund's base birth, 'I cannot conceive you' with the crude joke 'Sir, this young fellow's mother could; whereupon she grew round-womb'd, and had indeed, sir, a son for her cradle ere she had a husband for her bed' (*KL* 1.1.12–16). Similar bawdy innuendo surrounds the way Hortensio's **widow** understands or 'conceives by' Petruchio (*Shrew* 5.2.22–5).

Female conception, although natural, is perceived as threatening without the correct controls of husbandry. Burgundy describes the fertility of France as 'wanting the scythe' and thus 'losing both beauty and utility' as it 'Conceives by idleness, and nothing teems / But hateful docks, rough thistles, kecksies, burs' (*HV* 5.2.50–3). Polixenes patronisingly informs Perdita that the art of grafting is a natural process that can marry 'a gentler scion to the wildest stock, / And make conceive a bark of baser kind / By bud of nobler race' (*WT* 4.4.92–5), though his own violent reaction against his son's proposed match with a shepherd's daughter contradicts this philosophy. More extreme cases of misconception are found in *Henry VI Part I* and *Henry VIII*, where **Joan** La **Pucelle** pretends that she has been 'misconceived' and is not a shepherd's **daughter** but an immaculately-conceived **virgin** 'issued from the progeny of kings' (*1HVI* 5.4.38, 49–51). Henry VIII laments that fact that if Katherine 'conceived a male child by me', it died within the womb or shortly after birth (*HVIII* 2.4.189–94). Female conception becomes a grotesque metaphor for mistaken apprehension in *Julius Caesar* when Messala laments that mistaking of victory as defeat is like 'melancholy's child' which 'soon conceived / Thou never com'st unto a happy birth, / But kill'st the mother that engender'd thee!' (5.3.67–71).

(c) T. Raynalde, *The Birth of Mankind, otherwise named the womans booke* (1565) and extracts from other early modern medical texts which give an outline of early modern theories of conception are found in Aughterson (1995: 41–66).

concubine, (a) a kept mistress.

(b) The **widow** Elizabeth, Lady Grey regards it as a very demeaning status, telling King Edward IV, 'I know I am too mean to be your queen, / And yet too good to be your concubine' (*3HVI* 3.2.97–8). Her refusal to become his concubine obliges the King to make her his Queen, destroying his alliances with Lady **Bona**, France and the Earl of Warwick.

Constance, (a) the name of the **Duchess** of Bretagne, a title she inherited from her father. She was married to Henry II's son Geoffrey, to whom she bore a daughter

Elinor, and (shortly after she was widowed), a son Arthur. After Geoffrey's death, Constance ruled Bretagne but Henry II invaded and forced her to marry one of his favourites, the Earl of Chester, whom she eventually divorced, in order to marry Guy, Count de Thouars. She appears in *King John* as a **widow** and **mother** to Arthur.

(b) Perhaps Queen **Eleanor** speaks with reference to the historical figure when she warns King John 'that ambitious Constance would not cease / Till she had kindled France and all the world' to support Arthur's claims to the throne (1.1.32). In the play, Constance's ambitions are all focused on her son. Nevertheless, Eleanor presents a model of the widowed **dowager**'s power behind the throne. Anna Jameson argued 'the principal attribute of Constance is *power* – power of imagination, of will, of passion, of pride' (Jameson, 2005: 313), and much of her dramatic power derives from her status as **mother** and **widow**. John's first promise to 'create young Arthur Duke of Britain' is hardly likely to placate Constance since he inherited the title from her (2.1.551) and, indeed, she reacts passionately to the news of the match between Blanch and Lewis that will disinherit Arthur. She refuses to join the **wedding** procession and upstages it by staging herself as a proud queen of sorrow (3.1.67). Her acerbic reminders that the French King's lack of integrity makes him no more than 'a counterfeit / Resembling majesty' (3.1.99–100) and her claim that 'since the law itself is perfect wrong / How can the law forbid my tongue to curse?' (3.1.189–90) carry considerable moral and political weight. Constance lives up to her name in her sustained appeals on behalf of Arthur, thereby challenging the prejudice of inconstancy – so often levelled at women – by her maternal devotion and determination. When Arthur is taken prisoner to England, and the maternal role is gone, her life loses meaning. She uses her name to demonstrate the logic of her despair to others:

> My name is Constance, I was Geffrey's wife,
> Young Arthur is my son, and he is lost.
> I am not mad, I would to heaven I were!
> For then 'tis like I should forget myself.
>
> (3.4.46–9)

True to her name, Constance cannot 'forget herself' as a wife and **mother**. She persists in defining herself in relation to her husband and son, both of whom are now lost. As a widow, her despair leads her to court death (3.4.25–35); with the second loss of Arthur 'my widow-comfort' (3.4.105), nothing can 'fill the room up' (3.4.93).

(c) Anna Jameson, who was obviously very impressed by the example of female agency presented by the historical Constance, recounts her life in detail as a prelude to assessing Shakespeare's powerful character in her 1858 volume *Shakespeare's Heroines* (2005: 302–22). By contrast, Frank Harris (1912), with no evidence, reads Constance as a **scold** modelled on Shakespeare's shrewish wife, the only redeeming feature of the character being her maternal tenderness (Harris 1912: 43–9). Juliet Dusinberre (1989) and Howard and Rackin (1997: 119–33)

give good feminist readings of Constance's power to subvert male-directed historical narratives. Kelly Hunter (2004) discusses her impressions of the role in a 2001
Royal Shakespeare Company production.

contract, *see* **betrothal**

Cordelia, (a) the youngest **daughter** of Lear, legendary king of ancient Britain,
and a character in both versions of Shakespeare's play *King Lear.* Her celtic name
means 'of the sea' but is also closely related to the Latin *cor, cordis*, 'heart'.
(b) In Holinshed and Geoffrey of Monmouth's historical narratives, the **princess**
is named Cordeilla and in Higgins' *Mirror for Magistrates* (1574), she is Cordeile
or Cordell. In the anonymous tragicomedy *King Leir*, she is Cordell. Shakespeare
appears to have taken Cordelia from Spenser's version of the story in *The Faerie
Queene*, where she is called 'the wise *Cordelia*' (Spenser 1970: 121). The name's
connection to the heart is emphasized in Cordelia's response to Lear's love test
for his daughters: 'What shall Cordelia speak? Love, and be silent' (*KL* 1.1.62).
With a love 'more ponderous than my tongue', she protests she cannot 'heave /
My heart into my mouth' (1.1.78, 91–2). In predicting that she will give half her
love to her husband, she again speaks from the heart (1.1.105), and implicitly
claims this speech is more 'true' (1.1.107) than those proclaimed by her sisters.
As Cordelia knows, Lear does not wish to hear the hard truth that he does not
have the exclusive love of his daughters, especially when the youngest is about to
leave him for a husband. Cordelia's role may be doubled with that of the other
truth-speaker, the Fool. Carrying Cordelia's corpse, Lear says 'And my poor fool
is hang'd' (5.3.306). In spite of Lear's reaction, the King of France apparently
recognizes Cordelia's personal integrity and proves his own by marrying her
without a dowry. The idea of truth being located inside the body (near the heart,
as Cordelia's name implies) is borne out by subsequent events. While Lear seeks
to anatomize Regan's hard-heartedness (3.6.76), Cordelia's love is demonstrated
in her return to restore his kingdom to him, a tender care for his physical restoration, and an exchange demonstrating her unqualified love and forgiveness of the
parent who had previously banished her (4.7.25–83). Her position as leader of an
invading French army extends the tragic paradox she embodies as rebellious, self-
assertive virago and dutiful daughter (Millard 1989). The heart of unconditional
love she represents is broken when she is killed: Lear carries her on stage 'dead
as earth' (5.3.261–2), and dies seeking to find breath on her lips (5.3.308–12).
Kent's comment 'Break, heart, I prithee break!' (5.3.213) pinpoints the effects
of Cordelia's death on everyone. The only glimpse of hope that her sacrifice has
not been in vain is in the concluding vow to 'speak what we feel, not what we
ought to say' (5.3.325), which reiterates Cordelia's philosophy of speaking and
acting from the heart.
(c) Bullough (Vol. VII 1973: 269–420), reprints the sources including the anonymous play *The History of King Leir.* Spenser's short account of the Lear story is
given in Book 2, Canto X, Stanzas 27–32 in *The Faerie Queene* (Spenser 1970: 121).
R. S. White (1986) discusses Cordelia's role as sacrifice. Thomas A. Greenfield

(1977) argues for a change between the flawed Cordelia of Act 1 and the more mature heroine who returns in Act 4. Boose (1982) analyses Cordelia's position in the opening scene. Richard Knowles (1999) examines the political dimensions of Cordelia's return to England with an invading French army while Barbara C. Milllard (1989: 143–65) gives a striking reading of Cordelia's invasion, splitting her role between the stereotypical rebellious virago (condemned elsewhere in Shakespeare) and the dutiful daughter. Catherine S. Cox (1998) compares Cordelia and her sisters to the representation of virgos and viragos in early modern culture. The first chapter of Carol Rutter's *Enter The Body* (2000) concentrates on the representation of Cordelia's body in the final scene. Dympna Callaghan (1989) considers Cordelia's role in the contexts of *Othello*, tragedies by Webster, and feminist readings of women's place in early modern culture.

Cornelia, *see* **midwife**

countess, (a) a title used to indicate a woman holding a position in her own right equal to that of a count or an earl, or to indicate the wife or widow of a count. In the peerage of Great Britain and Ireland, 'countess' is also the correct term to refer to the wife or widow of an earl. The rank of countess is inferior to that of duchess or marchioness.

(b) Shakespeare's texts feature four speaking countesses: the Countess of Auvergne (*1HVI*), the Countess of Rossillion (*AWW*), the Countess of Salisbury (*EIII*), and **Olivia** in *Twelfth Night*. The first three characters are not named beyond their title and in *Twelfth Night* it still indicates formality when Orsino announces, 'Here comes the Countess, now heaven walks on earth' (*TN* 5.1.97), immediately demonstrating the emotional distance between him and Olivia. The title displays rank in *Henry VIII* where 'Certain Ladies or Countesses with plain circlets of gold without flowers' bring up the rear in the coronation procession following the crowned Queen and the Duchess of Norfolk, whose coronet does have flowers (*HVIII* 4.1.37 SD 'The Order of the Coronation'). The two gentlemen observers point out the magnificence of noble hierarchy: 'all the rest are Countesses. / Their coronets say so. These are stars indeed' (*HVIII* 4.1.53–4). Shakespeare's other uses of the title invariably invoke issues of class. In the first history tetralogy **Elizabeth**, formerly Lady Grey who married King Edward IV, feels threatened by 'The Countess Richmond', who does not appear on stage but whose reported 'proud arrogance' over Elizabeth (*RIII* 1.3.20–4) is unsurprising since **Margaret** Beaufort far outweighs her in rank, being daughter of a duke and great granddaughter of Prince John of Gaunt. She claimed the title Countess of Richmond in her own right from her first marriage to Edmund Tudor, Earl of Richmond, and is mother to Henry, Earl of Richmond who overthrows the Yorkist dynasty at the end of the play. Elizabeth arranges the marriage of her daughter to Richmond, thus subsuming the differences in blood between herself and the Countess.

Proud arrogance characterizes the Countess of Auvergne's plot to trap the English military hero Talbot, in *1HVI*. Through this comic battle between the sexes, the text critiques the French Countess's patronizing attitude to a lower-born soldier. She aims to imitate the military power of the Scythian queen Tomyris (and perhaps **Joan** La **Pucelle**), to deliver France and avenge the wrongs done to citizens, sons and husbands. She tells Talbot 'long time thy shadow hath been thrall to me' (*1HVI* 2.3.36), meaning his picture; so negative overtones of **witch**craft colour her feminine scheme to overthrow him. Parallels between the conquest of her castle, her body and of the nation are introduced when she seductively announces herself as: 'the virtuous **lady**, Countess of Auvergne', who 'with modesty', invites Talbot inside (*1HVI* 2.2.38–9). She then insults him by mocking his small stature. He is neither the Hector nor the Hercules she expected and appears to be at her mercy in the castle:

> Alas, this is a child, a silly dwarf!
> It cannot be this weak and writhled shrimp
> Should strike such terror to his enemies.
>> (*1HVI* 2.3.23–5)

The arrogant Countess wins only a hollow victory. Talbot claims he is overruled by 'a woman's kindness' and he will attend on her 'in submission' (*1HVI* 2.2.50–2), but secretly plots to bring his soldiers with him to the castle. In victory, he requests only that his 'soldiers' stomachs' can be satisfied with 'your wine' and 'what cates you have' (*1HVI* 2.3.79–80), although the potential for rape and pillage resonate beneath his courtesy.

The Countess of Rossillion, **a widow**, holds very different views about birth and rank. She is primarily a **mother**: to her son Bertram, the present Count, and to the orphaned gentlewoman **Helena**. In Act 1 Scene 2, Helena fears that the 'noble' Countess's 'honoured name' (*AWW* 1.3.156–7) will preclude any possibility of her marrying Bertram. The Countess, however, shows no social snobbery and assists Helena, writing to Bertram, presumably to promote the match (*AWW* 2.3.276–7). The Countess likewise engages in familiar exchanges with Rinaldo (her steward), and Lavatch, who used to be her husband's fool (*AWW* 4.5.64–7). She is the only character in Shakespeare to outwit a professional jester (in Act 2 Scene 2) (Freeman 2004: 77). Her one moment of social self-consciousness occurs when she rebukes herself for playing 'the noble huswife with the time / To entertain it so merrily with a fool' (*AWW* 2.2.60–1) and the rebuke is made half-jokingly (*see* **housewife**). Her most dramatic rejection of rank is to disown Bertram and 'wash his name' out of her blood (*AWW* 3.2.67–8) when he rejects Helena:

> There's nothing here that is too good for him
> But only she, and she deserves a lord
> That twenty such rude boys might tend upon,
> And call her hourly **mistress**.
>> (*AWW* 3.2.80–3)

The Countess, who is referred to as 'Old Lady' in the stage directions, almost collapses from grief and old age when she appears to have lost both her 'children'

(*AWW* 3.4.41–2). The play's conclusion allows her to see Bertram restored to the King's favour and Helena apparently restored to life and pregnant. The Countess's noble lineage allows her to identify the family ring, conferred 'Of six preceding ancestors' (*AWW* 5.3.195–8) and so unravelling the riddles.

In *Edward III*, the scenes with Countess of Salisbury are those in which critical opinion has most readily seen evidence of Shakespeare's hand. The Countess of Salisbury, renowned for her **beauty**, offers a parallel to the Countess of Auvergne in *Henry VI Part I*, in that she also invites the male hero into her husband's castle, but here with much more virtuous intentions. Under attack from the invading Scottish forces, she is the object of their acquisitive desire, but mocks them with spirit when news of the English King and his army is heard and her safety is assured:

> Say, good my lord, which is he must have the lady,
> And which her jewels? I am sure, my lords,
> Ye will not hence 'till you have shar'd the spoils.
>
> (EIII 1.2.62–4)

As **hostess** in her husband's absence, the Countess appeals to the King to accept her entertainment, explaining how this would honour them. She promises that the stern outside of the castle is exceeded by its beautiful interior: 'With bounty's riches and fair hidden pride' and 'where the golden ore doth buried lie' (*EIII* 1.2.145–9). This is a proper advertisement of her husband's wealth and the King formally accepts, addressing her as: 'Countess' (1.2.164–5). However, his desires for her make her lines seductive in corporeal terms as a metaphor for the Countess's body. Bounty's riches and fair hidden pride are qualities that emerge in the Countess's subsequent scenes in Act 2. She is generous, eloquent, witty, clever; loyal to her monarch, her nation and her husband. Rank is a prominent feature in wooing scenes between the King and the Countess; an awareness of the King's *droit de seigneur* lies behind their terms of address as 'Countess', 'my liege' or 'my thrice-dread sovereign' (*EIII* 2.1.208–11 and 2.1.217–220). At the same time, the King recognizes that his obsession gives her imperial power of command, as he accidentally conflates her with the Emperor of France:

> King Edward: Thus from the heart's abundance speaks the tongue:
> Countess for Emperor: and, indeed, why not?
> She is as imperator over me, and I to her
> Am as a kneeling vassal that observes
> The pleasure or displeasure of her eye.
> > *Enter Lodowick*
> What says the more than **Cleopatra**'s match
> To Caesar now?
>
> (EIII 2.2.35–44)

The Countess does not exploit her sexual power. The 'golden ore' at the centre of her strong character is a moral integrity and self-assurance that gives her confidence to resist the King's sexual advances, rebuff them and urge him to reform. She achieves this in an erotically charged exchange involving her **wedding**-knives as pledges of murder and suicide, through which she wittily out-manoeuvres him rhetorically. In spite of the formal ceremony of the coronation procession in *Henry VIII*, then, Shakespeare's countesses more often show that rank is unstable. Their exchanges with others above or below them in the social scale suggest that merit is a stronger mark of nobility than birth.

(c) Leggatt (1988: 3–4) argues that the Countess of Auvergne's role is designed to demonstrate the appeal of individual heroism associated with Talbot. James A. Riddell (1977: 51–7) offers detailed readings of the scenes in *Henry VI Part I*. Rackin (1990: 146–55) considers the Countess of Auvergne in the context of other female interventions into patriarchal historiography, while Semenza (2001) reads the scenes as a commentary on the move from sport to professionalization in military matters. Jane Freeman (2004) discusses the Countess of Rossillion as an aged figure open to compassion and life-long learning which gives her great wisdom. Charles Forker (2005), analyses Edward's seduction of the Countess of Salisbury in the light of other love plots in 1590s history plays, arguing that the King's desire causes a conflict between his body natural and body politic. Rackin (2002), pp. 79–81 reads the Countess as a paragon of both wifely virtue and military power. Thomas Leslie (2002) considers rhetoric in exchanges between the King and the Countess as a prelude to rhetorical patterns in the second half of the play.

country, (a) applied adjectivally to a woman, this means a dweller in a rural location, but it is often used with bawdy innuendo to refer to the vagina.

(b) Prefixed to **girl**, **mistress**, **woman** or servant, the term is ambiguous, sometimes referring to a supposed innocence not found in the court or the city as in **Elizabeth**'s claim 'I had rather be a country servant maid / Than great queen with this condition' (*RIII* 1.3.106–7) which echoes her real-life counterpart who protested she had rather be a milkmaid than Queen of England. The bawdy innuendo, as in Hamlet's coarse joke with **Ophelia** on 'country matters' (*Ham.* 3.2.116), is resonant in references to **Jaquenetta**, the 'country girl that I took in the park' (*LLL* 1.2.117–8) and the 'country maid' (*LLL* 3.1.131) who becomes pregnant to Don Armado. Sexual innuendo likewise colours Diomedes's view of **Helen** of Troy the '**whore**' when Paris tells him 'you are too bitter to your country-woman' and he replies 'She's bitter to her country' (*T&C* 4.2.67–9). The erotic flirtations between the mistaken lovers in *Midsummer Night's Dream* are brought to a conclusion with the 'country proverb' that 'every man shall take his own' (*MND* 3.2.458–9) and the tension between Posthumus's boasts of **Imogen**'s chastity amidst each man's praises of their 'country mistresses' (*Cym* 1.4.57–8) rely on the implicit allusion to female sexual organs.

(c) Elizabeth I's reference to being a milkmaid, in a 1576 speech to Parliament, is in Elizabeth I, *Collected Works* (2000: 170).

courtezan, (a) a court or high-class mistress or prostitute, deriving from an Italian term for the learned officers of the papal court. The *cortegiane* type was identified particularly with Venice. In early modern English it marks a social distinction from the **whore**, **strumpet** or **harlot**.

(b) Fynes Moryson described the relative freedom of courtezans in Venice saying that 'While Curtizans walke and ride in Coaches at liberty and are freely saluted and honored by all men passing by them theire wives and virgins are locked up at home' (Rosenthal 2006: 61). In Shakespeare the term is associated with Italy, or with wealth and the court. **Imogen**, hurt by Posthumus's belief that she has been unfaithful, believes that 'some Roman courtezan' has plotted to slander her (*Cym.* 3.4.122). In Ephesus the Courtezan, whose only title 'courtezan' appears in the stage directions of the Folio text and the *dramatis personae* of the Douai manuscript copy of the play, is described along the lines of the learned, higher-class mistress as a woman of some means. She is 'Pretty and witty; wild, and yet, too, gentle' (*Err.* 3.1.110). As **hostess** of the Porpentine, she is associated with the town rather than the court. The **jewels** promised and exchanged give an initial impression that this is a house of some wealth, not unlike Antipholus's own house, The Phoenix. For his entertainment at the Courtezan's, Antipholus of Ephesus intends to give her the jewelled gold chain he'd intended for his wife. She mistakenly asks Antipholus of Syracuse for 'the ring of mine you had at dinner / Or, for my diamond, the chain you promis'd' (*Err.* 4.3.68–9). The Courtezan goes on to point out that she can't afford to lose a ring worth 40 ducats, and, in the play's resolution, it is returned to her by Antipholus of Ephesus (*Err.* 5.1.393). Jardine (1996: 25) argues that **Bianca** in *Othello* should be read as a Venetian courtezan.

In all English-dominated settings, the term carries courtly associations playing out the distinction given in Sharpham's play *The Fleire*. 'Your whore is for everie rascal, but your Curtizan is for your Courtier' (Sharpham 1607: sig. D2v). **Joan La Pucelle** is called 'shameless courtezan' for her association with Charles and the nobles of the French court in defeating the English (*1HVI* 3.2.45). Richard, Duke of York imagines pirates revelling like lords and giving away their stolen treasure to courtezans (*2HVI* 1.1.232–4). Buckingham points out that Richard of Gloucester is worthy to be king since, unlike his brother Edward, he is not 'dallying with a brace of courtezans' (*RIII* 3.7.74). Once Lear's court has been disbanded and he has gone out into the storm, the Fool jokes 'This is a brave night to cool a courtezan' (*KL* 3.4.79).

(c) Feldman and Gordon's collection of essays on *The Courtesan's Arts* (2006) includes essays on early modern examples of spectacle and music used by courtezans in Italy. See especially Margaret F. Rosenthal's essay 'Cutting a good figure the fashions of Venetian courtezans in the illustrated albums of early modern travelers' (pp. 52–74). Rosenthal's *The Honest Courtesan* (1992) is a case study of Veronica Franco which illuminates the wider fashioning and self-fashioning of the courtezan as independent intellectual in Venice. Jardine (1996: 165–6) argues for Bianca's recognizability as a courtezan of Venice. Kehler (1987) considers Adriana's rejection by her husband and the courtezan's role. Maguire (2007: 166–8) discusses the Courtezan and the Abbess as female stereotypes, with the

Courtezan excluded from family structures by her lack of name. Candido (1990) considers the relationship between food and adultery with the Courtezan in *Errors*.

Cressida, (a) lover of the Trojan Prince Troilus in medieval legend and a character in Shakespeare's *Troilus and Cressida*. Having begun a relationship with Troilus, through the mediation of her uncle Pandarus, she is sent into the Greek camp to be restored to her father Calchas, a Trojan priest who defected to the Greeks. Although Cressida is not part of classical sources on the Trojan war, from the medieval accounts of Boccaccio and Chaucer her name becomes a byword for female infidelity since she breaks her pledge to Troilus and begins another relationship with the Greek soldier Diomedes. The name *Criseida* in Boccaccio is based on Greek *Khryseis* (a derivative of *khrysos* 'gold'), a Trojan girl who is prisoner of the Greeks at the beginning of Homer's *Iliad*.
(b) Although Cressida's name is always already tainted by her sexual infidelity in Shakespeare's texts, references also depict her, often with irony, as a prized object of desire. She is 'sweet Cressid' (*T&C* 3.2.140) 'Fair' Cressid (*T&C* 4.1.38; 4.4.118 and 4.5.283) and Troilus vows that her name will carry the power to protect in the ensuing battle. He tells Diomedes, 'If e'er thou stand at mercy of my sword / Name Cressid, and thy life shall be safe / As Priam is in Ilion' (*T&C* 4.4.114–16). Most spectators already know that Troy will fall, so Cressida's name is likewise doomed to bring death and destruction.

The love affair between Troilus and Cressida, brought about with the help of Pandarus, was famous in its own right as an example of successful matchmaking and secret liaison, as Troilus's words at the opening of *Troilus and Cressida* make clear. He points out 'I cannot come to Cressid but by Pandar' and romantically imagines that since Cressida is a typically 'stubborn chaste' **mistress** (*T&C* 1.1.95–7), he must quest against impossible odds:

> Her bed is India, there she lies, a pearl;
> Between our Ilium and where she resides,
> Let it be call'd the wild and wand'ring flood,
> Ourself the merchant, and this sailing Pandar
> Our doubtful hope, our convoy, and our bark.
> (*T&C* 1.1.100–4)

As he waits, giddy with expectation, Troilus asks Pandarus to pluck Cupid's wings to 'fly with me to Cressid!' (3.2.16). Feste in *Twelfth Night* wryly alludes to the story in order to solicit another coin from **Viola**. 'I would play Lord Pandarus of Phrygia, sir, to bring a Cressida to this Troilus', be begs, and follows this with 'Cressida was a beggar' (*TN* 3.1.51–5), an allusion to *The Testament of Cresseid* by Robert Henryson in which Cressida became a leper and a beggar after her infidelity (Henryson 1593: sigs. B3–B3v). Cressid's name carries erotic overtones to suggest a secret liaison between Helena and the French King in Lafeu's words, 'I am Cressid's uncle, / That dare leave two together; fare you well' (*AWW* 2.1.98–9).

Lorenzo chooses the Troilus and Cressida love story as the first in a series of ill-chosen examples to compare to his and **Jessica**'s story (*Mer.* 5.1.3–6).

In a gendered response to Troilus's masculine, positive vow to be 'As true as Troilus' (*T&C* 3.2.182), Cressida can only define herself in negative terms, promising not to be false. With a prophetic insight shared by **Cassandra** and **Andromache**, she predicts her own future as a byword for female unfaithfulness:

> yet let memory,
> From false to false among false maids in love,
> Upbraid my falsehood! When th' have said as false
> As air, as water, wind, or sandy earth,
> As fox to lamb, as wolf to heifer's calf,
> Pard to the hind, or step-dame to her son,
> Yea, let them say, to stick the heart of falsehood,
> 'As false as Cressid.'
>
> (*T&C* 3.2.191–6)

Cressida appears to see no escape from her fate, describing herself as 'A woeful Cressid 'mongst the merry Greeks!' (*T&C* 4.4.56), an object to be handed over and 'kiss'd in general' (*T&C* 4.5.21). Troilus is famously unable to recognize the false Cressida, fearing that 'to square the general sex / By Cressid's rule' would be deprave all of womankind. He would 'rather think this not Cressid' and that 'This is Diomed's Cressida' (*T&C* 5.2.132–7). How much licence Cressida gives him to assert this is up to how the **boy actor** performs on stage with the actor playing Diomedes. We are told 'she strokes his cheek' (*T&C* 5.2.51) and by the end of the exchange he has the sleeve pledge, though apparently he has snatched it (*T&C* 5.2.89). Ultimately Troilus cannot sustain a dual vision that 'This is and is not Cressid' (*T&C* 5.2.146). His horror at what has happened is expressed in terms just as hyperbolic as his earlier praise of Cressida:

> **Cressid!** O false Cressid! false, false, false!
> Let all untruths stand by thy stained name,
> And they'll seem glorious.
>
> (*T&C* 5.2.178–80)

This is the reputation that Cressida carries with her, and, arguably, is determined by throughout the play. Pistol calls Doll Tearsheet a 'lazar kite of Cressid's kind' (*HV* 2.1.76) referring again to her degradation as a beggar and leper in Henryson's poem.

(c) Robert Henryson's *The testament of Cresseid* (1593), is a 20-page ballad complete with moral coda for women readers and details how the gods took revenge on Cressida for scorning them for her fate, by making her a leper. Greene (1983) argues that Cressida deliberately fashions a 'kind of self' in relation to others, thus explaining her vulnerability to the market of male values and her apparent inconsistency. Adelman (1992: 45–63) reads Cressida as the necessary scapegoat for Troilus's own betrayal of bonds to others, a means for him to achieve a hyper-masculine individuality. Maguire (2007: 109–12) parallels Cressida and Helen as victims. Paul Yachnin (2005) discusses the appeal of the love story as high entertainment.

Cynthia, (a) the goddess of the **moon**, another name for **Diana**. Her name is derived from Mount Cynthus (*Kynthos* in Greek), the mountain on the island of Delos, on which she was supposed to have been born along with her twin brother Apollo, god of the sun.
(b) References to Cynthia in Shakespeare's texts all pair the moon with the sun, following the gendered pattern of twinning in myth. Adonis's beauty has been created by the goddess **Nature** 'To shame the sun by day and her [Cynthia, the moon] by night', by outshining them so that 'Cynthia for shame obscures her silvery shine' (*V&A* 728–32). Romeo denies the approach of day by saying the grey dawn is 'but the pale reflex of Cynthia's brow' rather than the 'morning's eye' whose approach determines his exile (*R&J* 3.5.19–20). In other instances, Cynthia is invoked with reference to **chastity**. When the knights bid 'Good mor-row' to Simonides in the hopes of wooing his daughter, he tells them **Thaisa** has sworn herself to 'Diana's livery' and 'by the eye of Cynthia hath she vowed' to remain chaste (*Per.* 2.5.1 and 10–11). The Jailer's **daughter**, mad with love for Palamon in *Two Noble Kinsmen*, implicitly rejects wooers with two songs beginning 'May you never enjoy the light' and 'When Cynthia with her borrowed light' (*TNK* 4.1.152). In the scenes ascribed to Shakespeare dramatizing Edward III's wooing of the Countess of Salisbury, the opposition of chaste moon and ardent sun carries extra resonance because of the sun's royal associations. The King is not pleased when his secretary Lodowick begins a commissioned love poem 'More fair and chaste than is the queen of shades' (*EIII* 2.1.141). Edward objects: 'Comparest thou her unto the pale queen of night?', protesting 'I did not bid thee talk of chastity' (*EIII* 2.1.143 and 151). Instead, he urges a comparison with the sun:

> Out with the moon-line! I will none of it;
> And let me have her liken'd to the sun . . .
> And in this application to the sun
> Bid her be free and general as the sun.
> (*EIII* 2.1.154–63)

References to Cynthia as a powerful **virgin** figure may allude to Queen **Elizabeth**'s use of the goddess as part of her iconography.
(c) Helen Hackett (1995: 174–7 and 183–7) analyses Elizabeth I's associations with Cynthia and the moon and their representation in early modern literature.

Cytherea, (a) another name for **Venus**.
(b) Shakespeare's texts associate this name with flowers in describing female physical desirability. Cytherea's breath is as sweet as violets in *The Winter's Tale* (*WT* 4.4.122) and her purity is like that of the lily in *Cymbeline* where Iachimo addresses

Imogen as 'Cytherea / How bravely thou becom'st thy bed, fresh lily, / And whiter than the sheets' (*Cym.* 2.2.14–16). She is a more desiring figure when Christopher Sly is promised erotic pictures with 'Cytherea all in sedges hid' looking on Adonis with 'wanton' breath that fans the reeds (*Shrew* Ind. 2.51–3).

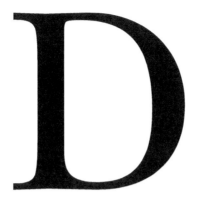

dam, (a) a female parent, used of animals (correlative to 'sire') and, archaically, of humans; a contemptuous term for **mother**, especially the devil's mother.

(b) In Shakespeare's texts, the word connotes otherness and generally carries a pejorative sense. Referring to a woman as the devil's dam implies transgressive sexual alliance (with an incubus or spirit). *The Tempest* offers an example in **Sycorax**, whom Prospero calls **witch**: he describes Caliban 'a born devil' as 'got by the devil himself / Upon thy wicked dam' (*Temp.* 1.2.319–20). When Caliban uses the insulting term himself to describe 'Sycorax, my dam' (*Temp.* 3.2.101), this may be to show he has internalized Prospero's views of his animality and illegitimate conception by an incubus, or to indicate his closeness to the animal and plant world. In the case of **Joan** La **Pucelle**, the imputation of sexual alliance with an incubus in 'Devil or devil's dam, I'll conjure thee' (*1HVI* 1.5.5) are also given some credence when she appears on stage with her familiars. More often, insults of this kind reveal the fears of the speaker rather than the sexual practices of the woman. For example, **Constance**, who believes that King John and Queen **Eleanor** conspire to dispossess her son, sees them as 'as like / As rain to water, or devil to his dam' (*KJ* 2.1.127). **Katherina**, who is not charged with any sexual transgression, is labelled 'a devil, a devil, the devil's dam' (*Shrew* 3.2.155) out of fear of her **shrew**ish temper, although it is noted that Petruchio's behaviour is even worse. The **Courtezan** in *Comedy of Errors* is jokingly referred to as 'Mistress Sathan', or 'the devil's dam' since she 'comes in the habit of a light **wench**' to tempt (*Err.* 4.4.49–51). Racial and religious otherness provokes pejorative use of 'dam' to suggest primitive, animalistic lack of enlightenment. The Goth **Tamora** and the mother of Shylock the Jew are both described as 'unhallowed dam' (*Tit.* 5.1.190 and *Mer.* 4.1.136, respectively).

The bestial associations of 'dam' make it an effective term to insult a character's physical make up or uncivilized behaviour. The two combine in Queen **Margaret**'s insults to Richard of Gloucester as 'neither like thy sire nor dam, / But like a foul misshapen stigmatic' (*3HVI* 2.2.135–8), and, like Caliban, Richard echoes this definition of himself as a bear-whelp (*3HVI* 3.2.161–2). A fear of maternal power to defend and destroy informs uses of the term. Snug reminds spectators of the mother lion's fierceness when reassuring the ladies he is not 'a lion fell, nor else no lion's dam' (*MND* 5.1.224). The name betokens female dominance in the Roman plays *Titus Andronicus* and *Coriolanus*, hinting at the potential for violence beneath the appearance of civilization. Titus warns that if **Tamora**'s sons, like bear-whelps, are threatened

> The dam will wake and if she wind ye once,
> She's with the lion deeply still in league,
> And lulls him whilst she playeth on her back,
> And when he sleeps will she do what she list.
> (*Tit.* 4.1.97–100)

In *Coriolanus*, Menenius refers back to the myth of Romulus and Remus, claiming that for Rome to attack one of her sons would be horrific 'like an unnatural dam / Should now eat up her own' (*Cor.* 3.1.291–2). Buckingham uses the term metaphorically describes the consequences of Wolsey's treacherous behaviour as 'a kind of puppy / To the old dam, treason' (*HVIII* 1.1.175–6).

The term is used with more positive connotations of maternal nurture but always with a tragic failure to protect, most famously in Macduff's desperate question about the murder of his family 'What, all my pretty chickens and their dam / At one fell swoop?' (*Mac.* 4.3.218–19). The same sense of guilt is found in King Henry VI's lament that he cannot protect his subject Gloucester from the butchery of the other nobles:

> And as the dam runs lowing up and down,
> Looking the way her harmless young one went,
> And can do nought but wail her darling's loss,
> Even so myself bewails good Gloucester's case
> (*2HVI* 3.1.214–17)

Mamillius, too, is a calf-like sacrifice to Leontes's savage delusions of cuckoldry in *The Winter's Tale* where **Paulina** defends **Hermione** in a redemptive use of the term by calling her the 'gracious dam' of his children (*WT* 3.2.198).

dame, (a) a female ruler, superior or head, and a formal mark of rank, from French *dame* ('lady'). The term was used to indicate the superior of a nunnery, the **mistress** of a household or of an elementary school ('dame school') and often carried associations of seniority in terms of age as well as status. It was the title or form of address for the **wife** of a knight, baronet, squire, citizen or yeoman.

(b) Princess **Katherine** uses the French '*dames*' to indicate her modesty and good breeding (*HV* 3.4.54 and 5.2.258). **Cleopatra**, **Empress** of Egypt is called 'dame', with the senses of female ruler and mistress of household when Antony takes leave of her in the most domestic scene of the play (*A&C* 4.4.29). Antipholus of Syracuse politely and formally refers to **Adriana** as 'fair dame' after she accidentally addresses him as her husband (*Err.* 2.2.147). The term (referring to social levels from yeoman's to baronet's wife but, significantly, not **queen**) becomes an especially heightened marker of rank in the status battle between **Margaret** of Anjou and Eleanor, **Duchess** of Gloucester. Suffolk woos the **dower**less beauty to be **queen**, claiming he is unworthy 'to woo so fair a dame to be his wife' (*1HVI* 5.3.124). Her rival, **Eleanor** of Gloucester imagines a reversal of status in which she sits on the throne 'Where Henry and Dame Margaret kneel'd to me / And on my head did set the diadem' (*2HVI* 1.2.39–40). She is promptly condemned with a reminder of her rank: 'Presumptuous Dame . . . Art thou not second woman in the realm?' (*2HVI* 1.2.42–3). Queen Margaret admits she is especially vexed that 'that proud dame, the Lord Protector's wife' sweeps through the court like 'an empress' (*2HVI* 1.3.75–79). When Margaret publicly asserts her senior authority, Eleanor responds 'She shall not strike Dame Eleanor unreveng'd' (*2HVI* 1.3.147). Humiliatingly, the public charge against Eleanor for conspiracy with witchcraft begins by formally insisting she confirm her title as second woman in the realm: 'Stand forth, Dame Eleanor Cobham, Gloucester's wife' (*2HVI* 2.3.1), and commanding her to do public penance for her ambitions in a white sheet (*2HVI* 2.4).

A more humorous reference to rank is Prince Hal's suggestion for a tavern entertainment where he will play Hotspur and Falstaff will play 'Dame Mortimer his wife' (*1HIV* 2.4.110), an early version of the pantomime dame. Both Mistress **Quickly** and **Paulina** are called 'Dame Partlet' for their fussy or overbearing commands of their households (*1HIV* 3.3.52 and *WT* 2.3.2.3.76, respectively).

'Dame' is a shorthand to conjure up aged housewives who do not appear on stage but represent the comforts of home. Mouldy appeals not to be press-ganged because his 'old dame' has 'nobody to do anything about her when I am gone, and she is old' (*2HIV* 3.4.112 and 229–32). More extensively, the Old Shepherd in *The Winter's Tale* gives a nostalgic picture of feast-day hospitality where his 'old wife' played high-status dame or mistress of the feast and as servant to the guests:

> Both dame and servant; welcom'd all, serv'd all;
> Would sing her song and dance her turn; now here,
> At upper end o' th' table, now i' th' middle;
> On his shoulder, and his; her face o' fire
> With labor, and the thing she took to quench it,
> She would to each one sip.
>
> (*WT* 4.4.57–62)

Lucrece is younger, but the title 'dame' clearly establishes her as the mistress of her household, offering hospitality to Tarquin in her husband's absence: 'Well was he welcom'd by the Roman dame' (*Luc.* 51). After she is raped, the signifier 'dame' emphasizes her continued loyalty and mature sense of responsibility to her husband's house. She is typified as a 'chaste dishonoured dame' (*Tit.* 4.1.90). Less complimentary references to the 'simpering dame' by King Lear (*KL* 4.6.118), and the 'sinful dame', Antiochus's **daughter** (*Per.* Gower. 1.31) suggest sexual maturity and a hypocritical false modesty not expected of a dame.

damsel, (a) a young unmarried woman, deriving from French demoiselle. Originally a young lady of noble or gentle birth, acting as a maid of honour, but extended as a respectful appellation to those of lower rank and country maids.
(b) The French appellation is used coyly by Princess **Katherine**, who tells Henry V that his tongue has false French enough to 'deceive de most sage demoiselle dat is in France' and who protests that it is not the custom of French maids to be kissed before they are married (*HV* 5.1. 219 and 258–9). The original French seems to have influenced Shakespeare's use of the word because instances of 'damsel' in the canon refer to French young women. **Joan** La **Pucelle** is arrested with the words 'Damsel of France' (*1HVI* 5.3.30) and Talbot challenges her 'Damsel, I'll have a bout with you again' (*1HVI* 3.2.56). In *Love's Labour's Lost*, set in Navarre, **Jaquenetta** the country wench is distinguised from the courtly French **Princess** and her ladies by the appellation 'damsel' and 'damosella, virgin' (*LLL* 4.2.132). Costard desperately moves between the English terms, **wench** (with connotations of wantonness) and **virgin** and the French 'damsel' in an attempt to evade punishment under the King's proclamation forbidding all his male courtiers the society of women:

> King: It was proclaimed a year's imprisonment to be taken with a wench.
> Costard: I was taken with none, sir, I was taken with a damsel.
> King: Well, it was proclaim'd damsel.
> Costard: This was no damsel neither, sir, she was a virgin.
> King: It is so varied too, for it was proclaim'd virgin.
> Costard: If it were, I deny her virginity.
>
> (*LLL* 1.1.287–96)

Jaquenetta's country origins are emphasized when Constable Dull reports 'for this damsel, I must keep her at the park' where she is to serve as a **dey-woman** or dairy woman (*LLL* 1.2.130–1).

Daphne, (a) a **nymph** from Greek mythology, the daughter of the river god Peneus. She was hit by Cupid's lead arrow and ran off into the woods disdaining marriage and the love of the god Apollo. He followed her into the woods and she escaped by being transformed into a laurel tree. Apollo continued to wear laurel as a wreath in his hair on his harp and bow to show his love for her.
(b) The story which appears in Ovid's *Metamorphoses* is erotically charged to tempt the lordly appetite of Christopher Sly, who is promised a picture of 'Daphne roaming through a thorny wood / Scratching her legs' and bleeding to make 'sad Apollo weep' (*Shrew* Ind. 2.57–9). The highly erotic shedding of blood probably makes a satiric jibe at the aristocratic tastes catered to by Shakespeare in *Venus*

and Adonis. Chasing after the impossible Daphne certainly holds strong appeal for Troilus who compares the 'stubborn-chaste' **Cressida** to the nymph (*T&C* 1.1.97–8). Daphne's story is alluded to in *A Midsummer Night's Dream* to point up the unconventionally assertive behaviour of **Helena** in pursuing Demetrius. When she determines 'the story shall be chang'd / Apollo flies and Daphne holds the chase', Oberon feels the need to intervene and restore the original pattern 'thou shalt fly him and he shall seek thy love' (*MND* 2.1.230–1 and 244).
(c) The story is in Ovid, *Metamorphoses*, translated by Golding, Book I, lines 565–700 (Ovidius 2000: 19–22). Lynn Enterline (2002: 1–38) reads the Daphne myth as a symbol of poetry's oral power. Bate (1993: 119–20) shows how the tragic rape of the Ovidian original still shadows the Shakespearian allusions.

Dark Lady, (a) the name ascribed to the addressee and subject of Sonnets 127 to 152 in the ordering of the collection printed by Thomas Thorpe in 1609. The woman has black eyes, black hair, and swarthy skin so does not conform to early modern fashionable ideas of **beauty**. Dark ladies also appear as characters in the plays: most notably, **Rosaline** in *Love's Labour's Lost*, and **Tamora** in *Titus Andronicus*. The identity of any real woman behind this figure cannot be established, though critics have argued for **A**emilia Lanyer and Mrs Jane Davenant as candidates.
(b) The appellation 'dark lady' comes from critics and never appears in the Sonnets themselves. Sonnet 127 introduces a mistress with 'raven black' eyes, a detail apparently typical of a dark, swarthy appearance that challenges tradition: 'it bore not beauty's name' (*Son.* 127.2, 9). It has, however, reversed the legacy of **beauty**, making fair looks now seem artificial and illegitimate, so usurping their position as 'beauty's successive heir' (*Son.* 127.3). Suggesting that the dark lady's looks slander conventional beauty 'with a bastard shame' (*Son.* 127.4) may contain a covert joke about **A**emilia Bassano, one of the real-life candidates. She was an Italian Jew who became pregnant with an illegitimate child when she was mistress to Henry Carey, Lord Hunsdon, the Lord Chamberlain (and patron of Shakespeare's theatre company). In 1592 she was married off to the musician Alphonso Lanier (Schnell 1997: 79). The sonnet speaker notes 'a thousand errors' in the dark lady's appearance (*Son.* 141.2) but Sonnet 130 plays out the thesis of Sonnet 127, showing how the dark lady whose hair is 'black wires' and whose breasts are 'dun' or swarthy, makes the **goddess**-mistress of Petrarchan tradition look false, an illusion (*Son.* 130.3–4). Having established that black is the new currency of beauty, Sonnet 131 draws attention to the **mistress**'s behaviour with the line 'In nothing art thou black save in thy deeds' (*Son.* 131.13). The dark **lady** in the Sonnets is promiscuous, unfaithful but nevertheless irresistible. In addition to breaking her **marriage** vows (*Son.* 152.3) she is unfaithful to the speaker. He is disgusted by his own delusory desire for her: 'For I have sworn thee fair and thought thee bright / Who art as black as hell, as dark as night' (*Son.* 147.13–14). It is her behaviour 'the refuse of thy deeds' rather than her looks which appals him (*Son.* 150.6). Sonnets 133 and 134 complain that the dark lady's 'cruel eye' and 'steel **bosom**' have made the young man 'slave to slavery' as well

(*Son.* 133.4–9). She is set in opposition to the 'man right fair': while he is the speaker's 'better **angel**', the '**woman** color'd ill' is the epitome of 'female evil' (*Son.* 144.3–4). She is, like Satan, a temptress, 'a devil' whose 'foul pride' threatens to transform the angelic young man into a 'fiend', consuming him and the speaker in 'hell', an allusion to her vagina (*Son.* 144.5–12).

(c) The works of Stephen Booth (1969) and (1977) remain the most detailed anatomization of the Sonnets. M. L. Stapleton (1993: 213–30) gives an excellent summary of critical responses to the Dark Lady and follows Joel Fineman's lead in *Shakespeare's Perjured Eye* (1986) to argue that the poems openly acknowledge the biased impressions of the Dark Lady, seen through the unreliable eyes of the speaker. James Joseph Davey (1986) gives a short account of her role while Hugh Richmond (1986) compares the figure with conventionally angelic beauty and to other characters in Shakespeare and beyond. Lisa Schnell (1997) traces interesting comparisons between Lanyer's dedications and Shakespeare's attitudes to patronage in the Sonnets. A. L. Rowse first argued that **Aemelia** Lanyer was the mysterious lady in the Sonnets in *The Poems of Shakespeare's Dark Lady* (1978). Martin Green (2006) identified the meaning 'dark' in the name and coat of arms of the Bassano family leading him to conclude that Lanyer is the Dark Lady. Weis (2007: 148–54, 173–4) discusses Lanyer's connections with the Dark Lady. For Jane Davenant see Acheson (1913).

daughter, (a) word expressing the relation of a female child to her parent or parents, or, more broadly, the female descendant of a family, race or country. The form 'daughter', with an 'a', appeared in the sixteenth century.

(b) Shakespeare uses 'daughter' and 'daughter-in-law' throughout his work to highlight family relationships. **Viola** in disguise as Cesario reaffirms her female identity and blood dynasty with the words 'I am all the daughters of my father's house' (*TN* 2.4.120). Although much is made of **Rosalind** and **Celia**'s identities as daughters to the banished and usurping Dukes to emphasize their status as heiresses in parallel with the status of Orlando and Oliver, neither seems to be 'daughter' to the malicious Duke Frederick 'if we judge by manners' (*AYLI* 1.2.271), a point proved when he judges that Rosalind's identity as 'thy father's daughter' is sufficient evidence to suspect her of treachery, and Celia declares herself a traitor too (*AYLI* 1.3.58 and 72–3). **Jessica** likewise distances herself from the kinship bond, claiming 'though I am a daughter to his blood, / I am not to his manners' (*Mer.* 2.3.18). Once reanimated, **Hermione** asks a blessing on **Perdita**: 'from your sacred vials pour your graces / Upon my daughter's head' (*WT* 5.3.122–3), subsequently defining the daughter as a redemptive figure, a typical characterization in Shakespeare's texts. Justice Shallow enquires after the welfare of 'your fairest daughter and mine, my god-daughter Ellen' (*2HIV* 3.2.5–6), demonstrating one of the ways in which daughters form alliances between families, another major preoccupation in Shakespearean texts. **Helena**'s quest in *All's Well That Ends Well* involves a delicate renegotiation of her position as 'a poor physician's daughter' (*AWW* 2.3.123) and adopted daughter to the **Countess** of Rossillion into that of her daughter-in-law:

> Helena: Can't no other,
>   But, I your daughter, he must be my brother?
> Countess: Yes, Helen, thou might be my daughter-in-law
>   (*AWW* 1.3.165–7)

'Daughter' features as a form of address in a pastoral context outside the family when used by priests. Friar Lawrence refers to **Juliet** as 'pensive daughter' (*R&J* 4.1.39) and goes on to tell her 'Daughter, I do spy a kind of hope' (*R&J* 4.1.68) when offering his advice. Duke Vincentio expands his role as father of the state of Vienna when disguised as a priest in *Measure for Measure*, and refers to Juliet as 'daughter' (*MM* 2.3.30), **Mariana** as 'gentle daughter' (*MM* 4.1.70), and **Isabella**, whom he later asks to be his wife, 'fair and gracious daughter' (*MM* 4.3.112). The plural 'daughters' appears in the canon to indicate a type. Master Ford 'curses all **Eve**'s daughters' a common name for **woman**kind (*MWW* 4.2.23–5), for example. Ulysses refers to whores or sluts as 'daughters of the game' (*T&C* 4.5.64), and in *The Rape of Lucrece* a matriarchal descent is established by Time who will 'show the **beldam**e daughters of her daughter' (*Luc.* 953).

Daughters are often characterized as vulnerable, especially when presented as babies or children. Leontes's determination to cast out his 'baby-daughter' (*WT* 3.2.191) means the figure of the baby is left alone on stage by Antigonus. The baby **Marina**, 'a little daughter', is 'too young for such a place' as the storm-tossed ship (*Per.* 3.1.15–21). We are told how Prospero's infant daughter, **Miranda**, was cast out with him in an open boat (*Temp.* 1.2.144–58). **Imogen** is defined to Cymbeline as 'The piece of tender air, thy virtuous daughter', although the Soothsayer's false etymology draws attention to what he has left out: her strength and resourcefulness (*Cym.* 5.5.446–8).

Daughters are also sexually vulnerable. Antigonus vows to rip out the ovaries of his daughters of eleven, nine and five years if Hermione is unchaste (*WT* 2.3.143–5). Lavinia is the victim of violent **rape** and dismemberment. Marcus presents her to Titus with the words 'This was thy daughter' (*Tit.* 3.1.63), equating the word with wholeness and an identity she has lost. Daughters are cited alongside **wives** as the victims of rape following military campaigns, as, for example, in *Coriolanus* (4.6.80) and *Henry V*. In a particularly graphic turn of phrase, the Duke of Bourbon says that for a Frenchman not to fight the English invaders would be to

>   hold the chamber-door
> Whilst by a slave, no gentler than my dog,
> His fairest daughter is contaminated.
>   (*HV* 4.5.14–16)

As it turns out, the truce rests on bargaining the body of the French King's daughter, **Katherine**.

Daughters are listed as part of the nuclear family 'the sire, the son, the dame, and daughter' who are victims of the Trojan war (*Luc.* 1477). At the same time, however, under patriarchal primogeniture, daughters are always outsiders to the family, property to be exchanged. The most blatant example is **Cressida** who is sent to the Greek camp by her father Calchas as a ransom for Antenor and a bargaining chip: 'he shall buy my daughter; and her presence / Shall quite strike off all service I have done' (*T&C* 3.3.28–9). Baptista's daughter **Bianca** is 'the prize' in what is effectively an auction (*Shrew* 2.1.342), while Katherina (*see* **Katherine**) exclaims 'Call you me daughter?' accusing Baptista of neglecting his 'fatherly regard' in matching her to a madman (*Shrew* 2.1.286). According to Solanio, Shylock equates the losses 'my ducats and my daughter!' as though they were inerchangable types of goods (*Mer.* 2.8.17). Polonius demands that **Ophelia** redefine herself as his **commodity**. 'You do not understand yourself so clearly / As it behooves my daughter and your **honour**', he complains, insisting that she 'tender' herself 'more dearly' (*Ham.* 1.3.96–7, 107). In the first history tetralogy, daughters are pawns used to negotiate political alliances. Both Prince Edward and the Duke of Clarence marry Warwick's daughters to secure his military and political support (*3HVI* 3.3.241–2 and 4.1.118–20). Richard III fully appreciates the dangers and advantages of dynastic alliances, selecting 'some mean-born gentleman / Whom I will marry straight to Clarence's daughter', thus ensuring she cannot be used to make a claim to the throne, and determining to 'be married to my brother's daughter' to strengthen his own claim (*RIII* 4.2.53–60). The widow Queen **Elizabeth** determines to prevent such a match: 'for my daughters, Richard, / They shall be praying **nuns**, not weeping **queens**' (*RIII* 4.4.201–2), and secretly marries Princess Elizabeth to his enemy, the Duke of Richmond. Perhaps the saddest alliance is that between Montague and Capulet at the end of *Romeo and Juliet*.

The daughter's position as an outsider makes her simultaneously an object of love and loss for fathers. Lear's reference to **Cordelia** as 'our sometime daughter' (*KL* 1.1.120) and Polonius's comment 'I have a daughter – have whilst she is mine –' (*Ham.* 2.2.106) capture the emotional complexity of the relationship. The intensity of love and loss is symbolized by Jephthah in the Old Testament, who met his beloved daughter and had to sacrifice her (Judges 11.30–40), and is referred to in *Hamlet* (2.2.403–12) and *Henry VI Part III* (5.1.90–1). The **betrothal** ritual, in which the father gives away his daughter as a gift, is a means to manage his emotional pain of loss (Boose 1982). Leonato formally tells Claudio 'take of me my daughter, and with her my fortunes' (*MAdo* 2.1.302), although Don John's plots disturb this rite. **Rosalind** as Ganymede refers to herself as a gift to be exchanged: 'Keep you your word, O Duke, to give your daughter; / You yours, Orlando, to receive his daughter' (*AYLI* 5.4.19). The rite can be violated if the daughter is taken rather than given, as **Ophelia** distractedly observes: 'it is the false steward, that stole his master's daughter' (*Ham.* 4.5.173). Page's possessive claim 'my daughter is disposed of' (*MWW* 3.4.70) is undercut when his own attempts to match her to Slender are crossed by Mrs **Page** and by **Anne** and Fenton. Serious crises, typical of Shakespearean drama, occur when the daughter herself rejects the passive role as gift to become an active, desiring subject. Both Egeus and Brabantio would rather believe that their daughters had been bewitched or stolen than acknowledge that the young women's desires might lie outside the family (*MND* 1.1.26–38 and *Oth.* 1.2.62–75, respectively). To Brabantio, this is 'treason of the blood!' He cautions: 'Fathers, from hence trust not your daughters' minds / By what you see them act (*Oth.* 1.1.169–71). **Jessica**'s elopement with a Christian, the embodiment of everything Shylock detests, represents the Shakespearean father's worst nightmare: 'I have a daughter – Would any of the stock of Barrabas / Had been her husband rather than a Christian!' (*Mer.* 4.1.295–7).

Portia, speaking from the daughter's perspective, condemns the injustice of a system where 'the will of a living daughter' must be 'curb'd by the will of a dead father' (*Mer.* 1.2.24–5). The daughter's viewpoint is advertised with sympathy in the roles of **Juliet, Cordelia, Desdemona** and **Miranda**. Desdemona explains the daughter's 'divided duty' (*Oth.* 1.3.181), owing loyalty to the father who gave her life and education up to the present, but now owing primary obedience to her husband:

> I am hitherto your daughter. But here's my husband;
> And so much duty as my mother show'd
> To you, preferring you before her father,
> So much I challenge that I may profess
> Due to the Moor, my lord.
>
> > (*Oth.* 1.3.185–9)

Cordelia's admission that she loves her father 'according to my bond' but is likewise bound to give half her love, duty and care to her husband (*KL* 1.1.93–104) echoes Desdemona's reasoned argument. *Cymbeline, Pericles* and *The Tempest* dramatize successful resolutions to the apparently irreconcilable tension between the daughter's duty and her exogamous desire. Simonides expresses surprise at the strength of **Thaisa**'s wish to marry Pericles: 'how absolute she's in 't, / Not minding whether I dislike or no!' (*Per.* 2.5.19–20) but, happily, agrees with her choice of suitor. The father's tendency to believe the suitor is 'a villain' who has 'bewitch'd my daughter' (*Per.* 2.5.49–50) is reduced to comedy since Simonides's anger is performed. Nevertheless, in public, he firmly maintains the appearance of controlling Thaisa, determining to 'bring you in subjection' and commanding his daughter to 'frame / Your will to mine'. He plays the gift-giving paternal role: 'Either be rul'd by me, or I'll make you – / Man and wife' (*Per.* 2.5.75–84). In *The Tempest*, **Miranda**'s freedom to fall in love with Ferdinand, tell him her name, and propose to him, all under the watchful eye of Prospero, is similarly stage-managed. It creates a similar fantasy of balance between the daughter's desire and the father's overarching prerogative to give her away to his liking as 'my rich gift' (*Temp.* 4.1.8). In spite of this harmonious resolution, Prospero claims he needs patience to bear a loss even more irrevocable than Alonso's supposed loss of his son: 'for I have lost my daughter' (*Temp.* 5.1.147–8).

Daughters become an even more intense focus for their father's hopes, desires and losses when they are an heiress or an only child, as is the case with Silvia (*TGV*), the **Princess** of France (*LLL*), **Portia** (*Mer.*), Hermia and Helena (*MND*),

Anne Page (*MWW*), Hero (*MAdo*), Rosalind and Celia (*AYLI*), Juliet (*R&J*), Desdemona (*Oth.*), **Goneril**, **Regan** and Cordelia (*KL*), and the daughters in the Romances, most intensely in Antiochus's incest with his daughter. Leontes's 'joy of his found daughter, as if that joy were now become a loss' (*WT* 5.2.49) may be based on Shakespeare's own experience, having two surviving daughters, **Susanna** and **Judith**, but having lost his son and heir, Hamnet. An anonymous old man summarises the father's intensely focused love on his daughter and heiress:

> One only daughter have I, no kin else,
> On whom I may confer what I have got.
> The **maid** is fair, a' th' youngest for a bride,
> And I have bred her at my dearest cost
> In qualities of the best.
>
> (*Tim.* 1.1.121–5)

A liberal attitude to educating daughters, implicit in the old man's words, is shown in *Taming of the Shrew* (2.1.55–83 and 108–10) and in *Love's Labour's Lost* where the parishioners' 'daughters profit very greatly' under Holofernes's instruction (*LLL* 4.2.75). Boyet asserts the equal value of daughters in mocking Moth's sexist praise of the ladies' 'sun-beamed eyes', with his words 'You were best call it "daughter-beamed eyes"' (*LLL* 5.2.170–2).

The pressures on daughters as heirs to perpetuate their father's patriarchal rule and simultaneously provide the 'kind nursery' (*KL* 1.1.24) of hospitality and care in the image of their mothers (as idealized by the Old Shepherd of *The Winter's Tale* 4.4.55–62), is explored most fully in *King Lear*. Goneril's failure to play the **hostess** to Lear and his hundred knights leads him to ask 'Are you our daughter?' (*KL* 1.4.218). Such un**housewife**ly behaviour recalls the apocryphal story of the **baker**'s daughter who refused Christ bread and was turned into an owl, as Ophelia remembers (*Ham.* 4.5.42). Lear defines his expectations of a daughter very clearly: 'the dear father / Would with his daughter speak, commands her service' (*KL* 2.4.102), and cannot understand why, as absolute rulers, Goneril and Regan 'owe me no subscription' (*KL* 3.2.18). In spite of – or perhaps because of – her assumption of authority, he cannot throw off kinship with Goneril:

> But yet thou art my flesh, my blood, my daughter;
> Or rather a disease that's in my flesh,
> Which I must needs call mine.
>
> (*KL* 2.4.221)

Lear's blaming the heavens for stirring 'these daughters' hearts' (*KL* 2.4.274) against him and his projection of his own suffering at their hands onto Poor Tom are all part of a failure to acknowledge what he has bequeathed them: a masculine will to absolute power that can not be reconciled with society's image of a daughter. Albany calls them 'Tigers, not daughters' (4.2.40) and 'dog-hearted daughters' (4.3.45). In contrast, Cordelia is the 'most dear daughter' (4.6.189), and the source of salvation for the type:

> Thou hast one daughter
> Who redeems nature from the general curse
> Which twain have brought her to.
>
> (*KL* 4.6.205–7)

In Cordelia's return and tragic death, Shakespeare dramatizes the redemption and inconsolable loss encapsulated by the daughter figure. The intensity of fatherly investment in a daughter and the injustice of a daughter's death are clear in Lear's anguish over Cordelia's corpse. It is expressed differently, but no less passionately in verse by the father of Lucrece, who describes his daughter as a lifeline that has been snatched away:

> 'Daughter, dear daughter,' old Lucretius cries,
> 'That life was mine which thou hast here deprived.
> If in the child the father's image lies,
> Where shall I live now Lucrece is unlived?
> Thou wast not to this end from me derived.
> If children predecease progenitors,
> We are their offspring, and they none of ours.'
>
> (*Luc.* 1751–7)

While **Perdita**, **Marina**, **Miranda** and **Imogen** are daughters who redeem their fathers and restore families and kingdoms, Shakespeare's texts never allow us to forget that possession of the happiness embodied by daughters is, at best, transient.

(c) Lynda Boose, 'The father's house and the daughter in it', in *Daughters and Fathers* (1989), Coppelia Kahn (1986) and Dreher (1986) all analyse the daughters with reference to the dynamic of power in family. Sharon Hamilton, *Shakespeare's Daughters* (2003), covers daughter characters with inept and wise mentors, rebelling and obedient daughters, scheming daughters, those who act in their father's place and forgiving daughters. Robert Tracy (1966) discusses Ophelia in 'The Owl and the Baker's Daughter'.

Desdemona, (a) the tragic heroine of *Othello*.

(b) Desdemona is a character apparently trapped by her name, which comes from Shakespeare's source, Cinthio's *Hecatommithi* (1565) and is spoken 42 times. Cassio's alliterative praise for the 'divine Desdemona' (2.1.74) not only flatters her **beauty** but points to the goodness and purity of her non-racist, non-sexist views. Nevertheless, under the perverse misogynistic influence of Iago, she is reconstructed as devilish, apparently an inherent quality since 'demon' is in her name. Desdemona's open expression of desire for Othello and her elopement tarnishes her reputation. Her public admission, 'That I did love the Moor to live with him / My downright violence and storm of fortunes / May trumpet to the world.' (1.3.248–50) elicits a warning from Brabantio: 'she has deceived her father and may thee' (1.3.292).

The play's escalating tragedy of suspicion makes it clear that the demon in Desdemona is the fantastic creation of male insecurities about women. These turn Desdemona's virtues into pitch. Othello points out that she 'feeds well, loves company, is free of speech, sings, plays and dances well. / Where virtue is, these are more virtuous' (3.3.187–8). Her appeals for Cassio's return to office are misconstrued as another example of outspoken desire with overtones of **shrew**ishness (3.3). Desdemona is trapped in the definition of 'fair devil' (3.3.481), since even her faithful conformity to traditional feminine virtues of modesty and submission is read as a mark of deception. **Bianca** the **courtezan**, who is asked to copy the embroidery of the handkerchief, is a doppelgänger for 'Desdemon' the 'subtle whore' (4.2.96) who is 'so delicate with her needle' (4.1.179–81). Shortening the character's name to 'Desdemon' (4.2.43), even when she humbly prays (4.2.155–65) emphasizes the gross moral inversion Iago has provoked. For women and enlightened male spectators, the tragedy is that Desdemona finally appears to accept this hard construction of her refreshingly liberal and honest behaviour. Although she dies 'guiltless' of infidelity, she blames her murder on 'Nobody, I myself' (5.2.132–3), apparently acknowledging the inappropriate nature of her former conduct. By blaming the anonymous 'Nobody', Desdemona exposes the smothering ideology, the master-narrative that has defamed and destroyed her.
(c) Emily C. Bartels (1996: 417–33) examines the unconvenional nature of Desdemona's love, while Michael D. Bristol (1990: 3–22) reads her as part of a carnivalesque satire of unconventionality. Stephen Greenblatt (1980: 222–54) traces the importance of narrative in the play. Holbrook (1989: 235–49), Lisa Jardine (1996: 19–35) and Valerie Wayne, in 'Historical Differences: Misogyny and *Othello*' (1991: 153–80), all discuss how the character becomes enmeshed in a net of misogynist discourse. Henry and Renée Kahane (1987) examine the significance of 'Desdemona' and its shortening.

despair, (a) complete loss of hope. Despair, the loss of belief in one's salvation, was a mortal sin in early modern England.
(b) The personification of despair is female in *Comedy of Errors*:

> comfortless despair,
> And at her heels a huge infectious troop
> Of pale distemperatures and foes to life.
>
> (*Err.* 5.1.80–2)

Destinies, (a) a name for the **Fates**, three goddesses who spin and cut the threads of human life.
(b) Touchstone jokes that Le Beau should answer 'as the Destinies decree' to make fun of **Rosalind** and **Celia**'s power to run verbal rings round him (*AYLI*

1.2.105). More often in Shakespeare, the Destinies are serious figures governing death and life. The **Duchess** of Gloucester points out that some of the lives of Edward III's descendants have been 'by the Destinies cut' (*RII* 1.2.15). Richard III has been 'marked by the destinies to be avoided' (*3HVI* 2.2.137). The **weird sisters**' powers of prophecy in *Macbeth* are a dramatic representation of the power of the Destinies or Fates. Launcelot Gobbo pretends he has died 'according to Fates and Destinies and such odd sayings' (*Mer.* 2.2.62); the term 'Fates' is used more extensively in Shakespeare.

(c) *See* under **Fates** for further information on how these goddesses are represented. *See also* **Furies** and **weird sisters**.

dey-woman (a) dairy-woman.

(b) This is Jaquenetta's job in *Love's Labour's Lost*. 'She is allow'd for the day-woman (*LLL* 1.1.131). It was a form of employment for women in areas with arable farming. Mopsa and Dorcas also perform milking as part of their daily duties (*WT* 4.4).

(c) See Gervase Markham's *Country Contentments* (1615: 107) for an account of dairy maids' typical routine of daily milking and churning cream and butter for market. McNeill (2007: 44) comments on the status of the dairy-woman as a maidservant.

Diana, (a) the Roman name for the **goddess** of the moon and of hunting, equivalent to the Greek goddess Artemis. The goddess appears as a character in *Pericles* and Diana is, significantly, the name of the young woman Bertram tries to seduce in Florence. In mythology Diana is characterized by beauty and chastity and is attended by a train of **nymph**s on her hunting expeditions. She carries a silver bow and is associated with the **moon**. She is reputedly hostile to men; when the young hunter Actaeon accidentally surprised her as she was bathing in a forest pool, she turned him into a stag and he was torn apart by his own hunting hounds. As a chaste huntress at the centre of a female community, Diana is closely identified with the **Amazons**; allusions to **Elizabeth** I as Diana emphasized beauty and chastity and sometimes wisdom, from Artemis. Ephesus, the site of Diana's temple, was also assumed to be the birthplace of the **Virgin Mary**, which led to some conflation of classical and Christian iconography. Diana was also praised as the guardian of pregnant women.

(b) Shakespeare's work does not follow the popular image of Diana as a three-faced goddess as set out by Robert Albott: '*Diana*, for her chast lyfe, vvas honoured for a Goddesse, she continually exercised her selfe in hunting wild beasts, in heauen she is called *Luna*, in earth *Diana*, in hell *Proserpina*' (Albott 1599: 143). Nevertheless, chastity, the moon and hunting are common characteristics in Shakespeare's allusions to Diana. Her name is a synonym for **chastity**. Posthumus remarks 'my mother seem'd / The Dian of that time' (*Cym.* 2.5.6–7) and **Portia** vows to die 'as chaste as Diana' (*Mer.* 1.2.106–7) if no one wins her by the terms of her father's will. Appropriately, her musicians play to the moon and 'wake Diana with a hymn' to welcome Portia home before she bids farewell to her virginity (*Mer.* 5.1.66). If **Hermia** refuses to marry Demetrius, she must dedicate herself to single life 'on Diana's altar' (*MND* 1.1.89–90) to sing 'faint hymns to the cold fruitless moon' (*MND* 1.1.73). As here, Diana's name is usually associated with coldness. In *Coriolanus*, **Valeria** is compared to the moon and to an icicle of purity that 'hangs on Dian's temple' (*Cor.* 5.3.65–7). When Orlando is late, **Celia** says he has lips like Diana since 'the very ice of chastity' is in his kisses (*AYLI* 3.4.15–17). Iachimo imagines Diana's votaresses living 'betwixt cold sheets' (*Cym.* 1.6.133).

The goddess's **beauty** and power are praised in allusions that indirectly compliment **Elizabeth** I. Orsino says 'Diana's lip / Is not more smooth and rubious' than **Viola**'s (*TN* 1.4.31–2) while Petruchio admiringly exclaims 'Did ever Dian so become a grove / As Kate this chamber with her princely gait?' (*Shrew* 2.1.258–60). An even more pointed patriotic allusion to the Virgin **Queen** is found in *Henry VI Part III*. In a feminised comparison King Henry is described surrounded by his faithful citizens, his island kingdom circled by the sea like 'modest Dian, circled with her nymphs' (*3HVI* 4.8.21). Oberon's spell 'Dian's bud o'er Cupid's flower / Hath such force and blessed power' perhaps includes a reference to the cult of chastity created by the queen in the Elizabethan court (*MND* 4.1.78–9).

Diana's power is imaged in references to her as an armed hunter. Romeo says **Rosaline** 'hath Dian's wit / And in strong proof of chastity well arm'd, / From Love's weak childish bow she lives uncharm'd' (*R&J* 1.1.209–11). In the brothel, **Marina** appeals to the goddess to 'aid her purpose' even if it means she must commit suicide with knives, fire or rope to keep her '**virgin** knot' (*Per.* 4.2.146–8). The stong, self-determined heroine of *All's Well* likewise muses that Diana, '**queen** of virgins', will be her protectress and will not 'suffer her poor knight surpris'd without rescue in the first assault or ransom afterward' (*AWW* 1.3.114–16). **Hero**, too, is Diana's 'virgin knight' (*MAdo* 5.3.12–13). Falstaff's allusion to Diana may include an appeal from Shakespeare's company for royal licence when he asks to be retitled and legitimized as one of 'Diana's foresters, gentlemen of the shade, minions of the moon' who are governed 'by our noble and chaste mistress the moon, under whose countenance we steal' (*1HIV* 1.2.25–9).

The myth of 'chaste Dian bathing' (*Cym.* 2.4.82) is painted on the chimney breast in **Imogen**'s bedchamber as if to preface her own assaulted modesty when Iachimo enters and then slanders her. *Titus Andronicus* stages a satirical rewriting of the Actaeon myth when Bassianus, surprising **Tamora** in the forest with her lover Aaron, wonders why the **Empress** is 'Unfurnish'd of her well-beseeming troop' and mockingly supposes it is 'Dian, habited like her / Who hath abandoned her holy groves / To see the general hunting in the forest' (*Tit.* 2.3.56–9). Tamora angrily retorts:

> Had I the pow'r that some say Dian had,
> Thy temples should be planted presently
> With horns, as was Actaeon's, and the hounds
> Should drive upon thy new-transformed limbs.
>
> (*Tit.* 2.3.61–4)

A few moments later, she does set Chiron and Demetrius to destroy Bassianus in revenge for his mockery.

Like the moon, Diana is an icon of changeability, especially in relation to her human **votaress**es. **Helena** freely admits that her passion for Bertram threatens to transgress her chaste wishes so that 'Dian / Was both herself and Love' (*AWW* 1.3.212–13). When the King grants her a choice of husband, she rejoices 'Now, Dian, from thy altar do I fly / And to imperial Love, that god most high' (*AWW* 2.3.74–5). Sonnet 153 likewise describes how a '**maid** of Dian's' who attempts to extinguish Cupid's fires is only temporarily successful (*Son.* 153.2). More cynically, Timon argues that gold has the power to 'thaw the consecrated snow / That lies on Dian's **lap**' (*Tim.* 4.3.385–6). Being changeable, Diana and moon are always potentially false. Claudio exclaims against Hero's appearance which 'seem'd to me as Dian in her orb / As chaste as is the bud ere it be blown' (*MAdo* 4.1.58). **Desdemona**'s supposed adultery has made the face which was 'as fresh as Dian's visage' now appear 'begrimed and black' (*Oth.* 3.3.386–7). There is cruel irony when **Cressida**, at the point of betraying Troilus, swears by the stars and moon: 'By all Dian's waiting-women yond / And by herself' (*T&C* 5.2.91–2).

In contrast to these prejudiced views of inconstancy, the character of Diana in *All's Well That Ends Well* redeems the name. Although slandered as 'a common gamester' (*AWW* 5.3.198) for supposedly yielding her virginity to Bertram, she remains chaste. The character may have originally been designated 'Violenta', as listed in the stage direction for Act 4 Scene 5. Her symbolic significance as Diana is quickly established, though:

> Bertram: They told me that your name was Fontibell.
> Diana: No, my good lord, Diana.
> Bertram: Titled goddess,
>   And worth it, with addition. But, fair soul,
>   In your fine frame hath love no quality?
>   (*AWW* 4.2.1–4)

Diana's answer, for all her willingness to take part in the bed-trick to help Helena, appears to be no. Having told Bertram 'my chastity's the jewel of our house' (*AWW* 4.2.46), she vows to remain true to her name and choose a single life: 'Marry that will, I live and die a **maid**' (*AWW* 4.2.74).

Diana's significance as a symbol of female strength is even more fully restored in the late plays *Pericles* and *Two Noble Kinsmen*. In the latter, the role of Diana's votaress is spectacularly presented in the figure of **Emilia** who, as a somewhat unwilling **bride**, makes an offering at Diana's altar. She appears '*in white*' followed by one of her maids '*in white holding up her train*' and another preceding her '*carrying a silver hind*' perfumed with incense, which is placed on the altar. To complement these visual signs referring to chastity and hunting and to the silver shrines in the Temple of Diana (Acts 19.24–41), Emilia addresses the goddess using the full panoply of associations:

> O sacred, shadowy, cold, and constant queen,
> Abandoner of revels, mute, contemplative,
> Sweet, solitary, white as chaste, and pure
> As wind-fann'd snow, who to thy female knights
> Allow'st no more blood than will make a blush,
> Which is their order's robe.

> (*TNK* 5.1.137–42)

The ritual's dramatic effectiveness depends partly on an awareness of the imminent loss of everything Diana represents. Although she appeals to her 'sacred, silver mistress' (*TNK* 5.1.146) to preserve her 'virgin flow'r', the single rose which appears in place of the silver deer '*falls from the tree*' (*TNK* 5.1.168 SD), symbolizing the de**flower**ing of Emilia.

A more expansive Diana: a goddess of pregnant women and fathers as well as of virgin women, appears in *Pericles*. When **Thaisa** revives from her premature burial at sea, her first words are, appropriately, to the divine patron of pregnant women: 'O dear Diana / Where am I?' (*Per.* 3.2.104). She speaks as if frozen in the midst of labour, not knowing whether she is safely delivered. In this state of suspended animation she vows to take a 'vestal livery' (*Per.* 3.4.10) as a votaress at Diana's temple in Ephesus. Pericles, too, identifies with the goddess, vowing 'by bright Diana, whom we honor' not to cut his hair until his infant daughter be married (3.3.28). Diana's appearance on stage as *dea ex machina* is a *coup de théâtre*: brief and completely unannounced. She is probably immediately recognizable by the 'silver bow' she refers to; Pericles calls her 'goddess argentine' (*Per.* 5.1.248–250). By telling him 'My temple stands in Ephesus, hie thee hither / And do upon mine altar sacrifice' (*Per.* 5.1.240–1), Diana initiates the family reunion in the final scene. At the Temple, the 'maiden priests' (*Per.* 5.1.242) give way to the restoration of husband to wife, wife to husband, and child to mother. Thaisa's childbed ends when she can finally greet the 'flesh of thy flesh' (*Per.* 5.3.46). This Diana of gentle restoration is a very different goddess from the cold, armed huntress whose exclusive chastity invoked the savage murder of Actaeon. Changing references across the Shakespeare canon accurately depict her as the moon goddess.

(c) Diana appears on many occasions in Ovid's *Metamorphoses*, as, for example, in the myth of Actaeon in Book III, lines 208–308 (Ovidius 2000: 67–9) and her significance is discussed by Warner in *Monuments and Maidens* (1985: 278–9). Albott (1599: 143), describes Diana as a three-faced goddess. Elizabeth F. Hart (2003) examines the cultural significance of the figure of Diana of Ephesus and her literary representations, including *Comedy of Errors* and *Pericles*. Hackett (1995: (esp.) 174–7 and 183–7) analyses Elizabeth I's associations with Diana, Cynthia and the moon and their representation in early modern literature.

Dictynna, (a) a name for the **moon**, a feminized object in much early modern writing, used typically to refer to **Diana**, goddess of chastity, and to Queen **Elizabeth** I. The name derives from a Cretan goddess who lived at the top of Mount Dicta and was sometimes identified with Britomartis, the Cretan goddess of hunting and fishermen, from the Greek word for net, 'dictynna'.

(b) This rather obscure name for the moon goddess is only used once in Shakespeare, appropriately by the pedantic Holofernes who explains to Dull that Dictynna is 'A title to **Phoebe**, to Luna, to the moon' (*LLL* 4.2.36–8).

Dido, (a) Queen of Carthage, in Virgil's *Aeneid*, ambiguously both a model of sacrificial widowhood and the lover of Aeneas. Also named Elissa, Dido fled to Carthage from Tyre when her brothers murdered her husband Sychaeus. Having founded Carthage, she is desired by Iarbus, a neighbouring king who promises to wage war on Carthage unless she become his wife. Preferring to stay faithful to her first husband, she builds a ceremonial funeral pyre to his memory, supposedly in preparation for her second marriage, and then sacrifices herself with a sword on it.

Virgil complicates the image of her as a loyal **widow** by depicting her falling in love with Aeneas when he arrives at Carthage from Troy. When Aeneas sails away from Carthage under command from the gods, Dido curses him and, with the help of her sister **Anna**, builds a pyre of all the objects associated with Aeneas, including the bed they have shared. According to Virgil's version of the story, she commits suicide with Aeneas's sword and in the underworld seeks the company of her first husband, Sychaeus.

(b) Dido is depicted as a sympathetic listener to Aeneas's sad tale of Troy's fall in both *Titus Andronicus* (*Tit.* 5.1.80–84) and *Hamlet* (*Ham.* 2.2.446). In *Henry VI Part II*, Margaret tries to persuade Henry VI that she really loves him more than he loves her, by woefully comparing herself to Dido as an eager but too-gullible listener bewitched by the false words of Aeneas's son:

> How often have I tempted Suffolk's tongue,
> (The agent of thy foul inconstancy)
> To sit and [witch] me, as Ascanius did
> When he to madding Dido would unfold
> His father's acts commenced in burning Troy!
> Am I not witch'd like her? or thou not false like him?
>
> (*2HVI* 3.2.114–19)

Although **Margaret** uses Dido as an emblem of fidelity, the more ambiguous dimensions of her identity as lover resonate through this speech since Suffolk is Margaret's lover. Lorenzo idealizes Dido as a figure of unrequited love in his image of her standing 'with a willow in her hand' hoping to 'waft her love / To come again to Carthage' (*Mer.* 5.1.10–12). Antony compares **Cleopatra** and himself to Dido and Aeneas to create an illusion of spectacular power and immortal love. In the Elysian fields, he says, 'Dido and her Aeneas shall want troops / And all the haunt be ours' (*A&C* 4.16.53). More ambiguously, **Tamora** compares herself and Aaron to Dido and Aeneas, who made love secretly in a cave (*Tit.* 2.1.21–6). References to the Queen of Carthage in *The Tempest* play on the ambiguous identity of Dido as lover, **Queen** and **widow**. Gonzalo sees 'widow Dido' as 'a paragon' but Antonio, Sebastian and Adrian all view her more as Aeneas's lover.

(c) The figure of Dido was made familiar in early modern England from the English translation of Virgil's *Aeneid* by Thomas Phaer and Thomas Twyne (London, 1584), although Shakespeare would probably have known the story, from Books IV to VI, in the original Latin. Marlowe's play *Dido, Queen of Carthage* (1594) also popularized the figure of Dido. Roger Savage's essay 'Dido Dies Again' (1998) discusses how allusions to Dido occur in works from across Shakespeare's career. Williams (2006) reads Dido as an icon of Elizabethan power and independence, embodied by the Queen and recalled in *The Tempest*. James (2001) reads her as the queen of sympathetic ears, a model for listening to tragedy that registers theatre's dangerous potential for generating subversive sympathies.

Dionyza, (a) a character from *Pericles*, the wife of Cleon, the governor of Tharsus, although the name is of Spanish origin, from Dionysus, god of wine.

(b) In spite of her name, the character has little to do with festivity; in *Pericles*, Act 1, Scene 4, Tharsus is suffering from a famine and Dionyza meekly echoes her husband's laments. When Pericles leaves his infant daughter **Marina** in their care, Dionyza is characterized as a **mother**, promising to give no less care to her charge than to her own **daughter** (3.3.32–4). Her heightened maternal feelings become destructive in Act 4 where, jealous of how Marina outshines Philoten ('beloved'), the 'cursed' Dionyza (4. Gower. 43) plots Marina's death. Dionyza's hypocrisy in pretending to nurture Marina and 'have a care of [her]' while sending her off to be killed (4.1.49) shocks Cleon but by Act 4 the cruelly impassioned Dionyza dominates him in the style of Goneril or Lady Macbeth:

> Dionyza: Why are you foolish? Can it be undone?
> Cleon: O Dionyza, such a piece of slaughter
>   The sun and moon ne'er look'd upon!
> Dionyza: I think you'll turn a child again.
>
>   (4.3.1–4)

She goes on to criticize him for 'not your child well loving', as she does (4.3.37). Perhaps the passion for her daughter which possesses and morally blinds Dionyza is what is recalled in the name linking her to Dionysus. Like **Goneril** and **Regan**, the 'wicked' Dionyza (4.4.33) is also an excellent liar, fully appreciating that 'soft and tender flattery' is the best mask for 'black villainy' (4.4.44–5), as is clear from the fulsome epitaph she hypocritically writes for Marina's tomb (4.4.34–43). Cleon aptly compares her to a **harpy** – seductively beautiful, but cruel (4.3.46).

(c) Marjorie Garber (1981: 36–7) and Suzanne Gossett (2003) discuss motherly love in *Pericles*.

distaff, (a) cleft stick about one metre in length, around which wool or flax was wound to prepare it for spinning, the primary occupation of a virtuous woman according to early modern patriarchy. The fibres were drawn from the distaff (held under the left arm) through the fingers of the left hand, and twisted in the finger and thumb of the right hand and wound onto a spindle. Because spinning was so culturally loaded an activity for women, the distaff also became a signifier of female authority or dominion.

(b) The distaff symbolizes dominant, maternal authority in **Hermione**'s determination to 'thwack' Polixenes 'home with distaffs' (*WT* 1.2.37). The distaff was also associated with a **housewife**'s flirtatious behaviour (Jones and Stallybrass 2000: 126); woman's sexual power in the domestic arena is telegraphed in Sir Toby's comment that Sir Andrew Aguecheek's hair is like 'flax on a distaff; and I hope to see a huswife take thee between her legs, and spin it off' (*TN* 1.3.101–4). The distaff is used metaphorically to indicate a fightening inversion of conventional gender roles in **Goneril**'s declaration, 'I must change names at home and give the distaff / Into my husband's hands' (*KL* 4.2.17–18) or in Richard II's rebellious population where 'distaff-women' take up arms to 'manage rusty bills' (*RII* 3.2.118). The courage of Belarius, Arviragus and Guiderius in battle has the power to inspire others and transform 'a distaff to a lance' (*Cym.* 5.3.34).

(c) Jones and Stallybrass (2000: 104–33) give a richly illustrated account of the significance of spinning and the distaff in early modern culture.

divorce, (a) a legal dissolution of marriage by a court or according to forms recognized in a nation or tribe. For early modern readers or spectators, the word would undoubtedly have had echoes of the divorce of Henry VIII from **Katherine** of Aragon, and of England from the Roman Catholic Church. In a wider, non-legal sense, divorce means a complete separation of things usually closely united.

(b) Unsurprisingly the word occurs most frequently in *Henry VIII*. Norfolk defines it: 'a divorce, a loss of her / That like a jewel, has hung twenty years / About his neck' (*HVIII* 2.2.30–2). Divorce's meaning spreads beyond the marital context to include **queen**ly status. Anne remarks that to divorce a queen from pomp is as painful 'as soul and body's severing' (*HVIII* 1.3.14–17) while Katherine determinedly vows 'Nothing but death / Shall e'er divorce my dignities' (*HVIII* 3.1.141–2). As Henry VIII's case showed, divorce was almost impossible to secure under English law. Separation *a mensa et thoro* (from bed and board) was the only form legally recognized in English law (charges of impotence of one of the parties under canon law were very difficult to prove (Lindley 1993: 89–96)), and people who legally separated had no right to remarry unless they were wealthy enough to secure a private Act of Parliament (Phillips 1988: 71). In line with the legal antipathy to divorce in early modern England, in Shakespeare's texts it is usually associated with pain and wrongdoing. In *Richard II*, for example, woman's suffering is foregrounded when Bolingbroke accuses Richard's followers, Bushy, Bagot and Green of having

> Made a divorce betwixt his **queen** and him,
> Broke the possession of a royal bed,
> And stain'd the beauty of a fair queen's cheeks
> With tears drawn from her eyes by your foul wrongs.
> (*RII* 3.1.12–15)

Physical separation of husband and **wife**, even without any legal divorce, is presented as unjust and painful. Attempts to separate **Imogen** and Posthumus are 'a lamentable divorce' and 'a horrid act' (*Cym* 1.4.20 and 2.3.61–2). Egeus recounts how the bad fortune of a storm and shipwreck has made 'unjust divorce' (*Err.* 1.1.104) between him and **Aemilia**. Divorce is often invoked negatively at a moment of ritual transition. In *The Winter's Tale*, Florizel's appeal for a witness to his and **Perdita**'s betrothal 'Mark our contract', is interrupted by Polixenes's angry 'Mark your divorce, young sir' (*WT* 4.4.416). In *All's Well That Ends Well* **Helena**, having fulfilled Bertram's terms and annulled their separation at bed if not board, reasserts their marriage contract with a chilling reminder of his attempts to escape it: 'If it appear not plain and prove untrue, / Deadly divorce step between me and you' (*AWW* 5.3.317–8). Her mention of 'deadly divorce' still hints at the possibility that all will not end well between them.

Whether a **woman** had the right to divorce her husband was a matter of heated controversy in early modern England as the case of Frances Howard proved (Lindley 1993: 89–93). Queen **Margaret** acts with characteristic disregard for conventional gender norms when she threatens King Henry with divorce in *Henry VI Part III* in retaliation for his agreement to disinherit his son. She declares: 'I here divorce myself / Both from thy table, Henry, and thy bed' (*3HVI* 1.1.247–8). Even though her vow is compromised by the fact she has already been Suffolk's lover, her use of the formal, legal terms of *a mensa et thoro* (from bed and board), gives weight to her lines.

(c) Phillips (1988) and Stone (1990) both provide detailed historical analyses of changing social and legal patterns. Laurence (1994: 51–4) gives a summary of women's position at the breakdown of marriage. Valbuena (2003) assesses the mental, emotional, political and religious meanings of divorce as division or self-division for English subjects after 1534. Lindley (1993: 85–93) analyses Frances Howard's attempts to divorce the Earl of Essex (current when Shakespeare and Fletcher's *Henry VIII* was staged), placing this in the context of the Jacobean court and contemporary writing about divorce including Elizabeth Cary's play, *The Tragedy of Mariam*.

Doll, *see* **Dorothy**

Dorcas, (a) a character in *The Winter's Tale*, in what appears to be friendly rivalry with **Mopsa** for the love of the Clown. Her name comes from the Greek *dorkas* meaning 'doe' or 'gazelle' and was popular among the Puritans because in the Bible it is given as the interpretation of the Aramaic name Tabitha, who became an early disciple of Christ after she was raised from death by Peter (Acts 9.36–41).

(b) Dorcas's country origins and those of the name may explain the choice for this character. She is certainly a lively tease, objecting that Mopsa must be the Clown's mistress in the dance and saying that she must have garlic to 'mend her kissing with' (*WT* 4.4.162–3). Dorcas goes on to insinuate that the Clown has promised to marry Mopsa, and Mopsa retorts with the insinuation that he may also have had sex with Dorcas: 'May be he has paid you more [than he promised], which will shame you to give him again' (4.4.237–41). Nevertheless, Dorcas joins Mopsa and the Clown in singing a ballad fittingly to the tune of 'Two **maid**s wooing a man' (4.4.289).

(c) Newcomb (2004) surveys literary representations of shepherdesses. Neely, *Broken Nuptials* (1993: 203–4) discusses the aggressive fertility of the Bohemian pastoral as a context for the song while Pafford (1959) comments on the ballad.

Dorothy, (a) the English form, via Latin derivation, of a post-classical Greek name, meaning 'a gift (*doron*) from God (*theos*)'. The shortened form of the name is Doll. This name is given generically to a female pet or mistress and is the origin for the image of a human as a plaything or dummy. Doll Tearsheet is a character in *Henry IV Parts I and II* and Doll Williamson is the character of the carpenter's wife in *Sir Thomas More*.

(b) Dorothy is the name of **Imogen**'s servant, who is named as 'Dorothy my woman' (*Cym.* 2.3.137), so distinguishing her as a lower-class character from **Helen** the **Lady**. Pistol's pompous form of address for Doll Tearsheet is '**Mistress** Dorothy' but he then offers to 'charge' her, playing on the bawdy inflection of 'Doll', and she defines herself as a sexual **commodity** in claiming 'I am meat for your master' (*2HIV* 2.4.121–7). Ben Jonson's *The Alchemist* spells out the name's generic meaning, to refer to a prostitute in the character of Doll Common, who is promised 'Thou shalt sit in triumph, / And not be styl'd Doll Common but Doll Proper, / Doll Singular' (Jonson 2011: 1.1.176-8). Doll Tearsheet is 'as common as the way between St Albans and London' (*2HIV* 2.3.167–8) and Falstaff reminds her 'you make the diseases, Doll, We catch of you Doll' (*2HIV* 2.4.44–6). In *Henry V*, Pistol disparagingly refers to her as 'the lazar kite of Cressid's kind' while recommending her as a wife for his rival Bardolph (*HV* 2.1.75–6). Outside the common structures of marriage, she and Mistress **Quickly** become 'the detritus of official history' (Howard and Rackin 1997: 179). Doll Tearsheet is, nevertheless, a source of pleasure and comfort in the tavern at Eastcheap, along with the food, drink and music. Mistress Quickly offers to serve her up to Falstaff: 'Wilt thou have Doll Tearsheet meet you at supper?' (*2HIV* 2.1.164). As well as simply providing sex, she is affectionate and loving. She compares Falstaff to Hector of Troy, wipes his face, sits on his knee and gives him 'flattering busses' or kisses 'with a most constant heart' (*2HIV* 2.4.216–28, 268–70). She is not afraid to disagree with Falstaff: they are, Mistress Quickly claims, as quarrelsome as two dry as toasts with each other. Nevertheless, her relationship with Falstaff is touchingly intimate and realistic in recognizing but refusing to see his faults or his age. As a common woman who brings diseases, she is well placed to bring a note of chilling realism into Falstaff's hyperbolic world. His refusal to heed her: 'Doll, do not speak like a death's head, do not bid me remember mine end' (*2HIV* 2.4.233–5) and his inability to relieve her when she is arrested by the beadles, forms part of the shift from carnival holiday to lenten work at the end of the play. Doll Williamson, in *Sir Thomas More* is a woman of the streets in a more political sense, a carpenter's wife who insists to have her demands heard.

(c) Mahood (1998: 250), considers whether Dorothy in *Cymbeline* is the same or a different servant from Helen. McNeill (2007), discusses Doll Tearsheet in the context of other working-class women in early modern England and represented in the drama. Howard and Rackin (1997: 177–80) offer an excellent reading of Doll Tearsheet as a double to Mistress Quickly, disrupting the aristocratic, masculine version of official history. Kurtz (1996: 267–88) examines the active role in civic politics taken by Doll Williamson in *Sir Thomas More*.

dowager, (a) a woman whose husband is dead and who is in possession of title or property that has come to her from him. The name dervies from **dower**, the portion of a deceased husband's estate which the law allows to his **widow** for her lifetime. The name was apparently first used of Mary Tudor, widow of the French King Louis XII, and then of **Katherine** of Aragon, divorced by Henry VIII.
(b) Dowager is primarily a term signifying wealth that distinguishes fortunate **widows** from the more impoverished majority. Because many women who survived childbirth also outlived their husbands, dowers are of particular concern when negotiating **marriage** contracts and **betrothals** in Shakespeare's texts (see, for example, *Shrew* 2.1.342–90). In *A Midsummer Night's Dream*, Lysander places his hopes of maintenance on his 'widow **aunt**, a dowager / Of great revenue' (*MND* 1.1.157) while the play opens with a more negative view of the 'dowager / Long withering out a young man's revenue' (*MND* 1.1.5–6). This view that a widow's longlevity unfairly deprives a younger man of his inheritance possibly includes an oblique allusion to the aged Queen **Elizabeth** who had still not named an heir to the throne.

The name is insulting as applied to **Katherine** of Aragon in *Henry VIII* since it explicitly re-designates her as widow to Arthur rather than wife to Henry. Henry raises questions about the validity of a marriage to 'the dowager / Sometimes our brother's wife' (*HVIII* 2.4.181–2) and Suffolk makes Katherine's demotion clear in his news that she will no longer 'be call'd **Queen**, but **Princess** Dowager / And widow to Prince Arthur' (3.2.70–1). A similar sense of vulnerability surrounds the three Queens in *Two Noble Kinsmen*, whose appeal to Theseus for military help is, they think, in vain. The first Queen says

> Dowagers, take hands.
> Let us be widows to our woes; delay
> Commends us to a famishing hope.
> (*TNK* 1.1.165–7)

It is only through the help of other women, **Hippolyta** and **Emilia**, that their fortunes are changed.
(c) Mendelson and Crawford (1998: 40–42) summarize widows' rights to property and their difficulties in securing it. Erickson (1993) gives a fuller account. Many of the essays in *Widowhood and Visual Culture in Early Modern Europe*, edited by Allison Levy (2003) discuss wealthy widows, including Bess of Hardwick. Panek's historicist reading (2007) focuses on dramatic representations of the rich and propertied widow.

dower, (a) portion of a deceased husband's estate which the law allows to his **widow** for her lifetime.

(b) As noted above, because wives frequently outlived their husbands, dowers featured strongly in **marriage** contracts and **betrothals**. Dowers and dowries are confused but for young women, the term implies they look forward to a third phase of life, as widows. Miranda swears by her modesty as 'The jewel in my dower' (*Temp.* 3.1.54).

dowry, (a) the property or sum of money given by a woman's family (usually her father) to her husband at her marriage. The dowry invariably operates as a price tag, defining a woman's value in material terms and reducing her to a **commodity**, a prize or an object to be exchanged between men.

(b) The travesty of valuing a woman according to her dowry is noted frequently in Shakespeare's texts. Most pointedly, when King Lear disinherits **Cordelia** with the words 'truth then be thy dow'r' (*KL* 1.1.108) and tells her suitors 'her price is fallen' (1.1.197), the King of France cannot believe that Lear's 'best object' (*KL* 1.1.214) could be so devalued. Unlike the Duke of Burgundy, France believes Cordelia 'is herself a dowry' and is 'most rich being poor' (*KL* 1.1.241 and 250). In *The Taming of The Shrew*, it is Petruchio's desire to 'wive it wealthily in Padua' (*Shrew* 1.2.75) that makes Katherina's dowry of twenty thousand crowns and the promise of half of Baptista's estate, sufficient grounds for making a match before even meeting her (*Shrew* 2.1.119–130). As if to emphasize the commodification of women, Katherina's submission to husbandly authority at the end of the play makes Baptista value her more and offer Petruchio a bonus twenty thousand crowns 'Another dowry to another **daughter**' (*Shrew* 5.2.114).

Cynicism about the value of a dowry and its cost to a woman in personal terms is evident in *King John*, where **Blanch** is set up as a political pawn with 'a dowry large enough' to make her an attractive marriage prospect to the French Dauphin (*KJ* 2.1.469). John promises 'Her dowry shall weigh equal with a **queen**' (*KJ* 2.1.486). The most famous queen's dowry was probably Aquitaine, 'a dowry for a queen' (*LLL* 2.1.8), the province that **Eleanor** of Aquitaine brought to the French and later the English crown. The Earl of Armaniak's offer of his daughter to Henry VI 'with a large and sumptuous dowry' (*1HVI* 5.1.20), including Aquitaine, probably makes Henry's marriage to **Margaret** 'without having any dowry' (*2HVI* 1.1.61–2) all the more offensive to the English nobles. The significance of one's dowry is recognized by Shakespeare's female characters. **Olivia** shows how much she values Malvolio by saying 'I would not have him miscarry for the half my dowry' (*TN* 3.4.63) while the cost of losing it is keenly felt by **Mariana** in *Measure for Measure*. When her brother is drowned she also loses what seems to be a physical connection to her future: 'the portion and sinew of her fortune, her marriage-dowry' (*MM* 3.1.221), and the love of her fiancé, Angelo.

(c) Erickson (1993) and Cook (1991) offer information on dowries. B. J. Sokol and Mary Sokol, *Shakespeare, Law and Marriage* (2003) includes sections on dowries. Chamberlain (2003) discusses Mariana's situation.

doxy, (a) a name from vagabonds' cant or dialect meaning an unmarried woman who is the **mistress** to a beggar or a rogue. Beyond this local context, it is a familiar term to refer to a paramour or prostitute.

(b) The sole use in Shakespeare is in Autolycus's song where he celebrates the spring and 'the doxy over the dale!' (*WT* 4.3.2). Since Autolycus is a rogue and trickster who sets himself up as a pedlar of fashion accessories, the reference is particularly appropriate given the definition of doxy in John Awdelay's guide to vagabonds' cant: 'Note especially all which go abroade working laces and shirt stringes, they name them Doxies' (Awdelay 1575: sig. A3).

(c) John Awdelay, *The Fraternity of Vacabondes* (1575); Gordon Williams (1994: 412).

drab, (a) a dirty or sluttish woman, a whore.

(b) The term is used pejoratively, and by male characters in Shakespeare except for the third witch in *Macbeth* who refers to the finger of a strangled child 'Ditch-deliver'd by a drab' (*Mac.* 4.1.30) as one of the ingredients in the cauldron. Unlike the **bona roba** or sound whore, drab is an expression of disgust, associated with poverty, dirt and contamination. In *Troilus and Cressida*, for example, Thersites refers to Cressida as a 'dissembling, luxurious drab' (*T&C* 5.4.8), and says of Patroclus that a 'parrot will not do more for an almond than he for a commodious drab' (*T&C* 5.2.193–4) like her. The Duke of Gloucester insults the poverty-stricken wife of the deceitful Simpcox as a 'drab' (*2HVI* 2.1.153). More forcefully, **Joan La Pucelle**'s father rejects her with contempt calling her 'cursed drab' (*1HVI* 5.4.32). Hamlet echoes this, condemning himself as a whore who 'fall[s] a-cursing like a very drab' instead of taking masculine revenge (*Ham.* 2.2.586). Reynaldo feels that allegations of 'drabbing' would dishonour Laertes (*Ham.* 2.1.26–7). More light-hearted instances still keep the sense of belittling or trivializing women, as when Autolycus claims he lost his fortune 'with die and drab' (*WT* 4.2.36–7) or when Pompey advises Escalus to restrain the 'drabs and the knaves' as the root cause of prostitution in Vienna (*MM* 2.1.234).

(c) Gordon Williams (1994: 412–13) notes the associations with dirt and the proverb 'Dicing, drabbing and drinking are the three Ds to destruction' (Tilley 1950: D324).

duchess, (a) the wife or widow of a duke or a woman holding a title equal to that of a duke in her own right. Duchess (and duke) are the highest titles beneath queen (or king). **Hippolyta**, Dame **Eleanor** Cobham, the **widow**ed Duchess of Gloucester in *Richard II* and the Duchess of Norfolk who carries Anne's train in the coronation procession in *Henry VIII* are named using this title. Other speaking characters who hold the title are **Goneril** and **Regan**; the wife of Edmund Langley, 1st Duke of York, mother of Aumerle and **aunt** to Bolingbroke in *Richard II*; Cicely Neville, wife of Edward, 3rd Duke of York and mother to Edward IV, Clarence and Richard in *Richard III*; and **Constance** who is Duchess of Brittany in *King John*.

(b) Shakespeare's depictions of duchesses are politically inflected to show the closeness to and difference from royal power. This is staged visually in **Anne**

Bullen's coronation procession in *Henry VIII* where she is followed by '*The old DUCHESS OF NORFOLK, in a coronet of gold, wrought with flowers, bearing the Queen's train*' (*HVIII* 4.1.36 SD), who is, in turn, followed by noble women of lower rank. In *A Midsummer Night's Dream*, Theseus's subordination of **Hippolyta**, formerly the autonomous **Queen** of the **Amazons**, is reflected in her new title as 'Duchess' (*MND* 1.2.6). In *Richard II*, the Duchess of Gloucester appeals against the King who murdered her husband on the grounds of consanguinity between the sons of Edward III or 'seven fair branches springing from one root' (*RII* 1.2.13). In spite of the appearance of sameness, she cannot challenge the difference of royal authority enjoyed by Richard II, descendant of one of those branches. As **aunt** to the usurping Henry IV, the Duchess of York comically subverts his royal authority (*RII* 5.3). After Richard II has been deposed and the Lancastrian monarchy judiciously retains the title of Duchy of Lancaster alongside the royal one (Dutton 2003b), the differences between a duchess and a queen are even more fragile. *Henry VI Part II* stages open rivalry between Queen **Margaret** and **Eleanor**, Duchess of Gloucester, conducted primarily through sartorial display. Sumptuary laws dictated that duchesses could wear 'cloth of gold or silver tissued and purple silk' (Jardine 1983: 144) like queens, a display of magnificence that inspires awe for the Duchess of Milan's gown in *Much Ado*: 'cloth a gold and cuts, and lac'd with silver, set with pearls' and 'underborne with a bluish tinsel' (*MAdo* 3.4.19–22).

It is presumably the Duchess of Gloucester's flamboyant display of costume like this that infuriates Margaret in *Henry VI Part II* who cannot bear that 'Strangers in court take her for the Queen' (*2HVI* 1.3.79). When **Eleanor** is condemned for consulting a **witch**, and forced to do public penance in a white sheet, she compares her former state as 'Duke Humphrey's wife' with the present where 'his forlorn duchess, / Was made a wonder and a pointing-stock / To every idle rascal follower' (*2HVI* 2.4.41–7). Stanley's promises to his prisoner that 'Like to a duchess and Duke Humphrey's **lady**, / According to that state you shall be used' (*2HVI* 2.4.98–9) are of no comfort to the Duchess who dreamed of being a Queen. In *Henry VIII*, Anne Bullen's usurpation of **Katherine** of Aragon's position is foreseen by the Old Lady who teases that since 'you would not be a queen', then 'What think you of a Duchess? Have you limbs / To bear that load of title', the joke being that the two are effectively synonymous since Henry VIII is King and Duke of Lancaster, a title which subsequently passed to Elizabeth and then to James (*HVIII* 2.3.34–39). It is the Duchess of Norfolk who, as godmother, presents **Princess** Elizabeth to be baptized in the final scene (*HVIII* 5.4.SD).

(c) The ambiguity of the titles of 'Duke' and 'Duchess' following the usurpation of Richard II are explained by Richard Dutton in 'Shakespeare and Lancaster' (2003). Sumptuary laws are discussed in Jardine (1983: 142–52). *See* **Eleanor** for studies of the Duchess of Gloucester's role in *Henry VI Part II*.

dug, (a) a name for the **breast** or **pap** of a female mammal, used in relation to suckling.

(b) Throughout Shakespeare's work, the term is used with reference to suckling. Juliet's **nurse**, remembering how she **suckle**d and weaned **Juliet**, makes a distinction between the nipple and the dug as breast, recalling that when the baby 'did taste the wormwood on the nipple / Of my dug and felt it bitter, pretty fool, / To see it tetchy and fall out wi' th' dug!' (*R&J* 1.3.30–2). Osric's affected behaviour is mocked as a perversion of nature by Hamlet who claims the supercilious courtier 'did comply' or reverence 'his dug before he sucked it' (*Ham.* 5.1.187–8).

The Duchesses of York in *Richard II* and in *Richard III* see the dug as a site of pollution. York accuses his wife of nurturing Aumerle's conspiracy to murder Henry IV: 'Shall thy old dugs once more a traitor rear?' (*RII* 5.3.90), while Richard of Gloucester's **mother** is quick to point out 'from my dugs he drew not this deceit' (*RIII* 2.2.30). In *Edward III*, the Countess of Salisbury uses poisonous breastfeeding as a metaphor for the worst kind of parental treachery, like that shown by her father who acts as a bawd to seduce her to the king's bed. 'No marvel when the leprous infant die, / When the stern **dame** envenometh the dug', she exclaims (*EIII* 2.1.420–1).

Because the term draws analogies between human and animal behaviour, as in Touchstone's lustful gaze at Jane Smile milking cows (*AYLI* 2.4.49–50), it can also signify primitive, instinctive passion. **Venus**'s overpowering, unfulfilled desire for Adonis makes her 'Like a milch doe, whose swelling dugs do ache' to feed him as a fawn (*V&A* 875). The dug is a source of both erotic excitement and infantile comfort for the banished Duke of Suffolk who longs to die in the arms of his lover **Margaret** 'As mild and gentle as the cradle-babe / Dying with mother's dug between its lips' (*2HVI* 3.2.392–3).

(c) Rachel Truebowitz (2000) surveys early modern attitudes to breastfeeding. The last two chapters of Gail Kern Paster's *The Body Embarrassed* (1993), Chapter 4 'Complying with the Dug' (pp. 163–214) and Chapter 5 'Quarreling with the Dug' (pp. 215–80), analyse literary representations. *See also* **breast** and **suckle**.

Earth, (a) the planet on which we live, frequently feminized as a **mother** to living things, a source of life and also the place to which they return after death.
(b) The image of Mother Earth as **womb**, nurturing **bosom** and tomb to living things is expressed most fully by Friar Lawrence:

> The earth that's nature's mother is her tomb;
> What is her burying grave that is her womb;
> And from her womb children of divers kind
> We sucking on her natural bosom find:
> Many for many virtues excellent,
> None but for some and yet all different.
>
> (*R&J* 2.3.9–14)

The paradox of earth as giving and taking life is based on the Greek goddess Gaia and the Roman goddess Terra. Neither of these appear in Shakespeare's texts; instead, the feminized earth personifies this natural process of nurturing and consuming. Sonnet 19 notes that time will 'make the earth devour her own sweet brood' (*Son.* 19.2). Human, especially male, fear of the mortal process is reflected in the earthy pits that swallow Titus's sons and in the grotesque feast where, he tells **Tamora**'s sons, 'your unhallow'd **dam**' will eat them in a pie and 'Like to the earth swallow her own increase' (*Tit.* 5.2.190–1). In contrast, **Venus** describes the mortal cycle as logical and reciprocal, telling Adonis, 'Upon the earth's increase why shouldst thou feed, / Unless the earth with thy increase be fed?' (*V&A* 169–70). Horatio (*Ham.* 1.1.137) and Othello (*Oth.* 4.1.245) both describe the earth as a fertile womb, and mother earth is the power Florizel calls on to counter his father's, protesting that **nature** will 'crush the sides o' the earth together / And mar the seeds within!' before Florizel will break his faith to **Perdita** (*WT* 4.4.478–9). Florizel's vow to stay true by all that 'the close earth wombs' (*WT*

119

4.4.490) puts him in touch with the organic patterns of death and renewal, winter and spring, and the allusions to **Ceres** and **Proserpina** in this play.

Earth's vast and somewhat frightening natural power is domesticated by Hotspur's pregnancy metaphors to describe a series of storms that he believes are perfectly natural rather than the supernatural proclamation of Glendower's birth. Hotspur's imagery attempts to manage female fertility by making the body of the earth comically vulnerable to wind:

> oft the teeming earth
> Is with a kind of colic pinch'd and vex'd
> By the imprisoning of unruly wind
> Within her womb; which, for enlargement striving,
> Shakes the old **beldam** earth and topples down
> Steeples and moss-grown towers. At your birth
> Our **grandam** earth, having this distemp'rature,
> In passion shook.
>
> (*1HIV* 3.2.27–34)

Less rudely, Puck dares to contain the female body of the earth by promising to put a girdle round it in 40 minutes (*MND* 2.1.175–6). Earth appears as a trope for nationhood or motherland when Richard II returns to greet the 'dear earth' of his native soil 'As a long parted mother with her child'. The 'gentle earth' is both Richard's child, as the kingdom for which he should care, and the mother that should not nurture his enemies (*RII* 3.2.6–26). Timon of Athens bitterly chastises the 'damn'd earth' for bringing forth gold instead of food (*Tim.* 4.3.42–5). However, he returns to the 'Common mother' whose 'infinite **breast** / Teems and feeds all' and is rewarded with a root (*Tim.* 4.3.177–9). The common association of maternity and the earth infuses Coriolanus's speech when facing the powerful figure of his mother. When she bows 'As if Olympus to a molehill should / In supplication nod', he surrenders himself to **Volumnia** with the words 'sink, my knee, i' the earth; / Of thy dear duty more impression show / Than that of common sons' (*Cor.* 5.3.30–1 and 50–2).

Mother Earth's affection for her children is given a sinister edge when **Venus** tells Adonis that the earth deliberately trips him up in order to make him fall and kiss her (*V&A* 721–3). More voracious images of the earth drinking the blood of her sons haunt the Yorkist soldiers (*3HVI* 2.3.15 and 23), and in *Richard III*, **Anne** appeals to the earth to swallow Richard of Gloucester who killed Henry VI: 'earth gape open wide and eat him quick, / As thou dost swallow up this good king's blood / Which his hell-govern'd arm hath butchered!' (*RIII* 1.2.65–7). The image of earth's gaping mouth as the womb and tomb that annihilates independent masculine identity recurs in tragic stage images such as the 'hole' or 'gaping hollow of the earth' (*Tit.* 2.3.246–9) in *Titus Andronicus*. It also lies behind the boast of Charles the wrestler: 'Come, where is this young gallant that is so desirous to lie with his mother earth?' (*AYLI* 1.2.200–1). By the end of this early scene in the comedy, Charles can no longer speak.

(c) Jeanne Addison Roberts (1991: 1–54). *See also* **nature** and **womb**.

Echo, (a) a **nymph** from classical myth who was punished by Juno with not being able to speak except in reply to others. Echo's babble had, previously, always forewarned Jupiter's paramours so that they could escape being caught. After she lost the power of independent speech Echo fell in love with Narcissus and her love was unrequited. As a result of her shame at rejection, she retired to caves, grew thinner and thinner until her body faded away completely and only her voice was left.

(b) Shakespeare would have known Echo's story from Ovid's *Metamorphoses*, Book III, lines 443–500 (Ovidius 2000: 73–5). Allusions to Echo in the canon signify intensity of frustrated passion. The figure of Echo lies behind the disguised **Viola** whose only expression of her love for Orsino is through relaying his suit to Olivia. She tells Olivia that she would not accept refusal but shout her name 'to the reverberate hills / And make the babbling gossip of the air / Cry out "Olivia"' (*TN* 1.5.272–4). Viola wistfully tells Orsino that the tune she hears 'gives a very echo to the seat / Where Love is thron'd' (*TN* 2.4.21–2). She functions as a kind of catalyst, intervening to disrupt the narcissistic tendencies of Olivia and Orsino. Unlike Viola, **Venus** does not escape the identity of Echo as the epitome of unrequited love. In spite of her high status, Venus is helpless in her unrequited passion for Adonis:

> And now she beats her heart, whereat it groans,
> That all the neighbor caves, as seeming troubled,
> Make verbal repetitions of her moans;
> Passion on passion deeply is redoubled:
> 'Ay me!' she cries, and twenty times 'Woe, woe!'
> And twenty echoes twenty times cry so.
>
> (*V&A* 829–34)

Juliet, too, compares herself to Echo. This time the frustration is that is she is not able to speak Romeo's name aloud as she wishes because of the danger. Otherwise, she says, she would 'tear the cave where Echo lies, / And make her airy tongue more hoarse than mine / With repetition of my Romeo's name' (*R&J* 2.2.161–3).

(c) Jonathan Bate (1993: 149–51) and A. B. Taylor, (ed.) *Ovid's Metamorphoses* (2000), pp. 7–9 both discuss the figure. Enterline's poststructural analysis (2002: 44–5 and 217–18) considers Echo as a disturbing figure whose presence demonstrates the citationality of all speech and dislocates a speaker's sense of presence. D. J. Palmer (1979) traces the presence of Echo and Narcissus in the interview between Viola and Olivia in *Twelfth Night*.

Elbow, Mistress (a) Constable Elbow's pregnant wife who is mentioned but does not appear on stage in *Measure for Measure*.

(b) Mistress Elbow is the butt of Pompey's lewd jokes and her husband's own limited command of language. Pompey explains that she entered Mistress **Overdone**'s brothel, because she was 'great with **child**' and had a sudden craving for stewed prunes (a favourite dish in brothels and so a slang term for prostitutes). Mistress Elbow appears to have spat in the face of Master Froth because he ate all but the last two prunes (2.1.84 and 95–102). The magistrates' critical attention is distracted from the brothel because Elbow's malapropisms inadvertently construct Mistress Elbow in bawdy terms as a woman he 'detest[s] before heaven' (2.1.70), who is 'cardinally given' and might indeed 'have been accus'd in fornication, adultery, and all uncleanliness there' (2.1.79–81). His linguistic blunders comically invert the norms of companionate **marriage** in which each spouse is respected by his or her partner. In desperately trying to clear her from the taint of the brothel as a suspected person, Elbow mistakenly asserts, 'The time is yet to come that she was ever respected with man, woman or child' and, furthermore, testifies 'If I was ever respected with her, or she with me, let not your worship think me the poor Duke's officer' (2.1.176–7).

(c) See DiGangi (1993) for a brilliant analysis of Mistress Elbow as the pivot of male anxieties in the play about wayward wives.

Eleanor, (a) the name used of **Dame** Eleanor of Cobham, the Duchess of Gloucester in *Henry VI Part II*. The name was introduced to England by Eleanor of Aquitaine (1122–1204), who came from south-west France to be the wife of King Henry II and who appears in *King John* as mother of the King. It was a name strongly associated with English queens consort, borne by Eleanor of Provence, the wife of Henry III, and Eleanor of Castile, wife of Edward I.

(b) In *King John*, Eleanor of Aquitaine is a dominant maternal figure, named in stage directions as 'Queene Elinor' 'Eleanor' and 'Queene', but she is not addressed by her Christian name on stage. Nevertheless, audiences may well have remembered her powerful presence in Peele's *Troublesome Reign of King John*, the play which was probably Shakespeare's source text. Here Eleanor of Aquitaine dominates her rival **Constance** with the words:

> Contemptuous dame, unreverent duchess, thou,
> To brave so great a queen as Eleanor.
> Base scold, hast thou forgot that I was wife
> And mother to three mighty English kings?
> (Peele 2009: I.7.7–10)

The queenly resonances of the name, and indeed the status battle between **queen** and **duchess** are played out in Shakespeare's *Henry VI Part II*. Eleanor, Duchess of Gloucester is haunted by the queenly power usually associated with the name. She recounts her dream of sitting on the English throne and being crowned with the 'diadem' by Henry VI and **Dame** Margaret (a title never used of queens). Her husband, whom she does not include in her transgressive coronation fantasy, chides her as 'Presumptuous dame, ill-nurtur'd Eleanor' (*2HVI* 1.2.39). Eleanor's challenge to Queen Margaret is essentially theatrical, relying on her assumption of the clothes and posture of a queen or an **empress** (Howard and Rackin 1997: 79; *2HVI* 1.3.75–86). It becomes physical, like the conflict between **Helena** and **Hermia** (*MND* 3.2), when Eleanor responds to a box on the ears with a threat to use all ten fingers to scratch: 'Could I come near your beauty with my nails / I could set my ten commandments in your face' (*2HVI* 1.3.241–2). Eleanor's fantasy of being 'your royal Majesty' (*2HVI* 1.2.70) tempts her into consulting the **witch**, **Margery** Jordan (*2HVI* 1.4), but the text frames this as a trap set so that 'Eleanor's pride dies in its youngest days' (*2HVI* 2.3.46), thus mitigating direct association between female ambition and evil. The Duke of Gloucester addresses her intimately and affectionately as 'sweet Nell' (*2HVI* 1.2.17), and 'gentle Nell' (*2HVI* 2.4.26 and 67). Nevertheless, when she is formally tried as 'Dame Eleanor of Cobham, Gloucester's wife' he resigns her to the law: 'Eleanor, the law, thou seest hast judged thee' (*2HVI* 2.3.1 and 15). The plot flamboyantly advertises the condemnation of Eleanor's queenly aspirations when she performs a public penance: appearing barefoot, in a white sheet with verses pinned to it, and carrying a taper. Nevertheless, the text allows room for considerable sympathy and the character encourages respect when she recognizes:

> My shame will not be shifted with my sheet,
> No, it will hang upon my richest robes,
> And show itself, attire me how I can.
> Go, lead the way, I long to see my prison.
> (*2HVI* 2.4.107–10)

Her final lines raise awareness about the lack of any legitimate arena for women's political ambitions. The damaging effects explored through Eleanor's role provide a prototype for the role of **Lady Macbeth**.
(c) On Eleanor of Aquitaine, see George Peele's *The Troublesome Reign of King John* (1591) (Peele forthcoming 2010) which gives a strong dramatic portrait of Eleanor of Aquitaine. Nina S. Levine, 'The case of Eleanor Cobham: Authorizing History in *2HVI*' (1994) is a detailed analysis of the political resonance of the role in relation to its historical context, to witchcraft and the subversion of patriarchal authority. Howard and Rackin's *Engendering a Nation* (1997: 74–7 and 119–33) reads the theatrical quality of Eleanor Cobham's ambitions, and discusses Queen Eleanor in *King John* in relation to women's power and knowledge.

Elizabeth (a) the name of Edward IV's **queen** and that of her daughter who married Henry VII, and of Elizabeth I, Queen of England from 1558 to 1603.
(b) Elizabeth of York (formerly the widow Elizabeth Woodville, Lady Grey) appears in *Henry VI Part III* where she is married to Edward IV and in *Richard III* where she is widowed. Elizabeth, their eldest child, does not appear on stage but is matched with Henry, Earl of Richmond, the founder of the Tudor dynasty. When Henry was crowned, the historical Elizabeth of York (1466–1503) embodied the process of uniting the houses of York and Lancaster in the new Tudor dynasty through their marriage and their offspring. The last Tudor monarch, Elizabeth I,

was named after her founding foremother and grandmother and appears as an infant in the final scene of *Henry VIII.*

Elizabeth I (1533–1603), daughter of Henry VIII and Anne Boleyn, was the most powerful woman in England during Shakespeare's lifetime, ruling from 1558 to her death in 1603. Having been declared illegitimate at the birth of her half-brother Edward VI (1537–53) who ruled from 1547, Elizabeth did not expect to accede to the throne and was subject to periods of imprisonment in the Tower of London and at Woodstock during the reign of her Catholic half-sister Mary Tudor (1516–1558). Since Elizabeth was literally the offspring of England's break with Rome, her survival and accession were, unsurprisingly, heralded by Protestants as a mark of divine Providence (Foxe 1583). The account of her 'Passage through the Cittie of London' before her coronation records that the first pageant, 'The uniting of the two houses of Lancaster and York', featured a family tree with actors personifying Henry VII with a red rose, Elizabeth of York with a white rose, Henry VIII, Anne Boleyn and Elizabeth herself. 'This pageant was grounded upon the Queen's Majesty's name. For like as the long war between the two houses of York and Lancaster was ended when Elizabeth, daughter to Edward IV, matched in marriage with Henry VII heir to the house of Lancaster so since that the Queen Majesty's name was Elizabeth, and forsomuch as she is the only heir of Henry VIII, which came of both the houses as the knitting up of concord, so she another Elizabeth might maintain the same among her subjects' (Mulcaster 1999: 23, ll. 134–99). The significance of 'Elizabeth' as a name signalling the inauguration and birth of a new peace may be linked to the biblical Elizabeth, mother of John the Baptist (Luke 1.5–58).

Elizabeth I received a strong humanist education under the direction of Roger Ascham with knowledge of Latin, Greek, French, Italian and a little Spanish. She undertook translations, wrote in verse and prose, enjoyed dancing, needlework, and played the lute and spinet. Diplomatic negotiations to arrange a marriage for Elizabeth all came to nothing, probably as a result of her determination to remain single for political reasons relating to both her own independence and that of the country. Her accession speech recorded 'in the end' it would be sufficient that a marble stone should declare 'that a Queene, having raigned such a tyme, lived and dyed a virgin' (Hartley 1981: 44–5).

In *Henry VIII*, Heaven is asked to send 'prosperous life, long and ever happy to the high and mighty Princess of England, Elizabeth' (5.4.1–3) and after Archbishop Cranmer names the baby, he is inspired to prophesy:

> This royal infant – heaven still move about her! –
> Though in her cradle, yet now promises
> Upon this land a thousand thousand blessings,
> Which time shall bring to ripeness. She shall be
> (But few now living can behold that goodness)
> A pattern to all princes living with her,
> And all that shall succeed.
>
> (*HVIII* 5.4.17–23)

Henry VIII thus self-consciously constructs the cult of Elizabeth in Jacobean England. The succession problems that plagued the virgin queen's old age are erased in a splendid picture of a 'bird of wonder' or '**maid**en phoenix' who creates an heir from her own ashes (*HVIII* 5.4.40–47). Cranmer rejoices that Elizabeth will live 'an aged **Princess**' whose many days of rule will bring good to England since there will be 'no day without a deed to crown it' (*HVIII* 5.4.57–8). He celebrates her saintly **virgin**ity: 'A most unspotted lily shall she pass / To the ground, and all the world shall mourn her' (*HVIII* 5.4.56–62).

Shakespeare's other plays make only oblique references to Elizabeth I via the words **Queen**, **Empress** of **England**, or via the royal iconography based on virginity and strength in references to Astraea, **Cynthia**, **Diana**, **Phoebe** and the **moon**, roses and the 'imperial **vot'ress**' (*MND* 2.1.163). When the name Elizabeth is used in *Richard III*, however, it always carries associations with peacemaking, unity and prosperity, as if dramatizing a living continuity between Elizabeth I and Elizabeth of York, the grandmother for whom she was named. Edward IV's queen is never named Elizabeth in the spoken lines so the name is reserved for Elizabeth of York. Richard III quickly recognizes that the 'knot' of marriage to 'young Elizabeth' is a way of cementing a claim to the crown (*RIII* 4.3.41–2) and so endeavours to wed her himself before Richmond can. Richard III's interview with her mother alludes wittily forward to Elizabeth I's successful reign. Richard begins his proxy wooing with the words: 'You have a daughter call'd Elizabeth, / Virtuous and fair, royal and gracious' and insists on her legitimacy 'Wrong not her royal birth, she is a royal princess' as though rehearsing the virtues and obstacles faced by Elizabeth I (*RIII* 4.4.204–5, 212).

Queen Elizabeth (Woodville) outmanoeuvres his attempts to trap her daughter in an unwanted **marriage** with a deftness that replays Elizabeth I's own diplomatic refusal of a match. Richard's declaration 'I love thy daughter / And do intend to make her Queen of England' is pointedly rebuffed with the words 'who dost thou mean shall be her king?' (*RIII* 4.4.263–5). Queen Elizabeth is determined that her daughter will not 'vail the title, as her **mother** doth' (*RIII* 4.4.348). Richard warns Queen Elizabeth, 'Without her, follows to myself and thee, / Herself, the land, and many a Christian soul / Death, desolation, ruin and decay' (*RIII* 4.4.407–10). Queen Elizabeth acts promptly by consenting that Richmond 'should espouse Elizabeth her daughter' (*RIII* 4.5.8). Richmond prays 'let Richmond and Elizabeth', the heirs of each royal house, 'conjoin together' to beget heirs that will 'Enrich the time to come with smooth fac'd **peace**, / With smiling plenty and fair prosperous days' (*RIII* 5.5.29–34). This is the same peace celebrated by Cranmer at Princess Elizabeth's christening: 'In her days every man shall eat in safety' and sing 'merry songs of peace to all his neighbors' (*HVIII* 5.4.33–5). By the time all these lines were spoken, England's young Princess Elizabeth, daughter to King James and Queen Anna, was married to the Elector Palatine, so perhaps this image of youthful, virginal regeneration stretching out to the future owes more to Shakespeare's hopes for his granddaughter, Elizabeth Hall, who was five in 1613.

(c) On Elizabeth of York see Rosemary Horrox (2004) and on Elizabeth I see Patrick

Collinson (2004) for biographical information. Queen Elizabeth's definition of herself as a virgin queen is in Hartley (1981: 44–5). For Elizabeth's cultural significance see H. Hackett (1995 and 2009), Carole Levin (1994), and the collection of essays *Elizabeth I: Always Her Own Free Woman*, edited by Carole Levin, Jo Eldridge-Carney and Debra Barrett-Graves (2003). An edition of *The Queens Majesties Passage Through the Cittie of London* (1559) by Richard Mulcaster is given in Kinney (ed.), *Renaissance Drama* (1999: 17–34). For studies of Elizabeth and her iconography see R. Strong (1977), Susan Doran and Thomas Freeman (2003), Louis Adrian Montrose, 'Elizabeth Through the Looking Glass: Picturing The Queen's Two Bodies' (2006), Archer (ed.) (2007) and Anneliese Connolly and Lisa Hopkins (eds), *Goddesses and Queens: The Iconography of Elizabeth I* (2007). Deanne Williams's essay in this volume (2007) and Jardine (1983: 169–79) both discuss Elizabeth as a strong role model. On Queen Elizabeth's role in *Richard III* see Dubrow (2000) and Susan Brown's account of a performer's experience of the role (2000).

Emilia, (a) the names of four characters in Shakespeare: the wife of Egeon, separated from him in a shipwreck, who becomes an **Abbess** at Ephesus in *Comedy of Errors*; the wife of Iago and female companion of **Desdemona** in *Othello*; one of Hermione's ladies in waiting in *The Winter's Tale*; and the younger sister of **Hippolyta**, former Queen of the Amazons, and beloved of both Palamon and Arcite in *Two Noble Kinsmen*. The name, with the variant form Aemilia, is a Latinized form of the Germanic *Amalia* (containing the word *amal* 'work') and is found in Plutarch where Shakespeare could have read it. **Princess** Emilia in *Two Noble Kinsmen* is also called 'Emily' to fit the metre of the verse. In addition to these fictional characters, Aemilia Lanyer is the name of the Venetian Jew who has been suggested by critics as a candidate for the **Dark Lady** of the Sonnets.
(b) Shakespeare appears to associate the name with female bonding, female community and strength. From her first line in *The Comedy of Errors*, when she orders, 'Be quiet people' (*Err.* 5.1.38) the Abbess Aemilia (First Folio) commands the stage, directing all other characters including the Duke. She brings order out of confusion by means of her maternal authority, which also solves the riddles of doubled identity in the twins. Her name has the power to unravel the play's web of errors and release her husband from imprisonment:

> Whoever bound him, I will loose his bonds,
> And gain a husband by the liberty.
> Speak, old Egeon, if thou be'st the man
> That hadst a **wife** once call'd Aemilia,
> That bore thee at a burden two fair sons.
> O, if thou be'st the same Egeon, speak,
> And speak unto the same Aemilia!
>
> (*Err.* 5.1.340–6)

Doubleness characterizes Aemilia too. As **Abbess**, she ventriloquizes patriarchal attitudes and condemns Adriana as a **scold** for railing against her husband's desire for other women (*Err.* 5.1.69–86). Immediately before, however, Aemilia assumes the opposite position, criticizing Adriana for not reprehending him 'rough enough' for his infidelity (*Err.* 5.1.58). Aemilia is a contradiction, an 'error' who confounds gender roles and 'begins to appear as a subtextual – and sexual – subverter' (Kehler 1991: 161). Such doubleness and subversive strength seems to go with the name in Shakespeare. Aemelia's critical attitude to the sexual double standard is shared by her counterpart in *Othello*, in what is arguably the most feminist speech in the Shakespeare canon. Emilia tells Desdemona that 'I do think it is their husbands' faults / If wives do fall' (*Oth.* 4.3.86–7) and gives a catalogue of male abuses ending with the argument:

> have not we affections
> Desires for sport, and frailty, as men have?
> Then let them use us well; else they may know
> The ills we do, their ills instruct us so.
>
> (*Oth.* 4.3.100–3)

Emilia's forthright proclamation of sexual equality contrasts markedly with her emotional subjection to Iago. There is deep sadness in her words 'I nothing but to please his fantasy' (*Oth.* 3.3.299); taking Desdemona's handkerchief is a desperate attempt to win Iago's love. This act has tragic consequences for Emilia as well as the protagonists: its futility is immediately apparent. Like the Abbess, this Emilia has a double role. Although initially she seems to be enslaved to male desires, she emerges as a powerful spokeswoman for the sex once Desdemona becomes the primary focus of her emotional energies.

The pairing of **mistress** and **waiting-gentlewoman** becomes closer throughout the play, beginning with the bedroom scenes where Desdemona repeatedly calls on Emilia by name, while Othello refers to her as a '**bawd**' who keeps the 'gate of hell' in guarding the door to Desdemona's supposedly adulterous body (*Oth.* 4.2.20 and 92). Emilia's loyalty to Desdemona is matched by a determination to speak out, thus defying the conventions of wifely modesty which 'cry shame against me' (*Oth.* 4.5.2.220–2). She openly disobeys Iago's injunctions of silence and his orders to go home. When he stabs her, Emilia's angry voice modulates into song as she dies beside her mistress, asserting Desdemona's chastity and reiterating her willow song.

Powerful female loyalty characterizes Shakespeare's other waiting-gentlewoman named Emilia, in *The Winter's Tale*. This small part provides a bridge between Hermione and **Paulina** during the former's confinement in childbirth and prison. Emilia takes on a midwife's role, delivering the baby Perdita from the prison to be presented to her father by Paulina (*WT* 2.2). Emilia's love and support for other women lends warmth to her few but significant lines. She praises Paulina's 'honor and goodness', believing '[t]here is no lady living / So meet for this great errand' (*WT* 2.2.41–4).

An even closer relationship between women is cherished by Emilia in *The Two Noble Kinsmen*. The name, unlike the previous examples, comes from the source text: Chaucer's *Knight's Tale*, but, in the scenes generally ascribed to him, Shakespeare's characterization intensifies the features of female loyalty and unconventionality shared by his earlier Emilias. As an **Amazon**, it is not surprising that Emilia finds more security in same-sex relationships. She does not want the third widowed queen to kneel to her; asserting instead that any distressed woman she can help 'does bind me to her' (*TNK* 1.1.37). Emilia declares 'Being a natural **sister** of our **sex** / Your sorrow beats so ardently upon me' that she must join their petition to Theseus (*TNK* 1.1.125–6), and a strong stage image of sisterly solidarity is created when **Hippolyta** and Emilia kneel with the queens. The word 'ardent' implies a passion in Emilia's sisterly affection that is elaborated when she speaks of the love she shared with **Flavina**, who died when the two girls were 11:

> The flow'r that I would pluck
> And put between my **breasts** (O then but beginning
> To swell about the blossom) she would long
> Till she had such another, and commit it
> To the innocent cradle, where phoenix-like
> They died in perfume.
>
> (*TNK* 1.3.66–71)

Although Emilia states this love is innocent, the language, including the innuendo of 'die' for orgasm, is overtly erotic. Hippolyta interprets her sister's words that 'true love 'tween maid and maid may be / More than in sex dividual' as a preference for same-sex love and a rejection of men (*TNK* 1.3.281–4). This proves prophetic since Emilia is attracted neither to Palamon nor to Arcite. Her heartfelt prayer to **Diana** is to 'Continue in thy band' (*TNK* 5.1.162). Emilia's open expression of individual desire and strong commitment to female community make her a fitting last characterization of the name in Shakespeare's work.

Kehler suggests that the real-life Aemelia Lanyer may have influenced Shakespeare's interpretation of the name in his plays. Lanyer was daughter to the Italian Jewish musician Bassano, whose family emigrated to England from Venice and were frequently called upon to provide music at court. Aemilia was mistress to Henry Carey, Lord Hunsdon, Lord Chamberlain, the patron of Shakespeare's company, and her reputation for sexual freedom was commented on in the diary of physician Simon Forman. When, in 1592, she became pregnant, she was swiftly married off to another accomplished musician, Alphonso Lanyer. Aemilia was probably musical herself and was also a published writer. Her poem *Salve Deus Rex Judaeorum* (1611) [Hail Christ, King of the Jews], shares several features with the speeches of the dramatic Emilias: a strong feminist sensibility and sense of female community. The religious poem contains a defence of Eve and the female sex, dedications to a powerful group of women and an idealization of Lanyer's relationship with her patrons the Countess of Cumberland and her daughter Anne.

(c) Plutarch's *Lives of the Noble Grecians and Romans* (1579) uses the name 'Aemilia' in the lives of Romulus (p. 21), Paulus Aemilius (p. 264), Sylla (p. 522) and, most extensively, Pompey, where she is a pawn in a 'cruell and tyrannicall' political marriage to Pompey and then dies in childbirth (p. 682). Dorothea Kehler (1991) compares the Emilias in Shakespeare's work, regarding celibacy and connections with widowhood as the most striking common characteristics. Rutter (2001: 142–77) is a fine analysis of Emilia's role in performance with a particular focus on Zoe Wanamaker's interpretations. Roberts, *Shakespearean Wild* (1991: 135–6) reads Emilia in *Two Noble Kinsmen* as an **Amazon**, Diana's knight who is ultimately stronger than Arcite since he cannot control her horses. Valerie Traub (2002: 172–5) agues that Emilia's separatism is a prototype for later plays and (p. 330) explores what kind of lesbian relationship her bond to Flavina represents. Laurie J. Shannon (2002: 90–123) reads the homoerotics of Emilia's relationship with Flavina in political terms as an assertion of female autonomy. A. L. Rowse (1978) first argued that Lanyer was the mysterious lady in the Sonnets in *The Poems of Shakespeare's Dark Lady.* Suzanne Woods' *Poems of Aemilia Lanyer: Salve Deus Rex Judaeorum* (1993) gives a fully annotated edition and introduction with detailed biographical information. René Weis (2007: 288–90) discusses Aemilia Lanyer and the character in *Othello*.

empress, (a) a female emperor, or the wife or widow of an emperor. The term is also used metphorically to mean a female potentate exercising supreme or absolute power.

(b) 'Empress' is a loaded title in Shakespeare's Roman plays, which exploit its double meaning to refer to both a consort and a woman exercising absolute power. It is sometimes disyllabic and sometimes, with an additional 'e', trisyllabic. At the opening of *Titus Andronicus*, Bassianus declares '**Lavinia** will I make my emperess / Rome's royal **mistress**, mistress of my heart' (*Tit.* 1.1.240–1), referring to her as a consort, but the title 'emperess' hints at the greater authority she carries as namesake of Aeneas's wife, the original ruler of Rome. The title becomes compromised when Saturninus elevates **Tamora**, previously 'prisoner to an emperor', as a substitute 'Emperess of Rome' (*Tit.* 1.1.258 and 320). Since Tamora 'prevail[s]' (*Tit.* 1.1.459) over Saturninus, the title 'empress' effectively refers to her as an absolute ruler. However, her selfish desire for revenge and her emotional enslavement to Aaron the Moor make a mockery of imperial rule. Aaron's phrase 'the empress of my soul' (*Tit.* 2.3.40) to flatter Tamora echoes the illusory power of the mistress in courtship as when Longaville extravagantly calls his beloved 'O sweet **Maria**, empress of my love' (*LLL* 4.3.54). Aaron knows that his so-called 'imperial mistress' is 'fett'red in amorous chains' to him (*Tit.* 2.1.15–16). He vows he will 'shine in pearl and gold, / To wait upon this new-made emperess' (*Tit.* 2.1.19–20) but quickly corrects himself:

> To wait, said I? to wanton with this **queen**,
> This goddess, this **Semiramis**, this **nymph**,
> This siren, that will charm Rome's Saturnine,
> And see his shipwreck and his commonweal's.
>
> (*Tit.* 2.1.21–4)

Tamora's exchange with the Clown makes it clear how Rome's government has now become a parody of imperial power because of her inversion of gender norms and just rule:

> Tamora: How now good fellow, wouldst thou speak with us?
> Clown: Yea forsooth, and your mistriship be emperial.
> Tamora: Empress I am, but yonder sits the Emperor.
>
> (*Tit.* 4.4.39–41)

Bassianus and Titus sarcastically refer to her as 'Rome's royal Emperess' (*Tit.* 2.3.55) and 'our proud Empress, mighty Tamora' (*Tit.* 5.1.26), Bassianus making an implicit unfavourable comparison between Tamora and the virginal English empress, **Elizabeth** I (*Tit.* 2.3.56–9). Titus grotesquely restores order by paying punctilious attention to hierarchy when inviting 'the Emperor and the Emperess too', Lucius and the Princes of the Goths to 'Feast at my house' (*Tit.* 5.2.127–8).

For **Cleopatra** the title 'Royal Egypt, Empress' (*A&C* 4.15.70) recalls the absolute power of Ptolemy and the Egyptian emperors, and thus functions as a reaffirmation of her sovereignty independent of Rome. The Italian play *Two Gentlemen of Verona* may refer back to the Roman tradition and to **Elizabeth** I in praising Valentine as 'worthy of an empress' love' (*TGV* 5.4.142). In an English context, empress again signifies absolute power. Queen **Margaret** complains that her rival, **Eleanor**, Duchess of Gloucester, sweeps through the court with trains of ladies 'more like an empress than Duke Humphrey's **wife**' and is taken for the **queen** by strangers (*2HVI* 1.3.78–9). Queen **Elizabeth** I's imperial ambitions, graphically advertised in the Ditchley portrait, are romanticized in *Henry V.* She is referred to as 'our gracious Empress' in *Henry V* (Chorus 5.30) with reference to Essex's campaign in Ireland. In the peacemaking scene, Henry tells **Katherine** to put off her **maid**en blushes and 'avouch the thoughts of your heart with the looks of an empress' (*HV* 5.2.235–6) to claim England, Ireland and France. He even imagines having a child who will 'go to Constantinople and take the Turk by the beard' (*HV* 5.2.208–10).

(c) *See* **Tamora**, **Isis** and **Cleopatra** and **queen** for further reading on female rule. On the Ditchley portrait and Elizabeth as an empress see Louis Adrian Montrose (2006) and Deanne Williams (2007).

England, (a) a country which now forms the southernmost part of Great Britain and in which Shakespeare was born, lived, worked and died. In the early modern period England, a feminized territory, was nominally and politically united to Wales, although the two had strongly different cultures. The crowns of England and Scotland were united under the rule of James in 1603. Attempts to bring Ireland under peaceful English rule were never wholly successful.

(b) John Hale's oration to Queen **Elizabeth** describing 'our naturall Mother Englande, whiche hath bene counted to be the surest, the richest, and of late also the most godly Nation of the earth' with 'louynge children', characterized the early modern patriotic feminization of England (Foxe 1583: 2116). The maternal trope for England continued into patriarchal Jacobean Britain; George Benson's 1609 sermon, for example, characterized Oxford and Cambridge Universities 'the two plentiful **breast**s of our mother England: they are deepe died and ingrained with knowledge from aboue' (Benson 1609: 57). Shakespeare's plays use feminized England as a trope to compliment Elizabeth. John of Gaunt's famously patriotic lines idealize a sacred Christian motherland: 'This blessed plot, this **earth**, this realm, this England, / This **nurse**, this teeming **womb** of royal kings' and 'This land of such dear souls, this dear dear land' (*RII* 2.1.50–6). When Bolingbroke is banished, he likewise bids a nostalgic farewell to England whose 'sweet soil' has imprinted him with true-born Englishness as 'My **mother**, and my nurse, that bears me yet' (*RII* 1.2.306–9). Such feminized images implicitly invoke **Queen** Elizabeth I, even though the idealized kingdom is apparently peopled exclusively by men (Howard and Rackin 1997: 147). Elizabeth's virginal independence is refracted in images of England as an island: 'that pale, that white-fac'd shore, / Whose foot spurns back the ocean's roaring tides / And coops from other lands her islanders' so that they remain secure from foreign invasion (*KJ* 2.1.23–8). The strong heart of monarch and nation, however weak the body of the queen, are recalled in *Henry V*'s Chorus. He addresses England as 'model to thy inward greatness / Like little body with a mighty heart', predicting great things for the nation if only 'all thy children' were 'kind and natural' or loyal (*HV* Chorus 2.16–19). To be disloyal to one's country and monarch is to be as 'bloody Neroes, ripping up the womb / Of your dear mother England' the rebels are told in *King John*. Their degeneracy is emphasized by the contrast with their 'own ladies and pale-visag'd **maids**' who 'Like **Amazons** come tripping after drums' to defend their motherland (*KJ* 5.2.152–8).

England and Elizabeth's enduring strength is imagined with reference to the eagle and to the **widow**. As a mother eagle, hunting for prey, England must protect her nest against the Scots, Ely warns (*HV* 1.2.169–70). Nevertheless, Canterbury refers back to the capture of King David of Scotland during Edward III's campaign in France to argue that the kingdom can defend herself. Even in the absence of her king and nobles, England has the threatening tenacity of a widow, to be 'more fear'd than harm'd':

> For hear her but exampled by herself:
> When all her chevalry hath been in France
> And she a mourning widow of her nobles,
> She hath herself not only well defended
> But taken and impounded as a stray
> The King of Scots; whom she did send to France
> To fill King Edward's fame with prisoner kings,
> And make her chronicle as rich with praise
> As is the ooze and bottom of the sea
> With sunken wreck and sunless treasuries.
>
> (*HV* 1.2.156–65)

131

Such powerful feminizations of England would have resonated strongly in the ears of spectators whose monarch still refused to name an heir or take advice on the succession.

(c) Hales's Oration to Queen Elizabeth is in John Foxe, *Actes and Monuments* (1583: 2116–19). George Benson's praise of the universities is in *A sermon preached at Paules Crosse the seauenth of May, M.DC.IX* (1609). Norman Jones, 'Shakespeare's England' (1999) gives a clear summary of the state of the nation while Howard and Rackin (1997: 117, 147, 151, 159, 211) give more detailed accounts of the emerging, feminized nation state.

Euriphile, (a) **nurse** to the Princes Arviragus and Cadwal, the lost sons of Cymbeline.

(b) Euriphile is dead before the action of *Cymbeline* begins but her actions are recalled by Belarius. He persuaded her to steal the royal infants, aged three and two, and take them into the country with him, marrying her as a reward for her actions (5.5.340–2). The Princes grew up believing she was their **mother**. Their faithful affection to her is clear since they remember mourning at her graveside (4.2.237–8) and 'every day do honour to her grave' (3.3.103–5). The beautiful song they sing to **Fidele** (4.2.258–81) was previously used for Euriphile's funeral.

Europa, (a) daughter of Agenor with whom Jupiter fell in love. He transformed himself into a bull to abduct her by taking her into the sea on his back and landing at Crete.

(b) Book II and the opening of Book III of Ovid's *Metamorphoses* briefly recount the rape of Europa. Falstaff alludes to the myth as a model for his own disguise as Herne the Hunter to seduce Mistress **Ford** and Mistress **Page** (and goes on to allude to **Leda** and the swan). His words advertise the grotesque nature of male lust: 'Remember, Jove, thou wast a bull for thy Europa, love set on thy horns. O powerful love, that in some respects makes a beast a man; in some other a man a beast' (*MWW* 5.5.3–6). In *The Taming of the Shrew*, the young Lucentio compares **Bianca** to this classical figure:

> I saw sweet beauty in her face
> Such as the daughter of Agenor had,
> That made great Jove to humble him to her hand
> When with his knees he kiss'd the Cretan strond.
> (*Shrew* 1.1.167–70)

This lengthy comparison, which allows Lucentio to display his classical education, makes him appear little more than a schoolboy in comparison with the worldly wooer Petruchio. The myth becomes a trope for residual male insecurities about female infidelity and illegitimacy in *Much Ado*. Claudio teases Benedick that, as a married man, he will have a cuckold's horns but these will be like Jove's 'And all Europa shall rejoice at thee / As once Europa did at lusty Jove'. Claudio's worrying assumption that Europa enjoyed being raped serves as a justification for male violence and for a sexual double standard. Benedick retorts 'some such strange bull leapt your father's cow', begetting Claudio, and so tunes into the fear of illegitimacy that lurks behind female **adultery** (*MAdo* 5.4.43–52).

(c) The account of Europa's rape is in Golding's 1567 translation of *Ovid's Metamorphoses*, Book II, lines 1058–96 and Book III, lines 1–3 (Ovidius 2000: 59–61).

Eve, (a) mother of humankind in Jewish and Christian religion, who, according to the Bible, was tempted by the serpent to take an apple from the Tree of Knowledge in the Garden of Eden. Having eaten the fruit forbidden by God in order to gain knowledge, Eve gave it to Adam (Gen 3.1–6). As a result of their actions, humankind lost innocence and, as a consequence of the Fall, became subject to the knowledge of good and evil, to desire, sin, mortality and labour. Eve was punished with the pains of **bear**ing children, desire for and subjection to her husband. Adam was punished with having to farm the earth and humans were sent out of the Garden of Eden.

(b) Early modern writing, that of Shakespeare included, engaged in different ways with the common assumption that Eve was responsible for the Fall. John Calvin preached 'women must needs stoop and understand that the ruin and confusion of mankind came in on their side, and that through them we be all forlorn and banished the kingdom of heaven' as an argument to justify 'the subjection that God hath laid upon them' (Aughterson 1995: 17). Eve's pride for wanting to have wisdom and to become like gods (Gen. 3: 5–6) is something that is, jokingly, supposed to be characteristic of woman. Launce points out that for a woman to be proud 'was Eve's legacy, and cannot be ta'en from her' (*TGV* 3.1.349). Shakespeare's texts refer to Eve as a shorthand for temptation. Feste's remark that Maria is 'as witty a piece of Eve's flesh as any in Illyria' (*TN* 1.5.28) draws on the name's associations with desire, temptation and the corporeal. The young man of the Sonnets is feminized in the warning 'How like Eve's apple doth thy beauty grow, / If thy sweet virtue answer not thy show' (*Son.* 93.13–14). Even female characters accept the guilt of Eve. Isabel, Richard II's **queen**, angrily asks the gardener, 'What Eve, what serpent, hath suggested thee / To make a second fall of cursed man?' (*RII* 4.1.75).

Alternative interpretations of the Fall and of Eve's responsibility did circulate in early modern England, however. **Aemelia** Lanyer's poem *Salve Deus Rex Judaeorum* argued that 'our Mother *Eve*' sinned out of ignorance and her 'fault was onely too much love' in giving the apple to Adam so that 'his knowledge might become more cleare' like hers (Lanyer 2003: 84–6, ll. 763–6 and 801–4). Rachel Speght mocked the anti-feminist pamphleteer Joseph Swetnam who 'on *Eues* sex he foamed filthie froth, / As if that he had had the falling euill'. Speght claimed that in the post-lapsarian world 'True *Knowledge* is the Window of the soule', the 'mother of faith, hope, and love (Speght 1621: 8). In most cases where Shakespeare's texts mention Eve, generalised prejudices about womankind are brought into question. Master Ford who 'so curses all Eve's daughters, of what complexion soever' (*MWW* 4.2.23–4) is caricatured as ridiculously suspicious. In a parodic version of the Fall, Don Armado reports that **Jaquenetta**, 'a child of our grandmother Eve, a female; or for thy more sweet understanding, a woman', has made Costard disobey the King's 'proclaimed edict and continent canon' or law-enforcing restraint (*LLL* 1.1.258–64). The rest of the play shows that it is men's will just as much as women's nature that causes disobedience against such an unnatural law. Indeed, Berowne radically reverses biblical history by claiming Boyet is so persuasive that 'Had he been Adam, he had tempted Eve' (*LLL* 5.2.322).

(c) Early modern views of Eve include *The Sermons of M John Calvin upon the Epistle of S. Paul to the Ephesians*, translated by Arthur Golding (1577), extracts reprinted in Kate Aughterson (1995), and in Aemelia Lanyer, *Salve Deus Rex Judaeorum* [1611] (1993). An extract from Rachel Speght's *Mortalities Memorandum with a Dreame Prefixed* (London, 1621) is in Greer et al. (eds), *Kissing the Rod* (1988: 68–78). On the nature of Eve's legacy and women's defences see Elaine V. Beilin, *Redeeming Eve* (1987: xiv–xv and 247–66). For its effect in drama see Findlay (1998: 11–48).

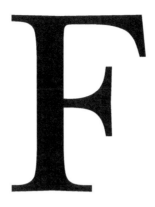

fame, (a) public reputation and esteem, frequently personified as female in early modern England. The goddess Fame often carried a trumpet, which she blew from her position on the top of a hill.

(b) Early modern English personifications of Lady Fame derived from Virgil's *Aeneid* (Book IV, ll. 173–4), from Chaucer's *The House of Fame* in which she is a malign **gossip**, magnifying details to monstrous proportions with her many mouths. She is an outright contradiction to the traditional feminine virtues of silence and modesty. Thomas Scot's 1616 description of 'The House of Fame' summarized this negative image, commenting that although previously Fame was 'a vagrant' without 'house and home', thanks to succceeding generations of poets she now had courts all over the world (Scot 1616: B2v). Her House of Fame is 'glazde al with eies' its doors are open ears and it is hung 'with nimble tongues, and couerd so without'. Thus 'All things are seene and heard the wide world ore / Which touch that place, and farthest off the more' (Scot 1616: sig. B3). Aaron's warning that 'The emperor's court is like the house of Fame, / The palace full of tongues, of eyes, and ears' (*Tit.* 2.1.126–7) follows this model of the court as Fame's natural home. Ben Jonson's *Masque of Queens* realized a reformed version of the model by staging **Anna of Denmark** and her ladies in the house of 'Good Fame', designed by Inigo Jones (Jonson 1995: ll. 413–40 and 621–44). Shakespeare's texts cite the traditional more ambiguous presentation of Fame as a gossip, a female equivalent of Rumour. Benedick says 'I have play'd the part of Lady Fame' in telling Claudio the rumour that his proposal to Hero has been successful (*MAdo* 2.1.213–4). Ulysses imagines that 'When Fame shall in our islands sound her trump', her mockery of Achilles' cowardice will be magnified by the songs of 'all the Greekish **girls**' (*T&C* 3.3.210–11). Fame's tendency to exaggerate informs Cassio's praise of Desdemona as 'a **maid** / That paragons description and wild fame' (2.1.61–2).

Even the Fame who praises and 'with her loud'st Oyes / Cries "This is he,"'

(*T&C* 4.5.143–4) is an unnerving figure because her speech is so unlike the soft, gentle and low voice that Lear thinks 'an excellent thing in woman' (*KL* 5.3.273–4). Fame can, however, distinguish between self-promotion and the praise of enemies, making sure it is the latter 'breath fame blows, that praise, sole pure, transcends' (*T&C* 1.3.243–4). Her voice is thus granted a measure of authority here and in *Love's Labour's Lost* where the Princess of France sharply observes that 'all-telling Fame / Doth noise abroad' the King of Navarre's vow to bar women from his 'silent court' (*LLL* 2.1.21–4).

When not personified, fame as public reputation carries a specific sexual resonance when applied to women. *The Rape of Lucrece*, for example, explicitly juxtaposes masculine military prowess and with women's beauty and chastity as gendered forms of fame. Collatine's bold advertisement of his **wife**'s fame incites Tarquin's desire. After being raped, **Lucrece** vows suicide as a means to restore her fame and displace shame onto her rapist. 'So of shame's ashes shall my fame be bred' (*Luc.* 1189), she vows, determining 'My shame be his that did my fame confound; / And all my fame that lives disbursed be / To those that live, and think no shame of me' (*Luc.* 1202–4). As Lucrece realizes, Fame is ultimately not under the command of the subject; it is multi-vocal, public and unpredictable.

(c) Chaucer's *House of Fame* c. 1374–85, is in *Works* (1968: 280–302). The reference to fame in the translation of Virgil available to Shakespeare, *The. xiii. bookes of AEneidos*, translated by Thomas Phaer and Thomas Twyne (1584), is in Book IV, sig. 4v. Ben Jonson 'The Masque of Queens' (1609), is in *Court Masques*, edited by David Lindley (1995: 35–53). Thomas Scot's 'The House of Fame' is in *The second part of Philomythie, or Philomythologie* (1616: sigs. B2–B6). Jonson and Jones's interpretation is discussed in Clare McManus (2002: 112–22). Fame's relationship with Rumour is considered by Warner (1987: 139–40, 234–5).

fan, (a) a fashion accessory used by women to cool or shield the face from the sun or from the gaze of others. Fixed fans, made out of feathers, and folding fans could be richly ornamented and valuable in material terms as well as being signifiers of gentle status. Royal or noblewomen such as Queen **Elizabeth**, Lady Chandos, the Countess of Nottingham and Lady Elizabeth Southwell were painted holding folding fans and fans made of feathers.

(b) Fans signified wealth and exoticism. Fixed feather fans may have developed from those brought from South America (Alexander 1984: 8) while folding fans, inspired by Chinese designs, became more popular at court following the foundation of the East India Company in 1600 which increased English trade with China (ibid.: 15–17). In Shakespeare, the fan is mentioned as a signifier of status or fashion-consciousness. Petruchio promises Katherina 'scarfs and fans' as part of her finery for the visit to Padua (*Shrew* 4.3.57). The cupids on Cleopatra's barge are equipped with 'divers colored fans' (*A&C* 2.2.208) which, like masks, increase desire rather than cooling (*see also V&A* 52).

The material value of fans is hinted at in *Merry Wives of Windsor*, where Pistol was apparently tempted to steal the handle of a fan belonging to one Mistress Bridget, sell it, and share out the profits (*MWW* 2.2.16). Othello imagines a fan as one of the adulterous **Desdemona**'s essential accessories (*Oth.* 4.2.8). Even Lady **Fortune** is imagined with a fan (*T&C* 1.3.26), while the Roman general and triumvir Antony is derided for having transformed his solider's heart into 'the bellows and the fan / To cool a gipsy's lust' in his relationship with **Cleopatra** (*A&C* 1.1.9). A lady's fan is carried by her follower as mark of deference and respect. Don Armado is mocked by Costard for walking before a lady to 'bear her fan' (*LLL* 4.1.168). In *Romeo and Juliet*, this status game is played out to comic effect when the servant Peter and Juliet's **Nurse** meet Romeo and Mercutio:

> Nurse: Peter!
> Peter: Anon!
> Nurse: My fan, Peter.
> Mercutio: Good Peter, to hide her face, for her fan's the fairer face.
> Nurse: God ye good morrow, gentlemen.
>
> (*R&J* 2.4.104–9)

The Nurse attempts to assert her high status and proper modesty in the public arena, in front of the young Montagues, by calling on a junior servant who carries her fan. Her endeavour is undermined by Mercutio's deliberate misreading of the need for a fan: not to protect her face from the sun, or from their immodest gazes, but to protect them from the sight of her. The fan is a vital stage prop with which to configure a status battle between women in *Henry VI Part II* where Queen **Margaret** deliberately drops her fan as a means to check **Eleanor, Duchess** of Gloucester's ambitious rivalry to her premier position in Court:

> [*The Queen lets fall her fan*]
> Queen: Give me my fan! What, minion, can ye not?
>   *She gives the Duchess a box on the ear.*
>   I cry your mercy, madam, was it you?
> Duchess: Was't I? yea, I it was, proud Frenchwoman.
>   Could I come near your beauty with my nails,
>   I could set my ten commandments in your face.
> King Henry: Sweet **aunt**, be quiet, 'twas against her will.
>
> (*2HVI* 1.1.138–43)

The **Queen**'s expectation that Eleanor will stoop like a 'minion' or servant to pick up her fan is thinly disguised by her pretence that she doesn't recognize the Duchess's nobility (itself insulting). There is no stage direction to indicate who picks up the fan. If Eleanor does so, it is quite possible that it could be returned aggressively on 'proud Frenchwoman!' and then used by Margaret as a shield against Eleanor ('could I come near your beauty with my nails'). The fan is cited as a weapon in *Henry IV Part I* where Hotspur's indignation at the letter warning him against rebellion makes him want to 'brain' the writer 'with his lady's fan' (*1HIV* 2.3.21–2). In the incident in *Henry VI Part II*, Eleanor may well be tempted to 'brain' or beat Margaret over the head with the fan. Alternatively, if King Henry picks it up and intervenes in a stand-off between the two women, this clearly telegraphs the inversion of conventional gender order and social order under his rule, a feature which runs strongly through this play.

(c) Alexander (1984) describes the two types of fan used in the late sixteenth and early seventeenth century. For examples of fans of both kinds in pictures of noble or royal women see Ashelford (1983: 102–3, 107, 11, 119–20, 136, 138) and Arnold (1988: 43, 45, 83, 114, 122–3, 136–7, 198–9).

Farthingale, (a) a hooped petticoat of various designs used to hold out the material of the skirt from the legs, originally a Spanish fashion. The English name 'verdingale' or 'farthingale', derives from the Spanish 'verdugado' and, in turn, from 'verdugos', the small, pliant twigs used for stiffening the hoops. In England, ropes were used instead, and, from 1580, whalebones, making the garment much lighter to wear.

(b) In *Two Gentleman of Verona*, Julia cites the farthingale as a definitive piece of female costume, in opposition to the male **breeches** (*TGV* 2.7.49–51), while Launce reports how he was shamed by his dog, who cocked his leg against Silvia's farthingale to make water (*TGV* 4.4.37–9). Petruchio defines the sartorial 'treasure' he orders for the feast at Baptista's as female fashions by including reference to a farthingale, a fan and a bracelet in his list of 'knav'ry' to be displayed:

> With silken coats and caps and golden rings,
> With ruffs and cuffs, and fardingales and things,
> With scarfs and fans, and double change of brav'ry,
> With amber bracelets, beads and all this knav'ry.
>
> (*Shrew* 4.3.55–8)

The half-farthingale, giving great width at the sides and the back and a flat front to the skirt, also became fashionable in England around 1580. Falstaff advertises it as an essential part of courtly fashion, telling Mrs **Ford** that her excellent posture would allow her to use a 'semi-circled farthingale' (*MWW* 3.3.63–4) to stylish effect as she walked. The so-called French farthingale, a wheel or drum-shaped frame to hold out the skirts in a hard-edged line, became more popular in the 1590s.

(c) Arnold (1988: 194–200) details the types of farthingale popular at the Elizabethan court.

Fates, (a) the Fates, also known as the **Destinies**, are classical goddesses, the daughters of Zeus and Nyx (Night) who, it was believed, governed life and death. Clotho, the youngest spun the thread of life; Lachesis, the second sister, measured the thread with a rod, while Atropos, the eldest, known as 'the inevitable', decided when to cut the thread of life with her shears. The sisters were also known as the Moriae and are sometimes confused with another female trio, the **Furies**.

(b) The Fates are never named individually in Shakespeare's texts but are pictured as a group. The comedies poke fun at these all-powerful goddesses by making heavy-handed references in inappropriate circumstances. Lancelot Gobbo, for example, teases his blind father that the 'Fates and Destinies, and such odd sayings, the Sisters Three' have decreed Lancelot's death and he is deceased (*Mer.* 2.2.62–4). Similarly, Bottom's rehearsal of lines from a Senecan-style tragedy 'in Ercles' vein' self-consciously advertises its comic effect to 'make and mar / The foolish Fates' (*MND* 1.2.37–8). Peter Quince's 'Pyramus and Thisbe' uses allusions as clumsy as the plodding verse. Thisbe ironically vows to be as loyal as **Helen** 'till the Fates me kill' (*MND* 5.1.197) and goes on to be destroyed by the lion. Pyramus's response to finding her blood-stained mantle is an appeal to the Fates for death:

> Approach, ye Furies fell!
> O Fates, come, come,
> Cut thread and thrum;
> Quail, crush, conclude, and quell!
>
> (*MND* 5.1.284–7)

Although comic in performance, these lines also draw attention to Bottom the weaver's role in twisting the strands of the three plots together, like the Fates. The death of Pyramus is effectively the end of Bottom's dreams and of a particular style of tragedy, so the Fates here tinge the lines with associations of loss.

References to the Fates in other texts are also ambiguous. 'Hapless Egeon' appears to be one whom 'the fates have mark'd / To bear the extremity of dire mishap' (*Err.* 1.1.140–1), although the death threat is lifted at the end of the comedy. Ariel announces himself and the spirits of 'Destiny' as 'ministers of Fate' but Prospero is able to grant forgiveness and release his enemies (*Temp.* 3.3.53 and 61). Leonato ominously asks Fate to lay the 'heavy hand' of death on the slandered Hero, but she is restored from a mock death (*MAdo* 4.1.115). Malvolio is ill advised by Maria's letter which proclaims 'Thy Fates open their hands, let thy blood and spirit embrace them' (*TN* 2.5.144–5).

The Fates are presented with more integrity in the histories, the Roman tragedies and to some extent the Romances. When Edward, Duke of York, is imprisoned by the Lancastrians he intones, 'What fates impose, that men must needs abide; / It boots not to resist both wind and tide' (*3HVI* 4.3.58–9). In *Richard II* the cutting of the sacred branches of Edward III's family tree is deemed to be work of 'the Destinies' (although the audience knows that Richard is indirectly responsible) (*RII* 1.2.15). The Fates appear to have even more control in *Julius Caesar.* Artemidorus suspects 'the Fates with traitors do contrive' (*JC* 2.3.16). Unlike the self-determined Cassius, who believes 'men are sometimes masters of their fates' (*JC* 1.2.139), Brutus resigns himself to their control: 'Fates, we will know your pleasures: / That we shall die, we know; 'tis but the time / And drawing days out, that men stand upon' (*JC* 3.1.98–100). In *The Winter's Tale* and *Pericles*, the Fates or Destinies do seem to control the plot. **Perdita** dreads the operation of 'the Fates' in bringing Polixenes to discover Florizel in shepherd's costume (*WT* 4.4.19–22), yet this disruption ultimately allows the oracle to be fulfilled. In

Pericles, Helicanus advises the hero to avoid Antiochus 'till the Destinies do cut his thread of life' (*Per.* 1.2.108) and shortly afterwards it is reported that he and his **daughter** are shrivelled up in their chariot by a fire from heaven (*Per.* 2.4.1–12).
(c) Bernard J. Paris, *Bargains with Fate* (1991) offers a psychoanalytic reading of Shakespeare's characters, who act as though they should be able to determine their own destiny as long as they live up to their own inner dictates. *See also* **Destinies** and **Furies** and the triad of mysterious **weird sisters**.

Faulconbridge, Lady (a) a character in *King John,* mother to an illegitimate son of Richard Coeur de Lion.
(b) Lady Faulconbridge does not appear in Shakespeare's historical sources but does feature in *The Troublesome Reign of King John* (1591), now attributed to George Peele, and Shakespeare's principle source. Her chief dramatic function is to confirm the paternity of the Bastard by admitting her **adultery** with Richard Coeur de Lion. In Peele's play, Lady Faulconbridge is present when her sons publicly declare the illegitimacy of the younger brother, Philip, since King John refuses her request to retire from the proceedings. In Shakespeare's text, Lady Faulconbridge enters with her servant James Gurney after the hearing, angry that her elder son 'holds in chase mine honor up and down' (1.1.223). The Bastard tactfully dismisses Gurney before insisting in private 'I was not Sir Robert's son' and asking his mother who his biological father is. She points out that, for his own good, he ought to defend her **honour** rather than undermine it but finally admits King Richard was his father: explaining that 'By long and vehement suit I was seduc'd' and that his love 'was so strongly urg'd past my defence' (1.1.254–8). The King's *droit de seigneur* excuses her adultery and ensures that her honour is not compromised, the Bastard explains:

> . . . your fault was not your folly;
> Needs must you lay your heart down at his dispose,
> Subjected tribute to commanding love. . .
>
> (1.1.262–4)

Lady Faulconbridge's situation is shared by the **Countess** of Salisbury, although in *Edward III,* the woman successfully resists the King's adulterous advances.
(c) For the treatment of the role in *The Troublesome Reign of King John* (I.1.65–118) see Peele ed. Forker (forthcoming 2010). For other examples of adultery validated by powerful paternity see Findlay (1994), pp. 173–84.

Fidele, (a) the name taken by the character **Imogen** in *Cymbeline* when she cross-dresses. It is derived directly from the Latin word for faith.
(b) Fidele is a perfect alternative identity for the character to inhabit in order to reassert her sexual fidelity after her identity as **Imogen** has been destroyed by Iachimo's slander and Posthumus's wish to murder her. Her adopted name 'well fits thy faith; thy faith thy name' as Lucius recognizes: 'Thou dost approve thyself the very same' (4.2.380–1). Her cross-dressed role resembles that of the

courageous maiden of folk tales who follows her lover into battle. More generally, her name signifies an escape from despair in the face of death or loss. When she consumes a sleep-inducing drug and even when she joins the Roman army, she functions as an agent for reuniting the British royal family.

(c) Margaret Jones Davies, '*Cymbeline* and the Sleep of Faith' (2003) reads the choice of name as an allegorical marker of the play's wider concerns with religious politics and the mysteries of faith.

Field, Jacqueline, (a) wife of a French Huguenot printer, Thomas Vautrollier, who had a shop in the Blackfriars and another printing business in Edinburgh. He died in 1587, leaving the business to her. The following year she married their apprentice, Richard Field, born in Stratford-on-Avon in 1561, who had recently been made a freeman of the Stationers' Company. Richard Field published editions Shakespeare's *Venus and Adonis* (1593) and *The Rape of Lucrece* (1594). An acquaintance with Jaqueline Field may have provided Shakespeare with the French that he used in the conversations between Princess Katherine, Alice and later Henry V (*HV* 3.4 and 5.1). Her name may also have been the starting point for the character of **Jaquenetta**. Jacqueline Field attended the same church as Madame Marie Mountjoy who became Shakespeare's landlady in 1604. Jacqueline and Richard Field moved to Wood Street, close to the Mountjoys' house in Silver Street in 1600 (Schoenbaum 260–1).

(c) Schoenbaum (1987: 262–3). C. C. Stopes (1918: 155) proposed Jacqueline Field as a character for the **Dark Lady** of the Sonnets and titled her 'Jaquenetta'.

fish, (a) a slang word for a **whore** or woman as sexual **commodity**.

(b) **Anne** Bullen is referred to as 'A very fresh fish here' for accepting the King's favour (*HVIII* 2.3.86) and of course Hamlet calls Polonius a 'fishmonger' with the suggestion that he is prostituting his **daughter**. **Ursula** and **Hero** refer to **Beatrice** as a 'fish' when they are trying to trick her into believing that Benedick loves her (*MAdo* 3.1.26). The proverbial phrase 'neither fish nor flesh' informs Falstaff's definition of Mistress **Quickly** as an otter because 'she's neither fish nor flesh, a man knows not where to have her' and her comic retort that 'thou or any man knows where to have me' (*1HIV* 3.3.125–30). Innuendo informs the word in *Merry Wives of Windsor* when Shallow remarks that 'the luce [pike] is the fresh fish' (*MWW* 1.1.22) and in Act 3 Scene 1 of *Comedy of Errors*, after Dromio of Syracuse accuses his twin of conjuring for **wench**es at the door of the house (*Err.* 3.1.34), the oddly-named maid **Luce** calls from within, and the men seek to force entry to the house using a crow (bar) to seek 'a fish without a fin' all seem to play on the bawdy sense of fish as whore (*Err.* 3.1.79–84).

Flavina, (a) childhood playfellow, remembered by **Emilia** in Fletcher and Shakespeare's *The Two Noble Kinsmen*.

(b) Flavina's name may derive from 'Flavia', the name of a character mentioned in Spenser's *Colin Clouts Come Home Againe* (1595) and a waiting-gentlewoman in Marston's *History of Antonio and Mellida* (1602). The 1634 Quarto text of *Two*

Noble Kinsmen has both 'Flavia' and 'Flavina'. The diminutive form 'Flavina' would appropriately reflect the character's youth. Flavina died aged 11 and so does not appear on stage. However, when her name is mentioned Emilia gives voice to a flood of memories about their loving relationship. Flavina's soul interacted with Emilia's in a process whereby their tastes and desires became one. At a superficial level, Flavina's casually chosen dress was assiduously copied by Emilia while Flavina copied Emilia's hairstyle and adored the same music (1.3.71–8). An erotic, corporeal attraction between the two is suggested by the identical **flowers** they plucked and held between their tumescent breasts to 'die in perfume' (1.3.66–71). The relationship convinces Emilia that 'true love 'tween maid and maid' can exceed heterosexual love (1.3.81–2). Memories of Flavina make Emilia 'out of breath' so **Hippolyta** concludes that she 'shall never (like the maid Flavina) / Love any that's called man' (1.3.82–85). Flavina may be absent but her name acts as a trigger for what is a more explicit cameo of adolescent female same-sex love than anywhere in Shakespeare's work, a return of what has been repressed in Athens under the rule of Theseus.

(c) The reference to Flavia, esteemed for chaste life and virtue in Spenser's *Colin Clouts Come Home Againe*, is in Spenser's *Poetical Works* (1970), pp. 535–45 (p. 542, ll. 572–3). Valerie Traub (2002: 330) explores what Emilia's emotional and possibly sexual bond to Flavina represents. Laurie J. Shannon (2002: 90–123) reads the homoerotics of Emilia's relationship with Flavina in political terms as an assertion of female autonomy.

flower(s), (a) In addition to the botanic meaning of the seed-bearing part of a plant, anatomically, the word 'flowers' was used for women's menses in early modern England. From this, 'flower' was used metaphorically to refer to a woman's virginity and, more widely, her sexuality. Shakespeare has no female characters named after flowers except **Viola** but flowers are used as props by Ophelia, Gertrude, Perdita, Marina, Emilia and Juliet. Metaphorically, a flower also signified a precious possession or ornament, or the choicest among a number of persons or things; the pick of the bunch.

(b) 'Fairies use flowers for their charactery [writing]' (*MWW* 5.5.73), Mrs **Quickly** observes and the symbolism of flowers, especially in relation to female sexuality, makes them complex signifiers in Shakespeare's texts. Occasionally flowers are associated with male characters. Lear enters crowned with flowers on the heath (*KL* 4.6.80), and Paris, for instance, is referred to as 'a flower; in faith, a very flower' amongst Verona's youth (*R&J* 1.3.77–8). After Adonis's death and metamorphosis into a flower, **Venus** inverts the seduction trope of deflowering a maiden as 'she crops the stalk, and in the breach appears / Green-dropping sap, which she compares to tears'. She promises not a minute will go by 'Wherein I will not kiss my sweet love's flow'r' (*V&A* 1175–6 and 1188).

More often flowers stand for women, especially **maids**, and the supposed fragility of their sexuality. Medical books such as *The Problemes of Aristotle* (1595) explained that 'the flowers of the woman are the materiall cause of the young one' (sig. E3), and although this term is probably a corruption of the French '*fleuve*' or 'flow', the connection between botanic flowers and female fertility seems to have been understood. Culpeper's *Dictionary of Midwives* (1662) explained that women's menses 'are called by some *flowers* because they do before conception as flowers do before fruit' (Keeble 1994: 29). Like Venus, **Emilia** and **Flavina** in *The Two Noble Kinsmen* cradle flowers as tropes of nascent adolescent desire, this time for each other, in their breasts (*TNK* 1.3.66–71). Emilia goes on to say that a rose is 'the very emblem of a **maid**' because when courted gently by the west wind it will open but if a rude and impatient north wind blows, she 'locks her beauties in her bud again' to retain her **chastity** (*TNK* 2.2.137–43). Orsino observes 'women are as roses, whose fair flow'r / Being once display'd, doth fall that very hour' (*TN* 2.4.38–9), implying that once women's sexuality has fully blossomed it has a very short life. Violets stand for sexual innocence in Angelo's confession of his lust (*MM* 2.2.165–7) and Laertes vows that violets will spring from Ophelia's unpolluted flesh (*Ham.* 5.1.239–40), while **Viola**'s is suggested by her name. The flower is, more specifically, a figure for **Diana**'s virginity after the bed-trick when the King tells her:

> If thou be'st yet a fresh uncropped flower,
> Choose thou thy husband, and I'll pay thy **dower**,
> For I can guess that by thy honest aid
> Thou kept'st a wife herself, thyself a maid.
>
> (*AWW* 5.3.327–30)

In contrast, the girl in *A Lover's Complaint* laments 'I might as yet have been a spreading flower, / Fresh to myself, if I had self-applied / Love to myself and to no love beside' (*LC* 75–7). Her beloved was so alluring that, as she now regrets, she 'Threw my affections in his charmed power, / Reserv'd the stalk and gave him all my flower' (*LC* 146–7).

Spring and summer scenes create a metaphoric landscape for the blossoming of female fertility in the comedies and romances. **Titania**'s open sexuality is evoked in the bower filled with thyme, cowslips, violets, honeysuckle and roses where she sleeps 'lull'd in these flowers with dances and delight' (*MND* 2.1.248–54). **Ophelia**'s anxiety about losing her **virgin**ity vocalized in her St Valentine song (*Ham.* 4.5.48–66) is dramatized kinetically as she distributes her flowers (*Ham.* 4.7.155–86) and then drowns herself with her 'fantastic garlands' (*Ham.* 4.7.168–83). Extending the idea of menses, flowers are also the fruit of the **womb** in Sonnet 16 where the young man is assured that 'many maiden gardens, yet unset, / With virtuous wish would bear your living flowers' (*Son.* 16.6–7). In *A Midsummer Night's Dream*, menstruation is metaphorically advertised in the detail of 'every little flower', that weeps as though 'Lamenting some enforced chastity' (*MND* 3.1.198–200) in the forest, where **Helena** and **Hermia** must remain chaste. Love-in-idleness, the flower dyed purple by the penetration of Cupid's arrow, eroticizes Helena as the new object of Demetrius's passion (*MND* 3.2.102–3). The tragedy of **Thisbe**, whose bloody mantle proves she has been 'deflow'r'd' by the lion (*MND* 5.1.292), plays out a violent alternative to the young women's imminent sexual initiation on the **wedding** night. *The Rape of Lucrece* argues that the 'wither'd flower', **Lucrece**, is not to blame for its devastation; instead, the aggressive male or rough winter 'that the flower hath killed' is at fault (*Luc.* 1254–5).

Because the chaste female fertility of an uncropped flower is so transitory, references to flowers and female graves occur in combination as if to capture the moment of perfection. It is this ideal that **Katherine** of Aragon seeks to recover in asking to be strewn 'with maiden flowers, that all the world may know / I was a chaste **wife** to my grave' (*HVIII* 4.2.168–70). Capulet romanticizes **Juliet**'s seduction by death that has left her apparently virginal: 'Flower as she was, deflowered by him' (*R&J* 4.5.37). Making the 'bridal flowers serve for a buried corse' (*R&J* 4.5.89) eroticizes Juliet's still perfect body; Paris tells her 'Sweet flower, with flowers thy bridal bed I strew' (*R&J* 5.3.12). Ophelia's corpse is likewise eroticized when Gertrude throws in the flowers she hoped to have used for the wedding bed, and both Hamlet and Laertes leap into the grave (*Ham.* 5.1.244–60).

The Romances move closer to the fantasy of sustaining the perfect flowers of female fertility. In *Cymbeline* **Imogen**'s sexuality is preserved beneath a disguise and a sleep that only mimics death. Guiderius laments

> O sweetest, fairest lily!
> My brother wears thee not the one half so well
> As when thou grew'st thyself.
>
> (*Cym.* 4.2.201–3)

The lily re-invokes **Imogen**'s female body, an effect heightened in the subsequent promises of flowers for her grave and the close-up focus on her face and eyelids which may even recall the desiring gaze of Iachimo (*Cym.* 4.2.218–24). **Marina** and **Perdita**'s fertility is staged in carrying of flowers. Marina's growth to sexual maturity as part of a maternal history is established in a short scene where she brings a basket of yellow summer marigolds and blue violets to strew on her **nurse**'s grave and remembers her mother and her own birth (*Per.* 4.1.12–20). **Thaisa**'s revival is deliberately feminized: 'see how she gins to blow / Into life's flower again!' (*Per.* 3.2.94–5). Early modern housewives were frequently responsible for preparing flowers for household use, including restorative medicines. Staging daughters carrying flowers in the romance plots advertises their regenerative qualities.

In *The Winter's Tale* **Perdita** is referred to as the goddess of flowers, 'Flora / Peering in April's front' (*WT* 4.4.2–3). Her distribution of flowers is juxtaposed with her thoughts of bearing Florizel's children. In spite of her dislike of grafted plants, she muses on his 'Desire to breed by me' and quickly tells her visitors 'Here's flowers for you; / Hot lavender, mints, savoury, marjoram / The marigold, that goes to bed wi' the sun / And with him rises weeping.' Since Prince Florizel is the royal sun, this list follows the train of Perdita's own desires and fears rather than addressing 'men of middle age' (*WT* 4.4.102–8). As with all other references to flowers in Shakespeare, even Perdita's are tinged with an awareness of loss. **Proserpina** dropped her daffodils when 'frighted' by the predatory Dis (*WT* 4.4.116–18), and Perdita cannot bring back the flowers of spring to give to those whose 'maidenheads' are still growing like blossom on their 'virgin branches' (*WT* 4.4.114–16). Nor can she give 'pale primroses / That die unmarried' before they feel the full heat of the sun '– a malady / Most incident to **maids**', she observes (*WT* 4.4.122–5). The fragility of virginal flowering is balanced against a larger seasonal cycle of sowing, maturing, reaping, death and rebirth, which is appropriate to the play's concerns with regeneration. The same seasonal pattern informs **Miranda** and Ferdinand's betrothal masque in *The Tempest* where the spring and summer flowers of **Ceres** (and implicitly Miranda) will be succeeded by a rich harvest (*Temp.* 4.1.65–7 and 78 and 106–17) followed by another spring. Female flowers are, Shakespeare's texts recognize, a powerful force of renewal, however fragile they may seem.

(c) *The Problemes of Aristotle* (1595: sigs E2v–E5v) discusses explanations for the function of female flowers or menses. Extracts from Culpeper's 1662 *Dictionary for Midwives* and from other early modern writings about the female reproductive body are found in Keeble (1994: 17–32 (esp.) 28–30). Ferber (1999) examines flower as a literary symbol of maidens and their sexuality from the earliest writings. Marjorie Garber (1981: 155–9) traces Shakespeare's uses of the term.

Ford, Mistress, (a) One of the two eponymous *Merry Wives of Windsor* who are wooed by Falstaff under the jealous eyes of Mistress Ford's husband.
(b) Mistress Ford's sense of fun as a merry **wife** is what raises Ford's suspicions about her reputation: that 'though she appear **honest** to me, yet in other places she enlargeth her mirth so far that there is shrewd construction made of her' (2.2.221–4). Ford acknowledges that she needs the pleasure of friendship and fun with Mistress **Page** who is going to visit her:

> Mrs Page: Is she at home?
> Ford: Ay, and as idle as she may hang together, for want of company. I
>   think if your husbands were dead, you two would marry.
> Mrs Page: Be sure of that – two other husbands.
>
> (3.2.13–15)

In the plots to take revenge on Falstaff and cure Ford of his jealousy, Mistress Ford plays the role of the potential **adulteress**, whose honesty might be forded or breached (in contrast to Mistress Page, the conduct-book model of wifely honesty). After his first attempt, Falstaff complains grievously 'Mistress Ford? I have had ford enough. I was thrown into the ford; I have my belly full of ford' (3.5.35–7). Mistress **Quickly** tells Falstaff that Mistress Ford has been the object of many courtiers' attentions but even earls and gentlemen of the royal bodyguard 'could never get an eye-wink of her', since she would not condescend to 'so much as sip on a cup with the proudest of them all' (2.2.71–6). Mr Ford's pseudonym, Mr Brook, conveys his own perverse behaviour: apparently plotting to drive her to adultery but then preventing it. At the end of the play, he tells Falstaff 'To Master Brook you yet shall hold your word / For he tonight shall lie with Mistress Ford' (5.5.244).

(c) Philip D. Collington (2000) argues that the play engages with anxieties about women's potential to commit domestic violence. Sandra Clark (1987) analyses the plotting of Mistress Page and Mistress Ford as wit in action rather than words and thus recuperative. Helgerson (2000: 57–75) argues that the wives combine domestic props and the beneficent witchcraft of wise women to reform Ford and Falstaff. Korda (2002: 76–110) reads Mistresses Page and Ford as part of the protective family economy. Wall (2003) shows how the wives stretch the protocols of domestic management to suit their own purposes.

Fortune, (a) a pagan **goddess** who appeared as an emblem of unpredictability in written and pictorial forms in early modern England. She was depicted as indifferent, blind or blindfolded, bringing both good and bad fortune, and held a wheel to symbolize the turns or revolutions and change she brought about. Fortune often stands on a sphere to represent her inconstancy. She is also associated with the sea, another unpredictable force, and with the inconstant **moon**.
(b) Fluellen summarizes the traditional attributes of Fortune as indifferent, inconstant and unstable:

> **Fortune** is painted blind, with a muffler afore his eyes, to signify to you that Fortune is blind; and she is painted also with a wheel, to signify to you, which is the moral of it, that she is turning, and inconstant, and mutability, and variation; and her foot, look you, is fixed upon a spherical stone, which rolls, and rolls, and rolls. In good truth, the poet makes a most excellent description of it. Fortune is an excellent moral.
>
> (*HV* 3.6.30–8)

The personification of Fortune from Roman philosopher Boethius's *Consolation of Philosophy* formed the bases of early modern representations such as emblem books, paintings and engravings. For example, emblem XX in Thomas Combe's *Theater of Fine Devices* (1614) remarked '*They that follow fortunes guiding / blindly fall with often sliding.*' The large painting of Fortune at one end of the Long Gallery at Little Moreton Hall, opposite the figure of Destiny, is copied from Robert Record's *The Castle of Knowledge* (London, 1556) and shows her blind and holding a wheel with the motto 'The wheele of Fortune, / Whose rule is ignorance' (National Trust 1998: 20–1). The conversation between a poet and painter in *Timon of Athens* advertises Shakespeare's awareness of the artistically fashioned image. The poet explains how he has 'upon a high and pleasant hill / Feign'd Fortune to be thron'd' and, amongst those trying to climb up the sphere, has depicted Timon: 'Whom Fortune with her ivory hand wafts to her' (*Tim.* 1.1.63–70). Fortune is a **queen** or **empress**, the trope suggesting the uncertainty of courtly favour and patronage. Indeed, the painter goes on to observe that '**Fortune**, in her shift and change of mood / Spurns down her late beloved' (*Tim.* 1.1.84–5). **Cleopatra** likewise comments that ''Tis paltry to be Caesar / Not being Fortune, he's but Fortune's knave / And minister of her will' (*A&C* 5.2.2–4).
 This is the 'moral' Fluellen refers to: unlike God, Fortune cannot be trusted. As

Robert Albott (1599: 144) summarized '*Fortune*, is faigned to dispose and change the good and euill haps of men, the daughter of *Oceanus*, or as *Orpheus*, of the blood, as a power not to be resisted; shee is painted blind, and drawne in a Coach with blind Horses, vainly honored for a **Goddesse**'. Mowbray's remark 'However God or fortune cast my lot' (*RII* 1.3.85) sets divine male providence against female, worldly uncertainty. Fortune is often invoked as a sponsor of those who have lost touch with providential destiny. Gower proclaims 'Let Pericles believe his **daughter**'s dead, / And bear his courses to be ordered / By Lady Fortune' (*Per.* 4.4.46–8). When **Perdita** asks 'O Lady Fortune, / Stand you auspicious!' to her unconventional match, the audience knows that something is about to go wrong since the prophecy has not yet been fulfilled (*WT* 4.1.52–3). Fortune is at best amoral; as Autolycus observes: 'If I had a mind to be honest, I see Fortune would not suffer me: she drops booties in my mouth' (*WT* 4.4.831–2). It is not surprising that the crafty and ambitious **Eleanor** of Gloucester determines that 'being a **woman**, I will not be slack / To play my part in Fortune's pageant' meaning that she must use **witch**craft (*2HVI* 1.2.66–7).

Male characters depict Fortune as irrational rather than coldly indifferent to human affairs. In military matters, she is a passionate – if moody – **mistress**, with the power to protect those whom she loves. Coriolanus is told 'Now the fair goddess Fortune / Fall deep in love with thee and her great charms / Misguide thy opposers' swords!' (*Cor.* 1.5.20–2) and Edgar wishes Albany 'Fortune love you!' in the oncoming battle (*KL* 5.1.46). After rousing the crowd in *Julius Caesar*, Antony believes 'Fortune is merry / And in this mood will give us any thing' (*JC* 3.2.266–7). Another amorous relationship, in which Fortune's power is like that of a monarch or **empress**, is imagined in *King John*, where the Bastard predicts

> in a moment, Fortune shall cull forth
> Out of one side her happy minion,
> To whom in favor she shall give the day,
> And kiss him with a glorious victory.
> (*KJ* 2.1.391–4)

In *Macbeth*, favouring Macdonwald made Fortune 'like a rebel's **whore**' (*Mac.* 1.1.14–15) in battle. Fortune is less likely to be a kind mistress in amorous and financial affairs. Launcelot Gobbo fantasizes a successful future of marrying eleven **widows** and nine **maids**, joking that 'if Fortune be a woman, she's a good **wench** for this gear' (*Mer.* 2.2.166–7). Antonio observes that, in sentencing him to death, Fortune perversely 'shows herself more kind / Than is her custom' which is to let 'the wretched man outlive his wealth' into an old age of poverty (*Mer.* 4.1.267–72). The speaker of Sonnet 111 chastises Fortune as 'The guilty goddess of my harmful deeds, / That did not better for my life provide' (*Son.* 111.1–4).

Juliet reiterates the archetypal image of Fortune as fickle, hoping that the faithful Romeo will not be to her taste:

> O Fortune, Fortune, all men call thee fickle;
> If thou art fickle, what dost thou with him
> That is renown'd for faith? Be fickle, Fortune:
> For then I hope thou wilt not keep him long,
> But send him back.
>
> (*R&J* 3.6.60–4)

The idea that the goddess has two faces is captured in Pandulph's view that when 'Fortune means to men most good, / She looks upon them with a threatening eye (*KJ* 3.4.119). Henry IV asks 'Will Fortune never come with both hands full, / But write her fair words still in foulest letters?' She is frustratingly perverse; she either gives an appetite and no food to the poor or banquets and no appetite to the rich – and to him she gives victory but no health to enjoy it (*2HIV* 4.3.103–8). Parolles and the Clown in *All's Well* both describe Fortune in grotesque bodily terms as a humiliating influence (*AWW* 5.2.116–32). Parolles, for example, smells since he has 'fall'n into the unclean fishpond of her displeasure' (*AWW* 5.2.20–21).

The most vehement criticisms of Fortune's inconstancy are expressed as sexual slander. She is called 'O **giglet** Fortune!' (*Cym.* 3.1.31) an 'arrant **whore**' (*KL* 2.4.52) and a '**strumpet**' (*Ham.* 2.2.493). This is partly because of her inscrutability, as Hamlet suggests when he jokes that Rosencrantz and Guildernstern live 'in the secret parts of Fortune? O, most true, she is a strumpet' (*Ham.* 2.2.235–6). **Constance** says that the 'strumpet Fortune' (*KJ* 3.1.61) has proved unfaithful to Arthur, 'adulterates hourly with thine uncle John' and has, moreover, used her 'golden **hand**' to corrupt the French King (*KJ* 3.1.55–9). Fortune's turning wheel conjures up identification with a **housewife** through the idea of spinning. **Cleopatra** wants to 'rail so high, / That the false housewife Fortune break her wheel, / Provoked by my offence' (*A&C* 4.15.43–4). Pistol ponders 'Doth Fortune play the huswife with me now?' (*HV* 5.1.80). **Celia** and **Rosalind** adapt the medieval idea of Fortune to describe her as a 'good housewife' who spins, and to criticize her as 'the bountiful blind woman' who is mistaken in her gifts, giving good looks to those who are unchaste and **chastity** to those who are not fair in looks. She bestows gifts of the world, whereas it is the goddess **Nature** who gives physical gifts. Touchstone, too, castigates 'Lady Fortune' (*AYLI* 2.7.16), implicitly labelling her influence as that of a whore in his account of time passing (*AYLI* 2.2.25–27).

Shakespeare picks up on associations with the sea to express the insecurity of Fortune. She is the presiding deity who divided Egeon's family in the storm and shipwreck typically leaving 'to both of us alike / What to delight in, what to sorrow for' (*Err.* 1.1.105–6). To Pericles too, she brings both good and ill: after his shipwreck, the sea miraculously washes up his father's armour: 'Thanks, Fortune, yet, that, after all my crosses, / Thou givest me somewhat to repair myself' (*Per.* 2.2.121–2). Nestor applies an elaborate nautical conceit to argue that Fortune's storms are a means of distinguishing between true and superficial valour of men (*T&C* 1.3.33–54). The redemptive possibilities of Fortune, as dramatized in *The Comedy of Errors*, *Pericles* and *Cymbeline* are summarized by Pisanio's line, 'Fortune brings in some boats that are not steer'd' (*Cym.* 4.3.46).

(c) Book 2 Part I of Boethius's *Consolation of Philiosophy* (1999) outlines the characteristics of Fortune, which were reproduced in emblem books such as Geffrey Whitney, *A Choice of Emblems* (1586), Thomas Combe's English translation of moral emblems by Guillaume de la Perriere, *Theater of Fine Devices* (1614), and described by Robert Albott, *Wits Theater of the Little World* (1599). Photographs of the picture of Fortune in Little Moreton Hall can be found in the National Trust Guidebook, *Little Moreton Hall, Cheshire* (1998). Frederick Kiefer's *Fortune and Elizabethan Tragedy* (1982) is the fullest study, arguing that Fortune maintained a distinctive place, independent of Protestant ideas of providence in works by Shakespeare, Jonson, Seneca, Plutarch and emblem books. His earlier article on 'Fortune and Providence in the *Mirror for Magistrates*' (1977: 146–65) is a useful introduction to the issues. Albott's *Wits Theater* (1599: 144) maligns Fortune's status as a goddess because she is blind. Peggy Munoz Simonds' illustrated article (1994) reads Cleopatra with reference to the iconographic tradition of the goddess Fortune. Clayton G. MacKenzie (2001) examines Shakespeare's varied uses of the personification. *See also* **spinster**.

France, (a) a feminized personification of the country.
(b) France is personified by Burgundy (*HV* 5.2.38–62) by association with Princess **Katherine**, and in *Love's Labour's Lost* by the French **Princess**. Costard, comically misunderstanding Don Armado's wish to 'enfranchise' him as 'marry me to one Frances' (*LLL* 3.1.120–1) goes on to play the part of Pompey the Great by announcing himself to the French Princess: 'I here am come by chance, / And lay my arms before the legs of this sweet lass of France' (*LLL* 5.2.554–5).

Francisca, (a) the nun who appears briefly as a companion to **Isabella** in *Measure for Measure*.
(b) Act I Scene 4 of *Measure for Measure* is set in a convent of the Sisterhood of St Clare. Francisca is not named in the dialogue; however, her name is an appropriate reminder of the Franciscan order of which the Poor Clares were the Second Order, founded by St Clare of Assisi in 1212. Francisca dutifully explains the Poor Clare rule of extreme austerity and seclusion: no communication with men except in the presence of the prioress and then either showing the face or speaking, but not both (1.4.10–13).
(c) Daryl Gless (1979) discusses the importance of the all-female community represented in the play and its relation to the Poor Clares. Claire Walker (2003) offers a historical analysis of English female religious communities on the Continent after the Reformation. *See* entry on **nun** for further reading.

froward, (a) an adjective applied primarily to women meaning 'perverse', 'difficult to deal with' or 'hard to please'; that is, disposed to go counter to what is demanded or what is reasonable (the opposite of 'toward') and in a wider sense, evilly disposed.
(b) Of the twelve occurrences of the word in Shakespeare, two-thirds are applied to women, the others being the Duke of Clarence (*3HVI* 4.7.84), the trouble-making

Bishop of Winchester (*1HVI* 3.1.18), and Adonis whose froward resistance is perversely opposite to **Venus**'s toward passion in *The Passionate Pilgrim*: 'Then fell she on her back, fair **queen**, and toward: / He rose and ran away; ah, fool too froward!' (*PP* 4.13–14). The word typically appears in a list of female vices or faults. **Julia** is 'peevish, sullen, froward / Proud, disobedient, stubborn' (*TGV* 3.1.68–9). **Katherina** is labelled as 'stark mad or wonderful froward' or 'intolerable curst / And shrewd and froward' (*Shrew* 1.2.90). At the end, she tells the other 'froward and unable' wives that it is not meet for a **wife** to be 'froward, peevish, sullen, sour / And not obedient' (*Shrew* 5.2.157). Hortensio's Freudian slip, when he says that if his **widow** be 'froward' he will be 'untoward' in correcting her, casts doubt on the legitimacy of the dominant / submissive binary (*Shrew* 4.5.78–9). Vincentio and Lucentio's rhyming couplet ''Tis a good hearing when children are toward / But a harsh hearing when women are froward' (*Shrew* 5.2.182–3) likewise seems to provide far too pat an answer to the complex dynamics of power within the family. Shakespeare's use of the word in *Shrew* seems thus to question rather than to reinforce the misogynist assumptions which it expresses.

(c) For further reading, *see* entries on **scold** and **shrew**.

Fulvia, (a) Antony's first wife, whose death is announced in the opening scene of *Antony and Cleopatra*.

(b) Even though Fulvia does not appear on stage her strong presence haunts the play and its protagonists in the opening scene. Details of Fulvia's military aggression, coming 'first into the field' against Antony's brother Lucius and then Octavius Caesar (*A&C* 1.2.88–93) remind readers and spectators of the account in Plutarch's 'Life of Antony' (Bullough V: 277). Shakespeare recasts Plutarch's account of Fulvia 'being of a peevish, crooked and troublesome nature' (Bullough Vol. V: 277) and stirring war in Italy to bring Antony away from Cleopatra, in Antony's guilty retort to the messenger:

> Rail thou in Fulvia's phrase, and taunt my faults
> With such full license as both truth and malice
> Have power to utter.
>
> (A&C 1.2.107–9)

This is followed almost immediately by news of Fulvia's death and Antony's admiration for her: 'There's a great spirit gone!' (*A&C* 1.2.122). As such a commanding, independent and assertive woman Fulvia is in fact a prologue to **Cleopatra**. Plutarch describes her as such, noting that (like Cleopatra) Fulvia is a **widow**:

> Fulvia that was Clodius widowe, a woman not so basely minded to spend her time in spinning and housewivery, and was not contented to master her husband at home, but she would also rule him in his office abroad, and commaund him, that commaunded legions and great armies: so that Cleopatra was to give Fulvia thankes for that she had taught Antonius this obedience to women, that learned so well to be at their commaundment.
>
> (Bullough V: 262)

Enobarbus's consolatory observation that Fulvia is not the only woman and that 'your old smock brings forth a new petticoat' (*A&C* 1.2.168–9) proves true in more than a superficial sense. Cleopatra is cut from the same cloth as Fulvia and Fulvia's commanding treatment of Antony in matters domestic, political and military, foreshadows Cleopatra's own.

(c) Details about Fulvia in Plutarch's 'Life of Antonius' in *Lives of the Noble Grecians and Romans*, translated by Sir Thomas North in 1579 are reprinted in Bullough, Vol V, pp. 262 and 277–8.

Furies, (a) the Furies or Erinyes were creatures of the underworld and goddesses of retribution in Greek mythology, depicted with hair made of snakes.

(b) When Tamora disguises herself as the goddess Revenge, Titus bids her 'Welcome, dread Fury, to my woeful house' (*Tit.* 5.2.82), associating her with retribution. Cleopatra tells the grim-faced messenger that he should 'come like a Fury crown'd with snakes' (*A&C* 2.5.40) since he appears to bring bad news. Visions of the Furies are a sign of mental instability when Parolles claims that Bertram was so madly in love with Diana that he 'talk'd of Sathan and of Limbo and of Furies' (*AWW* 5.3.260–1). Clarence's guilt is revealed when the ghost of Prince Edward, whom he stabbed, appears in a dream shrieking 'Sieze on him, Furies, take him unto torment!' (*RIII* 1.4.57). Bottom as Pyramus identifies the Furies with the Fates (*MND* 5.1.284–7), a term more often used in Shakespeare's work for this female triad also known as the Destinies.

(c) *See* **Fates** for further information about these figures and *see* **Destinies**, **hag**, and **weird sisters** as cognate female figures.

Gertrude, (a) a character in *Hamlet,* **mother** of Hamlet and **widow** of King Hamlet, now married to Claudius. The name is of Germanic derivation from *gar, ger* 'spear' and *þruþ* 'strength', though found in England from the later Middle Ages. In sources for the play, she is Gerutha (Saxo) or Geruth (Belleforest) and in *Amleth,* Amleth's second wife is Hermutrude. In the First Quarto, the character is named Gertred, in the Second Quarto she is Gertrard and in the Folio Gertrude. She is also referred to as 'Queen'.

(b) Gertrude's reputation as a malleable, weak character is promoted by the Ghost and Hamlet who both resent her remarriage as a 'falling-off' (1.5.47), a betrayal of her **widow**'s fidelity to King Hamlet's memory. Hamlet's prejudiced opinion 'Frailty, thy name is **woman**' (1.2.146), is played out in the dumbshow of 'The Mousetrap' where the Player **Queen** '*seems harsh awhile but in the end accepts love*' (3.1.135–6). Unlike the various sources, Shakespeare's texts do not imply Gertrude's culpability in either the murder of her husband or adultery before his death, although the sin of incest for marrying her brother-in-law may be a cause of her feelings of guilt. The issue was probably still topical following Henry VIII's divorce from **Katherine** of Aragon and Hamlet reminds Gertrude, 'You are the Queen, your husband's brother's wife, / And would it were not so, you are my mother' (3.4.15–16). The Ghost, in his nightgown, prompts Hamlet to help Gertrude's 'fighting soul' in her struggle against incest and widow's infidelity, since 'Conceit in weakest bodies, strongest works' (3.4.113–14). This gendered judgement is rendered immediately ironic since it is only Hamlet's conceit, or imagination, rather than Gertrude's that can perceive the ghost.

Descriptions by Hamlet, father and son, characterize Gertrude as lustful and therefore weak. Nothing in the texts indicates that Gertrude behaves with 'compulsive ardure' or ardour (3.4.86), though all three versions are open, providing opportunities for an actor to play Gertrude's love for Claudius as motivated by sensual appetite. This is only weak from a very particular, patriarchal perspective.

Similarly, Gertrude is only weak if we assign negative connotations to her divided loyalties to Claudius and to Hamlet. Claudius acknowledges the triangle, noting she 'lives almost by his [Hamlet's] looks', and claiming that he [Claudius] cannot live without her (4.7.12–16). In practical terms, her 'heart cleft in twain' (3.4.156) leads to inconsistent behaviour in trying to please both. She follows Claudius's directions for interviewing Hamlet in her closet but, at the end of the scene, follows Hamlet's directions in proclaiming he is mad in order to protect him. Even though Gertrude is the object of King Hamlet and Claudius's love and Hamlet's filial love, this does not bring high status. Rather, her impossible task of trying to please both husband and her son through submissive obedience is futile, leaving her 'bewildered and unhappy' (Smith, 1983: 194).

Gertrude is first introduced as 'th' imperial jointress to this warlike state' (1.2.9), an **empress** and a much stronger presence, more akin to the meaning of her name as 'strong spear'. Legally she does not hold part of the kingdom as her widow's jointure but symbolically she oversees the transfer of sovereignty between men (Aguirre 1996). Claudius claims she is 'conjunctive to my life and soul' (4.7.14); he cannot live without her, and when his state is threatened, he invokes her name as a source of strength: 'O Gertrude, Gertrude' (4.5.77) 'O my dear Gertrude' (4.5.94). Her words and actions are submissive but as an object of male sexual desire and an icon of sovereignty, Queen Gertrude's influence is extremely powerful. Her final actions in drinking from the cup enact the mythic pattern of Celtic tradition in which men receive death and renewed sovereignty from the hands of a powerful woman (Aguirre 1996: 168). Clutching the cup of death, Gertrude literally overrules Claudius with uncharacteristic independence:

> King: Gertrude, do not drink.
> Queen: I will, my lord, I pray you pardon me.
> *(Ham.* 5.2.290–1)

Gertrude introduces the imminent deaths of king and heir apparent, and the passing of Denmark's throne to Fortinbras, and of a feminine tradition to masculine modernity. Her sexuality also takes on a frightening symbolic dominance in the play as a reminder of maternal origins and mortality from which masculine identity vainly tries to escape. In both these senses, Gertrude's name stands for the strength of symbolic power which is absent from her own words and actions.

(c) Kehler (1995: 398–413) discusses the sympathetic characterization of Gertred in the First Quarto as a quasi-allegorical object lesson in remarriage. Akiko Kusunoki (1995) develops this. Rebecca Smith (1983) discusses the character's divided loyalties. Maxwell (1964) argues that Gertrude is weak until the end of the play where her one act of independence causes her death. Linda Bamber's *Comic Women, Tragic Men* (1982: 72–83), goes even further, claiming that the misogyny of the play reduces Gertrude to a 'vessel for Hamlet's feelings' with little independence as a character. By contrast, Aguirre (1996) attributes considerable mythic power to Gertrude as an embodiment of a literary ritual derived from Celtic origins, arguing that her death represents the passing of an ancient tradition of female-centred sovereignty to a masculine age of modernity. Adelman (1992: 11–37) reads Gertrude as the first in a series of female characters whose sexuality and reminders of maternal origin threatens masculine identity in the plays. G. B. Shand (1994) offers a performance-based approach, arguing that drinking the cup is an act of suicide to which Gertrude is driven. Greg Bentley (2003) contends that Gertrude's drinking at the end of the play is an assertion of her new, manly subjectivity and a rejection of female roles.

gift, (a) a noun used, among other meanings, to describe women as marriage partners in betrothal and wedding ceremonies. 'Gift' is thus a verbal indicator of the **commodity** status of women.

(b) The forest **wedding** of Audrey and Touchstone sets out the **marriage** ritual of gifting the woman to the husband. Sir Oliver Martext insists that 'she must be given or the marriage is not lawful' in spite of Toushtone's objections 'I will not take her on gift of any man', that imply the process reduces woman to second-hand goods (*AYLI* 3.3.67–70). Proxy wooing and wedding emphasizes that devaluation of the **bride** as gift when Suffolk hands over **Margaret** to Henry VI as 'the happiest gift that ever marquess gave / The fairest **queen** that ever king received' (*2HVI* 1.1.15–16).

Prospero refers to **Miranda** as 'my rich gift' and hands her over to Ferdinand with the words 'as my rich gift and thine own acquisition / Worthily purchas'd take my **daughter**' (*Temp.* 4.1.13–14). Since Miranda gave herself to Ferdinand (*Temp.* 3.2.83), this play manages a remarkable balance between fatherly possession and female autonomy.

When wedding ceremonies are disrupted, male pride as well as women's value is called into question. Claudio, believing that **Hero** is unchaste, mocks the ritual of giving away the bride, 'this rich and precious gift', by refusing to accept her at the altar and telling her father, 'Give not this rotten orange to your friend' (*MAdo* 4.1.27–33). Bertram is reprimanded by the King for his contemptuous behaviour in daring to object to the gift of **Helena**: 'Here, take her hand, / Proud scornful boy, unworthy this good gift'. The King goes on to commodify Helena still further by using imagery of scales to argue that his favour will counterbalance any inequality in birth: 'We poising us in her defective scale / Shall weigh thee to the beam' (*AWW* 2.3.150–5). Low-born Posthumus rejects the estimation of **Imogen** in terms of worldly value like a ring, arguing that 'the one may be sold or given' but 'the other is not a thing for sale and only the gift of the gods' (*Cym.* 1.4.82–5). However, he then gambles on her fidelity as though this were no different from the **bracelet** or **ring** used as pledges between them.

(c) Marcel Maus, *The Gift: The Form and Reason for Exchange in Archaic Societies*, translated by Ian Cunnison (1954) is the anthropological study from which theories about the exchange of women have developed. Singh (2000) analyses how gendered gifts operate in *Merchant of Venice* in an essay that provides a useful model for reading gift culture in other texts. Boose (1982) discusses gift exchange in betrothal and marriage in Shakespeare.

giglot, (a) a lewd, wanton woman, and derived from this, a giddy **girl**.
(b) The word is derogatory in Shakespeare. **Mariana** and **Isabella** are dismissed by Escalus as untrustworthy 'giglets' for slandering Angelo (*MM* 5.1.347). The self-advertised maiden warrior **Joan** La **Pucelle** reports Young Talbot's scornful refusal to fight with a 'giglot wench' like her (*1HVI* 5.1.41). 'Giglet **Fortune**' is an apt description for the inconstant **goddess** in *Cymbeline* (*Cym.* 3.1.31).

girl, (a) a young or relatively young woman, or used in a derogatory sense to a woman of any age to indicate social inferiority, such as a form of address to a female servant.
(b) The critical gendering of girls at birth is advertised in *Henry VIII* at the moment of **Anne** Bullen's delivery of an heir to the King. The Old **Lady** ambiguously refers to **Princess** Elizabeth as 'a lovely boy' asks God to bless 'her' and then announces ''tis a girl / Promises boys hereafter' (*HVIII* 5.1.164–6). Although Elizabeth may already have the heart and stomach of a boy, girl is unequivocally a second, inferior term. As well as denoting female infants, it also refers to adolescent or young women of marriageable age in Shakespeare. 'Between two girls, which hath the merriest eye' Warwick jokes (*1HVI* 2.4.15) while Lucentio announces his plan to woo 'this young modest girl', **Bianca** (*Shrew* 1.1.156). 'Girl' is used nostalgically by older male characters. Antony, admitting that grey hairs mingle with his brown, still calls Cleopatra 'girl' (*A&C* 4.8.19) and Capulet, recalling the days when he danced and wooed, bids his guests 'give room! and foot it, girls' (*R&J* 1.5.26). The perfection and inevitable loss of **youth** is beautifully captured in the lines 'Golden lads and girls all must, / As chimney-sweepers, come to dust' (*Cym.* 4.2.263–4).

Less idealized views of girls as immature and foolish are expressed by Polonius. He scolds **Ophelia** for speaking 'like a green girl / Unsifted in such perilous circumstance'. She is, he says, a 'baby' for believing Hamlet's professions of love (*Ham.* 1.3.101–5). Portia relies on more positive aspects of girlish innocence when she presents herself to Bassanio as

> an unlesson'd girl, unschool'd, unpractic'd;
> Happy in this, she is not yet so old
> But she may learn.
>
> (*Mer.* 3.2.159–61)

Her protestations disguise her power as a clever, rich heiress whose skill in directing others under a mask of deference becomes apparent in the play.

The opinions of girls are invariably dismissed as irrational and their affections as untrustworthy because governed by adolescent emotions. Caius Martius has no faith in 'the truth of girls and boys' notably listing girls first (*Cym.* 5.5.107). Costard's belief that **Jaquenetta** is 'a true girl' (*LLL* 1.1.312) proves ironically correct when she leaves him for Don Armado. The supposed emotional giddiness of girls is invoked by **Paulina**, mother to three daughters, in order to reprimand Leontes for jealous fantasies 'too weak for boys, too green and idle / For girls of nine' (*WT* 3.2.181–2). Her terms 'green and idle' allude to **green-sickness**, a condition supposedly suffered by **maids** or **virgins**. Ulysses imagines a chorus of 'all the Greekish girls' echoing **Fame**'s rumours by singing mocking rhymes about Achilles: 'Great Hector's sister did Achilles win, / But our great Ajax bravely beat down him' (*T&C* 3.3.211–13). **Cassandra**'s prophesies are brushed aside as the words of a 'foolish, dreaming, superstitious girl' rather than an adult (*T&C* 5.3.79). **Rosalind** acknowledges the giddy spontaneity of a girl when she anticipates the priest's lines and takes Orlando as her husband: 'there's a girl goes before the priest'. As if embarrassed by her immature behaviour, she qualifies this with 'and certainly a woman's thought runs before her actions' (*AYLI* 4.1.139–41).

Examples of strong will, especially when it contradicts fatherly authority, are explained as the result of girlish moodiness. Rather than acknowledge Silvia's desire for Valentine, Thurio patronisingly remarks 'this it is to be a peevish girl, / That flies her fortune when it follows her' (*TGV* 5.2.49–50). His view that such a 'girl' is not worth fighting for uncomfortably draws attention to how Silvia has been passed from Valentine to Proteus a few minutes earlier (*TGV* 5.4.133–5). The power of girls over young men is acknowledged in *All's Well* where the King of France warns his soldiers, 'Those girls of Italy, take heed of them' lest they make the men captive '[b]efore you serve' (*AWW* 2.1.19–22). Although 'girl' did not mean prostitute in Shakespeare's time, the innuendo of 'serve' lends it a sense of camp followers here.

The weakness of girls is set up as the negative opposite of mature masculinity in several plays. Cassius feels that Julius Caesar's illness in war and appeal for water 'As a sick girl' (*JC* 1.2.127–8) makes him unfit to govern with god-like power. Shocked by the ghost of Banquo, Macbeth strives to reassert his manhood by vowing to face any earthly challenge without trembling or else be thought 'The baby of a girl' (*Mac.* 3.4.104–5). Pericles apparently holds a more enlightened view, recognizing that **Marina** may have endured sufferings as great as his own. Unfortunately, though, he retains a sexist bias: if so, he says 'thou art a man, and I / Have suffered like a girl' (*Per.* 5.1.136–7). Antony's death constitutes a radical collapse of masculinity so that 'young boys and girls / Are level now with men' (*A&C* 4.14.65–6). Cleopatra's equation of boys and girls as men's binary opposites self-consciously alludes to the performance of female roles by boys.

'Girl', used by the **Nurse** to address **Juliet**, denotes an intimacy that goes back to Juliet's babyhood. Alongside the pet names 'lamb' and 'ladybird', it stands in stark contrast to the formal '**daughter** Juliet' used by her **mother**, Lady **Capulet** (*R&J* 1.3.3–4 and 64). The associations of social inferiority in 'girl' make it attractive to young men anxious to assert dominance over their mistresses. In *Love's Labour's Lost* Longaville re-groups the lords with the words 'Shall we resolve to woo these girls of France? (*LLL* 4.3.368), while the Clown condescendingly commands 'Follow me, girls' to **Mopsa** and **Dorcas** in *The Winter's Tale* (4.4.312–13). Othello suffocates and so silences **Desdemona** forever, and then diminishes her from adult to vulnerable child in his lament 'Cold, cold, my girl? / Even like thy **chastity**' (*Oth.* 5.1.275–6). When fathers refer to their daughters as 'girl', the term signifies subordination and ownership, vulnerability and intimacy. Shylock and

Brabantio call their daughters 'my girl' (*Mer.* 2.5.15) and 'unhappy girl' (*Oth.* 1.1.163), respectively. Joan La **Pucelle**'s refusal of the name and all it signifies is clear: 'Kneel down and take my blessing, good my girl. / Wilt thou not stoop? (*1HVI* 5.4.25–6). Baptista significantly differentiates between **Bianca**, his 'girl', and **Katherina** whom he calls 'dame'

> Why, how now, dame! Whence grows this insolence?
> Bianca, stand aside – poor girl! she weeps.
> (*Shrew* 2.1.23–4)

Once she has been sacrificed to Petruchio's dominance and abandoned on her wedding morning, however, Katherina becomes Baptista's vulnerable girl. He tells her 'Go, girl, I cannot blame thee now to weep' (*Shrew* 3.2.27). The ravished **Lavinia** is Titus's 'gentle girl' and 'sweet girl' (*Tit.* 3.2.34 and 4.1.51). Cressida, handed to the Greeks, is Pandarus's 'poor girl' (*T&C* 5.3.99–102).

When female characters call others 'girl' two different effects are achieved. Mistresses frequently address their servants as 'girl' following the common practice of registering social inferiority, but in all cases in Shakespeare, the intimacy of 'girl' also alludes obliquely back to the same-sex companionship of childhood. This can evoke a strong wish for **sister**ly solidarity in the face of male aggression or situations of vulnerability. **Lucrece**, for example, sees her **maid** weeping in sympathy and calls her 'my girl' and 'girl' although the maid's formal 'madam' reminds Lucrece of their difference, and she does not confide in her (*Luc.* 1226–85). Female friendship remains an unfulfilled possibility again in *Richard II*. Queen **Isabel**'s ladies-in-waiting are addressed as 'girl', and suggest bowls, dancing, storytelling or singing as possible pastimes that would bring shared comfort. However, neither of the ladies can break through the social etiquette of the court. A closer companionship exists between **Julia** and her gentlewoman **Lucetta**, who is addressed as 'gentle girl' and whose advice is sought 'in kind love' rather than commanded (*TGV* 2.7.1–2). Here the address 'gentle girl' announces a relationship of intimacy and friendship close to equality.

Such intimacy with 'girls' is not exclusive to gentlewomen. Immediately after Antony's death, Cleopatra erases social difference by appealing to **Charmian** and **Iras** as 'noble girls!' and 'women' to constitute a sisterhood of mourning (*A&C* 4.15.72–85). Against Caesar the 'girls' (*A&C* 5.2.191) become a same-sex conspiracy. The **Princess** of France also adopts the common term 'girls' to ally herself with her ladies in playful conspiracy against the group of men: 'we are wise girls to mock our lovers so' (*LLL* 5.2.58). The familiarity of 'girl' to denote same-sex bonding is strongest in **Celia**'s passionate appeal to **Rosalind**. Hoping that Rosalind does not lack the love 'Which teacheth thee that thou and I am one', Celia asks 'Shall we be sund'red? Shall we part, sweet girl?' (*AYLI* 1.3.96–7). The term 'girl' here registers both the power of female friendship and its imminent loss, something that haunts all uses of the word in Shakespeare.

(c) The outrageously sexist Edwardian critic Frank Harris (1912: 144) claims that 'Shakespeare seems to have known very little about girls and nothing about their natural modesty', arguing that the coarseness of characters like Helena in *All's Well* is 'a characteristic of the majority of Shakespeare's heroines' (ibid.: 137) that makes them utterly unbelievable.

glove, (a) an accessory worn by both men and women; gloves were a fashion item in early modern England as well as being functional. They were made of leather – washed with malmsey and then frequently perfumed – or sometimes of softer fabrics like linen. They were often given as gifts at new year or between lovers. Gloves carried symbolic value as a token of favour or to signal a pledge (as in challenging an opponent in a duel or making a tryst). As stage props in the early modern theatre, they could also carry an erotic, bawdy charge as a token of a woman's vagina.

(b) Othello lists **Desdemona**'s 'fan, her gloves, her mask' (*Oth.* 4.2.9) as the accessories of a **lady**, indicating how they probably formed a customary part of the **boy actors**' means of building up the image of a woman on stage. Gloves were worn indoors for warmth as well as being essential protection when riding in summer and winter (Arnold 1988: 217). Embroidered and perfumed gloves were luxury items, such as the pair given to Queen **Elizabeth** by Lady Mary Sidney 'one peir of perfumed gloves, with twenty four small buttons of golde, in every of them a small diamond' (Arnold 1988: 217). Gloves were frequently given at **wedding**s to the guests as well as the bride and groom. Henry Best noted 'sometimes the man gives gloves to the men, and the women to the women, or else he to her friends and she to his; they give them that morning when they are almost ready to go to church to be married' (Cressy 1997: 362). In *Much Ado About Nothing* **Hero** is sent a pair of perfumed gloves by Claudio (*MAdo* 3.4.62). While watching **Juliet**, Romeo fantasizes 'Oh that I were a glove upon that hand / That I might touch that cheek' (*R&J* 2.2.24). Gloves are used as a pledge by the Roman **matrons** in the people's championing of Coriolanus to be consul: 'Matrons flung gloves, / Ladies and **maid**s their scarfs and handkerchers' (*Cor.* 2.1.262–3).

Since John Shakespeare was a glover his son William would presumably have had close experience of glove manufacture. Mistress **Quickly** compares the Slender's beard to the breadth of 'a glover's paring knife' (*MWW* 1.4.21) and an allusion to John Shakespeare's craft may inform Feste's joke that 'a sentence is but a chev'ril glove to a good wit' (*TN* 3.1.11), kidskin being the most pliable leather and so easy to turn inside out, and 'whittawer' being a craftsman who prepared white leather. Feste goes on to discuss the **wanton**ness of his **sister**, associating the glove as a fetish for **woman**. No records of stage business in Shakespeare's plays make such bawdy use of gloves as Middleton and Rowley's *The Changeling* (1622), where De Flores picks up Beatrice-Joanna's glove and admits

> Now I know she had rather wear my pelt tanned
> In a pair of dancing pumps, than I should thrust
> My fingers into her sockets here.
> [*He thrusts his hand into the glove*]
>
> (Middleton 2007: 1.1.236–8)

Gloves are referred to as a symbol for the vagina in Shakespeare. When **Diana**'s chastity seems compromised, Lafeu comments 'This woman's an easy glove, my lord, she goes off and on at pleasure' (*AWW* 5.3.277). **Lucrece**'s chastity is advertised by the presence of a sewing needle stuck in her glove

> As who should say, 'This glove to wanton tricks
> Is not innur'd; return again in haste
> Thou seest our mistress' ornaments are chaste.'
>
> (*Luc.* 320–2)

A debased form of the troubadour love code is found in *King Lear*, where Poor Tom imagines himself a serving man who 'wore gloves in my cap; serv'd the lust of my **mistress**' heart, and did the deed of darkness with her' (*Lear* 3.4.86–8). **Cressida** gives her glove to Troilus as a pledge (*T&C* 4.4.71) signalling owner-ship of her body, in exchange for his pledge of his sleeve. The items of clothing symbolize Cressida's female infidelity in contrast to Troilus's faith at the moment where she promises herself to Diomedes. When he asks her for a token, she hands over Troilus's sleeve while imagining him 'thinking on his bed' where he 'takes my glove / And gives memorial dainty kisses to it' (*T&C* 5.2.71–80). Hector teases the cuckold Menelaus by telling him 'Your quondam wife swears still by **Venus**' glove' (*T&C* 4.5.179).

(c) Arnold (1988: 216–18) quotes and analyses the items relating to gloves in the records of Queen Elizabeth's wardrobe and quotes from Tommaso Garsoni on the perfuming of Spanish gloves 'treated with oil of jessamine and with ambergris, after they have been well washed with a little malmsey wine and anointed with a little odiferous grease' (ibid.: 217). Garsoni also lists cypress, cedar, musk oil, cinnamon, cloves, nutmeg; oils of lemon or civet, camphor, white lead, almonds, white ambergris, storax and rose water and white lead (biacca) as perfuming agents. Cressy (1997: 362–3) discusses the exchange of gloves at weddings. Middleton and Rowley's *The Changeling* (1622) is found in Middleton, *The Collected Works* (2007: 1632–78).

goddess, (a) female deity in polytheistic systems of religion, frequently with a phrase denoting her sphere of influence, as, for example, 'goddess of love'. **Venus** and **Diana** are the only goddesses who appear in Shakespeare although the spirits of Prospero's island present the goddesses **Juno**, **Ceres** and **Iris**.

(b) Juno, Ceres and Iris are not addressed as goddesses, but Pericles calls Diana 'goddess argentine', after her role as patroness of the silver merchants at Ephesus (*Per.* 5.1.250). Venus's longing for Adonis makes her appear a somewhat comic supernatural power who needs 'earth's sovereign salve to do a goddess good' (*V&A* 28). Charmian and Iras offer prayers to the Egyptian goddess **Isis** as a way to mock Alexas (*A&C* 1.2.68–71) and **Cleopatra** is closely identified with that goddess. In *Much Ado*, Claudio refers to Diana's sphere of influence by ask-ing, 'Pardon, goddess of the night / Those that slew thy virgin knight' (*MAdo* 5.3.12–13). The title gives a supernatural status to **Fortune**, **Nature** and '**Patience** herself, what goddess ere she be' (*T&C* 1.1.27) but these deities do not always command belief. In *Cymbeline*, **Imogen** is described in the image of the goddess Patience since 'She's punish'd for her truth, and undergoes, / More goddess-like than wife-like, such assaults / As would take in some virtue' (*Cym.* 3.2.7–9).

Referring to one's mistress as a goddess is a feature of Petrarchan courtship that Shakespeare's texts mock rather than follow. The over-effusive Pandarus praises Troilus by saying, 'Had I a sister were a grace, or a daughter a goddess, he should take his choice' (*T&C* 1.2.236–7). Longaville somewhat ridiculously tries to argue that he has not broken his vow in loving **Maria** since (like the **Virgin** Mary), she is divine rather than human. His assertion 'A woman I forswore; but I will prove, / Thou being a goddess, I forswore not thee' (*LLL* 4.3.62–3) is scorned by Berowne. To call 'a green goose a goddess' is, he protests 'pure, pure idolatry' (*LLL* 4.3.73–4), though he goes on to compare **Rosaline** to a goddess, too. Longaville's argument was published in the miscellaneous verse collection *The Passionate Pilgrim*, suggesting its popularity. Aaron's list of titles for **Tamora**, including **empress**, **queen** and goddess (*Tit.* 2.1.20–22), sceptically predicts her swift rise from worldly to supernatural power. Ironically, it is her overreaching impersonation of the goddess **Revenge** that causes her downfall (*Tit.* 5.2.1–148).

The magic juice love-in-idleness exposes the courtly convention with even more ludicrous effects when Demetrius hails Helena as 'goddess'. She logically assumes this is mockery: 'To call me goddess, nymph, divine and rare, / Precious, celestial? Wherefore speaks he this / To her he hates?' (*MND* 3.2.137 and 226–8). Sonnet 130 candidly points out 'I never saw a goddess go; / My mistress, when she walks, treads on the ground' (*Son.* 130.12). A more sinister effect is achieved in *All's Well* when Bertram tries to seduce Diana by calling her 'Titled goddess / And worth it, with addition!' (*AWW* 4.2.2–3). Ferdinand's reference to **Miranda** as 'the goddess / On whom these airs attend!' (*Temp.* 1.2.422) carries a genuine sense of awe at the wonders of the island rather than an attempt at flattery. Miranda's effect in generating wonder is repeated when Alonso asks 'Is she the goddess that hath sever'd us, / And brought us thus together?' (*Temp.* 5.1.187).

(c) Hackett (1995) and Connolly and Hopkins (2007) discuss how the cult of Elizabeth popularized the comparison of women to goddesses. Davies (1986: 111–74) traces a pattern of references to pagan goddesses through Shakespeare's work.

Goneril, (a) a character in *King Lear*, eldest daughter of King Lear and married to the Duke of Albany. The name is taken from Shakespeare's sources.

(b) The name Goneril (Gonoril in the Quarto text) is found in *The Mirror for Magistrates*, Geoffrey of Monmouth's history and Holinshed's chronicle, where it appears as Gonorilla. In *King Lear* it is used by the King to introduce the character: 'Goneril, / Our eldest born' (1.1.53–4) and she begins a series of flattering lies with the enigmatic line 'I love you more than [words] can wield the matter' (1.1.55). In the mock-trial scene, where she is represented by an object, a stool, her name becomes a focus for Lear's agonized recognition that emotional and kinship bonds no longer have any currency:

Lear: Arraign her first, 'tis Goneril. I here take my oath before this
honourable assembly, [she] kick'd the poor king her father.
Fool: Come hither, mistress. Is your name Goneril?
Lear: She cannot deny it.

(3.6.45–51)

Goneril's apparently hard-hearted behaviour to her father is accompanied by sibling jealousy, **adultery** with Edmund and plotting to murder her husband, a crime defined as petty treason in early modern England because of the analogy between household and state (Dolan 1994: 21–4). Her commands, even to Edmund, are pragmatic and terse, and Albany tells her, 'O Goneril / You are not worth the dust which the rude wind / Blows in your face' (4.2.29–31). She is condemned as demonic, a 'fiend' shielded by 'a **woman**'s shape' (4.2.66–7). Indeed, it is the aberration of gender norms that makes her so terrifying: 'See thyself, devil! / Proper deformity [shows] not in the fiend / So horrid as in woman' (4.2.59–61). By constructing an image of tyranny in a woman's shape, Shakespeare perhaps emphasized the exclusive, élitist violence of absolute monarchy (Alfar 2003). Nevertheless, in the first act, Goneril can also be read as a careful **housewife** or manager of the kingdom. She objects to Lear's train of a hundred knights (a remnant of feudal government), on the grounds that they bring disorder to the 'wholesome weal' of the early modern court and nation (1.4.201–14).

(c) Frances E. Dolan (1994: 21–4) explains the legal classification of domestic crime. Janet Adelman's *Suffocating Mothers* (1992) argues that the play demonstrates that Goneril and Regan are the creation of Lear's fantasy of monstrous **mother**s but simultaneously embraces his view to present them as such. In contrast, Christina Alfar (2003: 79–110) argues the play locates evil and monstrosity in the tyranny of patrilineal absolute monarchy, which Goneril and Regan learn to imitate and are finally subjected by. Hazel Sample Guyol (1966) offers a linguistic study of Goneril's pragmatic, sparse speech. Philippa Kelly (2004) discusses theatrical interpretations including a selection of those seeking to give a fuller voice to Goneril and Regan's perspectives on events.

gossip, (a) A spiritual sponsor to a baptized person and a companion to her or his parents such as a godfather or godmother. Although originally a unisex term, by the sixteenth century it was increasingly used of women and conflated with the female **midwife** and a woman's friends invited in to give advice and keep her company during her confinement. Additionally, gossip is idle or familiar talk, especially of a personal or social nature such as that shared in the all-female space of the **birth**room. The conflation of such talk with the godparent's role as familiar companion becomes gendered as part of the female stereotype of the talktative woman, probably fuelled by male anxieties.

(b) The unisex tradition of the gossip is invoked, perhaps nostalgically, in *Henry VIII* when the King thanks the Archbishop of Canterbury, **Duchess** of Norfolk and **Marchioness** Dorset for their rich gifts to **Princess** Elizabeth: 'My noble gossips, ye have been too prodigal' (*HVIII* 5.4.12). More non-gendered

161

gossips along with the idea of tale telling appear at the other end of Shakespeare's writing career in *Comedy of Errors*. **Aemilia** describes the reunion with her husband and sons as a second delivery and **birth**, inviting everyone, 'Go with me to a gossips' feast' and the Duke promises to 'gossip' with the rest (*Err.* 5.1.406–8). Gossiping is associated with mirth and emotional warmth in *King John* (*KJ* 5.2.58–9). It can also be an arena of indecorous female behaviour, a festival in which gossips celebrated the messy process of birth with their own demonstrations of the 'leaky' or uncontained female body. Puck remembers the carnivalesque scene where he sips at a gossip's bowl making her spill her drink and fall from her chair (*MND* 2.147–55). Act 3 Scene 2 of Middleton's *A Chaste Maid in Cheapside* comically realizes such female incontinence on stage. Allwit comments 'How hot they have made the rooms with their thick bums' and notices 'Nothing but wet' under the stools (Middleton 2007; 3.2.193–5).

When a gossip is gendered female, the name is usually disparaging. Capulet roughly silences the vocal **Nurse** who challenges his authority by ordering 'my **Lady** Wisdom' off stage to 'smatter with your gossips'. He tries to belittle her maternal knowledge with the demand 'Peace you mumbling fool! / Utter your gravity o'er a gossip's bowl' (*R&J* 3.5.169–74). Benedick derides the 'gossip-like humor' of Don Pedro and Claudio about romance as a diversion from the proper manly business of his challenge to fight (*MAdo* 5.1.186). Launce doubts his mistress's **virgin**ity by taking a very literal understanding of the word, saying ''tis not a **maid**, for she hath had gossips', meaning godparents to her child rather than talkative friends (*TGV* 3.1.270). The secrets of the bedchamber shared and potentially communicated by the gossip can be dangerous as the fate of the **nurse** in *Titus* shows. Aaron demands 'Shall she live to betray this guilt of ours, / A long-tongu'd babbling gossip? No, lords, no' (*Tit.* 4.2.149–50). He murders her to conceal the secret of Tamora's **adultery**, boasting that afterwards 'Then let the ladies tattle what they please' (*Tit.* 4.2.168). An acknowledgement that gossips do speak weighty truths, even if these are uncomfortable, is seen in *Merchant of Venice* where Salerio discusses the reputation of the Goodwin Sands for shipwrecks

> . . . where the carcasses of many a tall ship lie buried, as they say, if my gossip
> Report be an honest woman of her word.
> *Sol.:* I would she were as lying a gossip in that as ever knapped ginger or
>   made her neighbors believe she wept for the death of a third husband.
> (*Mer.* 3.1.5–10)

The gossip Report, like **Fame**, can speak either true or false. The domestic nature of her usual chat is juxtaposed with the outside world of male travel, implicitly levelling the differences between these two gendered spheres.

Positive senses of the gossip as a familiar friend and companion inform Titania's line 'Full often hath she gossip'd by my side' to describe herself and the pregnant **votaress** (*MND* 2.1.125). **Titania** seems to have been present at the birth, vowing to take care of the **child**. Companionship, neighbourliness, everyday chat and volubility is glimpsed in Mistress **Quickly**'s snapshot of 'goodwife Keech, the butcher's wife' who came in to 'call me gossip Quickly'. Mistress **Page** addresses her co-conspirator 'What, ho, gossip Ford! what, ho!' (*MWW* 4.2.9). **Paulina** plays on both meanings of the word to undermine Leontes's view of her as a **scold**. She brushes aside his protest about her voice by presenting the new baby with the witty response, 'No noise, my lord; but needful conference / About some gossips for your highness' (*WT* 2.3.38–40). The loquaciousness of gossip is clearly exemplified in **Viola**'s promise to 'halloo your name to the reverberate hills / And make the babbling gossip of the air / Cry out "**Olivia**"' (*TN* 1.5.272–4). Gossip here is **Echo**. The prejudice against gossips' speech as a form of female conspiracy is exploited by Richard III to attack Jane **Shore** and **Elizabeth**, queen to Edward IV.

> The jealous o'erworn **widow** and herself,
> Since that our brother dubb'd them gentlewomen,
> Are mighty gossips in our monarchy.
>
> (*RIII* 1.1.81–3)

His objections pick up on the idea of the gossip's power, but also her outspokenness.

(c) Thomas Middleton, *A Chaste Maid in Cheapside* in *Collected Works* (2007: 907–58 (esp.) 932–7) dramatizes the gossips drinking and wetting the stools in Allwit's house. Woodbridge (1984: 224–43) outlines the literary representations of female gossips. Patricia M. Spacks (1985) reads female gossip as a crucial resource for the subordinated while Bernard Capp's *When Gossips Meet* (2003) is a detailed analysis of the type in early modern English life. Caroline Bicks (2000) discusses the conflation of gossips with midwives as part of an exclusively female-centred culture whose authority caused anxiety in early modern England. Rutter (2001: 142–77) gives a brilliant analysis of the appropriation and ultimate failure of female gossip in *Othello*, focussing on the role of **Emilia** in performance.

gown, (a) a long garment worn by men as a mark of office (such as for a schoolmaster, lawyer or a court appointment), but more usually by women. The gown is an important piece of costume in the construction of male authority and of woman on the early modern stage.

(b) Male characters who wear gowns include Angelo in *Measure for Measure*, the Doge and lawyers in Venice, Evans in *Merry Wives*, and, more ludicrously, Malvolio, who imagines himself in his 'branch'd velvet gown' (*TN* 2.5.47). Dogberry boasts he is man who 'hath two gowns' (*MAdo* 4.2.85). Gowns appear as fashion items in *Much Ado* and *Taming of the Shrew* where the word seems to cover all the separate pieces that make up the whole: sleeves, skirts and bodices, which were all fastened together by **laces**. **Margaret** compares **Hero**'s **wedding** dress of 'fine, quaint, graceful and excellent fashion' (*MAdo* 3.4.22) to the **Duchess** of Milan's magnificent gown, which is 'cloth a' gold and cuts, and lac'd with silver, set with pearls, down sleeves, side sleeves, and skirts, round underborne with a bluish tinsel' (*MAdo* 3.4.19–22). Margaret's view that this splendid garment is 'a night-gown' beside Hero's, perhaps unconsciously betrays her guilt at wearing Hero's clothes for the night-time assignation with Borachio (*MAdo* 3.4.18). Female rivalry over clothing energizes the friction between Queen **Margaret** and **Eleanor** of Gloucester, who 'bears a duke's revenues on her back' and purportedly boasts that 'the train of her worst wearing gown' was worth more than all Margaret's **dowry** (*2HVI* 1.3.80–6).

In *Taming of the Shrew*, the sartorial construction of the fashionable gentle-woman is deconstructed on stage when the tailor presents the 'loose-bodied gown' with its 'small compass'd cape' and two trunk sleeves 'curiously cut' (*Shrew* 4.3.133–43). Loose-bodied gowns, cut to hang from shoulder to hem without a waistband, with a loose **kirtle** underneath, were very fashionable in the sixteenth century in addition to being comfortable and practical during pregnancy (Arnold 1988: 121). It is certainly to **Katherina**'s taste; she declares she 'never saw a better-fashion'd gown' (*Shrew* 4.3.101). Petruchio, however, mocks the fashion of the very full sleeves, slashed so that a layer of satin or silk could be seen through the cuts in the surface layer of material: ''tis like a demi-cannon. / What, up and down carv'd like an apple tart?' (*Shrew* 4.3.88–9).

Falstaff's disguise in the gown of the 'fat Woman of **Brainford**' (*MWW* 4.2.75) also parodies the fashion, perhaps picking up on his earlier joke 'my skin hangs about me like an old lady's loose gown' (*1HIV* 3.3.3–4). Designed to fit a very large woman, this garment must be large and loose, without requiring lacing at the back since Falstaff is expected to put it on without help.

The gown, as a disembodied construction of woman by male actors is subject to serious scrutiny in *The Two Gentlemen of Verona* where the cross-dressed **Julia** invents a history where 'I was trimm'd in Madam Julia's gown' which fitted 'As if the garment had been made for me' (*TGV* 4.4.161–3). Gowns were, of course, all made for the original wearer although they were also given as gifts and legacies. At one level, the joke is that the gown was made for the character and so obviously fitted perfectly, but behind this the **boy actor** marvels that, even though it has been passed down to him, either by a woman or by another boy actor, and yet the Julia costume fits him perfectly.

As with other female garments, 'gown' can also carry bawdy associations, as a metaphor for female sexuality. Comically, it is **Katherine**, Princess of France, who spells this out most blatantly, mistaking the English translations for the French *foutre* ('to fuck') and *coun* ('cunt'):

Katherine: Comment appelez-vous le pied et la robe?
Alice: Le foot, madame, et le count.
Katherine: Le foot et le count! O Seigneur Dieu! ils sont les mots de son
    mauvais.

(*HV* 3.4.50–3)

Grumio uses similar innuendo in joking that the tailor's gown is for his mistress, not for his master's use, proceeding to be shocked at the impropriety in the suggestion that the tailor should 'Take up my mistress' gown to his master's use!' (*Shrew* 4.3.156–63).

(c) Arnold (1988: 110–40) gives a lavish description of the French, Italian, Spanish, Dutch and Polish fashions of gown popularized by Elizabeth's court. Details of sleeves, and loose gowns are also included.

grandam, (a) **grandmother** or ancestress and, more broadly, an old woman or a **gossip**.

(b) This term is less formal than 'grandmother' and offers more opportunity for satire and for conveying human intimacy. Reverence for the matriarch as point of origin is satirized in many fictional texts, including Shakespeare's. Hotspur's picture of 'our grandam earth' as a flatulent old woman (*1HIV* 3.2.33), Malvolio's citation of the Pythagoras's theory that 'the soul of our grandam might happily inhabit a bird' and Feste's warning to 'fear to kill a woodcock lest thou dispossess the soul of thy grandam' (*TN* 4.2.51–60) all make fun of the grandmother's assumed status of material and spiritual superiority, promulgated through many early modern texts. Lady Grace Mildmay, for example, addressed her grandson Mildmay with the words, 'I your loving and old grandmother, exhort you in the name of the Lord to receive my words acceptably' (Mildmay 1993: 42) and, later in the seventeenth century, Quaker women claimed that as 'Antient Women in Our Families' they 'do know in the Wisdom of God what will do in Families' (Mendelson and Crawford, 1998: 187). Satirizing the grandmother's spiritual wisdom is not peculiar to Shakespeare. Thomas Dekker, for example, introduces London as 'this ancient and reuerend Grandam of Citties', the matriarch of the seven deadly sins (Dekker 1606: 27).

Showing due respect to one's grandam was an important piece of social civility. As John Stephens noted, 'shee can speake wonders to grand-children of the third generation. If they please her, she hath *old harry soueraignes*, that saw no sunne in fiftie yeares, to giue away on her death bed' (Stephens 1615: 371). Gratiano outlines the model behaviour designed to please a grandmother:

> If I do not put on a sober habit,
> Talk with respect, and swear but now and then,
> Wear prayer-books in my pocket, look demurely,
> Nay more, while grace is saying hood mine eyes
> Thus with my hat, and sigh and say amen,
> Use all the observance of civility,
> Like one well studied in a sad ostent
> To please his grandam, never trust me more.
>
> (*Mer.* 2.2.190–7)

This account of a well-practised duty probably gained its comic effect from easy recognition on the part of spectators.

Richard III, although not a trustworthy speaker, hits on a general truth when he declares 'A grandam's name is little less in love / Than is the doting title of a **mother**' (*RIII* 4.4.299–300). When Queen **Eleanor** says 'I am thy grandame, Richard; call me so' (*KJ* 1.1.168) she makes an important offer of kinship and support to her illegitimate grandson. Unlike 'grandmother', used to support matriarchal lineage in Shakespeare, 'grandame' appropriately implies a less formal royal connection for a grandson who is 'the very spirit' rather than the letter of Plantagenet having been born 'something about, a little from the right' (*KJ* 1.1.167–70). In *Richard III*, the **Duchess** of York, mother of Edward IV, Richard of Gloucester and Duke of Clarence, takes on the role of surrogate parent to the children of Clarence and later of Edward IV. After Clarence has been murdered by Richard, she appears as caretaker of his son and daughter. The boy asks, 'Good, grandam, tell us is our father dead?' and his innocent question, 'Think you my uncle did dissemble, grandam?' clearly demonstrates how necessary her protection of these 'shallow innocents' is (*RIII* 2.2.1, 18 and 31). A playful affection is shown between her and Richard, Duke of York, when the Prince recounts how he has grown, 'Grandam, one night when we did sit at supper . . .' or jokes that since his uncle could bite a crust at two hours old but he did not have a tooth for two years 'Grandam, this would have been a biting jest' (*RIII* 2.4.10 and 30). While his mother scolds him for being 'too shrewd', his grandmother counsels 'be not angry with the child' (*RIII* 2.4.36–7). She has also transmitted important family wisdom to the Prince of Wales about Clarence and the Tower, 'My grandam told me he was murd'red there' (*RIII* 3.1.145).

Speed draws attention to typical affection across generations when he cites 'a young **wench** that hath buried her grandam' as a typical example of weeping (*TGV* 2.1.23–4) and Launce reports how 'my grandam, having no eyes, look you, wept herself blind at my parting' (*TGV* 2.3.12–13). Due to grandmothers frequently taking part in the care of their grandchildren and taking delight in them, 'grandam will give me' was a frequent refrain in early modern ballads (Mendelson and Crawford 1998: 192–3). **Constance** in *King John* satirizes this tradition when **Eleanor** asks Arthur 'Come to thy grandame, child':

> Do, child, go to it grandame, child.
> Give grandame kingdom, and it grandame will
> Give it a plum, a cherry, and a fig.
> There's a good grandame.
>
> (*KJ* 2.1.159–63)

Constance's parody sarcastically shows how Eleanor's 'cank'red grandam's will' (*KJ* 2.1.194) is perverting her position of indulgent protector to bribe the innocent Arthur into surrendering his kingdom. The secure domestic world in which the child is indulged is cited as a dangerous illusion, or delusion in *Macbeth*, where Macbeth is criticized at the royal banquet for shameful fits and starts that 'would well become / A woman's story at a winter's fire, / Authoriz'd by her grandam' (*Mac.* 3.4.63–5). Whatever the grandam's potential as a figure of fun, her role as the indulgent, comfortable and experienced head of the family is pictured as a desireable future for at least one young female character. In *Love's Labour's Lost*

Katherine sadly imagines that her dead sister 'might 'a' been a grandam ere she died' (*LLL* 5.2.17).

(c) The stereotypical grandmother is warmly described in John Stephens, *Essayes and Characters* (1615: 371). Dekker uses the metaphor of grandam for London in *The seuen deadly sinnes of London* (1606). Mendelson and Crawford (1998: 184–9, 192–3) give a broad overview of the grandmother's position. Lady Grace Mildmay's autobiography and advice to her grandchildren is a fine example of the authority and measured affection adopted by grandmothers as heads of the family (Mildmay 1993: 42–7). Lady Anne Clifford's diaries (1990) and Richard T. Spence's chapter about her as 'The Grand Matriarch' (1997: 231–53) give another case study of the grandmother and matriarch's rule. Weimann (1999) discusses 'grandam' as part of the dispute between Constance and Eleanor in *King John*, and Heather Dubrow (2000) considers grandmothers as one type of surrogate parent in *Richard III*.

grandmother, (a) the mother of a parent, a more formal term than **grandam**.
(b) Each of the four uses of 'grandmother' in Shakespeare conveys respect for matriarchal lineage. The Archbishop of Canterbury's famous defence of the Salique Law argues that King Lewis X bases his claim to the French crown on the fact that

> fair Queen **Isabel**, his grandmother,
> Was lineal of the Lady Ermengare,
> Daughter to Charles the foresaid duke of Lorraine:
> By the which marriage the line of Charles the Great
> Was re-united to the crown of France.
>
> (*HV* 1.2.81–5)

Don Armado's flamboyant rhetoric styles **Jaquenetta** as a child of the ancestress 'our grandmother Eve' (*LLL* 1.1.263). **Miranda** tells her father 'I should sin / To think but nobly of my grandmother / Good wombs have borne bad sons' (*Temp.* 1.1.118–20). Even Launce prioritizes matriarchal descent in explaining to Speed 'who begot thee' was not the son of his grandfather 'it was the son of thy grandmother' (*TGV* 3.1.294–7). In this case, supposed reverence for the matriarch is hollow since it points to a lack of certainty about wifely fidelity.
(c) *See* immediately above in the entry on **grandam** for further reading.

green-sickness, (a) An anæmic disease, chlorosis, which mostly affects young women about the age of puberty and gives a pale or greenish tinge to the complexion. It was believed to be caused by a longing for sex.
(b) Shakespeare does not follow the common idea that a young woman 'beeing at the age of twentie yeeres' would 'fall into the greene sicknes for want of a husband' (Greene, 1583: 8). Rather, 'green-sickness' appears as a symptom of obstinacy or wilfulness. The owners of the brothel curse the determinedly chaste **Marina**, declaring 'a pox upon her green sickeness' (*Per.* 4.6.13–14). Capulet tells the pale **Juliet** who refuses to marry 'Out, you green-sickness carrion'

167

and calls her 'you baggage! You tallow-face!' (*R&J* 3.5.156–7). 'Green-sickness baggage' seems to have been a stock phrase and the condition may even have been physically manifested on stage. In Middleton's *World Tossed at Tennis*, for example, White Starch refers to Green Starch, who is appropriately costumed, as 'my tansy-face, that shows like a pride / Served up in sorrel sops, green sickness baggage' (Middleton 2007; ll. 382–3). The love-sick maid 'look't greene as any leeke' in Armin's *Two Maids of Moore Clack* (Armin 1609: sig C4v). Shakespeare's company may have used cosmetics to indicate green-sickness. Saying that male characters have the green-sickness is to feminize and diminish them. Falstaff famously derides Prince John as one of those 'demure boys' who eat too much fish and drink no wine so 'fall into a kind of male green-sickness, and when they marry, they get wenches' (*2HIV* 4.3.92–4). On the other hand, Lepidus is said to be 'troubled / With the green-sickness' (*A&C* 3.2.5–6) when he is suffering the effects of too *much* alcohol and possibly sea-sickness.

(c) Helen King, *The Disease of Virgins* (2003) is a wonderful historical survey of how theories of green sickness were developed in the Renaissance from Hippocrates and Galen and how these carried into later centuries. Examples of contemporary literary references to green-sickness are Thomas Greene, *Mamillia, a mirrour or looking glasse for the ladies of England* (1593: 8); Robert Armin *The history of the tvvo maids of More-clacke* (London, 1609) and Thomas Middleton, *The World Tossed at Tennis*, in *Collected Works* (2007: pp. 1405–36).

Grissel, (a) or Griselda, a fictional figure who is the epitome of wifely patience and suffering. Daughter of a poor man, she marries the nobleman Lord Walter, who then tests her virtue by taking away their baby daughter and then son from her, supposedly to kill them. Next, Walter annuls the marriage sending Griselda home in her smock to her poor father, and secretly recalls their 12-year-old daughter as a new wife. Throughout these trials, Griselda does not speak a single word of complaint. Pleased with her dutiful resignation, Walter reveals the truth, congratulates her on passing the test and the couple live happily ever after with their children.

(b) Only one direct reference to Patient Grissel occurs in Shakespeare when Petruchio anticipates his own abuse of **Katherina** by proclaiming 'For patience she will prove a second Grissel' (*Shrew* 2.1.295). However, versions of the story, including Boccaccio's *Decameron*, Chaucer's *Clerk's Tale*, numerous ballads, a dramatization of 1395 and the play *Patient Grissil* (1603) ensured its popular currency in early modern England. For this reason, spectators or readers would have identified elements of the Griselda story in references to **patience** as a female virtue. The suffering of characters like **Viola** in *Twelfth Night*, **Helena** in *All's Well*, **Hero** in *Much Ado*, **Imogen** in *Cymbeline* and **Hermione** in *Winter's Tale* implicitly invoke Griselda as one of the stereotypes of female heroism (Jardine 1983: 184).

(c) Jardine (1983: 183–5) cites Griselda as the model for the characters listed above, plus Desdemona. Linda Woodbridge (1984), provides a comprehensive analysis of the type as part of the controversy over women's natures (see esp. pp. 211–17).

hag (a) an evil spirit, dæmon, or infernal being, in female form, a term applied to the **Furies** or **Harpies** and malicious fairies of Greek, Latin and Teutonic mythology.

(b) The Hag as a Fury is a feature of many early modern literary texts. Samuel Daniel, for example, compares Jealousy to a 'Pale Hagge, infernall Fury' (Daniel 1605: sig G5) and one of Greene's heroes asks himself 'art thou haunted with some hellish hagge, or possessed with some frantike furie?' (Greene 1608: sig. C4v). In Shakespeare, 'hags' in the plural signifies the **Furies** of the underworld when the Lieutenant tells Suffolk that after death 'wedded be thou to the hags of hell', as a revenge for matching Henry VI to the worthless **Margaret** (*2HVI* 4.1.79). Something of the same supernatural power informs Macbeth's address to the **weird sisters** and **Hecate** as 'secret, black, and midnight hags' and 'filthy hags' (*Mac.* 4.1, 48 and 115). 'Hag' is always used with pejorative connotations, in most cases alongside **witch**, to express disgust and fear on the part of male characters. Talbot refers to **Joan** as 'Foul fiend of France, and hag of all despite, / Encompass'd with thy lustful paramours!' (*1HVI* 3.2.52–3). Here and in *Romeo and Juliet* the hag symbolizes fertility, possibly connected with **Hecate** as a goddess of childbirth. Mercutio describes Queen **Mab**, the fairies' midwife, as 'the hag when maids lie on their backs, / That presses them and learns them first to bear' (*R&J* 1.4.92–3). Unregulated female sexuality is demonised in a comically exaggerated use of 'hag' when Ford furiously addresses the Wise Woman of **Brainford**:

> She works by charms, by spells, by th' figure, and such daub'ry as this is, beyond our element we know nothing. Come down, you witch, you hag, you; come down, I say!
>
> (*MWW* 4.2.176–9)

As well as promoting illegitimate sexual practices, the hag is also a **scold**. **Paulina**, who brings baby **Perdita**, is called 'a gross hag!' for her uncontrolled tongue by the deluded Leontes (*WT* 2.3.108). York commands **Joan** to stop her cursing: 'Fell banning hag, enchantress, hold thy **tongue**! (*1HVI* 5.3.42) and, in the only instance where 'witch' is not used alongside 'hag', Lear invokes the idea of monstrous disorder, calling his daughters 'you unnatural hags!' (*KL* 2.4.278). The witch **Sycorax** is 'a blue-ey'd hag' and is twice more anonymized as hag (*Temp.* 1.2.269, 283, 365). Since she is 'bent double', the term here conjures up age, a sense it holds in more modern parlance. Richard tells the aged, cursing Margaret 'Have done thy charm, thou hateful with'red hag!' (*RIII* 1.3.214).

(c) Samuel Daniel, *Certaine small poems lately printed* (1605) and Robert Greene *Greenes carde of fancie* (1608), give early modern examples of the hag as **fury**. For connections between hags, the goddess **Hecate** and the wider network of beliefs about magic see Briggs (1962). *See* further reading on the entries on **Furies**, **witch** and **weird sisters**.

hand, (a) in humans, the chiefest bodily instrument for the expression of intentions and actions, as symbolized in the metonymic use of 'a hand' to mean a sailor or a labourer or to mean a round of applause at a performance. The hand is a formal expression of intention in rituals such as betrothal or bestowal in marriage or ceremonial activities such as invitations to dance. In addition, the word refers to the action of the hand in writing and the handwriting thus produced. It signifies a style of writing belonging to a particular person.

(b) Although all these meanings are superficially non-gendered, in Shakespeare's texts and in early modern culture more widely there is a significant difference between the ways men and women's hands are perceived. Men's hands are expected to initiate action or undertake labour whereas women's hands are culturally restricted to a passive, decorative existence. While the request 'give me your hand' is very common between men, a symbol of same-sex bonding, women's hands are *to be given* by their menfolk, gesturally reducing them to the role of **commodity** or **gift**. **Portia** is a rich prize who cannot give away her hand in marriage, but once cross-dressed as Bellario, is welcomed to the courtroom by the Duke who asks, 'Give me your hand' (*Mer.* 4.1.169). **Anne** Page (*MWW* 4.6.34–45), **Hero** (*MAdo* 4.1.303–4), **Miranda** (*Temp.* 4.1.2–5) and **Cordelia** (*KL* 1.1.240–44) are also subject to male handling in betrothal or marriage. Significantly, 'hand' is the first English word Princess **Katherine** learns (*HV* 3.4.6–8) as if in preparation to be handed over, along with her country, to King Henry V, who tells her, 'Upon that I kiss your hand, and I call you my queen' (*HV* 5.2.251). The rule of exchange is maintained even where adverse circumstances prevail. Troilus dutifully promises to 'give up to Diomedes' hand / The Lady Cressida' in exchange for Antenor (*T&C* 4.2.62–6), but grimly predicts that the formal ceremony of delivering her 'to his hand' will break his heart (*T&C* 4.3.6–9). Lucio describes prostitution as a parallel case of handing over money for an utterly passive commodity: 'is there none of Pygmalion's images, newly made woman, to be had now, for putting the hand in the pocket and extracting it clutch'd?' (*MM* 3.3.44–7).

Helena in *All's Well* is acutely conscious of usurping the male role in choosing a partner, and tells one lord, 'Be not afraid that I your hand should take; / I'll never do you wrong for your own sake' (*AWW* 2.3.89). **Mariana** is likewise cautious, introducing herself to Angelo by offering her hand as the restoration of a legitimate male-authored contract: 'This is the hand which, with a vow'd contract, / Was fast belock'd in thine' (*MM* 5.1.208). Complete passivity may offer a subversive form of resistance for Isabella when the Duke proposes 'Give me your hand and say you will be mine' (*MM* 5.1.492). The **Princess** of France swears by 'this **virgin** palm now kissing thine' (*LLL* 5.2.806) that she will give her hand to the King of Navarre if he endures the 12 months' retirement to a hermitage. **Portia** and **Rosalind** presumably use manual gestures to give themselves in the **betrothal** or marriage at the ends of their plays.

The ideal female hand is white, indicating chastity, passivity or leisure on the part of the woman, with a possible allusion to **Elizabeth** I who was extremely proud of her white hands. **Olivia** (*TN* 2.3.27), **Helen** of Troy (*T&C* 1.2.119), **Juliet** (*R&J* 3.3.36), Orleans' **mistress** (*HV* 3.7.93) and **Rosalind** (*AYLI* 3.2.394) are all praised for their white hands while Berowne addresses his letter 'To the snow-white hand of the most beauteous Lady **Rosaline**' (*LLL* 4.2.131–2), even though she is elsewhere referred to as 'black as ebony' (*LLL* 4.3.43). Lorenzo puns on the different meanings of hand as writing style and body part to praise **Jessica**:

> I know the hand; in faith, 'tis a fair hand,
> And whiter than the paper it writ on
> Is the fair hand that writ.
>
> > (*Mer.* 2.4.12–14)

Jessica's agency is indicated by her ability to take up the pen and write, a skill shared by only a small proportion of women (including Shakespeare's daughter **Susanna**), much fewer than those who could read. Jessica's hand communicates her plan to elope, to give her hand to Lorenzo. Transgressive behaviour and writing are connected again in *Two Gentlemen of Verona* where **Julia**'s love letter to Proteus literally takes her choice of marriage partner into her own hand, 'the agent of her heart' (*TGV* 1.3.45–50). The 'sweet Roman hand' declaring **Olivia**'s love for Malvolio represents class and gender transgression on the part of Olivia (pursuing her desire for Cesario / Sebastian) and **Maria** (pursuing Sir Toby). In *As You Like It*, **Phoebe**'s readiness to declare her love in a letter makes **Rosalind** believe she has a brownish-yellow, working 'leathern hand' and thus a prostitute or 'huswife's hand' (*AYLI* 4.3.24–7). In *Merchant of Venice*, Lorenzo quickly counterbalances the dangerous potential of Jessica's agency in writing and plotting to elope, with the evidence that the jewess's hand is whiter than the paper. Shakespeare makes even more blatant mockery of the courtly blazon by extending it to ridiculous lengths in *Troilus and Cressida* (1.1.55–9) and in *A Midsummer Night's Dream* where Demetrius's hyperbolic praise asserts that **Helena**'s hand a 'princess of pure white' makes the 'pure congealed white' of mountain snow appear as black as a crow (*MND* 3.2.141–4).

171

Given the strong symbolic significance of the female hand, it is not surprising that the active hand is, with a few notable exceptions, a polluted hand in Shakespeare's texts. As an indicator of maternal control it is protective yet also dangerously infantilizing as in the famous stage direction in *Coriolanus*: *[He holds her by the* hand, *silent]* (*Cor.* 5.3.182SD). More acceptable by early modern standards is the hand that is active in submission. **Silvia** becomes an idealized icon of mediation like the Virgin **Mary** when she pleads for Valentine, weeping upon her knees, 'Wringing her hands, whose whiteness so became them / As if but now they waxed pale for woe' (*TGV* 3.1.229–30). The most blatant example of such submission is **Katherina**'s recommendation to wives to

> vail your stomachs, for it is no boot,
> And place your hands below your husband's foot;
> In token of which duty, if he please,
> My hand is ready, may it do him ease.
>
> (*Shrew* 5.1. 176–9)

In contrast, the most obvious example of the polluted, active hand is Lady **Macbeth**'s after she has participated in the murder of Duncan and is haunted by 'the smell of the blood still', lamenting that 'all the perfumes of Arabia will not sweeten this / little hand' (*Mac.* 5.1.50–2). **Tamora**'s demand for a weapon and her vow 'Your **mother**'s hand shall right your mother's wrong' (*Tit.* 2.3.121) likewise mark her out as a villain. Less aggressive forms of manual agency are those linked to masturbation and sexual pleasure, most obviously in Mercutio's bawdy comment that for 'the bawdy hand of the dial is now upon the prick of noon' (*R&J* 2.4.113). On **Cleopatra**'s barge 'the silken tackle / Swell with the touches of those flower-soft hands, / That yarely frame the office' (*A&C* 2.2.209–11). Touchstone is excited by the thought of how **Jane** Smile's 'pretty chapt hands had milk'd' (*AYLI* 2.4.50). Sexual innuendo resonates through musical imagery in Sonnet 128 where the speaker envies the jacks on a lute 'that leap / To kiss the tender inward of thy hand' (*Son.* 128.5–6), and in **Katherina**'s point-blank refusal to play with her teacher, Hortensio, in a way that pleases him:

> I did but tell her she mistook her frets,
> And bow'd her hand to teach her fingering,
> When, with a most impatient devilish spirit,
> 'Frets, call you these?' quoth she 'I'll fume with them.'
>
> (*Shrew* 2.1.149–52)

Hot and moist hands are a dangerously attractive sign of sexual desire on women's part. Othello sees **Desdemona**'s hot hand as 'a young and sweating devil / That commonly rebels'. She replies 'You may, indeed, say so; / For 'twas that hand that gave away my heart' (*Oth.* 3.4.39–42). The hot hand she gave in marriage physically marks her sexual boldness and rebellion against paternal authority, as she eloped from her father's house to give herself to Othello. **Venus**'s passion for

Adonis is advertised manually: 'My smooth moist hand, were it with thy hand felt, / Would in thy palm dissolve, or seem to melt' (*V&A* 159).

Touching hands with a woman on the Shakespearean stage or as an action in a narrative poem is highly eroticized, as the actors who performed these roles must have been aware. When Henry VIII takes **Anne** Bullen's hand in the dance he falls in love, declaring it is 'the fairest hand I ever touch'd!' (*HVIII* 1.4.75). Likewise, when Romeo and **Juliet** touch hands in an eroticization of saintly reverence, the 'holy palmers' kiss' (*R&J* 1.5.100) leads directly to a kiss with their lips. **Cleopatra** seductively offers a messenger 'a hand that kings / Have lipp'd, and trembled kissing' (*A&C* 2.5.29–30) and Antony is predictably infuriated by one who dare be 'So saucy with the hand of she here, – what's her name, / Since she was Cleopatra?' (*A&C* 3.13.98–9), implying she has made herself common. Even though **Lucrece**'s greetings 'She took me kindly by the hand' (*Luc.* 253) are chastely innocent, the erotic nature of touching hands fuels Tarquin's desire for her as she desires news of her husband:

> And how her hand, in my hand being lock'd,
> Forc'd it to tremble with her loyal fear!
> Which strook her sad, and then it faster rock'd,
> Until her husband's welfare she did hear;
>
> (*Luc.* 260–3)

Thus when Tarquin perceives her in bed, her hand 'whose perfect white / Show'd like an April daisy on the grass, / With pearly sweat, resembling dew of night' (*Luc.* 394–6) tempts him further with its promise of purity and passion. In the most extreme versions in Shakespeare, **Desdemona** and **Hermione** are both attacked for touching the hands of men who were not their husbands. Desdemona is accused of flirting 'see her paddle with the palm of his hand? didst not mark that?' (*Oth.* 2.1.254) and Hermione of 'paddling palms and pinching fingers' (*WT* 1.2.115) with Polixenes. This is all the more disturbing to Leontes because, he recalls, it took him three months before Hermione would 'open thy white hand / And clap thyself my love' to declare 'I am yours for ever' (*WT* 1.2.102 and 104). This refers back to their hand-fasting or **betrothal**, a process self-consciously managed by Pandarus for Troilus and **Cressida** (*T&C* 3.2.196–204). It is striking that, in *The Winter's Tale*, a repetition of the hand-fast is what marks the resolution of Leontes's sexual jealousy. **Paulina** fears that if she makes the passive statue move 'And take you by the hand' he will think she is 'assisted / By wicked powers' (*WT* 5.3.89). Instead, he must present his hand and his faith to restore her: 'When she was young you woo'd her; now in age / Is she become the suitor?' (*WT* 5.3.107–8). Even here, the active female hand holds the potential for transgression and condemnation but Paulina's solution is much more harmonious than the fate that befalls **Lavinia**. Marcus asks in horror 'what stern ungentle hands / Have lopp'd and hew'd and made thy body bare / Of her two branches', that 'kings have sought to sleep in' (*Tit.* 2.4.16–18). Even as he recalls their **beauty**, he recognizes their dangerous power to arouse and distract male action:

> had the monster seen those lily hands
> Tremble, like aspen-leaves, upon a lute,
> And make the silken strings delight to kiss them,
> He would not then have touch'd them for his life!
>
> (*Tit.* 2.4.44–7)

Shakespeare's radical thesis seems to be that if women's hands, with their potential for agency and arousal, are really so dangerous, then the only solution is to cut them off.

(c) David M. Bergeron (ed.), *Reading and Writing in Shakespeare* (1996) contains essays on women's writing in *As You Like It, Macbeth, Cymbeline, Pericles, Titus Andronicus, Two Gentlemen of Verona, Twelfth Night* and *Winter's Tale*. See especially Karen Robertson, *A Feminine Revenging Hand in* Twelfth Night (pp. 116–30), which considers early modern writing by women with a focus on Maria's skill as a forger. The instability of theatrical gestures like Hermione's 'paddling palms' is discussed by Howard Felperin (1986). For further reading on the use of hands in ritual exchanges, *see* **betrothal** and **wedding**.

hand-fast, (a) another name for **betrothal**.

handmaid (a) a female personal servant or attendant, though the word carries religious associations since the Virgin **Mary** is described as the 'handmaid of the Lord'.

(b) Other than the image of inanimate 'handmaid' vessels or ships, which dutifully follow the flagship in a crescent-moon formation (*EIII* 3.1.73), Shakespeare's handmaids are not what they seem. Catholic celebration of the Virgin Mary as the handmaid of the Lord (Luke 1.38) introduces a paradox of submission and empowerment that influences Shakespeare's four uses of the word. Valentine describes **Maria** as a 'handmaid' returning news of Olivia's determination to remain enclosed 'like a cloistress' (*TN* 1.5.23–7), but the rest of the play depicts Maria as a dominant **Penthesilea** whose social ambitions are fulfilled. 'Handmaid' signifies a false humility when the Catholic **Joan** La **Pucelle** deftly persuades the Duke of Burgundy to rejoin the French by introducing herself with the words 'let thy humble handmaid speak to thee' (*1HVI* 3.3.42). Submission is a direct route to power for **Tamora** the '**Queen** of Goths' who tells Saturnine she 'will a handmaid be to his desires, / A loving nurse, a **mother** to his youth' if he marries her (*Tit.* 1.1.330–2). Images of false humility and calculation thus haunt the term by the time **Anne** Bullen parodies the Annunciation to send a message of obedience to King Henry VIII, 'As from a blushing handmaid to his Highness' (*HVIII* 2.3.71–2).

(c) Mark Thornton Burnett (1997: 118–54) discusses the position of maidservants and Maria's usurpation of her mistress's role. *See also* the further reading under **maid**.

harlot, (a) originally a unisex term used to denote a vagabond, beggar or rascal, villain, low fellow, knave. In the sixteenth and seventeenth centuries it carried a pejorative sexual sense, as a fornicator, and denoted an itinerant jester.

Applied to a woman in the sixteenth and seventeenth centuries, 'harlot' meant an unchaste woman, prostitute or **strumpet**, but often with the theatrical sense of a juggler, dancing-girl or actress. In post-Reformation England its scriptural associations with the **Whore** of Babylon meant it was also used to derogate Catholic idolatry.

(b) Mistress **Quickly** uncharacteristically makes a technically correct use of the term to refer to an itinerant jester or an unlicensed vagabond player without a patron when she says of Falstaff's acting: 'O Jesu, he doth it as like one of these harlotry players as ever I see!' (*1HIV* 2.4.395–6). Leontes also uses it of a man, calling Polixenes 'the harlot king' (*WT* 2.3.4). All other cases in Shakespeare are applied to female or feminine subjects. William Lambarde gave a historical explanation for its gendered nature: 'Robert, the Duke of Normandie, had issue by a Concubine (whose name . . . was Harlothe, and after whom, as I coniecture, such incontinent women have ever since beene called Harlots)' (Lambarde 1826: 200). Richard III joins two terms together to express his contempt for 'that harlot **strumpet**', Jane **Shore**, (*RIII* 3.4.71). Timon refers to the prostitutes **Phrynia** and **Timandra** as 'a brace of Harlots' (*Tim.* 4.3.80). The term is an insult in Mercutio's description of the classical heroines **Helen** and **Hero** as 'hildings and harlots' (*R&J* 2.4.42), and Antipholus of Ephesus complains his wife 'shut the doors upon me, / While she with harlots feasted in my house' (*Err.* 5.1.205).

'Mother of Harlots and abominations of the earth' is the name branded on the forehead of the Whore of Babylon in Revelation (Rev. 17.5). Shakespeare's references to harlots follow these negative connotations rather than the more positive biblical model of the repentant or holy harlot such as **Mary** Magdalene.

Laertes fears that his calm blood 'brands the harlot / Even here between the chaste unsmirched brows / Of my true **mother**' (*Ham.* 4.3.119–20). Branding of harlots was threatened by Henry VIII in 1531, though it never actually came onto the statute books and remained a metaphor for shaming (Henning 2000). **Adriana** observes that were she unfaithful like her husband, he would 'tear the stain'd skin off my harlot brow' (*Err.* 2.2.136). In *Julius Caesar* **Portia** complains that Brutus is not treating her as a second self and confidante in companionate marriage, but as a harlot. Shakespeare picks up a detail from his source in North's *Plutarch* where Portia says she is not a 'beddefellowe and companion in bedde and at borde onlie, like a harlot' but rather a partaker of Brutus's whole fortune (Bullough Vol I 1964: 471).

> Am I yourself
> But, as it were, in sort or limitation,
> To keep with you at meals, comfort your bed,
> And talk to you sometimes? Dwell I but in the suburbs
> Of your good pleasure? If it be no more,
> Portia is Brutus' harlot, not his wife.
>
> (*JC* 2.1.282–7)

175

Portia's observation that the harlot metaphorically dwells in the suburbs of a man's life alludes to the actual dwelling places of prostitutes in London's suburbs. While a **wife** should have secure possession of her husband, the harlot does not, as Bianca's situation proves. Although Cassio 'sups to-night with a harlotry' (*Oth.* 4.2.232), Bianca has no power over his movements. 'What? keep a week away? seven days and nights? Eight score eight hours?' she complains, but ultimately recognizes 'I must be circumstanc'd' (*Oth.* 3.4.173–4 and 201).

'Harlot' is used to slander assertive female behaviour. Owen Glendower describes his **daughter**'s refusal to let go of her new husband, as 'a peevish self-will'd harlotry, / One that no persuasion can do good upon' (*1HIV* 3.1.196–7). Capulet uses the same phrase to make the same implication, that his daughter is behaving dangerously like a harlot; Juliet's reluctance to obediently and automatically wed Paris is 'A peevish self-will'd harlotry' (*R&J* 4.2.14).

Perhaps because of its performance-related meanings and its associations with the whore of Babylon and Catholic idolatry in Protestant discourse, the word frequently denotes deception. The 1563 'Homily against Peril of Idolatry', for example, condemned the Catholic church as 'not only a harlot, but also a foule, fylthye, olde withered harlot' who recognized her age and ugliness so she 'doth (after the custome of such harlottes) paynt her selfe, and decke and tire her selfe' in costly garments so that their 'outward beawtie and glory' may entice lovers 'to spirituall fornication with her' (Jewel 1571: 147). Echoes of this sermon are found in Shakespeare. Apemantus's satiric prayer of grace includes 'a harlot for her weeping' in his list of things not to be trusted (*Tim.* 1.2.66). Antipholus of Ephesus calls **Adriana** 'dissembling harlot, thou art false in all' (*Err.* 4.4.101). Claudius sees that the 'harlot's cheek, beautied with plast'ring art' is just as grotesquely deceptive as his false language (*Ham.* 3.1.50). Like Hamlet, shamed by his tendency to unpack his heart with words like a whore (*Ham.* 2.2.585), Coriolanus feminizes language as a prostitution of his proper masculine identity. Having to change his tune to woo the people, he says 'Away, my disposition, and possess me / Some harlot's spirit!' (*Cor.* 3.2.111).

(c) 'The III part of the homily against perill of Idolatrie', in John Jewel's *The second tome of homilees . . . to be read in euery parishe church agreeably* (1571), is an example of Protestant propaganda that would have been widely known across early modern England. William Lambarde's historical definition is in *A perambulation of Kent; conteining the description, hystorie, and customes of that shyre* (1596, reprinted 1826). Standish Henning (2000) discusses Henry VIII's threatened statute for branding harlots. Maria Margaret Scott's biography *Representing "Jane Shore": harlot and heroine* (2005), briefly traces the literary genealogy of the harlot/heroine type, while a more detailed discussion of the legacy of the holy harlot can be found in Patricia Cox Miller (2003).

harpy, (a) a fabulous female monster from Greek and Roman mythology, having a woman's face and body and a bird's wings and claws, and supposed to act as a minister of divine vengeance.

(b) The harpy's rapacious, vengeful nature is exploited by Benedick to mock

Beatrice's outspoken behaviour as monstrous. He tells Don Pedro he would travel to the ends of the earth 'rather than hold three words' conference with this harpy' (*MAdo* 2.1.270–1). The joke will have more impact in performance if Beatrice wears a beaked mask when she derides Benedick in the masked ball. The harpy's ruthlessness lent it a hermaphrodite quality. Thomas Lodge averred that the harpy looked like the man 'whome when shee hath deuoured, and whose bodie when she hath torne, beeing assailed wyth thirst, she flyeth to the water to drinke' in which she saw her own face and remembered with grief 'the similitude of him whome shee slew' (Lodge 1596: sig E4v). Gender reversal is implicit in *Pericles* where Cleon refers to **Dionyza** as a harpy for murdering Marina and concealing it with a show of grief:

> Thou art like the harpy
> Which, to betray, dost with thine **angel**'s face
> Seize with thine eagle's talons.
>
> (*Per.* 4.3.46–8)

Ariel, who plays a harpy to condemn the 'three men of sin' Antonio, Sebastian and Alonso, in *The Tempest*, is spectacularly attractive and simultaneously rapacious as he claps his wings to make the banqueting table vanish (*Temp.* 3.3.53–4). Prospero tells him 'Bravely the figure of this harpy hast thou / Perform'd my Ariel; a grace it had, devouring' (*Temp.* 3.3.83–4). Ariel goes on to play another feminine supernatural figure in **Ceres**.
(c) The origins of Shakespeare's presentation of Ariel as the harpy from Virgil's *Aeneid*, Book III, lines 209ff or possibly Sabinus's commentary on Ovid are discussed in Bate, *Shakespeare and Ovid* (2003: 244). Thomas Lodge (1596: sig. E4v) describes the harpy's hermaphroditic nature. Roberts (1991: 98–101) discusses the harpy as an example of the monstrous feminine wild in Shakespeare.

Hathaway, Anne, (a) Born in 1555 or 1556, Anne Hathaway, who is also called 'Agnes' in the records, was the eldest of eight children of Richard Hathaway, a yeoman farmer of the village of Shottery, located at the edge of the Forest of Arden just outside Stratford on Avon. She grew up on a farm called Hewlands (now known as Anne Hathaway's cottage) where sheep farming was combined with arable farming, probably strips of land of about 30 acres. In 1581 Richard Hathaway died and left 'unto Agnes my daughter six pounds thirteen shillings four pence to be paid unto her at the day of her marriage' (Greer 2007: 14–15). In the summer of 1582 Shakespeare, who was still a minor at the age of 18, made Anne Hathaway pregnant and on 27 November the couple were granted a special licence to marry, although the licence names the bride as Anne Whateley of Temple Grafton, a mystery which has baffled Shakespeare biographers. Weis suggests it may have been the maiden name and home of Anne's mother, Richard Hathaway's first wife (Weis 2007: 51–8). Anne gave **birth** to three children, **Susanna** Shakespeare, baptized six months after the marriage, on 26 May 1583 and the twins Hamnet and **Judith**, baptized on 2 February 1585. While Shakespeare was in London,

Anne probably lived in Henley Street until 1597 when he bought New Place. The house had two barns, gardens and two apple orchards and Anne was evidently left in charge of managing the household, probably making malt, **brew**ing ale, **baking** bread and lending money while bringing up her two **daughters** (Greer 2007: 217–21). When Shakespeare died, Anne (aged 60) was not an executor of his will from which she is absent apart from the detail 'Item I gyve unto my wief my second best bed with the furniture' (*Riverside Shakespeare*, p. 1957). Rather than assuming this is a deliberate attempt to disinherit Anne, it may be evidence that Shakespeare had made a settlement about her future, along with the rest of his property, at the time when their daughter Susanna married John Hall (Greer 2007: 314–25). Greer points out that, as a **widow**, Anne had a range of options about where to live in Stratford until her death in 1623. Her epitaph, probably written by John Hall on behalf of Susanna, expresses a strong, loving relationship between **mother** and daughter:

> Ubera, tu mater, tu lac vitamque dedisti;
> Vae mihi, pro tanto munera saxo dabo?
> Quam mallem amoveat lapidem bonus angelus ore!
> Exeat, ut Christi, corpus, imago tua!
> Sed nil vota valent; venias cito, Christe! resurget
> Clausa licet tumulo, mater et astra petet.

> **Breast**s, mother, milk and life thou gavest me;
> Woe is me, for so great a boon must I give stones?
> How much rather would I that the good angel remove this slab from the
>   grave mouth,
> And thine image come forth as did the body of Christ!
> But prayers avail nothing – come quickly, Christ,
> That though shut in the tomb my mother may rise again and seek the
>   stars.

> (Greer 2007: 343)

(b) The name **Anne** appears 82 times in Shakespeare's work, and it is possible that the dramatic portraits of Anne Page and Anne Bullen, or characters like **Ophelia** who sings of losing virginity before marriage, **Constance** who laments the loss of her son, the speaker of Sonnet 57 who watches the clock for the return of a lover, and the long-suffering **Hermione**, may echo aspects of the woman Shakespeare knew for longest. The one unmistakable reference to 'hathaway' in Sonnet 145 and its octosyllabic lines, unique in the sequence, suggest this is may be an early love poem addressed to Anne Hathaway. The beloved begins by rejecting the poet with the words '"I hate"', but seeing his woe, '"I hate" she alter'd with an end' of gentle mercy (*Son*. 145: 2 and 9): and '"I hate" from hate away she threw / And saved my life, saying "not you"' (*Son*. 145: 13–14). The sonnet plays with 'Hathaway' and 'hate away' as homophones, perhaps suggesting that as well as throwing away the emotion, Anne will alter the end of her name, throwing away Hathaway in order to become Mistress Shake-speare.

(c) Germaine Greer's *Shakespeare's Wife* (2007) gives the most detailed biographical account of Anne Hathaway's family background and, drawing on records of contemporary women's lives and work in Stratford and beyond, speculates on how Anne might have responded to bringing up children in Stratford in the periods when Shakespeare was absent in London. Throughout the book, Greer draws parallels between Anne's life experiences and incidents in the texts (e.g. the death of Hamnet, and **Constance** in *King John*) (pp. 197–200) and speculates on how Anne might have responded to the publication of *Venus and Adonis* (pp. 189–92) and *The Sonnets* (pp. 252–67). Weis (2007: 172–3) discusses Sonnet 145, and makes the suggestion that Hamlet's accusations of Gertrude may echo Shakespeare's discomfort at discovering that Anne had committed **adultery** with one of his younger brothers (pp. 275–6).

Hecate, (a) an ancient Greek goddess, one of the Titans. She was **Queen** of the **Night**, the dark side of the triple-goddess who ruled over the moon and heavens as **Cynthia** or **Phoebe**, the **moon**, over the world as **Diana** and in the underworld as Hecate. Hecate was goddess of **witch**craft, of the crossroads, and the cycle of loss and deliverance. With the ability to see into the underworld, she discovered that **Proserpina** had been abducted. She appears as a character in *Macbeth* in sections often attributed to Thomas Middleton.

(b) In *Macbeth* Hecate makes a spectacular appearance as goddess of witchcraft to the three **weird sisters** who anxiously greet her 'Why, how now, Hecat? you look angerly' (*Mac.* 3.5.1). She is a high-status figure, 'the **mistress** of your charms / The close contriver of all harms' and reprimands them volubly for failing to consult her over their dealings with Macbeth (*Mac.* 3.5.2–9). This is 'that railing Hecate' or **scold** (*1HVI* 3.2.64) referred to by Talbot in order to demonize **Joan** La **Pucelle**. In *Macbeth*, Hecate promises to bring a drop of liquid, distilled from the moon's vapour and 'raise such artificial sprites' to trick Macbeth (*Mac.* 3.5.23–5). This establishes her high status as the controlling figure behind the apparitions in Act 4 Scene 1. She may exit through the air and certainly instigates two songs, 'Come away' and 'Black Spirits', the full text of which is found in Middleton's *The Witch* (1617). Hecate's appearance here and in Act 4 Scene 1 were exploited in a tradition of spectacular adaptations, begun by Davenant (Rosenberg 1978: 1–19).

Even if Shakespeare did not write the Hecate character, her influence is felt strongly earlier in the play and elsewhere in the canon. Macbeth anticipates murdering Duncan under Hecate's aegis when 'Nature seems dead and wicked dreams abuse / The curtain'd sleep'. He describes how 'witchcraft celebrates / Pale Hecate's offerings' invoking 'wither'd Murder' as well as **rape** and nightmares (*Mac.* 2.1.50–6). Macbeth looks forward to the murder of Banquo 'a deed of dreadful note' with another reference to 'black Hecat's summons' to the night (*Mac.* 3.1.41–4). Hecate is also the patroness of murder, this time by poison, in Hamlet's additional lines to 'The Murder of Gonzago'. The villain Lucianus commits himself to 'thoughts black' in the 'confederate season' of night and says that his mixture of 'midnight weeds' has been 'With Hecat's ban thrice blasted,

thrice infected' so as to make their poison immediately fatal (*Ham.* 3.2.255–60).
Hecate as nocturnal goddess is presented more neutrally as part of a cycle of loss
and rebirth in the pagan world of *King Lear* where Lear vows

> by the sacred radiance of the sun,
> The mysteries of Hecat and the night;
> By all the operation of the orbs,
> From whom we do exist and cease to be;
>
> (*KL* 1.1.109–12)

The opposition between day and night is found again in *A Midsummer Night's
Dream* where Puck summons the 'fairies that do run / By the triple Hecat's
team, / From the presence of the sun, / Following darkness like a dream' (*MND*
5.1.383–5). Although Hecate's domain is one where graves open wide, it is also
where the bride beds and conception of offspring will be blessed.
(c) Briggs (1962) studies the network of beliefs in magic and the goddess Hecate
in early modern England. Rosenberg (1978); Wilders (2004: 168–77) outlines
stage productions of Act 4 Scene 1 of *Macbeth*.

Hecuba, (a) the legendary **Queen** of Troy, **wife** of Priam and **mother** of Paris,
Cassandra, Hector, Helenus, Deiphobus, Polyxena and Troilus. Witnessing the
fall of Troy and the murder of her husband and sons under the attack of the
Greeks, Hecuba is an icon of women's suffering and loss in war. She is referred
to by Pandarus and Cressida as she passes to view the battle in *Troilus and Cressida*
(1.2.1–4) but she does not speak and need not necessarily appear on stage.
(b) Euripides's play *Hecuba* is probably the earliest dramatization of Hecuba's
fate, following the account in Homer's *Iliad*. It had been translated into Latin
by Erasmus (Gillespie 2001: 162) but Shakespeare may simply have followed the
account in Ovid's *Metamorphoses*, Book XIII, ll. 484–688 (Ovidius 2000: 332–7)
where Hecuba is found amongst the tombs of her sons:

> Queen Hecub: who (a piteous cace to see) was found amid
> The tumbes in which her sonnes were layd. And there as Hecub did
> Embrace theyr chists and kisse theyr bones, Ulysses voyd of care
> Did pull her thence.
>
> (Ovidius Book XIII, ll. 509–12, 2000: 332)

Young Lucius and **Imogen** both see Hecuba's mourning as disturbing and angry
rather than simply pitiful. Lucius compares **Lavinia**'s frenzy to what he has read in
Ovid 'I have read that Hecuba of Troy / Ran mad through sorrow' (*Tit.* 4.1.21).
Imogen seizes on Hecuba as a model of angry grief when she believes she has
found Posthumus's murdered body and rages 'All curses madded Hecuba gave
the Greeks, / And mine to boot, be darted on thee!' (*Cym.* 4.2.313–14). Because
she is mistaken, there is something absurdly extreme about her reaction that
matches well with the image of Hecuba as mad.

More restrained but equally moving pictures of Hecuba's grief are self-consciously fashioned in the players' rehearsal in *Hamlet* and the painting of Troy in *The Rape of Lucrece*. For Hamlet, Hecuba's tears focus the blurred boundaries between art and life, leading him to question his own emotional engagement with the task of revenge. Hecuba's grief at seeing Priam slain 'would have made milch the burning eyes of heaven' (*Ham.* 2.2.517) and, in turn, the player's identification with Hecuba makes Hamlet ask, 'What's Hecuba to him, or he to Hecuba, / That he should weep for her?' If he had Hamlet's cause, he would 'drown the stage with tears' (*Ham.* 2.2.559–62). Hecuba's contagious tears lead to Hamlet's plot to catch the conscience of the king. In *The Rape of Lucrece*, Lucrece searches the painting 'to find a face where all distress is stell'd' (*Luc.* 1444) and identifies with Hecuba:

> In her the painter had anatomiz'd
> Time's ruin, beauty's wrack, and grim care's reign;
> Her cheeks with chops and wrinkles were disguis'd,
> Of what she was, no semblance did remain.
> Her blue blood changed to black in every vein,
> Wanting the spring that those shrunk pipes had fed,
> Show'd life imprison'd in a body dead.
>
> (*Luc.* 1450–6)

Identifying with Hecuba and using her own 'lamenting tongue' (*Luc.* 1465) to voice Hecuba's woes allows Lucrece to realize a new form of tragic subjectivity (Kietzman 1999).

Shakespeare's satiric rewriting of the fall of Troy in *Troilus and Cressida* seems to deliberately deny Hecuba any opportunity to complain in the traditional manner. Patroclus reports that 'Queen Hecuba' has sent a letter and 'A token from her daughter, my fair love' charging him to keep his oath and not attack Troy (*T&C* 5.1.39–44) and **Cassandra** does have a prophetic vision of 'how Troy roars, how Hecuba cries out' (*T&C* 5.3.83). The only tears we hear about, however, are a perverse parody of Hecuba's iconic tragic status. Pandarus says that at Helen's joke 'Queen Hecuba laugh'd that her eyes ran o'er' (*T&C* 1.2.142–3). **Volumnia** in *Coriolanus* refashions Hecuba in her own image, rejecting the tragic lament in favour of Hecuba's pride at Hector's valour (*Cor.* 1.3.40–3).

(c) Stuart Gillespie, *Shakespeare's Books* (Continuum 2001) outlines the possible influence of Euripedes' work on Shakespeare. Lynn Enterline (2002: 152–97) discusses how the tragic mother functions as a positive model to Lucrece and Hamlet, and Mary Jo Kietzman (1999) analyses Hamlet and Lucrece's use of Hecuba as a way to access the literary tradition of complaint and, through that, new forms of action.

Helen, (a) English vernacular form of the Greek name *Helene* or Latin *Helena*, possibly deriving from *helios*, the Greek word for sun. The name became synonymous with **beauty** from classical legend, where Helen, wife of the Greek Prince

Menelaus, was abducted by the Trojan prince Paris, causing the Trojan War.

(b) Helen of Troy appears as a character in *Troilus and Cressida* and another Greek Helen(a) features in *A Midsummer Night's Dream*. In common with the usage in other early modern texts, 'Helen' and 'Helena' are interchangeable in Shakespeare, and used to fit the metre of a line. It also appears in the shortened, intimate form 'Nell' to refer to Mistress **Quickly**, Poins's **sister** (*2HIV* 2.2.140), Dame **Eleanor**, Duchess of Gloucester (*2HVI* 1.2.) and serving women in *Comedy of Errors* (3.2.111) and *Romeo and Juliet* (1.5.9). The character of Helena in *All's Well that Ends Well* may draw on a different early Christian tradition, since St Helena was the name of the mother of the Emperor Constantine, credited with having found the True Cross in Jerusalem. A belief that she had been born in Britain flourished in mediaeval England, making the Christian name very popular. Concrete reminders, such as churches like St Helen's in Bishopgate in London, kept her memory alive in early modern Protestant England. The Dauphin in *Henry VI Part I* compares Joan La Pucelle, as saviour of France, to 'Helen, the mother of great Constantine', though immediately seems to confuse the saintly and sensual associations of the name by going on to call her 'Bright star of **Venus**' (*1HVI* 1.2.142–4).

The face 'that launch'd above a thousand ships' (*T&C* 3.2.82) usually carries negative associations of inconstancy. Orlando boasts that **Rosalind** has 'Helen's cheek but not her heart' (*AYLI* 3.2.145) and Imogen's lady-in-waiting, who is called Helen (*Cym.* 2.2.1), jokes bawdily with Cloten about selling her 'good name' for gold (*Cym.* 2.3.83–4). Following the well-known classical legend, Helen is a synonym for beauty and political disaster in *Henry VI Part III* where Edward of York insults **Margaret**, remembering how she entranced both Suffolk and Henry into making a match through which England's military conquests are given away:

> Helen of Greece was fairer far than thou,
> Although thy husband may be Menelaus;
> And ne'er was Agamemnon's brother wrong'd
> By that false woman, as this king by thee.
> (*3HVI* 2.2.146–9)

In *Troilus and Cressida*, **Cassandra**'s words 'Cry, Trojans, cry, a Helen and a woe!' (*T&C* 2.2.111) proclaim Helen's name as the harbinger of disaster. Helen's appearance, delayed until Act 3 Scene 1 after the Trojan council on whether to continue the war, appears to confirm Hector's doubts that 'she is not worth what she doth cost / The keeping' (*T&C* 2.2.51–2). Her grand introduction as 'the mortal **Venus**, the heart-blood of beauty, love's immortal soul' is immediately undercut by Pandarus's question 'Who, my cousin **Cressida**?' and the servant's retort 'No, sir, Helen. Could not you find that out by her attributes? (*T&C* 3.1.32–6). Helen's attributes do not appear to include any awareness of the terrible cost of the war waged for her. Her exclusive concern with the pleasures of love can be presented as either innocent or grossly ignorant. In either case, she provides no majestic focus like **Cleopatra** in this scene, which is her only appearance in the play. Frequent references to her as 'sweet' and Paris's use of the diminutive 'Nell' (*T&C* 3.1.52) trivialize the legendary figure. A similar satiric deflation is found in *Henry IV Part II* where the futility of Falstaff's grotesque ambitions and promises are encapsulated in a mini-Trojan epic as Pistol reports the arrest of Mistress **Quickly**, the 'Helen of thy noble thoughts, / In base durance and contagious prison', whom Falstaff must rescue in revenge like Menelaus (*2HIV* 5.5.33–4).

A Midsummer Night's Dream makes active use of the name's associations with Helen of Troy as a desired and detested figure. Throughout the wooing scenes, such associations serve to reinforce the blindness of desire in which the frantic lover 'sees Helen's beauty in a brow of Egypt' (*MND* 5.1.11). When Hermia greets 'Fair Helena', Helena bitterly rejects her name. 'Call you me fair? That fair again unsay. / Demetrius loves your fair' (*MND* 1.1.180–1). The inconstancy of male desire in the forest undoes the name as a signifier of female faithlessness. The love juice transforms Lysander and then Demetrius's eyes to see her as 'Helen, goddess, nymph, perfect, divine' (*MND* 3.2.137). Helen's name is repeated 14 times by her Greek suitors, as if to emphasize connections with the legendary figure. It is frequently associated with the light or the sun, as in Lysander's 'Transparent Helena' (*MND* 2.3.103), or 'Fair Helena, who more engilds the night / Than all yon fiery oes and eyes of light' (*MND* 3.2.187–8). Like her namesake, Helena becomes an object of violent rivalry as they exit to 'try whose right / Of thine or mine is most in Helena' (*MND* 3.2.337–8). In contrast to the male characters, Helena remains constant in her determined pursuit of Demetrius. **Thisbe** refers obliquely to Helena's rewriting of the legend of inconstancy when vowing she will be faithful 'Like Helen, till the **Fates** me kill' (*MND* 5.1.197).

While frequently challenging the name's negative associations of inconstancy, Shakespeare's texts use it to signify women's open pursuit of desire, vivacity and self-determination. The 'lively Helena' is one of the guests invited to Capulet's feast (*R&J* 1.2.70) and in *Cymbeline*, Helen the waiting woman who is awake at midnight and can 'awake by four o' th' clock' contrasts with the sleepy **Imogen** (*Cym.* 2.1.1–7). Helena in *All's Well That Ends Well*, named in opposition to the virgin character **Diana**, undertakes a quest to legitimize female desire. Her name's associations with both St Helena and Helen of Troy are used to re-evaluate women's self-determined pursuit of sexual drives. Helena declares her 'idolotrous fancy' (*AWW* 1.3.97) for Bertram in the first scene, using religious language for secular passion in the male Petrarchan tradition. Lavatch's song conflates her with the 'fair face' and cause 'Why the Grecians sacked Troy' (*AWW* 1.3.70–1) but claims he is trying to rewrite the legend by celebrating one good woman in ten. Helena's experience in the play bears some similarities to that of her named saint. St Helena was of relatively lowly birth in comparison with her husband, the Roman general Constantius, and was effectively divorced by him for political reasons. As Helena knows, her quest to cure the French King and win the high-born Bertram risks labelling her with 'a **strumpet**'s boldness' (*AWW* 2.1.171). Her actions certainly offended the critic Frank Harris who saw 'a coarseness' in Helen's advertisement and pursuit of her desire, and felt 'the whole story of the play is unsuited to the character of a young girl, and perhaps no care could have made a girl charming, or even credible, who would pursue a man to such lengths or win him by such a trick' (Harris 1912: 137, 146). On the other hand, Helena's cure of the King is also interpreted as a miracle: 'a heavenly effect in an earthly actor' (*AWW* 2.3.24). As a pilgrim of love to acquire Betram's ring, redeem him and her true role as **wife**, she enacts a secular parallel of St Helena's religious pilgrimage to Jerusalem to discover the true cross.

(c) Laurie Maguire, *Shakespeare's Names* (2007: 74–119) demonstrates in detail that Helen of Troy is a cultural ghost or shadow which haunts every woman or dramatic character called Helen, arguing that the name functions like a straight-jacket in the sixteenth century. This expands Jeanne Addison Roberts' idea of Helen as a deathly presence (1991: 145–8). Carol Rutter's performance-based approach (2001: 116–23) discusses Helen of Troy as an absent icon. Frank Harris's outra-geously sexist reading of Helena in *All's Well* in *The Women of Shakespeare* (1912) draws attention to contradictions in the role and makes a largely unpersuasive case for reading the romantic plot as Shakespeare's dramatization of his relation-ship with William Herbert and Mary Fitton (pp. 133–60). Susan Snyder (1988) and (1992) discusses the significance of Helen's name in opposition to that of **Diana**. Richard Levin (2006) draws a parallel between the social ambition of the heroine in *All's Well* and Shakespeare's own. Helen Wilcox (2007) and Alison Findlay (2007: 35–45) both consider religious aspects of Helena's role. Palfrey and Stern (2007: 422–34) analyse the part of Helena in *All's Well* from the roll or script received by the boy actor.

Helena, name used interchangeably with **Helen**, frequently of the protagonists in *All's Well That Ends Well* and *A Midsummer Night's Dream*. (*See* **Helen** above.)

Hen, (a) a female common domestic chicken or fowl, and in a wider sense, the female of any bird, used figuratively of a **wife** or **woman**.
(b) Shakespeare's uses of 'hen' to describe women define them in two different ways: as comforting **mother**s or as overbearing, dominant wives. The former type most famously characterizes Lady **Macduff** and her children, the 'pretty chickens and their **dam**' (*Mac.* 4.3.218), who are deserted by Macduff in their castle or nest, which is then raided by Macbeth's soldiers. More unusually, **Volumnia**, the mother of Coriolanus, compares herself to a doting hen:

> Thou has never in thy life
> Show'd thy dear mother any courtesy
> When she, poor hen, fond of no second brood,
> Has cluck'd thee to the wars and safely home,
> Loaden with honour.
>
> (*Cor.* 5.3.160–4)

Actually, in this scene, Volumnia is more like the second kind of hen: the over-bearing woman who forces her supposed male superior into following her

directions. This type derived from Chaucer's Dame Pertelot, from folk stereotypes and popular drama such as 'The Second Shepherds' Play' of the Townley
Cycle. Leontes, who is shaken by **Paulina**'s determination to assert baby Perdita's
legitimacy, tries to shame Antigonus by calling him 'Thou dotard, thou art woman
tir'd; unroosted / By thy dame Partlet here' (*WT* 2.3.75–6). In fact, this more
accurately describes Leontes's own position. Falstaff calls Mistress **Quickly** 'Dame
Partlet the hen' (*1HIV* 3.3.52), alluding to her fuss over the alleged picking of
his pocket, but possibly also to her dominance of the tavern and thus her control
over his supplies of food and drink. Since Lady Macduff is also an outspoken critic
of her husband who 'wants the natural touch' (*Mac.* 4.2.9) in unnaturally flying
from the nest, it is possible that the hen references also hint at her kinship to the
overbearing Dame Pertelot.
(c) Pertelot appears in Chaucer's *Nun's Priest's Tale* (Chaucer 1968: 199–205)
and the stereotype of the overbearing hen appears in *The Second Shepherds' Play*
(Townley Cycle 13) in *English Mystery Plays*, edited by Happé (1975: 265–94, lines
67–108).

Hermia, (a) a character in *A Midsummer Night's Dream* whose name is a feminine
derivative of the Greek god Hermes, son of Zeus and Maia, known as 'Mercury'
to the Romans. Hermes is associated with trickery, cunning, and speed. He is the
god of traders and thieves and a messenger of the gods, depicted as a herald with
winged sandals, a hat and a wand with serpents. The name's negative connotations
carried over into early modern condemnations of Hermia as a **whore** who seduced
the philosopher Aristotle away from his studies.
(b) As the object of Lysander and Demetrius's passion, which leads them beyond
the bounds of reason and into hyperbolic expressions of love (*MND* 3.2.136–44),
Hermia's name may carry echoes of 'the most fylthy whore' of 'bawdy Aristotle'
who 'made hymnes in her prayse' (Bale 1551: Part II, sig. VIr). Robert Albott
pointed out that, notwithstanding his 'deepe philosophy and knowledge',
Aristotle 'becam a slave to faire Hermia' (Albott 1599: 76), a pattern that the male
characters comically reproduce by vowing that reason and judgement directs their
desires (*MND* 2.2.115–122).
  Hermia is dark in complexion and hair colour and short, and was probably
written for the same actor who played **Hero** and **Celia**. In her diminutive stature
as a 'puppet', 'dwarf' or 'minimus' (3.2.288 and 327–8), she physically echoes
the youthful god Hermes, and is bold to argue her case in defiance of the
god-like authority of her father in the opening scene. She is willing to 'fly this
place' (1.1.203) to trick her father rather than go through with an arranged
marriage and, like Hermes, is familiar with the love assignations of the gods. She
vows by Cupid, **Venus** and **Dido**. For the most part, however, Shakespeare's play
emphasizes the irony of her name since much of her behaviour is diametrically
opposed to the qualities of trickery, speed and change associated with Hermes and
Mercury. It is Lysander who announces and subsequently proves the quicksilver
or changeable nature of desire as 'swift as a shadow, short as any dream, / Brief as
the lightning in the collied night' (1.1.144–5) by deserting his beloved. Hermia,

by contrast, remains constant, pledging her faith 'By all the vows that ever man have broke / (In number more than women ever spoke)' (1.1.175–6). Her dream of a serpent eating her heart away constructs her as a victim rather than a trickster wielding a wand like Hermes, even though Lysander tells her, 'I will shake thee from me like a serpent' (3.2.261). **Helena**'s opinion that Hermia has played a trick in setting her suitors to woo Helena in scorn is quickly countered by Hermia's accusation that Helena is the 'juggler' and 'thief of love' who has stolen her lover's heart away (3.2.232–3). Hermia's difference from the god becomes painfully obvious when Helena tells that though her hands are 'quicker for a fray', Helena's legs are longer 'to run away' and Hermia is left alone on stage 'amazed' and not knowing what to say (3.2.342–4). Hermia is invariably associated with sweetness; Lysander's sudden rejection of her since 'a surfeit of the sweetest things / The deepest loathing to the stomach brings' (2.2.137) therefore appears all the more perverse, demonstrating how her name and role function ironically to highlight the fickle nature of love in those around her.

(c) Hammond and Scullard (1970) outline the characteristics of Hermes while John Bale (1551: Part II, sig VIr) popularizes the idea of Hermia as Aristotle's whore. Robert Greene's *Philomela* (1592: sig D1) and Nashe's *Have With You to Saffron Walden* (1596: sig. R3r), and Robert Albott (1599) continue this misogynist tradition. J. J. M. Tobin (1979) comments on it while Norman F. Holland (1979) gives a psychoanalytic reading starting from Hermia's dream. The classic study of how the play stages the breaking of bonds sisterhood, including those between Hermia and Helena, is Louis Adrian Montrose's 'Shaping Fantasies', reprinted in Richard Dutton (ed.), *New Casebooks: A Midsummer Night's Dream* (1996: 101–38).

Hermione, (a) the **Queen** of Sicilia in *The Winter's Tale*, who is accused of adultery by her husband Leontes. Her name derives from the mythological Hermione, daughter of Menelaus and Helen, and was used as a title of Demeter and **Proserpina**, so had links to seasonal mortality and renewal.

(b) Hermione is named 17 times in *The Winter's Tale*, most prominently at her trial where she is accused as 'Hermione, queen to the worthy Leontes, King of Sicilia' of high treason 'contrary to the faith and allegiance of a true subject' (3.2.12–14). In effect, the accusation kills Hermione's identity as **chaste** wife and subject when Leontes rejects he oracle's pronouncement that 'Hermione is chaste' (3.2.132). By disappearing from the stage as though dead until the final scene of the play, she encourages everyone to believe 'Hermione hath suffer'd death' (3.2.42), and Antigonus dreams of her ghost. She haunts the play through memories and through material reminders: 'the mantle of Queen Hermione's, her jewel' which are recovered from the fardel (5.1.32–3). Hermione thus fulfils her titular connection with Demeter and Proserpina, goddesses of the underworld. Proserpina, absent from the earth for six months of the year while she lives in Hades, is mentioned by Perdita (4.4.116) and Hermione's own reanimation or resurrection includes appeals to her name. The sculptor 'so near Hermione hath done Hermione that they say one would speak to her and stand in hope of an answer' (5.2.100–02). Leontes's faith inspires him to address the apparently lifeless stone with the words, 'Thou art indeed Hermione', a first signal to invoke her return to life. His observation that the real 'Hermione was not so much wrinkled' acknowledges a corporeal reality that reanimates her identity as chaste **wife** (5.3.25–9).

(c) For details of Hermione's links to Demeter and Proserpina (or Persephone) see Hammond and Scullard (1970). Stevie Davies, *Idea of Woman* (1986: 152–74) reads Hermione's connections with the Demeter / Persephone myth. Gemma Jones (1985) and Alexandra Gilbreath (2003) give accounts of playing the role in two very different Royal Shakespeare Company productions.

Hero, (a) the name of the romantic heroine of *Much Ado About Nothing* and a figure in classical mythology: a priestess of Aphrodite who lived in a tower at Sestos on the banks of the Hellespont, the narrow strait of water now called the Dardanelles, running between Anatolia (Asia Minor) and Europe. Leander, from Abydos at the other side of the strait, fell in love with Hero. He swam across every night of the summer to be with her, guided by a lamp which she lit in her tower, and persuaded her to have sex with him even though they were not married. One winter night, the wind blew out the torch, Leander got lost as he swam across. He drowned, and Hero threw herself from the tower to drown as well.

(b) Shakespeare would possibly have known of Hero and Leander's love from Ovid's *Heroides* Letters XVIII and XIX. Valentine and Proteus quickly cite Leander as a model from a 'love-book' for their own heroic conduct as lovers (*TGV* 1.1.20–6). Valentine goes on to tell the Duke that that to gain access to **Silvia**'s chamber, a rope ladder 'would serve to scale another Hero's tow'r / So bold Leander would adventure it' (*TGV* 3.1.119–20). Edward III imagines rewriting the story in more grotesque terms when he compares the **Countess** of Salisbury to the classical heroine after she has challenged him to murder his wife and her husband before he can enjoy her love:

> Fairer thou art by far than Hero was,
> Beardless Leander was not so strong as I:
> He swom an easy current for his love,
> But I will [thorough] a [Hellespont] of blood
> To arrive at Sestos where my Hero lies.
>
> (*EIII* 2.2.152–6)

Edward's Hellespont is of blood because the Countess has vowed only to surrender to his lust on condition he murder their spouses first: his own queen and the Count of Salisbury, her husband. **Rosalind** expresses a comic scepticism towards the story, telling Orlando that Leander did not die of love for Hero; he 'would have liv'd many a fair year though Hero had turn'd **nun**' and rejected him. What happened, in fact, was that he 'but went forth to wash him in the Hellespont, and being taken with the cramp was drown'd' but the story was glamorized to make 'Hero of Sestos' the cause of his tragic death (*AYLI* 4.1.100–6).

Hero, who is named 59 times in *Much Ado About Nothing*, is for the most part a silent, modest and submissive character, most unlike the classical heroine. However, her overdetermined name maps out the men's ready construction of her as a deceptive and sexually experienced woman, like the lover of Leander. It prefigures the unchaste version of Hero as a 'contaminated **stale**' (*MAdo* 2.2.25) conjured up by Don John to destroy her marriage to Claudio: 'Leonato's Hero, your Hero, every man's Hero' (*MAdo* 3.2.106). It is possible that when **Margaret** plays at being Hero at her mistress's chamber window, she is also play-acting as the classical heroine in her tower. Borachio reports that the scene is staged so that Don Pedro and Claudio will 'see me at her chamber-window, hear me call Margaret Hero' (*MAdo* 2.2.42–4). Imitiating Hero of Sestos would give a logic to Margaret's willingness to be wooed 'by the name of Hero' as she 'leans me out at her mistress' chamber window, bids me a thousand times good night' as though she were bidding farewell to Leander (*MAdo* 3.3.146–8). Benedick is certainly familiar with the story claiming that 'Leander the good swimmer' was never 'so truly turn'd over and over' in love as himself (*MAdo* 5.2.30–5).

The classical heroine effectively functions as Hero's wanton doppelgänger. Indeed, in the continuation of Marlowe's poem by Chapman, Hero of Sestos is condemned for trying to conceal her loss of virginity, making 'never **virgin**'s vow worth trusting more' (IV.258–9). Claudio likewise rages 'out on thee seeming!' (*MAdo* 4.1.56) and tells his bride

> Hero itself can blot out Hero's virtue.
> What man was he talk'd with you yesternight
> Out at your window betwixt twelve and one?
>
> (*MAdo* 4.1.82–4)

Don Pedro also recalls the clandestine meetings of Hero and Leander in reporting that Hero talked at the window with 'a ruffian' who has 'confess'd the vile encounters they have had / A thousand times in secret' (*MAdo* 4.1.91–4). Once Hero's name is cleared, she returns from the concealment of supposed death in 'glorious fame' supposedly to rid herself of the classical namesake who committed suicide along with her lover: 'one Hero died defil'd, but I do live, / And surely as I live, I am a maid' (*MAdo* 5.4.64).

(c) Mihoko Suzuki (2000: (esp.) 130–6) discusses the universal anxiety concerning women's sexuality that is represented by Hero and her connections with Hero of Sestos. Hayes (1983: 79–99), Neely (1993: 23–57), C. Cook (1986), and Findlay (2003) analyse the insecurities that lie behind Hero's fate in *Much Ado*. Melinda J. Gough (1999) compares the image of the unchaste Hero to the literary tradition of the **siren**-sorceress.

Hippolyta, (a) a character in *Midsummer Night's Dream* and Shakespeare and Fletcher's *Two Noble Kinsmen*, based on the **Amazon** queen from Greek mythology. She is sometimes identified with Antiope and in most versions of the myths she is mother to Hippolytus, lover of horses, their names deriving from *hippo*, the Greek for 'horse'. Hippolytus rejected the love of Phaedra and was punished by being dragged over the ground to death by his own horses, which had been frightened by a sea monster.

(b) Shakespeare appears to have derived the character's name from Chaucer's *Knyghtes Tale*, although Seneca's *Hippolytus* may also have influenced the choice of name for the Amazonian queen. It appears to be what Peter Holland calls a 'back-formation, a name passed back from son to mother' (Holland 1994: 144). In *A Midsummer Night's Dream* there are five mentions of Hippolyta's name, most significantly in the opening lines when it is used twice: 'Now fair Hippolyta, our nuptial hour / Draws on apace' and 'Hippolyta, I woo'd thee with my sword' (*MND* 1.1.1–2 and 16). Between these nominations are references to the moon, a silver bow, and the deferment of desires, which recall **Diana**, goddess of the chastity and allude back obliquely to Hippolyta's past as Queen of the Amazons. Theseus's address at the end of the first scene, 'Come, my Hippolyta: what cheer my love?' (*MND* 1.1.122) suggests that she has not been cheered by Theseus's judgement on Hermia or his negative depiction of a life without the society of men, worshipping the 'cold fruitless moon' (*MND* 1.1.66–73). In some productions, she has registered this non-verbally by refusing to exit with him or even slapping his face.

Remnants of Amazonian insubordination in Hippolyta may be represented in her night-time equivalent, **Titania**, Queen of the Fairies. If so, then the shaming of Titania, being forced to love an ass, can be read as a feminized, degraded parody of Hippolytus's wilful love for horses rather than a relationship with Phaedra:

> Oberon: Now, my Titania, wake you, my sweet queen.
> Titania: My Oberon, what visions have I seen!
>   Methought I was enamor'd of an ass.
> Oberon: There lies your love.
> Titania: How came these things to pass?
>   O, how mine eyes do loathe his visage now!
>
> (*MND* 4.1.75–9)

Titania's acceptance of Oberon as her lord leads into the hunting scene with Hippolyta and Theseus and thence to the wedding that finally eclipses Hippolyta's Amazonian identity.

A much more explicit account of Hippolyta's Amazonian past is given in *Two Noble Kinsman*, a play in which hunting and horses feature strongly. Hippolyta's renowned power in the hunt is immediately highlighted in an account of the Calydonian boar hunt which features her instead of Atalanta as the Amazonian huntress who drew the first blood. Hippolyta is addressed as:

> Honored Hippolyta,
> Most dreaded Amazonian queen, that hast slain
> The scythe-tusk'd boar; that with thy arm, as strong
> As it is white, wast near to make the male
> To thy sex captive.
>
> (*TNK* 1.1.77–81)

The Queen continues to praise Hippolyta's superiority to Theseus in spite of his military victory which has

> shrunk thee into
> The bound thou wast o'erflowing, at once subduing
> Thy force and thy affection; soldieress
> That equally canst poise sternness with pity,
> Whom now I know hast much more power on him
> Than ever he had on thee.
>
> (*TNK* 1.1.83–8)

The Amazons' familiarity with horses as part of their hunting is seen when **Emilia** gives Arcite the choice of any of her horses (*TNK* 2.5.54). The next thing we hear is that 'The Duke hath lost Hippolyta' because each have taken a different route into the forest (*TNK* 3.1.1–2). The Schoolmaster's blessing on the stag hunt in which he hopes that 'the ladies eat his dowsets' or testicles (*TNK* 3.5.157) gives another alarming reminder of Hippolyta's Amazonian power once on her horse. After the hunt, Hippolyta kneels to Theseus in order to plead for mercy for Palamon and Arcite: 'by strength, / In which you swore I went beyond all women, / Almost all men, and yet I yielded' (*TNK* 3.6.205–7). These words rewrite Hippolyta's military defeat, suggesting that she was not conquered but instead yielded to Theseus by her own choice. Although Hippolyta is married and remains silent in the final scene, the final victory of love over war is brought about by Emilia's horse, which crushes its unwanted rider, thus recalling the restless Amazonian power that defied enforced coupling with men.

(c) Seneca's *Hippolytus* appeared in *Seneca His Tenne Tragedies*, trans. John Studley (London, 1581). Brooks (1979: lxii–lxiii) identified this as a significant source for the play. Peter Holland (1994) traces the elusive connections between the Hippolytus story and Theseus's in *A Midsummer Night's Dream*. Boehrer (1994: 130–2) links Hippolyta with her son Hippolytus a lover of horses, as part of the play's overall strategy to construct marital unions as analogues to the sexual conjunction of people and animals (p. 131). Roberts (1991: 125–35 and 137–9) discusses Hippolyta and horses as examples of a wild zone beyond male-centred conventions. Berry (2001: esp. 213) analyses the importance of the hunt.

Hisperia, (a) Celia's **waiting-gentlewoman** in *As You Like It* whose name appears to derive from the Hesperides, nymphs of the evening in Greek mythology.
(b) Hisperia is probably so named because she was responsible for attending on Celia at bed time (2.2.5–6). She apparently overheard Celia and Rosalind's discussion about Orlando, presumably in the wrestling scene in Act 1 Scene 2, so could have been a walk-on part (*AYLI* 2.2.10–16).
(c) *See* **nymph**.

hobby-horse, (a) in plays and entertainments such as the morris, the model of a horse worn by one of the performers to mimic the movements of a skittish animal.

In human terms, the name meant a ridiculous or frivolous buffoon and, when applied to women, a **whore** or licentious person.

(b) Moth explains to Don Armado that, in fact, the term is not appropriate for women since 'the hobby horse is but a colt', a young male, as the morris performer would have been, and **Jaquenetta** is 'perhaps a hackney', a horse to be ridden (*LLL* 3.2.30–2). The two derogatory uses in Shakespeare are also singularly inappropriate. When Leontes slanders **Hermione** as 'a hobby-horse' who 'deserves a name' as lustful as a woman who has sex before marriage, Camillo firmly rejects this definition (*WT* 1.2.276–8). **Bianca** echoes Othello's mistake in assuming that the handkerchief belongs to Cassio's whore. She returns it angrily with the words 'there give it your hobby-horse. I'll take out no work on't' (*Oth.* 4.1.154–5). The use of the term 'hobby-horse', as a skittish plaything, for a prostitute is an appropriate extension of the metaphor of a dutiful wife as 'a well-broken horse' that obeys her husband 'readily going and standing as he wishes that sits upon his back' (Whateley 1617: 43). Sexual innuendo suffuses Cleopatra's exclamation, 'O happy horse to bear the weight of Antony' (*A&C* 1.5.21) and in *Henry V* the Dauphin claims 'my horse is my mistress'. Picking up on the pun horse / whores, the Constable teases him, saying 'I had as live have my mistress a jade' another name denoting a prostitute (*HV* 3.7.44–60).

(c) William Whateley, *A Bride Bush* (1617), with excerpts in Keeble (1994: 150–2), describes the dutiful wife as a horse. David Cressy (1989: 22–6) describes morris dancing.

honest, (a) This is a gendered term in early modern England. Applied to women, it was a synonym for **chastity**, carrying positive moral resonance and a sense of sincerity and respectability (deriving from 'honest' to mean persons 'holding positions of honour'). The phrase 'to make an honest woman of' meaning to marry someone after seduction comes into use after Shakespeare.

(b) Shakespeare's most playful use of the word is by the Clown in *Antony and Cleopatra* who refers to a previous customer who used the asp as 'a very honest woman, but something given to lie; as a woman should not do, but in the way of honesty', punning on 'lie' as 'speak untruth' and 'have intercourse', thus breaking the woman's honesty or chastity (*A&C* 5.2.250–3). Gobbo likewise jokes about the Moor whom he has got pregnant: 'If she be less than an honest woman she is indeed more than I took her for' (*Mer.* 3.5.46). Mistress **Quickly**'s protestations of her honesty are comically suspect. Indeed, her name may be a pun on Quick-lie (Kökeritz 1950: 242–3) suggesting her readiness for dishonesty. In response to Falstaff's insults, she claims 'I am an honest man's wife' (*1HIV* 3.3.119), later asserting that the minister thinks she is 'an honest woman and well thought on' (*2HIV* 2.4.99). As a **bawd**, however, Mistress Quickly in *Henry IV Part I* is not honest in the sexual sense, a fact which colours Prince Hal's objections to Falstaff 'Charge an honest woman with picking thy pocket!' (*1HIV* 3.3.176) and for slandering him 'before this honest, virtuous, civil gentlewoman' (*2HIV* 2.4.302).

Vives famously pointed out that honesty was the most important virtue for a **maid**, a prescription echoed by **Diana** who points out that 'the **honour** of a maid is her name; and no legacy is so rich as honesty' and 'all her deserving is a rich honesty' (*AWW* 3.5.14 and 65). When Bertram promises to show off Diana like a **commodity** to one of the other soldiers in *All's Well*, her honesty is a drawback: 'But you say she's honest', he objects. 'That's all the fault', replies Bertram (*AWW* 3.5.112–13). **Anne** Page is praised as 'As honest maid as ever broke bread' (*MWW* 1.4.160) and **Hero** is careful to devise 'honest slanders' to 'stain my cousin with' (*MAdo* 3.1.84) not slandering **Beatrice**'s chastity. Honesty matters to women of all classes. 'Would you not have me honest?' **Audrey** asks Touchstone. His argument that 'honesty coupled to beauty is to have honey a sauce to sugar' (*AYLI* 3.3.30–35) is debated by **Rosalind** and **Celia** who argue that those women **Nature** 'makes fair she scarce makes honest' (*AYLI* 1.2.41) The dangers of beauty to a maid's honesty are noted more cynically by Hamlet. Both Ophelia's lack of truthfulness and chastity are probably suspected in his question 'Ha, ha! are you honest?' and his view that her honesty 'should admit no discourse to your **beauty**' or it will be corrupted (*Ham.* 3.1.103–1).

In the case of wives, honesty or **chastity** is crucial to maintain patrilinear inheritance lines. Lancelot Gobbo relies on this distinction between male and female honesty to identify himself as 'an honest man's son or rather an honest woman's son' (*Mer.* 2.2.17). Edmund distinguishes himself from any 'honest madam's issue' or legitimate children (*KL* 1.2.9). Diana claims that her **mother** 'then was honest' in begetting her, whereas she would not be in committing **adultery** with Bertram (*AWW* 4.2.11–13). It is by Diana's 'honest aid' in the bed-trick that **Helena** is restored to her rightful position as wife and Diana kept 'herself a **maid**' (*AWW* 5.3.329–30). Chiron and Demetrius seek to attack **Lavinia**'s respectability and sense of cultural superiority as well as her body when they tell her 'we will enjoy / That nice-preserved honesty of yours' (*Tit.* 2.3.135). Honesty remains important even for the **widow**. Elizabeth Woodville rejects Edward IV's advances with the assertion 'mine honesty shall be my **dower**' (*3HVI* 3.2.72).

More often in Shakespeare's work the honesty of married women in both sexual and cultural senses is suspected. Like Lear (4.1118–23), Timon cynically wishes to reveal the hypocrisy of 'the counterfeit **matron**; / It is her habit only that is honest, / Herself's a **bawd**: (*Tim.* 4.3.113–15). Wives' sexual honesty is bound up with truthfulness and overall integrity as a source of comedy in *Merry Wives of Windsor* and tragedy in *Othello*. Testing and trickery in the former proves that 'Wives may be merry, and yet honest too' (*MWW* 4.2.105). Mistress **Ford**'s sense of fun brings her honesty into question. Master Ford fears that, 'though she appear honest to me, yet in other places she enlargeth her mirth so far that there is shrewd construction made of her' (*MWW* 2.2.221–3). He thus charges Falstaff to 'make aimiable siege to the honesty of this Ford's wife' (*MWW* 2.2.234–5), believing that 'If I find her honest I lose not my labor; if she be otherwise, 'tis labor well bestow'd' (*MWW* 2.1.238–40). The plot re-affirms her integrity as 'Mistress Ford, the honest woman, the modest wife' (*MWW* 4.2.136). The tragic version of such testing in *Othello* places the false appearance of honesty in Iago against its true incarnation in **Desdemona**. Othello's uncertainty, 'I think my wife be honest and think she is not' (*Oth.* 3.3.384), deftly nurtured by Iago, quickly gathers weight, erasing all but a last hope 'she may be honest yet' (*Oth.* 3.3.433). Othello charges her 'Swear thou art honest' (*Oth.* 4.2.38); **Emilia** vows 'For, if she be not honest, chaste, and true' then 'the purest' **wife** is 'foul as slander' (*Oth.* 4.2.17–18). Doubts about Emilia's own honesty are raised in the words of **Bianca** who asserts 'I am no strumpet; but of life as honest / As you that thus abuse me' (*Oth.* 5.1.122–3).

Only in the late romance of *The Winter's Tale* is female honesty fully endorsed. The word has associations of respectability and high status as well as sexual honesty when Leontes challenges his courtiers to judge Hermione 'a goodly **lady**' but then to add ''Tis pity she's not honest, honorable'. Her appearance of respectability is only superficial 'without-door form' (*WT* 2.1.66–9). **Paulina**, too, links the word with **honour**able status, complaining against the injustice of locking up 'honesty / And honor from the access of gentle visitors' (*WT* 2.2.10). She uses her own honesty to refute Leontes's charge that she is a **bawd**, and challenges his authority:

> I am as ignorant in that as you
> In so entit'ling me; and no less honest
> Than you are mad; which is enough, I'll warrant,
> (As this world goes), to pass for honest.
>
> (*WT* 2.2.70–3)

Paulina's observation that all human honesty is compromised is taken up by Autolycus, who uses the term sarcastically to refer to **gossips** as 'five or six honest wives' (*WT* 4.4.273). In contrast, **Marina** maintains that honesty is a definitive characteristic of the sex insisting that the **Bawd** must be 'An honest woman or not a woman' (*Per.* 4.2.83–5). Marina asks to be placed 'amongst honest women' rather than at the brothel (*Per.* 4.6.205) and 'chances into an honest house' (*Per.* Gower 5.2).

(c) Amussen (1988: 104) notes the gendered nature of honesty in early modern England. Rosemary Kegl (1994: 77–126) argues that *Merry Wives of Windsor* sympathetically demonstrates women's resistance to the idea of measuring a wife purely by her sexual honesty. Helge Kökeritz (1950) argues for a pun on Mistress Quickly as 'quick-lie', conflating lack of sexual purity and falsehood. For further reading *see* **chastity**.

honour, (a) a word with the general meaning of high esteem, reverence or respect, especially to those of exalted worth or rank by birth or by office, including the term 'your honour' for judges. Honour is also a strict allegiance to what is due or right. Of women, honour was a synonym of sexual **chastity**, purity and reputation for virtue in early modern England. Occasionally 'honour' is used independently of the physical body as a mark of female integrity.

(b) Masculine and feminine honour are very different entities in Shakespeare's texts. For male characters, physical prowess – especially martial skill – and loyalty are marks of honour. The soldier is 'jealous of honor', seeking reputation 'even in the cannon's mouth' (*AYLI* 2.7.151–3) as Hotspur does, although interestingly, he feminizes honour. She is both the powerful **moon** and a drowning **damsel** that he must rescue. Like a chivalric hero, he will 'pluck up drowned honor by the locks / So he that doth redeem her thence might wear / Without corrival all her dignities' (*1HIV* 1.3.201–7). Masculine honour is action-based, to be 'plucked' (*1HIV* 1.3.201) or dismissed as insubstantial 'air' (*1HIV* 5.1.135) whereas for women in Shakespeare it is inherent and embodied. In a few cases it is not connected to sexuality. **Celia** swears loyalty to **Rosalind** 'by mine honor' (*AYLI* 1.2.21); it is a mark of status when Dame **Eleanor** Cobham, the 'nobly born' **Duchess** of Gloucester is to be 'Despoiled of your honor in your life' as a punishment (*2HVI* 2.3.9–10), and Aaron shrewdly observes of **Tamora** 'upon her wit doth earthly honor wait' (*Tit.* 2.1.10). Other references to female honour all allude implicitly to sexuality. There is undoubted irony in Troilus's description of **Helen** as 'a theme of honor and renown / A spur to valiant and magnanimous deeds'. As an adulteress, she cannot embody honour personally; she is therefore only a catalyst to produce honour in men (*T&C* 2.2.199).

Virginity is, without any need for activity, a mark of honour. 'The honor of a maid is her name' (*AWW* 3.5.12) **Mariana** counsels **Diana**. Honour expresses the **Princess** of France's pride in her chastity when she swears 'by my maiden honor, yet as pure / As the unsallied lily' (*LLL* 5.2.352). Diana says her honour is just as valuable as Bertam's ancestral family ring, arguing that for the sake of honour, he should respect it:

> Mine honor's such a ring,
> My chastity's the jewel of our house,
> Bequeathed down from many ancestors,
> Which were the greatest obloquy i' th' world
> In me to lose. Thus your own proper wisdom
> Brings in the champion Honor on my part,
> Against your vain assault.
>
> (*AWW* 4.2.45–51)

The physical metaphors of **jewel** and **ring** for honour (found also in *Cymbeline* 1.4.130–51 and in *Merchant of Venice* 5.1.223–32) draw attention to its material base and appropriately advertise the social resonances of the word: its associations with wealth and nobility. Queen **Elizabeth**'s virginity is miraculously immortal since 'from the sacred ashes of her honor' James I will arise (*HVIII* 5.4.45).

The idealization of virginity as honourable implicitly defines sex as dishonourable, a fall from perfection, a pollution of purity. When Bertram 'fleshes his will in the spoil of her honor' (*AWW* 4.2.16–17), Diana will be 'corrupt' (*AWW* 3.5.73). **Virgin** honour is thus very vulnerable. In flirting, one must be sure that 'with the safety of a pure blush thou mayst in honor come off again' (*AYLI* 1.2.28–9). Through no fault of her own, **Hero**'s reputation is damaged when Claudio claims 'She's but the sign and semblance of her honor' (*MAdo* 4.1.34). **Thaisa** coyly plays on the sexual meaning of 'honour' alongside the social meaning of 'honours' as civil courtesies, telling the knights that she will fulfil the 'honor' of introducing each of them 'to preserve mine honor' (*Per.* 2.2.13–16). Laertes warns **Ophelia** 'weigh what loss your honor may sustain' if she believes Hamlet's protestations of love too easily, loses her heart and her virginity (*Ham.* 1.3.29–32). **Julia**'s oath of love is 'her honor's pawn' (*TGV* 1.3.47) and she is anxious to know 'How with mine honor may I undertake / A journey to my loving Proteus' (*TGV* 2.7.6–7), referring to physical safety and public reputation. **Portia** manages more confidently by surreptitiously taking on the title 'your honour' through her disguise as Bellario, the lawyer. Thus when she tells Bassanio, 'Now by mine honor which is yet mine own' and vows she will take Bellario as her bedfellow, her honour refers here to the masculine authority she plans to keep as well as to the virginity she can opt to yield or retain as she chooses (*Mer.* 5.1.232–3).

Rape is the most violent means to dishonour a woman. Prospero condemns Caliban for seeking to 'violate / The honor of my child' (*Temp.* 1.2.348). Cloten likewise goes to 'violate' Imogen's 'honor' (*Cym.* 5.5.284–5). When Silvia is captured by outlaws, Proteus assures her they 'would have forc'd your honor and your love' (*TGV* 5.4.22). *The Rape of Lucrece* offers a detailed exploration of how a woman responds to her dishonoured state. Arguably, Lucrece does not own her honour at all. She realizes that in entertaining Tarquin to uphold Collatine's honour, she is paradoxically 'guilty of thy honor's wrack' (*Luc.* 841–2) since 'thine honor lay in me' (*Luc.* 834). Without it she has 'no perfection of my summer left' (*Luc.* 837). Although she is confident that she is still mentally chaste, she decides on suicide, the destruction of her polluted body, as the only means to regenerate her lost honour:

> My honor I'll bequeath unto the knife
> That wounds my body so dishonored.
> 'Tis honor to deprive dishonor'd life,
> The one will live, the other being dead.
> So of shame's ashes shall my **fame** be bred,
> For in my death I murder shameful scorn:
> My shame so dead, mine honor is new born.
> (*Luc.* 1184–90)

As Lucrece's fate demonstrates, the sexual integrity and reputation of married women affects others directly, lending honour a value above life. Hermione points out at her trial that life, like grief, is only a transient quality, 'not a straw' (*WT* 3.2.43) but 'for honor, / 'Tis a derivative from me to mine, / And only that I stand for' (*WT* 3.2.42–4). If Hermione is 'honor-flaw'd' (*WT* 2.1.143) her children will be dishonoured in a very literal way because of doubts over their royal birth. She is determined to defend 'mine honor / Which I would free' (*WT* 3.2.110–11). The Bastard in *King John* likewise exclaims 'Heaven guard my mother's honor and my land' (*KJ* 1.1.70) since his inheritance is at stake. Honour as public reputation must be protected. In *Comedy of Errors* Antipholus of Ephesus is warned that his suspicions 'draw within the compass of suspect / Th' unviolated honor of your wife' (*Err.* 3.1.87–8). In *Measure for Measure* the Duke assures Mariana his plot has been 'the safeguard of your honor' to protect her reputation (*MM* 5.1.419).

The maintenance of married women's honour is celebrated in *Edward III* and *Merry Wives of Windsor.* Edward promises that the **Countess** of Salsibury's refusal to yield to his sexual advances gives her 'honor's fame / Which after ages shall enrich thee with' (*EIII* 2.2.297–8). Ford assures his wife 'Now doth thy honor stand . . . As firm as faith' (*MWW* 4.4.8–10). Mistress **Ford**'s honour shines brightly: 'She dwells so securely on the excellency of her honor' that 'she is too bright to be look'd against' (*MWW* 2.2.242–5). In contrast, **Tamora**'s adultery with Aaron 'doth make your honor of his body's hue / Spotted, detested and abominable' (*Tit.* 2.3.73–4).

Olivia's vow 'by maidhood, honor, truth and everything' (*TN* 3.2.150) demonstrates not only the importance of honour, but how it functions as a broader signifier for female integrity (*TN* 3.1.162). **Isabella** 'having the truth of honor in her' rejects Angelo's proposal (*MM* 3.1.150) and is praised for keeping her 'well-defended honor' (*MM* 5.1.402). The term indicates high status as well as integrity. Olivia's very self-esteem is at risk, she complains, in telling Cesario 'Have you not set mine honor at the stake / And baited it with all the unmuzzled thoughts / That tyrannous heart can think?' (*TN* 3.1.118–20). Honour lasts beyond fertility into middle and old age. Caesar vainly tries to mitigate the insult of conquering **Cleopatra** himself by excusing her affair with Antony as an enforced love that made 'scars' upon her honour, 'constrained blemishes' to her integrity (*A&C* 3.13.62–3). Helena observes the **Countess** of Rossillion's 'aged honor cites a virtuous youth' (*AWW* 1.3.210). Diana's **mother** believes dishonour is contagious, that her own 'age and honor / Both suffer under this complaint we bring' publicly against Bertram (*AWW* 5.1.162). **Helena**'s honour is not gendered in the usual way but derives from assertive merit, a more masculine type of behaviour and integrity where 'honors thrive / When rather from our acts we them derive' (*AWW* 2.3.131–6). She recognizes that in daring to cure the King she risks being branded with 'a **strumpet**'s boldness', dishonoured (*AWW* 2.1.171). Helena's virtue 'Is her own dower' but the King must give 'honor and wealth' since her unconventional behaviour and ignoble birth means she has no honour in the traditional feminine or courtly senses.

Female honour is the glue that binds the State together in *Cymbeline*. Contemplating **Imogen**'s beleagured fortunes, an unnamed lord entreats 'The heavens hold firm / The walls of thy dear honor; keep unshak'd / That temple, thy fair mind' so that she may enjoy Posthumus and 'this great land' (*Cym.* 2.1.62–5). Nevertheless, because female sexual integrity is impossible to prove, it is an unstable foundation for honour. Desdemona is 'protectress' of her honour but 'her honor is an essence that's not seen' as Iago observes. His view that 'They have it very oft that have it not' (*Oth.* 4.1.14–17) capitulates a collapse of faith in female integrity that causes tragedy. The dishonouring of women by male violence or insecurity is a recurrent pattern in Shakespeare's texts, making examples of honour, even when compromised, all the more admirable.

(c) Dusinberre (1996: 33–9) discusses Humanist theories of honour as an influence on Shakespeare. More general studies are Watson (1960) and Council (1973). Alice Shalivi (1972) and Michael Hattaway (1994: 121–36) consider dishonourable treatments of women in the problem plays. Kehler (1996) reads Imogen as focus for the play's redemptive interrogation of honour. Carol Cook (1986) discusses the gendering of honour and reputation. *See also* **chastity** and **honest**.

hostess, (a) a woman who lodges and entertains guests, sometimes commercially in a public place such as a tavern or an inn. Commercial entertainment leads to the derogatory sense of the hostess as prostitute.
(b) Shakespeare's two tavern keepers are Mistress **Quickly**, hostess of the Boar's Head in Eastcheap, and **Marian** Hacket, the 'fat **ale-wife** of Wincot' who authoritatively beats Christopher Sly out of the doors of her house for breaking glasses and plans to have him arrested (*Shrew* Ind. 1–11 and 2.22–5). His revenge is to 'rail upon the hostess of the house' in his drunken sleep and to accuse her of selling short measures (*Shrew* Ind. 2.85–8). A 'hostess' is also the keeper of the George and Dragon, the public house alluded to in *King John* (*KJ* 2.1.289). As manager of the Boar's Head Tavern, Mistress Quickly, like Marian Hacket, has absolute authority over who enters or is ejected from the building. 'Hostess, clap-to the doors! Watch to-night, pray to-morrow' (*1HIV* 2.4.276–8), Falstaff asks her and she obviously has power to bar Pistol (*2HIV* 76–96). Launce vows that a man is 'never welcome to a place till some certain shot be paid and the hostess say "Welcome!"' (*TGV* 2.5.7).

John Earle's early seventeenth century character sketch of 'A Handsome Hostess' remarks that 'Her Lips are your welcome and your entertainment her company, which is put into the reckoning too, and is the dearest parcel in it' (Earle 1934: 71). As Earle's description implies, the hostess's involvement in commerce and entertainment often calls her **chastity** or **honest**y into question. Innuendo runs through Falstaff's jokes 'Is not mine hostess of the tavern a most sweet **wench**?', Hal's question 'What a pox have I to do with my mistress of the tavern?' and Falstaff's reply 'Thou hast call'd her to a reckoning many a time and oft' (*IHIV* 1.2.40–50). Thersites disparagingly says the stupid Ajax 'ruminates like an hostess that hath no arithmetic but her brain to set down her reckoning' (*T&C* 3.3.252–4). All these jokes betray an insecurity about the hostess as a figure who controls male pleasure. Antipholus of Ephesus directly connects the word with prostitution when he vows to give the gold chain to the **Courtezan** 'to spite my wife / Upon my mine hostess there' (*Err.* 3.1.219).

Diana's **mother** in *All's Well* is a cameo of the hostess who provides a different kind of lodging for holy pilgrims. She says 'I know your hostess / As ample as myself' (*AWW* 3.5.42–3) implicitly suggesting generosity as well the fact that she knows herself fully. High-born hostesses include the **Countess** of Salisbury who welcomes Edward III 'enter our homely gate' and thereby rouses his passion for her (*EIII* 1.2.124) and Queen **Hermione** who defines herself as Polixenes' 'kind hostess' rather than his gaoler in keeping him at the Sicilian court (*WT* 1.2.60). Duncan famously greets Lady **Macbeth** as 'our honor'd hostess!' a role she pretends to live up to in humbly offering service, but one which fits ill with her ambitions (*Mac.* 1.6.10–18). When he greets her 'by the name of most kind hostess' he defines her domestically. Lady Macbeth's betrayal of her role as 'Fair and noble hostess' (*Mac.* 1.6.24) is just as heinous as Macbeth's betrayal of his kinsman. Her parody of the high-status role reaches a climax in the banquet scene where 'our hostess keeps her state', sitting at the high table rather than descending to welcome the guests (*Mac.* 3.4.5–6). This is the role **Perdita** finds it difficult to fulfil. The Shepherd's wife, by contrast, was the ideal 'hostess of the meeting' at the sheepshearing festival:

> This day she was both pantler, butler, cook,
> Both **dame** and servant; welcomed all, serv'd all
> Would sing her song and dance her turn; now here,
> At upper end o' th' table, now i' th' middle;
>
> (*WT* 4.4.56–64)

Perdita reluctantly takes on 'the hostess-ship o' the day' to greets the guests (*WT* 4.4.71–2).

The difficulties of hospitality, a key issue in *Rape of Lucrece*, are summed up in Lucrece's words 'A woeful hostess brooks not merry guests' (*Luc.* 1125).

(c) John Earle's 'A Handsome Hostess' is Character L in *Microcosmographie* (1628, reprinted 1934: 71–2). Judith M. Bennett (1996: (esp.) 34–7) discusses women's contributions to the brewing industry and the cultural misogyny that blamed them for sins arising from drunkenness. Fiona McNeill (2007: 58–9) and Steven Earnshaw (2000: 22–8) include Mistress Quickly in their accounts of working class women and pub culture. Daryl W. Palmer (1992) presents a full-length study of dramatic representations of hospitality including discussions of women as hostess in the comedies and tragedies alongside work on royal progresses. J. P. Dyson (1963) examines the parody of hospitality in the banquet scene and Lady Macbeth's role as hostess.

housewife, (a) a woman, usually married, who manages the affairs of her household. The housewife is the **mistress** of a family although younger girls sent out to service learned the art of housewifery. In a positive sense, with the adjectives 'careful' or 'good', housewife carries associations of careful domestic economy. However, elision of *w* and of the final *f*, *v*, meant that the name was sometimes shortened to *huzzif* or *huzzy*, which, especially in combination with the words 'idle' or 'light' carried deprecatory meanings of lewdness or worthlessness.

(b) The opposition between good and bad housewives derived from the Bible where Proverbs 14 pointed out that 'every wise woman buildeth her house: but the foolish plucketh it down with her own hands' (Prov. 14.1). Proverbs defined a virtuous woman whose 'price is far above rubies' as the perfect housewife who feeds and clothes the inhabitants, spins and produces textiles, buys land and grows vines, is charitable to the poor and speaks only wisdom and kindness (Prov. 31.10–26). 'She looketh well to the ways of her household, and eateth not the bread of idleness. Her children arise up and call her blessed, her husband also and he praiseth her' (Prov. 31.27–8). Positive images of housewifery as maternal comfort in Shakespeare include Timon of Athens's reference to **Nature** as a 'bounteous huswife' who feeds her children (*Cym.* 4.3.420), and **Imogen** as **Fidele** whose 'neat cookery' (*Cym.* 4.2.51) justifies Belarius's insistence 'you must be our huswife' (*Cym.* 4.2.45). Sonnet 143 gives an affectionately realistic picture of the challenge women faced in trying to realize the ideal of the multi-tasking housewife:

> Lo as a careful housewife runs to catch
> One of her feather'd creatures broke away,
> Sets down her babe and makes all swift dispatch
> In pursuit of the thing she would have stay;
> Whilst her neglected child holds her in chase,
> Cries to catch her whose busy care is bent
> To follow that which flies before her face,
> Not prizing her poor infant's discontent
>
> (*Son.* 143: 1–8)

Women's domestic labour was accorded considerable value. Thomas Trusser, detailing *Five hundreth pointes of good husbandrie* (1573) for example, observed 'Where huswife and huswifery joineth with thease / there wealth in abundance is gotten with ease' (Trusser 1573: sig. Fol. 6). References in Shakespeare pick up on the housewife's productivity. Mistress **Quickly**, Dr Caius's maid, gives a full account of her housewifely duties: 'I keep his house: and I wash, wring, brew, bake, scour, dress meat and drink, make the beds and do all myself' (*MWW* 1.4.95–7). Even the high-born Countess of Rosillion accepts the need for labour to avoid being classified as the housewife who eats her bread in idleness. She reprimands herself for wasting time: 'I play the noble housewife with the time / To entertain's so merrily with a fool' (*AWW* 2.2.60).

Following Proverbs 13, spinning and **sew**ing were iconic signifiers of house-wifely virtue. Queen **Katherine**, fearing that she will lose her role as queen and as Henry's wife, pointedly tells the Cardinals Wolsey and Campeius, 'You Graces find me here part of a huswife / (I would be all) against the worst may happen' (*HVIII* 3.1.24–5). She refers not only to the sewing that would suit a 'poor weak woman' as well as a **queen**; in the words 'I would be all' she also clings to the idea of being bound to her husband. In *Coriolanus*, **Valeria** calls **Volumnia** and **Virgilia** 'manifest housekeepers' since they are sewing (*Cor.* 1.3.51–2), and warns that she must make them 'lay aside your stichery' and 'play the idle huswife' by going out of doors as a **gossip** to visit a lady in childbed (*Cor.* 1.3.69–70). John Dod and Robert Cleaver pointed out: 'wee call the wife Huswife, that is house-wife, not a street-wife, one that gaddeth up and down' (Dod and Cleaver 1598: 223).

The ambiguity of housewife as dutifully hardworking and **wanton** produces comic eroticizations of housework. Sir Toby Belch mocks Sir Andrew's hairstyle by saying 'I hope to see a huswife take thee between her legs, and spin it off'

(*TN* 1.3.103–4). Puck voyeuristically enjoys bewitching the milk to 'bootless make the breathless housewife churn' (*MND* 2.1.37). Rosalind says Phoebe 'has a huswife's hand' (*AYLI* 4.3.27), purportedly referring to its brown, rough texture but also meaning that Phoebe is wanton since she has written openly declaring her love. The 'overscutched huswives' that Swallow sings to are prostitutes (*2HIV* 3.2.341). These jokes tune into early modern insecurities about the housewife's power as the effective controller of goods coming in and going out of the house (Korda 2002: 49). Lady **Fortune**, renowned for her fickle inconstancy, is referred to as a 'huswife' (*HV* 5.1.85) and 'false housewife' (*A&C* 4.15.44) by male characters. Nevertheless, in **Rosalind**'s opinion, she is also the 'good housewife Fortune' for giving women gifts (*AYLI* 1.2.34). The more extreme analogy of housewife with concubine (Cawdry 1609: C2) informs Iago's claims that women are 'players in your huswifery and huswives in your beds' (*Oth.* 2.1.112–13). The bad housewife, like the **courtezan**, has an open house; good housewifery involves restricting access to the house and, by implication, to the woman's body. Pistol, about to depart for the wars, commands 'Let housewifery appear; keep close'. He insists that Mistress Quickly 'look to my chattels and my moveables', including herself it seems, and 'trust none' (*HV* 2.3.48–53). Although early modern women did exercise considerable authority as mistresses of their households, as this quotation wryly acknowledges, for most housewifely virtue was officially a protection of male interests.

(c) Cawdry (1609), Dod and Cleaver, *A Godly Forme of Householde Government* (1598), Markham, *The English Housewife* (1622), and William Gouge, *Of Domesticall Dueties* (1622) all discuss the housewife as an important but often unstable figure. Natasha Korda (2002: 15–51) gives an excellent introduction to the ways women contributed to the domestic economy and how they were perceived, before considering **Katherina** (*Shrew*), **Mrs Ford and Mrs Page** (*MWW*), **Isabella** (*MM*) and **Desdemona** (*Oth.*). Mario DiGangi (2003) discusses the role of hostess in the comic household in Shakespeare. Amy Louise Erickson (1993: 53–5) considers housewifery as a form of apprenticeship for young women sent out to learn in other families. See also Crane (2000) for discussion of women's productive and reproductive roles in the household.

Imogen, (a) a character in *Cymbeline*, daughter of the King and a name which appears for the wife of Leonato in the opening stage direction of *Much Ado* in the First Folio text. The name 'Imogen' is thought to be a misreading of the double 'nn' as 'm' by the compositors of the First Folio. The name may derive from Holinshed's *Chronicles*, where Innogen is the name of Brute's wife. It is of Celtic origin, from Gaelic *inghean*, '**girl**' or 'maiden'.

(b) It appears that Shakespeare abandoned the idea of characterizing **Hero**'s mother who appears in the primary source *Much Ado*, and that the stage direction for Innogen's entrance are a remainder of his original intention. In *Cymbeline*, the **Princess** introduces herself by name when she pledges herself to Posthumus with her **mother**'s ring, a token that he must only part with to woo another wife 'when Imogen is dead' (1.1.114). From the moment of this pledge, Imogen's faith is put on trial, first in the plot of Iachimo in which she is associated with **Lucrece** and **Philomel** (2.2.12–14 and 44–6). When Posthumus commissions her murder, believing her unfaithful, she undergoes a symbolic death and rebirth of identity like **Hero** and **Hermione**, adopting the name **Fidele**. Imogen is unworldly: 'divine' (2.1.57), the gods' 'own' (5.1.16), but also the '**mistress**' of Britain (5.1.20), a symbol of the nation. When Posthumus openly repents his sin in doubting and supposedly murdering her, his recitation of her name invokes the rebirth of her feminine identity:

> O Imogen!
> My queen, my life, my wife! O Imogen
> Imogen, Imogen!
>
> (*Cym.* 5.5.225–7)

When Cymbeline recognizes 'the tune of Imogen' (5.5.238) in her voice and

Posthumus takes her in his arms, the play concludes with the reunion of husband and wife and royal family.

(c) Anna Jameson (2005: 226–45) famously praised Imogen as 'the most perfect' of Shakespeare's heroines (p. 226), combining goodness, affection, intellect and passion (p. 245). Shapiro's *Gender and Play on the Shakespearean Stage* (1994: 173–98) considers the role's derivation from the folk myths of the mysterious shipwrecked boy who turns out to be a prince, and the faithful wife who cross-dresses to serve her lord as a page (p. 182). Harriet Walter (1993) writes about playing 'Imogen in *Cymbeline*'. Nancy K. Hales, 'Sexual Disguise in *Cymbeline*' (1980) examines Imogen's cross-dressing. Bonnie Lander, 'Interpreting the Person: Tradition, Conflict and *Cymbeline's* Imogen' (2008) gives an astute reading of Imogen as a contradictory site in which external forces acting on and shaping the interior life collide with internal forces acting on and shaping the external world. This argument for a politically informed humanist reading also surveys Victorian critical responses to Imogen and performers' impressions of the role.

Innogen, *see* **Imogen**

Iras, (a) one of Cleopatra's two women in *Antony and Cleopatra*, less voluble than **Charmian**.

(b) Plutarch's *Life of Antony*, Shakespeare's source, explains that as a woman of Cleopatra's chamber, Iras 'friseld her heare and dressed her head' and that Cleopatra is found dead with 'one of her two women, which was called Iras, dead at her feet' (Plutarch 1579: 295). Shakespeare combines these associations at the end of the play when Iras and Charmian dress the **Queen** in her royal attire for suicide. Although, earlier, Iras joins the lively Charmian in teasing Alexis (*A&C* 1.2.70–74), she appears more serious. More quickly than Charmian, Iras realizes the full significance of Antony's death for Cleopatra – 'she's dead too, our sovereign' (4.15.69) – and for her household. Iras sets the tone for the final tragedy with the words 'Finish, good lady, the bright day is done, / And we are for the dark' (5.2.193–4). Having attired the Queen and kissed her farewell, Iras leads the way to the dark, in being the first of the three women to die (5.2.292–8).

(c) Sir Thomas North, 'The Life of Marcus Antonius' (1579) in Bullough, Vol. V (1964) gives details of Iras's role. Elizabeth A. Brown (1999) offers a detailed analysis of the scenes featuring Charmian and Iras as part of Cleopatra's household in comparison with that of Elizabeth I and her waiting women in '"Companion Me with My Mistress": Cleopatra, Elizabeth I and their Waiting Women'.

Iris, (a) goddess of the rainbow who acts as Juno's messenger, and appears as a character in the betrothal masque for Miranda and Ferdinand in Shakespeare's *The Tempest*.

(b) Iris functions like a chorus and stage manager in the betrothal masque, introducing herself as **Juno**'s 'wat'ry arch and messenger' (*Temp.* 4.1.71–2). The design for Iris in Jonson's masque *Hymeniae*, the probable source for *The Tempest*, presents Iris as wearing a rainbow-coloured costume (Gardiner 1976: 25).

Although she does not sing, she has the most lines in the masque. Iris cues the entrance of **Ceres**, and then brings news of **Venus** and Cupid whom she met in the clouds (*Temp.* 4.1.92–101). The stage direction that Juno and Ceres '*send Iris on employment*' (*Temp.* 4.1.124 SD) confirms her role as she proceeds to summon the Naiads or **Nymphs** followed by the reapers, directs them to put on their straw hats, and dance 'in country footing' (*Temp.* 4.1.128–38). Shakespeare's texts seem to enjoy word play on the 'distempered messenger of wet / The many-color'd Iris' who brings tears to Helena's eyes (*AWW* 1.3.151–2). Queen **Margaret** assures her lover Suffolk that wherever they are in the world, 'I'll have an Iris that shall find thee out' (*2HVI* 3.2.407).

(c) Judith Gardiner, 'Shakespeare's *The Tempest* IV.1.76–82 (Iris and Hymen)' (1976) compares the character in Shakespeare to that in Jonson and to the figure of Hymen, usually costumed in yellow. For the representation of a court masque in *The Tempest*, see Wickham (1975), McNamara (1987) and Lindley, *The Court Masque* (1984: 47–59).

Isabella, (a) the name of a character in *Measure for Measure* and in the shortened form 'Isabel', an off-stage character who is the mistress of Lavatch in *All's Well*. 'Isabel' is a Spanish version of 'Elizabeth', imported into France and then to England. It was a royal name, borne by Edward II's French-born queen, Isabel of France (d. 1270), daughter of Philip le Beau, King of France, and mother of Edward III who is mentioned at the opening of *Edward III*. It is also the name of the French Queen, wife of Charles VI, who appears in the final scene of *Henry V*, though she is not named. Richard II's queen, again unnamed, is also called Isabel.

(b) Since Isabella is a version of **Elizabeth** it is possible that allusions to royal Isabellas in *Henry V* and *Edward III* paid compliments to Elizabeth I. In the former, the name is used to justify a claim to the throne via the female line starting with 'fair Queen Isabel' grandmother of King Lewis the Tenth X (actually St Louis IX), which Shakespeare took from Holinshed (Bullough Vol. IV, 1968: 379). Through a maternal line 'the line of Charles the Great / Was re-united to the crown of France' (*HV* 1.2.84–5). The Salique Law is abused again by the French in *Edward III*, where Isabel of France's claim to the French crown has been wrongly passed over because they believe the realm 'Ought not admit a governor to rule / Except he be descended of the male' (*EIII* 1.1.24–5). This implicit foreign threat to Elizabeth's right to rule and appoint an heir is roundly critiqued by the play. Indeed, Isabel's son Edward III who was born from 'the fragrant garden of her womb' lays his claim to France via the maternal line (*EIII* 1.1.11–25). This Isabel of France and Edward II were depicted in one of the banners in Elizabeth I's funeral procession (Chettle 1603: sig. F2v).

The memory of Elizabeth as powerful **Virgin** Queen may also have informed the depiction of Isabella in *Measure for Measure*. The character is introduced as 'Gentle Isabella' (*MM* 1.4.7), the name she uses to introduce herself (1.4.23), but her absolute commitment to chastity above even saving her brother's life seems to contradict the typical feminine virtues of softness, flexibility and self-sacrifice.

Charlotte Lennox, writing in 1753, for example, notes that 'Isabella absolutely refuses and persists in her refusal to give up her Honour to save her Brother's Life' thus becoming 'a mere vixen in her Virtue' (Thompson and Roberts 1997: 17–18). 'Isabella' and 'Isabel' are used interchangeably in the text to fit the metre. The character authorizes her apparently harsh decision by using her name: 'Then, Isabel, live chaste, and, brother, die; / More than our brother is our chastity' (*MM* 2.4.184–5). This, and her introduction at the beginning of this scene as 'Isabel, a sister' (*MM* 2.4.2) may invoke Isabel of France (sister of St Louis IX and daughter of Blanch who appears in *King John*), who was canonized in 1521. Like Elizabeth I, Isabel refused offers of marriage from several suitors to continue her life of virginity. She ministered to the sick and poor of Paris and founded a convent of St Clare's and followed their rule, but like Isabella in the play, never became a fully professed **nun** (Delaney 1983: 257–8). Isabella or Elizabeth of Portugal (1271–1336) also became a Franciscan tertiary and was canonized in 1626 (ibid.: 159). Shakespeare's Isabella probably recalls the cult of virginity and female agency fostered by these saints, and by Elizabeth I and its perpetuation in the recruitment of Englishwomen as nuns (Findlay 1998: 32–45). Dr Johnson recognized Isabella's integrity 'when we consider her not only as a virgin but as a nun' (Geckle 1971: 163). The text defines her in this religious tradition as 'a thing enskied and sainted / By your renouncement' (*MM* 1.4.34–5), and in the company of a sisterhood of 'fasting maids, whose minds are dedicate / To nothing temporal' (*MM* 2.2.154–5).

Although Richard II's queen is not named as Isabel, she is indirectly associated with the cult of sisterly enclosure when Richard tells her 'Hie thee to France, / And cloister thee in some religious house / Our holy lives must win a new world's crown' (*RII* 5.1.22–4).

Isabella's progress through *Measure for Measure* may dramatize the dissolution of Elizabethan virginal authority into Jacobean patriarchal rule in 1604. She is persuaded by Mariana to compromise her absolute commitment to chastity and plead on her knees for the life of Angelo:

> Mariana: Sweet Isabel, take my part!
> Lend me your knees . . .
> > Isabel!
> Sweet Isabel do yet but kneel by me,
> Hold up your hands, say nothing; I'll say all.
> They say best men are moulded out of faults . . .
> O Isabel! will you not lend a knee?
>
> > > (*MM* 5.1.436–42)

Isabella does kneel and asks 'Let him not die' (*MM* 5.1.448). Following this, an invitation to further compromise is offered in the Duke's proposal: 'for your lovely sake, / Give me your hand and say you will be mine' (5.1.491–2), although Isabella never replies and the text gives no clue as to her non-verbal response. The Victorian critic Jameson reads the proposal positively, as an escape from the cloistered convent 'which may stand here poetically for any narrow and obscure situation in which such a woman might be placed' (Jameson 2005: 109) and authorizing women's entry into public life.

Lavatch's request to marry Isbel (a Scottish variant of the name) in *All's Well* is similarly defined as 'to go to the world' or leave the **Countess** of Rosillion's household where they serve (*AWW* 1.3.17). There may be a joke on the usual royal associations of the name when he admits 'I have no mind to Isbel since I was at court' because 'our Isbels a' the' country are nothing like your old ling and your Isbels a' th' court' (*AWW* 3.2.12–14).

(c) Henry Chettle, *Englands Mourning Garment* (1603) describes Isabella of France's banner at Elizabeth's funeral. Diana E. Henderson (2000) labels Queen Isabel in *Henry V* as 'the disappearing queen' and, in an attempt to rectify this, examines interpretations of the role on stage and in film. Excerpts from Charlotte Lennox, *Shakespear Illustrated*, 3 Vols (London: 1753–4) appear in Ann Thompson and Sasha Roberts (eds), *Women Reading Shakespeare* (1997: 15–21). Anna Jameson's *Shakespeare's Heroines* (2005: 98–110) compares Isabella to **Portia** as a character of intellect and reads her marriage to the Duke positively as an entry to public life which Jameson sees as the proper sphere for Isabella's talents. Natasha Korda (2002: 159–92) reads Isabella in relation to poverty and property. Daryll Gless (1979), Barbara Baines 'Assaying the Power of Chastity in *Measure for Measure*' (1990: 283–301), Jessica Slights and Michael Morgan Holmes, 'Isabella's Order: Religious acts and personal desires in *Measure for Measure*' (1995: 263–93), and Findlay (1998: 32–45) discuss Isabella in the context of convents. Jeanie Grant Moore (1991) analyses the role of Queen Isabel in 'Queen of Sorrow, King Of Grief: Reflections and Perspectives in *Richard II*' and Helen Ostovich (2007) discusses the Marian iconography of Isabel and Elizabeth I in '"Here in this garden": The Iconography of the Virgin Queen'. Palfrey and Stern (2007: 434–52) analyse the part of Isabella in *Measure for Measure* from the roll or script received by the boy actor. Paola Dionisotti and Juliet Stevenson discuss their experiences of playing the role in Rutter (1988: 26–52).

Isis, (a) a goddess of ancient Egypt, wife and sister of Osiris, alluded to in *Antony and Cleopatra*. Isis was associated with resurrection and natural seasonal cycles in the myth of Osiris's murder, where she collected the scattered body parts that had been cast into the river Nile. Shakespeare would also have known the name as that of the upper part of the river which runs through Gloucestershire, Wiltshire and Oxfordshire, whose confluence with the river Thame at Dorchester (Oxfordshire) makes the Thames.

(b) The myth of Isis and Osiris as Queen and King of Egypt was included in Plutarch's *Philosophie* (1603) which Shakespeare probably read and St Augustine's *Of the City of God* (1610: 660–3). Her reputation for immortal and sovereign command was popularized in texts like *England's Parnassus* where Spenser calls her 'A goddesse of great power and soueraigntie' (Abbott 1600: 153). Isis's name was written with the hierglyphic sign for 'seat' or 'throne' suggesting that she may have personified the power of the throne (Wilkinson 2003: 146). When **Cleopatra** imitates Isis, this is therefore an expression of agency, independent of Rome. She and Antony are 'publicly enthron'd' (*A&C* 3.6.5) and:

> She
> In th' abiliments of the goddess Isis
> That day appear'd; and oft before gave audience,
> As 'tis reported, so.
>
> (*A&C* 3.6.16–19)

These details derive from Plutarch's *Lives*, which observes 'for Cleopatra, she did not onely weare at that time (but at all other times els when she came abroad) the apparell of the goddess Isis, and so gave audience unto all her subjects, as a new Isis' (Bullough Vol. V 1964: 291). Samuel Brandon's play *The Vertuous Octavia* (1598) also shows Cleopatra making herself into an 'immortall queene' by attiring herself as Isis (Brandon 1598: sig. D6).

Plutarch reports that Isis is 'no other thing but generation' (Plutarch 1603: 1304–5), her power over fertility and renewal is alluded to when **Charmian** prays to her as goddess of the Egyptian 'people' (*A&C* 1.2.70–1) in relation to Alexas's marriage, teasingly asking 'sweet Isis' to let him marry a sexually frigid or infertile woman who will die to be succeeded by even worse wives (1.2.63–9). Cleopatra's imitation of Isis is appropriate in the latter part of the play where she is responsible for mourning over Antony and rebuilding or re-membering his reputation, as Isis did in immortalizing Osiris by collecting his body parts and revivifying his generative power. The play's frequent references to the connection between sex and death in relation to Cleopatra probably draw on the duality of mourning and renewal in the Isis myth. Cleopatra's formal royal attire in the suicide scene where she says 'I have / Immortal longings in me' (*A&C* 5.2.280–1) is her Isis costume. Holland's translation of Plutarch comments on its dual significance: 'the habiliments of *Isis* be of different tinctures and colours: for her whole power consisteth and is emploied in matter which received all formes, and becometh all maner of things, to wit, light, darknesse, day, night, fire, water, life, death, beginning and end' (Plutarch 1603: 1318). The *Lives* also notes that Cleopatra's monument was next to the Temple of Isis (Bullough Vol. V 1964: 291). Since Isis was a famous Egyptian icon of motherhood nursing her son Horus (Wilkinson 2003: 147) or 'as one would say, the nourse that suckleth and feedeth the whole world' (Plutarch 1603: 1301), this image of the goddess may have been invoked by Cleopatra's line about the asp 'Dost thou not see my baby at my breast / That sucks the nurse asleep' (*A&C* 5.1.309–10). Isis's connection to the River Nile in the myth, and her identity as the source of renewal and wisdom is recalled in the name of the English river in Drayton's *Poly-Olbion* (1612) which describes the Muses sitting 'at *Isis* bountious head / As telling that her fame should through the world be spread' and 'tempted by this flood', her eager response 'to Oxford after came / There likewise to delight her bridegroom, lovely *Tame*' (Drayton 1612: 43).

(c) Richard H. Wilkinson, *The Complete Gods and Goddesses of Ancient Egypt* (2003) and Plutarch 'Of Isis and Osiris', which is in *The Philosophie, commonlie called the*

Morals, translated by Philemon Holland (1603: 1286–319), detail the range of meanings in the myth and the iconographic power of Isis as mourner, beneficent force, generative power, moon, mother and nurse. St Augustine (1610) tells how Isis was associated with the Nile, was the patroness of seasonal renewal equivalent to Ceres, and carried a horn of plenty. Allusions to Isis in Robert Abbott, *England's Parnassus* (1600), Brandon's *The Vertuous Octavia* (1598), a closet drama, and Michael Drayton's discussion of the River Isis in *Poly-Olbion* (1612: 43) illustrate her popular image in early modern England. Adelman (1992: 183–4 and 337) deepens the earlier analyses of Isis's significance in *Antony and Cleopatra* given by Harold Fisch, '"Antony and Cleopatra": The Limits of Mythology' (1970), Michael Lloyd, '"Cleopatra as Isis" (1959) and Barbara Bono, *Literary Transvaluation: from Vergilian Epic to Shakespearean Tragicomedy* (1984: 199–213).

Jailer's daughter, (a) an anonymous but significant character in the sub-plot of *The Two Noble Kinsmen*, a section for which Fletcher and Shakespeare do not appear to have worked from any existing source.

(b) The lack of proper name for this character may have something to do with her isolation from the social worlds of both the main and sub-plots in her passion for Palamon and her subsequent madness. Without a name, a social indicator and a means to interact with the other characters, she has no social identity and spends most of her scenes occupying an idioverse dominated by her own thoughts and particular speech forms. Even in the first scene, her extravagant praise of Palamon and Arcite marks her off from the more mundane discourse of her father and her wooer. She speaks in soliloquies. These are strikingly direct and emotive; a stream-of-consciousness effect is created by the juxtaposition of immediate sensory impressions and fantasy. Abandoned by Palamon in the wood at night, she reports, 'I am very cold, and all the stars are out too', then registers 'The sun has seen my folly' and moves to 'Where am I now? / Yonder's the sea, and there's a ship' (3.4.1–5). Her father is disturbed to hear her speak 'So far from what she was, so childishly, / So sillily, as if she were a fool' (4.1.39–40).

Another reason that the character has no name may be that, in spite of the emotive nature of her soliloquies, she is a generic type from ballad tradition. Ballads are what give structure to her consciousness (as they do for **Ophelia**) even in madness. In her first soliloquy, she writes herself into the tradition of ballads such as 'The Fair Flower of Northumberland' (1597) in which the daughter releases a prisoner (here Scots) who promises to marry her but then deserts her, telling her he is already married. The Jailer's daughter sets out her own situation knowingly, in terms of the typical ballad plot:

> Why should I love this gentleman? 'Tis odds
> He never will affect me. I am base,

My father the mean keeper of his prison,
And he a prince. To marry him is hopeless;
To be his **whore** is witless. Out upon't!

(2.4.1–5)

In spite of her protestation and her knowledge, she is unable to move outside the tragic ballad plot and, by the end of the speech, vows to set him free so that he will love her. After she has released him and is impassioned with love, she already imagines a tragic future to be sung over by 'honest-hearted **maid**s' who will 'tell to memory my death was noble, / Dying almost a martyr' to love (2.6.15–17). She even anticipates the lesson that will come from the dramatization of her story, echoing the ballad's message 'maids will not so easily / Trust men again' (2.6.20–1). When her wits turn, she turns to a ballad of the maid-turned-page type as an answer to her loss of Palamon, singing she will 'go seek him through the world that is so wide' (3.5.23) At the same time, her desire and her self-awareness come strikingly to the fore as she longs for 'a prick now' to push her breast against and sing like **Philomel** the nightingale (3.5.25–6). The wooer says he has heard her, like **Ophelia**, singing snatches of old songs, 'Palamon is gone / Is gone to th' wood to gather mulberries'. She continues to make sense of the world by referring a sea-ballad (3.5.59–71) and back to her fantasy of following Palamon across the seas (4.1.144).

The Jailer's daughter is diagnosed with melancholy (4.3.50), a condition the Doctor believes can be cured by sexual intercourse with her wooer impersonating Palamon. Throughout these wooing scenes, the Jailer's daughter insists on continuing in song (5.2.12) and in spite of the potential for comedy in the deception, the final lines as the couple exit to bed are remarkably poignant:

Daughter: But you shall not hurt me.
Wooer: I will not, sweet.
Daughter: If you do, love, I'll cry.

(5.2.111–12)

For all her bawdy fantasies, the Jailer's daughter remains innocent and nervous about losing her virginity. Her uncensored speech allows her to speak directly to the fears and hopes of adolescent spectators.

(c) The ballad 'The Flower of Northumberland' is found in Thomas Deloney's *The pleasant historie of John Winchcomb in his yonguer yeares called Jack of Newbery* (1626: sigs. F3–G1v). For discussion of early modern perceptions of madness, see Michael MacDonald, *Mystical Bedlam* (1981). Susan Green (1989) offers a study of the part. Carol Thomas Neely (1991) and (2004: 69–98), Maurice Charney and Hannah Charney (1977) draw comparisons with other mad women in Shakespeare's plays. Douglas Bruster (1995: 277–300) brilliantly argues that the character registers the change between traditions of folk-drama and the newer, court-based entertainments that Fletcher wrote.

Jane, (a) a name associated with poor women who were often involved in sexual service to higher-class men.

(b) Jane Nightwork is a whore whom Justice Shallow recalls from the Windmill, a brothel in St George's Fields, in his youth (*2HIV* 3.2.194–210). The fact that she had a husband, Old Nightwork, and a son, Robin Nightwork, when Shallow met her 55 years before, suggests that the brothel was a family buisness in which she was a **bawd**. Jane Smile is another poor woman, a milkmaid, with whom Touchstone had bawdy relations. He admits bringing his sword 'a night' to her and kissing of her batler (a butter paddle, used in dairy work, but here probably with bawdy innuendo), and the teats of the cows she milked (*AYLI* 2.4.48–50). He goes on to refer contemptuously to the chanting of rhymes by the 'butter-woman' on her way to market (*AYLI* 3.2.95).

(c) *See also* Jane **Shore**.

Jaquenetta, (a) the character of a dairy woman in *Love's Labour's Lost*, beloved of both Costard and Don Armado.

(b) The character is variously introduced as a '**wench**' (*LLL* 1.1.262, 283), 'a **child** of our grandmother **Eve**, a female' and 'a **woman**' (1.1.262–4); a '**damsel**' (1.1.290), a '**virgin**' (1.1.295); and a '**maid**' who will serve Costard's turn, or give him sexual satisfaction (1.1.297), before she is finally named as 'Jaquenetta, and Jaquenetta is a true girl' (1.1.312–13). What is clear, in spite of these various titles, is that Jaquenetta is not of the same class as the other women in the play. She is the '**dey-woman**', the dairy woman (1.2.131). Don Armado recognizes that her foot is 'basest' (1.2.169) and poses as King Cophetua addressing the beggar maid **Zenelophon**, 'as witnesseth thy lowliness' (4.1.79–80), but cannot help falling in love with her like Touchstone with **Audrey**. Possibly, like Audrey, 'the country maid Jaquenetta' (3.1.131) is meant to be 'foul' in which case her name may carry associations with the toilet like the male form Jaques / Jakes. It is also possible that the diminutive form 'Jaquenetta' was chosen to rhyme with 'a letter' in the scene where the letters are mistaken (4.1.53–8). The love token Don Armado carries is 'a dishclout of Jaquenetta's' (5.2.714). In spite of her low birth and her inability to read, 'Jaquenetta (so is the **weaker vessel** called)' (1.1.272), is still able to mock Don Armado with as sharp a tongue as the French noblewomen who visit Navarre's court (1.2.132–44). Whether virgin or not at the outset of the play, she is, by the end of it 'quick with child', and Don Armado vows to become a farmer and 'hold the plough for her sweet love three year' (5.2.884–5). Her involvement with Costard suggests that it may be his child, in which case Jaquenetta's story rewrites conventional ideas about female promiscuity and cuckoldry (Kehler 1997).

(c) Patricia Parker (1993: 435–83) discusses the importance of status inversion and scatalogical humour including reference to Jaquenetta's name (p. 472). Dorothea Kehler (1997: 305–12 (esp.) 306–7) argues that Jaquenetta's relationship with Armado inverts conventional condemnations of cuckoldry and female promiscuity.

Jessica, (a) a character in *The Merchant of Venice*, daughter to Shylock the Jew, who elopes to marry the Christian Lorenzo. The name may derive from *Jesca* or *Iscah* in the Bible and is first used by Shakespeare.

(b) The biblical name Jesca (Gen. 11.29) appears to refer to a niece of Abraham. It may be that Shakespeare chose Jessica as the name of Shylock's daughter because of its Jewish origins since it nearly always appears next to a term referring to her racial identity. Shylock, anxious to establish the difference between himself and the Christian Bassanio, punctuates his speech by calling Jessica's name, as though trying to imprison her linguistically as well as confine her to the house:

> What, Jessica! – thou shalt not gurmandize,
> As thou hast done with me – What, Jessica! –
> And sleep and snore, and rend apparel out; –
> Why, Jessica, I say!
>
> (2.5.3–7)

Although Shylock tells her 'lock up my doors, Jessica' and swears 'by Jacob's staff' (2.5.36), Lancelot prophetically warns her 'There will come a Christian by / Will be worth a Jewess' eye' (2.5.42–3). From the beginning of the play, Jessica's name has been sandwiched between references to her Jewish parentage and a Christian future. Lancelot refers to 'my old master the Jew' and 'my new master the Christian' before promising to deliver a message to 'gentle Jessica' (2.4.17–19). From her elopement with Lorenzo, Jessica's name marks her difference. At Belmont, Gratiano introduces them as 'Lorenzo and his infidel' (3.2.217) without even naming Jessica, and tells Nerissa to 'cheer yond stranger, bid her welcome' (3.2.237). Perhaps the role of 'stranger' draws indirectly on Shakespeare's acquaintances with Jewish women and interracial marriage. The name Barbara means stranger (*see* **Barbary**) and the cousin of **Aemilia** Lanyer (a candidate for the **Dark Lady**) was 'Barbario Bassanio', who was 'wieff of Iunerent Locatello, merchaunt of Venice' (Green 2006: 548). Aemilia Bassano was herself married to a Christian, Alphonso Lanyer. Aemilia's own doubtful parentage as the daughter of the Venetian Baptista Bassano and the Englishwoman Margaret Johnson 'my reputed wieff' (Lanyer 1993: xv) is perhaps the source of Lancelot Gobbo's jokes that the only 'bastard hope' of Christian salvation for Jessica is to hope that 'your father got you not, that you are not the Jew's daughter' (5.3.6–12). Lancelot teases Lorenzo for marrying a Jewess, converting Jews to Christians and raising the price of pork (3.5.33–5).

(c) Woods in Lanyer, *Poems of Aemelia Lanyer* (1993) and David Lasocki with Roger Prior (2005) and Martin Green (2006) give autobiographical details about the Jewish Bassano family. Ephraim (2008: 133–52) has a chapter on Jessica and Leah in her book-length study of stage representations of the Jewish woman. Nevo (1980: 115–41) reads Jessica's elopement as a focus of elements that trouble comic harmony while Camille Slights (1980) reads Jessica's elopement positively. Mary Janell Metzger (1998) provides a sensitive analysis of Jessica in relation to the perceptions of Jews in early modern England. Janet Adelman (2003) discusses the difficulties of conversion for Jessica. Paul Gaudet (1986) considers the options for staging Jessica's silences, especially in Act 5.

jewel, (a) a precious stone or other valuable material (gold or silver) fashioned into a decoration to wear, but also used as part of courtly discourse to praise a mistress and, metaphorically, to mean a woman's chastity.

(b) The jewel displays wealth and status in the metaphor 'on the finger of a throned **queen** / The basest jewel will be well esteem'd' (*Son.* 96.5–6), which may derive from Shakespeare's own observation of the bejewelled person of **Elizabeth** I. It is used as a simile to express the worth of a **mistress** in courtly love discourse, a tradition which Romeo follows faithfully by describing **Juliet** as one who 'hangs upon the cheek of night / Like a rich jewel in an Ethiope's ear; / Beauty too rich for use, for earth too dear!' (*R&J* 1.5.45–7). Orlando's praise of his mistress in such set terms is critically rendered somewhat stiff through the repetition of his forced rhymes by the living voice of **Rosalind**:

> From the east to western Inde,
> No jewel is like Rosalind.
> Her worth, being mounted on the wind,
> Through all the world bears Rosalind.
>
> (*AYLI* 3.2.88–91)

Jewels were given as tokens of loyalty and love in the rituals of courtship in both a romantic sense and in order to please Elizabeth I as royal mistress, although in Shakespeare's texts, the frequent misplacing of such valuable objects heightens the artifice involved. The French noblewomen in *Love's Labour's Lost* expose the superficial nature of the men's courtly wooing by swapping gifts. The King's claim to know the **Princess**: 'by this jewel on her sleeve' betokens a wider ignorance of the women as people rather than as objects (*LLL* 5.2.455). The jewel referred to is a pearl, symbolic of purity, and demonstrates how the word and object function as metaphors of female virtue. Pearls formed a significant part of Elizabeth I's iconography as **Virgin** Queen, for example.

The metaphoric description of female **chastity** as a jewel is an attempt to render something imperceptible into something concrete, tenable, exchangeable. **Diana** says 'My chastity's the jewel of our house, / Bequeathed down from many ancestors' (*AWW* 4.2.46–7), presumably referring to a line of chaste wives and daughters bequeathed by men. Baptista refers to **Desdemona** as his 'jewel' a beautiful ornament to be given rather than a desiring subject (*Oth.* 1.3.195). **Miranda** has been taught that her modesty – her chastity and reputation for chastity – is 'the jewel in my dower', the most valuable thing she owns (*Temp.* 3.1.54). **Marina** maintains her chastity so steadfastly that Boult determines to 'take from you the jewel you hold so dear' (*Per.* 4.6.155).

The value of a woman's virginity and the material wealth of her **dowry** are blurred in the jewel as fetish. Hortensio points out that 'in Baptista's keep my treasure is. / He hath the jewel of my life in hold, / His youngest daughter, beautiful Bianca' (*Shrew* 1.2.118–20). Hortensio's predatory interest in **Bianca** is perhaps not primarily financial, but his words do draw attention to her position as **commodity**: co-heiress to Baptista's wealth, and to the traffic in women that the play advertises so explicitly. Claudio's dual interest in **Hero**'s wealth and her person are clearly signalled when he asks 'Can the world buy such a jewel?' to which Benedick replies 'Yea and a case to put it into' (*MAdo* 1.1.181–2). Claudio's first question to Don Pedro is 'Hath Leonato any son my lord?' (*MAdo* 1.1.294). When, in *The Two Gentlemen of Verona*, Valentine effusively celebrates

> she is mine own,
> And I as rich in having such a jewel
> As twenty seas, if all their sand were pearl,
> The water nectar, and the rocks pure gold.
> (*TGV* 2.4.169–72)

The spectacular flourish of Petrarchan praise also recognises the material reality that **Silvia** is heiress to the Duke of Milan. The most notable reversal of the conventional romantic trafficking is in *A Midsummer Night's Dream* where **Helena**'s pursuit of her beloved leads to the happy but mystifying conclusion where 'I have found Demetrius like a jewel / Mine own and not mine own' (*MND* 4.2.191–2).

Because jewels are a fetish, a trope for sexuality, the physical giving (and receiving) of ornaments is more dangerous for women than for men. Jewel imagery in *Twelfth Night* shows that once **Olivia** sends her **ring** in chase of Cesario her sexuality is at large, likely to be appropriated by anyone, even her steward Malvolio who fantasizes about playing with 'some rich jewel', having left Olivia sleeping in bed (*TN* 2.5.48–60). When Queen **Margaret**'s lover Suffolk is banished, her passionate reference to taking 'a costly jewel' (a heart surrounded by diamonds) from her neck and throwing it in the sea implies that their affair started on the voyage to England (*2HVI* 3.2.106–8). He calls her heart 'a jewel lock'd into the woefull'st cask / That ever did contain a thing of worth' when saying goodbye (*2HVI* 3.3.409–10). The mnemonic power of jewels is exploited in Shakespearean plots when tokens are exchanged. The deft exchange of **rings** in the romantic plot of *Merchant of Venice*, for example, allows **Portia** to remain mistress of her sexuality, and implicitly her house, even though she is married to Bassanio. She teases him to not let the doctor near the house because 'Since he hath got the jewel that I loved' she will be as free as Bassanio in giving her body and wealth where she pleases (*Mer.* 5.1.223–8).

For married women, the jewel is a normally a husband's possession. **Helena**, described as 'the jeweller that owes the ring' in *All's Well* (5.3.296) is a rare exception, fashioning a plot (like Portia) and actively using her sexuality to achieve her own ends. Collatine is blameworthy for advertising 'that rich jewel he should keep unknown / From thievish ears, because it is his own' (*Luc.* 33–5). Once she has been raped, **Lucrece** asks him, 'Dear lord of that dear jewel I have lost / What legacy shall I bequeath to thee?' (*Luc.* 1191–2). The jewel metaphor is given concrete form in *Cymbeline*. Iachimo wagers: 'if I come off, and leave her in such honour as you have trust in, she your jewel, this your jewel, and my gold are yours' (*Cym.* 1.6.151–4). It is his theft of **Imogen**'s **bracelet**, 'a jewel that too casually / Hath left mine arm' (*Cym.* 2.3.141–2) as she laments, which constitutes evidence for the loss of her chastity. Iachimo produces it triumphantly, telling Posthumus 'be pale' before begging leave 'to air this jewel' (*Cym.* 2.4.96–6).

In the case of wives whose husbands neglect them, the jewel's mnemonic power is used to stress continued worth. **Adriana** employs an elaborate jewellery trope to describe her husband's infidelity as malleable gold encasing her, complaining 'I see the jewel best enamelled / Will lose his beauty; yet the gold bides still / That others touch' (*Err.* 2.1.109–12). In *Henry VIII* **Katherine**'s value is expressed in material terms. Divorce is 'a loss of her / That like a jewel, has hung twenty years / About his neck, yet never lost her lustre' (*HVIII* 2.2.30–32). Jewel as staged object and as fetish combine to bring a happier resolution in *The Winter's Tale* where **Hermione**'s 'jewel' is sent into banishment along with the baby **Perdita**. The recovery of Queen Hermione's lost 'jewel about the neck of it' (*WT* 5.2.33) precipitates her reincarnation from a statue-like form, frozen by Leontes' abuse, into the warm flesh of his chaste wife.

(c) Scarisbrick (1994), Arnold (1988: 93–8) and Felicity Heal, 'Giving and Receiving on Royal Progress' (2007: 46–62 (esp.) 55–62) give material details about early modern jewellery and its use in royal courtship. Spurgeon (1935: 242) considers jewel imagery in Shakespeare. Traub's chapter 'Jewels, statues and corpses: containment of female erotic power' (1992: 25–49 (esp.) 39–43), discusses fetishization of female sexuality in *Othello* and *Winter's Tale*.

Joan, (a) a generic name for a woman of the lower class, a feminine form of 'John' contracted from the Old French *Jo(h)anne*, and the name given to the character of the French saint Joan of Arc (Joan La **Pucelle**) in *Henry VI Part I*. Joan was also the name of four of Shakespeare's relatives and of a female English pope who, according to mediaeval anti-Catholic legend, reigned for three years in the 850s.

(b) Joan is the typical kitchen maid in the concluding song of *Love's Labour's Lost*, where 'greasy Joan doth keel the pot' (*LLL* 5.2.929). Berowne captures the name's generic, lower-class meaning in his maxim 'Some men must love my **lady**, and some Joan' (*LLL* 3.1.205), a distinction echoed by the newly knighted Bastard in *King John*, who boasts 'now I can make any Joan a lady' (*KJ* 1.1.84). There is comedy of paradox when the tinker Christopher Sly wonders whether he should address his lady 'Joan Madam?' (*Shrew* Ind. 2.110). Queen **Margaret** refers to a hawk called Old Joan in the competition between the nobles in *Henry VI Part II*. Given the very loaded status battle, this may be an oblique slight on her rival **Dame Eleanor**, the Lord Protector's wife, whose imminent downfall she has plotted.

The characterization of Joan of Arc in *Henry VI Part I* relies on the low-birth tradition. Joan La Pucelle (the **maid**) announces herself as 'by birth a shepherd's **daughter** / Untrained in any kind of art' (*1HVI* 1.2.72). While St Joan of Arc claimed to be guided by saints, the character claims her mission from the **Virgin**, who 'willed me to leave my base vocation / And free my country from calamity' (*1HIV* 1.2.80–1). The French victoriously delare that 'Joan La Pucelle shall be

France's saint' (*1HIV* 1.6.29) after capture of Rouen. Their belief in the 'holy maid' (*1HIV* 1.2.50–1) and her apparently miraculous defeat of Talbot makes her something of an enigma in the early part of the play, a quality suggested by her other name: 'Excellent Pucelle, if thy name be so' (*1HIV* 1.2.110). The pun on **pucelle** ('maid') and and puzzel (English for 'whore') encapsulates her as a puzzle. Although she repeatedly rejects the idea of the crown or marriage with the Dauphin, her modesty is brought into question when she appears with him at the counter-attack on Rouen. The Bastard of Orleans caustically remarks 'Tut, holy Joan was his defensive guard' (*1HIV* 2.1.49), possibly alluding to the legendary figure of Pope Joan, a primary target of Protestant anti-Catholic propaganda in the early modern period. Bale's *Pageant of Popes*, for example, describes how 'through the promptnesse of her wit and ready tongue, shee talked eloquently in publique lectours and disputations' (Bale 1574: 76), a skill borne out in the play in her conversion of Burgundy on behalf of 'fertile France' (*1HVI* 3.3.44–57). Bale, quoting Mantuan, commented scathingly that Joan of Arc had 'playde a shamelesse strumpettes parte in place of Popes degree' (Bale 1574: 77) and Shakespeare's Joan is, likewise, eventually shamed; pleading that she is pregnant in order to save her life at the hands of the English. The appearance of her spirits or familiars on stage allies her with **witch**craft rather than with miracles. The most sentimental part of her tragedy is the reminder of her humble origins in her father's appeals to her and her rejection of her name and the humble status it signifies.

> Shepherd: Ah Joan, sweet daughter Joan, I'll die with thee!
> Pucelle: Decrepit miser! base, ignoble wretch!
> I am descended of a gentler blood.
> Thou art no father no nor friend of mine
> > (*1HVI* 5.4.6–9)

The name probably held associations of kinship for Shakespeare since two of his sisters, his mother's sister and his mother-in-law, **Anne** Hathaway's stepmother, were all called Joan. Joan Hathaway continued to own land and farm from Shottery until her death in 1599 (Greer 2007: 18). Shakespeare's first-born sister who died in 1558 and his younger sister (b. 1569), who married a hatter, William Hart, were both called Joan (Weis 2007: 160). Joan Shakespeare had apparently not married a man from Stratford so she might have met William Hart in service. She reappeared in Stratford in 1600, the year before her father's death and continued to live in Henley Street with her three sons after she was widowed (Greer 2007: 206).

(c) McNeill (2007) gives an account of the lifestyle of the working class woman identified by the generic name (esp. p. 44). Early modern historical accounts of Joan of Arc in Hall and Holinshed's chronicles can be found in Bullough, Vol. III (1966). Early modern accounts of Pope Joan include John Bale, *The Pageant of Popes* (1574), Thomas Bell's *The Woeful Crie of Rome* (1605) and Henry Ainsworth's *An animadversion to Mr Richard Clyftons advertisement* (1613: 66). M. L. Stapleton (1994) reads the role in relation to the self-confident figure of **Medea** in Seneca.

Carol Rutter (2006: (esp.) 190–6), traces a brief theatre history of the role and Fiona Bell (2004) offers an actor's perspective on Joan of Arc's role played alongside that of Margaret of Anjou. *See also* **pucelle**. Information about Joan Hathaway and Joan Shakespeare are found in Greer (2007) and Weis (2007).

Judith, *see* **Shakespeare, Judith**

Julia, (a) a character in *The Two Gentlemen of Verona*. Julia is the feminine form of the old Roman family name 'Julius', associated with the seventh month of the year, July, which was named after Julius Caesar. A woman called Julia is mentioned in Paul's Epistle to the Romans (Rom. 16.15), and the name was borne by numerous early saints.

(b) The name's calendrical derivation associated it with heat and, with this, intense passion and madness (Berry 2003: 70). While medical advice recommended the regular letting of blood to preserve 'loue-sicke persons, from madnesse, by drawing humors from the head to the lower partes, and so expelling the same' (Gyer 1592: 36) it was quick to point out that the cure could not be administered 'in Sommer time, in an hote countrey, and in an hote and drie state of the aire: as vnder the dog-starre, and from mid Iuly to mid September; or rather to mid August' (ibid.: 89). Julia in *Two Gentlemen of Verona* seems to follow this cultural pattern. Her name functions as register of repressed passion and madness in herself and in others. The appellation 'Gentle Julia' (2.1.1) refers to her high birth, also signalled in the title 'Madam Julia' (2.5.12), rather than her personal qualities. 'Heavenly Julia' (1.3.50) draws attention to the dog-star Sirius, the supposed cause of madness when it ruled the heavens in July (Berry 2003: 76–9). Proteus names her as the origin of his distraction:

> Thou, Julia, thou hast metamorphos'd me,
> Made me neglect my studies, lose my time,
> War with good counsel, set the world at nought;
> Made wit with musing weak, heart sick with thought.
> (1.1.66–9)

Julia's name drives her to a form of madness, too. When she reads 'To Julia' on Proteus's love letter, she illogically returns it unread to Lucetta, calls her back and then tears up the letter, even though she longs to read it (1.2.35). Her name becomes a focus for her confusion as she gathers the scattered pieces noting:

> Look, here is writ 'kind Julia.' Unkind Julia
> As in revenge of thy ingratitude,
> I throw thy name against the bruising stones,
> Trampling contemptuously on thy disdain.
> (1.2.106–9)

She is poised to tear out the words 'To the sweet Julia' which Proteus's letter 'couples' to his own 'complaining names', but then folds them carefully together as if her written name can fulfil her desires to 'kiss' and 'embrace' (1.2.122–6). Proteus's wanton disregard of Julia, in spite of their protestations of love, is rhetorically figured in his casual substitution of Silvia's name for Julia's. He muses 'Julia I lose, and Valentine I lose' but focuses on what he will gain: 'For Valentine, myself, for Julia, Silvia' (2.6.19–22). When Julia cross-dresses as a page her name becomes a talisman of her original identity a verbal equivalent of the **ring** she gave to Proteus. Her name is repeated four times in as many lines when she returns the ring to Proteus and he is forced to recognize and re-acknowledge her as his betrothed:

> Proteus: At my depart
> I gave this to Julia
> Julia: And Julia herself did give it me;
> And Julia herself hath brought it hither
> Proteus: How? Julia?
>
> (5.4.96–100)

Since Julia is still cross-dressed as Sebastian, the repetition of her name is the essential signifier on which hangs the play's final celebration of heterosexual romance alongside male friendship. Julia's name thus functions as a register for the course of desire in the play through the madness of love-sickness, impetuous disguise, betrayal and misdirected passions, through to a superficial restoration of vows and faith and self-assurance.

(c) Nicholas Gyer, *The English phlebotomy* (1592: 36 and 89) outlines the connection between July and madness. Jeffrey Masten's essay on the play (2003: (esp.) 275–7) discusses Julia as a means of critically diffracting the misogyny of the play.

Juliet, (a) diminutive form of **Julia**. Name of the 13-year-old heroine of *Romeo and Juliet* and of the pregnant fiancée of Claudio, friend of **Isabella** and relation of the Provost in *Measure for Measure*.

(b) The calendrical associations of July with passion and madness (*see* **Julia**) are conjured up even more powerfully in the case of the tragic heroine Juliet. Juliet's birthday is on 31 July, Lammas Eve, which marked the official end of summer. The **Nurse**'s recollection of Juliet's weaning splits her name into the two syllables of the month, repeating the words 'Jule' and 'Ay' in a comic account that gives the impression of Juliet looking forward eagerly to sexual experience when she comes of age, even from her babyhood (*R&J* 1.3.38–57). Her childlike nature is signalled by the diminutive form Juliet. The Nurse appeals to her as 'lamb' and 'ladybird' before calling 'Where's this girl? What, Juliet!' (*R&J* 1.3.3–4). The Chorus then refers to her as 'tender Juliet' (*R&J* 2. Chorus. 4). Romeo identifies her with 'the sun' of July (*R&J* 2.2.3) rather than the chaste **moon**, implying the passion she later shows in impatiently anticipating Romeo's message 'Are you so hot?' (*R&J* 2.5.62) and his arrival at her bedchamber (*R&J* 3.2.1–31). The Friar's prophetic warning 'these violent delights have violent ends' and his caution 'Too

217

swift arrives too tardy as too slow' is immediately followed by Juliet's entrance with 'so light a foot' (*R&J* 2.6.14–16).

Juliet's connection with the month of July, a time replete with rituals of festive celebration and destruction, makes her a textual site through which linear and cyclical time converge in the drama (Berry 2003: 69). Juliet is supremely aware of the co-existence of life-creating passion and death, expressed most succinctly through the early modern pun of death as orgasm. Her corporeality is emphasized when Romeo points out that 'philosophy' cannot 'make a Juliet' (*R&J* 3.3.58) to satisfy him in banishment. Juliet appeals to the **matron** 'loving, black-brow'd **night**' to 'Give me my Romeo' and 'when I die' to cut him out as stars (*R&J* 3.2.20–1). Although Juliet's Christian name is not Romeo's enemy, on the morning after their **wedding** night, she is the herald of post-lapsarian mortality. Romeo says 'Come death and welcome! Juliet wills it so' (*R&J* 3.5.24). She threatens to stab herself in Friar Lawrence's cell, claiming 'I long to die' (*R&J* 4.1.66) and subsequently appears to have wedded Death on the morning of her marriage to Paris (*R&J* 4.5.39). When Romeo approaches the Capulet tomb, Juliet's name echoes through his lines like a knell until he beholds her 'and her beauty makes / This vault a feasting presence full of light' in a 'lightning before death' (*R&J* 5.3.85–90). Montague's promise of a memorial to ensure that there will 'no figure at such rate be set / As that of true and faithful Juliet' (*R&J* 5.3.301–2) exploits rhyme to establish her as the first of the two lovers in the tragic story of 'Juliet and her Romeo' (*R&J* 5.3.310).

The character in *Measure for Measure*, introduced as 'Madam Juliet' (*MM* 1.2.115) is processed across the stage bearing the signs of too much 'immoderate' liberty or passion in her pregnant body (*MM* 1.2.125–7). Claudio points out that their sexual encounter 'with character too gross is writ on Juliet' (*MM* 1.2.155). She admits freely that their sin was committed 'mutually' (*MM* 2.3.27) and the Provost implies the heat of her immoderate desire in his report that the 'flaws of her own youth / Hath blister'd her report: she is with child' (*MM* 2.3.11–12). Like her tragic namesake, this character is also a focus for the convergence of sex, conception and death. Her words 'Must he die tomorrow? O injurious love / That respites me a life whose very comfort / Is still a dying horror' draws attention to the cycle of mortality (*MM* 2.3.40–2).

(c) Anna Jameson (2005: 124–49) acknowledges that 'intensity of passion' and 'singleness of purpose' best characterize Juliet's tragic role (p. 125). Carolyn E. Brown (1996) surveys critical discussion of Juliet, reading maturity and skill in the character. Robert Watson and Stephen Dickey (2005) discuss Juliet in relation to Tereus and the legacy of rape.

Juno, (a) a Roman goddess, daughter of Saturn and Rhea, **wife** and sister of Jupiter (or Jove) and **queen** of the gods on Mount Olympus. Her name is the Latin feminine form of 'Jove' ('Hera' in Greek). Juno is the goddess of **marriage** and protector of wives. In classical mythology she is jealous of Jupiter's adulterous affairs with mortals. Her sacred bird was the peacock. She appears as a character in *The Tempest*.

(b) Juno's arrival in *The Tempest*'s betrothal masque is ceremoniously celebrated. She '*descends*', lowered in a small chariot supposedly drawn by peacocks (from the gods in the Globe or an equivalent elevated position in Blackfriars or Court venues). Her commanding status is emphasized by the titles 'her sovereign Grace' and 'Highest Queen of State' (*Temp.* 4.1.72 and 101), perhaps alluding to the role Queen **Anna of Denmark** played in court masques. Cleopatra wishes that she had 'great Juno's power' to lift Antony up to her monument (*A&C* 4.15.34). Shakespeare seems to have seen Juno's gait as a special mark of her majesty. This is what **Ceres** notes in *The Tempest* (4.1.102) and Pericles praises his wife **Thaisa**'s 'wand-like' straight stature and 'pace like Juno' (*Per.* 5.1.109, 111). These representations follow the popular image of the goddess as majestic, as outlined by Robert Albott: '*Iuno*, the daughter of *Saturne*, vvas the sister and wife of *Iupiter*, borne at Argos, some write at Samos, the Goddesse of marriage, and therefore called *Pronuba*, likewise *Lucina* for child-**birth**, the Queene of riches and honour, to whom the Pecocke is consecrated' (Albott 1599: 42).

Shakespeare's texts present Juno as a goddess of chaste married love and fertility like **Lucina**. Having excluded **Venus**, Cupid and the extramarital desire they represent from the masque, Juno confers 'honour, riches, **marriage**-blessing' on Ferdinand and **Miranda** and commands the 'temperate **nymphs**' to dance in celebration (*Temp.* 4.1.131). Thaisa's chaste desires for marriage with Pericles are signalled by her oath: 'By Juno, that is queen of marriage / All viands that I eat do seem unsavory / Wishing him my meat' (*Per.* 2.3.30–2). Although Hymen is the deity who presides over the final dance in *As You Like It*, his 'wedlock-hymn' (*AYLI* 5.4.136) begins '**Wedding** is great Juno's crown / O blessed bond of board and bed' (*AYLI* 5.4.141–2).

Juno's reputation as 'the jealous queen of heaven' (*Cor.* 5.3.46) is made most explicit in *Cymbeline* in the masque of Jupiter, whom she 'rates and revenges' for his 'adulteries' (*Cym.* 5.4.32–4). Kent and Lear swear by the opposing deities, as if to add fuel to their own conflict (*KL* 2.3.21–2). Juno is a fearful rather than a pitiful figure. Pisanio says that Imogen's feminine trimmings 'made great Juno angry' (*Cym.* 3.5.165), while **Volumnia** determines to lament 'in anger, Juno-like' (*Cor.* 4.2.53).

(c) Albott (1599) gives the popular image of Juno. Juno's jealousy is a cause of tragedy in Ovid's *Metamorphoses*, Book IV, lines 518–94 (Ovidius 2000: 100–2), a story that may lie behind the snake imagery in **Hermia**'s dream, as discussed by A. B. Taylor (2003). It was also popularized in the opening of Marlowe's *Dido, Queen of Carthage* (1594) and Thomas Heywood's plays *The Golden Age*, *The Silver Age* and *The Brazen Age*. On Juno and the representation of a court masque in *The Tempest*, see Glynne Wickham (1975), Kevin McNamara (1987) and David Lindley, 'Music, masque and meaning in *The Tempest*' (1984).

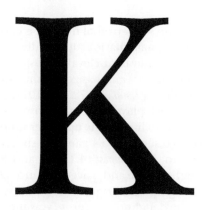

K

Kate and **Katherina**, variations on **Katherine** – *see* below

Katherine, (a) the name of five characters in Shakespeare's plays: Katherina Minola, the eponymous heroine of *The Taming of the Shrew*; Lady Percy, wife of Hotspur; Katherine of Alençon, companion to the Princess of France and beloved of Dumaine in *Love's Labour's Lost*; the French Princess Katherine of Valois in *Henry V*; and Katherine of Aragon in *Henry VIII*. Katherina is a continental form and Kate a common shortened form, a nickname indicating intimacy between speakers, and often carrying lower class associations, as in the taverns where Lucio's mistress 'Kate Keepdown' (*MM* 3.1.199) works as a prostitute. The common woman or prostitute referred to in Stephano's drinking song 'who had a tongue with a tang' (*Temp.* 2.1.50) is also called Kate, so, in Shakespeare's work at least, the name appears to carry associations of **shrew**ishness.

(b) The diminutive form is the only name we hear used of Lady Percy, wife of Hotspur. Historically, Mortimer's sister was called Elizabeth and Holinshed and Hall's chronicles call her Eleanor. Shakespeare's deliberate alteration to Kate intimates both affection and potential **shrew**ishness. From Hotspur's first address 'How now, Kate?' (*1HIV* 2.3.36) it establishes the strong sense of a genuinely companionate marriage in which Lady Percy can address her lord as 'you mad-headed ape!' command him 'come, you paraquito, answer me', and threaten to break his little finger in jest (*1HIV* 2.3.77, 85–9). The intimacy between them triumphs in spite of his unwillingness to reveal details of the conspiracy, when he promises she shall follow him to Wales. Here, their banter is conducted in a slightly more public arena, with an increasingly bawdy tone more typical of the tavern. Hotspur tells her 'Come Kate, thou art perfect in lying down' and invites her to sing (*1HIV* 3.2.236–45). When she refuses 'in good sooth', probably as a retort to his joke that he wants to sleep with Mortimer's wife, he criticizes the socially inferior discourse of 'Sunday-citizens' she is using:

Not yours, in good sooth! Heart, you swear like a comfit-maker's wife: 'Not
  you, in good sooth', and 'as true as I live' and 'as God shall mend me,'
  and 'as sure as day';
And givest such sarcenet surety for thy oaths
As if thou never walk'st further than Finsbury.
Swear me, Kate, like a lady as thou art,
A good mouth-filling oath.

(1HIV 3.1.246–63)

A distressing difference between them opens up: he can still talk down to her as
Kate, but she must speak and behave obediently, like a lady, and agree to sing. In
the company of others, the honour of husbandly authority must be preserved; the
equal banter of the bedchamber now appears shrewish and is no longer appropriate. She still refuses to sing and it is sad that they exit separately without mending
the rift since this is the last time they speak to each other before Hotspur's death.
When Lady Hotspur reappears as a **widow** in *Henry IV Part II*, she honours his last
words and speaks like a Lady in passionate blank verse, beginning with an oath
'O yet, for God's sake, go not to these wars' (*2HIV* 2.3.9). To do so would be to
dishonour Hotspur's name she tells his father Northumberland, fondly recalling
her husband's idiosyncratic habit of 'speaking thick (which nature made his blem-
ish)' (*2HIV* 2.3.24). Left without her companion to 'tilt with lips' (*2HIV* 2.3.92),
she refashions her power of speech and intelligence to chastise Northumberland,
and finally succeeds in persuading him to retreat to Scotland.

References in *Henry VI Part I* and *Henry VIII* invoke the name's Catholic derivation from St Katherine of Alexandria, the fourth-century martyr who was tortured
on a wheel and decapitated for converting Empress Faustina to Christianity. **Joan**
La Pucelle alludes to her as the patron saint of the church in which Joan finds
the 'keen-edg'd sword' to defeat the English (*1HVI* 1.2.98–100). As a guardian of
maids, St Katherine is an appropriate patron for Joan. St Katherine shadows the
saintly portrait of Katherine of Aragon in *Henry VIII*, who is conceived of primarily
as a staunchly Roman Catholic queen. She is announced as 'Katherine, Queen of
England' (*HVIII* 2.4.11), only to be demoted to '**Princess Dowager**' (*HVIII* 3.2.70),
in spite of her intelligence and political skill, seen in her plea against taxing the
people (*HVIII* 1.2) and her apparently submissive response to the Cardinals in Act
3 Scene 1. In the latter scene, where she **sew**s with her **women**, Katherine already
appreciates the inevitability of her fall and its injustice. Although Henry bids her
farewell with intimacy 'Go thy ways, Kate' and appreciation (*HVIII* 2.4.134–44),
there is undoubted irony when he vows to remain with 'Katherine our queen,
before the primest creature / That's paragon'd o' th' world' (*HVIII* 2.4.230–1);
firstly, because we know he will abandon her, and secondly because the play
shows him exchanging an earthly paragon in **Anne**, for the heavenly paragon
of Katherine. Katherine's vision of golden-masked heavenly spirits clad in white
offering her a garland of bays celebrates her spiritual apotheosis in its echoes of
Revelation 7.9 (*HVIII* 5.1.SD 83). The parallels with the virgin martyr St Katherine
are reinforced just before her death when she pleads for provision for her servants

and asks to be laid out with 'maiden flowers' (*HVIII* 4.2.169–70).

Katherine of Alençon and Katherine of Valois both demonstrate French wit in the wooing games of *Love's Labour's Lost* and *Henry V*. In the first play, the lady-in-waiting Katherine flirts with Boyet and cleverly escapes a kiss (*LLL* 2.1.221–224). Princess Katherine coyly tells Henry V that it is not the custom of French **maids** to kiss before they are married. Both Katherines are adept with words; indeed, the Princess has been learning English from the point of Henry's invasion as if in preparation for the wooing scene. The words she learns with Alice in Act 3 Scene 4 are all parts of her body which, in the final references to the foot and the gown, '*le coun*', become explicitly sexual when Katherine hears in them the French words *foutre* ('to fuck') and *con* ('cunt'). Her body has become a metaphor for the French territories Henry has invaded and intends to rule. Henry addresses her alternately as 'Katherine' and 'Kate', an onomastic marker of the juxtaposition of formal political alliance and intimate emotional engagement in the wooing, and perhaps a reminder of Henry's continued alliance to the common English of the tavern. The Princess responds to his suit carefully with a piquant reminder of the cost of war: 'Is it possible dat I should love de enemie of France?' (*HV*5.1.170) and awareness that, as a political pawn, her fate will be determined 'as it shall please de *roi mon père*' (*HV*5.2.47). When Henry flatters her as '*la plus belle Katherine du monde, mon très cher et devin déese*' she notes that comparison to the 'divine' St Katherine for whom she is named is seductively deceptive (*HV*5.2.216–7). Shakespeare uses the diminutive and socially inferior form to make an even more abrupt elision of mistress and saint in Dumaine's praise of Katherine of Alençon:

> Dumaine: O most divine Kate!
> Berowne: O most profound coxcomb!
>
> (*LLL* 4.3.81–2)

As Berowne observes, the effect is to comically undercut Dumaine's pose as Petrarchan lover.

Katherine of Alençon's wit, like that of **Beatrice**, is partly a defensive mask. She will not 'be friends' with Cupid, (and postpones Dumaine's suit at the end of the play even though she is attracted to him), because her **sister** died for love, becoming melancholy, sad and heavy' (*LLL* 5.2.13–14). **Rosaline**'s tactless reminder of this detail provokes Katherine to tease her about her dark beauty in an increasingly barbed exchange that the Princess stops (*LLL* 5.2.29).

In *The Taming of the Shrew* differences between the formal 'Katherina or Katherine' and the diminutive form 'Kate' are an initial point of contention between the protagonists, a major issue in a play in which, as Laurie Maguire has demonstrated, names and naming are of primary importance. Up until the wooing scene in Act 2, Katherine Minola is referred to by everyone in the play, including herself, by her formal name. When Baptista uses the intimate form 'shall I send my daughter Kate to you?' (*Shrew* 2.1.167), Petruchio takes advantage of this opening to insert himself as a family member in aggressively pursuing his suit, regardless of Katherine's own self-identification:

Petruchio: Good morrow, Kate, for that's your name, I hear.
Katherine: Well have you heard, but something hard of hearing.
            They call me Katherine that do talk of me.
Petruchio: You lie, in faith, for you are call'd plain Kate,
            And bonny Kate, and sometimes Kate the curst;
            But Kate, the prettiest Kate in Christendom,
            Kate of Kate-Hall, my super-dainty Kate,
            For dainties are all Kates, and therefore, Kate,
            Take this of me, Kate of my consolation –
            Hearing thy mildness prais'd in every town,
            Thy virtues spoke of, and thy beauty sounded,
            Yet not so deeply as to thee belongs
            Myself am mov'd to woo thee for my wife.
                                            (*Shrew* 2.1.182–94)

Petruchio deliberately ignores Katherine's own choice of name. Re-naming her as 'the prettiest Kate in Christendom' is a crucial tactic in his strategy to tame her from a shrew to 'a Kate / Conformable as other household Kates' (*Shrew* 2.1.277–8). The pun on the diminutive for 'cake' or sweetmeat emphasizes how re-naming refashions her as a consumable more palatable to men's tastes, an attractive **commodity**. Indeed, once she does conform to male desires and social expectations, she will achieve a limited autonomy as mistress of her own house: 'Kate of Kate-Hall'. As Maguire notes, Petruchio calls her 'Kate' 58 times through the action of the play. She has to endure the humiliation of his late, outlandish appearance at their wedding and is forcibly removed as one of his goods or chattels without being able to enjoy her primary position as mistress of the feast at her own wedding breakfast. At Petruchio's house, the taming-school, she has no cates or meat, or sleep or clean clothes (*Shrew* 4.3) until she answers to his version of a household Kate and accepts his god-like authority to rename even the sun and moon according to his will (*Shrew* 4.5.12–20). Even his own servants agree he is more shrew than she (*Shrew* 4.1.85–6). Petruchio's soliloquy claiming that 'this is how to kill a wife with kindness' (*Shrew* 4.1.188–211) registers the destruction of her identity and its reconstruction in bestial terms. However dubious the politics of Petruchio's taming, it does have the effect of detaching meaning from signifiers, and so self-consciously disrupts the very authority on which male dominance is based. He can insist Kate kisses him in the street (*Shrew* 5.2.143–50), but when she obeys his commands at the end of the play, he refers to her as Katherine again (*Shrew* 5.2.130). It is not clear whether Katherine's rehearsal of wifely duties in her final speech (*Shrew* 5.2.136–79) is evidence of her internalization of the ideology of subjection or a playful performance of being a household Kate. Either way, the speech should be uncomfortable in performance to varying degrees depending on period of performance and the beliefs of individual spectators. For the female protagonist, the text certainly offers the possibility of a marriage in which she can still be her own woman: Katherine within the Kate of Kate Hall.

(c) Lynda E. Boose (1994), and Laurie Maguire's *Shakespeare's Names* (2007: 120–50) discuss Katherine Minola's loss of name. Natasha Korda (2002: 52–75) considers the pun on Kate / cate and her domestication in the context of insecurities about the household economy. Carol Rutter's *Clamorous Voices* (1988: 1–25), records the impressions of female actors playing the role of Katherine Minola. Nancy Carroll (2004), analyses the role of Lady Katherine Percy from the perspective of an actor. Jean E. Howard and Phyllis Rackin (1997: 190–4, 209–15) look at Princess Katherine's role as a political pawn. Anna Jameson (2005: 336–57) gives a positive reading of Katherine of Aragon's role. Linda McJ. Micheli (1987), Kim H. Noling (1988) and Gordon McMullan (2000: 120–36) contrast Katherine with her rival Anne.

kicky-wicky, (a) an extraordinary name for a beloved or wife.
(b) In *All's Well* Parolles criticizes the young man 'That hugs his kicky-wicky here at home' in time of war (*AWW* 2.3.280).

kirtle, (a) originally an overgarment of bodice and skirt but after 1545, more frequently a separate woman's skirt or overskirt, worn over the petticoat. French kirtles were cut to hang longer at the back to create a train while round kirtles reached to the ground with a level hemline.
(b) In order to comfort Doll Tearsheet, Falstaff asks her 'What stuff wilt have a kirtle of? I shall receive money a' Thursday' (*2HIV* 2.4.274–5). Looser kirtles with bodices and without a waist seam, to be worn under the fashionable loose-bodied gown, are seen in several portraits so probably remained fashionable, as well as being comfortable and suitable to wear during pregnancy. The actors playing Hermione at the opening of *The Winter's Tale* and Helena in *All's Well* would probably have worn loose kirtles and loose-bodied gowns to demonstrate pregnancy.
(c) Arnold (1988: 120–2).

laces, (a) forms of decoration and fastening for clothes and accessories. In the singular, lace is an open-work fabric of threads made by attaching bobbins or bones to the threads and passing them over each other on a pillow or cushion to make delicate patterns. Laces are decorative braids made by intertwining a number of threads, sometimes silk, gold and silver, together. The term is also used of cords used to fasten garments together; in the case of women, lacing at the back of the bodice or gown; to attach the sleeves to the bodice; and to attach the **kirtle** to the bodice.

(b) Lace was a luxury item although its production was usually a low-paid craft undertaken by women. Orsino cites the 'free **maids** that weave their thread with bones' and sing alongside the **spinsters** and knitters, as examples of plain or common people (*TN* 2.4.45). What kinds of lace or decorative braid could be worn by different classes of people was rigorously controlled. The payments for Alice Montague, Queen Elizabeth's silkwoman, detail decorative 'lase of sundry sortes & colours made of jean satten silke' and 'loupes of venice golde bone lase edgid with silver pinkes' (Arnold 1988: 220). James I issued an edict in 1613 'prohibiting all his Subjects from using any Gold or Silver, either fine or counterfeit; all Embroiderie, and all Lace of Millan, or of Millan Fashion' (*OED*). On stage, however, the circulation of clothes meant that **boy actors** playing the parts of noblewomen or **queen**s could wear elaborate lace and laces. In January 1598, for example, Henslowe laid out the considerable sum of 29 shillings to buy 'copr lace for the littel boye & for a valle for the boye' who were to play in *Dido and Aeneas* (Henslowe 2002: 86). In July he paid another 33 shillings and four pence for 'white satten for a wommons gowne layd with whitte lace' (ibid.: 94). Selling laces or braids was a pedlar's job. Autolycus, vaunting courtly fashions, asks 'Will you buy any tape, / Or lace for your cape' (*WT* 4.4.315–16) and the Clown promises to buy gifts for Mopsa and Dorcas. When Jack Cade claims his wife is descended from the Lacies, Dick undercuts his social pretensions with the joke 'she was, indeed, a pedler's daughter, and sold many laces' (*2HVI* 4.2.45).

The laces referred to in Shakespeare's texts are more often the cords that fasten women's garments together. 'Lac'd mutton' (*TGV* 1.1.96–9) refers to a prostitute with a laced bodice in *Two Gentlemen of Verona*. Laces fastening the bodice or bodies of a costume could restrict if pulled too tight to allow for quickened breathing during times of heightened emotion or physical activity. Since the laces could not be easily be reached by the wearer, help was required in such emergencies. **Cleopatra**, wearing early modern costume, commands 'Cut my lace, **Charmian**, come; / But let it be: I am quickly ill, and well' (*A&C* 1.3.71). Failure to cut laces could result in collapse. Before the Tower where her sons are imprisoned, Queen Elizabeth asks 'cut my lace in sunder, that my pent heart / May have some scope to beat / Or else I swoon' (*RIII* 4.1.32–4). Just after Hermione swoons at news of Mamillius's death because 'her heart is but o'ercharged' (*WT* 3.2.150), Paulina predicts a similar fate for herself in reporting Hermione's death:

> Woe the while!
> O, cut my lace, lest my heart, cracking it,
> Break too.
>
> (*WT* 3.3.172–4)

What happens on stage at this moment? Does someone come to her aid and loosen her laces? A Lord certainly intervenes to ask her 'What fit is this good lady?' (*WT* 3.3.174). If so, then the lace detail may be a significant turning point: by stopping Paulina's heart from breaking, the Lord's care reverses the tragic process and allows her to orchestrate the restoration of Hermione (whose laces are presumably loosened off-stage) and the repentance of Leontes.

(c) Arnold (1985: 53–9, 72, 77, 84, 103, 108–9) illustrates the elaborate process of lacing. Jones and Stallybrass (2000: 23–6) analyse laces as fastenings and lace as decoration. Arnold (1988: 110, 220–3) and Greer (2007: 177–83) give records of the production of laces and Henslowe (2002) their deployment in the theatre for costumes. The extract from the *King's Edict prohibiting all his Subjects from using any Gold or Silver, either fine or counterfeit; all Embroiderie, and all Lace of Millan, or of Millan Fashion'* (London, 1613) is found in the *OED*.

lady, (a) a term referring to a woman to indicate social superiority, as the head of a household or one who rules over subjects, servants or attendants. The title was honorific, referring to a woman of high rank, especially a member of the nobility, usually addressed as 'your ladyship'. 'Lady' constituted a polite form of address to a woman of elevated or higher social standing and, additionally, to a genteel or refined woman having the characteristics traditionally associated with the social élite. Paradoxically, it was also used to signify a servant to a woman of high rank, such as those who waited on a queen or noblewoman, and might well be nobly born themselves.

(b) That Shakespeare uses the term more than 700 times (as opposed to about 400 occurrences of 'woman') indicates how many of his female characters are members of the social élite. 'Lady' is used to indicate command or rule in a range of different contexts. **Cleopatra** as **Empress** is defined to all her court as 'the lady whom you serve' (*A&C* 1.2.31). Queen **Katherine** is 'a royal lady' (*HVIII* 2.4.154). The commanding figures of **Fortune** and **Queen** Margaret are referred to as 'sovereign lady' (*Tim.* 1.1.68 and *2HVI* 3.1.161), though in the latter case with some irony since **Margaret**'s powerful plotting contradicts the honourable behaviour expected of a lady. Lear promises **Goneril** to 'make thee lady' or ruler of his divided kingdom (*KL* 1.1.66). A**emilia** who rules over the Abbey at Ephesus is likewise designated as 'the Lady **Abbess**' and 'a reverend Lady' (*Err.* 5.1.166 and 134). **Olivia** and Lady **Capulet** are both referred to as the 'the lady of the house' to indicate their command of the household as well as noble birth (*TN* 1.5.167 and *R&J* 1.5.113). Celia's 'ladies, her attendants of her chamber' (*AYLI* 2.2.5) are examples of servants who are nobly born.

'Lady' and 'your ladyship' continue to be used as a mark or rank, as in the case of **Portia**, 'a lady richly left' (*Mer.* 1.1.161) whose birth makes her a worthy match for the Prince of Morocco (*Mer.* 3.1.31–2). **Jessica** formally addresses Portia as 'your ladyship' (*Mer.* 3.4.42). The **Princess** of France (*LLL* 2.1.101), the **Countess**es of Rossillion (*AWW* 1.3.17), Auvergne (*1HVI* 2.3), **Duchess** of Gloucester (*2HVI* 1.4.4) and the Countess Olivia (*TN* 1.5.89) are called 'your ladyship'. The title is also used to show respect to the Roman 'ladies' (*Cor.* 5.5.6) **Valeria**, **Virgilia** and **Volumnia**, and Young Lucius apologizes for running away from his distracted 'sweet aunt' **Lavinia** by promising to 'willingly attend your ladyship' (*Tit.* 4.1.26–8). Cassio shows a careful formality and Iago a false respect in addressing **Desdemona** as 'lady' and 'your ladyship' (*Oth.* 2.1.85 and 105).

Often, however, the honorific title 'Lady' refers to older characters, as if Shakespeare is drawing attention to the decline of a feudal order in which rank is foremost. The Clown in *All's Well* makes a pointed distinction between **Helena** 'my most fortunate lady', whose title is the result of fortune, and 'my old lady' the nobly-born Countess of Rossillion (*AWW* 2.4.14–19). The two gentlemen in Henry VIII note that **Anne** Bullen's train is carried by 'that noble old lady, Duchess of Norfolk' (*HVIII* 4.1.52). Anne's servant is designated by the title 'Old Lady' presumably because, as a Lady-in-Waiting, she is nobly born. Rank is the subject of playfulness in juxtapositions of 'Lady' with 'Lord'. **Rosalind** says that to see 'the Lady the epilogue' is no more 'unhandsome than to see the lord the prologue' (*AYLI* Epilogue. 1–2). **Hermione** teases 'A lady's "verily" is / As potent as a lord's' (*WT* 1.2.50–1). **Beatrice** admits Benedick is 'a good soldier to a lady, but what is he to a lord?' implying severe limits to his chivalric military prowess (*MAdo* 1.1.52–3). In *Midsummer Night's Dream*, the pairing of Lord and Lady is one rejected by Titania because of the domineering attitude Oberon takes and because of his infidelity:

> Oberon: Am not I thy lord?
> Titania: Then I must be thy lady; but I know
> When thou hast stolen away from fairy land
> And in the shape of Corin sat all day,

> Playing on pipes of corn, and versing love
> To amorous Phillida.
>
> (*MND* 2.1.63–8)

Some uses of 'Lady' expose the artificiality of rank. The newly knighted Bastard in *King John* boasts 'now I can make any **Joan** a Lady' (*KJ* 1.1.184) and when Hal is addressed as 'my lord the Prince', he responds 'How now, my lady the **hostess**!' (*1HIV* 2.4.284–5). Mistress **Quickly** later reminds Sir John Falstaff that he promised 'to marry me and make me my lady thy **wife**' (*2HIV* 2.1.92). When he promises the same to Mistress **Ford**, her protestation that she 'should be a pitiful lady!' (MWW 3.2.51–2) is quickly dismissed. The fragile boundary between citizens and nobility lies behind Hotspur's insistence that his wife Lady **Katherine** Percy, speaks 'like a lady, as thou art' (*1HIV* 3.2.253). The social and ethical degeneration of Lear's kingdom is criticized in the Fool's image of 'Lady Brach', a dog who can rest by the fireside 'and stink' while Truth is whipped out of the household (*KL* 1.4.11–3).

The title often invokes moral authority by association with 'our Lady' as a name for the Virgin **Mary**. **Hermione**, for example, is referred to as 'my most sacred lady' (*WT* 1.2.76) and 'our gracious lady' (*WT* 2.2.19). It also signals social deference and respect on the part of a speaker, signalled forcefully in the formal appellation 'your Ladyship'. **Perdita** appeals to 'Lady Fortune' (*WT* 4.4.52) in soliciting her help. Hamlet (*Ham.* 3.4.179), **Juliet** (*R&J* 3.5.107) and Bertram (*AWW* 4.3.88–9) use formal address to their **mother**s to show special respect when they have been impolite or disobedient. The convention is open to abuse, however. Hotspur is infuriated by the 'lady-terms' with which the affected messenger addresses him on the battlefield (*1HIV* 1.3.46) and Benedick addresses Beatrice with mock deference as 'my dear Lady Disdain' (*MAdo* 1.1.119) and 'my Lady Tongue' (*MAdo* 2.1.284).

In the discourse of courtly love, which Benedick parodies, the title of 'Lady' conventionally conveys the reverence and deference of a lover. Romeo exclaims 'It is my lady, O it is my love!' (*R&J* 2.2.10). Mercutio mockingly seranades the **Nurse**: 'Farewell, ancient lady, farewell [*singing*] "lady, lady, lady"' (*R&J* 2.4.142–3). Honourable rank and Petrarchan elevation of the **mistress** are conflated in *The Two Gentlemen of Verona*, in which the repeated appellations 'lady' and 'your ladyship' construct Julia and Silvia as nobly born and as Petrarchan mistresses. The ancient code of chivalry is ultimately upheld by neither of the two young gentlemen but by Sir Eglamour who gallantly offers morning greetings and his service to the 'worthy lady' Silvia:

> According to your ladyship's impose,
> I am thus early come to know what service
> It is your pleasure to command me in.
>
> (*TGV* 4.3.8–10)

The high status of a lady as mistress is dramatized in *Love's Labour's Lost* where praise is offered 'To any lady that subdues a lord' (*LLL* 4.139–40). The confused exchange of compliments 'From which lord to which lady? (*LLL* 4.1.102–3) exposes the superficial nature of such courtship. A deliberately strategic use of 'lady' occurs in the wooing scenes of *Edward III*, where the King addresses his beloved as '**Countess**' more frequently than as 'Lady' until he overcomes his passion and celebrates her as a 'true English lady' for maintaining her integrity (*EIII* 2.2.193).

The transfer of gentility of birth to personal qualities of honour, gentleness and delicacy recurs frequently in Shakespeare. **Imogen** is admired because 'she hath all courtly parts more exquisite / Than lady, ladies, women, from every one / The best she hath' (*Cym.* 3.5.71–3). She regrets that the fool Cloten has made her 'forget a lady's manners / By being so verbal' and telling him bluntly she hates him (*Cym.* 2.3.103–11). The delicacy of ladies' sensibilities preoccupies the rude mechanicals who fear the violent elements of their play 'should fright the ladies out of their wits' (*MND* 1.2.79) and so construct an additional prologue to assure 'You gentle ladies, you whose gentle hearts do fear / The smallest monstrous mouse that creeps on floor' (*MND* 5.1.219–20). Similarly, Touchstone believes that wrestling and 'breaking of ribs' is hardly suitable 'sport for ladies' (*AYLI* 1.2.138–9). Given such sensibilities, 'Lady' can signify women's weakness, their need for chivalric protection. Edward III scorns King David of Scotland for attacking 'silly ladies', meaning defenceless women (*EIII* 1.1.137). Hector argues that there is 'no lady of more softer bowels / More spongy to suck in the sense of fear' (*T&C* 2.1.11–12), than himself. Gloucester exclaims against **Regan**'s absolute violation of gentility as gentleness in the phrase 'Naughty lady', meaning 'wicked' (*KL* 3.7.36).

King Lear draws attention to the sartorial construct of noble ladies on the Shakespearean stage. He tells Regan 'Thou art a lady; / If only to go warm were gorgeous, / Why, nature needs not what thou gorgeous wear'st / Which scarcely keeps thee warm' (*KL* 2.4.267–70). The appearance of honour projected by her clothes is emptied out by her betrayal of the feudal code that would honour her father's royal right to his knights. Metatheatrical references to the **boy players** remind spectators that all the ladies of rank and romantic idols are constructs of performance. Christopher Sly's illusions that he is a lord are bolstered by Bartholomew the page 'dress'd in all suits like a lady' (*Shrew* Ind. 1.106), whom Sly must address as 'Madam' since 'so lords call ladies' (*Shrew* Ind. 2.61). In an even more explicit deconstruction of status, Hamlet greets the **boy actor** as 'my young lady and mistress! by' lady, your ladyship is nearer to heaven than when I saw you last by the altitude of a **chopine**' (*Ham.* 2.2.424–6). The social elevation invoked by the term 'Lady' and its association with moral superiority 'nearer to heaven' and association with the Virgin ('by' lady'), is parodied by reduction to the physical growth of the boy actor and his use of high-soled shoes.

(c) Ralph Berry (1988) gives a general overview to the topic with useful brief observations on some of the female roles. Richard Hosley (1967) discusses the age and naming of Lady Capulet as 'Lady', 'Ladyship', 'Wife' and 'Old Lady', while Thomas Merriam, 'The Old Lady or All is Not True' (2001) examines the

Lady-in-Waiting as an untrustworthy figure. Mahood (1998: 75–6) comments on the Old Lady's splendid political realism.

ladyship, a form of address to one of high or superior rank; a member of the nobility. *See* **lady**.

lap, (a) the area between the waist and knees when sitting, usually with maternal associations when applied to women, but also a synonym for the vulva.
(b) Helkiah Crooke's *Mikrokosmographia* (1615) used 'lap' as a general term for the female genitals in his chapter 'Of the lap or privities' where he defined the vulva as a floodgate:

> The last dissimilar part of the wombe, *Galen* . . . calleth in Latine *pudendum muliebre*, that is, the womans modesty, of some *Vulua*, as it were *vallis* a valley, or *Valua* a Flood-gate, because it is diuided into two parts by a cleft, which like Flood gates or leafedoores are easily opened or shut as neede is. We will call it the lappe.

> (Crooke 1615: 237)

In Shakespeare, women's laps follow this definition as an entrance to the womb, the site of male sexual desire and the point of return to one's maternal origins. As the object of male desire, the lap is a target. Romeo complains that the obstinately chaste **Rosaline** will not 'ope her lap to saint-seducing gold' (*R&J* 1.1.214). Titus bids the young Lucius shoot his arrow 'in Virgo's lap' (*Tit.* 4.3.65). In contrast, the lap also represents rest, a cessation of masculine activity and struggle for self-assertion. In the case of Antony, this means the neglect of military endeavour; Pompey sees it as a challenge to pluck him 'from the lap of Egypt's **widow**', **Cleopatra** (*A&C* 2.1.37–8). Glendower's **daughter** tempts Mortimer to forget the wars by lying down on the '**wanton** rushes' to 'rest your gentle head upon her lap' and sleep (*1HIV* 3.1.211–19). The active Hotspur, however, regards his wife's lap in terms of desire, commanding **Katherine** 'Come, quick, quick, that I may lay my head in thy lap' (*1HIV* 3.1.227). The two meanings of 'lap' are brought together most passionately and movingly in the words of Suffolk. Banished from Queen Margaret, he says he cannot live 'And in thy sight to die, what were it else / But like a pleasant slumber in thy lap?' (*2HVI* 3.2.388–90). He describes self-annihilation as a return to the fulfilment of a 'cradle-babe' dying at its mother's **breast** (*2HVI* 391–3).

Hamlet physically shifts the focus of his desire, refusing the offer of Gertrude's lap and moving to Ophelia who is 'metal more attractive'. He asks to sit in her lap, deliberately punning on country / cunt with bawdy associations:

> Hamlet: Lady, shall I lie in your lap?
> Ophelia: No, my lord.
> Hamlet: I mean, my head upon your lap.
> Ophelia: Ay, my lord.

Hamlet: Do you think I mean country matters?

(*Ham.* 3.2.112–16)

Benedick, invoking the pun of death for orgasm, also uses the word in a bawdy sense to tell **Beatrice**, 'I will live in thy heart, die in thy lap and be buried in thy eyes' (*MAdo* 5.2.102). Richard of Gloucester sarcastically devalues romance as a poor substitute for possessing the kingdom when he claims 'I'll make my heaven in a lady's lap' (*3HVI* 3.2.148).

Used anthropomorphically in feminizations of the **earth** and the nation, 'lap' indicates fertility. The 'fresh green lap' of Richard II's kingdom promises spring and rebirth (*RII* 3.3.47 and 5.2.47). In a rare same-sex occurrence of the metaphor, Joan La Pucelle recognizes that France must 'let her fair head fall into **England**'s lap' (*1HVI* 5.3.26), though the conquering English force is male.

(c) Helkiah Crooke, *Mikrokosmographia* (1615), defines lap anatomically and discusses it on pp. 237–9.

Lavinia, (a) a character in *Titus Andronicus*, sole **daughter** of Titus. Her name is resonant with echoes of Roman mythology in which Lavinia is the wife of Aeneas and thus the mother of the Roman people.

(b) Shakespeare's text advertises Lavinia's symbolic status as 'Rome's rich orna-ment' (*Tit.* 1.1.52), an embodiment of the State, whose arms 'kings have sought to sleep in' (2.4.19). In the opening scene, she is the object of a struggle between the rivals competing to be Emperor. The newly elected Saturninus pointedly claims her with the lines 'Lavinia will I make my **empress**, / Rome's royal **mistress**' (1.1.240–1), as though using the legacy of her name to buttress his own leadership of Rome. His brother Bassianus snatches her, claiming to have been formerly betrothed to her. Saturninus regards this '**rape**' as a form of treachery (1.1.403–4) and can only reconcile the fact that he is not married to this 'changing piece' (1.1.309), this potential mother of the Roman people, by inviting her and Bassianus to a joint wedding celebration with him and his bride **Tamora**, Queen of the Goths. Lavinia is also an object of desire for the **Queen**'s sons Chiron and Demetrius. Because of the political resonances of her name their possessive lust again signifies rival heirs greedily competing for rule. This time, however, Rome is threatened by alien invasion, as the brothers rape Lavinia. Lavinia prides herself on her **chastity**, following the model of **Lucrece** (2.1.108–9), so her rape is a pollution in personal and political terms. When they cut off her tongue and her **hands**, her body becomes a living metaphor of the dismembered Roman State, reflected in the quarrels between Saturninus and Tamora and the family of Titus.

Lavinia's personal tragedy echoes that of **Philomel** as the play's numerous references to Ovid explicitly foreground. These are introduced via her uncle's beautifully poised description of the piteous spectacle of her mutilated body (2.4.11–57). Previously, Lavinia's tongue had been critically sharp of Tamora's adultery so, after Bassianus has been murdered, her eloquent appeals to Tamora for mercy, on the grounds of common **woman**hood, are unsurprisingly rejected

(2.1.136–84). After her mutilation, as a silent presence on the stage she is a persistent reminder to Titus and his sons of the injuries they have suffered (5.2.170–7). She chooses an active role by revealing the names of her rapists using Philomel's story in a copy of Ovid's *Metamporphoses* (4.1.47–9) and, when Titus takes revenge by slitting their throats, by holding the basin to catch their blood. Titus's decision to kill his daughter since her shame also symbolizes his wider sorrow seems at once shocking, sacrificial and highly emblematic. It launches his destruction of the Roman emperor and his family to make way for Lucius who vows to teach the people to knit 'these broken limbs again into one body' (5.3.72).

(c) Heather James (1995: (esp.) 285–7) and Kahn (1997: 46–76 (esp.) 52) discuss Lavinia as a personification of Rome. Liz Oakley-Brown (2006: 23–42) considers the ways in which Lavinia's rape configures the sexual politics of translation, from body to text and from Ovid to the stage, with Shakespeare's Lavinia as a translator and reference to Ravenscroft's 1678 adaptation *The Rape of Lavinia*. Katherine Rowe investigates, 'Dismembering and Forgetting in *Titus Andronicus*' (1994). *See also* entries on **Philomel** and on **rape**.

lead apes in hell, (a) a proverbial phrase meaning 'to die a virgin'.

(b) Shakespeare's texts draw on a common knowledge of the proverb. In *The London Prodigall* (1605), a play performed by his company, Master Weathercock points out "tis an old prouerbe, and you know it well, / That women dying maides, lead apes in hell.' The view of both male characters that this is 'a foolish prouerbe, and a false' indicates how the commonplace is challenged in Shakespeare's own texts (*London Prodigall*, sig. B1v). In *The Taming of the Shrew*, Katherina sees it as a mark of shame; she complains that her father's unjust favouring of **Bianca** will make her a **spinster** who must 'dance barefoot' at Bianca's wedding 'And for your love to her lead apes in hell' (*Shrew* 2.1.33–4).

Beatrice expresses a very different view. To avoid **marriage** which would subjugate her to a man, she would rather 'even take sixpence in earnest of the berrord' (the bear-ward whose job included the training of apes as well as bears) 'and lead his apes into hell'. She will not be damned in hell, she argues, but sent to heaven 'so I deliver up my apes to Saint Peter' to sit with the bachelors 'and there live as merry as the day is long' (*MAdo* 2.1.39–49).

(c) Anon. *The London prodigall As it was plaide by the Kings Maiesties seruants. By VVilliam Shakespeare* (1605). Although this text was performed by Shakespeare's company there is nothing more substantial to support its attribution to him. Tilley (1950: M37) details the proverb for which no explanation has yet emerged.

Leda, (a) the daughter of Thestius and wife of Tyndareus in mythology. She was raped by Zeus in the figure of a swan. From the egg hatched **Helen** of Troy, Clytemnestra and possibly also Castor and Pollux.

(b) The myth of Leda and the swan was a popular subject for Renaissance art by Leonardo da Vinci, Michelangelo and Rubens. Elegy 10 of Ovid's *Elegies* glorified Jupiter's transformation 'In snow-white plumes of a false swanne' (Ovidius, 1603:

B2v) while literary interpretations like Spenser's *Faerie Queene* also romanticized the rape, admiring the 'wondrous skill' and 'sweet wit' of Jupiter in transforming himself 'To win faire *Leda* to his lovely trade' while she slept:

> Whiles the proud Bird ruffing his fethers wyde,
> And brushing his faire brest, did her inuade:
> Shee slept, yet twixt her eyelids closely spyde,
> How towards her he rusht, and smiled at his pryde.
> (Spenser 1970: 203. Book III, Canto XI, Stanza 32)

Shakespeare's two references to Leda both point up the grotesque nature of the rape rather than the male prowess of Jove. Tranio, preparing to woo **Bianca**, comically attempts to show off his learning by saying that 'Fair Leda's daughter had a thousand wooers, / The well one more may fair Bianca have' (*Shrew* 1.2.242–3). Unfortunately his roundabout way of naming Helen via her mother Leda has the effect of associating him and his suit with the aggressive Jupiter. The grotesque, even ridiculous nature of the rape is pointed up by Falstaff wearing the buck's head of Herne the Hunter and trying to seduce Mistresses Ford and Page. He recalls Jupiter's 'foul fault' done 'in the semblance of a fowl' in becoming 'a swan for the love of Leda' (*MWW* 5.5.6–11).

(c) The myth is recounted in N. G. L. Hammond and H. H. Scullard (1970). *Ouid's elegies three bookes* (1603), and Spenser (1970: 203) are early modern references. Nelson (2007) examines artistic representations of Leda as indicative of early modern attitudes towards the female body.

Luce, (a) a female character in *Comedy of Errors* who is a member of **Adriana** and Antipholus's household and who speaks out of the window or door. Luce is also a name for a pike, from Latin.

(b) Luce seems to be the same character as the fat kitchen maid **Nell**, referred to by Dromio (*Err.* 3.2.81–114) since Antipholus and Dromio identify the person who shouted at them as a kitchen **maid** (*Err.* 4.4.73–5). However, her name also suggests an abbreviation of **Luciana**, who appears in the next scene. The character that speaks from the house is named three times as 'Luce', and the name draws on the bawdy associations of pike. Fish being a metaphor for woman as sexual partner (Williams 1994: 126), 'luce' probably means a loose woman or whore. In *Merry Wives*, Shallow obscurely points out that 'the luce is the fresh fish, the salt fish is an old coat' (*MWW* 1.1.22–3). Luce in *The Comedy of Errors* engages in bawdy banter at the door, which makes Dromio of Syracuse remark 'If thy name be called Luce – / Luce thou hast answered him well' (*Err.* 3.1.53). She is certainly berated as a 'baggage' (*Err.* 3.1.55) and a 'minion' (*Err.* 3.1.54 and 58) for not letting Antipholus and Dromio of Ephesus into the house. As guardian of the gate, Luce may have links to **Lucina** as goddess of childbirth.

(c) Thomas P. Hennings (1986: 98–101) points out strange similarities between the characters of Luciana and Luce. Mahood (1998: 6, 247–8) outlines the possible staging of the role. Richard Dutton (2003a) suggests that the character's name may have been prompted by Lucian's essay on *The Calumny of Apelles*, a source for the play.

Lucetta, (a) the lady-in-waiting or maid to Julia in *Two Gentlemen of Verona*, a diminutive of Lucy or Lucia (*see* **Luciana**), with similar derivation from the Latin *lux*, or light.

Lucetta is introduced by name as soon as she appears, and acts as a guide or adviser to Julia; her commentary serving to illuminate or cast light on each of the suitors. Julia also accuses her of wantonness in acting as a go-between for Proteus and herself: 'Dare you presume to harbor wanton lines? / To whisper and conspire against my youth?' (1.2.42–3). The mistress and maid's exchange over reading Proteus's love rhyme like a song includes some innuendo that furthers the idea of Lucetta as a genteel pandar or go-between. Julia conjures Lucetta 'Who art the table wherein all my thoughts / Are character'd and engrav'd' (2.7.3–4). Although Lucetta does not make independent suggestions, true to her name, she has an invaluable role in helping Julia to acknowledge her feelings for Proteus and advising on how to pursue him. She also illuminates the possible outcomes of Julia's audacious plan, hinting with insight at the unwelcome reception Julia will receive from Proteus (2.7.79).

(c) Lori Schroeder Haslam (1994) analyses Lucetta's role in taking Julia through her romantic options in a kind of catechism that relies on female intimacy. The intimacy between mistress and **maid** is the subject of Carole McEwin's (1983) discussion. Rodney Stenning Edgecombe (2004: 12–14) analyses the wit an innuendo of the proposed song.

Luciana, (a) a character in *Comedy of Errors*, the unmarried sister of **Adriana**, who lives at her house in Ephesus. Her name is the feminine form of a Roman given name, 'Lucius', which is probably a derivative of Latin *lux*, meaning 'light'. The English derivation was 'Lucy'.

(b) The play's setting in Ephesus and its links to Syracuse suggest that, in addition to its associations with light, Luciana's name might invoke memories of St Lucia of Syracuse, who remained a well-known saint in early modern England in texts such as John Donne's poem 'A Nocturnal Upon St Lucy's Day' (Donne 1990: 116–17). St Lucy was often associated with sight and the eyes because of the derivation of her name. She was martyred in AD 304 because she refused marriage to a Roman suitor, and was sentenced to imprisonment in a brothel, to be burned to death and was finally stabbed through the throat (Delaney 1983: 323). Shakespeare's character is named only twice in the script: on her first appearance (*Err.* 2.1.3) and after Antipholus of Syracuse has wooed her (4.2.1). Like her saintly namesake, she seems reluctant to marry (2.1.26–9). When Antipholus declares what appears to be an adulterous passion for her, she advises him to conceal his love, 'Apparel vice like virtue's harbinger' and 'teach sin the carriage of a holy **saint**' (3.2.11–14), exposing a duplicity which troubles the associations of light and purity conjured by her name and that of Saint Lucy. Antipholus of Syracuse regards her as divine, full of grace and wonder (3.2.31–2) but he also hints at more subversive aspects of her identity as a seductive **siren** with golden hair (3.2.47–8). The possibility of another sexually active version of Luciana existing alongside the saintly one is projected in the bawdy figure of **Luce** (Hennings 1986). Later, Dromio of Syracuse mixes the associations of St Lucy and Luce and implicitly parallels Luciana with the **Courtezan**, pointing out that light **wench**es 'appear to men like **angel**s of light, light is an effect of fire, and fire will burn: *ergo*, light wenches will burn' (4.3.56–7).

(c) John J. Delaney (1983: 323) and John Donne, 'A Nocturnal upon St Lucy's Day, being the shortest day' in *John Donne* (1990: 116–17) give details about St Lucy. Thomas P. Hennings points out strange similarities between the characters of Luciana and Luce in 'The Anglican Doctrine of Affectionate Marriage in *Comedy of Errors*' (1986: (esp.) 98–101). Richard Dutton (2003) suggests that the character's name may have been prompted by Lucian's essay on *The Calumny of Apelles*, a source for the play.

Lucina, (a) the Roman goddess of childbirth, possibly linked to the Latin word *lux* or light, representing the emergence from confinement for both mother and child.

(b) The sense of Lucina as a gatekeeper from confinement to birth is suggested in *Pericles*, where Antiochus imagines his daughter's conception and gestation 'till Lucina reigned' (*Per.* 1.1.8). **Thaisa**, who appears to die in childbirth but is revived from her coffin by Cerimon, has the name 'Lucina' in Shakespeare's source, Twine's *Patterne of Painefull Adventures* (1607). Lucina is not a beneficent deity in the vision in *Cymbeline*. Posthumus's mother reports 'Lucina lent me not her aid, / But took me in my throes / That from me was Posthumus ripp'd' (*Cym.* 5.4.43–6) while she died.

(c) Laurence Twine's *Patterne of Paineful Adventures* (London, 1594) is reprinted in Bullough, Vol. VI (1966: 423–82).

Lucrece, (a) the wife of Collatine in Roman legend, famous for her chastity even though she was raped by Tarquin. Her story is told in Shakespeare's poem *The Rape of Lucrece* (1594) and references to her as a model of married **chastity** are found in the plays.

(b) Lucrece is introduced as 'Lucrece the chaste' in *The Rape of Lucrece* (7), which immediately establishes her iconic status as a paragon of wifely fidelity following a tradition which included St Augustine, Chaucer, Gower, Titian and Raphael. Petruchio boasts that Katherina will prove a 'Roman Lucrece for her chastity' as a wife (*Shrew* 2.1.296) and Aaron claims that Lavinia is unassailable since 'Lucrece was not more chaste' to her husband (*Tit.* 2.1.108). In the poem, Lucrece's 'incomparable chastity' (*Luc.* Argument. 12), her 'sov'reignty' (*Luc.* 36), as advertised by Collatine, is the cause of the tragedy. Constructed as a **commodity**, a 'rich **jewel**' (*Luc.* 34) and blazoned under the gaze of Tarquin in the descriptions of her golden hair (*Luc.* 399–406), white **breasts** (*Luc.* 407–13) classic **beauty**, blending red and white (*Luc.* 386), she becomes a prize to be stolen. The competitive desire and voyeuristic male gaze which animate the poem's account of Tarquin's approach and the rape provide a prototype for dramatized bed scenes with **Desdemona** (*Oth.* 5.2.1–83) and **Imogen** (*Cym.* 2.2.12–15).

Lucrece's 'sovereignty' (*Luc.* 69) as mark of her high-principled integrity also makes her heroic. In terms of virtue and innocence she is an 'earthly saint' (*Luc.* 85). She is also an ideal **hostess** (*Luc.* 50–3): she pleads with Tarquin not to abuse the hospitality she has offered (*Luc.* 575–6) and, after the **rape**, still maintains the necessity of offering it on her husband's behalf: 'Yet am I guilty of thy honour's wrack / Yet for thy honour did I entertain him' (*Luc.* 841–2). The **Countess** of Salisbury in *Edward III* likewise welcomes a lustful King into her husband's castle, though her fate is happier since he repents of his dishonourable intentions and compares her to the legendary Lucrece:

> true English lady, whom our isle
> May better boast than ever Roman might
> Of her, whose ransack'd treasury hath task'd
> The vain endeavour of so many pens.
>
> (*EIII* 2.2.193–6)

If Shakespeare did write this scene, the final line probably contains a self-conscious reference back to *The Rape of Lucrece*, published a year earlier: a piece of blatant self-publicity. The poem's description of Lucrece as a maiden city, entered and conquered by the enemy (*Luc.* 412–13 and 462–9) nevertheless preserves the sense of her sovereignty. Even as the 'spotted princess' or ruler (*Luc.* 721), she declares 'For me, I am the mistress of my fate' (*Luc.* 1069).

Lucrece's voice is essential to sustain her sovereignty. She speaks with 'modest eloquence' to dissuade Tarquin (*Luc.* 563), pointing out his violation of the laws of hospitality and the ruin of his honour as 'a sovereign king' (*Luc.* 652). After the rape, her voice dominates the poem, debating rationally in the literary tradition of the complaint, apostrophizing **Night**, Opportunity and Time, and appealing to the latter to punish Tarquin. (Kietzman 1999). She also identifies with **Hecuba** and **Philomel** 'that sing'st of ravishment' (*Luc.* 1128). She rejects her bodily pollution without assuming guilt: 'Though my gross blood be stain's with this abuse / Immaculate and spotless is my mind' (*Luc.* 1655–6). In spite of her eloquence and self-assurance, Lucrece is, as she recognizes, trapped within a patriarchal ideology that values women's bodies above their minds. 'In vain I cavil with mine infamy' (*Luc.* 1025), she admits. Suicide, the separation of her physically polluted self from 'she that was thy Lucrece' (*Luc.* 1682) is ironically the only means left to preserve her self-integrity. Lucrece's suicide is a curious parallel to Othello's murder of **Desdemona** so she will not corrupt more men. It is to preserve women's chastity in the future: 'No dame hereafter living / By my excuse shall claim excuse's giving' (*Luc.* 174–15). By stabbing herself (a symbolic repetition of the rape), Lucrece confirms the male definition of **chastity** as an absolute, offering no blurred boundaries that might provide loop-holes to women of less strict principles. Olivia in *Twelfth Night* adopts an image of Lucrece as her personal seal and is constructed along similar absolute terms in **Maria**'s letter:

'silence, like a Lucrece knife, / With bloodless stroke my heart doth gore' (*TN* 2.5.105–6). In the poem, the two streams of blood which flow 'pure and red' and 'black' from Lucrece's violated body, graphically demonstrate the dismemberment of woman by patriarchal ideology (*Luc.* 1742–3).

(c) Full length studies of Lucrece are given by Ian Donaldson (1982), Mercedes Maroto Camino (1995) and Stephanie Jed (1989). Jocelyn Catty (1999) puts the poem's representation of rape in a wider literary and legal context. Diana Vickers considers the Petrarchan framing of Lucrece (1985), while Jane O. Newman's work (1994) demonstrates how Shakespeare edits the classical models of Philomel and Hecuba to construct a heroine who conforms more easily to patriarchal models. Mary Jo Kietzman (1999: 21–45) analyses the poem's representation of Lucrece's voice with reference to the literary tradition of complaint. Catherine Belsey (2001) examines the context of the poem, its narrative constructions of Lucrece and Tarquin. Margo Hendricks (2000) considers Lucrece's speech and her suicide in relation to St Augustine and Christian ideas of confession.

Lychorida, (a) a character in *Pericles* who acts as midwife to **Thaisa** and **nurse** to **Marina**.

Lychorida's name is taken from Shakespeare's sources in Gower and Twine and George Wilkins's *Painefull Adventures of Pericles*; the latter lists 'an aged Nurse called *Lychorida* a midwife, with other handmaides' (Bullough Vol. VI: 518), though it is not clear whether Lychorida is both nurse and midwife as she is in *Pericles*. Pericles asks 'O, how, Lychorida! / How does my queen?' (*Per.* 3.1.6–7) and links her with Lucina, goddess of childbirth (*Per.* 3.1.10 and 14). As both midwife and nurse Lychorida functions to strengthen the tenuous bonds between Marina and her mother Thaisa which are apparently severed by death. She announces the death of Thaisa by presenting Marina as 'all that is left living of your queen' (*Per.* 3.1.20). Associated closely with weeping, Lychorida draws attention to dangers and loss in the midst of new birth. She sheds tears when she and Marina are left in the care of Cleon and Dionyza (3.3.38–9) and Lychorida's own death produces further weeping from Marina (4.2.11–12), who strews Lychorida's grave with flowers in mourning for her nurse and, by association, her lost mother (4.1.13–17).

(c) George Wilkins' *Painfull Adventures of Pericles, Prince of Tyre* (London, 1608) and Twine's *Patterne of Painefull Adventures* are both found in Bullough, Vol. VI (1966: 423–82 and 492–546). In Twine the character is called Ligozides and the narrative details how her death leaves the princess Tharsia (Marina's equivalent) alone and defenceless (Bullough Vol. VI: 452–5).

Mab, Queen, (a) a name invented by Mercutio for the fairy who creates nightmares. The OED lists mab as meaning slattern or promiscuous woman and **witch**. (b) According to Mercutio, Queen Mab is minute:

> She is the fairies' midwife and she comes
> In shape no bigger than an agate stone
> On the forefinger of an alderman,
> Drawn with a team of little atomi
> Over men's noses as they lie asleep.
>
> (1.4.54–8)

As well as commanding her coach with a whip, this fantasy queen commands the fantasies of sleeping people, men and women. The detail of her clothing: 'Her collars of the moonshine's wat'ry beams' (1.4.65) suggests this may be a nightmare version of Queen Elizabeth, supreme commander of both church and state in England. She inspires courtiers to 'dream on cur'sies' and of preferment (1.4.72 and 77); parsons to dream of 'another benefice' and soldiers to defend the nation with dreams of 'cutting foreign throats' (1.4.83). Queen Mab, who gets angry when ladies dream on kisses (1.4.74–5) as Elizabeth did with her ladies-in-waiting, bears an uncanny resemblance to the 'little old woman in a coarse white petticoat all unready' and yet ready enough to entertain Simon Forman's advances in his erotic dream about the Queen (Montrose 1996). Mab the slattern is the Virgin Queen's own nightmare alter-ego: the scandal of promiscuity. Like Queen Elizabeth, Queen Mab's power to shape literary fantasies almost immediately is evidenced by the fact that she reappeared in Jonson's *Alchemist*, and his court entertainments *Oberon, the Fairy Prince* and *Particular Entertainment of the Queen*, written for Anna of Denmark's visit to Althorpe (Buccola 2006: 231), in Brown's *Brittanias Pastorals*, Milton's 'L'Allegro', and she starred in *Queen Mab*, *or the Fairies Jubilee* at Garrick's celebration of Shakespeare as a national poet in 1797 (Reeves 1902: 20).

(c) W. P. Reeves (1902) traces possible origins for the name in Welsh, Irish and French folk lore, favouring the latter. The account of Simon Forman's dream is in Louis Montrose's 1983 essay on *A Midsummer Night's Dream* (Montrose 1996) which, surprisingly, does not mention Queen Mab. Regina Buccola (2006) is a full length study of fairies, fairy queens and their relationship to Catholicism in early modern literature, with a brief mention of Queen Mab (pp. 71 and 231). *See* **midwife** and **mare**.

Macbeth, Lady, (a) wife and Scottish queen consort to the eponymous hero in *Macbeth*.

(b) The character is introduced, via Macbeth's letter, as his partner and later his **wife**, but she is never named in the script. She shifts anonymously from a variety of different subject positions as **hostess**, **mistress** or **lady** of the house, **Queen** of the Scottish court and, finally, patient. As such she exemplifies Belsey's argument that women have no unified subject position from which to speak in tragedy (Belsey 1985: 160). The closest Lady Macbeth's role gets to a secure subject position is as Macbeth's 'dearest partner of greatness' (1.5.11). In order to murder Duncan and grasp their desires the two have to work as a team: 'What cannot you and I perform upon / Th'unguarded Duncan?' (1.7.69–70). The regicide is a *folie à deux*, an emotional chemistry between two people through which they can commit impassioned acts of violence they would not be able to enact alone (Symons 1985: 168). Lady Macbeth pours her 'spirits' into Macbeth's ear, while he wields the dagger to do 'the deed' (2.2.14). When Macbeth greets her as 'my dearest love', and she incites him to murder or threatens 'From this time / Such I account thy love' (1.7.38–9), the two are fused in erotically driven desire for violence. After the murder, she is still his 'love', his 'dear wife' and his 'dearest chuck' (3.2.29, 36 and 45) but is henceforth excluded from his confidence and his plot to shed further blood.

Lady Macbeth is described as 'fiend-like' (5.9.35) and allies herself with the de-feminized **witches** or **weird sisters** by invoking spirits to 'unsex' her and fill her 'from the crown to the toe topful / Of direst cruelty' (1.5.40–43). This is not a subject position she can maintain, however, since the human bonds that tie her to Macbeth and to her other social roles, continue to contradict its illusion of absolute unity and absolute power. The character is addressed as a hospitable 'hostess' (1.6.10 and 31), as the 'mistress' of the household and its servants (2.1.31 and 3.2.2). Her reaction to news of the murder, 'Woe alas / What, in our house?' (2.3.87–8) is either a supremely well-managed improvization of the role or an internalization of its demands.

As Queen and royal householder, Lady Macbeth continues to 'keep her state' (3.4.5) at the banquet in spite of the breakdown of decorum brought by Banquo's ghost. Once Macbeth moves on to confide in the weird sisters, the futility of her social and emotional roles becomes apparent: 'Nought's had, all's spent / Where our desire is got without content' (3.2.4–5).

The character's final coherent subject position as woman is one she has tried to deny. Macduff's appellation is heavily ironic, given what spectators have just witnessed in the previous scenes:

> O gentle lady
> 'Tis not for you to hear what I can speak:
> The repetition in a woman's ear
> Would murther as it fell.

> (2.3.83–6)

A crucial part of denying 'access and passage to remorse' is an attempt to destroy the maternal origins which are refigured in her own body as **breasts**, vagina and **womb** and the potential for **mother**hood (1.4.44) The **boy actor** in the role already advertises their absence. Without these features essential to the construction of womanly identity in early modern England, Lady Macbeth has no place and certainly no future. She has 'in effect, sold Macbeth's heir for a little, fleeting power' (Chamberlain 2005: 84). Her final scene as a mad patient (5.3.37) cruelly mocks her own impatience with those womanly characteristics by replaying fragmented memories of the *folie à deux* and the illusion of completeness it offered. She acknowledges the annihilation of the Other woman, as mother, in a reference to Lady Macduff's murder: 'The Thane of Fife had a wife; where is she now?' and her now tragic recognition that 'What's done cannot be undone' (5.2.42 and 68).

(c) Joan Larsen Klein, 'Lady Macbeth: "Infirm of Purpose"' (1983) is a foundational essay tracing the character's tragic progress, along with Huston Diehl's excellent 'Horrid Image, Sorry Sight, Fatal Vision: The Visual Rhetoric of *Macbeth*' (1983), which analyses Lady Macbeth's material focus and her deliberate moral blindness. Adelman (1992: 130–46) reads the play as a temporary escape from the maternal matrix. Anna Jameson (2005) notes Lady Macbeth's 'amazing power of intellect, her inexorable determination of purpose, her superhuman strength of nerve' without condemning these un-Victorian feminine virtues and Alfar (2003: 111–35) offers another positive political analysis. Chapter 3 of Valbuena (2003: 79–112) identifies anxiety about history, blood, and matriline inheritance in the play as a legacy of Henry VIII's divorce while Arthur Kinney (2001) looks at Lady Macbeth and Lady Macduff with reference to lexias of family in 1606. Phyllis Rackin (2005: 120–34) discusses the historical specificity and timelessness of Lady Macbeth's role. Stephanie Chamberlain (2005) examines the part with reference to early modern attitudes to infanticide. Inga-Stina Ewbank (1966) discusses the classical origins of this in Medea. Crime writer Julian Symons (Sales 1985: 167–73) gives a dated but interesting short introduction to *folie à deux* as a way into reading the relationship between the Macbeths. Frederick Kiefer (1996) argues that Lady Macbeth's memory functions like a conscience book. John Russell Brown (2005) gives a detailed account of staging possibilities and key productions; Judith Cook (1980: 121–30) outlines a stage history for the 'fiend-like queen'; Carol J. Carlisle (1983) analyses Helen Faucit's performance; Sinead Cusack's approach to the role is detailed in 'Lady Macbeth's Barren Sceptre' in Rutter (1988: 53–72) and Schafer (1998: 149–61 (esp.) 154–7) discusses female directors' interpretations.

Macduff, Lady, (a) wife of Macduff, the Thane of Fife in *Macbeth* and **mother** of his children and relative of Rosse.
(b) Deserted by her husband, who flies to England in search of Malcolm, Lady Macduff is defenceless against the attacks of Macbeth's murderers. Although Rosse and the messenger show respect of her 'state of honor' (*Mac.* 4.2.66) she is presented more in the role of a protective mother, helplessly trying to defend her 'little ones' (4.2.69). Imagery of nests and fledglings (connecting back to Banquo's words in Act 1 Scene 6 line 4) makes her a symbol of Macbeth and Lady Macbeth's destruction of fertility. Lady Macbeth muses 'The Thane of Fife had a **wife**; where is she now?' (5.2.42–3) in her madness, strengthening the idea that Lady Macduff is the image of domesticity and motherhood that Lady Macbeth has annihilated in herself and in Scotland in an attempt to secure Macbeth's crown.
(c) Rackin (2005: 134–6) and Kinney (2001: 163–9) read Lady Macduff with reference to early seventeenth century ideals of female domesticity. Robert Lanier Reid, *Shakespeare's Tragic Form: Spirit in the Wheel* (2000: 120–2) offers a Freudian interpretation of Lady Macduff and her children as the objects of Macbeth's desire to destroy the maternal matrix.

madonna, (a) a respectful or mock-respectful form of address to an Italian woman. With the definite article, it is a name for the Virgin **Mary** or an icon representing her. It is thus often a complimentary term, noting a likeness to the **Virgin**. However, it was also used to mean 'prostitute' in early modern England.
(b) The term refers to only one character in only one conversation in Shakespeare: the exchange between Feste and **Olivia** over her grief for her brother's death. It is thus part of the Fool's set piece, a mock-catechism to entertain her. 'Madonna' is an appropriate title for Olivia since she is the most important person in the house and Feste depends upon her forgiveness for his absence, in the same way that a Catholic sinner approaches the Virgin as a mediatrix to aid in the forgiveness of sins. Feste's use – eight times – of the appellation 'madonna', is therefore bold. Perhaps he chooses it to drive home the necessity of accepting death and seeing it as a cause for celebration (as the Virgin had to at the crucifixion). He tells Olivia she is 'the more fool, madonna, to mourn for your brother's soul being in heaven' (*TN* 1.5.70–1). Feste's mock-authority as a priest-like figure effectively legitimizes Olivia's abandonment of mourning in the ensuing scene when she meets Cesario. It may also cleverly expose her mourning as a convenient way to avoid engaging romantically with Orsino. However Olivia understands it, she evidently 'takes delight' in it (*TN* 1.5.83). It is part of a wider network of Catholic allusions in the play including references to St **Anne**, the name **Maria** and Feste's later role as Sir Topas the priest.
   The derogatory sense of 'madonna' is clear in Dekker's *Blurt Master-Constable* (1602 sig. C2) where the whore, who is well known (in the sexual sense) by both

men, is referred to as 'the freckle cheeke *Madonna*'. In *Twelfth Night* it may convey Feste's prophetic insight that Olivia will not only come out of mourning but openly offer herself to Cesario.

(c) Anne Lecercle, 'Country House, Catholicity and the crypt(i(c) in *Twelfth Night*' (2003) traces the network of caltholic allusion in the play.

maid, maiden (a) a virgin or person without sexual experience, usually applied to women and specifically to the Virgin or to Joan La **Pucelle** as the Maid of God. Also used more generally to signify a young or unmarried woman and a female servant or attendant. **Maidenhead** is the condition of being a maid, the state of virginity.

(b) At its simplest level, 'maid' distinguishes a younger from an older woman in Shakespeare, the youngest being 'A maid-child call'd Marina' (*Per.* 5.3.6). In *Coriolanus* 'matrons flung gloves, / Ladies and maids their scarfs and hand-kerchers' (*Cor.* 2.1.263). The juxtaposition of maid and matron occurs again in *Cymbeline* (3.4.39) and *All's Well* (3.5.97). Set in opposition to the title '**mother**', 'maid' usually means '**virgin**'. Lady **Capulet** tells **Juliet** 'I was your mother much upon these years / That you are now a maid' (*R&J* 1.3.72). **Margaret** of Anjou's presentation of herself as 'a maid / A virgin and his servant' (*1HVI* 5.3.177–8) draws attention to two strands of meaning in the term.

'Maid' identifies a character's inferior status and social dependency in the case of female servants. Sly remembers 'a woman's maid of the house'; Mistress **Quickly** is 'this honest gentlewoman, your maid', (*MWW* 1.4.82) and **Perdita** calls herself a 'poor lowly maid' in recognition of her social difference from Prince Florizel (*WT* 4.4.9). Caesar is horrified that **Octavia** is come 'a market-maid' to Rome instead of with the pomp and circumstance befitting Antony's wife or Caesar's **sister** (*A&C* 3.6.51). Female servants were called 'maid' because their period of service lasted only until they married and set up a household of their own. Whether this actually reflected their virginity was open to question since masters often abused their dominant position (Jones 1999: 23). Timon refers to this: 'Maid, to thy master's bed; / Thy **mistress** is o' the brothel!' (*Tim.* 4.1.12). In *King John*, poor maids are the most likely victims of 'That smooth-faced gentle-man, tickling **Commodity**'; the maid 'having no external thing to lose / But the word "maid,"' is cheated of even that (*KJ* 2.1.572–3).

Even when the master did not threaten her sexually, a maid remained vulner-able to the criticism of her employers, even when unjustified, and she needed outstanding diplomatic skill. The double standard for maidenly behaviour between mistresses and servants is anatomized in *Two Gentlemen of Verona*. **Julia** excuses her own petulant, perverse behaviour on the receipt of Proteus's love let-ter as the result of her status as **maid**, apparently oblivious to the sensitivities – or insight – of her maidservant **Lucetta**:

> What a fool is she, that knows I am a maid,
> And would not force the letter to my view!
> Since maids, in modesty, say "no" to that

Which they would have the profferer construe "ay."
(*TGV* 1.2.53–56)

Julia acknowledges 'how churlishly I chid Lucetta hence' (*TGV* 1.2.60) and calls her back. When she returns, Lucetta tellingly wishes 'That you might kill your stomach on your meat, / And not upon your maid' (*TGV* 1.2.69), perhaps speaking for many female spectators who had experience of having to tolerate similar experiences.

Shakespeare's references to serving maids often invoke the sexual meaning of the word to doubly emphasize differences between women. In *Rape of Lucrece*, for example, Lucrece's unnamed maid who 'sorts a sad look to her lady's sorrow', is set alongside the polluted heroine to mark difference (*Luc.* 1221). Although both weep alike, the maid is innocent of sexual experience and of what has happened (*Luc.* 1220–36). In *Othello* the 'maid call'd **Barbary**' remained a maid since she died forsaken by her lover (*Oth.* 4.3.26–30). Given Gratiano's usual bawdy style, his simple statement 'You saw the mistress, I beheld the maid' (*Mer.* 3.2.198) could imply that Portia, the mistress, is not a maid.

Shakespeare's texts make no direct reference to the Virgin using this word; indeed Joan La **Pucelle** undermines the tradition of divine maidenly perfection. She is introduced as 'a holy maid' inspired by a heavenly vision (*1HVI* 1.2.51) and claims to be 'Chaste and immaculate in very thought' (*1HVI* 5.4.51). However, at her execution, her self-definition as a virgin martyr whose 'maiden blood' will 'cry for vengeance at the gates of heaven' is subverted by her life-saving claim to be pregnant. York mocks 'Now heaven forfend! the holy maid with child!' (*1HVI* 5.4.52–65).

Apart from respect for the 'maiden pilgrimage' of **nun**s (*MND* 1.1.75), Shakespeare's idealizations of maids are secular and, for the most part, feminized even though 'maid' was used of both sexes to mark virginity. Sebastian tries to alleviate Olivia's potential embarrassment in wooing another woman by casting himself as 'both a maid and a man' (*TN* 5.1.263), for example. Maidenhood is a mark of outstanding excellence for young female characters. The **Princess** of France is 'A maid of grace and complete majesty' (*LLL* 1.1.137); **Desdemona** is 'a maid / That paragons description and wild fame' (*Oth.* 2.1.61–2) and **Helena** is 'a maid too virtuous / For the contempt of empire' (*AWW* 3.2.31–32). **Marina** is conscious of her special status when she arrives 'with my companion maid' (both a servant and virgin **sister**) to offer service in the healing of Pericles (*Per.* 5.1.77):

I am a maid
My lord, that ne'er before invited eyes
But have been gaz'd on like a comet.
(*Per.* 5.1.84–6)

For women, maidenhood is iconic. **Diana**'s determination 'Marry that will, I live and die a maid' makes her 'no maiden, but a monument', no better than a living statue or corpse in Bertram's view (*AWW* 4.3.6 and 74). Rigid adherence to

chastity appears morbid when 'our cull-cold maids' call erotic 'long purple' flowers 'dead men's fingers' (*Ham.* 4.7.171). Other negative impressions of maiden isolation are found in the Petrarchan mistress, 'a fair cruel maid' who slays her lover (*TN* 2.4.54). **Beatrice** abandons single life with the words 'Contempt, farewell! and maiden pride, adieu! / No glory lives behind the back of such' (*MAdo* 3.1.109–1).

There are, however, many examples where maids are celebrated as glorious examples of innocence. The most striking is **Miranda**. Ferdinand's first question to this 'wonder' is 'If you be maid or no?' to which she replies 'No wonder, but certainly a maid' (*Temp.* 1.2.428–9), and it is this which gives her the courage to propose:

> prompt me, plain and holy innocence!
> I am your **wife**, it you will marry me;
> If not, I'll die your maid: to be your fellow
> You may deny me; but I'll be your servant,
> Whether you will or no.
>
> (*Temp.* 3.1.82–6)

Miranda plays on the dual meaning of maid as virgin and as servant. Petruchio's play-acting in addressing Vincentio as a 'Fair lovely maid' with 'fresher' youth and heavenly beauty, mocks the ready idealization of maidenly innocence (*Shrew* 4.5.29–33). Rosalind likewise observes that 'maids are May when they are maids, but the sky changes when they are wives' (*AYLI* 4.1.148).

Nevertheless the type has an enduring appeal as a link to childhood virtue and security. Evans imagines 'a maid / That, 'ere she sleep, has thrice her prayers said' can now sleep 'sound as careless infancy' (*MWW* 5.5.49–53). Helena implies that the maid's name is itself a tower of strength, asserting 'I am a simple maid, and therein wealthiest, / That I protest I simply am a maid' (*AWW* 2.3.66–67).

The term's associations with youth and innocence carry implications of vulnerability and weakness. Rome's contempt for the Egyptian military potential is shown in the belief that 'Photinus an eunuch and your maids / Manage this war' (*A&C* 3.7.14–15). In *As You Like It*, **Celia** is 'a young maid with travel much oppress'd', who 'faints for succour' (*AYLI* 2.4.73–74). **Ophelia** proves that 'a young maid's wits' are as fragile as 'an old man's life' (*Ham.* 4.5.160–1). **Helena** invokes the maid's traditional weakness, claiming 'I have no gift at all in shrewishness; / I am a right maid for my cowardice' (*MND* 3.2.301–2). The maid's vulnerability thus needs protecting. Bianca 'must live a maid at home' where her father has 'closely mew'd her up' (*Shrew* 1.2.182 and 183).

Moreover, a 'Maid's mild behaviour and sobriety' is the prescribed behaviour for the type (*Shrew* 1.1.71). **Hermia** primly follows 'maiden modesty' (*MAdo* 4.1.179), insisting that Lysander lie apart from her in the wood: 'Such separation as may well be said / Becomes a virtuous bachelor and a maid' (*MND* 2.2.58–9). However, as she admits, Demetrius drives her 'past the 'bounds / Of maiden's patience' (*MND* 3.2.65–6). Whatever her desires, a young maid's enforced

patience makes time move slowly 'between the contract of her marriage and the day it is solemniz'd' (*AYLI* 3.2.314). Modesty extends to speech as well as deportment. Properly, 'a maiden hath no tongue but thought' (*Mer.* 3.2.8) so Pandarus wishes he could help all the 'tongue-tied maidens here' in the audience (*T&C* 3.2.210) reach their desires. Modesty demands that the expression of a maid's desire can only be perversely achieved through denial. Buckingham counsels Richard III to 'Play the maid's part, still answer nay, and take it' (*RIII* 3.7.51).

The traditional mark of a maiden's modesty is her blush, a convention Shakespeare reiterates in several texts. Although King Henry tells **Princess Katherine** to 'Put off your maiden blushes' (*HV* 5.2.234–5) she supposedly cannot face direct discussion of love 'Being a maid yet ros'd over with the virgin crimson of modesty' (*HV* 5.2.295–6). Desdemona is likewise supposedly 'A maiden never bold; / Of spirit so still and quiet, that her motion / Blush'd at herself' (*Oth.* 1.3.94–6). Neither of these is estimates is accurate, however. Katherine knowingly flirts with Henry V and Desdemona runs away with Othello. Juliet takes comfort in the fact that it is dark when she declares her love to Romeo, 'Else would a maiden blush bepaint my cheek / For that which thou hast heard me speak to-night' (*R&J* 2.1.86). The convention of the virgin's blush is comically reversed in *Love's Labour's Lost* and *Venus and Adonis*. Don Armado admits 'I do betray myself with blushing' when he addresses the less-than-virginal Jaquenetta as 'Maid!' (*LLL* 1.2.133). She is a country **dey-woman** or dairy woman (*LLL* 3.1.131) rather than a virgin. Adonis 'burns with bashful shame' while **Venus** 'with her tears / Doth quench the maiden burning of his cheeks' (*V&A* 49–50). Moreover, the blush is an untrustworthy sign of maidenhood since it is a mark of shame as well as modesty. This is how Claudio reads it on Hero's face:

> Behold how like a maid she blushes here!
> O, what authority and show of truth
> Can cunning sin cover itself withal!
> Comes not that blood as modest evidence
> To witness simple virtue? Would you not swear,
> All you that see her, that she were a maid,
> By these exterior shows?
>
> (*MAdo* 4.1.34)

The impossibility of deciphering the blush for Claudio and the other men on stage (to say nothing of spectators who presumably have to imagine it) draws attention to an ambiguity that runs through Shakespeare's texts. Whether a maid is really a maid is ultimately concealed, a secret. As Viola points out, 'What I am and what I would are as secret as maidenhead' (*TN* 1.5.216). Shakespeare's texts play with the ambiguity of the word to emphasize this. Mopsa and Dorcas are not virginal maids but they enjoy singing the ballad 'Two maids wooing a man' (*WT* 4.4.289). Launce muses about his beloved ''tis a milkmaid; yet 'tis not a maid, for she hath had gossips; yet 'tis a maid, for she is her master's maid, and serves for wages' (*TGV* 3.1.271). **Gossips** traditionally attend a woman in childbirth, meaning the milkmaid cannot be a maid, and the innuendo of 'serves for wages' heightens doubts about her virginity. Diana teases Bertram and the court with a series of contradictions and puns on 'knowing' as carnal knowledge that constitute a riddle of her virginity: 'He knows I am no maid, and he'll swear to 't; / I'll swear I am a maid, and he knows not' (*AWW* 5.3.290–1).

Ophelia's song of the maid at her valentine's window who 'let in the maid, that out a maid / Never departed more' (*Ham.* 4.5.54–5) gives a narrative framework to the loss of maidenhood, an experience frequently presented as traumatic for female characters. The tragic fates of Romeo and **Juliet** chart the loss of maidenhead with special focus on Juliet's experience. Romeo uses 'maid' of Juliet to mean both virgin and servant of Diana, goddess of chastity, when he urges, 'Be not her maid, since she is envious' (*R&J* 2.2.5–9). Juliet appeals to **night**, a 'sober-suited matron' for help in pursing her desires and losing her maidenhood without the loss of modesty:

> learn me how to lose a winning match,
> Play'd for a pair of stainless maidenhoods:
> Hood my unmann'd blood, bating in my cheeks,
> With thy black mantle.
>
> (*R&J* 3.2.11–15)

When Romeo is exiled on their wedding night, Juliet's sexual frustration is palpable in her line, 'I, a maid, die maiden-widowed' and her determination to let 'death, not Romeo, take my maidenhead!' through suicide, a pattern that the play fulfils after their wedding night (*R&J* 3.2.135 and 137).

Male characters' attitudes to maidenhood and its loss are expressed in voyeuristic and predatory terms in Shakespeare's work. Prince John of Lancaster's first taste of battle is celebrated with the words 'Come, brother John; full bravely hast thou flesh'd / Thy maiden-sword' (*1HIV* 5.4.130), drawing a comparison between male initiation into battle and to sex. Joan La **Pucelle** challenges such male dominance in the person of Young Talbot with her words 'Thou maiden youth, be vanquish'd by a maid' (*1HVI* 4.7.38). Tullus Aufidius makes a remarkable comparison between his wedding night and the thrill of meeting Coriolanus:

> Know thou first,
> I loved the maid I married; never man
> Sigh'd truer breath; but that I see thee here,
> Thou noble thing! more dances my rapt heart
> Than when I first my wedded **mistress** saw
> Bestride my threshold.
>
> (*Cor.* 4.5.113–19)

The aftermath of war is a more or less violent male conquering of the female maiden body. Henry V warns the citizens of Harfleur that if they do not surrender 'your pure maidens' will 'fall into the hand / Of hot and forcing violation' (*HV*

3.3.20), a realization of his earlier words to Falsaff 'if there come a hot June and this civil buffeting hold, we shall buy maidenheads as they buy hob-nails, by the hundreds' (*1H1V* 2.4.362). **Mariana** in *All's Well* warns that the soldiers' arrival in the city following war begins a pattern of seduction that cannot be resisted:

> many a maid hath been seduced by them; and the misery is, example, that so terrible shows in the wreck of maidenhood, cannot for all that dissuade succession, but that they are limed with the twigs that threaten them.
>
> (*AWW* 3.4.20–4)

In *Henry V* the King's wooing of Katherine constitutes a sexual colonization of the unconquered cities of France in which 'the cities turn'd into a maid: for they are all girdled with maiden walls that war never enter'd' (*HV* 5.2.320–2). This echoes the English colonial project proposed by Sir Walter Ralegh, who had recently described Guiana as 'a Countrey that hath yet her Maydenhead' (Ralegh 1997: 196). In *The Rape of Lucrece*, Tarquin sees Lucrece's breasts as 'A pair of maiden worlds unconquered', or a maiden city to be invaded by him (*Luc.* 408 and 463–9).

Maidenhood continues to fall subject to masculine sexual aggression in peacetime as part of the traditions of patriarchal kingship, most crudely when Jack Cade, a pretender to the throne, determines to exact his *droit de seigneur* so that 'there shall not a maid be married, but she shall pay to me her maidenhead ere they have it' (*2HVI* 4.7.121–3). Rape by servants is sanctioned by the uncivil conflict between their masters in *Romeo and Juliet* where the Capulet Sampson threatens to 'thrust' Montague's 'maids to the wall' and cut off 'the heads of the maids, or their maidenheads' (*R&J* 1.1.17–26). Even apparently comic moments contain a threat of violence, as when the Fool suddenly warns female spectators 'She that's a maid now, and laughs at my departure, / Shall not be a maid long, unless things be cut shorter (*KL* 1.5. 51–2).

Agricultural images of husbandry present the taking of a woman's maidenhood in gentler, more creative terms although it could be argued that acts of ploughing constitute a no-less-violent invasion of the female body. The young man of the Sonnets is urged that 'many maiden gardens yet unset' would bear the living flowers of his children (*Son.* 16.6). There is a predatory voyeurism in the way Burgundy regards maids as ripening fruit when he says 'fair maids, well summer'd and warm kept, are like flies at Bartholemew-tide' and will 'endure handling which before would not abide looking on' (*HV* 5.2.295–311). The Bawd says of Marina: 'Such a maidenhead were no cheap thing, if men were as they have been' (*Per.* 4.2.60). Such comments are disturbing because they naturalize a heightened male attraction to virgins and the ripe fruit of their virgin sexuality. Angelo's perverse fascination with the 'virtuous maid' (*MM* 2.2.30) Isabella is explicitly condemned as unjust. Many of Shakespeare's other texts advertise the maid as tempting ripe fruit and interpellate male spectators to sanction the plucking of such fruit via invitations like Petruchio's to 'Carouse full measure to her maidenhead' (*Shrew* 3.2.225).

(c) The relationship between sexual and territorial colonization is in Sir Walter Ralegh's 1596 *Discoverie of the Large, Rich and Bewtiful Empyre of Guiana* (1997: 196). For discussion of maids as servants see Susan Frye and Karen Robertson (eds.), *Maids and Mistresses, Cousins and Queens* (1999), especially Ann Rosalind Jones's excellent essay 'Maidservants of London: Sisterhoods of Kinship and Labor' (pp. 21–32) and Natasha Korda, *Women and Property in Early Modern England* (2002: 49–60). See also Laurie Ellinghausen's case study of Isabella Whitney's text as a representation of maidservants' lives in London (Ellinghausen 2008: 20–35). Tracey Sedinger, 'Working Girls: Status and Sexual Difference' (2003) compares mistresses and maids. The linguistic manipulation of maidenhood and maidens' sexuality in Shakespeare is analysed by William C. Carroll (2001: (esp.) 21) and Angus Easson discusses Boult's puns in 'Marina's Maidenhead' (1973: 328–9).

Maiden and **maidenhead** – *see* **Maid** above

mammet, (a) a false image or idol or, in secular terms, a doll or a puppet.
(b) The *OED* does not suggest that this was a particularly gendered term in general, and Shakespeare seems to have been the first dramatist to use it in the derogative sense of doll or infantile woman. Hotspur belittles human love, seeing his wife as an idol or distraction from the real business of war and telling her, 'This is no world / To play with mammets and to tilt with lips' (*1HIV* 2.3.95). Capulet uses it to trivialize **Juliet**'s distress at the prospect of marrying Paris. He ventriloquises her as a spoilt child:

> a wretched puling fool,
> A whining mammet, in her fortune's tender,
> To answer 'I'll not wed; I cannot love,
> I am too young; I pray you, pardon me.
> (*R&J* 3.5.183–6)

Here the word may well prefigure the *OED*'s examples of 'mammet' as a regional word meaning 'child'. It is used again in a similar situation by Dekker in *The Shoemaker's Holiday*, where Rose is scolded as a 'mammet' for refusing to marry Hammon (Dekker 1600: sig C2), and in *The Alchemist*, where the angry Kastril tells his sister; 'you are a mammet!' for marrying Lovewit (Jonson 2010: 5.5.128).
(c) Thomas Dekker, *The Shoemaker's Holiday* (1600: Sig. C2) and Jonson, *The Alchemist* (2011) give uses following Shakespeare's.

marchioness, (a) the wife or widow of a marquess; a woman holding the rank of marquess in her own right. **Anne** Bullen is made Marchionesss of Pembroke in her own right in *Henry VIII* and a non-speaking character, the Marchioness of Dorset, is a godmother to the Princess **Elizabeth** in the final scene of the play.
(b) 'Marchioness' is a contested title in *Henry VIII*. The Old **Lady** who attends on Anne Bullen teases her at the news of her new title because her acceptance of it

exposes her desire to be **queen**. The King's Majesty's approval of Anne is formally announced in his wish to bring

> honor to you no less flowing
> Than Marchioness of Pembroke; to which title
> A thousand pound a year, annual support,
> Out of his grace he adds.
>
> (*HVIII* 2.3.62–5)

The terms make it clear that this is a very material **honour** (as opposed to the spiritual honour garnered by Queen Katherine) and the Old Lady shrewdly defines Anne's potential to rise from Marchioness to **Duchess** at least (*HVIII* 2.3.93–9). Cardinal Wolsey is outraged, emphasizing Anne's plain surname 'Bullen? / No, we'll no Bullens' in contrast to her title 'The Marchioness of Pembroke?' (*HVIII* 3.2.88–90). Anne's absence from the text after her coronation and the replacement of a different Marchioness as godmother to Elizabeth (5.4.0SD) may have served to relegitimate the title.
(c) Thomas Merriam, (2001), Kim H. Noling (1988) and Paul Dean (1988) discuss Anne's title.

mare, (a) a female horse and a derogatory name for a woman, but also the name of a type of throw in wrestling where the opponent is jerked over one's shoulder from behind. Derived from this, a 'night-mare' is female spirit supposed to settle on a sleeping person or animal and cause bad dreams.
(b) Puck's pat phrase 'The man shall have his mare again / And all shall be well' (*MND* 3.2.463) advertises how heterosexual coupling reduces women to subjection as inferior beings. Petruchio's treatment of his horse gives a dark suggestion of how he intends to treat Katherina and the same idea of female subjection informs Nym's words, 'Though patience be a tired mare, yet will she plod' (*HV* 2.1.26). Enobarbus draws on the specialized meaning of the word in wrestling to suggest an inversion of gender order. The 'Mare' was one of many 'sleights and tricks' appertaining to the sport of wrestling (Carew 1602: Vol. 1, fol. 76). Enobarbus explains that if Cleopatra joins the army to fight against the Romans, she will overthrow Antony's power:

> If we should serve the horse and mares together,
> The horse were merely lost; the mares would bear
> A soldier and his horse.
>
> (*A&C* 3.7.7–9)

The inversion of gender norms between **Venus** and Adonis is also symbolized with reference to horses. Adonis's horse escapes to be led off by the mare while he is physically restrained by Venus. He is powerless in 'how to get my palfrey from the mare' (*V&A* 384).

Shakespeare employs a specialized derivative, 'night-mare', to expose masculine insecurity. Night-mares are defined by Topsell as a manifestation of female super-natural evil, 'spirits of the night, called Incubi or Succubi' (Topsell 1608: 173). Poor Tom describes his night-mare in similar terms:

> He met the night-mare and her nine-fold;
> Bid her alight,
> And her troth plight,
> And aroint thee, witch, aroint thee!
>
> (*KL* 3.4.121–4)

Queen **Mab** who 'gallops night by night' (*R&J* 1.3.70) over sleeping people is a night-mare. Mercutio's preoccupation with her activities betrays his own insecurity as the group of young men head towards the Capulet ball and romance. Mistress Quickly, determined to have her debt repaid by Falstaff, theatens to haunt him: 'I will ride thee a' nights like the mare'. He replies with a jest: 'I think I am as like to ride the mare, if I have any vantage of ground to get up' (*2HIV* 2.1.76–9), implying that he will get the better of her again, but he is under pressure at this point.

(c) Robert Carew, *Survey of Cornwall* (1602: Vol. 1. fol. 76) lists the 'mare' as one of the tricks used in wrestling. Edward Topsell's *Historie of Serpents* (1608) describes night-mares.

Margaret, (a) the name of three characters: Margaret of Anjou, Queen to Henry VI; the gentlewoman to **Hero** in *Much Ado* and the niece of Richard III, Lady Margaret Plantagenet, who is never named in the text other than as Clarence's **daughter**. Shakespeare had two aunts called Margaret, one a sister of Mary Arden and the other the wife of his uncle Henry Shakespeare. An elder sister to Shakespeare, who died only months after she was born, was named Margaret, probably after these aunts (Weis 2007: 10). Margaret, a name popular since medieval times, means 'pearl' and derives via the old French *Marguerite*, Latin *Margarita* and the Greek *Margarites*, from the Hebrew word *margaron* 'pearl'. The pearl is a symbol of purity. It was also a royal name. St Margaret of Scotland (d. 1093) was daughter of Edmund Ironside of England and Margaret Tudor (1489–1541), sister of Henry VIII, married James IV of Scotland and ruled as regent there after his death.

(b) The only Margaret in Shakespeare's canon to live up to the purity of her name is the child Margaret Plantagenet who appears with her brother to lament their father's death (*RIII* 2.2.) and then with **Anne**, her **aunt**, in a scene of **sisterly** solidarity (*RIII* 4.1.) where she does not speak. Both other Margarets are false in some way. The character Margaret of Anjou appears to embody the classic model of **beauty**, her entrancing physical appearance reflecting a divine purity suggested by her name. She offers Henry VI a **maid**'s token of 'a pure unspotted heart, / Never yet taint with love' (*1HVI* 5.3.177–82). However, the fact that she is quite willing to submit to Suffolk's infatuated kiss immediately belies the appearance of innocence. King Henry's own spiritual purity points up her hollowness; even when she laments his lack of love for her, her tears are not pearls like Cordelia's (*KL*

4.3.22) or the innocent Prince Arthur's (*KJ* 2.1.169), but crocodile tears conjured for theatrical effect (*2HVI* 3.2.73–121). Real tears are shed at the banishment of Suffolk in a passionate exchange that re-casts her as victim of a political match rather than simply a strategist (*2HVI* 3.2.300–412). When Suffolk is killed King Henry argues 'Come Margaret, God, our hope, will succour us' but Margaret only replies, 'My hope is gone now Suffolk is deceas'd' (*2HVI* 4.6.55–6), cradling his head in her arms.

Margaret of Anjou's worldly focus is evidenced in a 'valiant courage and undaunted spirit / (More than in women commonly is seen)' (*1HVI* 5.5.70–1). She takes up arms herself to defend her son's rights, having verbally **divorce**d King Henry who disinherited him (*3HVI* 1.1.247–50). Her cruelty to the defeated Duke of York, showing him the handkerchief soaked in his son Rutland's blood, elicits the famous condemnation that she is 'opposite to every good' and has a 'tiger's heart wrapp'd in a woman's hide!' (*3HVI* 1.4.134–7). While the men all weep, she remains sternly dry-eyed (*3HVI* 1.4.150–74), showing her lack of so-called womanly virtue. Defeat, followed by the murder of her son, does bring tears (*3HVI* 5.4.73–5) and a wish for death. She remains a powerfully prophetic, cursing presence in *Richard III*, however, invoking hell, **revenge** and destruction in a complete inversion of the purity associated with her name, which Gloucester speaks to turn her curses back on her (*RIII* 1.3.233–9).

Margaret in *Much Ado*, who is named 17 times in the script, is not as pure as Benedick's appellation 'Sweet Mistress Margaret' (*MAdo* 5.2.1) implies. She is instrumental in betraying her mistress, however unwillingly, by agreeing to dress up in Hero's clothes and imitate her (or the classical heroine **Hero**) at her balcony on the night before the wedding. Borachio reports 'she leans me out at her mistress' chamber-window, bids me a thousand times good night' (*MAdo* 3.3.146–8). Leonato points out that Margaret 'was pack'd in all this wrong, / Hired to it by your brother' (*MAdo* 5.1. 208–9) and thus 'in some fault' even though she later protested that she was party to Don John's villainy 'against her will' (*MAdo* 5.4.4–5).

(c) Patricia-Ann Lee (1986: 183–217) gives a detailed account of the historical figure of Margaret of Anjou and her representations in the English chronicle histories, with a brief suggestion that Shakespeare's character is a comment on the sovereignty of **Elizabeth** I. Carol Rutter (2006), and Stuart Hampton-Reeves and Carol Chillington Rutter, *Shakespeare in Performance: The Henry VI Plays* (2006: 74–9 and 197–201) discuss Margaret of Anjou in production. Fiona Bell (2004) offers an actor's perspective in 'Joan of Arc in Part I of *Henry VI* and Margaret in Parts 1, 2, and 3 of *Henry VI* and *Richard III*'. Tracy Sedinger (2003) discusses women who disguise themselves as mistresses, including Margaret in *Much Ado*.

Margery (a) the medieval vernacular form of **Margaret**.

(b) 'Margery' is associated with working women in Shakespeare. It is the name of Launcelot Gobbo's mother (*Mer.* 2.2.84–6), who is referred to but does not appear; of 'Margery Jordan, the cunning **witch**' (*2HVI* 1.2.75), and, in Stephano's song, one of the girls who keeps sailors company (*Temp.* 2.1.48). Its assocations with lower-class **gossip** may be why Leontes mocks Paulina as 'Lady Margery, your **midwife**' (*WT* 2.3.160).

Maria, (a) a character in *Love's Labour's Lost*: one of the ladies attending the Princess of France, and **Olivia**'s gentlewoman in *Twelfth Night*. The name is the Latin for 'Mary', a formation from the early Christian name 'Mariam' which came from the Hebrew name 'Miriam'. In early modern England the name had obvious associations with the Virgin Mary and Catholicism in rituals such as the *Ave Maria*.

(b) Longaville's attempts to woo the French lady-in-waiting in *Love's Labour's Lost* are a romantic adaptation of the *Ave Maria*. He invokes her as 'O sweet Maria, **empress** of my love' and praises the 'heavenly rhetoric of thine eye', claiming that he is not foresworn or guilty of perjury because 'my vow was earthly, thou a heavenly love' (*LLL* 4.3.54–64). Like the Virgin Mary (or the Virgin Queen **Elizabeth**), Maria can offer 'grace' which 'cures all disgrace' in Longaville. Breaking his vow of celibacy to worship her is a fortunate fall since it was done 'to win a paradise' (*LLL* 4.3.65–71). Because of her name, Maria exemplifies the idolatry of Petrarchan courtship through which a woman becomes a **goddess**. Amongst Longaville's many fair virtues Maria recognises 'a sharp wit match'd with too blunt a will' (*LLL* 4.3.47–9), a fault evidenced in the clumsy wooing. She plays her part in mocking this when Longaville sends her pearls, also associated with the Virgin Mary's purity (*LLL* 5.2.53). Maria promotes a more emotionally sincere form of secular love at the end of the play by promising to change her mourning attire 'for a faithful friend' (*LLL* 5.2.834) after a year.

The name's religious associations are tested more daringly in *Twelfth Night* where Maria tells Sir Andrew Aguecheek 'My name is Mary, sir', but the foolish knight compounds his earlier mistake that her name is Mistress Accost by addressing her as 'Good Mistress Mary Accost' (*TN* 1.3.53–5). These names introduce her as a paradox of modest humility following the model of the Virgin, and a figure of bawdy assertiveness. The ensuing dialogue in which she totally outwits Sir Andrew repeatedly puns on her name with the oath 'Marry' (by the Virgin Mary), playing this against the probably bawdy physical business of getting him to bring his hand 'to th' butt'ry bar and let it drink' (*TN* 1.3.67–79).

The name's Catholic associations may inform Sir Toby's reference to Mistress Mall's picture (*TN* 1.3.127) which has been hidden, like so many Catholic icons in Protestant England. Malvolio's English address 'Mistress Mary' is a sharp reproof when Sir Toby orders 'a stoup of wine, Maria' (*TN* 2.3.120–1). The association of Catholicism with seasonal festive sports make Maria a natural opposite to Malvolio, whom she identifies as 'a kind of puritan' (*TN* 2.3.125). When he swallows the bait of her trick letter, she compares his gullibility to sectarian blindness: 'there is no Christian that means to be sav'd by believing rightly can ever believe such impossible passages of grossness' (*TN* 3.2.70–2). It is Maria who first suggests Malvolio is 'possess'd' (*TN* 3.4.9) and in need of exorcism, following Catholic tradition. She then sets up a parody of the ritual, costuming Feste as Sir Topas the priest.

Maria's position in Olivia's household is that of a '**handmaid**' (*TN* 1.1.24), again with Catholic resonances, and a 'chamber**maid**' (*TN* 1.3.52) but she is also referred to as a 'gentlewoman' (*TN* 1.5.163–4). As Olivia's companion, she represents a class of young ladies sent into neighbouring noble families as a means of broadening their social connections and preparing to take on the role of **housewife** themselves (Lindheim 2007: 705). Maria is an ally as well as a dependent; she works alongside Olivia to secure her female authority in the household. Indeed, Maria's plotting can be read as a scheme to restore her authority by subordinating Malvolio and undermining Cesario who threatens to usurp her position as Olivia's chosen confidante (Tvordi 1999: 124). Maria's gentle status makes her courtship and marriage of Sir Toby look less like social ambition. He does suggest their different financial situations, vowing 'I could marry the wench for this device . . . and ask no other **dowry** but such another jest' (*TN* 2.5.182–5). As this implies, her value as his 'metal of India' (gold) is in her wit (*TN* 2.5.14); she is 'noble' because she is a 'gull-catcher' (*TN* 2.5.187). Maria's superior intelligence makes her a natural leader, a '**Penthesilea**' (*TN* 2.3.176), adept at directing others through her plots. It is not social difference that renders her dominance over the knights comically absurd, but her diminutive stature, which is made fun of in the names 'giant' (1.5.180), 'little villain' (2.5.13) and 'the youngest wren of nine' (3.2.66).

(c) Lecercle (2003) discusses Shakespeare's technique of encrypting Catholic references. Karen Robertson, 'A Feminine Revenging Hand in *Twelfth Night*' (1996) considers Maria's skill as a forger and revenger via letter writing. Nancy Lindheim (2007: 704–8) reads against the view that Maria is socially ambitious. Jessica Tvordi (1999: (esp.) 121–30) reads Maria and Olivia as close to being equals and allies.

Marian, (a) the name of Robin Hood's mistress in folk tradition, and a character who appeared in May Day festivities, played by a man. Maid Marian was the butt of ribald jokes in such entertainments.

(b) Falstaff compares Mistress **Quickly** to Maid Marian in derogatory terms, claiming that 'for womanhood, Maid Marian may be the deputy's wife of the ward to thee' (*1HIV* 3.3.114–15). Since Maid Marian was already a disreputable figure, **Mistress** Quickly, the Hostess of the Tavern, does not come off well by the comparison. 'Marian' appears to be a name Shakespeare associated with drink and festivity, perhaps in association with the Maid Marian figure. 'Marian Hacket, the fat **ale-wife** of Wincot' (*Shrew* Ind. 2.21) is the **hostess** named by Christopher Sly, and the Winter song concluding *Love's Labour's Lost* celebrates how 'Marian's nose looks red and raw / When roasted crabs hiss in the bowl' (*LLL* 5.2.924–5). Roasted apples floated in ale were popular at all-hallows celebrations. Marian Hacket, the ale-wife of Wincot, may have had local associations for Shakespeare since E. K. Chambers discovered that the family name 'Hacket' is recorded in the parish register for Wincot at Clifford Chambers-Quinton, just south of Stratford (Weis 2007: 410). Elsewhere, Marian appears as a generic lower-class woman's name. Dromio of Ephesus calls out to the household servants, 'Maud, Bridget, Marian, Cic'ly, Gillian, Ginn' (*Err.* 3.1.31) and in Stephano's drunken song, the sailors

enjoy the company of 'Mall, Meg and Marian and Margery' (*Temp.* 2.1.48).
(c) On Maid Marian as part of the Robin Hood festivities, see Lois Potter (1998: 21–90), especially Alexandra J. Johnston's essay on 'Robin Hood of the Records' (pp. 27–44); Weis (2007: 153–5 and 410) examines the evidence for local references in the Induction of *Shrew.*

Mariana, (a) a character in *Measure for Measure,* betrothed to Angelo but deserted by him, and finally married to him at the play's dénouement, and a friend of Diana and her mother, who appears briefly in Act 3 Scene 5 of *All's Well.* The name seems to be derived from 'Marian', originally a diminutive of the French name 'Marie'.
(b) Mariana, the friend in *All's Well,* is worldly wise and, having apparently had some knowledge of Parolles, warns **Diana** to beware of the seductive promises, oaths and 'engines of lust' of soldiers like he and Bertram (*AWW* 3.5.16–28). Her naming may draw on the associations of Marian in early May Day Robin Hood plays. Mariana in *Measure for Measure* exemplifies both the quasi-religious connotations of the name in her imitation of the **Virgin** Mary's role as mediatrix for human sins, and the bawdy associations of the name 'Marian' in presenting herself publicly as an unmarried, sexually experienced woman. Her name is Shakespeare's invention and may, like 'Marina', carry associations with the sea that reflect her situation. After her brother is shipwrecked and drowned at sea along with her dowry (*MM* 3.1.209–18), she is marooned on the 'moated grange' (*MM* 3.1.263): surrounded by water but unable to transform her betrothal to her 'combinate-husband' or contracted fiancé Angelo into marriage because he pretends 'discoveries of dishonor' in her (*MM* 3.1.222–8). Although Mariana is geographically located as a marginal figure, she is 'at the heart of the play, structurally, morally and psychologically' (Neely 1993: 96). In structural terms, she is the mediatrix for the other two women: her situation mirrors that of the condemned **Juliet** and she acts as a surrogate for **Isabella**. She provides legitimation for the former's pre-nuptial sex by repeating this act under the Duke's authority and saves Isabella's **chastity** through the bed-trick. Her most obvious imitation of the Virgin Mary's mediatory role is when she intercedes to save Angelo's life:

> They say best men are moulded out of faults
> And, for the most, become much more the better
> For being a little bad. So may my husband.
> (MM 5.1.439–41)

By her own admission, however, Mariana kneels to save Angelo in pursuit of her own desire. She 'crave[s] no other nor no better man' (*MM* 5.1.426). The violence of her passion, which has grown 'more violent and unruly' (*MM* 3.1.243) since Angelo originally rejected her, combined with her readiness to leave the moated grange and have sex with Angelo in a secret assignation, lays her open to the ribaldry traditionally directed at the Maid Marian figure of folk tradition. The ambiguity of her identity is advertised when she appears **veil**ed, and Lucio comments, 'My lord, she may be a punk, for many of them are neither **maid**, **widow** nor **wife**' (*MM* 5.1.179–80). In keeping with her physical home on the moated grange, she is marooned between the conventional designations of **woman**. She boldly deconstructs the **blazon** used in male courtship to reveal the perversity of male desire:

> This is that face, thou cruel Angelo,
> Which once thou swor'st was worth the looking on;
> This is the hand which with a vow'd contract,
> Was fast belock'd in thine; this is the body
> That took away the match from Isabel,
> And did supply thee at thy garden house.
>
> (*MM* 5.1.207–12)

In the final two lines, Mariana publicly constructs herself as **Marian** the **whore**, victim to Angelo's lust unless he marries her. Even after Mariana has intervened on his behalf, he 'crave[s] death more willingly than mercy' (*MM* 5.1.476) so the ending of the play highlights only the difference between his desires and hers. Her brave actions finally combine both aspects of her name in advertising the healing powers of love (in both carnal and spiritual senses), forgiveness and self-sacrifice. It is, however, unclear from the text whether her example does teach others to acknowledge repressed sexual desires and seek the redemptive potential offered at the end of the play.

(c) Neely (1993: 93–102) gives a brilliantly nuanced reading of Mariana's central role in *Measure for Measure*. Adelman (1992: 100–2) emphasizes the subordination of her role as part of the Duke's plan. Theodora A. Jankowski (2003) discusses Mariana as a victim of the commericalized nature of marriage and traffic in women. James Black (1973: 119–28) reads Mariana's role in the bed-trick in positive terms. Marliss C. Dessens, *The Bed-Trick In English Renaissance Drama* (1994) provides a discussion of the context for Mariana's involvement in the plot. Chamberlain (2003: 12–22) discusses Mariana's situation following the loss of her dowry.

Marina, (a) the daughter of the protagonist in *Pericles*, named after her birth at sea during a storm in which her mother Thaisa appears to die. She is brought up by Cleon and **Dionyza** in Tharsus, threatened with murder, captured by pirates, taken to a brothel in Mytilene where she reforms its governor, Lysimachus, whom she finally marries. She is responsible for redeeming her father from lethargy and despair so that he can be reunited with his wife at Ephesus.

(b) Pericles introduces his daughter to Cleon and Dionyza as 'My gentle babe Marina, whom / For she was born at sea, I have nam'd so' (3.3.12–13). Since **Thaisa** was buried at sea, such naming identifies Marina as a figure of rebirth. The storm in which Marina was born is not just a watery element. Pericles tells the baby:

> Happy what follows!
> Thou hast as chiding a nativity
> As fire, water, earth and heaven can make
> To herald thee from the **womb**.
>
>   (3.1.31–4)

It is the hotter element elements of fire and air, alongside solid earth and malleable water that give Marina her redemptive power in the play. Dionyza, who plots her murder, does not take account of these personal qualities in the premature epitaph she writes for Marina. Marina appears as a young woman in conventionally feminine terms, weeping for the death of **Lychorida** her nurse and holding a basket of flowers 'to strow thy green with **flowers**' (4.1.14), an action that links her to the **earth**. Although Marina defines herself in terms of water, 'Born in a tempest when my mother died / This world to me is a lasting storm' (4.1.18–19), she does not, like Pericles, passively accept suffering. When Leonine threatens to kill her, the pirates create an immediate form of escape via the sea. In the brothel in Mytilene, Marina vows she will actively use the elements to defend her virginity, and take matters into her own hands: 'If fires be hot, knives sharp, or waters deep / Untied I still my virgin knot will keep' (4.2.146–7).

Dionyza's ignorance of these passionate elements in Marina's character is clear in the epitaph she composes for Marina's grave. She emphasizes Marina's kinship with the sea to create a myth (in which **Thetis**, a sea-**nymph**, is mistakenly substituted for Tethys, wife of Oceanus), to explain Marina's death.

> Marina was she call'd; and at her birth,
> Thetis, being proud, swallow'd some part a' th' earth:
> Therefore the earth, fearing to be o'erflow'd,
> Hath Thetis' birth-child on the heavens bestow'd.
> Wherefore she does, and [Thetis] swears she'll never stint,
> Make raging battery upon shores of flint.
>
>   (4.4.38–43)

The story of the Thetis's threat to consume the earth, and the earth's revenge in killing the sea-child hints at Dionyza's own motivation for plotting the murder to free her own **daughter** from the overpowering influence of Marina. Although the play continues to define Marina in terms of earth and water, it acknowledges external forces in the sea's unremitting power.

The fluidity of the element in which she was born gives Marina the power to adapt to her circumstances and survive. Indeed, her freedom from normal family structures, 'not of any shores' (5.1.103), allows her more than the usual freedom to use her rhetorical skills to transform Lysimachus, and her **sewing** skills to make her own living (Moore 2003: 41). Marina's longing to be transformed into the 'meanest bird / That flies i' th' purer air' (4.6.101–2) points to the transcendent qualities that allow her to redeem Lysimachus and then Pericles. He identifies her with 'modest Justice', with 'crown'd Truth' and 'Patience' (5.1.119–21 and

138) but the transcendent moment of the scene is the revelation and repetition of her name:

> Marina: My name is Marina.
> Pericles: O, I am mock'd . . .
>   Thou little know'st how thou dost startle me
>   To call thyself Marina . . .
>   How, a king's daughter?
>   And call'd Marina?
> Marina: You said you would believe me,
>   But not to be a troubler of your peace,
>   I will end here . . .
> Pericles: . . . Well, speak on. Where were you born?
>   And wherefore call'd Marina?
> Marina: Call'd Marina
>   For I was born at sea.
>
>   (*Per.* 5.1.141–56)

The chiasmus in these lines on Marina's name is reiterated when Pericles appeals to her as 'thou that beget'st him that did thee beget; / Thou that wast born at sea, buried at Tharsus / And found at sea again' (5.1.195–7). The circling rhetorical pattern encapsulates Marina's redemptive agency: transforming death into rebirth as it precipitates the revelation of her parentage, Pericles's sensitivity to the music of the spheres, and Diana's summoning voice which brings him to Ephesus and Thaisa.

(c) Inga-Stina Ewbank (1980) discusses Marina's name and the language of recognition in Act 5 Scene 1. Jeanie Grant Moore (2003), analyses Marina as redemptive figure rescuing family relationships perverted by incest and jealousy. Holbrook (1989: 191–206) offers a psychoanalytic reading of Marina as a symbol of hope and continuity, with reference to T. S. Eliot's poem 'Marina'. Deanne Williams (2002) discusses how the Marina plot deflects the threat of father–daughter incest, which is apparent in the scenes depicting Antiochus's daughter and Thaisa. Palfrey (1997) reads Marina in the context of other restorative daughters in the late plays.

marriage, (a) for women in early modern England, probably the most important life-changing event, consisting of a move away from their birth home and the establishment of themselves as **mistress** of their own household. At the same time, this legal, physical and cultural shift meant the **woman** was subsumed under the identity of her husband, becoming a *feme covert*.

(b) In Shakespeare's work, marriage is an event around which the majority of female characters construct themselves. More than 50 characters speak as married women, a further 36 are looking forward to marriage or betrothal by the end of the text, and a further 15 speak as widows. Marriage is not presented as happy in Shakespeare's texts. The comic and tragic effects of 'Fell jealousy / Which troubles oft the bed of blessed marriage' (*HV* 5.2.363–4) are seen in *The Merry Wives of Windsor*, *Merchant of Venice*, *The Winter's Tale*, *Othello* and *The Rape of Lucrece*, for example. Othello voices a typical male insecurity, 'O curse of marriage, / That we may call these delicate creatures ours / And not their appetites' (*Oth.* 3.3.268). However, the potential for women's marital misery, based on the double sexual standard, is blatantly exposed in Antony's confession 'Though I make this marriage for my peace / I' th' east my pleasure lies' (*A&C* 2.3.39). *Comedy of Errors* shows poignantly how **Adriana** has to suffer her husband's infidelity and neglect. It is presumably this example of 'troubles of the marriage bed' (*Err.* 2.1.27) that makes her sister **Luciana** wish to avoid marriage.

Nevertheless, marriage was an expected rite of passage. Lady **Capulet** tells **Juliet** to 'Think of marriage now' (*R&J* 1.3.69) and Juliet thinks of little else once she has met Romeo, promising that if his love 'be honorable / Thy purpose marriage' he should send her word of the arrangements and she will find a way to be there (*R&J* 2.2.144). **Rosalind** notes the excitement of anticipation, where Time 'trots hard with a young maid between the contract of her marriage and the day it is solemnised' (*AYLI* 3.2.53). She reports the impatience of **Celia** and Oliver who have 'made a pair of stairs to marriage which they will climb incontinent, or else be incontinent before marriage' (*AYLI* 5.2.41). This rewrites the religious doctrine of peace of conscience and spiritual joy as degrees or 'so manie steppes and staires, make vs to clime vp to that perfect and eternall happines which is reserued for thy Saintes in heauen' (Finch 1589: sig. G1v).

Through marriage a woman's legal status changed from *feme sole* (theoretically equal to man), to *feme covert*, where her identity was subsumed into that of her husband; he became her 'head' in the new family structure (Mendelson and Crawford: 1998: 37). With bawdy innuendo, Pompey jokes that he cannot execute a married man for 'if he be a married man, he's his wife's head, and I can never cut off a woman's head' (*MM* 4.2.3–5). However, the cultural advantage of marriage for women was increased status. Henry Smith's *Preparative to Marriage*, for example, commended the honour of marriage since it was ordained of God for the primary purpose of propagation and 'for this cause marriage is called *matrimony*, which signifeth *mothers*, because it maketh them **mothers** which were **virgins** before' (Keeble 1994: 120). Married life thus was an improvement on the situation of maids who, 'being desolate and unmarried' remained 'pensife without your marriage songs and lived solitarie, sitting at home among the soote of pots' as Thomas Bentley noted (Bentley 1582: 342). Dromio of Syracuse alludes to the security associated with marriage when he describes the kitchen **maid** Nell as 'a wondrous fat marriage' (*Err.* 3.2.94). Unlike the foolish virgins in the biblical parable who did not have enough oil to keep their lamps burning until the bridegroom arrived (Matt. 25.1–13), she will bring enough fat to 'burn a week longer than the whole world' (*Err.* 3.2.93).

Whatever material or social improvements marriage brought women, it did not necessarily bring happiness. Fenton refers to the potential miseries for **Anne** Page: 'A thousand irreligious cursed hours / Which forced marriage would have brought upon her' (*MWW* 5.5.243). **Portia**'s vehement protest, 'I will do any thing, Nerissa, ere I'll be married to a sponge' (*Mer.* 1.2.98–9) and **Juliet**'s plea 'Delay this marriage for a month' (*R&J* 3.5.201) convey the desperation faced by some women matched against their will. The commodification of woman in marriage, even in romantic situations of elopement, colours Lucentio's wish to 'steal our marriage' in order to 'keep mine own' (*Shrew* 3.2.140–2). He later confesses to **Bianca**'s father that he has 'by marriage made thy **daughter** mine' (*Shrew* 5.1.116). The two gentlemen of Verona rather than the heroines of that play arrange the romantic conclusion so 'our day of marriage shall be yours / One feast, one house, one mutual happiness' (*TGV* 5.4.172–3), although this situation is neatly reversed in *Twelfth Night* when **Olivia** promises to celebrate the marriages jointly 'Here at my house and at my proper cost' (*TN* 5.1.319). The picture of female control echoes what Malvolio reports in this play about the **Lady** of the Strachy marrying the yeoman of the wardrobe (*TN* 2.5.39–40) and Feste's joke that Olivia 'will keep no fool till she be married' (*TN* 3.1.33). **Diana** ventriloquizes **Helena**'s marriage vows to emphasize women's control of the plot in *All's Well*:

> If you shall marry,
> You give away this **hand**, and that is mine;
> You give away heaven's vows, and those are mine;
> You give away myself, which is known mine;
> For I by vow am so embodied yours,
> That she which marries you must marry me.
> (*AWW* 5.3.169–74)

Although Diana notes that she is subsumed into Bertram's legal identity, or 'embodied yours', her repetition of the vows serves to secure Helena's claim on Bertram. Women's subversion of normal marriage practices is taken to comic extreme in *Merry Wives of Windsor* where Ford meets Mistress **Page** on her way to visit his wife and quips anxiously, 'I think if your husbands were dead, you two would marry' (*MWW* 3.2.15).

The sanctity of marriage is used politically in several plays. Richard II accuses his captors of violating 'a twofold marriage', by dividing him from his **wife** and his kingdom (*RII* 5.1.72), though previously, he had prevented Bolingbroke's marriage to the Duc de Berri's daughter (*RII* 2.1.168). Henry VIII claims that he is wracked with conscience about the sanctity of his marriage to his brother's widow Queen **Katherine** (*HVIII* 2.2.27–8), as a pretext for dissolving it. The gentlemen appear shocked to hear that Katherine was swiftly 'divorc'd, / And the late marriage made of none effect' (*HVIII* 4.1.32–3). More vehemently, Hamlet believes that the 'o'erhasty' marriage between his mother and uncle desecrates the rite, and 'Makes marriage vows / As false as dicers' oaths' (*Ham.* 3.4.44). He vows 'we will have no more marriages' (*Ham.* 3.1.154).

The solemnity of the occasion as life-changing event for women and men is registered in the decree that Portia's suitors must 'never to speak to lady afterward / In way of marriage' (*Mer.* 2.1.42) if they fail the casket test. Touchstone is told that the woman must be given according to protocol 'or the marriage is not lawful'

(*AYLI* 3.3.71). Jacques advises they go to church and find 'a good priest that can tell you what marriage is' (*AYLI* 3.3.87). He has in mind a sermon such as Henry Smith's *Preparative to Marriage* (1591) which observed that in a companionate marriage, a woman should model herself round the names *comforter, **housewife*** and *yoke-fellow* assigned to wives 'to show that she should help her husband to bear his yoke, that is, his grief must be her grief; and whether it be the yoke of poverty, or the yoke of envy, or the yoke of sickness, or the yoke of imprisonment, she must submit her neck to bear it patiently with him' (Aughterson 1995: 82). Suffolk, somewhat hypocritically, but perhaps thinking of his own loveless match, argues that 'Marriage is a matter of more worth / Than to be dealt in by attorneyship' (*1HVI* 5.4.55–6). King Lewis is infuriated by Edward IV's impromptu match to **Elizabeth** Woodville and vows to teach him a lesson 'For mocking marriage with a **dame** of France' (*3HVI* 3.3.255).

As You Like It and *The Tempest* both mark the solemnity of marriage by the appearance of its patron deities: Hymen and **Juno** 'that is queen of marriage' (*Per.* 2.3.30). Prospero's masque for the betrothal of Ferdinand and **Miranda** looks forward to their marriage where, provided they remain chaste, 'Hymen's lamps shall light you' (*Temp.* 4.1.23). Again with reference to the parable of the **virgins**, **Iris** reminds everyone that 'no bed-right shall be paid / Till Hymen's torch be lighted' (*Temp.* 4.1.96–7). **Juno** confers 'Honor, riches, marriage-blessing / Long continuance, and increasing / Hourly joys . . .' (*Temp.* 4.1.106–8). A much more female-centred marriage ceremony is planned in *As You Like It* where **Rosalind** makes the arrangements, beginning 'in sober meanings' (*AYLI* 4.2.69) with a ritualistic series of the promises and the repeated phrases 'And I'll be married tomorrow', 'and you shall be married tomorrow' (*AYLI* 4.2.113–18). After she appears to give herself to Duke Senior and then to Orlando, seemingly on her own terms, she hands over the **wedding** ceremony to Hymen.

The emotional and cultural charge of such ceremonial moments means that their disruption makes for tense drama in *The Taming of the Shrew* and *Much Ado About Nothing*, and, to a lesser extent, in *King John* where **Constance**'s fury is followed by a metaphorical dismemberment of the bride, **Blanch**, as her loyalties to her husband and her birth family are set against one another (*KJ* 3.1.300–30). In *Taming of The Shrew*, Baptista gives voice to everyone's unease at Petruchio's non-appearance: 'What mockery will it be, / To want the bridegroom when the priest attends / To speak the ceremonial rites of marriage' (*Shrew* 3.2.4–5). Katherina is understandably the most upset at his cruelty in appointing 'the day of marriage', setting in train all the preparations and then shaming her by arriving late and in outlandish costume (*Shrew* 3.2.15). Petruchio's protest, 'To me she's married, not unto my clothes' (*Shrew* 3.2.117) may well emphasize the solemnity of marriage as a meeting of two minds and souls, rather than a superficial spectacle, but it hardly excuses the insult to his bride and guests, who feel 'such a mad marriage never was before' (*Shrew* 3.1.182).

An even more disturbing disruption of the conventional ceremony occurs at **Hero**'s wedding to Claudio. The preparations for the marriage, played out through a scene of excitement and all-female intimacy (*MAdo* 3.4) and news of the success of Don John's plot (*MAdo* 3.5) build up the suspense. Leonato asks for 'the plain form of marriage' to be used, thereby emphasizing the bluntness of Claudio's responses in desecrating the ceremony:

> Friar: You come hither, my lord, to marry this lady.
> Claudio: No.
> Leonato: To be married to her. Friar, you come to marry her.
> Friar: Lady, you come hither to be married to this count.
> Hero: I do.
> Friar: If either of you know of any inward impediment why you should
>   not be conjoin'd I charge you on your souls to utter it.
> Claudio: Know you any Hero? . . .
>   . . .
> Leonato: What do you mean, my lord?
> Claudio: Not to be married,
>   Not to knit my soul to an approved **wanton**.
>   (*MAdo* 4.1.1–16 and 43–4)

At the end of the play, the solemnity of the occasion is re-established in Benedick's formal request to 'be conjoin'd / In the state of honorable marriage' with **Beatrice** (*MAdo* 5.4.29–30) and the subsequent ritual in which the **brides** appear veiled. Other immediate disruptions to marriage are the fight that disturbs Othello and **Desdemona**'s wedding night (*Oth.* 2.3) and the appeal of the mourning **queens** which interrupts Theseus and **Hippolyta**'s formal marriage procession in the opening scene of *Two Noble Kinsmen*. The scene opens with '*Hymen with a torch burning*', a boy strewing flowers, and a **nymph** and then Hippolyta as bride, both with their hair loose and displaying wheaten garlands (*TNK* 1.1.1SD).

Rosalind's enthusiasm to play out a mock marriage with Orlando testifies to the enduring appeal of the ceremony and the institution to Shakespeare's female characters, and, no doubt, to many of the first spectators and readers of the texts. She asks for Orlando's hand and appeals to **Celia** to be the priest:

> Orlando: Pray thee marry us.
> Celia: I cannot say the words.
> Rosalind: You must begin, "Will you Orlando" –
> Celia: Go to! Will you Orlando, have to **wife** this Rosalind?
> Orlando: I will.
> Rosalind: Ay, but when?
> Orlando: Why, now, as fast as she can marry us.
> Rosalind: Then you must say, "I take thee, Rosalind, for wife."
> Orlando: I take thee, Rosalind, for wife.
> Rosalind: I might ask you for your commission, but I do take thee,
>   Orlando, for my husband. There's a **girl** goes before the priest, and
>   certainly a woman's thought runs before her actions.
>   (*AYLI* 4.1.127–41)

The woman-directed marriage ceremony tells us a lot about what marriage might mean to early modern women. Rosalind's eagerness for marriage, as her thoughts run before her actions, leads her to substitute a female priest and to give herself away since there is not one to do this for her ('I might ask you for your commission'). For so many women trapped in marriages arranged and directed by men, Rosalind's marriage game plays out their deepest desires to control what was probably the most important life-changing moment of their lives.

(c) Extracts from the Puritan preacher Henry Smith's sermon *A Preparative To Marriage* (1591) are printed in Aughterson (1995: 82–3) and Keeble (1994: 119–21) amidst other examples of early modern attitudes to marriage. Cressy (1997: 285–376) gives a detailed account of varied types of ceremony, rituals and customary celebrations relating to marriage. Thomas Bentley's *Monument of Matrones Conteining Seven Severall Lampes of Virginitie* (1582), Sir Henry Finch's *The sacred doctrine of diuinitie gathered out of the worde of God* (1589) offer examples of early modern views of marriage in spiritual terms. Mendelson and Crawford (1998: 37–9 and 126–48) give a broad survey of early modern women's experiences of marriage. Ranald (1979) explains the need for a basic grasp of early modern matrimonial law to understand *Shrew*, *Much Ado*, *All's Well* and *Measure for Measure*. Sid Ray (2004) discusses *Titus*, *Othello*, *Tempest*, *Shrew*, Lisa Hopkins (1998) and Irene Dash (1981) provide good full-length studies of the topic. For more on operations of the matrimonial ceremony, *see* entries on **gift** and **hand** and **wedding**. For more on woman's status within marriage, *see* **wife**.

Mary, (a) the English version of **Maria**, the name of the **Virgin**, mother of Christ, and also of Shakespeare's mother, Mary **Arden**.

(b) Ironically, the only character in the Shakespeare canon to swear 'By holy Mary', the anglicized oath (*HVIII* 5.2.33) is Henry VIII, originally entitled Defender of the Faith but cause of England's break with the Roman church. Since by the time play was written (1613) **Anna of Denmark**'s Catholic sympathies were well known, the use of such an oath would appear more acceptable. Earlier in the play, Henry opens up the legitimacy of his marriage to **Katherine** by pointing out that proposals for a match between 'the duke of Orleans and / Our daughter Mary' (*HVIII* 2.4.175–6) were subject to questions over the **Princess**'s legitimacy. This reminds spectators and readers that Mary Tudor along with **Elizabeth** had indeed been declared illegitimate while their brother Edward VI was alive. John of Gaunt's nostalgic speech about **England** as a 'blessed plot' with a great tradition of crusading kings fighting for 'blessèd Mary's son' (*RII* 2.1.56) looks back idealistically to the unity of religion before the Reformation. In *King John*, an overtly Protestant play, King Philip of France announces that **Blanch** and Lewis will marry in 'Saint Mary's Chapel' (*KJ* 2.1.538).

Olivia's gentlewoman announces herself with 'My name is Mary' (and is addressed with the anglicized name in her first scene and follows this up with punning on her name and the weakened oath '**Marry**' (by the Virgin Mary) (*TN* 1.5.54–67) but is thereafter referred to as **Maria**. Both names are part of a network of Catholic discourse in the household including **Madonna** for Olivia herself.

(c) Mary E. Fissell (2004) discusses how images of the pregnant Virgin Mary and Elizabeth raised the status of childbearing in post-Reformation England. Ruth Vanita (2000) discusses Mariological Memory in *The Winter's Tale* and *Henry VIII.*

mask, (a) a covering for the face, worn on or held in front of the face by women for protection against the sun and by both sexes for disguise. Decorative masks made of fine leather, velvet or silk, made to conceal the whole face or the upper part of it (except the eyes), were worn at balls and masques and by actors as a form of disguise. Figuratively, a mask signified a pretence, a front, an outward show intended to deceive.

(b) **Julia** refers to the mask as a ladylike protection from the sun, lamenting how, since she has put on male disguise

> And threw her sun-expelling mask away
> The air hath starv'd the roses in her cheeks
> And pinch'd the lily-tincture of her face,
> That now she is become as black as I.
> (*TGV* 4.4.153–6)

Cressida too, says that she relies upon 'my mask, to defend my beauty' (*T&C* 1.2.26).

Moryson's *Itinerary* remarked of the French style that 'Gentlemen and Citizens wiues when they goe out of dores, weare vpon their faces little Maskes of silk, lined with fine leather', and unpin them to greet each other (Moryson 1617: 177). Autolycus advertises 'Masks for faces and for noses' as courtly fashion accessories in his pedlar's pack (*WT* 4.4.221).

In addition to serving as protection against the weather, the mask, like the veil, is a fashionable advertisement of female modesty but in Shakespeare's texts it always does more. **Juliet** is relieved that 'the mask of **night** is on my face / Else would a **maid**en blush bepaint my cheek' (*R&J* 2.2.84–6). As Romeo perceptively points out, to conceal the face actually serves to provoke desire: 'These happy masks that kiss fair ladies' brows / Being black, puts us in mind they have the fair' (*R&J* 1.1.230–1). In *Love's Labour's Lost* when the French ladies cover their faces to greet the French King and his companions, the mask is a tool for flirting:

> Berowne: Now fair befall your mask!
> Katherine: Fair fall the face it covers!
> Berowne: And send you many lovers!
> (*LLL* 2.1.23–5)

A fetishistic aspect to **beauty**'s erotic attraction is women's use of masks, seen in *Love's Labour's Lost* and *Much Ado*, for example. Cressida relies on her mask 'to defend my beauty' (*T&C* 1.2.262) but Angelo perceptively points out that to conceal is to provoke desire: 'as these black masks / Proclaim an enshield beauty ten times louder / Than beauty could' (*MM* 2.4.79–81).

In his account of masks and scarves, the puritan writer Stubbes complained that, far from being necessary protection against the sun, these accessories were 'flagges of pride'. In addition, the 'Masks & visors made of velvet' made for riding abroad, could utterly conceal 'so that if a man that knew not their guise before, should chaunce to meet one of them, he would thinke he met a monster or a Devil' (Stubbes 1595: 50). Even though Flute is assured that since he has a beard coming he can play the role of Thisbe in a mask (*MND* 1.2.49–50), there is no textual evidence to suggest that **boy actor**s used full masks to play female roles. However, female characters use masks as tools of deception in *Love's Labour's Lost* where the Princess and the ladies swap identities and woo by proxy. Longaville complains to **Katherine** 'You have a double tongue within your mask' (*LLL* 5.2.245). In this case, they blur class hierarchies too. When Rosaline and the Princess of France swap places, they play out the truth that 'Degree, being vizarded / Th' unworthiest shows as fairly in the mask' (*T&C* 1.3.83–4). Like the French Ladies, **Beatrice** in *Much Ado* takes full strategic advantage of the freedom the mask gives her to insult Benedick in the masked ball (*MAdo* 2.1.125–50). In the final scene, when the ladies enter 'masked' (*MAdo* 5.4.12), the masks or **veil**s force Claudio to take his new **bride** on trust, the quality in which he was so singularly deficient at the **wedding**.
(c) Stubbes, *The Anatomie of Abuses* (1595), Fynes Moryson, *An Itinerary*, Book 4 Part III (1617: 177), Arnold (1988: 12, 202–3) and Ashelford (1983: 128 and 141) give examples of masks as early modern fashion accessories and decorative costumes. Meg Twycross and Sarah Carpenter's book *Masks and Masking in Medieval and Early Tudor England* (2002) offers a detailed account of masks in theatrical traditions.

matron, (a) an older married woman, usually with experience of a large family and expertise in matters of child**birth**, so able to act as a **midwife**. The term connotes dignity and propriety, a secure sense of social rank. 'Matron' in early modern English also referred to a woman responsible for managing the domestic arrangements in a charitable hospital and was the title of a married female saint.
(b) Robert Cawdry's *Table Alphabeticall* (1604) defined a matron as an 'auncient, sober, and a discreete woman', a list to which Cotgrave (1611) added the terms 'sage', 'modest' and 'motherlie'. Matron distinguishes an older, post-menopausal woman when listed alongside maid and wife. Examples are found in the report that 'Matrons flung gloves, / Ladies and maids their scarfs and handkerchers' to honour Coriolanus (*Cor.* 2.1.263–4), or in Malcolm's list of wives, daughters, matrons and maids as types of woman his lust will consume (*Mac.* 4.3.61–2). Posthumus Leonatus's mother is described in the stage directions for her brief appearance as '*an ancient* MATRON' (*Cym.* 5.4.29SD). **Juliet** refers to the matron's typical sobriety by personifying 'civil **night**' as 'Thou sober-suited matron, all in black' (*R&J* 3.2.10–11). Juliet, who is passionate and yet sexually inexperienced, looks to the matron as a teacher, a source of wisdom based on experience (*R&J* 3.2.12). Male characters in other texts find the matron's mature sexuality offensive. For the mistanthropic Timon, the degeneracy of human behaviour is shown

when 'Matrons, turn incontinent!' (*Tim.* 4.1.3). He is revolted by what he feels is hypocritical sobriety on the part of 'the counterfeit matron' insisting that 'It is her habit only that is honest, / Herself's a **bawd**' (*Tim.* 4.3.113–15). Hamlet, too, is famously revolted by mature female sexual desire. He constructs its awakening as demonic:

> Rebellious hell,
> If thou canst mutine in a matron's bones,
> . . . Proclaim no shame
> When the compulsive ardour gives the charge,
> Since frost itself as actively doth burn,
> And reason panders will.
>
> (*Ham.* 3.4.82–9)

Since Hamlet confesses that his own wit is diseased, the text may encourage spectators to challenge rather than to accept such a prejudiced viewpoint.
(c) Robert Cawdry, *A Table Alphabeticall* (London, 1604) and Randle Cotgrave's *Dictionarie of the French and English Tongues* (1611) offer examples of early modern definitions of the matron.

Medea, (a) niece of the enchantress Circe, and the wife of Jason in Greek myth, Medea is an archetype of female sorcery and pitiless revenge. She was a priestess of the witch **Hecate** and used her skill with herbs to restore the youth of Jason's father, Aeson, and to help Jason win the Golden Fleece. She escaped with Jason, killing her brother Absyrtus in order to distract her father. When Jason deserted her for Glauce, Medea took **revenge** by sending his second wife a poisoned dress and coronet and by killing the sons she (Medea) had borne to Jason. She later tried to poison Theseus as well.
(b) The apparently restorative qualities of Medea's magic are invoked by **Jessica** who imagines 'In such a night / Medea gather'd the enchanted herbs / That did renew old Aeson' (*Mer.* 5.1.12–14). However, since Medea then went on to murder Pelias with the same potion by leaving out a vital ingredient, the power alluded to here in Ovid is also dangerous and bloody (Bate 1993: 155–6). Shakespeare cites Medea as an archetype of pitiless murder. Young Clifford, discovering his father's body on the battlefield, vows:

> Henceforth I will not have to do with pity.
> Meet I an infant of the house of York,
> Into as many gobbets will I cut it
> As wild Medea young Absyrtus did;
> In cruelty will I seek out my fame.
>
> (*2HVI* 5.2.56–60)

Allusions to Medea's murders of her brother and her young sons resonate through these lines. The account of Medea in Ovid's *Metamorphoses* probably contributed to the memories of **Sycorax** in *The Tempest*. Inga-Stina Ewbank (1966) draws attention to similiarities with Lady **Macbeth**.

(c) Shakespeare would have known Ovid's account of Medea in *Metamorphoses* Book VII, ll.1–580 in the original Latin and in Golding's 1567 translation (Ovidius 2000: 161–76) and probably Seneca's *Medea* in *Seneca His Tenne Tragedies*, translated by John Studley (1581: fols. 119–39). For the influence of Medea in *The Tempest, see* **Sycorax**. Other influences are traced by M. L. Stapleton (1994: 229–51) and Rosalind S. Meyer, '"The Serpent Under't": Additional Reflections on *Macbeth*' (2000: 86–91) on Lady Macbeth. Jonathan Bate, *Shakespeare and Ovid* (1993: 151–7) compares Portia to Medea and discusses Prospero, Sycorax and Medea. Susan C. Staub (2000: 249–56) examines understandings of Medea and child murder in popular culture.

mermaid, (a) a fabulous, partly human sea creature with a woman's head and upper body and a scaly fish's tail, often identified with the **Nereids**, the 50 sea-nymphs who were the attendants of Poseidon or Neptune. The mermaid is presented as beautiful, with long flowing hair, and she holds a mirror in her right hand and a comb in her left. She was also identified with the **Siren** of classical mythology as a dangerous figure capable of luring sailors and ships to their destruction.

(b) Pliny's *Historie of the world* claimed that 'As for Mere maides called Neriedes, it is no fabulous tale that goeth of them: for looke how painters drawe them, so they are indeed: onlie their bodie is skaled all over, even in those parts wherein they resemble a woman' (Pliny 1601: Vol. 1, 236). The appeal of the mermaid as a curiosity in early modern culture is evident from its use in early modern decoration and narrative. Lady Anne Bacon Drury, for example, had an image of a mermaid with comb and looking glass as one of the paintings decorating the inside of her closet (Meakin 2008). The fabulous nature of the mermaid emphasizes the gossipy nature of Lucio in *Measure for Measure*, who reports of Angelo that 'a sea-maid spawned him', his weird conception in the cold sea supposedly explaining his antipathy to sex (*MM* 3.2.108). The mermaid is identified with the **Siren** as a deceptive creature whose destructive power Richard of Gloucester wants to imitate, vowing that he will 'drown more sailors than the mermaid shall' with his artificial tears (*3HVI* 3.2.186). The motif's usual effects are comically reversed in *Venus and Adonis* where, first, Venus tells Adonis 'Thy mermaid's voice hath done me double wrong' (*V&A* 429) and later, he tells her that even if love had given her twenty thousand tongues, 'Bewitching like the **wanton** mermaids' songs' (*V&A* 777), he would not be tempted by her charms.

Antipholus of Syracuse, enchanted by the beauty of **Luciana**, distinguishes between the 'sweet mermaid' who, in solidarity with her **sister**, would make him drown in **Adriana**'s tears, and the dangerous **Siren** who woos for herself (*Err.* 3.1.45–52). For **Lucrece**, the mermaid's voice represents her own potential to call for war and thus incite revenge for what has happened to her. She imagines all the Greek soldiers on the painting of Troy listening to Nestor's appeal for them to fight, 'As if some mermaid did their ears entice' (*Luc.* 1411).

Shakespeare conflates the fish-tailed mermaid with the fully human figures of the **Nereids** (Edgcombe 2000: 181) in his detailed pictures of mermaids' erotic power on Cleopatra's barge. The mermaids are in charge of the ship luring the land-bound Antony, rather than tempting sailors. Cleopatra's gentlewomen, 'so many mermaids' attend on her while 'At the helm / A seeming mermaid steers', Enobarbus's description focusing particularly on her 'flower-soft hands' that gracefully control the vessel (*A&C* 2.3.206–11). Shakespeare's mermaids may draw on Daniel's 'Letter from Octavia' to Antony, in which she dreams about a powerful mermaid (Cleopatra) commanding two sea horses (Antony and Caesar). **Octavia** sees the first sea horse: 'Vpon whose backe a wanton Mermaid sate, / As if she ruld his course and steerd his fate' (Daniel 1605: D2v). In the ensuing battle, where the water is dyed purple, the mermaid shifts her loyalty to the second sea horse (Caesar) and the first (Antony) 'se'ing her gone straight after her he hies / As if his hart and strength laie in her eyes' (ibid.: D3). The similarity to what happens in the first sea battle of *Antony and Cleopatra* (3.11.53–61) suggests Shakespeare had this mermaid story in mind when writing the play.

Because of their power to seduce, mermaids were associated with **wanton**ness and prostitution. Dekker's play *Satiro-mastix* refers to the gentlemen's practice of sneaking 'into a Tauerne with his Mermaid' (Dekker 1602: H2). The 'Mere-Mede Tavern in Bread Streete in London' was a popular hostelry in Shakespeare's day (Coryat 1776: Vol. 3, Sigs L8v–M2). The most powerful mermaid in Shakespeare's canon is the one Oberon recalls when

> once I sat upon a promontory
> And heard a mermaid on a dophin's back
> Uttering such dulcet and harmonious breath
> That the rude sea grew civil at her song,
> And certain stars shot madly from their spheres,
> To her the sea-maid's music.
>
> (*MND* 2.1.149–54)

This mermaid's music can command the stars and seas. Oberon's use of 'sea-maid' rather than 'Nereid' emphasizes virginity, suggesting that this figure may be identified with the 'fair **vestal**' and 'imperial' **votaress** who cannot be touched with Cupid's arrow as she passes by (*MND* 2.1.158–64), and who is probably a compliment to **Elizabeth** I. The Queen's entertainment at Kenilworth (1575) had featured a sea pageant complete with a 'Triton upon a swimming mermaid' (Edgecombe 2000: 181) as part of its tribute to royal power. The Armada Portrait had depicted Elizabeth with a statue of a mermaid (Traub 2002 127–8), so the compliment would not be out of place. **Fortune**, who also rode upon a dolphin's back, was another powerful goddess associated with the sea (Simonds 1994: 139–40).

In contrast to these figures, the mad **Ophelia** presents a more serene type of mermaid. 'Mermaid-like' she floats in the brook, chanting 'snatches of old lauds' or hymns as though she were 'a creature native and indued / Unto that element'

(*Ham.* 5.1.176–80). Although – or perhaps *because* – she is passive, this image of Ophelia as mermaid has exercised considerable seductive power over readers, writers and artists (Romanska 2005).

(c) Pliny the Elder, Vol. 1, (1601: 326) describes mermaids. Samuel Daniel, *Certaine small poems lately printed with the tragedie of Philotas* (1605), Thomas Dekker, *Satiro-mastix* (1602) and Heather Meakin, *The Painted Closet of Lady Anne Bacon Drury* (2008) offer sample early modern views of mermaids. Thomas Coryat, *Coryat's Crudites* Vol. 3 [1615] (1776) gives details of the Mermaid Tavern. Traub (2002: 131–2) analyses the mermaid's early modern significance with reference to Elizabeth. Rodney Edgcombe (2000) discusses the reference in *A Midsummer Night's Dream*, suggesting that the mermaid is Amphitrite. Leeds Barroll (2005: 278) discusses allusions to the mermaid and Circe in *Antony and Cleopatra*. Belsey (1996) analyses Cleopatra in the barge pageant while Simonds (1994) discusses Cleopatra's link to Fortuna and mermaids. Magda Romanska (2005) considers Ophelia as mermaid.

midwife, (a) a person – almost exclusively a woman in Shakespeare's day – who helps in the process of childbirth.

(b) The midwife was regarded as an expert assistant in the **birth** process. A woman's contractions were helped by 'the skilfull hand of the heads-woman or Midwife as we cal them, for she setteth the woman in a due posture or position of parts, receiueth the Infant gently which falleth from betwixt her knees, directeth it if it offer it selfe amisse; and finally draweth away as easily as is possible the after-birth which stayeth behinde' (Crooke 1615: 269). References to midwives in Shakespeare's plays acknowledge the intrinsic role they played. **Lucina**, the **goddess** of childbirth is described as a 'midwife gentle' (*Per.* 3.1.11) whose help Pericles solicits. When Jack Cade claims his mother was a Plantagenet, Dick undercuts his claims to status with the remark 'she was a midwife' (*2HVI* 4.2.42–3), possibly punning on 'Plantagenet' to imply she was not a good one (*gêner* meaning 'to impede' or 'to obstruct'). Leontes refers disparagingly to **Paulina** as 'Lady **Margery**, your midwife there' (*WT* 2.3.160) since she has taken responsibility for delivering the baby **Perdita** from the prison and taking care to preserve it.

The midwife's importance lay not just in physically delivering the baby, but in being the first to culturally define it. Richard of Gloucester feels he has been marked at birth by the stories of the midwife and the **gossips**. He is determined to prove a villain since 'The midwife wonder'd and the women cried / "O Jesus bless us, he is born with teeth!"' (*3HVI* 5.6.74–5). Cornelia the midwife, an off-stage character who is important enough to be named, delivers the black-skinned child of Tamora and Aaron, and presumably begins the definition of the baby as 'a devil' and 'a joyless, dismal, black and sorrowful issue' (*Tit.* 4.2.63–66). The only way Aaron can undo this stigmatized **blazon** is to kill the **nurse** and trace back its point of origin in the midwife to kill her as well.

According to Prince Hal, midwives usually have a more liberal attitude to illegitimate children: 'the midwives say the children are not in the fault, whereupon the world increases, and kinreds are mightily strengthen'd' (*2HIV* 2.2.24–7).

Hal's satiric view that midwives help to strengthen kindred bloodlines by secretly delivering illegitimate children gives rise to male distrust of the type. The midwife who avouches the truth of a ballad telling how a usurer's wife 'was brought to bed of twenty money bags at a burthen' is, significantly, 'one Mistress Tale-porter', an obvious liar (*WT* 4.4.262–70).

The secrecy of the midwife's work in the all-female space of the birthroom breeds insecurity in the minds of male characters as seen in Mercutio's nightmare vision of Queen **Mab**. She is, he says, 'the fairies' midwife' who helps to give birth to fantastic dreams, 'which are the children of an idle brain' and presses maids who 'lie on their backs' and 'learns them first to bear' (*R&J* 1.4.54–98). Male midwives did not come to dominate the profession until later in the seventeenth century but Queen **Isabel** in *Richard II* prophetically imagines a man-midwife in another fantastic birth metaphor to describe her sadness. Green, who brings news of Bolingbroke's invasion, is the 'midwife to my woe', the 'unborn sorrow' she feels (*RII* 2.2.10 and 62). Although a midwife helps to bring forth new life, the word is a trigger to male insecurity, danger and sorrow in Shakespeare.

(c) Helkiah Crooke *Mikrokosmographia* (1615) and Jane Sharp's 1671 *The Midwives Book* (1999) give early modern views of the midwife's specialist role. Sharp's text is based on more than 30 years of practice. Doreen Evenden, *Midwives of Seventeenth-Century London* (2000) gives a detailed study of early modern midwives as carefully trained for the task of child delivery and explores the relationships between the midwife and her clients. Caroline Bicks, 'Midwiving Virility in Early Modern England' (2000) discusses how midwives occupied the centre of a female-centred culture in the birthroom with the authority to control male virility through the operation of cutting the umbilical cord. Her book-length study, *Midwiving Subjects in Shakespeare's England* (2003) discusses midwives as participants in cultural production, with reference to kingship and history, and male desire for control.

Minerva, (a) Roman name for Athena, Greek goddess of wisdom, weaving, music, poetry and medicine. In Roman tradition, she was also celebrated as a patron of warriors.

(b) Lucentio demonstrates his enchantment with **Bianca** and his own sense of values by comparing her to the goddess of wisdom and music when she obeys her father and retires to the house. Her words 'to your pleasure humbly I subscribe / My books and instruments shall be my company' make Lucentio exclaim, 'Hark, Tranio, thou mayst hear Minerva speak' (*Shrew* 1.1.81–2). The idea that Minerva was a living woman rather than a deity had been strongly advocated by Christine de Pisan who claimed that 'this mayde was of so great excellence in wytte that the lewde people of that countree' said 'she was a goddesse comen from heaven' because she invented or discovered so many things. These included working in 'certayne lettres' or shorthand; 'the crafte of wolle and to make clothe'; how to make armour, chariots and olive oil; discovery of the first 'pypes, shalmes & trompes & instruments of mouthe (Pisan 1521: sig Mm IIIr–v). To crown these achievements she was also celebrated for 'grete chastyte', remaining 'alwayse a vyrgyn' (ibid.: sig. Mm III–v). In the Italian settings of *Cymbeline* she is an icon of perfect physical and moral posture, referred to as the 'straight-pight Minerva' (*Cym.* 5.5.164).

(c) Christine de Pisan, *The Boke of the Cyte of Ladyes* (1521) cites Minerva as one of the examples of female virtue. For more on Pisan's work as a precursor to early modern English women writers' work, see Beilin (1987: xiii–xv)). Warner (1985: 201–8) examines representations of Minerva.

minx, (a) a pet dog or puppy and, figuratively, a pert, sly or boldly flirtatious young woman. In a more derogatory sense, a lewd or **wanton** woman or a prostitute.

(b) The original meaning of minx as 'dog' came from Erasmus: 'There been litle mynxes, or puppees that ladies keepe in their chaumbers for especiall iewelles to playe withall' (Erasmus 1542: fol. 127). The sense of impertinence associated with the name is found in Nashe: 'Mistris Minx a Marchants wife, that will eate no Cherries forsooth, but when they are at twentie shillings a pound' (Nashe 1592: sig C4v). Shakespeare's texts do not use the proper name but nevertheless draw on this sense in *Twelfth Night* where Malvolio calls Maria 'minx' for her cheekiness in counselling him to pray (*TN* 3.4.120). In *Othello*, 'minx' is sexually derogatory. Othello believes Desdemona is a 'lewd minx' and Bianca believes the handkerchief is 'some minx's token' (*Oth.* 3.4.476 and 4.1.153).

(c) Erasmus *Apophthegmes* (1542: 127b) and Nashe, *Pierce Penilesse* (1592: sig. C4v) give early modern definitions.

Miranda, (a) a character in *The Tempest*, **daughter** of Prospero. Her name derives from the Latin *mirari* 'to wonder at', or 'to admire', and is the feminine form of the gerundive *mirandus* 'admirable' or 'lovely'.

(b) Ferdinand puns on her name, calling her 'Admir'd Miranda / Indeed, the top of admiration' (*Temp.* 3.1.37–8) when she forgets her father's command and tells Ferdinand her name. Miranda is certainly a cause of wonder and admiration. On first seeing her, Ferdinand exclaims 'O, you wonder!' (1.2.427), assuming she is a '**goddess**' (1.2.422). Prospero regards her as a 'nonpareil' (3.2.100) and draws attention to her as lovely, an object of love, by calling her 'dear heart' (1.2.305). Caliban's desire for Miranda as a mate to people 'This isle with Calibans' (1.2.350) is a more savage version of Stephano, Ferdinand and Prospero's construction of her as the lovely object of their desires to breed future generations. She also inspires spiritual awe. Prospero wondered at his infant daughter's **angel**ic smiles when they were cast off in the boat, claiming she was 'infused with a fortitude from heaven' (1.2.152–4), and so preserved him from the sin of despair.

As well as attracting admiration, Miranda embodies her name by her admiration for other human beings, most famously in the line 'O brave new world / That hath such people in it!' Sight of the 'goodly creatures' makes her exclaim 'O wonder!' (5.1.181–4). Earlier in the play, Ferdinand's 'brave form' leads her to call him 'A thing divine, for nothing natural / I ever saw so noble' (1.2.419–20). Her innocence of gender difference logically leads her to believe that lifting logs 'would become me / As well as it does you', as she tells Ferdinand (3.1.28–9) and enables her to propose to him. Miranda acts as a focus for the opportunities all the characters on the island share in looking anew at the world, themselves and their values. She may likewise make spectators wonder about the sexism of an inheritance system where she must lose all to Ferdinand when she protests 'You play me false' in the chess game (5.1.172). Her innocence recalls pre-lapsarian equality and, protected within the confines of the island and the play, her quest for knowledge leads to an image of harmony and reconciliation, although that depends on her subjection.

(c) Jameson (2005: 189–96) reads Miranda as a blend of 'the purely natural and the purely ideal', the 'very elements of womanhood' (p. 189), while Harris (1912) finds her modesty 'mawkish' (p. 270). Harris (pp. 247–51) and Weis (2007: 336–7) rehearse the argument that the role relates to Shakespeare's daughter **Judith**. Mary B. Moore, 'Wonder, Imagination and the Matter of Theatre in *The Tempest*' (2006) considers the character as part of the play's contributions to the early modern debates on wonder. Lorie Jerrell Leininger, 'The Miranda Trap: Sexism and Racism in Shakespeare's *Tempest*' (1983) is an early feminist reading. For a postcolonial reading see Jyotsna G. Singh (1996). Melissa E. Sanchez (2008) gives a political reading of Miranda and her **marriage** as a metaphor for the play's investigation of the relationship between political rule, subjection and love in the State. Jessica Slights (2001) surveys a range of critical responses from the nineteenth to twentieth centuries to show how Miranda embodies alternative models of selfhood, moral agency and community life.

mistress, (a) a woman having control or authority, in material and political terms as the female head of a country or household, including a woman working alongside a male counterpart. 'Mistress' is also the commanding and controlling beloved of courtly love discourse. From this, the word also denotes a ruling female patron. In addition to the superior Petrarchan mistress, the term also signified a carnal lover, often a woman in a long-term relationship with a married man. 'Mistress', usually with a surname or first name, is a form of polite address to a married woman or an unmarried woman or girl.

(b) As a form of address, mistress is used for characters from the **Empress Cleopatra** to the housekeeper Mistress **Quickly**, ranging in age from the **Countess** of Rossillion to the baby **Marina**. Bottom uses it to show respect in Titania's bower, asking Peaseblossom to 'commend me to Mistress Squash, your mother, and to Master Peascod, your father' (*MND* 3.2.186–7). Sir Andrew likewise comically blunders in formally addressing Maria as 'Good Mistress Accost, I desire better acquaintance' (*TN* 1.3.52). Unsurprisingly, Shakespeare's texts play with the different meanings of 'mistress' when it is used as a form of address. In *Merry Wives of Windsor*, for example, Falstaff woos the two wives Mistress **Page** and Mistress **Ford** as courtly mistresses with the aim of making them his sexual mistresses. In addition, the younger Mistress Anne Page, the daughter, is the love object of Caius, Slender and Fenton; and Mistress **Quickly** is the housekeeper to Dr Caius. Falstaff's attempt to transform Mistress Page into his romantic ideal on the grounds that she, like him, is 'not young' but is 'merry' and 'love[s] sack', is amusing (*MWW* 2.1.6–10). Mistress Quickly deftly flatters Falstaff and provokes his desire for Mistress Ford by constructing her as the cold Petrarchan mistress of a range of suitors. Not even 'the best courtier of them all' could succeed with her in spite of their letters and gifts 'in silk and gold' and sweetened wine 'that would have won any woman's heart' she claims (*MWW* 2.2.61–78).

Loss of identity and confusion arise from the slippage of the important social marker 'mistress' in *Comedy of Errors*, as Dromio of Ephesus complains

> 'My mistress, sir' quoth I; 'Hang up thy mistress!
> I know not thy mistress; out on thy mistress!' . . .
> 'I know' quoth he 'no house, no wife, no mistress'
>
> (*Err.* 2.1.67–71)

Adriana, diagnosing the infidelity of her own husband, ruefully points out 'Some other mistress hath thy sweet aspects; / I am not Adriana nor thy wife' (*Err.* 2.2.111). Even the **Courtezan** is mistaken as 'Mistress Sathan' (*Err.* 4.3.49). The illusion of command offered by the title in a romantic scenario is quickly punctured by **Rosalind** who calls **Phoebe** 'proud mistress' and then tells her, 'mistress, know yourself, down on your knees, / And thank heaven, fasting, for a good man's love' (*AYLI* 3.5.45 and 57–8). True to his nature, Lucio mocks both the romantic and commanding senses of the word by asking enquiring after the **bawd** Mistress Overdone 'How doth my dear morsel, thy mistress? Procures she still? (*MM* 3.1.54–5).

Because of the relative formality of the title, 'mistress' can mark disapproval or emotional distance. Malvolio cautions 'Mistress Mary' to remember her place in Olivia's household (*TN* 2.3.121). Duke Frederick abruptly orders **Rosalind**, 'Mistress, dispatch you with your safest haste / And get you from our court' (*AYLI* 1.3.41). Othello refers to **Desdemona** as 'mistress', to show the withdrawal of his love and his belief that, like an **adulteress**, 'she can turn, and turn, and yet go on / And turn again' (*Oth.* 4.1.250–4). **Bianca** is sharply addressed as 'mistress' along with '**strumpet**' by Iago, who casts suspicions about her involvement in Cassio's stabbing (*Oth.* 5.1.100, 105 and 125). It is certainly derogatory in Ajax's mocking address 'Mistress Thersites' (*T&C* 2.1.36). Fathers use 'mistress' as a means to chastise or talk down to their daughters. Capulet deals with **Juliet**'s challenge to his paternal authority by calling her 'you mistress minion' (*R&J* 3.5.151). Simonides, secretly pleased with the initiative **Thaisa** has taken in determining to marry Pericles, asks 'Yea, mistress, are you so peremptory?' and commands 'hear you, mistress . . . frame / Your will to mine' (*Per.* 2.5.73–82). Even though he is scolding her like a child, 'mistress' also registers paternal pride in her self-determination.

To be mistress of oneself denotes agency on the part of Shakespeare's female characters. Deciding on suicide allows the raped **Lucrece** to declare, 'For me, I am the mistress of my fate' (*Luc.* 1069). Rosalind is less confident, telling Celia 'I show more mirth than I am mistress of' (*AYLI* 1.2.3). For **Viola**, command over where to give her love represents the only area of control that remains to her. She tells Olivia her heart, body and integrity are her own and no woman 'Shall mistress be of it, save I alone' (*TN* 3.1.158–60). Hamlet expresses himself in a similar way, saying that 'since my dear soul was mistress of her choice' she has chosen Horatio as a friend (*Ham.* 3.2.63). Shylock refers to affection as 'mistress of passion' swaying emotions 'to the mood / Of what it likes or loathes' (*Mer.* 4.1.50–1) and the Duke in *Othello* calls opinion 'a sovereign mistress of effects' (*Oth.* 1.3.224–5).

In material terms, 'mistress' signalled command over kingdoms, households and people. **Elizabeth** I was mistress of England and, after her coronation, Aylmer's *Harborowe for faithfull and true subjects* (1559) depicted Mother **England** advising subjects to 'Obey your mistress and mine which God hath made lady over us' (Aylmer 1559: R2r). **Lavinia** is both a love object and the symbolic matriarch of the empire: 'Rome's royal mistress, mistress of my heart', as Saturninus proclaims (*Tit.* 1.1.241). Posthumus believes that 'Britain, I have kill'd thy mistress' in plotting the death of his own beloved **Imogen** (*Cym.* 5.1.20). Cardinal Wolsey is horrified by the breach of social hierarchy in promoting **Anne** 'the late **queen**'s gentlewoman' and 'a knight's daughter / To be her mistress' mistress! the queen's queen!' (*HVIII* 3.2.94–5). The title has imperial connotations too when Antony promises to piece **Cleopatra**'s throne with kingdoms so that 'all the east' shall 'call her mistress' (*A&C* 1.5.45–7).

Perhaps the central, or commanding position of the royal mistress is what helped to popularize the name to refer to the jack or target ball in the game of bowls in the early modern period. As the bowls are aimed to get as near to the mistress as possible, so courtiers compete to get as close to their royal mistress as they can. Pandarus makes a reference to the game, telling the lover Troilus 'so, so, rub on, and kiss the mistress' (*T&C* 3.2.49). The role of teacher or instructress is another type of female command signalled by 'mistress'. **Hecate** pointedly reminds the other **witch**es that she is 'the mistress of your charms' (*Mac.* 3.5.6). **Perdita** is admired because 'she seems a mistress / To most that teach' (*WT* 4.4.583–4) in spite of her youth.

In the domestic context, Shakespeare uses mistress to signify the female head of a family or household, sometimes in conjunction with a male counterpart. Perdita has been made 'mistress o' th' feast' (*WT* 4.4.68), responsible for welcoming guests to the sheepshearing. **Portia** is significantly still 'mistress of the house' (*Mer.* 5.1.38 and 52) even after surrendering herself and her fortunes to Bassanio. **Helena** addresses the **Countess** of Rossillion formally as 'honourable mistress' and 'noble mistress' (*AWW* 1.3.139 and 186) and the Countess, in turn, greets Helena as a daughter-in-law 'That twenty such rude boys might tend upon / And call her hourly mistress' (*AWW* 3.2.81–3). **Goneril** uses the word to mean both lover and absolute commander of the royal household. She tells Edmund that she will change roles 'at home' with Albany so that Edmund is 'like to hear' before long 'A mistress's command' (*KL* 4.2.17–21). Even the baby **Marina** holds future command over a royal household. **Lychorida** must 'Look to your little mistress, on whose grace / You may depend hereafter' (*Per.* 3.3.40–1). Leontes tragically confuses two meanings of mistress and Hermione's proper role as gracious hostess with jealous fantasies of her adultery when he hears Polixenes will stay to 'Satisfy? / Th' entreaties of your mistress? Satisfy?' (*WT* 1.2.232–4).

Feste's song 'O mistress mine, where are you roaming?' (*TN* 2.4. 39) is one of many Shakespearean references to a female sweetheart as a mistress. **Rosalind** playfully sets Orlando to 'imagine me his love, his mistress' and 'every day to woo me' in her changing moods 'longing and liking, proud, fantastical, apish, shallow, inconstant, full of tears, full of smiles, for every passion something, and for no passion truly any thing' (*AYLI* 3.2.408–14). The intimacy of this wooing, allowed by Rosalind's male disguise, is uncommon. More often, addresses to a mistress are much more formal, public events, even involving more than one suitor simultaneously as in *Taming of the Shrew* and *Two Gentlemen of Verona.* **Bianca** is referred to as 'our fair mistress' (*Shrew* 1.1.117) and Hortensio is particularly anxious to provide 'a fine musician to instruct our mistress' so as not to fall 'behind in duty / To fair Bianca, so beloved of me' (*Shrew* 1.2.173–5). When Valentine asks his 'mistress' to entertain Proteus as a 'fellow-servant', **Silvia** jokes about the high status she is supposed to occupy as the celestial object of their adoration:

> Silvia: Too low a mistress for so high a servant.
> Proteus: Not so, sweet lady, but too mean a servant
> To have the look of such a worthy mistress
> (*TGV* 2.4.103–8)

The Petrarchan mistress of courtly love assumes the same level of command over the beloved as the commanding mistress over household or kingdom. In troubadour tradition she was always of a higher social status, the wife of a nobleman, so any imagined relationship was transgressive in more ways than one and she usually remained out of reach, idealized as a paragon. Queen **Katherine** recalls how she was 'the Lily / That once was Mistris of the Field' (*HVIII* 3.1.151–2). These power dynamics are reflected in Shakespeare's texts in the dramatized wooing of Silvia or of the French ladies in *Love's Labour's Lost,* and in shorter allusions. In *Twelfth Night,* for example, Orsino promises Viola that since she called him master for so long, 'you shall from this time be / Your master's mistress' (*TN* 51.324–6).

The mistress's transforming influence is expressed powerfully by Shakespeare's lovers. Lucentio tells Bianca 'you, sweet dear, prove mistress of my heart' (*Shrew* 4.2.10). Even men such as Coriolanus can emulate the mistress's magnetic power; Tullus Aufidius's servants comment 'our general himself makes a mistress of him: sanctifies himself with's hand and turns up the white o' the eye to his discourse' (*Cor.* 4.5.194–6). For Ferdinand, the mistress transforms night to day and hard labour to delight: 'The mistress which I serve quickens what's dead, / And makes my labors pleasures' (*Temp.* 3.1.6–7). Indeed, Troilus notes that lovers think it is 'harder for our mistress to devise imposition enough than for us to undergo any difficulty imposed' (*T&C* 3.2.78–80). Lafeu recalls that, in addition to commanding others through her astonishing beauty and enchanting speech, **Helena** possessed a 'dear perfection' so that even 'hearts that scorn'd to serve / Humbly call'd [her] mistress' (*AWW* 5.3.15–19). The romantic mistress thus has power to be a patron, inspiration or guiding influence for a whole way of life. Speed claims that now Proteus is 'metamorphis'd with a mistress, that, when I look on you, I can hardly think you my master' (*TGV* 2.1.30–2).

Mistresses represent emotionally transgressive as well as idealized, transformative love in Shakespeare. **Dorcas** jealously asks the Clown, '**Mopsa** must be your mistress: marry, garlic, / To mend her kissing with' (*WT* 4.4.162–3). **Bianca** is jealous that Cassio's handkerchief 'is from some mistress, some remembrance' (*Oth.* 3.4.185–6). **Titania** knows that **Hippolyta** is Theseus's 'buskin'd mistress and your warrior love' (*MND* 2.1.71). Female figures who have long-lasting extra-marital sexual relationships with men are referred to as 'mistresses' in Shakespeare. Jane **Shore**, mistress of Edward IV, for example, is an open secret in court:

> Gloucester: Naught to do with mistress Shore! I tell thee, fellow,
> He that doth naught with her, excepting one,
> Were best he do it secretly, alone.
>
> (*RIII* 1.1.98–100)

Falstaff's mistress, Doll, is repeatedly called 'Mistress Tearsheet', 'Mistress Dorothy' and 'Mistress Doll' (*2HIV* 2.4.11, 41, 121, 127, 152). Walter Whitmore uses the word in this sense referring to Suffolk's lover **Margaret** as 'the Queen his mistress' (*2HVI* 4.1.143). Mistress Overdone exposes Lucio's long-standing affair with 'Mistress Kate Keepdown' who 'was with child by him in the Duke's time; he promis'd her **marriage**' and he is forced to marry her (*MM* 3.2.199–201 and 5.1.509–11). In spite of the long commitment shown in these affairs, such mistresses never command the same absolute commitment demanded in marriage, as is shown in *Titus Andronicus*. When Demetrius asks Aaron, 'Wilt thou betray thy noble mistress thus?' by preserving the baby, he has no doubts about where his loyalties lie: 'My mistress is my mistress; this myself' (*Tit.* 4.1.106–7).

(c) John Aylmer, *An Harborowe for faithfull and trewe subiectes* (London, 1559: sigs. R2r), discussed by Hackett (1995: 49–52) considers the construction of Elizabeth I as ruling mistress of England.

Montague, Lady (a) a character in *Romeo and Juliet*; wife to Montague and mother to Romeo.

(b) Lady Montague is not named in the text other than as the *wife* of *old* Montague (1.1.78SD) who enters brandishing his sword at Capulet. She is, however, a forceful peacemaker, physically restraining her husband and reprimanding him 'Thou shalt not stir one foot to seek a foe' (1.1.80), in the dominant role of a mother. She likewise expresses her relief that Romeo 'was not at this fray' (1.1.117). Benvolio's account of Romeo's love-sickness and his parents' concern about his reclusive behaviour prefigures that of Gertrude for Hamlet. Lady Montague may be a prototype of the doting, potentially suffocating mother. She has no verbal reaction when Romeo's life is demanded by Lady **Capulet** or when he is banished (3.1.180–97), but, like Gertrude with her son, seems to live only by his looks. At the end of the play Montague reports 'my wife is dead tonight / Grief of my son's exile hath stopp'd her breath' (5.3.210–11).

(c) The anonymous *The True Ophelia: And Other studies of Shakespeare's Women by An Actress* (1913), gives an account of the relationship between Lady Montague and Lady Capulet, arguing that the latter is jealous of Lady Montague as mother of a son (pp. 69–70).

Moon, (a) the satellite of the earth, created alongside the sun by God on the fourth day of creation according to the Bible. The moon was feminized from classical times and associated with **Diana** (or Artemis), the goddess of **chastity**, and named **Cynthia** and **Dictynna**. In early modern England the moon formed an important part of Queen **Elizabeth**'s royal iconography.

(b) The moon is a complex feminized figure – the heavenly aspect of the triple-faced goddess – and known by many titles, including **Cynthia** and **Diana**. As the pedantic Holofernes explains, the name **Dictynna** is 'A title to **Phoebe**, to Luna, to the moon' (*LLL* 4.2.38). The moon's changes governed the tides absolutely, making it impossible to 'forbid the sea for to obey the moon' (*WT* 1.2.427). She is, **Titania** points out, 'the governess of floods'; a powerful environmental force who, 'Pale in her anger, washes all the air / That rheumatic diseases do abound' (*MND* 2.1.103–5). Othello, believing that the 'error of the moon' has caused his madness, expresses a common view that it influenced human behaviour too: 'She comes more nearer earth than she was wont / And makes men mad' (*Oth.* 5.2.109–11). The moon and its cycles were thought to have a particularly strong influence over women's bodies and emotions. Mulcaster's educational treatise explained that girls were subject to 'a moonish influence' (Hackett 1995: 182). Olivia warns Cesario ''tis not that time of moon with me to make one in so skipping a dialogue' (*TN* 1.5.200–1). **Elizabeth** in *Richard III* identifies her tearfulness as the result of lunar influence: 'I, being governed by the watery moon / May send forth plenteous tears to drown the world' (*RIII* 2.2.69–70).

Given Elizabeth I's self-conscious adoption of the moon as part of her virgin iconography, it is not surprising that many Shakespearean references emphasize the power of the moon. The myth of the moon goddess who fell in love with the shepherd Endymion had been dramatized by John Lyly for the audience of **Elizabeth** I's court (Lyly 1996), a play which is recalled in **Portia**'s reference to the lovers Jessica and Lorenzo: 'The Moon sleeps with Endymion, / And would not be awak'd' (*Mer.* 5.1.108–9). Falstaff's comparison of himself and his followers to 'squires of the night's body' and followers or 'minions' of Diana the moon probably carries an oblique reference to the Queen's protection of legitimized piracy by courtiers like Sir Walter Ralegh. Falstaff hopes that, like Ralegh, he and his followers will be accounted 'men of good government' since they are governed by 'our noble and chaste mistress the moon, under whose countenance we steal'. Prince Hal reminds him that 'the fortune of us that are the moon's men doth ebb and flow like the sea, being govern'd, as the sea is, by the moon' (*1HIV* 1.2.24–33), perhaps referring obliquely to Ralegh's 1592 imprisonment in the Tower after his secret marriage to Elizabeth Throckmorton (Hackett 1995: 184). Hotspur's reference to the 'pale-fac'd moon' as the keeper of 'bright honor' (*1HIV* 1.3.201) again casts her in a very superior position. Falstaff refers to the 'full moon' looking down on others like 'pins' heads' (*2HIV* 4.3.52–3).

The darker side of the moon, linked to **Hecate** and **witch**craft, is alluded to in several texts. Edmund claims that Edgar mumbled wicked charms and was 'conjuring the moon / To stand's auspicious **mistress**' (*KL* 2.1.39–40). In *Macbeth*, Hecate creates magic spirits by the power of the moon (*Mac.* 3.3.22–9) and **Sycorax** is so powerful a witch that she 'could control the moon', and mimic her power to 'make flows and ebbs' in the tides (*Temp.* 5.1.269–71). Puck explains that fairies who run 'by the triple-Hecate's team' work when 'the wolf behowls the moon' and flee the presence of the sun, 'Following darkness like a dream' (*MND* 5.1.372–86). The moon is an ominous portent to the Welsh captain in *Richard II* whose soldiers believe the king is dead since 'The pale-fac'd moon looks bloody on the earth' (*RII* 2.4.10). Enobarbus, too, views the 'blessed moon' as 'sovereign **mistress** of true melancholy' (*A&C* 4.9.7–11). More positively, the moon's associations with **Diana** make it a trope for female modesty. Coriolanus's pride for daring to 'bemock the modest moon' (*Cor.* 1.2.257) is not tolerated in Rome. In contrast, Menenius flatteringly compares the 'noble ladies' **Volumnia**, **Virgilia** and **Valeria** to 'the moon' (*Cor.* 2.1.97–8) and Valeria is referred to as 'The moon of Rome' for her exemplary cold chastity (*Cor.* 5.3.65). Laertes warns Ophelia that a careful **maid** does not even 'unmask her **beauty** to the moon' (*Ham.* 1.3.37). Romeo says that since Juliet's sun-like beauty outshines the 'envious moon / Who is already sick and pale with grief', she should finish serving the chaste Diana as a virgin and love him instead (*R&J* 2.2.3–9).

In courtly love discourse, the moon is a favourite trope for the cruelly chaste mistress. Ferdinand sees the **Princess** of France's face as the bright 'silver moon' (*LLL* 4.3.) and raises her above the other ladies by saying she is 'a gracious moon' presiding over attending stars (*LLL* 4.3.226–7 and 5.2.204–6). The women play with the trope by masking and swapping identities, then perversely saying they have changed their minds and do not wish to dance: 'not yet, no dance: thus change I like the moon' (*LLL* 5.2.212). The trope allows Rosaline to artfully expose and reject the King's wish to dominate the French Princess when she quips, 'You took the moon at full, but now she's changed'. The French Princess is not the moon; like the King, she is properly symbolized by the sun to mark her sovereignty. His insistence 'Yet she is still the moon, and I the man' implies that he plans to overrule the French Princess by virtue of his sex (*LLL* 5.2.214–15). Perhaps here the play glances back at **Elizabeth** I's earlier reluctance to submit to a French royal suitor, the Duke d'Alençon. Petruchio plays similar games when asserting his dominance over **Katherina**, provoking her to identify the masculine sun and perversely insisting it is the moon, as though to demonstrate the ridiculousness of believing in the illusion of female mastery in a blatantly patriarchal universe:

> Petruchio: I say it is the moon
> Katherine: I know it is the moon.
> Petruchio: Nay then you lie; it is the blessed sun.
> Katherine: Then God be blest, it is the blessed sun,

> But sun it is not, when you say it is not;
> And the moon changes even as your mind.
> (*Shrew* 4.5.16–20)

Katherine appears to accept Petruchio's superiority, like that of Adam, to name and direct, although her final quip about his mind changing like the moon suggests she has not internalized a belief in male superiority.

As a gendered symbol, the moon emphasizes feminine changeability. **Juliet** tells Romeo not to swear not by 'th' inconstant moon, / That monthly changes in her circled orb' in case his love should likewise prove changeable (*R&J* 2.2.109–11). Henry V compares his heart to 'the sun and not the moon; for it shines bright and never changes, but keeps his course truly' (*HV* 5.2.163–4). **Cleopatra** rejects both her gender and the moon in her 'marble constant' resolution for suicide, claiming 'I have nothing / Of woman in me' so that 'now the fleeting moon / No planet is of mine' (*A&C* 5.2.238). Nevertheless, the moon has perpetual power that outlasts the linear life of man, as shown in the answer to Dull's riddle about the age of the moon. Holofernes explains that because of her cycles 'The moon was a month old when Adam was no more, / And raught not to five weeks when he came to five score' (*LLL* 4.2.39–40).

References to the moon as a feminine, changing and yet mysteriously enduring power, with local reference to **Elizabeth** I, figure most strongly in *A Midsummer Night's Dream*. Theseus complains that the old moon wanes slowly lingering his desires like a '**stepdame** or a **dowager**' whose long life diminishes 'a young man's revenue' (*MND* 1.1.2–6). **Hippolyta**, by contrast, thinks that the four nights will pass quickly 'And then the moon, like to a silver bow / New bent in heaven' will see their wedding night (*MND* 1.1.7–11). Her references to **Diana**'s bow and her **Amazon**ian identity create a powerful image of female rule about to be eclipsed by patriarchy in the form of Theseus, a situation with obvious parallels to late Elizabethan England and the imminent death of the ageing **Virgin** Queen. Shakespeare appears to have made a direct connection between Elizabeth and the moon in an oblique reference to her death in Sonnet 107: 'the mortal moon hath her eclipse endur'd' (*Son.* 107.5).

A Midsummer Night's Dream prophetically stages the eclipse as a clumsy male appropriation of the moon. Theseus regards a chaste single life 'chanting faint hymns to the cold fruitless moon' as less happy or useful for women (*MND* 1.1.73). Oberon, likewise, suggests the coldness of single life pursued by the 'fair **vestal** throned by the west' at whom Cupid's dart is aimed. When his arrow is 'Quench'd in the chaste beams of the wat'ry moon' his failure to hit the 'imperial **votaress**' alludes to Queen Elizabeth's powerful but threatened position as an independent virgin **queen** (*MND* 2.1.157–64). The mechanicals' production of 'Pyramus and **Thisbe**' parodically enacts the encroachment of patriarchy in the fairy and human worlds. Although originally anxious to 'find out moonshine' (*MND* 3.1.54) and present it naturally by leaving the window of the chamber open, they resort to having Starveling 'disfigure' the 'person of Moonshine' (*MND* 3.1.60–1) by coming on as the man in the moon. The stupidity of male attempts to appropriate the traditionally feminine power of the moon are suggested by the courtiers' mocking comments 'this is the greatest error of all the rest' and Hippolyta's pointed comment 'I am a-weary of this moon. / Would he would change' (*MND* 5.1.246–51). The parody continues in Caliban's ludicrous worship of Stephano as 'the Man i' th' Moon' (*Temp.* 2.2.137–41). Puck's reminder that the power of 'triple **Hecat**'s team' (*MND* 5.1.384) will return with the moon cautions spectators that although Elizabeth's reign might be eclipsed by death, it would not be so easy to exorcize the potent symbols of female sovereignty conjured by the moon.

(c) Ferber (1999: 127–9) gives a brief survey of the moon as a symbol in Western literature. John Lyly's court plays, *Endymion or the Man in the Moon* [1591] (1996) and *The Woman in the Moon* [c. 1595] (2006) both play to Queen Elizabeth's choice of the moon goddess as part of her iconography. Hackett (1995: 174–6, 178–87 and 191–7) analyses the many aspects of moon imagery associated with the Queen in literary culture. Her essay on '*A Midsummer Night's Dream*' (2003: (esp.) 347–50) discusses links between the moon and menstrual cycles.

Mopsa, (a) a character of a milkmaid and shepherdess in *The Winter's Tale* with whom the Clown says he is in love.

(b) The Clown dances with her in the *dance of Shepherds and Shepherdesses* at the sheepshearing feast and has apparently promised to marry her, although she suspects he has also had sex with her rival, **Dorcas** (4.4.162–5 and 239). Mopsa reminds him that he promised her **gloves** and ribbons as love tokens for the feast (4.4.237–41). She is a lover of ballads, exhibiting what appears to be a rural naivety in wondering whether they are true (4.4.260–7). Although she expresses irritation with Dorcas, she does not object to the three of them singing a ballad fittingly to the tune of 'Two **maid**s wooing a man' (4.4.289), and urges the Clown to buy it.

(c) Newcomb (2004) surveys literary representations of shepherdesses. Neely, *Broken Nuptials* (1993: 203–4) discusses the aggressive fertility of the Bohemian pastoral as a context for the song, while J. H. Pafford (1959), includes comments on the ballad.

Mortimer, Lady, (a) a character in *Henry IV Part I*, who appears in only one scene: Act 3 Scene 1. She is the Welsh daughter of Glendower and is married to Lord Mortimer, nominated by Richard II as heir to the English throne.

(b) Lady Mortimer speaks no English and her husband speaks no Welsh so the **boy actor** must have had to communicate how she 'doteth on her Mortimer' (*1HIV* 3.1.144) by non-verbal means (gestures, kisses and tears) and the unscripted speeches '*in Welsh*' noted in the stage directions. Although the couple have apparently been married as part of a political alliance, they seem to be infatuated with each other. Lady Mortimer weeps at the thought of his parting for battle and he says he is in danger of weeping too. Lady Mortimer's Welsh speech and song is credited with a magical power over Mortimer. She sings like 'a fair **queen** in a summer's bow'r, / With ravishing division to her lute', threatening to charm his blood 'with pleasing heaviness' and send him to sleep on her **lap** on the '**wanton** rushes' (3.1.207–15). Lady Mortimer's power to enchant through song is like the emasculating power of the **Siren** whose 'pleasures are emblematically understood, from which unless a man abstain, or at least use moderately, he shall be devoured in their waves' (Blount 1656). Rackin and Howard suggest that Shakespeare uses Lady Mortimer's seduction of her husband to reconfigure more brutal scenes from the augmented 1587 edition of Holinshed's *Chronicles* (that Shakespeare used) in which the Welshwomen are responsible for castrating the dead bodies of the English soldiers on the battlefield: 'the women of Wales cutt off their privities, and put one part thereof into the mouthes of every dead man' (Howard and Rackin 1997: 171). Mortimer's Welsh-speaking wife certainly threatens to distract him from the battle since he is 'slow' (*1HIV* 3.1.263–4) to leave in contrast to the honourable fiery Hotspur.

(c) Howard and Rackin (1997: 169–74) discuss the role with reference to Abraham Fleming's additions to the 1587 edition of Holinshed's *Chronicle. See* **siren** for more on Blount.

mother, (a) The female parent of a human being; and a name used by children to address a parent. 'Mother' is sometimes used as a respectful or mock-respectful form of address to an older woman, or metaphorically to a female ancestor such as **Eve** (the mother of humankind) or the **Virgin** Mary (mother of God or Christ). It signfied the female head of a religious community, the senior woman in charge of the maids of honour in a royal household (Mother of the Maids), and, bawdily, a woman in charge of a brothel. With the definite article, the word signifies womanly attributes inherited from the mother.

(b) It is a critical commonplace that Shakespeare's texts are characterized by the absence of mothers (Rose 1991; Kahn 1986). Prince Hal appears typical in making a single dismissive reference to a mother who died before the action begins (*1HIV* 2.4.291). The mothers of **Beatrice, Goneril, Regan, Cordelia,** Edmund, Edgar, **Celia and Rosalind, Hermia** and **Helena, Silvia** and **Julia, Portia, Katherina** and **Bianca,** Claudio and **Isabella, Cressida, Imogen** and **Miranda,** to name just a selection, are noticeably absent. Innogen, possibly Hero's mother, is no more substantial than a name in the early stage directions of *Much Ado* while Edmund's remains anonymous, the subject of bawdy jokes in *King Lear* (1.1.13). However, the presence of absent mothers is felt in the texts. In *Othello,* for example, both protagonists remember their mothers. Othello's imbues the handkerchief with the strange authority of maternal wisdom (*Oth.* 3.4.56–65); Desdemona remembers her mother's love-lorn maid **Barbary,** whose fate uncannily predicts Desdemona's own (*Oth.* 5.3.26–33). Treasured objects carry maternal traces. Imogen gives Posthumus the diamond ring that 'was my mother's' (*Cym.* 1.1.112–13), while Shylock is disturbed to hear that **Jessica** traded her mother's ring for a monkey (*Mer.* 3.1.118–19). Even more poignantly, Young Lucius's mother is remembered through the gift of a book:

> Boy: Grandsire, 'tis Ovid's Metamorphosis
> My mother gave it me.

> Marcus: For love of her that's gone,
>   Perhaps, she [Lavinia] cull'd it from amongst the rest.
>
> *(Tit.* 4.1.42–4)

The absent mother's influence, excluded by male characters in their attempts to prove their masculine difference, is dangerous. Exeter depicts it is as a weakening yet suffocating force: 'But I had not so much of man in me, / And all my mother came into mine eyes / And gave me up to tears' (*HV* 4.6.30–2). Sebastian, too, feels that he is 'yet so near the manners of my mother, that upon the least occasion more mine eyes will tell tales of me' (*TN* 2.1.40–2). Cassius believes that the Romans are 'govern'd with our mothers' spirits' because they are subjected under Caesar's rule (*JC* 1.3.83) and later describes his own emotional behaviour as the 'rash humour which my mother gave me'. Brutus promises to excuse any future passionate outbursts with the thought 'your mother chides' (*JC* 4.3.120–3). The most striking example of a return of repressed maternal influence is Lear's declaration:

> O, how this mother swells up toward my heart!
> Hysterica passio! Down, thou climbing sorrow!
> Thy element's below!
>
> *(KL* 2.4.56–8)

In addition to Lear's return to an ungoverned emotional state linked to the wandering **womb**, the return of the absent mother is played out with violent results in Lear's wish to make his daughters into mothers who will take responsibility for the kingdom and care for him (Kahn 1986).

Early modern English women's experience of motherhood did not usually begin as early as Lady **Capulet** says is customary in Verona where ladies of 13 'Are made already mothers' (*R&J* 1.3.71–3). Nevertheless, the canon does give glimpses of the frightening experiences of **birth** by new mothers. Imogen jokes 'ne'er long'd my mother so / To see me first, as I have now' a longing to see Posthumus (*Cym.* 3.4.2). **Beatrice** reminds Don Pedro, 'sure lord, my mother cried' perhaps referring to her death in childbirth (*MAdo* 2.1.334). Mistress **Quickly** jokes 'I'll be sworn, / As my mother was, the first hour I was born' (*MWW* 2.2.37–8). Facing a new-born baby could be a source of dread if the baby was not perfect, as Queen **Isabel** anticipates: 'I, a gasping new-deliver'd mother, / Have woe to woe, sorrow to sorrow join'd' (*RII* 2.2.65). The Duchess of York 'felt more than a mother's pain, / And, yet brought forth less than a mother's hope' in Richard of Gloucester, 'To wit, an indigested and deformed lump' (*3HVI* 5.6.49–51). **Anne** wishes that his children prove 'abortive', premature births 'Whose ugly and unnatural aspect / May fright the hopeful mother at the view' (*RIII* 1.221–4). **Constance** in *King John* catalogues the full range of fears of an expectant mother, suggesting that mothers do not love children born with physical differences. This is, however, an exaggerated explanation of why she does feel such extreme maternal grief at the perfect Prince Arthur's misfortune:

> If thou that bid's me be content were grim,
> Ugly, and sland'rous to thy mother's **womb**,
> Full of unpleasing blots and sightless stains,
> Lame, foolish, crooked, swart, prodigious,
> Patch'd with foul moles and eye-offending marks,
> I would not care, I then would be content,
> For then I should not love thee.
>
> (*KJ* 3.1.43–9)

In spite of the dangers and fears surrounding birth, the male wish to emulate the creative power of mothers comes through strongly in Cymbeline's words when he recovers his three lost children and declares himself 'A mother to the birth of three', vowing that 'Ne'er mother / Rejoiced deliverance more' (*Cym.* 5.3.369–70).

Shakespeare's texts register the irony that, without any proof of paternity in early modern England, a mother provided the most secure origin of identity in a patriarchal society. Simon Shadow introduces himself via his mother:

Falstaff: Shadow, whose son art thou?
Shadow: My mother's son, sir.
Falstaff: Thy mother's son! like enough, and thy father's shadow. So the son of the female is the shadow of the male.

> (*2HIV* 3.2.126–30)

Mothers have unique access to the truth of a child's paternity. Joan La **Pucelle**'s father asserts that 'her mother liveth yet, can testify / She was the first fruit of my bachelorship' (*1HVI* 5.4.12–13). For **Marina** (and **Perdita**), identification with a lost mother restores identity. Marina tells Pericles, 'Is it no more to be your daughter than / To say my mother's name was **Thaisa**?' and advertises a typical maternal cycle of loss and perpetual renewal: 'Thaisa was my mother, who did end / The minute I began' (*Per.* 5.1.209–14). For male characters, the mother's word guarantees their identity. The Bastard Falconbridge repeats the term 'mother' in his quest to find his true paternity, both as an appeal to her and as a form of securing his identity. He begins 'mother, I am not sir Robert's son' and concludes 'good my mother, let me know my father; / Some proper man, I hope. Who was it, mother?' (*KJ* 1.1.246–50). Richard of Gloucester insults Prince Edward by saying 'Whoever got thee, there thy mother stands, / For well I wot, thou hast thy mother's **tongue**' (*3HVI* 2.2.133–4). Since a mother's chastity or honour is the only guarantee of a son's link to his father, male characters are understandably preoccupied with it. Seeing **Cressida**'s infidelity, Troilus determines

> Think, we had mothers; do not give advantage
> To stubborn critics, apt, without a theme,
> For depravation, to square the general sex
> By Cressid's rule:
>
> (*T&C* 5.2.132–5)

Hamlet, Laertes (*Ham.* 1.2.146 and 4.5.118–20) and Posthumus (*Cym.* 2.5.2–5) are tortured in a similar way.

Ironically in patriarchal societies, maternal lines represent a more secure basis for claims to the throne as examples from Shakespeare's histories show. In *Henry VI Parts 2* and *3*, for example, Mortimer is heir to the English throne since 'by my mother I derived am / From Lionel Duke of Clarence, the third son / To King Edward the Third' (*1HVI* 2.5.74). Richard Plantagenet, Duke of York, bases his claim on this lineage via '**Anne**, / My mother, being heir unto the crown' since she was the granddaughter of Mortimer and **Philippe**, daughter to Lionel, Duke of Clarence. 'By her I claim the kingdom', York confidently asserts (*2HVI* 2.2.43–7). A reminder of the powerful challenge maternal claims make to male rule sounds in Caliban's complaint 'This island's mine by **Sycorax** my mother' (*Temp.* 1.2.331).

For many male characters, the mother represents an image of absolute security and fulfilment. The Duke of Suffolk fantasizes about an infantile return to the maternal breast and **lap** where he could be

> As mild and gentle as the cradle-babe
> Dying with mother's **dug** between its lips:
> Where, from thy sight, I should be raging mad,
> And cry out for thee to close up mine eyes,
> To have thee with thy lips to stop my mouth;
>
> (*2HVI* 3.2.392–6)

As his words suggest, everything that follows such a perfect sense of completeness feels like loss or lack. The male character can try to recreate it through a love relationship or the creation of a family around him, as Edward IV does in imagining a united family with **Elizabeth** Woodville as the maternal head, a microcosm of a kingdom united from differences (*3HVI* 3.2.101–6). The unnaturalness of trying to preserve the state of infantile dependence is shown in the incestuous relationship between Antiochus and his **daughter** who describes herself as feeding 'On mother's flesh which did me breed' and becoming Antiochus's 'mother, **wife**, and yet his **child**' (*Per.* 1.1.65).

Elizabeth Grymeston wrote to her son 'there is nothing so strong as the force of love; there is no love so forcible as the love of an affectionate mother to hir naturall childe' (Travitsky 1989: 52). Mothers' typical indulgence of their children is noted in several texts. Polonius feels that 'nature makes them partial' (*Ham.* 3.3.32), which seems to be the case with Hamlet's mother (*Ham.* 4.7.12), and with the **Duchess** of York, who pleads for the pardon of her son Aumerle (*RII* 5.3). Lady **Capulet** shows no such bias, however, and there is something desperate in Juliet's agonized cry, 'O, sweet my mother, cast me not away!' (*R&J* 3.5.198). Richard II compares his reunion with his kingdom to 'a long-parted mother with her child' who 'Plays fondly with her tears and smiles in meeting' (*RII* 3.2.8–9). Idealized scenes of intimacy between mothers and sons are presented in *The Winter's Tale*, where Mamillius tells Hermione his tale of sprites and goblins (*WT*

2.1.23–32), and in the Macduff household in *Macbeth* where Lady Macduff, like a **hen** bird, tries to protect her chicks (*Mac.* 4.2.30–85). Both scenes are, of course, rudely broken up by aggressive male invasions. In Tarsus, famine causes another shocking violation of the natural child and mother bond where

> Those mothers who, to nousle up their babes,
> Thought nought too curious, are ready now
> To eat those little darlings whom they loved.
>
> (*Per.* 1.4.42–4)

Mothers give political guidance and protection too, often with a thinly disguised degree of self-interest as when **Tamora** promises Saturnine she will be 'a mother to his youth' (*Tit.* 1.1.332) with the intention of ruling according to her will. Undoubtedly **Elizabeth** I's styling of herself as the maiden mother to her kingdom helped to legitimize and popularize images of maternal political power. The widowed Queen Elizabeth in *Richard III* must be 'a careful mother', protecting the interests of her son, herself and her Woodville relations (*RIII* 2.2.96). In *King John*, **Constance** and **Eleanor** prove to be powerful champions of their sons' rights to the throne. The loss of these mother figures is a profound shock to King John. When he misses his 'mother's care' over his estate in France, the news that she died on April 1 and 'The Lady Constance in a frenzy died / Three days before (*KJ* 4.2.117–23) arguably begins the traumatic collapse which results in his death. 'What? mother dead?' he asks, apparently concerned about France, but the repetition 'My mother dead!' betrays how emotionally devastating the loss is (*KJ* 4.2.127–8 and 181).

'Mother' signifies maternal authority in a religious, especially Catholic, context in Shakespeare. In *Measure for Measure* it refers to the **Abbess** of the convent when Isabella says she will 'give the Mother' notice of her absence (*MM* 1.4.86). Joan La **Pucelle** vows that the **Virgin** Mary, 'God's Mother deigned to appear to me' in a 'vision full of majesty' (*1HVI* 1.2.78–9). Gloucester believes he has been commissioned by 'God's Mother' to save the kingdom from calamity (*2HVI* 2.1.49). Richard III uses it hypocritically, saying of Margaret, 'by God's holy Mother, / She hath had too much wrong; and I repent / My part thereof that I have done to her' (*RIII* 1.3.305–7). The Virgin and the institutional power of the Catholic church are invoked by the Cardinal in *King John* who uses the term to suggest that the kings John and Lewis are behaving like disrespectful and unnatural sons 'against the church, our holy mother' (*KJ* 3.1.141). In this explicitly Protestant play, the maternal imagery implies that England's Reformation is a natural maturing process of splitting from the mother Church. Lewis is warned that defection would make 'the Church, our mother, breathe her curse, / A mother's curse, on her revolting son' (*KJ* 3.1.256–7).

In secular contexts, the name of mother conjures authority as a mark of seniority, experience or household command. Juliet's mother is matriarch of the Capulet household, although this comically subverted in Juliet's exchange with the Nurse 'How oddly thou repliest! "Your love says, like an honest gentleman

'Where is your mother'"?'(*R&J*2.5.59–62). Likewise, Rosalind challenges **Phoebe** 'Who might be your mother, / That you insult, exult, and all at once, / Over the wretched?' (*AYLI*3.5.35–7). **Margery** Jordan, the oldest woman and the **witch** in the gathering at **Eleanor** of Gloucester's house, is addressed by the title 'Mother Jordan' (*2HVI*1.4.10). Mistress **Page** sustains the trick of Falstaff's disguise as the old woman of **Brainford** by apparently addressing him respectfully as 'Mother Prat' (*MWW* 4.2.182), although the name 'prat' (meaning trick and buttock) comically anticipates his beating by Ford. The code of honour and respect properly paid to a mother appears to be strong in Shakespeare's texts, possibly deriving from the respect paid to Mary **Arden** and other matriarchs in his home environment. In the midst of the political negotiations over the Roman empire, Pompey curiously reminds Antony, as a point of honour, that 'Your mother came to Sicily and did find / Her welcome friendly' (*A&C* 2.6.45–6), a point Antony concedes. Robert Falconbridge and **Helena**, however, are accused of failing to observe the proper code of honour. **Eleanor**, the Queen Mother, scolds the former for defaming his mother's **chastity** in a public arena. Parolles wittily tells Helena that to 'speak on the part of virginity, / is to accuse your mothers' (*AWW* 1.1.181). Bertram later tries to use the same argument on **Diana** (*AWW*4.2.9–11). Doll Tearsheet attempts to shame the officers who come to arrest her with the words 'thou wert better thou hadst struck thy mother, thou paper-fac'd villain' (*2HIV* 5.4.9–10). The dangers of slighting a mother are dramatized powerfully through the relationship of Richard of Gloucester and his mother. Richard's belated greeting makes a mockery of his show of respect:

> Gloucester: Madam, my mother, I do cry you mercy;
> I did not see your grace: humbly on my knee
> I crave your blessing.
> Duchess: God bless thee, and put meekness in thy breast,
> Love, charity, obedience and true duty!
> Gloucester: Amen. [aside] and make me die a good old man!
> That is the butt-end of a mother's blessing.
> (*RIII* 2.2.104–10)

Richard's contempt for his mother and the traditional moral values she stands for come back to haunt him, literally, when he receives her curse later in the play. The Duchess of York's parting words to her son are to give him 'my most grievous curse' to weigh him down on the battlefield. She then tells him 'My prayers on the adverse party fight' with the souls of those has murdered (*RIII* 4.4.188–94).

Hamlet's lack of respect for his mother threatens to subvert the ghost's command to not 'let thy soul contrive / Against thy mother aught' but to 'Leave her to heaven' (*Ham.* 1.5.85–6). He responds to her 'mother's commandment' with sarcasm 'O wonderful son, that can so stonish a mother! / But is there no sequel at the heels of this mother's admiration?' and acquiesces with mock deference 'We shall obey were she twenty times our mother', implying contempt for her authority as a mother (*Ham.* 3.2.311–34). For Hamlet the word 'mother' signifies corruption and infidelity. He pointedly refuses to call Claudius his father, referring to him instead as 'dear mother' and 'My mother!' (*Ham.* 4.2.49–51). Hamlet uses 'mother' out of a desire to separate the pure but insubstantial nature of paternity from the corrupt, corporeal reality and mortality he associates with his mother. His disgust at Gertrude moves him close to physical violence against her. He is conscious of matricidal feelings that liken him to Nero, who arranged the murder of his mother Agrippina: 'O heart, lose not thy nature; let not ever / The soul of Nero enter this firm bosom', and steels himself to 'speak daggers to her, but use none' (*Ham.* 3.2.392). On a national scale the rebels in *King John* are shamed as 'degenerate' matricides in the comparison to 'bloody Neroes' who will rip 'up the **womb** / Of your dear mother **England**' (*KJ* 4.2.151–3).

In Shakespeare, as in most Western culture, mothers are defined in terms of loss. While sons and daughters experience the loss of maternal plenitude, mothers have to reconcile themselves to loss of their children: in death, in physical separations as they grow up and in the transfer of their affections. The most immediately shocking of these is invoked in Burgundy's poignant vision of a mother watching her child die:

> As looks the mother on her lowly babe
> When death doth close his tender dying eyes,
> See, see the pining malady of France!
> (*1HVI* 3.3.47–9)

Since about one in five children died in the first 12 months of life and another one in five were likely to die before their fifth birthday, child mortality was a painful fact of life for most families. Undoubtedly Burgundy's words would have echoed the sentiments of many early modern women. Lady Elizabeth Cavendish Egerton, for example, prays for her sick daughter Frances 'restore her, I beseech thee, to be a healthfull child, and bring her out of the jawes of death' but without success and prays again, when she is pregnant 'lay not thy heavy hand of Justice and affliction on me, in takeing away my Children in their youth, as thou wast pleased to take my last Babe Frances' (Egerton 1999: 177–8).

The emotional violence of losing a child is figured in images of physical violence in Shakespeare's texts. Mothers repeatedly figure losing their children in war. Coriolanus pities 'mothers that lack sons' in Corioli (*Cor.* 2.1.179). In *King John* the citizens of Angiers are warned that the fighting has made 'Much work for tears in many an English mother, / Whose sons lie scattered on the bleeding ground' (*KJ* 2.1.303–4). Richard II fears that 'Ten thousand bloody crowns of mothers' sons' (*RII* 3.3.96) will stain England's ground and Henry V threatens that the Dauphin's jest will 'Mock mothers from their sons' (*HV* 1.2.286). The most violent of these nightmares of loss are imagined as a repetition of Herod's slaughter of the innocents:

> Your naked infants spitted upon pikes,
> Whiles the mad mothers with their howls confused

> Do break the clouds, as did the wives of Jewry
> At Herod's bloody-hunting slaughtermen.
>
> (*HV* 3.3.38–41)

Antony promises that the savage butchery following Caesar's murder will be so common 'That mothers shall but smile when they behold / Their infants quarter'd with the hands of war' (*JC* 3.1.267–8). Queen **Margaret** gives what is perhaps the most emotionally raw expression of maternal loss in Shakespeare. The fierce military leader is suddenly exposed at a human level as she holds the dead body of her son Prince Edward and bids him 'Ned, sweet Ned! speak to thy mother, boy! / Canst thou not speak?' She determines to speak for him 'that so my heart will burst', condemning the Yorkists as 'Butchers and villains! bloody cannibals!' who have no children and therefore no remorse (*3HVI* 5.5.51–67).

In non-military contexts, Shakespeare's texts register mothers' experiences of losing children through political plotting or even just the process of growing up beyond the maternal realm. **Constance** becomes distracted with grief at the loss of Arthur and gives voice to the various experiences of loss shared by so many mothers amongst Shakespeare's readers or audiences, including perhaps his own wife who watched their son Hamnet Shakespeare die in August 1596. Constance refutes the imputation of madness by giving a perfectly logical explanation for her distraction: 'Young Arthur is my son, and he is lost. / I am not mad, I would to heaven I were!' (*KJ* 3.4.47–8). She then points out, 'If I were mad, I should forget my son, / Or madly think a babe of clouts were he' but instead she feels 'too well, too well' the calamity of her loss and his impending death (*KJ* 3.3.57–60) Perhaps this is something Anne and William Shakespeare felt about Hamnet too (Weis 2007: 182–4):

> Grief fills the room up of my absent child,
> Lives in his bed, walks up and down with me,
> Puts on his pretty looks, repeats his words,
> Remembers me of all his gracious parts,
> Stuffs out his vacant garments with his form;
> Then, have I reason to be fond of grief?
> Fare you well! Had you such loss as I,
> I could give better comfort than you do . . .
> . . .
> O Lord, my boy, but Arthur, my fair son!
> My life, my joy, my food, my all the world!
>
> (*KJ* 3.4.93–104)

A repeated pattern in which women are transformed from 'joyful mother' to 'one that wails the name' (*RIII* 4.4.99) is summed up by the Duchess of York who imagines herself as 'the mother of these griefs' of loss shared by the family. 'Pour all your tears! I am your sorrow's **nurse**, / And I will pamper it with lamentation' she tells Elizabeth and Anne (*RIII* 2.2.79–88). The three women all invoke the name of mother as a passport to see the Princes imprisoned in the

Tower. **Elizabeth**'s bold claim 'I am their mother, who shall bar me from them?' followed by the **Duchess**'s authority as 'their father's mother', and **Anne**'s claim that she is 'in love their mother' (*RIII* 4.1.21–4) are tragically powerless. It is a 'mother's lamentation' (*RIII* 4.4.14) of loss that finally brings the rival Yorkist and Lancastrian queens together in a shared pain and sorrow.

The roles of **Volumnia** and **Dionyza** show how passionate maternal love can be destructive in nature. Volumnia seems to share Imogen's view that 'Plenty and peace breeds cowards: hardness ever / Of hardiness is mother' (*Cym.* 3.6.21–2). She has thus encouraged her son to seek danger and honour, even though this contradicts the mother's conventionally protective role. She remembers how 'When yet he was but tender-bodied and the only son of my womb', a time when 'a mother should not sell him an hour from her beholding', she sent Coriolanus to 'a cruel war'. His honourable delivery from this bloody war, the birth of his manhood, gave her no less joy than 'at first hearing he was a man-child' at his birth (*Cor.* 1.3.5–17). Volumnia tells him 'Thy valiantness was mine, thou suck'dst it from me', suggesting that she is displacing her own frustrated masculine energies onto him and living them through her son (*Cor.* 3.2.127–30). He repeatedly recalls her sayings of motherly wisdom and reminds her affectionately, 'My mother, you wot well / My hazards still have been your solace' (*Cor.* 4.1.2–4 and 27–8).

The full power of maternal love to destroy a man's self-crafted independent identity becomes clear when Volumnia speaks on behalf of Rome, the mother-country, mocking Coriolanus's unnatural attempt to attack it and stand 'As if a man were author of himself / And knew no other kin' (*Cor.* 5.3.36–7). She says his purpose is no better than to tread on his mother's **womb** (*Cor.* 5.3.124–5). Volumnia claims 'there's no man in the world / More bound to 's mother' (*Cor.* 5.3.158–9), and casts herself as a protective mother **hen**, doing the 'duty which / To a mother's part belongs' in pleading for Rome (*Cor.* 5.3.162–8). The simple, telling gesture where Coriolanus '*holds her by the hand silent*' graphically marks the collapse of his adult identity, accompanied as it is by the words 'O mother, mother' and again

> O my mother, mother! O!
> You have won a happy victory to Rome;
> But, for your son, believe it – O, believe it –
> Most dangerously you have with him prevail'd,
> If not most mortal to him.
>
> (*Cor.* 5.3.185–9)

The Volscians' facile view that Coriolanus 'no more remembers his mother now than an eight-year-old horse' (*Cor.* 5.4.16–18) shows the shallow understanding, the unwillingness of the military community to acknowledge the power of maternal influences.

The fierceness of maternal love for her son leads the Queen in *Cymbeline* to adopt the stereotypical cruelty of a **stepmother**, 'A mother hourly coining plots' (*Cym.* 2.1.59) towards Imogen. In *Pericles*, the foster-mother **Dionyza** justifies her plotting to murder **Marina** as an expression of maternal love towards her own child Philoten:

> She did distain my child, and stood between
> Her and her fortunes. None would look on her,
> But cast their gazes on Marina's face . . .
>   It pierc'd me through
> And though you call my course unnatural
> You not your child well loving, yet I find,
> It greets me as an enterprise of kindness
> Perform'd to your sole daughter.
>
> (*Per.* 4.3.31–9)

The **Countess** of Rosillion in *All's Well* is a very different kind of adoptive mother to **Helena**. Her role as a mother, foster-mother and mother-in-law is carefully developed through the twists and turns of the plot, which trace a typical Shakespearean pattern of maternal loss but follow this through to miraculous recovery. The Countess is grief-stricken at 'delivering' her son from home to the court in the play's opening line, but sends him off with benediction and maternal advice (*AWW* 1.1.61–70). Her role as surrogate mother, protectress of Helena and prospective mother-in-law is carefully negotiated in an interview between the two women:

> Countess: Why not a mother? When I said 'a mother,'
>   Methought you saw a serpent: what's in 'mother,'
>   That you start at it? I say, I am your mother;
>   And put you in the catalogue of those
>   That were en**womb**ed mine: 'tis often seen
>   Adoption strives with nature and choice breeds
>   A native slip to us from foreign seeds:
>   You ne'er oppress'd me with a mother's groan,
>   Yet I express to you a mother's care:
>   God's mercy, maiden! does it curd thy blood
>   To say I am thy mother?
>
> (*AWW* 1.1.140)

Helena's initial refusal to accept the Countess as her mother leads the Countess to delicately negotiate the possibility of reconfiguring Helena's role as daughter-in-law. When Bertram rejects Helena, the Countess rejects him, telling her, 'He was my son / But I do wash his name our of my blood / And thou art all my child' (*AWW* 3.2.66–8).

Having lost Bertram to the wars, she then faces the loss of Helena who 'If she had partaken of my flesh, and cost me the dearest groans of a mother I could not have owed her a more rooted love' (*AWW* 4.5.10–12). At this low point of the play, the pains of motherhood seem to outweigh any benefits. The worldly experience of Diana's mother, telling her just how Bertram would woo and flout his **marriage** vows, makes Diana choose single life (*AWW* 4.2.69–74). For the Countess, however, the dénouement allows her to see both children restored: Bertram to the King's favour and Helena apparently to life and to her rightful place as a wife, with the promise of motherhood in the future. For the Countess, the resolution is complete when Helena addresses her with the term she had been previously unwilling to use: 'O my dear mother!' (*AWW* 5.3.319). The Countess's role thus appears to offer Shakespeare's most comprehensive account of the pains and pleasures of motherhood and surrogacy.

(c) Mendelson and Crawford (1998: 148–74), Valerie Fildes (ed.), *Women as Mothers in Pre-Industrial England* (1990: (esp.) 3–38, 139–78), and Linda Pollock, *Forgotten Children: Parent Child Relations from 1500–1900* (1983) give very good historical accounts of early modern women's experiences of motherhood. Accounts of motherhood and writings to children by early modern women clearly disprove the theory that little emotional bonding existed between parents and children in the period. A selection of extracts, including Elizabeth Grymeston's *Miscelanae Meditations, Memorative* (1604), can be found in Travitsky (1989: 55–71). Booy (2002: 105–29), E. Brown (1999) and Egerton (1999) give examples of early modern women's writings about motherhood, including edited texts of mothers' legacies. Kristen Poole (1995) provides a good reading of these. Mary Beth Rose's classic essay asks 'Where Are the Mothers in Shakespeare?' (1991); Coppélia Kahn's, 'The Absent Mother in *King Lear*' (1986) and Adelman's *Suffocating Mothers* (1992) provide answers for the tragedies, looking especially at the return of the repressed mother figure who haunts the early modern male psyche. Chamberlain (2005) considers Lady Macbeth as an unnatural mother. Jane Freeman (2004), reads the Countess of Rossillion as a maternal guiding force in *All's Well*. Naomi J. Miller and Naomi Yavneh (eds), *Maternal Measures: Figuring Caregiving in the Early Modern Period* (2000), offers a range of useful representations of motherhood including Heather Dubrow's (2000) essay on surrogate parents in *Richard III*. Kathryn M. Moncrief and Kathryn R. McPherson's edited collection, *Performing Maternity in Early Modern England* (2007) includes essays on dramatic representations of motherhood in *All's Well*, *Antony and Cleopatra*, *Macbeth*, *Merchant of Venice*, and *Winter's Tale*.

Mountjoy, Marie (a) French landlady to Shakespeare from 1604 in Silver Street, London. Marie Mountjoy was married to Christopher Mountjoy, a maker of **tires** – fashionable ornamental headdresses. Shakespeare may have got to know the Mountjoys through Mme Monutjoy's acquaintance with Jaqueline **Field** (née Vautrollier), who attended the French church in London. If Shakespeare had met the Mountjoys before lodging with them, Mary's French background may have influenced *Henry V*, which includes extensive dialogue in French between women as well as the herald Mountjoy. Shakespeare must have gained first-hand awareness of women's fashion accessories, especially headwear, from lodging in the Mountjoys' house and in Silver Street. He also had first-hand experience of a dispute over a marriage **dowry**, since in 1612 he was called to testify at the Court of Requests about the portion assigned to their daughter Mary, who married their apprentice Stephen Belott (the son of a French widow) on 19 November 1604. Shakespeare appears to have been part of the matchmaking process. A witness, Joan Johnson, recalled that 'the defendant [Mountjoy] did send and persuade one Mr Shakespeare that lay in the house to persuade the plaintiff [Belott] to the same marriage' (Schoenbaum 1987: 262). When Belott, who had been holding out for a larger portion, only received £10.00 and some furniture and household goods instead of the expected £60.00 and an inheritance of £200, relations between the couple and Christopher Mountjoy became increasingly bitter, in spite of Marie Mountjoy's attempts to find a reconciliation up to her death in 1606.

(c) Schoenbaum (1987: 260–4).

Muse, (a) an inspiration for artistic or intellectual creative endeavour, especially poetry or song. The Muse is often invoked at the beginning of a work. In Greek mythology, the nine Muses were the daughters of Zeus and Mnemoyne, the **goddess** of memory. By the early modern period they had become more closely associated with specialist branches of the arts and learning: Clio (history); Calliope (epic poetry); Thalia (comedy); Melpomene (tragedy); Terpischore (dance); Euterpe (music); Urania (astronomy); Erato (love poetry); and Polyhymnia (songs to the gods).

(b) Theseus is not tempted by 'The thrice three Muses mourning for the death / Of Learning, late deceas'd in beggary', one of the courtly entertainments offered for his **wedding**. He believes it will be 'some satire keen and critical', and therefore unsuitable (*MND* 5.1.53–5). The title probably alludes to Spenser's 1591 poem *The Tears of the Muses*, a lament rather than a satire. However, the title does make a prophetic satiric comment on the decease of learning exhibited in the 'tedious brief scene' and 'very tragical mirth' of Pyramus and **Thisbe** as performed by the mechanicals (*MND* 5.1.56–7). It perhaps prompts the keen and critical comments of the male courtly spectators on the performance. Another reference to the Muses as a group occurs in Sonnet 38 where the poet tells his lover that he is a source of infinite inspiration for the poet's Muse, and then goes on to conflate the two, addressing his lover as more powerful than all the nine traditional Muses:

> How can my Muse want subject to invent
> While thou dost breathe, that pour'st into my verse
> Thine own sweet argument . . .
>
> Be thou the tenth Muse, ten time more in worth
> Than those old nine which rhymers invoke.
> (*Son.* 38.1–3 and 9–10)

The poet self-consciously admits that 'so oft have I invok'd thee for my Muse' that rival poets have now adopted the young man and 'my sick Muse doth give another place' (*Son.* 78.1 and 79.4). Thus betrayed, the speaker's poetic Muse develops as a separate identity, its detachment pointedly acknowledged in the remark 'I grant thou wert not married to my Muse' (*Son.* 82.1). The betrayed Muse adopts a tone of bitter, silent regret:

> My tongue-tied Muse in manners holds her still,
> While comments of your praise, richly compil'd,
> Reveal their character with golden quill
> And precious phrase by all the Muses fil'd.
>
> (*Son.* 85.1–4)

In Sonnet 100, the poet charges his 'forgetful Muse' and 'truant Muse' for poetic infidelity in neglecting to maintain praise of the youth (*Son.* 100.5 and 101.1). Whatever the circumstances, the poetic Muse must not fail to 'do thy office' which is to keep the beloved alive through verse (*Son.* 101:13–14). Two instances in Shakespeare's plays invoke the creative Muse. The Chorus of *Henry V* longs for 'a Muse of fire, that would ascend / The brightest heaven of invention!' (*HV* Prologue. 1–2). Iago regards his personal Muse in specifically maternal terms as the invisible partner to his male inventions: 'my Muse labors / And thus she is deliver'd' (*Oth.* 2.1.127–8). Although he is joking with Desdemona and Emilia, the phrase, which draws on a common trope of literary parthenogenesis (where the poet intellectually begets and gives birth to a poetic offspring), reveals the misogyny that displaces his other evil plots onto a female origin.

(c) H. L. Meakin (1998: 24–84) gives an impressive, detailed analysis of the feminized Muses as figures associated with inspiration and poetic decadence in the early modern period. Jane Hedley's *Power in Verse* (2008: (esp.) 96) offers a broader account of the dynamics of lyric poetry. Stephen Booth (1977: 273–4) and Helen Vendler, *The Art of Shakespeare's Sonnets* (1999: 198–200, 354–6 and 426–32) analyse the Muse figure in Sonnets 38, 79, 101–2.

naiad, *see* **nymph**

nature, (a) the creative and regulative power operating in the earth and over all its animate and inanimate objects: plants and creatures (including humans), landscape, weather; frequently personified as a maternal force, **Dame** Nature and as a **goddess**. As the material point of origin for all living things, Nature was also credited with giving them their inherent or essential qualities.

(b) Shakespearean references to Nature's maternal and life-giving qualities follow a common early modern view. For example, Thomas Raynalde's much reprinted **midwife**ry book argued 'nature created the wombe or matrix to be the sayde receptacle, & house of office wherin she mought at her leasure worke her devine feates about the seede once conceaved'. To nurture the foetus, 'prudent Lady nature full wisely hath provided that there shoulde alwayes be prest and redye a continuall course and resort of blood' (Raynalde 1565: fol. xxvii r and v).

Such associations with midwifery and fertility inform Parolles' argument to **Helena** that 'it is not politic in the commonwealth of nature to preseve **virgin**ity' (*AWW* 1.1.138), and the idea that Thaisa (who has no human mother in *Pericles*) is 'beauty's child, whom nature gat' (*Per.* 2.2.6–7). Nature's power over fertility lies behind King Lear's appeal

> Hear, Nature, hear, dear goddess, hear!
> Suspend thy purpose, if thou didst intend
> To make this creature fruitful.
>
> (*KL* 1.4.275–7)

He calls on Nature to punish **Goneril** for her unfilial (and thus unnatural) behaviour with the curse of sterility or the birth of a monstrous child (*KL* 1.4.278–81). Nature is likely to break out in 'strange eruptions' herself from the pregnant

womb of the **earth**, producing climactic conditions which male characters like Hotspur or Glendower find threatening (*1HIV* 3.1.27–34). On a smaller, human scale, Cerimon can 'speak of the disturbances / That nature works, and of her cures' through his study of human physiology and medicine (*Per.* 3.2.37–8).

More positive views of Nature as a maternal force occur in *Richard II* and *Timon*, where, in both cases, nature's protective care is set in contrast to the destructive energies of human beings. Nature is geographically creative in John of Gaunt's view of **England** as a 'fortress built by Nature for herself / Against infection and the hand of war' (*RII* 2.1.43–4) to nurture kings and people. Timon of Athens sees her as a provider: 'The bounteous **housewife** Nature on each bush / Lays her full mess before you' (*Tim* 4.3.420–1). As a powerfully creative and potentially disruptive female force, the goddess Nature is a perfect patroness of those born outside patriarchal law: bastards, who were known as 'natural' children. Edmund in *King Lear* rejects the culture which disadvantages him and vows 'Thou, Nature, art my goddess; to thy law / My services are bound' (*KL* 1.2.1–2). Achilles, anticipating the bizarre depictions of Nature as a cook in Margaret Cavendish's poetry (Cavendish 1653), describes the irascible bastard Thersites as 'Thou crusty batch of nature' (*T&C* 5.1.5).

Nature, as a maternal point of origin, prompts what male characters view as feminized, childlike, behaviour. Laertes, for example, weeps at news of **Ophelia**'s death and explains: 'Nature her custom holds, / Let shame say what it will; when these are gone, / The **woman** will be out' (*Ham.* 4.7.187–9). Lucius, too, admits that 'nature puts me to a heavy task' in weeping over the body of his father, Titus (*Tit.* 5.3.150). Henry V advises his soldiers to 'Disguise fair nature with hard-favour'd rage' before Harfleur (*HV* 3.1.8). Antony has a more flexible view of masculinity, arguing that Julius Caesar's life was gentle and 'the elements / So mix'd in him that Nature might stand up / And say to all the world "This was a man!"' (*JC* 5.5.73–5).

Shakespeare's texts illuminate the quality of nature to prompt human love between family members, especially parents and children. Lady **Macbeth** seeks to stop up her **womb** to avoid 'compunctious visitings of nature' that would shake her masculine purpose to murder (*Mac.* 1.5.45). In *Coriolanus* Sicinius argues that 'Nature teaches beasts to know their friends' (*Cor* 2.1.6), and despite Menenius's reminder that Nature is savagely individualist, making the lion eat the lamb (*Cor.* 2.1.7–10), at a family level her influence dominates Coriolanus. He is ultimately powerless to resist the appeals of his mother Volumnia, **wife** and son, since 'Great Nature cries "Deny not"' (*Cor.* 5.3.33). In the **mother**-figure of **Volumnia**, Nature forces Coriolanus to reject masculine, splendid isolation 'As if a man were author of himself / And knew no other kin' (*Cor.* 5.3.36–7). Acting to save Rome at the cost of his own life is simultaneously 'an unnatural scene' (*Cor.* 5.3.184–5), its absurdity drawing attention to the contradictions set up when the symbolic power of Nature is made to function ideologically. A straightforward example is Belarius's belief that Nature invests his foster sons with royalty, a symbolic use of the goddess's name to justify social hierarchy as natural difference:

> O thou goddess,
> Thou divine Nature, thou thyself thou blazon'st
> In these two princely boys! They are as gentle
> As zephyrs blowing below the violet,
> Not wagging his sweet head; and yet as rough,
> Their royal blood enchafed, as the rud'st wind,
> That by the top doth take the mountain pine,
> And make him stoop to the vale.
>
> (*Cym.* 4.2.169–76)

More often, the plays engage actively with 'the violence and ideological complexity of nature as a cultural concept' (Dollimore 1991: 115). In *The Winter's Tale* Nature starts off as the primary, creative power when **Paulina** presents the baby **Perdita** as the handiwork of 'thou, good goddess Nature, which hast made it / So like to him that got it' (*WT* 2.3.104–5). Men's distrust of Nature's creativity leads to her subordination to male artistic control. Polixenes tells Perdita that that art of husbandry (implicitly male) improves and substitutes itself for imperfect Nature, and that, furthermore, this process is natural: 'this is an art / Which does mend Nature – change it rather; but / The art itself is Nature' (*WT* 4.4.95–7). The same idea of female defectiveness governs the French court in *All's Well* who despair that their physicians' art 'can never ransom nature / From her inaidible estate' (*AWW* 2.1.118–19). Male artistic arrogance in daring to 'beguile Nature of her custom' is exposed in the figure of Julio Romano, whose supposed statue is in fact the natural body of Hermione (*WT* 5.3.99).

Julio Romano's reputation as the 'ape' of Nature (*WT* 5.3.100) draws attention to the goddess's role as a bridge between the divine and human as illustrated in Robert Fludd's *Utriusque Cosmi Historia* (*see* p. 297). Here, Nature's creative artistry is directly chained to the controlling hand of God, and she in turn controls the human artist as her imitative 'ape'. Northumberland refers to Nature as an instrument of control in his words, 'Now let not Nature's hand / Keep the wild flood confin'd! Let order die!' (*2HIV* 1.1.153–4). Shakespeare's depictions of Nature's artistry frequently have a subversive edge rather than faithfully reproducing such a hierarchy. In *Venus and Adonis*, Nature's 'curious workmanship' (*V&A* 734) includes 'stealing moulds from heaven that were divine' in order to create Adonis (*V&A* 730).

Images of Nature 'forging' (*V&A* 729) implicitly suggest she intrudes on a male province of craftsmanship. In Sonnet 20 she subverts the myth of Pygmalion, falling in love with the young man she has 'wrought' and painted, but then altering him for women's sexual pleasure (*Son.* 20.1–14). Her creativity is often mischievous or perverse. Solanio points out 'Nature hath framed strange fellows in her time' (*Mer.* 1.1.51), and **Juliet**, believing Romeo killed Tybalt, blames the goddess for deceiving her in creating a man whose divine beauty conceals a spirit from hell (*Rom.* 3.2.80–2). Richard of Gloucester believes he has been 'cheated of feature by dissembling nature' because he is deformed (*RIII* 1.1.19). **Margaret** too labels him the 'slave of nature' (*RIII* 1.3.229). Nature cheats Aaron's bastard son of his imperial birthright by making his skin black (*Tit.* 5.1.29–30). Characters also complain of Nature's harsh indifference. After **Thisbe**'s death, Bottom, as the desperate lover Pyramus, asks 'O wherefore, Nature, didst thou lions frame?' (*MND* 5.1.291), a sentiment echoed by Titus who can see nothing but malice in a goddess who creates 'gloomy woods' that make an ideal venue for rape and murder: 'O why should nature build so foul a den, / Unless the gods delight in tragedies?' (*Tit.* 4.1.59–60).

Even when Nature is not perverse, she is still a hard and threatening taskmistress whose creative investment must be repaid. The Duke in *Measure for Measure* observes:

> Nature never lends
> The smallest scruple of her excellence
> But, like a thrifty goddess, she determines
> Herself the glory of a creditor,
> Both thanks and use.
>
> (*MM* 1.1.36–40)

The *Sonnets* repeatedly show this aspect of Nature. Since she has 'best endow'd' the young man and 'carved' him with her 'seal' or signature, he must return such bounty through reproduction (*Son.* 11.11–14). Indeed, having invested everything in him, 'Nature now bankrout [bankrupt] is' (*Son.* 67.9). Nevertheless, she retains a high-status position, commanding mortality as well as birth. He must give account of himself, and is asked 'when Nature calls thee to be gone, / What acceptable audit canst thou leave?' (*Son.* 4.11–12). Sonnet 126 aches with dread of mortality at Nature's hand. She is the 'sovereign mistress' to whom the young man is subject as 'minion of her pleasure' (*Son.* 126.1 and 5). Ultimately, she must call him in to make her books balance: 'Her audit (though delay'd), answer'd must be, / And her quietus is to render thee' (*Son.* 126.11–12).

Women are likewise subject to Nature's strict accounting. Boyet advises the **Princess** of France, 'Be now as prodigal of all dear grace / As Nature was' in giving all graces 'to you' (*LLL* 2.1.10–11). **Phoebe**, who is not the most outstanding of 'nature's sale work' must 'sell when you can' (*AYLI* 3.5.43 and 60). Female characters' relatively passive position gives them distance to make a typical comparison between the 'lineaments' or endowments of the goddess Nature against those of the more fickle **Fortune** who 'reigns in gifts of the world' (*AYLI* 1.2.41–2). **Constance** in *King John* tells her son Arthur that at his birth 'Nature and Fortune join'd to make thee great'. Fortune, having deserted Arthur, comes off worse in this comparison while Nature is constant: 'Of Nature's gifts thou mayst with lilies boast, / And with the half-blown rose' (*KJ* 3.1.52–4).

A strikingly different allusion to Nature, which suggests her complexity, is found in *Othello*. Drawing on a common Shakespearean analogy between shadows and actors, Othello describes Nature acting, arguing that the goddess could not support the illusion of **Desdemona**'s infidelity (and its effect on Othello) without some foundation: 'Nature would not invest herself in such shadowing passion without some instruction' (*Oth.* 4.1.39–41).

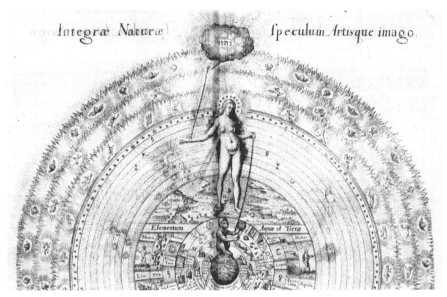

From Fludd, Robert, *Utriusque Cosmi majoris scilicet et minoris metaphysica atque technica historia in duo volumina secundin cosmic differentiam divisa*, Vol. 1 Plate 'Integra Natura' (Oppenheim, 1617)
Photograph by Douglas A Lockard, courtesy Roy G. Neville Historical Chemical Library, Chemical Heritage Foundation

(c) Lady Nature as an agent of divine creativity appears in Thomas Raynalde's *The birth of mankinde* (1565: folio xxvii). John F. Danby's important early study of contradictory meanings of the term in *Shakespeare's Doctrine of Nature* (1948), is developed by Jonathan Dollimore (1991: 106–16) who reads nature as an ideological bridge between the divine and the social, identifying complexities verging on contradictions in its uses. Eagleton *Shakespeare* (1987: 92–3) examines Polixenes Perdita's exchange on nature, though neither Dollimore or Eagleton dicuss nature's feminization. Jeanne Addison Roberts *The Shakespearean Wild* (1991: 25–8), outlines the equation of women and nature, tracing a pattern of male retreat, return and incorporation with it across the canon. Gabriel Egan (2006) and Bruce Boehrer (2002) are examples of more recent ecocriticism.

needle, *see* **sew**

Nell, (a) a shortened version of **Helen** and the name of the kitchen wench in *Comedy of Errors*.
(b) Dromio of Syracuse puns on the character's name and the measurement of an ell (45 inches) as indicative her size:

S. Antipholus: What's her name?

S Dromio: Nell, sir; but her name and three quarters, that's an ell and three quarters, will not measure her from hip to hip . . . she is spherical like a globe.

(*Err.* 3.2.109–11)

The kitchen **maid** speaks in the previous scene and is referred to several times as 'Luce' (*Err.* 3.1.48–53); her renaming here is designed to set up a comic routine by Dromio who compares her body parts to the countries of the world. As a familiar shortening of Helen, Nell is an appropriate starting point to deconstruct the **blazon** of **beauty** embodied most famously by Helen of Troy. Nell is the grotesque other to the classical female body celebrated in courtly love discourse. She is 'all grease', with a swart, as opposed to white face, buttocks like the bogs of Ireland, a work-hardened **hand** rather than a smooth white one, and is balding rather than having hair like silk or gold (*Err.* 3.2.96, 102, 116–20). Dromio cannot find the traditionally emblazoned white teeth in his mistress and subverts the traditional comparison of body parts to precious stones in his report that Nell's nose is 'embellish'd with rubies, carbuncles, sapphires' or skin blemishes (*Err.* 3.2.126–37). 'Nell' usually signifies lower social status in Shakespeare. It is the name of one of the servants in the Capulet household (*R&J* 1.5.9) and of Poins's sister (*2HIV* 2.2.129) who is not a suitable match for Prince Hal. It is used familiarly of Mistress Quickly (*HV* 2.1.18 and 31) by Pistol, although she is referred to more formally as **Ursula** by Falstaff. Shakespeare uses the familiar term strategically to mark the degradation of higher-born characters when Paris addresses Helen of Troy as Nell (*T&C* 3.1.56 and 150) and when Gloucester tells his wife **Eleanor** doing penance in the streets, 'Sweet Nell, ill can thy noble mind abrook / The abject people gazing on thy face' (*2HVI* 2.4.10–11).

(c) Hennings (1986: 98–101) and Maguire (2007: 168–9) consider the kitchen maid character's divided identity as Luce / Nell, Maguire linking her to the other sexually loose and assertive Helens in Shakespeare's canon. Jonathan Gil Harris (2003: 40–1) reads Nell's anatomized body as a critique of the corruption of the colonial economy in early modern Europe.

nereids, (a) in mythology, **nymphs** of the sea. Usually referred to in the plural, they were the daughters of Oceanus and Tethys.

(b) Shakespeare equates these aquatic beings with **mermaids** when comparing **Cleopatra**'s attendants on the royal barge to 'the Nereides' who 'tended her i'th'eyes / And made their bends adornings' (*A&C* 2.2.206–8). In addition to idealising the courtly relationship between a powerful queen and her ladies-in-waiting (perhaps recalling Elizabeth I's household), this comparison effectively raises Cleopatra to divine status, in line with her self-stylization as **Isis**. Robert Albott's 1599 guide to mythology pointed out that '*Nereus*, was likewise a God, and *Nereides* the Faieries of the Sea, borne of *Oceanus* and *Tethis*' (Albott: 1599, 154v).

(c) *See* entries on **nymph, mermaid** and **Thetis** for further information.

Nerissa, (a) the waiting-gentlewoman to **Portia**. Her name may derive from the Greek *nereis* 'sea sprite' or from the Italian feminine form for black '*nerricia*'.

(b) Nerissa – whose name indicates her dark hair – would stand in opposition to the fair Portia in a typical pairing in Shakespeare's comedies where the fair **boy-actor** was taller than the dark-haired one, thus creating a joke from Portia's reference to her 'little body' (*Mer.* 1.2.1). Nerissa's link with the **Nereids** or sea-nymphs who lived in the Mediterranean, is appropriate since Portia's suitors are compared to Jasons, journeying across the sea to win her. Portia later compares herself to Hesione who was chained to a rock in the midst of the sea (3.2.55–9). Nerissa, like **Lucetta** in *Two Gentlemen of Verona*, functions as a confidante and leads her mistress through a ritual consideration of each suitor (1.2) As the title '**waiting-gentlewoman**' suggests, her status is that of a lady rather than a low-born maidservant. Nerissa's future appears to be bound to that of her mistress. Their hopes are staked on Bassanio's success (2.7.101) and Nerissa's contract to Gratiano acts as a mirror of her mistress's marriage. The disguises and the **ring** plots likewise bind the two women together almost as strongly as the men and may suggest that they intend to remain close after marriage (Jankowski 2000: 309).

(c) Haslam (1994) discusses the ritual of considering suitors that relies on female intimacy. Karen Newman (1987) considers Portia and Nerissa as mistresses of the structures of exchange while Jankowski (2000: 308–9) reads Nerissa and Portia's relationship as intimate, lasting and potentially erotic.

night, (a) Corin wryly defines night as 'lack of the sun' (*AYLI* 3.2.29) but the term is frequently feminized in Shakespeare's texts with interesting effects.

(b) Spenser referred to Night as the 'most auncient Grandmother of all / More old than Jove' (Spenser 1970: 1.5.22) and personifications of Night as female in Shakespeare link to the myth of the triple goddess ruling as **Phoebe** or **Cynthia**, the **moon** in the heavens; **Diana**, **chastity** and hunting on earth; and **Lucina** or **Hecate**, death and child**birth** in the underworld. Orlando refers to the triple goddess as 'thrice-crownèd Queen of Night' (*AYLI* 3.2.2). Lear vows by 'the mysteries of Hecat and the night' (*KL* 1.1.110). Night is an authoritative maternal figure for **Juliet** – 'Come, civil night, / Thou sober-suited **matron** all in black' (*R&J* 3.2.10–11) – but one who can be wooed as patroness of desire to bring Romeo: 'Come, gentle night, come, loving, black-brow'd night, / Give me my Romeo' (*R&J* 3.2.20–1). Romeo sees night as an exotic mistress where Juliet 'hangs upon the cheek of Night / Like a rich jewel in an Ethiope's ear' (*R&J* 1.5.47). Less flatteringly, the lover in Sonnet 27 describes Night as a crone when he dreams of his beloved who 'like a jewel hung in ghastly night' making 'black night beauteous, and her old face new' (*Son.* 27.11–12). Adonis insults 'black-fac'd night' as 'desire's foul nurse' (*V&A* 720 and 773).

Night is invariably the feminized negative opposite of daylight, a trope for the fears and mysteries demonized by patriarchal culture. **Lucrece** addresses Night as the origin of chaos, death and infamy; the nurturer of **rape**, illicit sexual activity and treason:

> O comfort-killing night, image of hell,
> Dim register and notary of shame,
> Black stage for tragedies and murthers fell,
> Vast sin-concealing chaos, **nurse** of blame!
> Blind, muffled **bawd**, dark harbor of defame,
> Grim cave of death, whisp'ring conspirator
> With close-tongu'd treason and the ravisher.
>
> (*Luc.* 764–70)

Blame for the tragedy of *The Rape of Lucrece* is partly shifted from Tarquin, 'Night's child' (*Luc.* 785) onto the maternal influence of 'sable Night, mother of Dread and Fear' who rules over time and 'in her vaulty prison stows the Day' (*Luc.* 114–17).

Night is a terrifying mother, a harbinger of destruction to the soldiers in *Henry V* who await the birth of morning and battle from the 'foul **womb** of night' (*HV* Chorus 4.4.4). 'Black-brow'd Night' is a **Hecate**-like figure in *Midsummer Night's Dream*, mistress of the dead, damned spirits and shame (*MND* 3.2.379–87). Hamlet, too, welcomes the 'very **witch**ing time of night' when 'hell itself breathes out / Contagion to this world' (*Ham.* 3.2.388–90). Night is a majesterial power whose 'palace' is the entrance to eternity for Romeo (*R&J* 5.3.107). Lady **Macbeth** invokes 'thick night' to dress 'in the dunnest smoke of hell' to hide the wicked murder of Duncan (*Mac.* 1.4.50–4).

More postively, Falstaff associates the night with pleasure: implicitly sexual pleasure with **Doll** Tearsheet but also the delights of drink, food, company and relaxation, in his regret that 'now comes in the sweetest morsel of the night and we must leave it unpick'd' (*2HIV* 2.4.367–8). Pericles casts night in maternal terms as a longed-for site of rest and safety. 'Careful night', he says, 'seem'd my good protector' in covering him with darkness to escape but he is now distressed that 'peaceful night / The tomb where grief should sleep' cannot 'breed me quiet' (*Per.* 1.2.4–5 and 81–2).

(c) Ferber (1999: 135–6) traces Night's classical origins in Hesiod's *Theogeny* as mother of sky, day, heaven, the hills and the sea, and lists later literary representations. An extended personification of Night appears in Book 1, Canto V, stanzas 20–31 in Spenser's *Faerie Queene* [1596] (Spenser 1970: 26–7). Night also appeared in the ante-masque of Daniel's *Vision of the Twelve Goddesses* (1604). Diana Vickers considers the Petrarchan framing of Lucrece in '"The blazon of sweet beauty's best": Shakespeare's *Lucrece*' (1985), and she and Kahn (1997: 38–40) both briefly consider Lucrece's apostrophe to Night. *See also* **Lucrece**.

night-mare, *see* **mare**

Northumberland, Lady (a) wife of the Earl of Northumberland who appears in Act 2 Scene 3 of *Henry IV Part II*.
(b) Lady Northumberland is afraid of losing her husband in battle in the rebellion against Henry IV and has been 'troublesome' to him in arguing against

his participation. Perhaps afraid of being labelled a **scold** at the opening of the scene, she is resigned to the fact that her pleas have not been heard: 'I have given over, I will speak no more; / Do what you will, your wisdom be your guide' (*2HIV* 2.3.4–6). She gives place to the arguments of her daughter-in-law **Katherine** Percy, **widow** of Hotspur. Lady Northumberland's comparative lack of emotion at Hotspur's death is explained by the fact that the historical Lady Northumberland, Maud de Lucy, the widowed Countess of Angus, was not Hotspur's mother, being Northumberland's second wife (Davis and Frankforter 2004: 348). This also explains why she recommends that they 'fly to Scotland' her homeland, for safety (2.3.50).

(c) Davis and Frankforter (2004) explain the historical origins of the character in Maud de Lucy. *See* **wife**.

nothing, (a) a crude and reductive term for the vagina and signifying woman as lack.

(b) Blatant examples of this reductive definition of woman as her vagina and her lack of penis in Shakespeare are Hamlet's crude comment that nothing is 'a fair thought to lie between maid's legs' (*Ham* 3.2.117–21) and in the play about **Hero**'s virginity *Much Ado About Nothing*. Further bawdy innuendo surrounds Speed's account of the apparently worthless delivery of Proteus's letter to **Julia**: 'I (a lost mutton) gave your letter to her (a lac'd mutton), and she (a lac'd mutton) gave me nothing for my labor' (*TGV* 1.1.96–9). The gift of nothing from a 'lac'd mutton', a **whore** with a laced bodice, adds to Speed's slander of Julia. The Duke's view that **Mariana** is 'nothing then: neither maid, widow nor wife' leads straight into Lucio's suggestion 'she may be a punk' (*MM* 5.1.177–9). Richard III's joke about having 'naught to do with Mistress Shore' (*RIII* 1.1.98–103) and Flute's definition of a 'paramour' as '(God bless us!) a thing of naught' (*MND* 4.2 14) rely on the same bawdy innuendo. The invisible slippage from risqué amusement to disparaging woman as a disposable **commodity** is clear when Enobarbus casually jokes that 'it were a pity to cast them [women] away for nothing, though between them and a great cause there should be esteem'd nothing' (*A&C* 1.2.138–9). Even **Cleopatra** uses it against **Octavia**, claiming she is 'nothing' in comparison with Cleopatra's positive 'majesty' (*A&C* 3.4.24 and 41–2). When **Rosalind** claims that she will 'weep for nothing, like **Diana** in the fountain' (*AYLI* 4.1.153–4) this may refer to a loss of virginity.

Bertram's refusal to consummate his marriage and accept Helena as his wife is seen in the contents of his letter protesting, ''Till I have no **wife**, I have nothing in France' and the **Countess**'s objection, 'Nothing in France until he have no wife! / There's nothing here that is too good for him / But only she' (*AWW* 3.2.75–81). The foundational nature of the female vagina as an utterly unknowable cornerstone to human identity is seen in *The Winter's Tale*. Once Leontes loses faith in his wife's chastity, his deluded focus on 'nothing' (her vagina) marks the collapse of his identity in the family, the state and the cosmos, into a state of lack:

> Is this nothing?
> Why then the world and all that's in't is nothing,
> The covering sky is nothing, Bohemia nothing,
> My wife is nothing, nor nothing have these nothings,
> If this be nothing.
>
> (*WT* 1.2.292–6)

The use of 'nothing' to define woman in terms of lack informs Queen Isabel's speech in *Richard II*. Helpless to aid her husband, she feels swollen with an indefinable grief 'for nothing hath begot my something grief / Or something hath the nothing that I grieve' (*RII* 2.2.31–40). Richard, too, moves into this feminized space of lack once he has surrendered the crown to Bolingbroke (*RII* 4.1.201 and 5.5.40–1). **Cordelia**'s determination to retain her integrity, and vow 'nothing' beyond her bond of child to father is a sign of strength in *King Lear*. Lear's superficial view that 'nothing will come of nothing' (*KL* 1.1.87–90) expresses the wider problem of patriarchy in the Lear world where the repressed m(other), reduced to 'nothing', will always return to trouble those in power. The Fool points out that Lear (like Richard II) is become 'an O without a figure' (*KL* 1.4.192–3). Since the word 'nothing' signifies the woman's vagina, the use of this word in the Sonnets to the young man gives a literal truth to the lesson that 'Nothing 'gainst Time's scythe can make defence / Save breed to brave him when he takes thee hence (*Son.* 12.13–14).
(c) *See also* **thing**.

nun, (a) a member of a religious community of women typically living by vows of **chastity**, poverty and obedience. A**emilia**, the **Abbess** of the convent in Ephesus and Francesca, who appears in the convent in *Measure for Measure*, are nuns and **Thaisa** in **Diana**'s Temple in Ephesus is also described as a nun.
(b) Since the dissolution of the monasteries by Henry VIII, nuns were not a visible part of early modern English society although strong links remained between Catholic families and continental convents especially in France and the Low Countries (Walker 2003). Unlike overtly Protestant texts such as Peele's *The Troublesome Reign of King John*, Shakespeare's plays do not give extended satiric dramatizations of nuns as lustful or corrupt. Lavatch does say he has answers that fit all circumstances as naturally as 'the nun's lip to the friar's mouth, nay, as the pudding to his skin' (*AWW* 2.2 26–7) and Hamlet, a student of Wittenberg, undoubtedly draws on the tradition of Protestant satire when he cruelly directs **Ophelia** to 'Get thee to a nunnery!' (*Ham.* 3.1.120–49). The contexts immediately suggest that such negative views are biased and inaccurate. In *A Lover's Complaint*, published alongside Shakespeare's Sonnets, the false lover's lies of seduction include boasting to the young woman that he had the power to charm a highly disciplined 'sacred nun' (*LC* 260–4). This 'sister sanctified, of holiest note' had previously 'kept cold distance' from all her glamorous suitors and retired from Court 'To spend her living in eternal love' (*LC* 232–8). Even if Shakespeare did not write these lines, the effect of conventual non-accessibility perversely

provoking male desire is what drives Angelo's lust for Isabella in *Measure for Measure.*

More often in Shakespeare's texts, nuns are simply 'othered' or depicted as being culturally as well as geographically removed from normal life. **Isabella**'s view 'More than our brother is our chastity' (*MM* 2.4.185) was designed to sound extraordinary to early modern ears as well as to modern audiences. Theseus's description of conventual life is not a positive one when he asks **Hermia** if she can

> endure the livery of a nun,
> For aye to be in shady cloister mew'd,
> To live a barren **sister** all your life,
> Chanting faint hymns to the cold fruitless **moon**.
>   (*MND* 1.1.70–3)

Although he accords admiration to women 'that master so their blood, / To undergo such **maid**en pilgrimage' it is definitely an unusual, extreme option (*MND* 1.1.74–5). Unsurprisingly, **Venus** also rejects the 'fruitless chastity' as selfish choice of 'Love-lacking **vestals** and self-loving nuns' (*V&A* 751–2). There is gentle mockery in Celia's joke that Orlando 'hath bought a pair of cast lips of **Diana**. / A nun of winter's **sister**hood kisses not more religiously' with 'the very ice of chastity' (*AYLI* 3.4.15–17). The basis of her humour is the difference, the oddness of the nun's life rather than an attack on its hypocrisy. Her association of nuns with the figure of Diana recalls the links between the Virgin Mary and Diana at Ephesus, which inform Shakespeare's depictions of the Abbey and Diana's Temple in *Comedy of Errors* and *Pericles*. Rosalind's suggestions that Leander would have survived his passion for **Hero**, even if she had 'turn'd nun' likewise suggests the nun's choice as unusual but not necessarily negative (*AYLI* 4.1.101). In more positive references, the protection offered by conventual life is hinted at. The widowed **Elizabeth** tells Richard III that her **daughter**s 'shall be praying nuns, not weeping **queens**; / And therefore level not to hit their lives' (*RIII* 4.4.202–3). Friar Lawrence plans to provide for **Juliet** in a convent telling her 'Come, I'll dispose of thee / Among a sisterhood of holy nuns' (*R&J* 5.3.156–7). Thaisa in *Pericles* chooses service to Diana as a refuge following the loss of her husband and child.

(c) Silvia Evangelisti (2007) surveys the experiences convent life offered to women including analysis of cloistered spaces, writing, theatre and music. Walker (2003) analyses the establishment of new religious houses for English women after the dissolution of the monasteries. Van Wyhe (ed.) (2008) provides an excellent collection of essays on female monasticism in Early Modern Europe. Weaver (2002) surveys convent drama in early modern Italy while Gless (1979) considers the convent in *Measure of Measure*.

nurse, (a) (**v.**) to breastfeed a child, or care for someone in sickness; (**n.**) a woman, often an employee wet-nurse, responsible for breastfeeding a child. Also a person responsible for caring for a child or children or caring for someone in sickness on a day-to-day basis. These jobs were women's tasks in early modern England.

(b) Breastfeeding continued until the child was anything from nine months up to about two years old, although some writers record breastfeeding up to three years – so **Juliet**'s weaning, at just less than three, is not exceptional (*R&J* 1.3.37–8). Breastfeeding was unconventional amongst upper-class mothers, possibly because of fears that nursing would mar the appearance of the nipple and **breast**; because of the inconvenience and early discomfort involved; or because of the belief that sexual intercourse could corrupt the milk. Wealthier households often employed a wet nurse to **suckle** the baby instead. However, most medical guidebooks and conduct books on female behaviour encouraged women to suckle their own children, appreciating the power of emotional bonding and the protective powers of the mother's own milk. In the late sixteenth and early seventeenth centuries some of the nobility began to accept this line of thought, which was strongly associated with the Puritan tradition. Elizabeth Clinton's *The Countess of Lincolnes Nurserie* (Oxford 1622) exhorts other women, 'I pray you set no more so light by God's blessing in your own breasts, which the Holy Spirit ranketh with other excellent blessings . . . be not so unnatural to thrust away your own children; be not so hardy as to venture a tender babe to a less tender heart; be not accessory to the disorder of causing a poorer woman to banish her own infant for the entertaining of a richer woman's child, as it were bidding her unlove her own to love yours' (Aughterson 1995: 119–20).

The divided opinion on nursing by upper-class women is represented in Shakespeare's plays. Lady **Macbeth** has 'given suck' (*Mac.* 1.5.54), as has the Duchess of York in *Richard III* (2.2.28). Hermione 'did not nurse' (*WT* 2.1.58) Mamillius in *The Winter's Tale* (in spite of the associations of his name with the nurturing breast), but has fed **Perdita** with her own breastmilk (*WT* 3.2.98–100). Lady **Capulet**'s daughter Juliet has a **nurse** (*see* below) and Cymbeline's sons also had a wet nurse, **Euriphile**. Her actions in stealing the children away telegraph the dangers of entrusting the country or family's future to an outsider. The fact that they reverenced their nurse as a natural mother conversely shows the strength of emotional bonding established in the surrogate family group (*Cym.* 3.3.104) in contrast to the hostile court dominated by the royal **step-mother**. The practice of sending children out to be nursed away from home is extended in the pre-play history, and when Belarius returns the sons at the end of the play, he jokes that Cymbeline must 'pay me for the nursing of thy sons' (*Cym.* 5.6.323).

It was thought that the breastmilk imparted qualities to the child. So **Rosalind** quips, of the woman who is not clever enough to outwit her husband, 'never let her nurse her child herself, she'll breed it like a fool' (*AYLI* 4.1.155). In *Henry VIII*, the Princess **Elizabeth**'s virtue as a daughter of the Reformation is confidently predicted in the idea that 'Truth shall nurse her' (*HVIII* 5.4.28), a pertinent contrast to Wolsey's earlier view that Rome is the 'nurse of judgement' (*HVIII* 2.2.123).

The figure of the nurse represents security, care and comfort. Sonnet 22 promises to keep the lover's heart as carefully 'as tender nurse her babe from faring ill' (*Son.* 22.12). Unnamed nurses appear in the final scene of *Henry VI Part III* (with the young Prince Edward) and in *Titus Andronicus* (4.2.60ff). In the latter, the nurse's view that **Tamora**'s blackamoor child is monstrous and must be killed is a striking contrast to the usual caring role, and to the protection offered by its father Aaron. Aaron's murder of the nurse, while savage in itself, continues his usurpation of the aggressively protective maternal instinct. *Pericles* represents the character of **Lychorida**, nurse to the Princess **Thaisa**. She acts as **midwife** to her mistress at sea and is then cares for baby **Marina**. The most fully characterized example of the type is Juliet's Nurse. As well as breastfeeding and weaning Juliet from the **dug**, the Nurse has cared for her up until just short of her fourteenth year. The scene in which she describes the weaning process (*R&J* 1.2.26–34) makes it clear that she fills the maternal role of emotional and physical carer more easily than Lady Capulet. Juliet fills the place of the Nurse's own daughter Susan (*see* **Susanna**) who died in infancy (*R&J* 1.3.21–22). The Nurse's nurturing, comforting role within the Capulet household is suggested by the name Angelica (*R&J* 4.4.6), her duties in the pantry and her teasing of Lord Capulet (*R&J* 1.3.103–4, 4.4.1–10). She is responsible for putting Juliet to bed (*R&J* 2.1.149–53 and 4.3.2–3) and for choosing her **wedding** clothes (*R&J* 4.2.33–5). The Nurse is elderly and moves with some difficulty (*R&J* 2.4). A comic warmth related to her self-confidence and material physicality is evident in her fondness for bawdy innuendo and in the scene with Peter and Romeo where her **fan** is the cause for comic business (*R&J* 2.4.104–115). She is also a valued confidant who informs **Juliet** about the people present at the ball (*R&J* 1.5.111–43), gives her opinion on the suitors Paris and Romeo (*R&J* 2.4.38–44). She takes a considerable risk in furthering Juliet's relationship with Romeo by taking messages and bringing the rope ladder. Her maternal concern parallels that of the Friar for Romeo (*R&J* 3.3). Advising Juliet to marry Paris constitutes a return to the Capulet household but a betrayal of the emergent adult who has formed new emotional bonds outside. It forms a fracture point in the relationship from which Juliet emerges as an isolated but independent woman (*R&J* 3.5.204ff). Coming to dress Juliet on her wedding morning, the Nurse is the first to discover her supposed death; her grief for the loss of the Capulet **daughter** looks back to her own loss of Susan, and joins with the parental lamentations as an expression of wider cultural phenomenon of the inevitable loss of the daughter from the family through exogamous **betrothal** and **marriage** (*R&J* 4.4).

The image of the nurse is employed in a range of contrasting ways through the canon. Mothers draw on it to express their emotional reactions. The **Duchess** of York sees herself as a pampering figure who will envelop the sorrows of her daughter-in-law and grandchildren (*RIII* 2.2.97). In contrast, Queen **Elizabeth** calls the Tower of London a 'rude ragged nurse' to which she unwillingly surrenders the young Princes (*RIII* 4.1.122).

From an adult perspective, the security offered by the nurse is often looked back to with longing. The troubled king in *Henry IV Part II* says sleep is 'Nature's soft nurse' (*2HIV* 3.2.6) and the Doctor in *King Lear* says repose is a 'foster-nurse of nature' (*KL* 4.5.15). Fun is made of the man who is still dependent on the material comforts provided by a 'dry-nurse' (as opposed to a wife) in *Merry Wives of Windsor* (1.2.4), and in *Lucrece* the nursing of life with 'honour, wealth and ease in waning age' is scorned as the goal of acquisitive lust (*Luc.* l. 141). The nurse's professions of care can be tinged with an unsettling matriarchal dominance, as when **Tamora** promises that, as Empress of Rome, she will be 'a loving nurse' and 'mother' to her husband Saturninus's youth (*Tit.* 1.1.388). Fears of the dominant nurse inform Lucrece's image of Tarquin's monstrous name being used to terrify a crying child (*Luc.* 927). The limits of the nurse's power to protect are shown in the apparent failure of **Lychorida** to save Thaisa's life in childbed (*Per.* 2.3.58 and 3.1.21–4). Lychorida's own death leaves Marina vulnerable to the cruel plots of Dionyza (*Per.* 4.4.43).

The active role of the carer is seen in **Adriana**'s determination to 'attend my husband, be his nurse / Diet his sickness' (*Err.* 5.1.99) as a way of re-establishing her conjugal rights in the face of the **Abbess** who has taken Antipholus into her abbey. The irony of this moment is only apparent when it is revealed that the Abbess, as his **mother**, has literally pre-empted Adriana's role. An idealization of the active nurse is seen in the picture of cross-dressed **Imogen**. Although she is disguised as a page to Lucius, her feminine qualities shine through as

> so kind, so duteous, diligent,
> So tender over his occasions, true
> So feat, so nurse-like.
>
> (*Cym.* 5.5.86–8)

The dangers of irresponsible nursing are suggested by pictures of those who will sleep through a baby's cries (*MAdo* 3.3.60) or let it cry 'into a rapture' while she **gossips** (*JC* 2.1.207).

On a national level, the nurse offers a sense of native security. **Volumnia** laments that if Coriolanus attacks Rome, 'we must lose / The country, our dear nurse' (*Cor.* 5.3.125). In *Richard II*, the kingdom is described as a nurse by Gaunt (*RII* 2.1.55) and Bolingbroke (*RII* 1.3.326). Nursing is associated with a pre-lingual state when the banished Mowbray laments that he can no longer 'fawn upon a nurse' and must accept the loss of his native tongue (*RII* 1.3.188). The nurse as educator features in many texts. The Duchess of York imagines herself as a nurse teaching Bolingbroke's tongue how to speak the word 'pardon' (*RII* 5.3.135). In France, Burgundy longs for **peace** as a 'nurse of arts, plenties and joyful births' (*HV* 5.2.35). Night perverts such nurturing power as 'desire's foul nurse' (*V&A* 773) in *Venus and Adonis* while in *The Rape of Lucrece* night is the 'nurse of blame' (*Luc.* 767) and in *The Taming of the Shrew* melancholy is the 'nurse of frenzy' (*Shrew* Ind. 2.141). A dramatic inversion of care, hierarchy and decorum is shown where 'the baby beats the nurse' (*MM* 1.3.34). Less dramatically the 'tetchy' babe who scratches the nurse only to submit to authority provides an apt metaphor for **Julia** to describe her own childishly peevish behaviour (*TGV* 1.2.62).

(c) The standard studies of breastfeeding and wet nursing, which include sections on the early modern period are two books by Valerie Fildes, *Breasts, Bottles and*

Babies: A History of infant feeding (1986) and *Wet Nursing: A history from antiquary to the present* (1988). Examples of early modern medical and spiritual tracts and conduct books recommending breastfeeding are Desiderius Erasmus, *The Colloquies* (1519: 301–2); John Jones, *The Art and Science of Preserving Body and Soul* (1579), Henry Smith, *A Preparative to Mariage* (1591; 99–101); William Gouge, *Of Domesticall Duties* (1622), Treatise VI, and *The Countess of Lincolns Nurserie* (1622). Extracts from these are found in Aughterson (1995) and Keeble (1994). A full text of *The Countess of Lincolns Nurserie* is available from the Brown Women Writers' Project's 'Renaissance Women Online' at http://www.wwp.brown.edu/texts/rwoentry.html. On Puritan discourse and breastfeeding see David Leverenz (1980). *See also* entries on **suckle**, **breast** and **dug**.

nymph, (a) a female deity associated with natural features usually trees or water, often acting as an attendant to a senior deity such as **Diana**. There were several groups of nymphs: **Nereids** were the guardians of salt and fresh water, and Oceanids nymphs of the sea; Naiads were associated with springs, rivers and lakes; Dryads with forests; Oreads with mountains; Napiae with glens and dells; Alseids with groves, Hesperides with gardens and with the evening. Nymphs were mortal, beautiful and eternally young. Nymphs appear on stage in *The Tempest*.
(b) Shakespeare uses the word to indicate **beauty** in Hamlet's address to 'The fair **Ophelia**!' as 'Nymph' (*Ham.* 3.1.88) and seductive, sprightly delicacy in Richard of Gloucester's regret that he will never be able to charm 'a wanton ambling nymph' (*RIII* 1.1.17). Warwick suggests King Henry VI's unsuitability for masculine leadership by describing him as waiting passively in London like 'modest Dian circled with her nymphs' (*3HVI* 4.8.21). Allusions to Diana and her nymphs here are probably compliments to Elizabeth I and her maids-of-honour, as in Saturninus view that Tamora 'like the stately **Phoebe** 'mongst her nymphs / Dost overshine the gallant'st dames of Rome' (*Tit.* 1.1.316). Chastity features again in Sonnets 153 and 154 which imagine one of Diana's 'many nymphs that vow'd chaste life to keep' attempting to quench Cupid's firebrand in a 'cool well' (*Son.* 154.3 and 9) or a 'cold valley fountain' (*Son.* 153.4) like Naiads. The enduring power of the nymph as a symbol of **chastity** is seen in Shakespeare and Fletcher's *Two Noble Kinsmen* where '*a* NYMPH *encompass'd in her tresses*' (her loose hair advertising her virginity) and '*bearing a wheaten garland*' followed by two others, appear in Theseus and **Hippolyta**'s wedding procession. Emilia fashions herself as a nymph of Diana by appearing before her altar '*in white, her hair about her shoulders, and wearing a wheaten wreath*' (*TNK* 5.1.SD187). Nymphs were part of spectacular courtly culture in numerous masques and entertainments. A baptismal masque for James VI (1566) featured Naiads and Oreads, representing the streams, rivers and mountains of Scotland, for example, and in Daniel's *Tethys Festival* (1610) Anna of Denmark's noble ladies and her daughter Princess Elizabeth appear as nymphs of the English Rivers (Findlay 2006: 112 and 130–1).

Since specific types of nymph featured in early English maps as well as in literature, it is unsurprising that Shakespeare's other references to nymphs link to precise natural locations. In the wood outside Athens, **Helena** is a 'nymph' in a 'grove' and Demetrius's hyperbolic praise begins by calling her 'goddess, nymph, perfect, divine' (*MND* 2.1.245 and 3.2.137). All four lovers are referred to as 'nymphs' by Theseus (*MND* 4.1.127). When **Tamora** proposes a hunting party in the woods outside Rome, Aaron looks forward to a wanton assignation with this 'nymph' (*Tit.* 2.1.22). Alone in the 'unfrequented woods' at the end of *Two Gentlemen of Verona*, Valentine prays 'Repair me with thy presence, Silvia; / Thou gentle nymph, cherish thy forlorn swain!' (*TGV* 5.4.11–12) Her name, linked to the Latin for 'wood', immediately associates her with a Dryad. Prospero commands Ariel to 'make thyself like a nymph o' the sea' apparently for the benefit of Prospero and the audience since he is to be invisible to other characters (*Temp.* 1.2.301–3). Ariel cues in a chorus of 'Sea-nymphs' whose voices produce a knell of mourning for Alonso (*Temp.* 1.2.403). In order to seduce Adonis and prove her youthful beauty and sprightliness, the dominant **Venus** offers to take the shape of a sea nymph and 'with long dishevell'd hair / Dance on the sands, and yet no footing seen' (*V&A* 147–8).

Naiads are brought to the stage by **Ceres** in *The Tempest* to dance in **Miranda** and Ferdinand's betrothal masque. **Iris** describes them as 'cold nymphs' who gather spring flowers from banks of the streams to make 'chaste crowns' (*Temp.* 4.1.64–6). She summons them as

> You nymphs, call'd Naiades, of the windring brooks,
> With your sedged crowns and ever-harmless looks,
> Leave your crisp channels and on this green land
> Answer your summons; **Juno** does command:
> Come, temperate nymphs, and help to celebrate
> A contract of true love; be not too late.
>
> (*Temp.* 4.1.128–33)

As they are symbols of chaste temperance, their dance with the 'sunburn'd sicklemen of August' (*Temp.* 4.1.134) represents the ideal balance of restraint and sexual energy required to make a legitimate, fruitful, **marriage**. In addition to the royal nymphs in the recent *Tethys Festival* (1610) by Daniel the nymphs in Prospero's masque are probably modelled on *Hymeniae*, Jonson's 1606 masque for the wedding of Frances Devereux and Robert Carr. A spectator commented that a ritual uniting feminine cool water and masculine fire was drawn from Roman marriage tradition (Lindley 1984: 51).

(c) Jennifer Larson, *Greek Nymphs: Myth, Cult, Lore* (2001) is a broad survey of the type in ancient culture. Daniel's *Tethys Festival* was performed on 5 June 1610 and is found in Lindley (ed.), *Court Masques* (1995: 54–65). Lindley (1984: 149–52) and McNamara (1987: 183–203) analyse Ariel's song and the betrothal masque with reference to Jonson's masque. Bowerbank (2004) considers the nymph within the eco-politics of early modern England. Traub (2002: 1–5, 18, 125) looks at the erotic dimension of nymphs and same-sex communities.

Octavia, (a) a character in *Antony and Cleopatra*, widowed sister to Octavius Caesar and married to Antony.

(b) Shakespeare's sympathetic characterization of Octavia prioritizes the torn loyalties signifed by her name. She is introduced as Octavius's '**sister** by the mother's side / Admir'd Octavia' (2.2.119–20). Octavius bequeaths her in marriage to Antony with a handshake while she is off stage, making her Octavia '**wife** of Marcus Antonius' (2.6.112). She is a political pawn 'to join our kingdoms and our hearts' (2.1.149–51), and to conduct love between the two men and the population: 'Her love to both / Would each to other and all loves to both / Draw after her' (2.2.134–6). Significantly, stage directions indicate that she is to enter '*between them*' (2.3SD). Octavia is thus placed the impossible position of being torn between the two men standing 'between, / Praying for both parts' (3.4.13–14) and later admitting she is wretched for having 'my heart parted betwixt two friends / That does afflict each other' (3.6.77–8). Plutarch's 'Life of Antony' highlights her dilemma 'For now, said she, everie mans eyes doe gaze on me, that am sister of one of the Emperours and wife of the other' and when the two come into conflict, she laments: 'But for me, on which side soever the victorie fall, my state can be but most miserable still' (Bullough Vol V: 282). Plutarch recounts her strong handling of the situation much more fully than Shakespeare's play. Indeed, Sir Thomas North's marginal note to his translation, which Shakespeare read, noted her 'wise and womanly behavior' (Bowling 1957: 253). When she returns to Rome as 'go between' (3.6.25), Caesar's greeting firmly splits her identities as 'Caesar's sister' and 'The wife of Antony' into two separate sentences (3.6.43).

Plutarch's Octavia threatens to usurp Cleopatra's control over Antony 'having an excellent grace, wisdom, and honestie, joined unto so rare a beawtie' (Bullough Vol. V: 278). In *Antony and Cleopatra* the model of wifely duty she presents is much less attractive. Being 'of a holy, cold and still conversation'

(2.6.123–4), Octavia contrasts dramatically with **Cleopatra**, who uses the messenger to conduct a comparison. Octavia is smaller, 'low voic'd', round faced and low browed, with brown hair (3.4.11–35) probably playing against a taller **boy actor** in a typically contrasted pairing as with **Celia** and **Rosalind** and **Viola** and **Olivia**.

(c) Plutarch's 'Life of Antony' (Bullough Vol. V: 254–317) focuses considerable attention on Octavia as the anchor of Roman hopes for peace, pp. 278–82, 288–9. Samuel Brandon's *The Vertuous Octavia* (1598) and Samuel Daniel's 'Letter From Octavia to Mark Antony' in *Certaine small poems lately printed* (1605), both offer representations of Octavia that may have contributed to Shakespeare's. Raber (2001: 52–110, esp. 107–10) considers these and Mary Sidney's *Antonie* (Herbert 1592). Rodney Simard (1986: 65–74) examines Plutarch's discussion of Octavia and Shakespeare's changes. Bowling (1957) analyses her as one of four minor characters who are set between Antony and Caesar. Kahn (1997: 115) briefly mentions her.

Olivia, (a) a character in *Twelfth Night*, whose brother and father have died leaving her as **Countess** and head of the household. Her name (possibly derived from the Latin for 'olive') closely mirrors that of **Viola**.

(b) Olivia is introduced as a Petrarchan **mistress** whose **beauty** purges 'the air of pestilence' but who cruelly rejects Orsino's love (1.1.19). She is 'a virtuous **maid**' (1.2.36) whose cloistered seclusion in **veil**ed mourning for her brother is presented as pseudo-Catholic. Feste refers to her as **madonna**; her gentlewoman's name is **Maria**. Feste hints that Olivia's mourning may be superficial (1.5.57–70), merely a protection for her own independence. She occupies a high-status position in her own right as a countess and has apparently sworn 'she'll not match above her degree, neither in estate, years, nor wit' (1.5.109–11). Her attraction to Cesario (the cross-dressed **Viola**) is invoked by Viola's passionate invocation of her name to 'make the babbling gossip of the air / Cry out "Olivia!"' (1.5.273). In printed texts, this allusion to the figure of Echo in Golding's translation of Ovid, part of the Narcissus myth, possibly draws attention to Olivia and Viola as reflections of each other (Palmer 1979). Their names are essentially anagrams (Parker 1987: 33).

Olivia proclaims a loss of self-determination in falling for Cesario: 'ourselves we do not owe' (1.5.310), but, nevertheless, as a page he is very firmly her social inferior. She astutely wonders, 'How shall I feast him, what bestow of him / For **youth** is bought more oft than begg'd or borrow'd?' (3.4.2–3). Olivia's initial proposal to the lower-born and possibly younger Sebastian: 'Would'st thou be rul'd by me?' (4.1.64), suggests her intention to retain a commanding position even in **marriage**.

(c) Richard A. Levin, *Love and Society in Shakespearean Comedy*, reads Olivia unsympathetically as a selfish and arrogant character who fails to learn very much through the play. Mihoko Suzuki (2000: (esp.) 136–42), argues that Olivia fiercely protects her independence, even in marriage. D. J. Palmer (1979) and Douglas H. Parker (1987) discuss the Ovidian echo and Viola's mirroring of Olivia. Jami Ake (2003) elaborates a lesbian poetics in the same-sex dialogue between Olivia and Viola. Palfrey and Stern (2007: 415–22) analyse the part of Olivia as received in the roll or script by the Elizabethan **boy actor**.

Ophelia, (a) a character in *Hamlet*, daughter of Polonius, sister of Laertes and beloved of Hamlet.

(b) The name is probably a feminine derivation of the Greek name 'Ophelos', meaning 'helper'. Given Hamlet's love for her, Ophelia is probably the only figure who could help to move the hero into the future beyond the death of his father and **Gertrude**'s remarriage. Perhaps his reported appearance in her closet where he takes her 'firmly by the wrist' and gazes into her face is a silent appeal for her help (2.1.84–97). Laertes calls her a 'minist'ring **angel**' (5.1.240), constructing her as spiritual helper, and her lines and actions show her as devout, modest and obedient to her father and brother. Nevertheless, she quickly challenges the sexual double standard, ministering to Laertes and for equality on behalf of her sex:

> Do not, as some ungracious pastors do,
> Show me the steep and thorny way to heaven,
> Whiles, like a puff'd and reckless libertine
> Himself the primrose path of dalliance treads
> And recks not his own rede.
>
> (1.3.47–51)

Ophelia helps Polonius and Claudius in a practical way, as a pawn to test whether love is the cause of Hamlet's madness (3.1). **Gertrude** gives her more agency as a source of help for Hamlet: 'I hope your virtues / May bring him to his wonted ways again / To both your honors' (3.1.39–41). This probably matches Ophelia's own motivation, which is encouraged by his initial request to pray for him: 'The fair Ophelia. **Nymph** in thy orisons / Be all my sins remember'd' (3.1.88–9). Given her role as helper, Ophelia's reaction to his tirade: 'Heavenly powers, restore him!' (3.1.141), and her grief at failing in her task are desperate. After rejection and insult at his hands, her primary focus is still Hamlet, the 'form and stature of blown youth / Blasted with ecstasy' (3.1. 156, 159–60), and not herself.

Hamlet's aggressive questioning of Ophelia's **honesty** or **chastity** in this interview is followed by the sexual innuendo about lying in her **lap** to watch 'The Mousetrap' (3.2.112–16). The bawdy meaning of '**nothing**', as a reference to the vagina ('a fair thought to lie between maid's legs'), may take its cue from 'O', the first sound of Ophelia's name. Hamlet ends his speech 'For O, for O, the **hobby horse** is forgot' (3.2.117–21). Under the diametrically opposed pressures of sexual invitation from Hamlet and the need for chastity, it is not surprising that Ophelia's sanity collapses. Her entrance '*distracted, with her hair down, playing on a lute*' (4.5.21SD), her snatches of song and speech all advertise her preoccupations with the loss of **chastity**, with death, and with a sense of helplessness to prevent either. That Ophelia cannot, finally, help herself to avoid drowning, is all the more tragic given her name's meaning. Her final line is a prayer for divine help: mercy

311

for her father 'And of all Christians' souls, I pray God' (4.5.199).

(c) Anna Jameson's *Shakespeare's Heroines* (2005: 176–88), first published in 1858, reads Ophelia's 'helplessness arising from her innocence, and pictured without any indication of weakness' (p. 178) as emotionally moving. Frances Barber (2001: 146) describes how she played the role as 'strong and spirited'. The character's iconographic status and openness to interpretation is considered in Elaine Showalter's important essay 'Representing Ophelia: women, madness and the responsibilities of feminist criticism' (1985) and Carol Rutter discusses the on-stage presence of Ophelia's corpse in *Enter The Body* (2001: 27–56). Richard Finkelstein (1997) and Gabrielle Dane (1998) consider how Ophelia's subject position is constricting and challenges the stability of gendered identity. Ranjini Philip (1991) and Alison Findlay (1994a: 189–205) discuss Ophelia's mental breakdown. *The True Ophelia* (1913) offers an actress's perspective.

Overdone, Mistress (a) a character in *Measure for Measure*.

(b) The character is a **bawd** or keeper of a brothel and her name 'Mistress Overdone' comically reflects her wide sexual experience since she has had nine husbands 'Overdone by the last', leaving her as a **widow** (*MM* 2.1.200–2). Elbow defines her as 'a bad woman' whose first brothel in the suburbs has been pulled down and so 'now she professes a hot-house' (2.1.65). This bath-house or 'common house' (2.1.44) provides premises for sexual assignations. Lucio's nickname for the character, 'Madam Mitigation' (1.2.45) therefore proves appropriate since, in continuing her trade as bawd, she continues to covertly manage excessive male desire in the play. Indeed, as she points out, she has also provided maintenance for the bastard child of Lucio and **Kate** Keepdown, one of her **whore**s (3.2.199–203). Mistress Overdone is, appropriately, arrested at the point where Duke Vincentio finalizes his own plan for containing Angelo's desire and saving Claudio (3.2.205). Lucio asks Pompey, 'How doth my dear morsel, thy **mistress**? Procures she still?' but is told 'she hath eaten up all her beef, and she is herself in the tub' (3.1.54–7). In prison Pompey feels at home: 'one would think it were Mistress Overdone's own house, for here be many of her old customers', all suffering from various sexually transmitted diseases as 'great doers in our trade' (4.3.2–4 and 17–18). Because the Duke condemns the 'corruption' that he has seen 'boil and bubble / 'Till it o'er run the stew' (5.1.318–9), and reforms the State through enforced marriages, we can assume that the widow Mistress Overdone is more likely to be married to one of her customers rather than being allowed to resume her former trade when she is released from prison.

(c) DiGangi (1993) comments on Mistress Overdone's house as a place of pleasure and danger for Mistress Elbow.

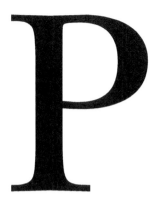

Page, Mistress, (a) one of the two eponymous protagonists of *The Merry Wives of Windsor*, married to Master Page and mother of **Anne**.

(b) Mistress Page is a **housewife**. Page directs her to 'bid these gentlemen welcome' to a dinner of a hot venison pasty (1.1.194–5). In everything but the question of matching their daughter, Mistress Page appears to enjoy a companionate, mutually trusting relationship with her husband. They address each other familiarly, 'How now Meg? / Whither go you, George, hark you?' and 'You'll come home to dinner George?' (2.1.148–9). Mistress **Quickly** observes the freedom and control Mistress Page enjoys as home 'do what she will, say what she will, take all, pay all, go to bed when she list, rise when she list, all is as she will and truly she deserves it, for if there be a kind woman in Windsor, she is one' (2.2.117–21). When Mistress Page requests Falstaff's page, Shakespeare may use the pun on her name to point up her identity as a model wife, a living page from a conduct book, or to refer to the **boy actor** playing this stereotype. 'Mistress Page would desire you to send her your little page' (2.2.113–14) seems designed as a pun, reiterated when the page announces 'here's Mistress Page at the door' (3.3.85–6).

Falstaff is convinced that she controls the household finances and is thus 'a region in Guiana, all gold and bounty'. He compares her to the East Indies and Mrs **Ford** to the West in his plan of sexual conquest to 'trade to them both' (1.3.69 and 71–2) by sending them nearly identical love letters. In contrast to her friend, Mrs Page appears more assured and able to easily dismiss Falstaff's suit (2.1.22–32). She assures Mistress Ford that she is 'an unmeasurable distance' from giving her husband cause for jealousy (2.1.103–5). She is, however, immediately concerned about how her conduct could have given Falstaff reason 'that he dares in this manner to assay me', remembering that on meeting him she was modestly 'frugal of my mirth' (2.1.25–8). Mistress Quickly commends Mrs Page's virtue as 'a civil modest wife, and one (I tell you) that will not miss morning or evening prayer' (2.2.98–9). On the matter of tricking her husband over the match of their

daughter Anne, she takes a pragmatic attitude: 'better a little chiding than a great deal of heart-break' (5.3.10). She ends the play by blessing the match of Anne and Fenton and offering housewifely hospitality again: 'let us every one go home, / And laugh this sport o'er by a country fire – / Sir John and all' (5.5.241–3).
(c) Philip D. Collington (2000) proposes that the play rewrites the well-publicized murder of George Page of Plymouth by his wife Eulalia in 1591 and engages with anxieties about women's potential to commit domestic violence. Sandra Clark (1987) analyses the plotting of Mistress Page and Mistress Ford as wit in action rather than words and thus recuperative. Helgerson (2000: 57–75) argues that the wives combine domestic props and the beneficent **witch**craft of wise women to reform Ford and Falstaff. Korda (2002: 76–110) reads Mistresses Page and Ford as part of the protective family economy. Wall (2003) shows how the wives stretch the protocols of domestic management to suit their own purposes.

Parca, (pl. **Parcae**) (a) a Roman name for the three **Fates**.
(b) Pistol ostentatiously uses this term, challenging Fluellen 'Dost thou thirst, base Troyan, / To have me fold up Parca's fatal web?' (*HV* 5.1.19–20). The 'fatal web' referred to is the threads of destiny spun and cut by the Fates, and shows that this is a threat to kill Fluellen. It is couched in the flamboyant classical rhetoric typical of the braggart soldier, in contrast to Fluellen's idiomatic Welsh.
(c) *See* **Fates** and **Destinies**.

patience, (a) the calm, uncomplaining endurance of pain, affliction, inconvenience, and the capacity for such endurance, often personified as a female virtue. The name of a minor character in Shakespeare and Fletcher's *Henry VIII*.
(b) The feminized personification of patience can be traced back in English at least to *Piers Plowman* and the anonymous alliterative poem *Patience*, and appeared on stage in morality dramas such as *The Castle of Perseverance* (c. 1410). Othello describes Patience as 'thou young and rose-lipp'd cherubin' who would be transformed by **Desdemona**'s adultery to 'look as grim as hell' (*Oth.* 4.2.63–4). It is a virtue idealized in lines like **Viola**'s description of her imaginary sister who 'never told her love' but let it grow unrequited until it consumed her:

> she pined in thought,
> And with a green and yellow melancholy
> She sat like Patience on a monument,
> Smiling at grief. Was not this love indeed?
>   (*TN* 2.4.112–15)

These lines simultaneously monumentalize extreme female passivity and acknowledge its self-destructive nature. A more positive picture is **Marina** who, in spite of her sufferings, 'dost look / Like Patience gazing on kings' graves, and smiling / Extremity out of act' (*Per.* 5.1.137–9). **Cordelia**'s serene acceptance of events is of this heavenly character. 'Patience and sorrow strove / Who should express her goodliest', and she smiles and weeps 'Sunshine and rain at once' (*KL* 4.3.16–17).

Male characters do not embrace it so easily. Alonso displaces his inability to bear the loss of his son onto the feminized Patience: 'Irreparable is the loss, and patience / Says it is past her cure' (*Temp.* 5.1.140–1). Troilus boasts that 'Patience herself, what goddess e'er she be' would endure suffering less stoically than he, waiting to meet Cressida (*T&C* 1.1.27). **Rosalind**, in receipt of **Phoebe**'s haughty insulting love letter, asserts 'Patience herself would startle at this letter, / And play the swaggerer' (*AYLI* 4.3.13–14). In *Cymbeline*, **Imogen** is compared to the personified virtue Patience since 'She's punish'd for her truth, and undergoes, / More goddess-like than wife-like, such assaults / As would take in some virtue' (*Cym.* 3.2.7–9).

Feminine patience is not a gift but a virtue that has to be learned through hard discipline, with greater or lesser success, by Shakespeare's female characters. **Hermia** complains that Demetrius has driven her 'past the bounds / Of maiden's patience' (*MND* 3.2.65–6). **Helena**, too, feels that to 'extort / A poor soul's patience, all to make you sport' (*MND* 3.2.160–1) falls short of noble behaviour. Petruchio boasts of Katherina that 'For patience she will prove a second **Grissel**' (*Shrew* 2.1.295) and spends much of the play trying to prove his point. The complete passivity of Grissel or Griselda as a model of patience sometimes devalued it as feminine weakness. Clifford complains 'Patience is for poltroons, such as he' [Henry VI] (*3HVI* 1.1.62), for example. Shakespeare's texts invariably show that this is not the case, however. Patience to endure suffering is a hard lesson for Katherina to learn, though she pleads for Petruchio's servants 'Patience, I pray you, 'twas a fault unwilling' (*Shrew* 4.1.156). Similiarly, the advice Caesar gives to **Octavia**, 'Be ever known to patience: my dear'st sister!' (*A&C* 3.6.98) would not be easy to follow in the light of Antony's desertion. **Hero**, too, must learn to 'have patience and endure' following Claudio's rejection of her at the altar (*MAdo* 4.1.254). The Countess of Rossillion advises the rejected Helena to 'think upon patience' (*AWW* 3.2.48).

'Patience' can also mean physical endurance. When **Portia** wounds herself in the thigh to prove her secrecy to Brutus, she advertises her virtue as patience rather than strength: 'can I bear that with patience / And not my husband's secrets?' (*JC* 2.1.361–2). More often, female characters' patience is proved by enduring loss. The Duke tells **Isabella** that her brother has been killed and counsels 'show your wisdom, daughter, / In your close patience' (*MM* 4.3.118). When it seems that even her cause will not be heard, she asks 'O you blessed ministers above, / Keep me in patience' (*MM* 5.1.115–6). Other female characters are far less patient, however. **Juliet** will not 'bear this work of heaven with patience' when she finds Romeo is dead and commits 'violence on herself' (*R&J* 5.3.261–4). The more mature **Cleopatra** is singularly lacking in this feminine virtue. When Antony dies she immediately thinks of suicide, declaring 'Patience is sottish, and impatience does / Become a dog that's mad' like herself (*A&C* 4.15.79–80). **Lucrece** struggles to remain patient but cannot bear the image of the treacherous Sinon (a painted substitute for her rapist Tarquin) and 'all enraged, such passion her assails, / That patience is quite beaten from her breast. / She tears the senseless Sinon with her nails' (*Luc.* 1562–4).

Patience is perversely strong in adversity. Frederick is enraged by **Rosalind**'s, claiming that she is 'too subtle' and 'Her very silence and her patience, / Speak to the people, and they pity her' (*AYLI* 1.3.78–9). In anticipation of revenge, **Tamora** calmly endures the taunts of **Lavinia** and Bassianus, saying 'Why, I have patience to endure all this' (*Tit.* 2.3.88). **Adriana** speaks from experience when she warns her **sister** that putting patience into practice when 'bruised with adversity' is extremely difficult and 'helpless' (*Err.* 2.1.32–41). Nym hints at how Shakespeare's texts often show the stoic power of women's patience, even if it may not be glamorous: 'though patience be a tired mare, yet she will plod' (*HV* 2.1.23). **Hermione** confidently believes her innocence will eventually make 'False accusation blush and tyranny / Tremble at patience' (*WT* 3.2.30–2). The fate of Queen **Katherine** in *Henry VIII* dramatises another endurance test where, although the courtiers 'vex me past my patience!' (*HVIII* 2.4.131), she will add 'an honour, a great patience' to her **wif**ely virtues of truth, honesty, obedience and care (*HVIII* 3.1.137–8). Fittingly, as she resigns herself to her fate, she is attended by a lady-in-waiting called Patience. Katherine asks this allegorical figure 'be near me still; and set me lower: / I have not long to trouble thee' (*HVIII* 4.2.75–6). She calls her by name: 'Patience, is that letter / I caus'd you write yet sent away?' (*HVIII* 4.2.127–8) and, appropriately, Patience is the instrument inscribing Katherine's last requests to the King. Katherine appeals, 'Patience / You must not leave me yet' as she awaits her death, and leaves instructions for her burial with the 'good wench' (*HVIII* 4.2.165–70).

(c) Mark Sardona's unpublished dissertation 'Patience and the Agents of Renaissance Drama' (Harvard University Press, 1989) surveys the use of this allegorical character. An extracted essay 'Patientia Regina: Patience as Character from the Morality Play to Jacobean Tragedy' is available online at the Centre for Medieval and Renaissance Studies (Los Angeles, University of California), http://repositories.cdlib.org/cgi/viewcontent.cgi?article=1129&context=cmrs/comitatus

Paulina, (a) A character in *The Winter's Tale*, married to Antigonus and **mother** of three daughters, friend and defender of **Hermione**. Paulina is **widow**ed during the play and becomes a counsellor to King Leontes, stage-managing Hermione's reappearance, after which Paulina is married to Camillo. Her Latin name *Paulina* (feminine of *Paulinus*, a derivative of the family name *Paulus*, 'small'), is a feminization of 'Paul' and thus associated with St Paul, a founder of the Christian church.

(b) Much of Paulina's behaviour bears similarities to the controversial activities of the biblical Paul. Just as Paul's preaching aroused considerable official hostility leading to his execution, Paulina's outspoken defence of **Hermione** enrages Leontes, leading to her condemnation as a **callet** for her **shrew**ish behaviour. She insists on baby **Perdita**'s legitimacy to the tyrannical Leontes, speaking in direct, unflattering terms that make him threaten 'I'll ha' thee burnt', to which she replies, 'I care not. It is an heretic that makes the fire, / Not she which burns in't' (2.3.114–15). When she comes to announce the death of Hermione, Paulina presents herself to Leontes as a martyr to his tyranny:

> What studied torments, tyrant, hast for me?
> What wheels? racks? fires? What flayling? boiling
> In leads or oils? What old or newer torture
> Must I receive, whose every word deserves
> To taste of thy most worst?
>
> (3.2.175–9)

Told 'you have made fault / I' th' boldness of your speech' (3.2.218–20), she says she will answer this in heaven, but Leontes admits, 'Thou did'st but speak well / When most the truth' (3.2.232–3) and from this point she becomes his guide in repentance. Her counsels against re-marriage until the oracle is fulfilled and Hermione is 'again in breath' seem harsh to the other courtiers (5.1.83–4) though they are prophetic. Paulina's refusal to be frightened by Leontes does not go as far as Paul's recommendations to bless those who persecute you, but she subsequently works to bring good out of evil (Rom. 12.14–21).

Paulina is referred to as 'Lady **Margery**' a '**midwife**' (2.3160), an appropriate title since she is responsible for delivering the baby from prison to the air, insisting that it was 'prisoner to the **womb**' therefore rightly 'Freed and enfranchis'd' by the processes of **Nature** and not subject to legal imprisonment (2.2.57–8). Her joy at Perdita's return, locking her into an embrace 'as if she would pin her to her heart, that she might no more be in danger of losing' shows her embrace of things new-born and the future, alongside her sorrow at 'the loss of her husband' (5.2.72–8). Paulina imitates her biblical namesake in stage-managing the miraculous scene in which Hermione is transformed from statue to living woman. Acts 19 reports that God wrought special miracles through the hand of Paul, so that even Paul's handkerchiefs and aprons could drive out diseases and evil spirits (Acts 19.11–12). More importantly, Paul points out that the gifts of healing the sick, of working miracles, and of prophecy are gifts of the spirit given to humans to profit everyone (1 Cor. 12.9–10). Such is the authority that Paulina relies on to protest she is not 'assisted / By wicked powers' (5.2.90). The miracle of resurrection and cure she directs, having told everyone 'it is required / You do awake your faith' (5.2.94–5), can be read on both literal and metaphoric levels. Even though Mamillius has perished, it results in a healing of the kingdom.

(c) Huston Diehl (2008: 69–82) argues persuasively that Shakespeare creates a female Paul whose rebukes match early modern Protestant views and whose theatricality appropriates Pauline authority in defence of the theatre. Roy Battenhouse (1980) traces connections between Paulina and St Paul. Paulina's links with **Proserpina** and regeneration are examined in Janet S. Wolf (1994: 32–44). Michael D. Friedman, *The world must be peopled: Shakespeare's comedies of forgiveness* (2002: 218–27) discusses Paulina as a **shrew**. *See also* **hen**, **scold** and **witch**.

Peace, (a) personified as female in a morality tradition dating back to medieval literature.

(b) Burgundy gives an extended, idealized picture of Peace in order to encourage the French and English monarchs to reach a reconciliation that will achieve it, following the war which has ravished **France**. The personification 'naked, poor, and mangled Peace' is a victim of the war. Instead, she should be a nurturing figure: 'Dear nurse of arts, plenties and joyful births' (*HV* 5.2.34–5). 'Gentle Peace' is also a gardener with a 'lovely visage' who has been exiled from France 'And all her husbandry doth lie on heaps' (*HV* 5.2.37, 39 and 60). Burgundy implicitly allies the future fertility of Peace with that of **Katherine** who is a political pawn in the proposed alliance. Any threat to **Elizabeth** I's kingdom by rebels is implicitly depicted as barbaric rape in the view that **England** should not wish to

> Change the complexion of her maid-pale peace
> To scarlet indignation, and bedew
> Her pasters' grass with faithful English blood.
>
> (*RII* 3.3.98–100)

The harvest of Peace is depicted more cynically in *Hamlet* and *Henry IV Part II*. Claudius's letter to England asks that 'peace should still her wheaten garland wear / And stand a comma 'tween their amities' (*Ham.* 5.2.41–2). To harvest such peace, the English monarch must execute Hamlet. Civil peace brings prosperity in monetary terms to the Archbishop of York's territories. He should not want to raise troops against King Henry IV since his beard has been touched by 'the silver hand of peace' and he has been tutored by her in diplomacy 'learning and good letters'. As a churchman, his white robes should 'figure innocence' like the dove, the 'very blessed spirit of peace' (*2HIV* 4.1.41–6). The irony of these lines is that Prince John uses the ideal image of Peace to bring about a peaceful resolution to the conflict by verbally tricking the Archbishop and his allies, only to arrest them and send them to be executed once their army has been dismissed.

Penelope, (a) the wife of Odysseus in classical mythology who waited for him for ten years while he fought in the Trojan war and another ten while he returned home. In order to repel each of her 100 suitors, she promised to marry them only when she had finished weaving a shroud for Odysseus's father, and after each day's weaving, she unpicked what she had done. She is a model of female virtue, especially loyalty and patience. Her weaving symbolizes woman's never-ending work.
(b) A single reference to Penelope occurs in the sewing scene in *Coriolanus* when Valeria tells **Virgilia**, 'You would be another Penelope: yet, they say, all the yarn she spun in Ulysses' absence did but fill Ithaca full of moths' (*Cor.* 1.3.82–4). Like Penelope, Virgilia has refused to leave the house 'till my lord return from the wars' (*Cor.* 1.3.75), even to visit another woman in labour.
(c) Crawford (1984) and Jones and Stallybrass (2000: 104–33) examine the significance of Penelope as a stereotype of female virtue.

Penthesilea, (a) in mythology, the Queen of the Amazons who led troops in defence of King Priam and Troy in the final year of the Trojan war. She was admired for combining exceptional martial strength and beauty. When Achilles defeated her, he fell in love with her and immediately regretted having killed her.

(b) Shakespeare makes no reference to Penthesilea in *Troilus and Cressida*, probably because this is set before her entry to the Trojan war. However, Sir Toby Belch bids Maria 'Good night, Penthesilea' in *Twelfth Night* (2.3.177), as a mark of his love and his admiration for her plot against Malvolio. The name is appropriate in setting her up as an Amazonian rival to Malvolio.

(c) Blundell (1995), pp. 60–1 discusses Penthesilea in the context of other Amazons as a figure who exemplifies the connection between violent military domination and sex in ancient Greek culture.

Percy, Lady Katherine *see* **Katherine**

Perdita, (a) a character in *The Winter's Tale*, daughter of King Leontes and Queen **Hermione**, who is banished as illegitimate by him, and is reared by an old shepherd in Bohemia. Her name, 'meaning she who was lost' derives from the Latin *perdo*, meaning lose, destroy, ruin or waste.

(b) Perdita is nameless in Sicilia, as befitting her supposed status as a bastard (Findlay 1994: 18–21) but she is named by Antigonus following the directions of Hermione who appeared to him in a dream and asked him to leave her baby in Bohemia:

> . . . and for the babe
> Is counted lost for ever, Perdita
> I prithee call't. For this ungentle business
> Put on thee by my lord, thou ne'er shalt see
> Thy wife **Paulina** more.
>
> (3.3.32–6)

Perdita thus personifies the condition of loss in the play. She is the answer to the Delphic oracle's mysterious pronouncement that 'the King shall live without an heir if that which is lost be not found' (3.2.134–6). Through being 'found' after 16 years in Bohemia, Perdita brings new life to the Sicilian royal family and to her mother Hermione, whose reanimated statue turns to speak to her on hearing the words 'our Perdita is found' (5.3.121). Perdita's identity as a spirit of regeneration and restoration is closely linked to her rural upbringing, celebrated in the sheepshearing festival over which she presides as a carnival queen. The choric figure of Time announces the passing of 16 years and the winter season of the play, and introduces a nubile 'Perdita, now grown in grace / Equal with wond'ring' (4.1.24–5). Perdita's references to flowers recall **Proserpina** and a seasonal cycle that includes death as well as rebirth. Even while she grows in grace, her appearances bring to the scene reminders of loss. Counselling Perdita on her role as mistress of the feast, the Old Shepherd recalls his dead wife. Florizel and Perdita face loss of each other in the light of Polixenes' threats. Perdita's reappearance at the Sicilian court reawakens memories of Hermione and of Mamillius. While Hermione and Perdita are restored, Mamillius is dead, typifying the play's staging of gender difference: women are symbols of regeneration but men are subject to mortality. By saving Perdita, Antigonus too loses his life. Perdita thus brings to the Sicilian court the restoration of Hermione to Leontes and a confirmation of Antigonus's death, heralding the third phase of female life, widowhood. She starts the play hidden or lost in embryo as Hermione 'rounds apace' (2.1.16) and Leontes refuses to recognise her. Her 'lost years' in Bohemia dramatise her as an agent of seasonal restoration and regeneration; her return to the Sicilian court transplants that rural myth to a courtly context, but not without poignant reminders of the loss of sons and husbands.

(c) Dash (1983) traces the representations of Perdita in eighteenth-century stage adaptations. Davies (1986), pp. 152–65 reads Perdita with reference to the seasonal myth of Demeter / Ceres. Simon Palfrey (1997), pp. 221–9 and Amy L. Tigner (2006) consider Perdita's associations with rural fruitfulness; Tigner sees her as a virginal garden that can redeem the play from the post-lapsarian garden represented by Hermione's body. David Kaula (1976) compares Perdita with Autolycus as representatives of Protestant simplicity as opposed to popish idolatry.

Persephone, *see* **Proserpina**

petticoat, (a) a skirt or underskirt, often padded or richly decorated and intended to be seen. The word derives from the male garment, a short (petit) padded undercoat worn over a shirt and under a doublet or armour. Women's petticoats were usually made out of warm fabrics such as flannel, bayes and kersey or the more expensive velvet or silk, or could be lined. Summer petticoats were made out of lighter materials such as taffeta. They were either fastened at the waist or made with unstiffened bodies or bodices for the upper body, to take some of the weight of the fabric on the shoulders.

(b) The petticoat is a synecdoche for woman, even more obviously on the stage where the **boy actor** begins to put on female identity with the garment. **Rosalind** sets it in opposition to breeches as a marker for appropriately gendered behaviour: 'doublet and hose ought to show itself courageous to petticoat' (*AYLI* 2.4.6–7). It is used to criticize **Queen Margaret**, who leads her husband's Lancastrian forces in battle, for her subversive behaviour: 'You might have still worn the petticoat, / And ne'er have stol'n the breech' (*3HVI* 5.5.23). Even more starkly, Antony's former wife **Fulvia** and his mistress **Cleopatra** are reduced to pieces of disposable underclothing when Enobarbus tells him, 'Your old smock brings forth a new petticoat' (*A&C* 1.2.168–9).

An example of the richness of women's petticoats is indicated in the 1600 Stowe inventory which lists: 'Item one Peticoate of white Satten embroidered allover like peramydes [pyramids] and flowers of venice golde and silke' (Arnold 1988: 86). **Rosalind**, betraying her courtly origins, refers to a richly decorated garment like this when she says she and Aliena live 'in the skirts of the forest, like fringe upon a petticoat' (*AYLI* 3.2.336–7). However decorative, the petticoat does remain an undergarment. **Bianca**, thinking that Katherina might be jealous of the ornaments she wears, tells her 'I'll pull them off myself, / Yea, all my raiment, to my petticoat' (*Shrew* 2.1.4–5), a potentially flirtatious line for the off-stage audience. Making holes in a woman's petticoat carries sexual innuendo in *Henry IV Part II* (2.2.81–3 and 3.2.166).

(c) Arnold (1988: 86–9, 153–5) describes petticoats that formed part of the royal wardrobe.

Philippe, Queen, (a) a character in the anonymous *Edward III*, some scenes of which may have been composed by Shakespeare. Historically, Philippe is the daughter of William, Earl of Hainault, wife and **queen** consort of Edward III, and **mother** to Edward the Black Prince, six more sons and five daughters. Her name, spelt 'Philip' in the First and Second Quartos is an English vernacular name which was borne by women as well as men in the Middle Ages.

(b) Philippe does not appear until Act 5 of the play. However, the report of her in Act 4 introduces a culturally androgynous figure who gives **birth** and leads armies at the same time, a medieval concept of **queen**ship. Edward is told that at the Battle of Newcastle Philippe 'big with child, was every day in arms' (4.2.45). Giving birth and vanquishing the enemy are equated as Philippe's work: 'the painful travel of the Queen' (4.2.44) which will secure the future of the kingdom. Within the space of 200 lines, she is presented as an angry consort; a spokeswoman for **peace**; a mourning and then joyous mother. Each phase of the action is punctuated by the speaking of her name, which signals typically feminine and masculine subject positions. The scene opens 'No more, Queen Philippe, pacify your self' (5.1.1) and she then adopts the typically feminine subject position of peacemaker, following a Marian tradition of intercession later used by **Mariana** and **Isabella**. She recommends Edward show mercy since 'It is a glorious thing to stablish peace, / And kings approach the closest unto God / By giving life and safety unto men' (5.1.41–2). Her plea for the burghers of Calais draws on Froissart's chronicle in which 'The quene being great with chylde, kneled downe and sore wepyng, sayd, A gentyll sir, syth I passed the see in great parell, I have desyred nothyng of you; therfore nowe I humbly reqyre you, in honour of the Son of the Virgyn Mary and for the love of me that you woll take mercy of these six burgesses' (Melchiori 1998: 213). The turning point of the sequence is when Edward tells her, 'Philippe prevail: we yield to your request; / These men shall live to boast of clemency' (5.1.53–5). As if taking a cue from this, in the following confrontation with Copland, Philippe adopts a high-status, masculine role as consort and substitute for the King. She tells him: 'Copland, thou did'st scorn the king's command, / Neglecting our commission in his name' (5.1.83–4) an objection to which the play offers no answer. Edward intervenes this time to ask, 'I pray thee, Philippe, let displeasure pass' (5.1.88). The action moves on to news of Prince Edward's death, at which Philippe (again following Froissart) recreates herself in the role of grieving mother: 'Sweet Ned, I would thy mother in the sea / Had been prevented of this mortal grief' (5.1.160–1). Edward's third and final use of her name, 'Content thee, Philippe, 'tis not tears will serve / To call him back if he be taken hence' prompts further action in his suggestion that she 'Comfort thyself' with thoughts of revenge (5.1.162–5). The surprise return of Edward moves her to kiss him 'to express my joy' since her passion is beyond further speech (5.1.190–1). The threat of **revenge** and war now removed, it seems appropriate that the final word of the play refers to Philippe as the English return victorious 'three kings, two princes and a queen' (5.1.243).

(c) Giorgio Melchiori (ed.), *King Edward III* (1998) and Rackin (2002), pp. 81–4 discusses Philippe's military activities as unremarkable in the context of a medieval tradition of queenship.

Philomel, (a) a tragic **rape** victim from classical mythology. Philomel was raped in the forest by her brother-in-law, Tereus, who then cut out her tongue so that she could not speak of the crime. Philomel contrived to send her sister Procne a piece of embroidery into which she had woven her story and the two sisters took revenge by serving Tereus a meal of the flesh of his and Procne's son. Philomel was transformed by the gods into a nightingale, who supposedly sings sadly because she forces her breast onto a thorn in order to sing.

(b) Philomel's story was probably known to Shakespeare from North's translation of Ovid's *Metamorphoses* (Ovidius 2000: 151–9). Philomel is a very important icon for **rape** victims in the Shakespearean canon, as a figure of pity, of enduring suffering, and as an inspiration for **revenge**. In *Titus Andronicus*, Aaron predicts that **Lavinia**, soon to be raped by the villains Chiron and Demetrius, will follow the path of Philomel (*Tit.* 2.3.43–4), but as well as ravishing her and cutting out her tongue, they also cut off her hands. Her uncle Marcus's lyrical lament over the piteous spectacle points out

> Fair Philomela, why she but lost her tongue,
> And in a tedious sampler sew'd her mind.
> But, lovely niece, that means is cut from thee.
> A craftier Tereus, cousin, hast thou met,
> And he hath cut those pretty fingers off
> That could have better **sew**'d than Philomel.
> (*Tit.* 2.4.38–43)

Here Philomel becomes a silent spectacle of female tragedy, the object of eloquent male literary composition. Nevertheless, the frighteningly destructive power of Philomel as a figure of revenge is played out by Lavinia, who literally appropriates the classical story for her own purposes by snatching her nephew's copy of Ovid's *Metamorphoses* and turning to the story of Philomel to communicate her fate to her father, uncle and nephew (*Tit.* 4.1.1–57). She adopts the elevated masculine register of Latin to rewrite the ending, using the stumps of her arms to write '*stuprum*' and the names of her rapists (*Tit.* 4.1.75–7). The rest of Philomel's revenge story is enacted with her father Titus adopting the role of Procne, to serve the flesh of Chiron and Demetrius in a pie to their mother.

The heroine of *The Rape of Lucrece* makes an extended comparison between herself and Philomel the nightingale as dawn breaks after the terrible night in which she is raped by Tarquin. **Lucrece** bids the dawn chorus be silent and calls 'Fair Philomel that sing'st of ravishment, / Make thy sad grove in my dishevelled hair' (*Luc.* 1128–9). She sees herself as a bird of night, like Philomel, because of the shame she now feels, and models herself on the nightingale's supposedly masochistic behaviour:

> And whiles against a thorn thou bear'st thy part
> To keep thy sharp woes waking, wretched I
> To imitate thee well, against my heart
> Will fix a sharp knife to affright mine eye
> Who if it wink, shall thereon fall and die.
>
> (*Luc.* 1135)

Lucrece's subsequent public suicide, by stabbing herself in front of the Roman generals, ultimately brings revenge onto Tarquin and his family.

Philomel is pictured as a figure of mournful stoicism in Sonnet 102 where the sonneteer compares his own enduring, painful but quiet love with that of the bird whose 'mournful hymns did hush the night' (*Son.* 102.10) only in the early summer. Philomel's 'sweet melody' ominously occurs in the fairy lullaby of Act 2 Scene 2 of *A Midsummer Night's Dream*, implicitly suggesting that Oberon's planned seduction of **Titania** by a monstrous lover constitutes a form of **rape** no less tyrannical than that of Tereus. Equally ominous is **Imogen**'s choice of reading matter before she falls asleep to be dishonoured, verbally rather than physically, by Iachimo in *Cymbeline*. He creeps up to her bedside to discover 'here the leaf's turned down / Where Philomel gave up' (*Cym* 2.2.53). The literary legacy of this tragic figure seems to haunt vulnerable women in Shakespeare's plays although some are able to remodel the story to escape the status of passive victim. For example, while Edward III knows that Philomel, the nightingale, 'sings of adulterate wrong' that echoes his intent, the **Countess** of Salisbury rhetorically manoeuvres herself out of his lustful advances (*EIII* 2.1.110).

(c) Ovid's account of Tereus's rape of Philomel and the revenge taken by her and Procne is in Book 6, lines 578–853 of the *Metapmorphoses* (Ovidius 2000: 151–9). How the violence of the myth is translated on stage in *Titus* is explored by Eugene M. Waith (1957), Jessica Lugo (2007) and Liz Oakley-Brown (2006: 25–8), while Ann Thompson (1978) discusses traces of the Philomel myth in *Titus* and *Cymbeline*.

Phoebe, (a) a character from *As You Like It*, a shepherdess from the Forest of Arden and beloved of Silvius. Her name derives from the Latin form of a Greek deity, *Phoibe* (from *phoibos*, 'bright'), and is identified with **Diana**, goddess of the **moon**, and indirectly with Queen **Elizabeth** I, whose iconographic self-representation included this lunar personification.

(b) Florio's *World of Words* (1611) explained that Phoebe 'the Moone' was 'so called because she is Phebus sister'. References to Phoebe the moon in *Midsummer Night's Dream* and *Titus Andronicus* allude indirectly to Elizabeth I. Lysander and Hermia plan to meet when 'Phoebe doth behold / Her silver visage in the watery glass' (*MND* 1.1.209), one of many lunar references in this play. In *Titus*, Saturninus praises Tamora, as one who 'like the stately Phoebe 'mongst her nymphs / Dost overshine the gallant'st dames of Rome' (*Tit.* 1.1.316–17), an indirect compliment to Elizabeth who has the power to overshine any Roman woman (or indeed, the Roman church). Jonathan Bate confidently asserted that Phoebe in *As You Like It* is neither Ovid's Diana nor Elizabeth (1993: 162). However, in the light of Juliet Dusinberre's persuasive thesis that *As You Like It* was performed at Richmond Palace at Shrovetide for Elizabeth I and her court (Dusinberre 2003), the character must have created some kind of connection with the royal mistress.

Phoebe's name comes from Shakespeare's source in Thomas Lodge's *Rosalynde*. It is first proclaimed by Silvius, 'O Phoebe, Phoebe, Phoebe!' (*AYLI* 2.3.43), and is spoken 16 more times in the text, once as a verb (*AYLI* 4.3.39). Although Shakespeare takes the name from Lodge, he changes Phoebe's appearance. She has 'no more' illuminating beauty than 'without candle may go dark to bed' (*AYLI* 3.5.38–9) and 'has a leathern hand / A freestone-colored hand' (*AYLI* 4.3.24–5), in contrast to Elizabeth I who was justly proud of her white, long-fingered hands. Shakespeare omits the hymns of praise in Lodge that compare Phoebe to the purity of the spheres and so could have flattered Elizabeth I (Bullough Vol. II 1958: 186). What remains is a guarded defence of the mistress's absolute power. Silvius pleads with his 'Sweet Phoebe' not to kill him with bitterness

> The common executioner,
> Whose heart th' accustom'd sight of death makes hard,
> Falls not the axe upon the humbled neck
> But first begs pardon. Will you sterner be
> Than he that dies and lives by bloody drops?
>
> (*AYLI* 3.5.3–7)

Phoebe gamely defends herself against the charges, ridiculing the Petrarchan conceit that there is 'murder in mine eye' and challenging him to 'show the wound mine eye hath made in thee' (*AYLI* 3.5.10–20). This comic disavowal of the harsher effects of queenly authority may have flattered Elizabeth as a compliment to her natural gentleness to others. Essex was present at Richmond and was already playing the role of a scorned lover by 1599 so Silvius's complaints and Phoebe's reply would have fitted the Shrovetide performance well. The joke is furthered by Rosalind's comment that the cruel shepherdess 'Phoebes me' with a 'boisterous' (spelt 'boysterous' in the original text) tyrannical masculine style (*AYLI* 4.3.31–9). Elizabeth's reputation for masculine, princely, ruthlessness is immediately undercut by the love letter: 'Art thou god to shepherd turn'd / That a maiden's heart hath burn'd?' (*AYLI* 4.3.40–1). Might this Phoebe have been designed as a carnival queen for the Shrovetide performance? Might the powerful **mistress** now condemned to an unobtainable love also appeal covertly to a queen who could not publicly pursue her desires? Whatever the case, the play finishes with Phoebe remaining the object of her swain's absolute devotion. Silvius may not be the ideal husband, but he is the ideal courtier:

> All adoration, duty, and observance,
> All humbleness, all patience, and impatience,
> All purity, all trial, all obedience;
> And so am I for Phoebe.
>
> (*AYLI* 5.2.96–9)

Shakespeare's decision to retain the name 'Phoebe' but rewrite her in more complex, less immediately attractive terms may have been part of a strategic pattern of carnivalesque inversions designed for the Shrove Tuesday performance at Court.

(c) Lodge's full romance text *Rosalynde or Euphues' Golden Legacy* (London, 1590) appears in Bullough, Vol. II (1958: 158–256). Sections with reference to Phoebe are found on pp. 180–191, 227–33, 239–46 and 248–52. Juliet Dusinberre (2003) sets out the case for a court Shrovetide performance at Richmond Palace, on 20 February 1599. Her edition of the play discusses Phoebe's role as a parallel to Audrey's (pp. 34–6) and examines the words 'boystrous' and 'Phoebes' in the text (Dusinberre 2006: 131–2, 135–6). Newcomb (2004) surveys the figure of the shepherdess with reference to Elizabeth I and with brief reference to Phoebe.

Phrynia, (a) a character in *Timon of Athens* who is a **courtezan** to Alcibiades and appears with him and with **Timandra**, another **courtezan**, in one scene of the play.

Her name derives from Phryne, a famous courtezan of Athens, fourth century BC, who was called by this name (Greek for 'toad') because of her yellow complexion.

(b) Phryne, whose real name was Mnesarete, was 'Phryne in meriment because she looked pale or yellow like unto a kinde of frogge named in Greeke Phryne' (Plutarch 1603: 1195). Her nickname and colouring associate her with the imagery of gold and disease in *Timon*. Phryne was renowned for her beauty; Plutarch wondering 'what great dowry was it that she had all her lovers in such subjection under her?' (Plutarch 1603: 1137). Popular stories told how she earned so much as a courtezan that she promised to rebuild the walls of Thebes, 'vpon this condition, that vpon euery gate of the Citty, this sentence should be set; This Citty Alexander the great threw downe, and Phryne the Curtezan builded vpon againe' (Albott 1599: 51). She inspired and modelled for Apelles' painting of Aphrodite rising from the sea, having walked in naked with her hair loose. The preacher John King cites her as an archetypal **Venus**, saying that 'Al the Painters of Thebes painted her after the image of Phrine, a beautiful, but a notorious **harlot**' (King 1594: 109). When tried for blasphemy, Phryne persuaded her judges to be merciful to her by showing them her **bosom**. Plutarch recounts that when 'the famous courtisan' was about to be condemned to death for atheism, the orator

Hyperius 'brought the woman foorth in open court before the judges, rent her clothes, and shewed unto them her bare brest; which the judges seeing to be so white and faire, in regard of her very beautie absolved and dismissed her' (Plutarch 1603: 936).

Unlike Timandra, Phrynia is not named in the dialogue of *Timon of Athens* but is addressed first by Timon as a 'fell **whore**' who 'Hath in her more destruction' than Alicbiades' sword in spite of her 'cherubim look' (*Tim.* 4.3.62–3). Shakespeare may have named her Phrynia in the speech prefixes to invoke, with irony, the famous, wealthy Athenian courtezan who wanted to rebuild the walls of Thebes. Readers of the text would have known of her through reading or listening to texts by Plutarch, Montaigne, King and Albott. Shakespeare's Phrynia is hardly an example of outstanding oratory: her one line is a curse to Timon 'Thy lips rot off' (*Tim.* 4.3.64).

(c) Popular ideas about Phryne in the early modern period can be found in Plutarch (1603), pp. 936, 1137, 1195, John King's divine teachings (1594), p. 109, Robert Albott's popular guide to mythology (1599), p. 51 and Montaigne's, *Essays*, trans. John Florio. Kahn (1997), pp. 154–6 gives a critical reading of Phrynia and Timandra and the gold in this scene.

placket, (a) an opening at the front of a woman's skirt or petticoat which gives access to a pocket or to her genitals so it is often used metaphorically in the sense of vagina.

(b) Thersites uses placket in the vulgar sense to refer to **Helen** when he castigates the Greeks and Trojans as 'those that war for a placket' (*T&C* 2.3.20). Edgar as Poor Tom warns Lear to 'Keep thy foot out of brothels, thy hand out of plackets' (*KL* 3.4.96–7). Shakespeare's texts associate plackets with open sexual appetite. Berowne calls Cupid the 'prince of plackets, king of codpieces' (*LLL* 3.1.184). The shameless desire of Mopsa and Dorcas is likened to the opening in a skirt when the Clown complains, 'Will they wear their plackets where they should bear their faces?' (*WT* 4.4.242–4) and Autolycus uses it as a symbol of appetite and ravishment, saying that the crowd was so rapt with his wares that 'you might have pinch'd a placket, it was senseless' (*WT* 4.4.609–10).

(c) Arnold (1988: 148–9) discusses how the placket fitted with the other pieces of female costume.

Portia, (a) name of the heroine of *Merchant of Venice* and the wife of Brutus in *Julius Caesar*, whose name derives from the Roman family name 'Porcius', related to the word for 'pig'.

(b) Portia is a name that evokes strength and initiative in Shakespeare. The Roman Portia was the daughter of the hero of the Republic, Marcus Porcius Cato Uticensis who ultimately committed suicide rather than submitting to Caesar. According to Plutarch, Portia proved she had inherited her father's stoic qualities by wounding herself in the thigh. Shakespeare's character offers the same proof to Brutus but here specifically as a means to refute the assumptions about female inconstancy, weakness and loquaciousness:

> Think you I am no stronger than my sex,
> Being so father'd and so husbanded? . . .
> I have made strong proof of my constancy,
> Here, in the thigh; can I bear that with **patience**,
> And not my husband's secrets?
>
> (*JC* 2.1.296–302)

Not to share his secrets would make her, she claims, Brutus's **harlot** rather than his wife (*JC* 2.1.287), a detail taken from Plutarch (Bullough Vol. V 1964: 471). Appealing for constancy, Shakespeare's Portia duly overcomes the urge to talk even though she feels 'I have a man's mind, but a woman's might' (*JC* 2.4.6–8) and retreats inside to the traditionally domestic space with the words 'How weak a thing / The heart of **woman** is!' (*JC* 2.4.39–40). Portia's next actions show this is far from the case. As her father had famously committed suicide, Portia is true to her family name and Brutus learns she 'swallow'd fire' (*JC* 4.3.156). Albott gives the popular account of her: 'Portia the wife of Brutus, and daughter of Cato, when she heard that they both were deade, beeing carefully watched of her seruants, tooke the fire from the harth & swallowed the coales.' (Albott 1599: 103). North's translation of Plutarch, used by Shakespeare creates a headline in the marginal note: 'Porcia, Brutus wife, killed her selfe with burning coles' (Bullough Vol. V 1964: 131–2). Portia and her father thus both provide suicide models for Brutus.

The heroine of *Merchant of Venice* has the same admirable qualities of strength and determination as the Roman Portia. Jameson remarks on her 'high mental powers' and 'decision of purpose' (Jameson 2005: 79). Bassanio compares the two: 'Her name is Portia, nothing undervalu'd / To Cato's daughter, Brutus' Portia' (*Mer.* 1.1.165–6). The value of Portia in *Merchant of Venice* is measured in material terms. Because of her status as an heiress, she is a **commodity**, a golden fleece in a Venetian version of Jason's quest:

> her sunny locks
> Hang on her temples like a golden fleece,
> Which makes her seat of Belmont Colchis' strond,
> And many Jasons come in quest of her.
>
> (*Mer.* 1.1.169–72)

Portia (like the Roman Portia), shows respect for her father, obeying the terms of his will concerning the suitors. Her continued respect for the institutions of paternal authority is seen in her deft impersonation of Balthazar, the 'young doctor or Rome', and her strict adherence to the laws of Venice (*Mer.* 4.1.53–4). Her paternal inheritance from the Porcius family may even be hinted at in Launcelot's joke that in 'converting Jews to Christians you raise the price of pork' (*Mer.* 3.5.34–6). The model of self-sacrifice represented by Cato's daughter is also resonant when she compares herself to Hesione, the Trojan Princess offered to the sea-monster (*Mer.* 3.2.55–9). Her ostentatious self-surrender to Bassanio continues this role (*Mer.* 3.2.149–74). When Bassanio receives news of the threat to Antonio's life, Portia insists on sharing this grief, using the same arguments as her classical namesake: 'I am half yourself / And I must freely have the half of any thing / That this same paper brings you' (*Mer.* 3.2.248–50). Like the Roman Portia, the Venetian character works within the boundaries of patriarchal society to realize a form of agency. Winning back her **ring** from Bassanio and then giving it again on her own terms allows her to keep a sense of equality, or possibly even dominance, within **marriage**. To the late Victorian critic M. Leigh-Noel, Portia is a model of progressive female agency who retains 'the independence of her nature' and 'assumes the place of partner and not that of servant' with respect to her husband (Thompson and Roberts 1997: 180).

(c) North's translation of Plutarch's 'Life of Brutus' in which Portia is a prominent and integral part of his life, is in Bullough Vol V (1964: (esp.) 131–2). Albott (1599: p. 103) is an example of the early modern popular view of Portia. Martin Mueller (1991) examines how the figure of Portia in Plutarch influences her namesake in *Merchant* and other Shakespearean female characters, including a persuasive comparison of Hotspur and Kate but less convincing examples like Lady Macbeth and Cleopatra. Coppelia Kahn (1997: 98–103) reads Portia as constructing herself via her father in order to win Brutus's trust. Anna Jameson (2005: 75–97) sees Portia of Belmont as an admirably gifted character of intellect who 'discovers besides talents and powers she has also passions and affections' (p. 88). M. Leigh Noel in *Shakespeare's Garden of Girls* (1885) (extracts in Thompson and Roberts 1997: 179–81) believes Portia fails to see Bassanio's mercenary motives and regards him as unworthy of her. Jyotsna G. Singh (2000: 144–59) reads Portia's elegant subversion of gift exchange between men. Karen Newman (1987) considers Portia and Nerissa as mistresses of the structures of exchange while Jankowski (2000: 308–9) reads Nerissa and Portia's relationship as intimate, lasting and potentially erotic. Palfrey and Stern (2007: 392–408) analyse the part of Portia received by the **boy actor**. The actor Deborah Findlay (1993) gives an account of her approach to the role; Schafer (1998: 119–27) records the comments of Jude Kelly and Deborah Paige on directing the play with an emphasis on the staging of Portia.

princess, (a) a female member of a royal family, usually the daughter or granddaughter of a monarch. It is also used as a title for the wife of a prince or for a sibling or cousin of a monarch, and occasionally for a queen. Metaphorically, it is a term of praise for a woman or feminized object that surpasses all others.

(b) Shakespeare's texts use 'Princess' as a mark of status to signify both older and younger women. Although the historical Queen **Elizabeth** preferred the title 'Prince', at the christening in *Henry VIII* the Porter announces, 'Make way there for the Princess' and Garter King-At-Arms acclaims her as 'the high and mighty Princess of England, Elizabeth' (*HVIII* 5.3.87 and 5.4.2–3). Cranmer prophesies that the baby Elizabeth will be 'to the happiness of England / an aged princess' (*HVIII* 5.4.57). Cleopatra, another ruling sovereign past her salad days commits suicide in a manner 'fitting for a princess / Descended of so many royal kings' (*A&C* 5.2.326–7). To Kent, **Cordelia** is 'Kind and dear princess' (*KL* 4.7.28) rather than Queen of France, the title prioritizing her status as Lear's daughter. 'Princess **Dowager**' is a drop in status for **Katherine** of Aragon, formerly Queen of England but now titled as the **widow** of the former king (*HVIII* 3.2.70). **Imogen**'s status as 'Princess', a title by which she is introduced as the heir to the throne, is what makes her marriage to Posthumus so socially transgressive. Iachimo's appeal to her, 'Be not angry / Most mighty Princess' (*Cym.* 1.6.172), may be made from fear of her power as well as in flattery. He identifies her with Britain, 'I have belied a lady, / The princess of this country' (*Cym.* 5.3.3–4) and refers to her as 'the truest princess / That ever swore her faith' (*Cym.* 5.5.416–17). By the time all these lines were spoken, England had a young Princess Elizabeth (b. 19 August 1596), daughter to King James and Queen **Anna**. She had made appearances at court, taking part in the celebrations for her brother Henry's installation as Prince of Wales in 1610, including playing the part of **Nymph** of the Thames in Daniel's masque *Tethys' Festival* (Daniel 1995: 54–65). The idealized princesses of Shakespeare's late plays may include compliments to the marriageable young Elizabeth. **Marina**, for example, is idealized by Cleon as a lady 'Much less in blood than virtue, yet a princess / To equal any single crown o' the earth / I' the justice of compare!' (*Per.* 4.3.6–9).

In *The Winter's Tale*, 'princess' is the title that the young **Perdita** loses at her birth when Leontes rejects her as a bastard. **Paulina** forbids her husband to legitimize Leontes's slander, warning 'For ever / Unvenerable be thy hands, if thou / Takest up the princess by that forced baseness / Which he has put upon't!' (*WT* 2.3.77–80). Perdita gradually recovers her title: first as queen of the sheepshearing, then by masquerading as Princess of Lybia, until she is restored as Princess of Sicilia (*WT* 4.4, 5.1.86 and 157). Her romantic marriage to Prince Florizel may have appealed as court entertainments for Princess Elizabeth, since it was performed at court in the Christmas revels just before her wedding to Prince Frederick, Elector Palatine, in 1613.

In earlier plays, 'princess' still acts as a marker of status for younger women. When Henry woos Katherine in *Henry V*, for example, the two titles 'Princess' and 'Kate' neatly signify the mixture of political formality and romantic flirtation in the wooing scene (*HV* 5.2). **Celia**, the heir to Duke Frederick is referred to as 'Fair Princess' (*AYLI* 1.2.99). It is rather an empty title used for effect in the case of **Margaret**, daughter of the Reigner, King of Naples. Suffolk attempts to cover her lack of dowry with the flamboyant title of 'Princess Margaret' (*2HVI* 1.1.4). The use of 'princess' in Shakespeare's texts also draws on the romance tradition with a fairytale princess as the object of admiration. In *King John*, for example, Prince Arthur sentimentally recalls that his best handkerchief was a token: 'a princess wrought it me' (*KJ* 4.1.43). The title carries connotations of purity and value when the raped **Lucrece** is called a 'spotted princess' (*Luc.* 721). As a figure of pre-eminence, the fairytale princess is idealized as beautiful, learned, highly born and rich. **Blanch** is constructed as such by King John. He promises to

> gild her bridal bed and make her rich
> In titles, honours and promotions,

> As she in beauty, education, blood,
> Holds hand with any princess of the world.
>
> (*KJ* 2.1.491–4)

Miranda is probably the best-educated princess in Shakespeare but, interestingly, she is referred to as a 'prince' (perhaps reflecting Elizabeth I's choice of title to mark the masculinity of her learning and authority). Prospero tells her that as her 'schoolmaster' he has 'made thee more profit / Than other princes can that have more time / For vainer hours' (*Temp.* 1.2.172–4). Marina, who is idealised as the 'heir of kingdoms, and another life' to Pericles is to be acknowledged by Helicanus as 'thy very princess' (*Per.* 5.1.207 and 218).

The Princess of France in *Love's Labour's Lost* is never given any other name, perhaps to point up her political authority as the diplomatic representative of the King of France, and her suitability as a future bride of Ferdinand, King of Navarre. The most likely source for the character is a combination of the married Marguerite de Valois, who paid a diplomatic and romantic visit to Navarre in 1578, and Queen Elizabeth I on progress (Campbell [1925] in Londré 1997: 85–6; Hunt 1992). The Princess immediately points out the emptiness of Navarre's supposed greeting to a 'Fair Princess' (*LLL* 2.1.90) since he refuses her access to his palace. By remaining outside the gates in his park, however, she offers a lively representation of Elizabeth I's delights in hunting. 'The Princess comes to hunt here in the park' (*LLL* 3.1.163), Berowne announces and her subsequent banter with the Forester 'First praise me and again say no?' (*LLL* 4.1.14) may comment on the ways in which Elizabeth's courtiers continued the dangerous game of flattering an older princess. Costard cuts through all pretence of flattery by bluntly asking to speak to 'the head lady', to which she replies, 'Thou shalt know her, fellow, by the rest which have no heads' (*LLL* 3.1.44–5) alluding jokingly to Elizabeth's power over her subjects. Holofernes, like the writer of entertainments laid on for Elizabeth's royal progresses, renders all her activities into art: 'The preyful princess pierced and prick'd a pretty pleasing pricket' (*LLL* 4.4.56). The Princess's wry response to such entertainments is to disguise Rosaline to take her place and subvert the King's mask of Muscovites.

The French Princess deconstructs her name as a marker of absolute pre-eminence. The lover Demetrius, *Midsummer Night's Dream* offers a prime example of such courtly praise in calling **Helena**'s hand 'this princess of pure white, this seal of bliss' (*MND* 3.2.144). In *Love's Labour's Lost*, when Berowne teases the King that 'There is no certain princess that appears' (*LLL* 4.3.154) in his verses and tears, the princess is both heir of France, and the beloved, unparalleled mistress. The plot of masking and exchanging tokens so that each man woos the wrong mistress makes the Princess one of a group rather than an élite, distanced figure. Boyet asks, 'What would you with the Princess?' (*LLL* 5.2.178), and introduces Rosaline, the princess of Berowne's heart. The Princess's role-swapping device thus exposes the hyperbolic praise of the young men as superficial (*LLL* 5.2.220).

(c) Oscar J. Campbell's 1925 essay reproduced in Londré (ed.), *Love's Labour's Lost: Critical Essays* (1997: 83–116) sets out the possible combination of sources for the French Princess's role (pp. 85–8). Hunt (1992) traces a double representation of Queen Elizabeth in *Love's Labour's Lost*. Julie Campbell (2008) reads the French Princess and her ladies as a palimpsest of witty Continental female performance by French courtly women, based on Italian actresses. Palfrey (1997: 199–204) analyses the role of the princess in the late plays with brief reference to Princess Elizabeth. Ann Thompson (1990) considers Imogen as Princess of Britain. Yates (1975) discusses how Elizabeth I set the fashion for the nationally embodying Princess.

Progne, (a) Shakespeare's spelling of the name of the mythological character Procne, who conspired with her sister of Philomel, after the latter's rape by Tereus, Procne's husband (*see* **Philomel** above).
(b) Titus adopts the role of Procne in order to take revenge on Tamora by baking her sons in a pie, telling them 'For worse than Philomel you used my daughter / And worse than Progne will I be revenged' (*Tit.* 5.2.194–5).

prophetess, (a) a female prophet, someone with insight into the future.
(b) Shakespeare represents one unequivocally gifted prophetess in Cassandra and two more equivocal figures in Joan La **Pucelle** and Queen **Margaret**. In *Troilus and Cressida*, **Cassandra** enters '*raving with her hair about her ears*' with 'shrikes' [shrieks] to tell the Trojans she will fill their eyes 'with prophetic tears' for the fall of Troy. She correctly predicts a 'mass of moans to come', prophesying that 'Troy must not be, nor goodly Ilium stand' (*T&C* 2.2.101–9). Since the men dismiss her as 'mad' or infected with 'brain-sick raptures' (*T&C* 2.2.122), Cassandra's identity as a prophetess contributes to the play's project to satirize masculine honour and authority. In *Othello* the sybil who created the handkerchief personifies a similar threat to masculine authority with her ability to transcend time. Othello believe 'there's magic in the web of it' since she is 200 years old and 'in her prophetic **fury** sew'd the work' (*Oth.* 3.4.69–72).

The Catholic Joan La Pucelle's power of prophecy is strategically represented as ambiguous in *Henry VI Part I*. She is introduced as a holy maid with prophetic powers:

> The spirit of deep prophecy she hath
> Exceeding the nine sybils of old Rome
> What's past and what to come she can descry.
> (*1HVI* 1.2.55–7)

She gains a reputation as a national icon: 'a holy prophetess new risen up' who 'is come with a great power to raise the siege' of Orleans (*1HVI* 1.3.102–3). After the siege has been lifted, Charles calls France to 'triumph in thy glorious prophetess!' (*1HVI* 1.6.8). In 1597 she was condemned – from a Protestant perspective – by comparing her with the English prophetess, Elizabeth Barton, the Holy Maid of Kent, infamous for her proclamations: 'The hypocrisie of two counterfait holy maids, one of Kent in England, called Elizabeth Barton, the other of France, called Ioane la Pucelle (Beard 1597: 111). Queen **Margaret** is cast as an aged 'wither'd hag' with prophetic powers in *Richard III*. Marginalized from the Court, she intervenes to curse them all and bid them remember her warnings about Richard 'another day / When he shall split thy very heart with sorrow / And say poor Margaret was a prophetess' (*RIII* 1.3.298–300). Buckingham does remember this when he is sentenced to death in Act 5:

> Now Margaret's curse is fallen upon my head;
> "When he," quoth she, "shall split thy heart with sorrow,
> Remember Margaret was a prophetess."
>
> (*RIII* 5.1.25–7)

The actor Fiona Bell highlighted Margaret's prophetic, unworldly power by delivering her curses over the bones of her dead son, which she carried round in a black bag and laid out on the floor.

(c) Thomas Beard's *The Theatre of Gods Judgement* Vol. 1 (1597: xxii, 111). Diane Watt (2001) outlines the mediaeval and early modern tradition of English female prophets up to the outbreak of civil war, focusing on Margery Kempe, Elizabeth Barton, Anne Askew and Lady Eleanor Davies. Phyllis Mack (1992) and Hilary Hinds (1996) discuss later seventeenth-century female prophets. Fiona Bell (2004: (esp.) 179–82) describes connections between the two prophetesses Queen Margaret and Joan of Arc developed though productions of the first tetralogy.

Proserpina, (a) Roman name for Persephone, the daughter of the Greek gods Zeus and Demeter (Ceres in Roman mythology), who was abducted by Hades (or Dis) and taken to be queen of the underworld. **Ceres** wandered the earth, appealing to the gods to restore Proserpina to earth, which they granted, provided she had not eaten anything. Because she had consumed six pomegranate seeds, Proserpina was obliged to remain for six months below the earth but could return for the other six. Her story thus provides a narrative to explain the seasonal cycle; she is usually associated with the spring and the return of life to the earth.

(b) Perdita, whose own return from the Bohemian countryside to the Sicilian court turns the winter's tale of tragedy to comic resolution, appropriately invokes Proserpina as goddess of springtime flowers:

> O Proserpina,
> For the flowers now, that frighted thou let'st fall
> From Dis's waggon! daffodils,
> That come before the swallow dares, and take
> The winds of March with beauty; violets, dim,
> . . .   pale primroses
> That die unmarried ere they can behold
> Bright Phoebus in his strength
>
> (*WT* 4.4.116–24)

Because **flowers** are a metaphor for female virginity, Perdita's reference to Proserpina prophesies the loss of her virginity in marriage with Florizel as well as the impending disaster of Polixenes's discovery and refusal to grant their match. The Greek Thersites also refers to Proserpina as a model of beauty and thus envied by Cerberus (*T&C* 2.1.33–4).

(c) Janet S. Wolf (1994) discusses Paulina's appropriation of the mythological triple-headed goddess with Persephone / Proserpina as queen of the underworld. Stevie Davies (1986: 152–65) reads the Ceres / Demeter / Proserpina myth in relation to *The Winter's Tale*.

pucelle, (a) a maid or girl implicitly a virgin (from the French '*pucelle*'). With the definitive article, 'the Pucelle' was a name for Joan of Arc, the Holy Maid of France. In complete contrast, the early modern English 'puzzel' was a term for a **drab**, a **harlot** or a **courtezan**.

(b) The text of *Henry VI Part I* plays on the different meanings of the word to suggest the equivocal nature of Joan La Pucelle as young girl, holy maid (or **prophetess**), and **courtezan**. Thomas Churchyard, punning on pure and '*puer*' the Latin word for 'boy', had described Queen Elizabeth as 'Lyke pucell puer, a perll in peace and warrs.' (Churchyard 1575: fol. 94v). **Joan** cleverly conflates images of humble purity and kinship with the Virgin Mary when she introduces herself. Although by birth 'a shepherd's daughter' she has been touched by the **Virgin** and transformed from 'base vocation' and equally base 'black and swart' complextion as a divinely inspired champion of the French forces (*1HVI* 1.2.72–86). She is immediately a puzzle to the English forces because of her gender ambiguity:

> Burgundy: But what's that Pucelle whom they term so pure?
> Talbot: A maid, they say.
> Bedford: A maid? and be so martial?
> Burgundy: Pray God she prove not masculine ere long.
> (*1HVI* 2.1.20–2)

As a woman with a sword (making a pun on pucelle and the phallic term 'pizzle' meaning penis), Joan is both a **maid** and a man.

Minsheu's dictionary defined 'a Pusle' as '*trull, or stinking wench*' (Minsheu 1617: 393). The derogatory meaning of 'puzzel' may have derived from Protestant propaganda against Joan La Pucelle as a Catholic champion. Henri D'Estienne, for example, noted 'Some filthy queans, especially our puzzles of Paris' were disreputable women of the streets who picked purses (D'Estienne 1607: 98). In Shakespeare's play, 'Pucelle and her practisants' trick the English with disguises to sneak into Rouen (3.2.20). She is an object of erotic interest for the Dauphin: 'Impatiently I burn with thy desire; / Excellent Pucelle, if thy name be so / Let me thy servant not thy sovereign be' (1.2.109–11). She has power to defeat Talbot, making his mind whirl like a potter's wheel (1.6.19). Talbot captures all these ambiguities by memorably referring to her as 'Pucelle or puzzel, Dolphin or dogfish' (1.6.107). The derogatory associations of the name become dominant as the English dominate the action. Joan is demonized as 'Pucelle, that **witch**, that damned sorceress' (3.2.38), a view supported when she appears on stage with her fiends (5.3.1–23). She no longer refers to herself as Pucelle but as 'Joan', although the ambiguous associations of pucelle / puzzel remain until her last scene. She claims she is inspired by celestial grace, has been 'a virgin from tender infancy' and will die a virgin martyr but then claims that she is pregnant in order to save her life (5.4.36–91).

(c) The word is glossed in Minsheu (1617: 393) and used by Churchyard (1575) and D'Estienne (1607: 98) as noted above. Bloom (1992) compares dramatic representations of Joan La Pucelle, including Shakespeare's. Burns (2000: 25–7) analyses the dramatic character as an 'optical paradox', an anamorphic figure who can be viewed in two ways at once. Eggert (1999: 57–67) examines the construction of Joan La Pucelle in detail. Productions which challenged the English Protestant definition of Joan as a harlot are described in Knowles (2003: 272), Goy-Blanquet (2003) and Hodgdon (1991: 91).

punk, (a) a prostitute, originally a young man kept as a catamite or lover of an older man.

(b) The term is always derogatory in Shakespeare's texts. Lavatch claims there is nothing more perfectly matched than 'your French crown for your taffety punk' (*AWW* 2.2.22); the coin pays the taffeta-clad prostitute and she gives the customer a bald head, a symptom of the so-called 'French disease', syphilis. Taffeta was a fabric popular with prostitutes. The term 'punk' conjures up the plague of uncontrolled sexual activity in the Vienna of *Measure for Measure*. Even Mariana is diseased with it after her sexual assignation with Angelo. Lucio tells the Duke 'she may be a punk; for many of them are neither maid, widow, nor wife', characteristically speaking with a grain of truth here (*MM* 5.1.179–80). Even when the Duke remits his death sentence, Lucio dreads having to marry the prostitute whose baby he has fathered, arguing that 'Marrying a punk, my lord, is pressing to death, whipping, and hanging' (*MM* 5.1.522–3). The term also seems to include a **bawd**. As go-between for Falstaff and the merry wives, Mistress Quickly gains a reputation as a 'punk' who is 'one of Cupid's carriers' (*MWW* 2.2.135). Since the term also signified a catamite, it might well have implied a sexual relationship between apprenticed boy actors and their older masters.

(c) Williams (1994: 300) details taffeta as a cloth of the trade. Scott McMillin (2004) discusses **boy actors** as young men maintained by older masters.

Puzzel, *see* **pucelle**

quean, (a) a hussy or **harlot**.

(b) 'Quean' is a term associated with dirt in Shakespeare. Mistress **Quickly** angrily challenges Falstaff's order to 'throw the quean into the channel' (*2HIV* 2.1.47). Ironically, this is the fate that befalls Falstaff himself when disguised as the Old Woman of **Brainford** 'a **witch**, a quean, an old cozening quean!' (*MWW* 4.2.172). Read as an ironic reference to himself, Falstaff's line in *Henry IV Part II* suggests that *Merry Wives* was indeed composed between the two parts of *Henry IV*. The qualifying 'old' may support the idea that 'quean' usually referred to younger women, as in Middleton's *Your Five Gallants* (1604) where Bungler suggests that a quean is an apprentice whore: 'none goes in there [to Bridewell] but she comes out an arrant whore' (Middleton 2007: 3.4.143–4). 'Quean' is used in derogatory terms again in *All's Well* where Lavatch pairs up 'a scolding quean to a wrangling knave' as a perfect match (*AWW* 2.2.25–6). The comparison makes an additional common pairing between illegitimate female sexuality and disorderly speech. Shakespeare's references to 'queen' (*see* below) frequently exploit the pun on quean to suggest sexual innuendo or give a subversive derogatory edge to comments or forms of address.

(c) Middleton, *Your Five Gallants* [1608], in *Works* (2007: 594–636). Gordon Williams (1994: Vol 3, p. 127).

Queen, (a) a female sovereign such as a **goddess** of mythology, a female ruler of an independent state, or the **wife** or consort of a king. The term is also applied to a mock sovereign on a festive occasion, such as a May Queen. Metaphorically it signifies a female whose authority or pre-eminence is comparable to that of a queen. In Shakespeare's canon the characters Titania, Hippolyta, Hecuba, Helen, Margaret, Elizabeth, Anne (consort of Richard III), Isabel (consort of Richard II), Eleanor, Constance, Isabel (consort to King of France), Katherine of Aragon, Anne Bullen, Philippe of France (consort to Edward III), Tamora, Gertrude,

Cordelia, Cleopatra, Lady Macbeth, Thaisa, Hermione, the three Theban queens in *Two Noble Kinsmen*, Venus and Juno occupy the position of queens.

(b) Shakespeare's texts entitle goddesses as queens, as a mark of pre-eminence. **Juno** is referred to as 'queen of marriage' (*Per.* 2.3.30) by **Thaisa** who is herself 'queen a' th' feast' (*Per.* 2.3.17) in honour of her birthday and will soon become Pericles's wife and Queen of Tyre. As the pre-eminent goddess, Juno is welcomed to the stage in Prospero's masque as 'Highest Queen of state / Great Juno' (*Temp.* 4.1.101–2). **Diana**, the moon, is honoured as the 'pale queen of night' (*TGV* 4.2.100) and as 'silver shining queen' (*Luc.* 786). These goddess queens are represented exercising absolute power. John Knox had provoked debate over female rule by declaring that, on earth, things were very different. His infamous statement that 'to promote a woman to bear rule, superiority, dominion or empire above any nation of city is repugnant to nature, contumely to God, a thing most contrarious to his revealed will and approved ordinance, and finally it is the subversion of good order and all equity and justice' (Aughterson 1995; 138) did not go unchallenged. Defences of female rule were published by John Aylmer, John Leslie, Lord Henry Howard and Sir Thomas Smith (Shephard 1994: 26–37 and 86). Shakespeare's references to queens contribute to the debate, which continued throughout Elizabeth's lifetime. The absolute power of queenship, like that wielded by the goddesses, is regarded with some degree of cynicism. In *Richard III*, for example, Richard undermines Queen **Elizabeth**'s authority with the comment 'We are the queen's abjects, and must obey' (*RIII* 1.1.106). **Eleanor** argues that **Constance** wants to put her son Arthur on the throne 'That thou mayst be a queen, and cheque the world!' (*KJ* 2.1.123). A glimpse of queenly ambition for absolute power (perhaps with a backward glance to the rivalry between Elizabeth I and Mary Queen of Scots) is found in the description of **Lucrece**'s complexion where red and white fight for supremacy to be 'the other['s] queen' and 'The sovereignty of either being so great, / That oft they interchange each other's seat' (*Luc.* 66–70). The unfairness of power dynamics in a Queen's court is glanced at in Sonnet 96 which complains:

> As on the finger of a throned queen
> The basest jewel will be well esteem'd,
> So are those errors that in thee are seen
> To truths translated and for true things deem'd.
>
> (*Son.* 96.5–8)

Venus and Adonis creates a somewhat sadistic pleasure in removing the usual pre-eminence of **Venus** by showing the 'Poor queen of love, in thine own law forlorn / To love a cheek that smiles at thee in scorn' (*V&A* 251). The Fairy Queen, a title associated with Queen Elizabeth I since the publication of Spenser's poem *The Faerie Queene* (1590 and 1596), is another supernatural sovereign in Shakespeare's texts. Mercutio imagines Queen **Mab**'s pervasive power in shaping human fantasies (*R&J* 2.3); **Titania** is referred to four times as 'fairy queen' in *A Midsummer Night's Dream* (2.1.8, 2.2.12, 3.1.80 and 4.1.75) as part of the play's fantasy of a transfer of queenly power to patriarchal rule. A parodic representation of Titania's power is seen when Mistress **Quickly** appears as 'the Fairy Queen' in *Merry Wives of Windsor* (4.6.20 and 5.5.50). This comic turn probably inspired the appearance of Doll Common as the fairy queen in Jonson's *The Alchemist* (Jonson, 2011).

As a title of state, 'queen' carries resonance of tradition, power and romance. In a curiously patriotic reference, Boyet counters **Rosaline**'s tale of King Pippen of France with 'one as old, that was a woman when Queen Guinover of Britain was a little wench' (*LLL* 4.1.122–4). *The Tempest*'s imperial concerns are highlighted with references to the consorts **Claribel** as 'Queen of Tunis' and **Miranda** as future 'Queen of Naples' (*Temp.* 2.1.71 and 1.2.449–50). **Hermione**, Queen of Sicilia, is formally called to her trial as 'Hermione, queen to the worthy Leontes, king of Sicilia' (*WT* 3.2.12–13), although her subjection to the so-called worthy Leontes is rendered questionable. **Paulina** insists to the tyrant Leontes that Hermione is a 'Good queen, my lord, / Good queen; I say good queen' (*WT* 2.3.59–60). **Cleopatra** is 'the queen of Ptolemy' (*A&C* 1.4.6) exercising her power as 'dread queen' (3.3.8) over servants and messengers. By giving her 'the stablishment of Egypt' and making her 'Of lower Syria, Cyprus, Lydia, / Absolute queen' (*A&C* 3.6.11), Antony betrays the Roman imperialist ideal that would subordinate her. Cleopatra mocks this in her message to Caesar:

> If your master
> Would have a queen his beggar, you must tell him,
> That majesty, to keep decorum, must
> No less beg than a kingdom. If he please
> To give me conquer'd Egypt for my son,
> He gives me so much of mine own as I
> Will kneel to him with thanks.
> (*A&C* 5.2.15–21)

Cleopatra identifies with Egypt so strongly that she imagines her suicide as a means to ransom or save her people, bidding death 'come, and take a queen / Worthy many babes and beggars!' (*A&C* 5.2.47–8). Ritualized gesture and deportment are strategic means to mark the presence of a queen. When Queen **Margaret** visits France in *Henry VI Part III*, for example, King Lewis tells her

> Fair Queen of England, worthy Margaret,
> Sit down with us: it ill befits thy state
> And birth, that thou shouldst stand while Lewis doth sit.
> (*3HVI* 3.3.1–3)

She protests she must 'learn awhile to serve / Where kings command' since she can no longer count herself 'Great Albion's queen' (*3HVI* 3.3.7) but King Lewis refuses to accept her physical performance of subjection, possibly because it exposes the fragility of his own authority. Insisting she sit with him is a kinetic, ritualistic expression of support, prefiguring his verbal promise of soldiers to defend her position as Lancastrian Queen of England. In *Edward III* Copland's refusal to surrender his prisoner to Queen **Philippe** is seen as an insult. He will only kneel to the King, refusing to recognize more than 'his name' in the person of the consort (*EIII* 5.1.85–8). However, Philippe's pre-eminence as queen is implied in the play's last line. The play looks forward to the victorious return to England of 'three kings, two princes and a queen' (*EIII* 5.1.243).

Shakespeare's texts frequently emphasize the importance of spectacle as a means to establish queenly identity. Cleopatra's last commands to 'Show me, my women, like a queen: go fetch / My best attires' (*A&C* 5.2.226–7) are to recreate herself for death as Queen of Egypt and the Nile, a flamboyant spectacle of alterity to defy Octavius Caesar, who wishes to lead her in triumph through Rome. Although **Thaisa**'s burial at sea is rushed, Pericles uses the rites to re-establish her identity as 'this queen, worth all our mundane cost', when he requests 'give her burying; / She was the daughter of a king' (*Per.* 3.2.71).

Coronations are pivotal moments of spectacle in *Henry VI Part II* and *Henry VIII*. In the former, Henry VI thanks his court for their 'great favour' in entertaining the dowerless Margaret as 'my princely queen' and seeks to ratify this through her coronation: 'Come, let us in, and with all speed provide / To see her coronation be perform'd' (*2HVI* 1.1.73–4). The most elaborately staged coronation in Shakespeare is that of **Anne** Bullen who has been secretly married to the King and is then 'view'd in open as his queen' and processes across the stage to her coronation:

> *A canopy borne by four of the CINQUE-PORTS; under it, the* QUEEN *in her robe; in her hair richly adorned with pearl, crowned. On each side her, the Bishops of* LONDON *and* WINCHESTER. *The old* DUCHESS OF NORFOLK, *in a coronal of gold, wrought with flowers, bearing the Queen's train.*
>
> (*HVIII* 4.1.36SD)

The visual spectacle is supplemented by a detailed account of the off-stage sacred ceremony of coronation in which Anne kneels to her people and the Archbishop of Canterbury gives her 'all the royal makings of a queen', including the holy oil, 'Edward Confessor's crown, / The rod, and bird of peace, and all such emblems' (*HVIII* 4.1.85–89). For Richard III's consort Anne, the coronation ceremony is a perverted or maimed ritual that will bring pain. She declares:

> O would to God that the inclusive verge
> Of golden metal that must round my brow
> Were red-hot steel, to sear me to the brains!
> Anointed let me be with deadly venom,
> And die, ere men can say, "God save the Queen!"
>
> (*RIII* 4.1.58–62)

Less extreme forms of parody are the carnival recreations of queenship that emphasize its performative nature. Falstaff, the carnival king, tells the **bawd** Mistress Quickly 'weep not sweet queen' (*1HIV* 2.4.391). **Perdita** bitterly regrets her dream of being Florizel's queen, a role she has played as queen of the sheepshearing feast, and insists 'I'll queen it no inch farther, / But milk my ewes and weep' (*WT* 4.4.448–50). This recalls Elizabeth I's celebrated declaration 'if I were a milkmaid with a pail on mine arm, whereby my private person might be little set by, I would not foresake that single state to match myself with the greatest monarch' (Elizabeth I 2000: 170). Edward IV's consort **Elizabeth** makes a similar claim:

> I had rather be a country servant maid
> Than a great queen, with this condition,
> To be so baited, scorn'd, and stormed at.
> (*RIII* 1.3.106–8)

In the case of characters whose claims to sovereignty are tarnished or unstable, the rhetoric of majesty (both verbal and sartorial) is paradoxically a means of exposing their illegitimacy. Pandarus's effusive praise of **Helen** of Troy as 'Sweet queen, sweet queen! that's a sweet queen, i' faith' plays on the pun with **quean** meaning whore, to undermine her value (*T&C* 3.1.70). The Old **Lady** in *Henry VIII* simultaneously exposes Anne Bullen's ambition for the crown and delegitimizes her right to be queen using the same pun. Anne declares she 'would not be a queen' for all the riches under heaven but the Old Lady says that a bent threepence coin would hire her 'Old as I am to queen it', implicitly referring to Anne's status as the King's **courtezan** (*HVIII* 2.3.24–37). Hamlet bitterly undermines **Gertrude**'s sovereignty by telling her 'You are the Queen, your husband's brother's wife / And would it were not so, you are my mother' (*Ham.* 3.4.15–16). When Claudius carefully sets out Gertrude's status as 'our sometime sister, now our queen, / Th' imperial jointress to this warlike state' (*Ham.* 1.2.8–9) as a supplement to his own claim to the throne, the resonance of **Katherine** of Aragon's match to Henry VIII and the arguments about divorce would undoubtedly have sounded a note of rottenness at the heart of the Danish monarchy for some spectators.

The queen with the most insecure foundations to her rule in Shakespeare is **Margaret**, consort to Henry VI. Immediately after the formal welcome, 'Long Live Queen Margaret, England's happiness!' (*2HVI* 1.1.37), her lack of dowry transforms her from the nation's happiness, to 'England's dear-bought queen' (*2HVI* 1.1.252). Although her father is King of Naples, his lack of wealth compromises Queen Margaret throughout the four plays in which she appears. She resents the Duke of Gloucester's power: 'Am I a queen in title and in style, / And must be made a subject to a duke? (*2HVI* 1.3.48–9). Margaret's claim to sovereignty exposes it as performative and she is threatened by the queenly performances of others. The extravagant dress of **Eleanor**, **Duchess** of Gloucester means 'Strangers in court do take her for the Queen' (*2HVI* 1.3.79). York deconstructs Margaret's authority as 'proud queen' to insult the English nobility with the reminder that although her father 'bears the type of King of Naples, / Of both the Sicils and

Jerusalem', he is 'not so wealthy as an English yeoman' (*3HVI*1.4.121–3). Finally, in *Richard III*, Margaret remains on stage as a ghost queen, a vocal register of the emptiness of queenly power. When Elizabeth complains, 'Small joy have I in being England's queen' (*RIII* 1.3.153), Margaret asserts her pre-eminent claim to sorrow and authority:

> A little joy enjoys the queen thereof,
> For I am she, and altogether joyless.
> I can no longer hold me patient. *[Comes forward]*
> Hear me, you wrangling pirates, that fall out
> In sharing that which you have pill'd from me!
> Which of you trembles not that looks on me?
> If not, that, I being queen, you bow like subjects,
> Yet that, by you depos'd, you quake like rebels?
>   (*RIII* 1.3.154–61)

Although the rise and fall of kings is the immediate subject of Shakespeare's history plays, these texts also dramatize a similar, no less tragic pattern for queens. Weeping queens appear as potent symbols of loss in *Richard II* and *Two Noble Kinsmen*. While Richard II is unkinged by Bolingbroke, his consort is unqueened by grief. The royal gardener vows to plant rue 'in the remembrance of a weeping queen' (*RII* 3.4.107) and Richard calls her 'Good sometime queen' (*RII* 5.1.37). The '*three Queens*' of Thebes who appear before Theseus '*in black, with veils stain'd, with imperial crowns*' come to plead not only as **widows** for their husbands' bones but for protection of their own regal status since 'for our crowned heads we have no roof' (*TNK* 1.1.24SD and 52).

Queen Margaret expresses most feelingly the emotional pain of falling from power. The greatest curse she can place on her successor Elizabeth 'poor painted queen, vain flourish of my fortune!' (*RIII* 1.3.239) is to wish that

> Thyself a queen, for me that was a queen,
> Outlive thy glory like my wretched self!
> Long mayst thou live to wail thy children's death,
> And see another, as I see thee now,
> Deck'd in thy rights as thou art stall'd in mine!
>   (*RIII* 1.3.201–5)

Elizabeth, the **widow** of a knight who brings no substantial dowry or political alliance, threatens and infuriates Margaret because they are so alike. By Act 4, Margaret fully appreciates the grand mechanism of monarchy from a female perspective and advertises the theatricality of queenship, calling it 'The flattering index of a direful pageant; / One heav'd a-high, to be hurl'd down below' (*RIII* 4.4.85–6). Shakespeare takes the pattern of rise and fall further in *Titus Andronicus* where **Tamora** enacts a spectacular change of fortunes that appears to offer another critique of absolute female rule. Formally and formerly 'Queen of

Goths / (When Goths were Goths and Tamora was queen)' (*Tit.* 1.1.139–40), she opens the play as a 'distressed queen' (*Tit.* 1.1.103), imprisoned and pleading in vain to save her son's life. Once established as **empress** by **marriage** to Saturninus, she is transformed to the 'dread queen' who is deaf to Lavinia's plea 'O Tamora, be call'd a gentle queen, / And with thine own hands kill me in this place!' (*Tit.* 5.3.26 and 2.3.168–9) and finally overreaches herself by trying to mould herself as Vindicta, the goddess of **Revenge**.

Katherine of Aragon presents a more positive example of queenly resilience in *Henry VIII*. Her response to falling from power and being put on trial is to assert her royal integrity and transcend worldly misfortune by having her preeminence as 'queen of earthly queens' (*HVIII* 2.4.142) divinely legitimated through the heavenly vision which implicitly likens her to the **Virgin** queen. Katherine responds with spirit when she is formally summoned to the court: 'Say, Katharine Queen of England, come into the court' (*HVIII* 2.4.10), ignoring the summons, making her own way through the court and appealing on her knees to her husband (*HVIII* 2.4.11–12SD). She tells Wolsey

> I am about to weep; but, thinking that
> We are a queen (or long have dream'd so), certain
> The daughter of a king, my drops of tears
> I'll turn to sparks of fire.
>
> (*HVIII* 2.4.70–3)

For Katherine, queenship is the spark for female agency. Margaret makes the same argument to Suffolk, telling him that 'To be a queen in bondage is more vile / Than is a slave in base servility; / For princes should be free' (*1HVI* 5.3.112–14), suggesting the relative autonomy enjoyed by Elizabeth as both queen and prince. The word indicates exemplary emotional self-control as well as royal status and autonomy for Cordelia who is 'a queen / Over her passion, who, most rebel-like, / Sought to be king o'er her. (*KL* 4.3.13–15). Most inspiringly, once **Portia** has been won in marriage according to the terms of her father's will she still manages to remain 'Queen o'er myself' (*Mer.* 3.2.271), an autonomous agent rather than a subordinate **wife**.

Some Shakespearean references to 'queen' intertwine the rhetoric of majesty and that of courtly love to suggest the pre-eminence of a **mistress**. **Mortimer** romantically imagines that his wife's tongue makes Welsh sound like poetry, 'Sung by a fair queen in a summer's bower, / With ravishing division, to her lute' (*1HIV* 3.1.207–8). The perfectly matched turtle-dove and phoenix in Shakespeare's poem are an ideal picture of platonic love where 'Distance and no space was seen / 'Twixt this Turtle and his queen' (*PT* 30–1). More satirically, the King of Navarre's hyperbolic praise glorifies the **Princess** of France: 'O queen of queens, how far dost thou excel / No thought can think, nor tongue of mortal tell' (*LLL* 4.3.39–40). Orsino claims that it is not **Olivia**'s lands but her person, 'that miracle and queen of gems' that attracts him (*TN* 2.4.85), yet quickly redirects his attentions to **Viola** as his 'fancy's queen' (*TN* 5.1.388). The class differences between Count Orsino and his so-called queen are erased by the power of love here. When Parolles calls **Helena** 'queen', in *All's Well*, though, the term is loaded with reminders of what she is not:

> Parolles: 'Save you, fair queen!
> Helena: And you, monarch!
> Parolles: No.
> Helena: And no.
>
> (*AWW* 1.1.106–9)

As these direct lines make clear, although the word 'queen' and its synonym 'quean' are often used to deconstruct female royal authority, they invariably retain traces of power. It was perhaps inevitable during the last decade of **Elizabeth**'s reign and the early years of James's that, even when exposed as a figure of performance, the name 'queen' continued to resonate with a ghostly power on Shakespeare's stage.

(c) Extracts on female rule from John Knox's *First Blast of the Trumpet against the monstrous regiment of women* (1558), John Aylmer's *An Harborow for faithful and true subjects* (1559), John Leslie's *Defence of the honour of the right high, mighty and noble princess, Marie Queen of Scotland* (1569), Thomas Smith's *Commonwealth of England* (1589) are given in Aughterson (1995: 138–45). The debate provoked by Knox is discussed fully by Shephard (1994). Elizabeth I's 1567 comparison of herself to a milkmaid is in her *Collected Works* (2000: 170). Orgel's essay 'Gendering the Crown' (1996a) gives a short illustrated account of the hermaphrodite nature of sovereignty in England and France. Liz Oakley-Brown and Louise Wilkinson (eds.), *The Ritual and Rhetoric of Queenship: Medieval to Early Modern* (2009), is a selection of essays analysing representations of queenship. Findlay (1998: 164–201) deals with queenship and subjection in a selection of renaissance drama. Eggert (1999: 1–21 and 51–169) discusses queenship in the history plays (pp. 51–99), *Hamlet* (pp. 100–31), *Antony and Cleopatra* and *Winter's Tale* (pp. 132–69). Patricia Ann Lee's essay, 'Reflections of Power: Margaret of Anjou and the Dark Side of Queenship' (1986) is a useful account of Margaret of Anjou and sovereignty. For further reading on Elizabeth I *see* entry on **Elizabeth**.

Quickly, Mistress, (a) a character who appears in *Henry IV Parts I* and *II*, *Merry Wives of Windsor* and *Henry V*.

(b) Mistress Quickly is a character whose marital status and name change across the four plays in which she appears, so her name, meaning 'lively' as well as 'fast-moving', is an appropriate signifier of her shifting, fluid identity. In *Henry IV Part I* she is married to the tavern keeper. Prince Hal asks 'How doth thy husband? I love him well. He is an honest man' (*1HIV* 3.3.92–3). In *Henry IV Part II* she is **widow**ed and her first name appears to be '**Ursula**' (*2HIV* 1.2.240). Falstaff has long promised to marry her, proposing to her, as she remembers, in the dolphin chamber of her tavern. At the beginning of *Henry V*, she is married to Pistol, who refers to her as 'Nell'. Her role as **hostess** includes boarding 14 women who live by 'the prick of their needles' in the tavern (*HV* 2.1.33–4) so she is also a **bawd**, as suggested by reading her name as quick-lie (a quick route to 'laying', or having sex with, a partner, see Kökeritz 1950). Falstaff refers to her as a **quean** or **harlot** (*2HIV* 2.1.47). Her unintended sexual innuendo and considerable material assets make her the focus of the play's anxieties about sexualized female entrepreneurship and the 'levelling lawlessness' it represents (Howard and Rackin 1997: 179). In *Merry Wives of Windsor*, if not a bawd, Mistress Quickly is certainly a trickster and matchmaker. 'Send Quickly to Sir John to know his mind', says Mistress **Page**, punning on the name of their helper (*MWW* 4.2.82). Quickly follows this up by urging Sir John Falstaff, 'I must carry her word quickly' (*MWW* 3.5.46–7). She also plays off one suitor against another, taking money from Slender and Master Fenton to further their suits to **Anne** Page, even as she is fooling her master, Dr Caius, that Anne loves him (*MWW* 1.4). Pistol calls her a 'punk', and 'one of Cupid's carriers' (*MWW* 2.2.136). Mistress Quickly is characterized in maternal terms as Dr Caius's **maid**, 'in the manner of his **nurse**' (*MWW* 1.2.2–5) and his **housewife**: 'I keep his house: and I wash, wring, **brew**, **bake**, scour, dress meat and drink, make the beds and do all myself' (*MWW* 1.4.95–7). As a character whose name carries associations with sleight, deception and speed, she is an appropriate figure to preside over the gulling of Falstaff and the suitors at Herne's Oak. 'Dispatch it quickly' (*MWW* 5.3.3). Mistress Page directs Caius, little knowing that she will be outmanoeuvred. As 'radiant **Queen**' of the Fairies who 'hates **sluts** and sluttery' (*MWW* 5.5.46), Quickly is so different from the hostess of the history plays as to become a metaphor for the magical transformation from Eastcheap to Windsor which this domestic comedy makes, perhaps at the request of the Fairy Queen of the **Elizabeth**an court. If so, Quickly functions to 'debunk some of the most cherished and dangerous images of the reign' (Purkiss 1996: 94).

(c) Kökeritz (1950) discusses Mistress Quickly as 'quick-lie'. Purkiss (1996: 193–4) analyses her supernatural role; Anderson (2005) reads her as a servant, Forse (2004: 75) suggests the part of Quickly may have been a hit with theatregoers, so explaining the character's reappearance in four different plays. Howard and Rackin (1997: 176–85) offer a detailed reading of Quickly as a register for the disorderliness and social marginality that disrupt the hermetically sealed world of aristocratic masculine history. Edward Berry (2001: 133–58 (esp.) 140 and 156–7) sees Mistress Quickly's fairy role in *Merry Wives* as parodying the role of peacemaker. Peter Erickson (1987) and Freedman (1994) mention Mistress Quickly in their discussions of the evidence for a court performance of this play.

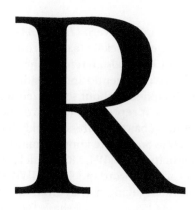

rape, (a) the act or crime, committed by a man, of forcing a woman to have sexual intercourse with him against her will, especially by means of threats or violence. (b) *The Rape of Lucrece* and *Titus Andronicus* constitute the most extensive treatments of this crime in the canon. These and other briefer references present rape as a savage act on the part of the male perpetrator; one which dishonours the woman and often the man as well. The legal guidebook *The Lawes Resolutions of Womens Rights* (T. E. 1632) reviewed centuries of legislation to find a remedy against 'so damnable a crime' which had been 'a cause of bitter complaint' for 'the whole Realme'. Elizabethan law 'for repressing of felonious rapes, and rauishments of women, and of felonious Burglaries', removed any exceptions to the death penalty for those found guilty of these crimes (ibid.: 401). The classification of burglary with rape demonstrates how, up until 1597, women's bodies were legally defined as property. The trivialization of female suffering implicit in such a definition is highlighted in the comparison of rape to a boyish trick: 'He will steal, sir, an egg out of a cloister. For rapes and ravishments he parallels Nessus' (*AWW* 4.3.250–1). Nessus was the Centaur who attempted to rape Deianeira, the wife of Hercules.

Rape was of two kinds: the first 'when a woman is enforced violently to sustaine the furie of brutish concupiscence' and the second being 'rape by abduction' of a woman, motivated as much by avarice as by lust (T. E. 1632: 387 and 381). In spite of the 1597 Act which moved some way to redefining rape as a defiling of the woman's person, 'to the disparagement of the said women' (Wynne-Davies 1991: 131–2), male characters in *Titus Andronicus* continue to define **Lavinia** as property. Saturninus refers to his brother's abduction of Lavinia as a rape: 'Traitor, if Rome have law or we have power, / Thou and thy faction shall repent this rape' (*Tit.* 1.1.403–4). However, Bassianus claims that Lavinia was already betrothed to him:

> Rape call you it, my lord, to seize my own,
> My true betrothed love, and now my wife?
> But let the laws of Rome determine all,
> Mean while am I possess'd of that is mine.
>
> (*Tit.* 1.1.405–8)

Following this model, where rape is an expression of male acquisitive power rather than lust, **Constance** accuses King John of having 'done a rape / Upon the maiden virtue of the crown' in seizing it (*KJ* 2.1.97–8). Paris defines his abduction of **Helen** in what sounds (to modern ears) a contradiction in terms as 'the soil of her fair rape' which he wants 'Wiped off, in honourable keeping her' (*T&C* 2.2.148–9). Regarded as a theft of male property, rape incites revenge in *Troilus and Cressida, The Rape of Lucrece* and *Titus Andronicus*. In *Lucrece* the Greeks are determined 'For Helen's rape the city to destroy, / Threat'ning cloud-kissing Ilion with annoy' (*Luc.* 1369–70). The Greeks' passing round **Cressida** to be 'kiss'd in general' (*T&C* 4.5.21) can also be read or played as a gang rape, a form of revenge for the Trojan rape of Helen. Lucrece's father and husband, Lavinia's father, brother and uncle all regard rape, the physical invasion of the female body, as a reason to launch military invasions which change the political structure. The male Andronici ally themselves with 'the woeful fere / And father of that chaste dishonoured **dame**', who swore revenge 'for Lucrece' rape' (*Tit.* 89–91). The Andronici swear 'mortal revenge upon these traitorous Goths' as though Lavinia's rape physicalizes the political invasion of the Roman state by Tamora and her sons (*Tit.* 4.1.93).

Lavinia's biological rape by Chiron and Demetrius highlights the crime as the violation of a person: emphasizing its emotional and physical consequences for the female victim. The move beyond the walls of Rome to the forest's 'unfrequented plots' that are 'Fitted by kind for rape and villany' (*Tit.* 2.1.115–16) stages a re-definition of rape from abduction to the violent enforcement of brutish concupiscence. This follows the archetypal story of **Philomel**'s rape in Ovid, in the 'ruthless, vast and gloomy woods' that nature has made 'for murders and for rapes' (*Tit.* 4.1.54–8). Lavinia's bloody appearance on stage with '*her **hands** cut off, and her **tongue** cut out, and ravish'd*', turning away her face 'for shame' physicalizes the violence of rape and its erasure of her identity (*Tit.* 2.4.1SD and 28). Taking a prompt from Ovid, her male relatives read her as 'the tragic tale of Philomel', the victim of 'Tereus' treason and his rape' (*Tit.* 4.1.47–8). Once Chiron and Demetrius are identified or 'decipher'd', as 'villains mark'd with rape' (*Tit.* 4.2.8–9), Chiron becomes a personification of Rape or Rapine (*Tit.* 5.1.61–2, 103 and 134), telling Titus 'Show me a villain that hath done a rape / And I am sent to be revenged on him' (*Tit.* 5.2.94–5). Their role as 'bloody villains' (*Tit.* 4.2.17), literally covered with Lavinia's blood, is finally inverted when she catches theirs after their throats are cut. *The Rape of Lucrece* concentrates on the emotional and psychological effects of rape and, while the heroine's apostrophe to Opportunity chastises it as fostering 'Wrath, envy, treason, rape and murther's rages', the word is not used directly of the heroine at all (*Luc.* 909). Its absence mirrors Lucrece's own determination to transcend her bodily pollution and reconceive of herself as pure: 'Though my gross blood be stain'd with this abuse, / Immaculate and spotless is my mind' (*Luc.* 1655–6). This revisionary self-definition, beyond ideas of woman as property, is so radical that there is, arguably, no place for Lucrece in the Rome of the poem. She compares her pain to that of the **ravish**ed Philomel, and imitates the mythical nightingale by stabbing herself in the breast (*Luc.* 1127–39).

(c) T. E. *The Lawes Resolutions of Women's Rights* (1632: 377–401) gives a lengthy account of English rape legislation. Catty (1999) surveys early modern writings of rape. See Robertson and Rose (2001) for a broader survey of medieval and early modern representations, especially pp. 189–241 for essays by Robin L. Bott and Karen Robertson on rape and revenge in *Titus*. Oakley-Brown (2006: 23–43) considers the importance of Ovid as a means of translating the experience of rape from body to rhetoric. Velz (1986) considers the difference between silent victims of rape in Ovid and those in Shakespeare's texts. Wynne-Davies (1991) reads Lavinia's rape with reference to the changes in Elizabethan legislation. Wilbern (1978) relates rape to revenge in a psychoanalytic reading of *Titus*. Belsey (2001) looks at how Lucrece is constructed as both person and property and Kietzman (1999) discusses Lucrece's redefinition of herself after the rape while Kahn (1997: 63–7) compares Lavinia and Lucrece. Mann (2008: 189–200) analyses stage representations of rape and Aebischer (2003: 24–54) considers stage and screen performances of Lavinia's rape.

ravish, (a) to carry away a woman by force or with violence. In early modern England the verb always implied rape. It also meant to plunder, rob, steal from or devastate, thus implicitly defining woman as property or territory when used in a sexual sense. Figuratively, it meant to draw a person forcibly into a condition or action, even to transport them from earth to heaven.

(b) T. E.'s legal guidebook *The Lawes Resolutions of Womens Rights* (1632) teased out the question 'what the difference is betwixt rauishment with force, and without force' citing one source which claimed 'all rauishment to bée forcible'. While conceding that 'no woman is rauished in this sort only by parroll, or influence of Rhetoricke', the guidebook went on to distinguish the 'more detestable villainy' where a man overcome with lust 'ouercommeth a woman hand to hand, by length of breath, and strength of his owne sinewes' (T. E. 1632: 396–7). Physical force is certainly implied when the word is used in military contexts in Shakespeare. War 'may be said to be a ravisher' (*Cor.* 4.5.226) in the Roman plays and history plays. Cominius warns the Roman citizens, 'You have holp to ravish your own daughters' (*Cor.* 4.6.81) by driving Coriolanus to fight with the Volscians. The superior political and physical power of the feudal *seigneurs* or masters is what allows them to oppress the common people 'take your houses over your heads, ravish your wives and daughters before your faces' (*2HVI* 4.8.29–31).

In private contexts, ravishing and murder are still closely linked. Macbeth imagines himself like 'wither'd murder' moving stealthily 'With Tarquin's ravishing strides' towards his design (*Mac.* 2.1.52–5). For Cloten, forcing himself on

Imogen and destroying and replacing his rival Posthumus carry a related erotic charge. He determines to put on Posthumus's clothes and 'with that suit upon my back, will I ravish her: first kill him, and in her eyes there shall she see my valour, which will then be a torment to her contempt' (*Cym.* 3.5.137–40). Ravishment also carries a magical, less tangible sense of force in Shakespearean references to speech. Don Armado, who loves 'the music of his own vain tongue' is transported since it 'Doth ravish like enchanting harmony' (*LLL* 1.1.166–7). Berowne's 'fair tongue' also threatens to enchant his listeners 'And younger hearings are quite ravished; / So sweet and voluble is his discourse' (*LLL* 2.1.75–6). These references may derive from the classical tradition of Jupiter ravishing mortals by means of his supernatural power.

Although women cannot rape in the biological sense they do have the power to ravish, even by force. **Regan** is condemned as a 'Naughty **lady**' for plucking Gloucester by the beard as a violation of the rules of hospitality and gentle conduct: 'These hairs which thou dost ravish from my chin / Will quicken, and accuse thee' (*KL* 3.7.37–9). **Margaret** of Anjou's power over Suffolk is likewise presented as forceful and deceptive since she has no **dowry**. Describing her 'chief perfections' would make 'a volume of enticing lines, / Able to ravish any dull conceit' (*1HVI* 5.5.12–15). When Henry VI meets her in person 'Her sight did ravish' and her speech was even more powerful (*2HVI* 1.1.32). In the description of **Rosaline** in *Love's Labour's Lost* the word 'ravish' is explicitly linked to deception. Her dark beauty shames the artifice of painted faces and artificial hair that 'ravish doters with a false aspect' (*LLL* 4.3.256).

(c) T. E. *The Lawes Resolution of Women's Rights* (London, 1632), outlines legal definitions of ravishment. For other further reading, *see* above under **rape**.

Regan, (a) second daughter to King Lear and wife to the Duke of Cornwall in *King Lear*. Her name can be identified with the Irish Gaelic word *ríogan*, 'queen', an identity she embraces when Lear resigns his kingdom.

(b) From the beginning of the play Regan is set in competition with her sister, cleverly overreaching Goneril's extravagant praise by saying she 'comes too short' (1.1.72). Although Regan avows she is 'made of that self metal as my sister' (1.1.69), she uses her new-found power as co-ruler differently. Regan finds it less easy to assume the queenly authority implied by her name and resorts to more extreme forms of cruelty as if to outdo her older sister. While **Goneril** acts out the role of careful **housewife** (1.4), Regan blatantly rejects it, refusing hospitality to Lear and Kent as she bids Gloucester 'shut up your doors' (2.2.134–5 and 2.4.304). Perhaps from anger and jealousy at Goneril's departure with Edmund, Regan then turns on her host, and supervises the binding and blinding of Gloucester. Her physical actions are confined to pulling his beard, the symbol of his manhood and power to rule. He calls her 'unmerciful' and wicked or 'Naughty lady' (3.7.32–36), a judgement apparently borne out by her demand that he be turned out of the gates as a traitor to 'smell / his way to Dover' (3.7.93–4). After Cornwall's death, Regan is queen and co-ruler in her own right, living up to her name *ríogan*. She is also free to marry Edmund and thwart her older sister's relationship with him. In a spontaneous betrothal she gives herself and her estate to Edmund before being poisoned by Goneril (5.3.74–8).

(c) The sources for the role are identified in Bullough, Vol. VII (1973: 269–402). Adelman (1992) argues that the play demonstrates that Regan and Goneril are the creation of Lear's fantasy of monstrous mothers but simultaneously embraces his view to present them as such. Alfar (2003: 79–110), argues the play locates evil and monstrosity in the tyranny of patrilineal absolute monarchy which Goneril and Regan learn to imitate and are finally subjected by. Waldo F. McNeir (1968) traces the love rivalry between the sisters and Regan's relative weakness.

Revenge, (a) a female personification, based on Tisiphone (the avenger), one of the three **Furies** in Greek mythology, and adopted as a disguise by Tamora in *Titus Andronicus*.

(b) Book 6 of Ovid's *Metamorphoses* recounts how Tisiphone helps Juno to take revenge on the house of Cadmus. Ovid's description of Tisiphone's appearance 'with horie ruffled heare', dangling snakes which twine round her hair, shoulders, breasts and 'hisse and spit out poyson greene' (Ovidius 2000: IV.587–8 and 610), offers a wonderful model for Tamora's disguise as 'Revenge, sent from th'infernal kingdom / To ease the gnawing vulture of thy mind' (*Tit.* 5.2.30–1). Tisiphone carries a poisoned syrup boiled in new-shed blood, a precursor of the stage image of Lavinia, holding the 'hateful liquor' of Chiron and Demetrius's blood (*Tit.* 5.2.199). Titus greets Revenge, 'Welcome, dread Fury, to my woeful house' (*Tit.* 5.2.82) and directs her to find a queen like herself and subject her to 'some violent death' (*Tit.* 5.2.106–9). Leaving her sons to be slaughtered by Titus, Tamora unwittingly fulfils her promise as Revenge to 'bring in the Empress and her sons', and make them 'stoop and kneel' (*Tit.* 5.2.116–17). By outwitting her, he appropriates the persona of 'sweet Revenge' (*Tit.* 5.2.146–7), and compares himself to the female figure of Progne avenging Lavinia as **Philomel**. The female personification Revenge probably derives from the feminine gender of the Latin term *vindicta*. The ghost in Marston's *Antonio's Revenge* (1600), asks that 'stern Vindicta towereth up aloft / That she may fall with a more weighty peise' [blow] (Marston 1978: 5.1.4). Since revenge operates outside the law or in its absence, the emergence of female revenge figured in the text of *Titus* dramatizes how the system of masculine justice has broken down in Rome.

(c) The description of Tisiphone is found in Ovid's *Metamorphoses*, Book 4, Lines 585–630 (Ovidius 2000: 101–3). Janet Clare (2006) discusses the satiric, farcical and improvisatory nature of revenge in Renaissance revenge tragedies. For more on the feminine character of revenge see Findlay (1998: 49–86). *See also* **Furies**.

ring, (a) a piece of jewellery worn on the finger by both sexes for ornamental purposes. Rings are also used to plight a troth between lovers and in the ceremony of marriage. Because of such rituals, a ring symbolizes a character's sexuality; its shape makes it an obvious metaphor for a woman's vagina.

(b) The **Courtezan** in *Comedy of Errors* draws on the sexual connotations of the term when she says she gave Antipholus of Syracuse her ring at dinner, in return for a gold chain (*Err.* 4.4.68). When payment is not made, she criminalizes the sexual act as theft or **rape**, telling **Adriana** that her enraged husband 'rush'd into my house, and took perforce / My ring away' (*Err.* 4.4.94–5 and 137–8). Because of the sexual meanings of the term, to be a 'ring-carrier' (*AWW* 3.5.92) is to be a **bawd** as well as a matchmaker. The most explicit definition of female sexuality as a ring occurs in Field's play, *Amends for Ladies* (1618), where Lord Proudly remarks 'Sure shee has an inuisible ring' and Feesimple replies 'Marrie she's the honester woman, for some of their rings are visible enough, the more shame for them' (Field 1618: sig. D3). Since Field was an actor later associated with the King's Men (Gurr 2004: 227), it is possible that his crude reference to women's sexual organs as rings was informed by the gentler but persistent sexual innuendo in Shakespeare's references to women and rings. It is intriguing to wonder whether Hamlet's hope that the visiting **boy actor**'s voice (and implicitly virginity) is not 'crack'd within the ring' may have been addressed to Field (*Ham.* 2.2.428). For a woman to offer a ring as a love token is a high-risk strategy. Olivia recognizes that in sending 'a ring in chase' of Cesario, she has abused her chaste reputation and set her 'honor at the stake' (*TN* 3.2.111–14).

The exchange of rings in troth-plighting is invariably a time of greater risk for female than for male characters. In *As You Like It* spring time is 'the only pretty ring time' for lovers, a time for sexual activity and the plighting of vows (*AYLI* 5.3.19). Between lovers a ring is a signal that 'May token to the future our past deeds' (*AWW* 4.2.63). **Juliet**'s ring represents comfort and hope to Romeo (*R&J* 3.3.165) when she sends it with the message 'Give this ring to my true knight / And bid him come and take last farewell' (*R&J* 3.2.142–3). It symbolically reaffirms their marriage pledge in spite of Tybalt's death, though her words are also chillingly accurate given the tragic conclusion. Romeo pretends he wants to enter the 'bed of death' or tomb 'chiefly to take thence from her dead finger / A precious ring' that he 'must use' but of course he will 'use' the precious ring of her sexuality by committing himself to death, with the early modern pun for orgasm, in the tomb with her (*R&J* 5.3.28–31). The most painful test of **Julia**'s love for Proteus comes when she has to offer the troth-plight ring she gave him to his new beloved, Silvia:

> This ring I gave him when he parted from me,
> To bind him to remember my good will;
> And now am I (unhappy messenger)
> To plead for that which I would not obtain,
> To carry that which I would have refus'd,
> To praise his faith which I would have disprais'd.
> (*TGV* 4.4.97–102)

It is a mark of **sister**ly solidarity in this play that **Silvia** refuses the ring, saying that 'Though his false finger have profaned the ring, / Mine shall not do his Julia so much wrong' (*TGV* 4.4.136–7). When Julia produces both Proteus's ring and her own, this final risk in revealing her true identity and shaming him does achieve a superficial romantic resolution, though its instability is signalled in the ease with which rings are exchanged or mistaken (*TGV* 5.4.88–115). The fashion of wearing rings on chains or ribbons round the neck or attached to the clothing or hair (Arnold 1988: 41) would have been an alternative way to display a token that belonged to a lover whose hands were of a different size from the wearer's.

Rings as pledges are emotionally significant objects lasting across time, perhaps most poignantly in Shylock's dismay at the loss of a ring Jessica traded for a monkey: 'Thou torturest me, Tubal. It was my turkis [turquoise], I had it of Leah when I was a bachelor. I would not have given it for a wilderness of monkeys' (*Mer.* 3.1.120–3). **Thaisa**'s reunion with her long-lost husband Pericles is confirmed when she recognizes the ring he was given at their wedding (*Per.* 5.3.38). More sadly, the death of Antigonus is confirmed by 'rings of his that **Paulina** knows' (*WT* 5.2.66). A grotesque ritual of troth plight is taken by the despairing **Constance** in *King John* who promises to kiss the 'carrion monster' death 'And ring these fingers with thy household worms' (*KJ* 3.4.29–31) since she has lost her son. When Richard of Gloucester tricks **Anne** into accepting his ring, his comment, 'Look, how this ring encompasseth thy finger', ominously predicts the claustrophobia and murder that will await her in **marriage** (*RIII* 1.2.203).

The most elaborate use of rings as props in Shakespeare occurs at the point between marriage and its consummation, a period which is lengthened in *The Merchant of Venice* and *All's Well That Ends Well*. In the former, the ring's significance is telegraphed unmistakeably to spectators and readers. **Portia** hands over

> This house, these servants, and this same myself
> Are yours – my lord's! – I give them with this ring,
> Which when you part from, lose, or give away,
> Let it presage the ruin of your love,
> And be my vantage to exclaim on you.
>
> (*Mer.* 3.2.170–4)

Nerissa's ring is likewise valuable for its symbolic significance rather than its material value. It is 'a hoop of gold, a paltry ring' inscribed with the words 'Love me, and leave me not' (*Mer.* 5.1.147–50). In spite of nominally occupying the subordinate position in marriage, Portia maintains control of her property and her sexuality by winning back her ring from Bassanio after the court scene. Antonio's insistence that Bassanio give the ring to the learned doctor as a token of his love to Antonio ''gainst you're wive's commandement' (*Mer.* 450–1) signals the continued emotional threat his love for Bassanio poses to the marriage. Bassanio's excuse and Portia's reply makes the competition between same-sex and heterosexual love explicit. He argues that her anger would be mitigated

> If you did know to whom I gave the ring,
> If you did know for whom I gave the ring,
> And how unwillingly I left the ring.
>
> (*Mer.* 5.1.193–5)

She, however, appreciates what is really at stake in this alternative pledge and spares no emphasis on Bassanio's betrayal of their marriage vows:

> If you had known the virtue of the ring,
> Or half her worthiness that gave the ring,
> Or your own honor to contain the ring,
> You would not then have parted with the ring.
>
> (*Mer.* 5.1.199–202)

Both Portia and Nerissa invoke the sexual associations of 'ring' to reclaim ownership of their sexuality and their agency in choosing where to bestow it. By threatening to sleep with the doctor and clerk who have the rings instead of their husbands, they raise the possibility of lesbian pairings as well as provoking male fears of cuckoldry. It is only Antonio's vow that Bassanio will be faithful to Portia that assures her sufficiently to give herself to him in marriage and, significantly, Antonio is the one who must ritually seal the **marriage** by giving the ring to his friend. Gratiano's concluding vow, 'while I live, I'll fear no other thing / So sore as keeping safe Nerissa's ring' (*Mer.* 5.1.306–7) comically accepts the need for care throughout marriage and the potentially dangerous agency which animates female sexuality.

An even more elaborate exchange of rings is found in *All's Well That Ends Well* as a trope for the mingled yarn of sexual desire, intimacy and marriage contracts. Rings point up the double sexual standard. Bertram's ring is the symbol of 'my house, mine honor, yea, my life' (*AWW* 4.2.52) his paternal family blood 'bequeathed down from many ancestors' (*AWW* 4.2.43) which should by rights be **Helena**'s. Diana argues that her **virgin**ity is just as valuable: 'Mine honor's such a ring: / My **chastity**'s the **jewel** of our house, / Bequeathed down from many ancestors' (*AWW* 4.2.45–7). The sexual exchange of the bed-trick to trap Bertram is symbolized when Diana promises 'on your finger, I'll put another ring', namely Helena's vagina (*AWW* 4.2.61–2). The possibility of an erotic dimension to Helena's cure of the King is signalled when he recognizes the ring and in it a curative power to bring life from death, a value 'That I have in this ring. 'Twas mine, 'twas Helen's, / Whoever gave it you' (*AWW* 5.3.101–5). Diana's refusal to claim the ring as her own prepares for the entrance of Helena with Bertram's ring as a confirmation that their marriage has been consummated (*AWW* 5.3.310).

In **marriage**, the ring is a symbol of faith, 'a token of our purposed endless continuance in that which we never ought to revoke' according to the Anglican theologian Richard Hooker, although some stricter reformers objected to wedding rings in the marriage ceremony as remnants of Catholic superstition. Nevertheless, their popularity as symbols persisted. In the words of Matthew Griffith, the ring signalled that the wife's heart 'is shut up, and sealed from love, or thought in that kind, of any other man' (Cressy 1997: 342–4). Adriana claims that if she committed adultery, her husband would 'from my false hand cut the wedding ring' (*Err.* 2.2.137). Although no Shakespeare play dramatizes this symbol of divorce, it is grotesquely realized in Heywood and Brome's *The*

Late Lancashire Witches (ll. 2445–6), and Middleton and Rowley's *The Changeling* (3.2.25–6). It is no accident that Iachimo's prize in the wager over Imogen's chastity is Posthumus's ring. Iachimo warns 'Your ring may be stolen too' in anticipation of his plot. Posthumus's willingness to gamble it demonstrates a male tendency to objectify and advertise female **chastity** which causes tragedy in *Lucrece* and *Othello*. Iachimo refers to both Imogen's vagina and the jewel when he confesses his goal was to 'win this ring / By hers and mine adultery' (*Cym.* 5.5.185–6) and ends the play by returning both the pledges: 'your ring first; / And here the **bracelet** of the truest princess / That ever swore her faith' (*Cym.* 5.5.415–17).

(c) Cressy (1997: 263–6, 273–4) details the use of rings in courtship and betrothal and the controversy over using rings in the marriage service is outlined on pp. 342–7. Arnold (1988: 15, 22, 41.53, 116–17) contains examples of pictures where rings are displayed on fingers, round the neck and on costume. Nathan Field, *Amends for Ladies* (1618) and Williamson (1972) and (1986: 49–52) offer early modern examples of explicit references to rings as figures for the vagina. Karen Newman's essay 'Portia's Ring' (1987) sets out the sexual commodification of women encapsulated by the ring metaphor.

Rosalind, (a) the heroine of *As You Like It*, and the longest female role in Shakespeare's plays. The name, from Latin and Spanish *rosa linda*, means 'beautiful rose' and may allude to Elizabeth I, whose iconography included the wild rose or eglantine. It is taken from Thomas Lodge's *Rosalynde* (1590), the most immediate source for the play.

(b) In a conversation encouraging Rosalind to remember happiness, **Celia** alludes to the floral origin by calling her cousin 'sweet Rose' and 'my dear Rose, be merry' (1.2.23), perhaps making a second pun on rosemary, 'for remembrance' (*Ham.* 4.5.175). Celia's reminder that she and her cousin are 'coupled and inseparable' also unconsciously assumes her name in saying they 'Rose at an instant, learned, played, ate together' (1.3.73–6) and indeed her father comments, 'She robs thee of thy name' (1.3.80).

Rosalind's name is crucial in the wooing scenes with Orlando: it is a demonstration of his obsession, a means of mocking the formalities of Petrarchan courtship and in moving beyond those in role play when, as Ganymede, she asks him to imagine her as Rosalind in order to test and develop his love for her. Orlando plays with Rosalind's name in the verses he hangs on the trees. At several points in Act 3 Scene 2 her name rhymes with long vowel sounds, 'lined' and 'mind', which Touchstone takes up and mocks in his additional lines ending with a bawdy reference to her name and deflowering her: 'He that sweetest rose will find / Must find love's prick – and Rosalind' (3.2.111–12). In other verses, Orlando rhymes Rosalind with 'Inde' and 'wind' (3.2.88–91; probably short vowels) and then promises to finish every sentence with 'Rosalinda' (3.2.137), punning poetry and legal sentences, a challenge that is (perhaps fortunately for spectators), not fulfilled. When Jaques remarks he does not like the name 'Rosalind', Orlando retorts 'there was no thought of pleasing you when she was christen'd'

(3.2.266–7). Rosalind takes him to task for carving the trees and 'deifying the name of Rosalind' in their barks (3.2.359–63) before proposing the role-play game in which 'Rosalind' will become an assumed identity by both the **boy actor** and the cross-dressed character (3.2.426–35). The action of the following wooing scene (4.2) demonstrates this deconstruction of woman as a 'beautiful rose' or silent object, when Rosalind shows Orlando a sample of the woman's wit and vivacity with which he must learn to be happy. Rosalind's faint on seeing Orlando's bloody handkerchief further demonstrates the complexity of 'counterfeiting' and essentialist gendered behaviour (4.3.165–82). The chanted pledges of the lovers, ending each time with 'And I for Rosalind' and 'And I for no woman' (5.2.85–102), assert the fictional female identity and, simultaneously, her absence from the all-male stage, something that the play's epilogue points up as a final reminder of the character's and the text's witty games with gender.

(b) Thomas Lodge, *Rosalynde: Euphues Golden Legacy* (1590) is the prose source of the play. Clare R. Kinney (1998: 291–315) compares the Rosalind of the play with those in Lodge's prose romance and Spenser's pastoral. Margaret Boerner Beckman (1978: 44–51) reads the role optimistically as a vehicle for magically harmonizing opposites in the play. Juliet Dusinberre (ed.), *As You Like It* (2006: (esp.) 9–31) and '*As You Like It*' (2003a) and 'Pancakes' (2003b) discusses connections between Rosalind and Queen Elizabeth, the play and the Elizabethan court. Palfrey and Stern (2007: 408–14) briefly analyse the part of Rosalind in from the roll or script received by the Elizabethan boy actor. Fiona Shaw and Juliet Stevenson (1988) describe the relationship between Celia and Rosalind in their performances of the roles and Carol Rutter, *Clamorous Voices* (1988: 97–121) gives actors' impressions of the part and the importance of the cousins' friendship. Penny Gay offers a brief stage history of interpretations from 1952–90 in *As She Likes It* (1994: 48–85). Stephen Orgel (1996: 53–82) reads Rosalind's disguise via the Ganymede figure in early modern culture. The role's multiple opportunities for transgressing or dissolving gender boundaries are explored in Catherine Belsey's pioneering essay, 'Disrupting sexual difference: meaning and gender in the comedies', focusing on the epilogue (1988) and in Valerie Traub's *Desire and Anxiety* (1992: 117–44).

Rosaline, (a) name of a character in *Love's Labour's Lost*, a maid of honour to the **Princess** of France, and beloved of Berowne. Rosaline is also the name of Romeo's first love in *Romeo and Juliet*. She is invited by name to the Capulet ball so may appear in the dance as a comparison to **Juliet**.

(b) Shakespeare's choice of this version of the name rather than the anglicized Latinate '*Rosa linda*' may allude back to the Old French name deriving from *hros* (horse) and *lind* (weak, tender, soft) (*ODN*). Neither Rosaline is tender, weak or soft however. They conform rather to Colin Clout's cruel mistress Rosalind in *The Shepheardes Calender* (1579), who is of 'hardest flint', 'voide of grace' and 'roote of all' his 'ruthlesse woe' so that finally, he bids her adieu as the year comes to an end (Spenser 1970: 442 and 466). Rosaline in *Romeo and Juliet* is Capulet's niece, advertising – even before he meets **Juliet** – Romeo's attraction to the unobtainable mistress. Although she is 'right fair', endowed with beauty and wisdom, she refuses to 'stay the siege of loving terms' and 'hath forsworn to love' (*R&J* 1.1.207, 212 223). Benvolio's promise to make the fair Rosaline look more like a crow than a swan in comparison with other beauties is fulfilled when Romeo sees Juliet, and echoes the lengthier inversion of romantic stereotypes in *Love's Labour's Lost*. In this play, Rosaline is introduced as wedded 'to her will' and plays up to role of hard-hearted, scornful mistress (*LLL* 2.1.212). Berowne challenges her to 'bruise me with scorn, confound me with a flout' and 'Cut me to pieces with thy keen conceit' (*LLL* 5.2.397–9). He romanticizes her as a 'gentle lady', saying 'When tongues speak sweetly, then they name her name / And Rosaline they call her' (*LLL* 3.1.165–7). Where she differs from the traditionally rose-like Rosalind, however, is in her looks: 'a velvet brow / With two pitch-balls stuck in her face for eyes' (*LLL* 3.1.196–7). While Berowne boasts that all the best complexions meet in her fair cheek, the King retorts 'thy love is black as ebony' (*LLL* 4.3.230–1 and 243). Berowne's only defence is to argue that her dark hair and eyes deconstruct the ideal of rose-like **beauty**:

> Her favor turns the fashion of the days,
> For native blood is counted painting now;
> And therefore red, that would avoid dispraise,
> Paints itself black, to imitate her brow.
> (*LLL* 4.3.258–61)

Rosaline's command to Berowne to 'move wild laughter in the throat of death' through the cold winter echoes the cruelty of Spenser's Rosalind, but Shakespeare's looks forward to 'reformation' (*LLL* 5.2.869) of an ultimately heartless wooing style. The Rosalind of *As You Like It* completes the reformation process with wit and love in her courtship of Orlando.

(c) The etymology of 'Rosaline' is found in the *Oxford Dictionary of Names*. Rosalind's cruelty to Colin Clout is detailed at the end of the June Eclogue in Spenser's *The Shepheardes Calender* (Spenser 1970: 415–67 (p. 442)). Peter Erickson (1981) argues that the play shows the unworkable nature of heterosexual relationships when they are cramped by the pure idolatry of women in courtship rituals. Lewis (2008) comments on Rosaline's reassessment of Berowne's wit as part of a process of reckoning or re-evaluation that this comedy addresses, as part of its own work in progress on courtship and romantic love.

ruff or ruff-band, (a) a gathered style of neckwear worn in early modern England by both men and women, in which a starched linen collar or band was gathered, often using heated sticks or pieces of steel to shape the material into figure-of-eight shapes. In the 1570s these were worn very close to the neck. By about 1586 the fashion changed to wider ruffs spreading further out from the face. From 1587 a shallower ruff also became more popular, sometimes worn with a slight opening at the front. In the 1590s deeper ruffs were worn open at the front, framing the neckline.

(b) Petruchio promises Katherina 'ruffs and cuffs' (*Shrew* 4.3.56), both starched items, among the many fashionable accessories of a lady, to wear for their visit to Baptista's house for Bianca's **wedding** feast. The haberdasher's 'ruffling treasure' (*Shrew* 4.3.60) refers to the gathers or pleats in the material of the gown and sleeves. The whore **Doll Tearsheet** probably wears an open-necked ruff since it is the subject of much sexual innuendo as Pistol promises to 'murther your ruff' (*2HIV* 2.4.135), implying that he will tear his way into her bodice, and Doll comments derisively that he cannot deserve the rank of captain simply 'for tearing a poor **whore**'s ruff in a bawdy house' (*2HIV* 2.4.144–5). Ruffs designed for women would have been important distinguishing features of the **boy actors**' costumes for female parts.

(c) Janet Arnold (1988: 15, 26–7) gives an illustrated account of the changing fashions in styles of ruff worn at Queen Elizabeth's court.

saint, (a) a person formally recognized by the Church for exceptional holiness of life, believed to occupy an elevated place in heaven and entitled to veneration of the faithful. In post-Reformation England, the celebration of saints was much reduced, although under Roman Catholicism they remained powerful influences with the ability to enact miracles from heaven. On earth, 'saint' could be used, sometimes ironically, to describe a person of extraordinary goodness, long-suffering tolerance and holiness of life. It was appropriated as part of secular courtly love discourse as a term of veneration for a mistress.

(b) Thomas Wilson's *A Christian Dictionarie* (1612) defined a saint in very Protestant terms as 'An holy one, or a person called to holinesse: such is euery faithfull person, hauing the perfect holinesse of Christ put vppon him, by imputation of Faith, and the quality of imperfect holinesse, powred into his heart, by the Spirit of sanctification' (Wilson 1612: 419). In line with this definition, there are no representations of canonized saints in Shakespeare's work (with the possible exception of the equivocal figure of Joan La **Pucelle**) but the term is applied to human characters to indicate goodness or mark veneration, especially in romantic contexts in which women are praised as saints. Echoes of Catholic veneration for saints occur in the canon in references to St **Anne**, St Crispian, St Denis, St **Katherine**, St Michael, St Nicholas, St Paul, St Peter, St Philip, St Valentine, and to the patron saints St David, St George and St James, and in numerous references to place names named after saints.

Lucio refers to **Isabella**, a novice intending to become one of the 'votarists of Saint Clare' (*MM* 1.4.5) as 'a thing enskied, and sainted, / By your renouncement an immortal spirit' (*MM* 1.4.34–5). She is thus to be talked with 'in sincerity / As with a saint' (*MM* 1.4.36–7). Her subsequent role interceding on behalf of her brother to save his life, and then to save Angelo's, reinforces the image set up by Lucio. Isabella herself sees a greater difference between humanity and the saints. Although 'Great men may jest with saints; 'tis wit in them, / But in the less, foul profanation' (*MM* 2.2.127–8). Angelo commits such profanation in regarding both Isabella and himself as saints: 'O cunning enemy that to catch a saint / With saints doth bait thy hook!' (*MM* 2.2.179–80). If Isabella is an instrument of the devil, then Angelo's subsequent behaviour certainly allies him with a false saintliness. **Luciana** takes the associations of religious hypocrisy one stage further: suggesting that Antipholus should disguise his adulterous desires and 'teach sin the carriage of a holy saint; / Be secret-false' to deceive his wife (*Err.* 3.2.14–15). The patriotic, protestant tone of *Henry VI Part I* likewise serves to discredit the French veneration of **Joan** La **Pucelle** as one who should replace 'Saint Denis' as 'France's saint' (*1HVI* 1.6.28–9). Since she was burned as a lapsed heretic and not canonized until 1920, original viewers of the play, whatever their beliefs, would not have credited Alençon's promise that 'We'll set thy statue in some holy place, / And have thee reverenc'd like a blessed saint' (*1HVI* 3.3.14–15) as prophetic. Even here, her humanity as being '*like* a blessed saint' is emphasized.

Katherine of Aragon in *Henry VIII* is much easier to read as saint-like because of her **patience** through suffering (a quality that even saints run short of, according to Baptista (*Shrew* 3.2.28)). This has been preceded by a life of 'saint-like' meekness; she is both 'Sovereign and pious' (*HVIII* 2.4.139–41). **Anne** Bullen tries to usurp this role at her coronation where 'she kneel'd, and saint-like / Cast her fair eyes to heaven, and pray'd devoutly' (*HVIII* 4.1.83–4), perhaps in imitation of Saint Anne, who gives birth to the Virgin Mary. Anne will give birth to the Virgin Queen, who, although mortal, will be claimed as an unspotted virgin by the saints after death (*HVIII* 5.4.60). However, Anne's reported performance of devotion is immediately and spectacularly upstaged by Katherine's heavenly vision. The stage spirits perform a pseudo-canonization, holding a '*spare garland over her head, at which the other four make reverend curtsies*' a process which is enacted three times as though dramatizing the approval of the Trinity. Katherine responds with '*rejoicing*' and *holdeth up her hands to heaven*' (*HVIII* 4.2.82SD). She thus exits life and the play looking forward to recognition in heaven for her saint-like behaviour. **Hermione** is another abused wife described as being saint-like. Anxious that Leontes does not marry again, **Paulina** conjures up an imagined scenario where Hermione's 'sainted spirit' will again 'possess her corpse' and 'on this stage' complain that her less worthy successor is better treated by Leontes (*WT* 5.1.57).

Secular uses of 'saint' in Shakespeare's work serve to venerate a romantic love object. Romeo's youth and the intense reciprocation of his love for Juliet lends their religious discourse integrity. Romeo, whose name is an Italian word for 'pilgrim', takes Juliet's hand as though touching a sacred statue: 'If I profane with my unworthiest hand / This holy shrine . . .'. When she tells him 'saints have hands that pilgrims' hands do touch', her speech animates her as a living 'dear saint' rather than a cold icon and leads gradually to their kiss (*R&J* 1.5.93–106). The imagery of worship allows Juliet to retain her modesty, to intercede as a saint to save her pilgrim from despair and to pursue her own desire: an earthly love that does not, in this case, seem profane. A more sceptical attitude to courtly love is voiced by Proteus who regards Silvia, the object of Valentine's 'worship', as an 'idol':

Valentine: Is she not a heavenly saint?
Proteus: No; but she is an earthly paragon.
Valentine: Call her divine.
Proteus: I will not flatter her.

(*TGV* 2.4.145–7)

The Rape of Lucrece repeats the idea that women cannot be saints, however virtuous and admirable their lives. Lucrece is praised for her innocence as 'this earthly saint' who 'little suspecteth the false worshipper', the 'devil' Tarquin (*Luc.* 85–6). The religious language of courtship serves to highlight mixed monetary and moral values in *The Merchant of Venice*. Morocco says that Portia's suitors come like pilgrims 'To kiss this shrine, this mortal breathing saint' (*Mer.* 2.7.39–40). The play's Christian framework is further undermined by Portia's racist observation that even if Prince of Morocco has 'the condition of saint, and the complexion of a devil', she would not like to marry him. Sonnet 144 plays out the most extreme inversion of the courtly love convention by presenting the young man as the 'saint' corrupted by the 'devil' in the form of the dark lady who woos his 'purity' with her 'foul pride' (*Son.* 144.7–8). The proud mistress is sexually active rather than remote and so loses her qualification to pose as a saintly icon of male worship, becoming instead the corporeal location of hell.

(c) Thomas Wilson, *A Christian Dictionarie* (1612) gives the definition above citing biblical authority. Eamon Duffy *The Stripping of the Altars*, (1992: 155–205) analyses the cult of the saints in early modern England before and after the Reformation. Bell (1998: 15–32) considers the poetics of Elizabethan courtship; Maassen (2005) uses Romeo and Juliet's exchange to explore the use of religious rhetoric in sonnets.

school-maid, (a) a girl who attends school.

(b) Although in general girls had fewer opportunities for formal education than boys, some girls did attend local dame schools where they were taught to read, sew, spin and knit (Greer 2007: 53–4). **Isabella** refers to herself and **Juliet** as former 'school-maids' who swapped confidences and adopted the title of 'cousins' to show their close friendship (*MM* 1.4.47–8). **Helena** likewise refers to the 'school-days friendship, childhood innocence' she shared with **Hermia**. Their education seems to have involved needlework, singing and the study of heraldry, all useful skills in attracting a husband from an appropriate family (*MND* 3.2.202).

(c) Greer (2007: 53–4) describes dame schools and Charlton (1999) gives a broader survey of educational opportunities for women.

scold, (a) an outspoken woman whose verbal insubordination was frequently accompanied by other forms of unruly behaviour designed to flout the male authority which sought to control her. In early modern England, such behaviour was swiftly identified as a symptom of disorder and could be punished by public shaming rituals using the cucking stool or the scold's bridle. The former was a cart with a chair mounted on it, used to take the scold or **shrew** through the streets and duck or lower her into the water (a pond or river), so silencing her. The scold's bridle was an iron framework that fitted over the head to enclose it with a sharp metal gag or bit which entered the mouth and restrained the tongue to stop speech completely. Less brutally, a wisp of straw was given as a mark of disgrace for a scold.

(b) The Clown in *All's Well* thinks that a 'scolding **quean**' is the perfect match for 'a wrangling knave' (*AWW* 2.2.25–6), and Shakespeare tests out this thesis in the romantic plots of *The Taming of the Shrew* and *Much Ado About Nothing*. Petruchio knows Katherina by reputation as 'an irksome brawling scold' (*Shrew* 1.2.187), since she is 'renowned in Padua for her scolding **tongue**' (*Shrew* 1.2.100). As Grumio appears to know from experience, however, and as Katherina finds when she reaches Petruchio's house, his scolding tongue is even worse than hers, so 'she would think scolding would do little good upon him' (*Shrew* 1.2.108–9). In the less disturbing plot of the merry war between Benedick and **Beatrice**, Beatrice's sharp tongue has animated even Benedick's mask to retaliate with scolding. He complains 'while she is here a man may live as quiet in hell' since 'all disquiet, horror, and perturbation follows her' (*MAdo* 2.1.257–61). Women's outspokenness in the history plays is tolerated even less. Richard of Gloucester condemns Queen **Margaret** as a 'scold' who has usurped her husband's breeches and should not be allowed to live 'to fill the world with words' (*3HVI* 5.5.29, 44). Edward claims she should be given 'a wisp of straw' to shame her as a scold (*3HVI* 2.2.144). Female characters slander each other with the name too. In the battle for their sons' claims to the throne, Queen **Eleanor** refers to **Constance** as 'Thou unadvised scold' (*KJ* 2.1.191) in an attempt to discredit her protest that King John's claim is illegitimate. The **mother**s dominate the stage in this exchange, leaving the kings who supposedly have authority looking somewhat powerless. Paulina's assertive speech in *The Winter's Tale* leads the tyrannical Leontes to condemn her as 'a **callet** / Of boundless tongue', this being another term for a scold.

(c) David Underdown, 'The Taming of the Scold: The Enforcement of Patriarchal Authority in Early Modern England' (1987) details early modern practices for dealing with scolds. Boose's illustrated article (1991), examines how literary representation of scolds engage with the condemned social type. *See* **tongue**, **shrew**, **callet**.

Scylla, (a) a rock between Italy and Sicily near **Charybdis**, the whirlpool. Scylla was the daughter of Phorcys, transformed by **Circe** from a beautiful nymph into a sea monster with dogs about her lower limbs, and then into a rock.

(b) Shakespeare would have known the story from Golding's translation of Ovid's *Metamorphoses*, Book 14, lines 1–88 (Ovidius 2000: 350–2). The dangers of sailing here are alluded to by Launcelot Gobbo who tells Jessica that she cannot avoid being damned, because if she clings to the hope she is not Shylock's daughter, she will be damned by the adultery or sins of her mother: 'thus when I shun Scylla, your father, I fall into Charybdis, your mother. Well, you are gone both ways' (*Mer.* 3.5.16–18). Sylla, a Roman dictator, is phonetically conflated with the female sea monster when Suffolk is compared to 'Sylla, overgorged / With gobbets

of thy mother's bleeding heart' (*2HVI* 4.1.83–5).
(c) The reference to Scylla in Golding's 1567 translation of Ovid's *Metamorphoses*, is in Book 14, lines 1–88 (Ovidius 2000: 350–2).

Semiramis, (a) an Amazonian queen from Greek myth.
(b) Although Semiramis was a well-known figure in early modern England, celebrated in texts like Pisan's *Book of the City of Ladies* and included in Jonson's *Masque of Queens*, she is only mentioned once in Shakespeare, and the reference is derogatory to Tamora. By arranging the brutal stabbing of Bassianus, Tamora has outdone even Semiramis's cruelty. Lavinia says: 'Semiramis, nay barbarous Tamora / No name fits thy nature but thy own!' (*Tit.* 2.3.118). Jeffrey Kahan (2005) points out that this reference may, in turn, have inspired Massinger, another King's Men playwright, to use it in his play *The Picture* (1629).
(c) Christine de Pisan, *The Boke of the Cyte of Ladyes*, translated by Bryan Ansley (1521) gives an account of Semiramis as a virtuous figure (GG1–GG2). Jeffrey Kahan, 'A Further Note on Semiramis' (2005: 27–8) considers Massinger.

sew, (a) to create or repair something out of fabric by making stitches using a needle and thread. To be able to handle a needle and sew well was deemed a feminine virtue in early modern England, often associated with the arts of spinning and weaving.
(b) Scenes of women sewing occur in *Coriolanus* and *Henry VIII*, both with the intention of representing the characters as models of female **housewife**ly virtue. Queen **Katherine** is staged with '*her Women as at work*' while her enemies plot in court (*HVIII* 3.1.1SD). She cleverly uses the needlework to introduce herself as a 'huswife' (*HVIII* 3.1.24) and advertise her innocence and virtue to the Cardinals:

> I was set at work
> Among my **maid**s, full little, God knows, looking
> Either for such men or such business.
>
> (*HVIII* 3.1.74–6)

Essentially a domestic activity, sewing showed that woman's industry, identity and place were in the home rather than in the public sphere of male activity. While Coriolanus fights abroad, his wife and mother sit down on two low stools to sew and to care for the child Martius. Valeria praises them as 'manifest housewives', admiring the 'fine spot' or piece of embroidery worked by **Virgilia** (*Cor.* 1.3.51–3). Virgilia's refusal to leave the house and her frenzied commitment to domestic industry emphasizes her **wife**ly modesty. Valeria comments, 'I would your cambric were as sensible as your finger, that you might leave pricking it for pity' (*Cor.* 1.3.84–6). For **Volumnia**, sewing is a substitute for the epic military world enjoyed by her son. Chapman described sewing for women as a means of ordering and releasing emotions: 'That their plied wits in numbred silks might sing / Passions huge conquest and their needels leading / Affection prisoner through their own built citties' (Jones and Stallybrass 2000: 142). Sewing is an essential mode of female expression. **Philomel** who 'lost her **tongue**, / And in a tedious sampler sew'd her mind' (*Tit.* 2.4.38–9) symbolizes the culturally silenced women who used samplers and embroidery to speak creatively. Such expression is denied to **Lavinia** whose rapists have cut her **hand**s and 'pretty fingers off, / That could have better sew'd than Philomel' (*Tit.* 2.4.42–3), so she must finally resort to a massive stump or pen to write their names. As a form of passionate female expression, sewing is potentially subversive (Parker 1984). The embroidered handkerchief in *Othello*, for example, is woven with ancient feminine wisdom. A **sibyl** 200 years old 'in her prophetic fury sew'd the work' and Othello believes 'there's magic in the web of it' (*Oth.* 3.4.69–72).

Sewing is a feminine accomplishment that crosses class boundaries. In addition to royal **Katherine** and the Roman nobility, the court lady **Ophelia** says that she was surprised by Hamlet as she was 'sewing in her closet' (*Ham.* 2.1.74). **Bianca**, wealthy co-heiress of Baptista, is directed to sew (*Shrew* 2.1.25) and, further down the social scale '*Item*, She can sew' is listed as one of the accomplishments of the servant Launce's girlfriend (*TGV* 3.1.306). Thomas Trusser's *Hundred Good Points of Housewifery* included sewing and mending:

> Good sempsters be sowing of pretty fine knacks
> good housewives by mending and piecing their sacks
> Though making and mending be housewifely ways
> yet mending in time is the housewife to praise.
> Though ladies may rend and buy new every day,
> good housewives must mend and buy new as they may.
> (Quoted in Aughterson 1995: 202)

For **Marina**, and **Bianca**, sewing is a financial asset. Marina says her ability to 'sing, weave, sew and dance' (*Per.* 4.6.183) should recommend her for employment in an honest house and she is the only Shakespearean heroine to earn her own living. The work she undertakes and teaches is embroidery, the craft of gentle and noble women which uses expensive silk thread. The skill and imagination it requires is clear from Gower's description of Marina, who

> with her needle composes
> Nature's own shape of bud, bird, branch, or berry,
> That even her art **sisters** the natural roses;
> Her inkle, silk, twin with the rubied cherry,
> That pupils lacks she none of noble race,
> Who pour their bounty on her;
> (*Per.* Gower 5.6–10)

Bianca in *Othello* also works in silk embroidery, we assume, since Cassio asks her to copy the handkerchief. She is a 'huswife that by selling her desires / Buys herself bread and clothes' (*Oth.* 4.1.94–5), or 'cloath' as the Folio text says, meaning cloth, and so possibly indicating that she maintains herself through sewing or embroidery as well as by selling her sexual favours (Callaghan 2001: 64–5).

(c) Excerpts from Thomas Trusser's *Hundred Points of Housewifery* (1557: sigs 29r–35v) are reprinted in Aughterson (1995: 198–203). Chapman's verse, describing Hero's embroidery of a scarf in his translation of *Hero and Leander* (1616), is quoted in Jones and Stallybrass (2000: 134–44 (esp.) 142) in a section detailing attitudes to sewing and embroidery as important female tasks. Roszika Parker's *The Subversive Stitch* (1984) considers the making of the feminine through needlework. Lisa Klein (1997) analyses Elizabethan needlework. Callaghan (2001) discusses the importance of textiles in *Othello*. *See also* **spinster**.

sex, (a) a mark of distinction between male and female humans and many other living creatures, based on their biological reproductive functions.

(b) Robert Cawdry's *Table Alphabeticall* (1604) glosses 'sex' simply as 'kind' but Wilson's *Christian Dictionarie* employs a more modern sense, the act of copulation, when defining **chastity** as an abstinence 'from all strange and roving lusts, about the desire of Sex' (Wilson 1612: sig. 50). Shakespeare's texts use it in the former sense as a marker of kind. 'Sex' is used exclusively of women, by both male and female characters, as though male identity is the invisible norm. The extreme forms of anxiety about sexual difference that preoccupy male characters produce views designed to derogate the female sex. Benedick, for example, declares himself a 'professed tyrant to their sex' (*MAdo* 1.1.169) though his supposed misogyny moderates during the play. Arising from the male need to overmaster the opposite sex, references invariably define female inferiority. **Cleopatra** is to be led in triumph by the victorious Octavius Caesar 'like the greatest spot / Of all thy sex (*A&C* 4.12.35–6). 'Their gentle sex to weep are often willing' (*Luc.* 1237) we are told, denoting an emotional rather than rational or active response to events. **Cressida** relies on such misogyny to make an excuse for her own behaviour. 'Ah, poor our sex! this fault in us I find, / The error of our eye directs our mind' (*T&C* 5.2.109–10). The text may even hint that she is moulded by the stereotype of woman's inconstancy. Cleopatra uses misogynist assumptions more cunningly, confessing 'I have / Been laden with like frailties which before / Have often shamed our sex' merely as a performance to deceive Octavius Caesar (*A&C* 5.2.122–4).

Troilus is anxious not 'To square the general sex / By Cressid's rule' (*T&C* 5.1.132), a principle that Shakespeare's texts follow in showing that women's supposed frailties are not biologically determined. **Helena** in *All's Well* has reversed the violent hierarchy of male supremacy. Lafeu, adopting the conventionally feminine position, reports that 'in her sex, her years, profession, / Wisdom and constancy' she 'hath amaz'd me more / Than I dare blame my weakness' (*AWW* 2.1.83–5). Helena's namesake in *A Midsummer Night's Dream* defies the stereotypical gendered behaviour in courtship. Her determined romantic pursuit of Demetrius and conflict with **Hermia** gives the lie to her protestation

Your wrongs do set a scandal on my sex.
We cannot fight for love, as men may do.
We should be wooed and were not made to woo.

(*MND* 2.1.240–2)

By this score, **Viola**'s wooing of Olivia, to say nothing of her forced handling of a weapon in Toby's duel, are actions 'much against the mettle of your sex' (*TN* 5.1.321). **Joan** La **Pucelle** works against the mettle of her sex by military means: 'My courage try by combat, if thou darest, / And thou shalt find that I exceed my sex (*1HVI* 1.2.89–90), something she proves by defeating the Dauphin and Talbot. In battle, Queen **Margaret** inverts the assumption that 'Their gentle sex to weep are often willing' (*Luc.* 1237) by failing to show any emotion or pity over Rutland's murder while Northumberland and York are 'weeping-ripe'. York tells her 'How ill-beseeming is it in thy sex / To triumph, like an **Amazon**ian **trull**, / Upon their woes whom **fortune** captivates!' (*3HVI* 1.4.113–15). More positively, **Hermione** stoically declares 'I am not prone to weeping, as our sex / Commonly are' (*WT* 2.1.108–9).

Even though such positive and negative examples show that behaviour is not biologically determined, female attempts to transcend the supposed limitations of their sex invariably constitute something of a betrayal. 'Think you I am no stronger than my sex?' says Roman **Portia** (*JC* 2.1.296), inevitably devaluing the gentler qualities held by women who choose not to give themselves voluntary wounds by thrusting knives into their thighs or swallowing coals. **Imogen** wants to 'change my sex' to be companion with her brothers (*Cym.* 3.6.87). Betraying one's sex, a repeated pattern in Shakespeare, holds dangers for women. Lady **Macbeth**'s invocation of spirits to 'unsex me here, / And fill me from the crown to the toe top-full / Of direst cruelty!' is deemed demonic and leads only to madness and death (*Mac.* 1.5.41–3). **Isabella**'s more positive betrayal in attempting to transcend women's faults in the cloister still has the crucially damaging effect of separating her from other women, to whom she refers in the third person. They are, she says, as frail 'as the glasses where they view themselves' (*MM* 2.4.125). This gives Angelo the weapon he needs to undermine her authority as an agent of religious and moral authority. Using 'this testimony of your own sex' he insists she conform to the 'destined livery' of subjection (*MM* 2.4.28–38). **Rosalind**'s male disguise likewise separates her from her own sex and its interests. As Ganymede, she refers to 'their sex' adopting a misogynist tone to 'thank God' she has escaped the 'many giddy offences' her uncle 'hath generally tax'd their whole sex withal' (*AYLI* 3.2.348–50). By contrast, **Celia**'s reproach *includes* Rosalind as a woman who has 'simply misus'd our sex', like a bird destroying her own nest (*AYLI* 4.1.201–4). Helena complains to Hermia 'Our sex, as well as I, may chide you for it, / Though I alone do feel the injury' (*MND* 3.2.218–19). Loneliness in the absence of other women is hinted at when **Miranda** tells Ferdinand, 'I do not know / One of my sex; no woman's face remember' (*Temp.* 3.1.48). Poignantly, this exclusively male-moulded woman still sees no one of her own sex in the 'brave new world' she greets (*Temp.* 5.1.183).

(c) Aughterson (1995: 41–56) and Keeble (1994: 33–43) give extracts from a selection of publications on female physiology that show early modern ideas of sexual difference. *See* under **woman** for broad-ranging research relating to the sex in general.

Shakespeare, Judith, (a) Shakespeare's second daughter, baptized along with her twin brother Hamnet, on 2 Febraury 1585. Her biblical name, meaning 'Jewess' or 'woman from Judea', was that of the Jewish heroine and widow in the Book of Judith in the Apocrypha. Judith delivers her people from the invading Assyrian army by gaining the confidence of their commander, Holofernes, and cutting off his head while he is asleep.

(b) Judith Shakespeare and her twin Hamnet were undoubtedly named after the Shakespeares' friends Hamnet and Judith Sadler. The name 'Judith' does not appear anywhere in Shakespeare although the pedant Holofernes in *Love's Labour's Lost* is told 'their daughters profit very greatly under you' and he reponds, 'if their daughters be capable I will put it to them: but *vir sapit qui pauca loquitur* [that man is wise who speaks little]' (*LLL* 4.2.75–80), perhaps alluding to Shakespeare's deliberately cautious paternal role in relation to teaching his daughter Judith, in fear of having his own head metaphorically cut off. Holofernes is shamed, out-fac'd' and 'baited' in the cruel reception of his pageant of the Nine Worthies (*LLL* 5.2.622, 629 and 631). If Shakespeare played Holofernes, and did teach his children that 'Ovidius Naso was the man' following Shakespeare's own love for Ovid (*LLL* 4.2.123), there would be added humour in his comment 'I do dine to-day at the father's of a certain pupil of mine' (*LLL* 4.2.153–5).

Judith Shakespeare was 16 when Shakespeare wrote *Twelfth Night*, a play that dramatizes the experience of losing a brother. She, as much as Susanna, may have influenced the strong father–daughter relationships in the late plays since she was still living at home when these were written (Weis 2007: 266–7). She did not get married to Thomas Quiney (whom she would have known as a neighbour and childhood playmate from Henley Street) until 1616, when she was 31, and the marriage was conducted quickly with a special licence to marry in Lent and without reading of the banns (Greer 2007: 311). The swift ceremony, following what appears to be a carefully planned match, may have been prompted partly by Shakespeare's illness, and a more urgent reason: the discovery that Quiney had also had an affair with Margaret Wheeler who became pregnant. After his marriage to Judith, on 10 February 1616, Quiney was presented at court and confessed; Margaret Wheeler died in childbirth along with the baby and they were buried on 15 March 1616. Probably as a consequence of this scandal, and to ensure the financial well-being of his younger daughter, Shakespeare altered his will, bypassing Quiney in favour of Judith (Weis 2007: 350–2 and 60–1).

(c) As noted above, Weis (2007) and Greer (2007) devote attention to the emotional dimensions of Judith's loss of her brother Hamnet, her continued presence in the family home until she was married aged 31, and the shock of the scandal involving her husband Richard Quiney, just before Shakespeare's death.

Shakespeare, Susanna, *see* **Susanna**

Shore, Jane, (a) an historical figure referred to in *Richard III* but not represented on stage.

(b) **Mistress** of Edward IV and afterwards of William, Lord Hastings, she would have been well known to audiences from Thomas Heywood's play *Edward The Fourth* and possible Thomas Churchyard's poem *The Tragedy of Shore's Wife* (1593). In *Richard III*, she functions to set up the decadent atmosphere of King Edward's court. Her status as royal mistress is a source of smutty humour and uneasy laughter reflecting the insecurity of the court in the opening scene. Richard of Gloucester tells Brakenbury that they speak no treason in talking about her physical attributes 'a pretty foot, / A cherry lip, a bonny eye, a passing pleasing tongue' (1.1.93–4). The open secret of her liaison with the king is, nevertheless, dangerous to speak of:

> Gloucester: Naught to do with Mistress Shore? I tell thee, fellow,
> He that doth naught with her (excepting one)
> Were best to do it secretly alone.
> Brakenberry: What one, my lord?
> Gloucester: Her husband, knave. Wouldst thou betray me?
> (1.1.98–102)

References to her become increasingly sinister because her name is repeatedly associated with those about to die. Gloucester mockingly bids Hastings 'Give Mistress Shore one gentle kiss the more' in celebration of the death of his enemies (3.1.185) while planning to arrest him. Richard then uses her as a pawn to condemn Hastings to death. He accuses the '**harlot, strumpet** Shore', of having conspired with the Queen **Elizabeth** in **witch**craft to wither up his arm (3.4.71). Buckingham implies to the Mayor of London that she is a source of corruption, saying that Hastings became a dangerous man 'After he once fell in with Mistress Shore' (3.4.51).

(c) Thomas Heywood, *The First and Second Parts of Edward the Fourth* [1599] (2009) dramatizes Jane's relationship with King Edward IV sympathetically. Thomas Churchyard's 'Howe Shores Wife, Edward the fowerthes concubine, was by king Richarde despoyled of all her goodes, and forced to do open penance' (1938) notes the political exploitation of Jane Shore. Churchyard's subversive treatment of the figure and its links to Shakespeare's character are analysed by Mary Steible, 'Jane Shore and the Politics of Cursing' (2003). Maria Margaret Scott's biography (2005) compares Shakespeare's dramatic cameo with other representations from the sixteenth, seventeenth and twentieth centuries.

shrew, (a) a woman given to railing or **scold**ing or other perverse or malignant behaviour, frequently a scolding or turbulent **wife**, although the *Oxford English Dictionary* also lists the term to mean a wicked, evilly disposed or vexatious man. The shrew is a female stereotype, often the creation of misogynist discourse.

Outspoken or domineering behaviour from a woman in early modern England would certainly attract the name and the accompanying censure. Men married to so-called shrewish wives were permitted to beat them or to solicit public punishment by means of the **scold**'s bridle or cucking stool.

(b) The most fully depicted example of the shrew stereotype in Shakespeare is in the play-within-the-framing-plot of *The Taming of the Shrew*. **Katherina**'s short temper is indicated in the label 'so hot a shrew' (*Shrew* 4.1.21) while her reputation as a 'curst shrew' (*Shrew* 5.2.188) connotes the immorality associated with the transgressive female stereotype, advertised in an earlier reference to the 'curst and shrewd' **Xantippe** (*Shrew* 1.2.70). 'Curst' also hints at the burden under which the woman suffers from such stereotyping. Petruchio's wooing of Katherina perversely ignores her shrewish behaviour, and puts forward the argument that it is a politic performance rather than an inherent quality. He argues that in private, even a timid man can tame 'the curstest shrew' (*Shrew* 2.1.313) and that Katherina's shrewishness is a public show: 'If she be curst, it is for policy' (*Shrew* 2.1.292). What Katherina's policy could be is never made explicit, although her shrewishness effectively excludes her from the **marriage** market until Petruchio arrives in Padua. The text continues to explore the performative nature of the stereotype and the misogyny which invariably accompanies it by setting up Petruchio as more shrewish than his bride. His apparent failure to appear for the **wedding**, so shaming Katherina, would 'vex a **saint**, / Much more a shrew of thy impatient humor' (*Shrew* 3.2.28–9) her father acknowledges. Grumio's account of Petruchio's behaviour on the journey to his country house prompts spectators to agree with Curtis's view 'By this reck'ning he is more shrew than she' (*Shrew* 4.1.85), effectively deconstructing the exclusively female stereotype. Petruchio's tactics for taming Katherina involve physical humiliation: depriving her of clean clothes, water to wash in, food and sleep, in addition to his rhetorical trickery and lying. The process is compared to taming a hawk in order to subdue it to obedience to its master's call (*Shrew* 4.1.187–96). Petruchio's soliloquy in Act 4 Scene 1 openly challenges the audience with the ethical problems it raises:

> This is a way to kill a wife with kindness,
> And thus I'll curb her mad and headstrong humor.
> He that know better how to tame a shrew,
> Now let him speak; 'tis charity to shew.
>
> (*Shrew* 4.1.208–11)

The hawking and hunting metaphors continue in the final scene where the **Widow** challenges Katherina with being a shrew who troubles her husband, a slander that Katherina condemns as 'very mean' (*Shrew* 5.2.28–31). When the men wager on their wives' obedience, Katherina demonstrates the success of the taming process by coming to her husband's call and subsequently counselling the other **brides**, **Bianca** and the Widow, on wifely duty. To what extent this speech is another performance in contrast with an earlier public display of shrewishness, or whether it expresses Katherina's own thoughts is not clear, although both are certainly possible in performance. The 'wonder' (*Shrew* 5.2.189) of the taming in the play-within-the-play closes Shakespeare's play but is extended in a closing framing scene in *The Taming of A Shrew*, a probable source. In this text, Christopher Sly wakes up from a brave dream in which he has learned how to tame a shrew and confidently prepares to go home and tame his own wife (*Riverside Shakespeare*, p. 175).

Shrewishness is most frequently linked to verbal transgression or **scold**ing in Shakespeare's work. Petruchio's taming school is designed to 'tame a shrew and charm her chattering **tongue**' (*Shrew* 4.1.58), while the 'curst' **Beatrice** is counselled 'thou wilt never get thee a husband if thou be so shrewd of thy tongue' (*MAdo* 2.1.18–20). In this case, as often in Shakespeare, 'shrewd' means both shrewish and sharp-witted. After listening to Beatrice's arguments against marriage and self-subordination, Leonato acknowledges that she 'apprehends passing shrewdly' (*MAdo* 2.1.81). Antipholus of Ephesus explains that his wife is 'shrewish' if he is late for dinner (*Err.* 3.1.2), and the Abbess later scolds **Adriana** for criticizing Antipholus incessantly in bed and at dinner and in public assemblies, which has driven him mad (*Err.* 5.3. 60–73). Antipholus slanders the goldsmith Angelo for his importunate speech demanding payment: 'like a shrew you first begin to brawl' (*Err.* 4.1.51). In this case the term is not explicitly gendered.

Its misogyny as part of popular culture is made clear in the snatch of a ballad sung drunkenly by Silence in *Henry IV Part II*: 'Be merry, be merry, my wife has all, / For women are shrows, both short and tall' (*2HIV* 5.3.32–3). In the light of such prejudice, Sir Andrew Aguecheek's paradoxical greeting to **Maria**, 'fair shrew' (*TN* 1.3.47), quickly establishes his folly. 'Shrew' is, however, used affectionately and teasingly by Lorenzo of **Jessica**: 'In such a night / Did Jessica (like a little shrow) / Slander her love, and he forgave it her' (*Mer.* 5.1.20–2) and by the **Princess** of France to condemn **Rosaline**'s impertinence (*LLL* 5.2.46). More spitefully, **Helena** invokes the term's negative associations to increase Demetrius and Lysander's hostility to the angry **Hermia**. She coyly claims that, while she 'was never curst' and has 'no gift at all in shrewishness' herself (*MND* 300–1), Hermia is 'keen and shrewd / She was a vixen when she went to school' (*MND* 3.2.323–4).

(c) Empson [1961] (1996: 27–33), Bean (1983), Brooks (1960), Fineman (1985), Karen Newman (1991: 33–50) and Brown (2003) all give readings of the representations of Katherina as a shrew. Michael D. Friedman (2002: 200–27) considers the taming of shrews within the genre of comedy as forgiveness. Leah Marcus (1992) and Ann Thompson (2001) both discuss the issues faced by feminist editors of the play. Paola Dionisotti, Sinead Cusack and Fiona Shaw discuss playing the part of Katherina in Rutter (1988: 1–25). Penny Gay (1994) considers the challenges that directors, performers and spectators face in staging or watching this play and Elizabeth Schafer (1998: 57–72) interviews Gale Edwards, Di Trevis and Jude Kelly about some of these.

Silvia, (a) a character in *Two Gentlemen of Verona*, the daughter of the Duke of Milan, and beloved of Valentine and later Proteus. Her name derives from the

Latin *silva*, meaning 'wood' or 'forest'. In Roman legend, Rhea Silvia was the **vestal** virgin seduced by Mars in the Temple of Mars, who became the mother of the twins Romulus and Remus, founders of Rome.

(b) Silvia's name is simultaneously invoked and mocked when Valentine grasps her **glove**, calls her 'a thing divine' and in the best tradition of the courtly lover calls out 'Ah, Silvia, Silvia!' only to be echoed by Speed's call 'Madam Silvia! Madam Silvia!' (2.1.4–6). Her identity as 'a construction evolved and then circulated among male image-makers' (Estrin 1994: 178) is highlighted by Speed who calls her an 'exceeding puppet!' (2.1.95), 'deform'd' (2.1.54) by male admiration. She is the love object of Valentine, Thurio, and Proteus and commands the chivalric service of Sir Eglamour. Silvia is defined by her absence; she is the 'shadow of perfection' on which Valentine and the other men feed (3.1.177). Repeating her name, Valentine believes 'Silvia is myself', there is no light 'if Silvia be not seen' and there is no joy 'if Silvia be not by' (3.1.174–5). The objectification of Silvia reaches a climax in the song:

> Who is Silvia? what is she,
> That all our swains commend her?
> Holy, fair, and wise is she;
> The heaven such grace did lend her,
> That she might admired be.
> Is she kind as she is fair?
> For beauty lives with kindness.
> Love doth to her eyes repair,
> To help him with his blindness;
> And, being help'd, inhabits there.
> Then to Silvia let us sing,
> That Silvia is excelling;
> She excels each mortal thing
> Upon the dull earth dwelling.
> To her let us garlands bring.
>
> (4.2.39–53)

The answer to the first two questions is that Silvia is a romantic icon, constructed as such by the men to be beloved and worshipped by many rather than being the mistress of one, whatever her personal feelings. Shakespeare's play may set an English trend for the name, which is used again in Daniel's *Hymen's Triumph*, where she is beloved of Thyrsis (Daniel 1615: 1–2).

The answer to the second stanza's question moves her beyond the status of beautiful object. She carefully manages to remain polite and gentle to all her suitors, no mean feat since she is so 'hard beset' (2.4.49). She expresses warm sympathy with **Julia**'s plight, again showing kindness in sending her picture or 'shadow' to Proteus and refusing the ring with a reprimand. She is daring enough to plot to run away from her father: originally with Valentine and latterly with Sir Eglamour to find Valentine. Given her name, it is unsurprising that Silvia flees to the 'shadowy desert' of 'unfrequented woods' (5.4.2). The woods hold dangers for her, dramatized in her capture by the outlaws who, Proteus claims 'would have forc'd your honor and your love' (5.4.22). Valentine's references to the nightingale (5.4.5–6 and earlier at 3.1.178–9) recall the story of **Philomel**, who was raped in the forest by Tereus. The threat of **rape** is transmuted to a less physically violent form of commodification. First, Valentine hands Silvia over to his friend and rival 'All that was mine in Silvia I give thee' (5.4.83) and, after Julia's self-revelation has resolved the romantic plot, the Duke formally gives Valentine 'thy Silvia, for thou hast deserved her' (5.4.147). Throughout this process, she does not speak, perhaps in imitation of Philomel.

(c) Dowland's *Second book of songs or airs* (1600), Plutarch's Life of Romulus in *Lives* (1579: 20–40) and *The Queenes Arcadia* (1605), a masque presented to Queen Anna and her ladies all use 'Silvia' as the name of a mistress or beloved. See also Daniel's *Hymen's Triumph* (London, 1615). Barbara Estrin (1994) briefly considers Silvia as the object of male courtship in her study of female figures constructed in the Petrarchan tradition. See also William C. Carroll (2004: 13–16; 92–107).

siren (a) in mythology, one of the sea goddesses responsible for luring sailors to their destruction on the rocks by their enchanting, irresistible song. They were often referred to as **mermaid**s. More generally the term was used of a beguiling, seductive woman.

(b) The encounter between Ulysses and the Sirens, during which he stopped his sailors' ears with wax and had himself strapped to the mast to resist their song, is found in Book 12 of Homer's *Odyssey* but was already common knowledge to the early moderns (Vredeveldt 2001). Sir Arthur Golding referred to it when introducing his translation of Ovid's *Metamorphoses* (Golding 1567: A4v). In early modern texts the words 'mermaid' and 'siren' are used interchangeably. Ovid's *Metamorphoses* describes the 'Meremaides' as half-bird 'with yellow feathers' and half-maiden with 'countnance of virginitie', moving 'upon the waves with hovering wings' and singing (Ovidius 2000: 131–2). Blount's 1656 *Dictionary* said that, according to the poets, there were three sirens, Parthenope, Leucosia and Ligea:

> the first used her voyce, the second a Citern, the third a Pipe; and so are said to entice Marriners and Sea men to them, by the sweetness of their musick, and then to destroy them. The upper part of their bodies, was like a beautiful **Virgin**, the neather was fishy. By these Syrens, pleasures are emblematically understood, from which unless a man abstain, or at least use moderately, he shall be devoured in their waves.
>
> (Blount 1656)

Shakespeare does not number or identify individual sirens or associate them with birds but he does appear to distinguish the siren from the mermaid as a more deceptive, beguiling type. Antipholus of Syracuse, who has just completed a long sea-journey to Ephesus, thinks he has been enchanted by a siren when Luciana speaks to him. As a 'sweet mermaid' she would drown him in Adriana's tears, out of sisterly solidarity, but he bids her

> Sing, siren, for thyself, and I will dote;
> Spread o'er the silver waves thy golden hairs,
> And as a bed I'll take them, and there lie,
> And in that glorious supposition think
> He gains by death that hath such means to die.
>
> (*Err.* 3.2.47–51)

'Siren' is a derogatory term to describe the false enchantments of **Tamora**: 'this siren that will charm Rome's Saturnine' (*Tit.* 2.1.23) to gain absolute control of Rome while pursuing her passionate affair with Aaron. Even more intense loathing is suggested in Sonnet 119 where the speaker complains, 'What potions have I drunk of Siren tears / Distilled from limbecks foul as hell within' (*Son.* 119.1–2). The Siren, presumably the Dark Lady, has beguiled him into losing himself 'when I saw myself to win'. It is, as the speaker recognizes, a 'distraction' or 'madding fever' (*Son.* 119.3–4 and 8). Here, as in both other occurrences, the siren is a figure for the loss of masculine self-control and complete self-abandonment to pleasure, as outlined by Blount.

(c) Arthur Golding's introduction to his translation of Ovid includes a reference to Homer's account of the sirens (Golding 1567: sig A4v). This and the description of the sirens as hybrid creatures is in Book 5, lines 5.689–98 (Ovidius 2000: 131–2) would certainly have been known to Shakespeare. Harry Vredeveld's article (2001) gives a detailed account of sirens' encounter with Ulysses as a literary commonplace, one that informed Antipholus of Syracuse's words in *Comedy of Errors*. Thomas Blount, *Glossographia or A Dictionary* (1656), gives a retrospective impression of what the sirens meant, allegorically.

sister, (a) in a family context, a woman or **girl** in relation to other sons or **daughters** of the same parents. In early modern England a sister-in-law by **marriage** was commonly referred to simply as 'sister'. 'Sister' also denoted a member of a religious community of women, and, used by a female character of another, it signified a close female friend or ally, a proto-feminist bond.

(b) Shakespeare's texts represent sisterhood in sibling relations between sisters, between sisters and brothers, and in references to communities of women. Sibling bonds of opposition, rivalry and sameness are related to mythic origins in references to the pagan gods and goddesses. The **moon** is the sister of Apollo the sun (*Tim.* 4.3.1–2), an opposition in which the sister occupies the subordinate position. **Juno**, who greets **Ceres**, 'How does my bounteous sister?' (*Temp.* 4.1.103), is the superior sister in a relationship of sameness. Bonds between sisters such as **Katherina** and **Bianca**, **Adriana** and **Luciana** in Shakespeare combine common interests and rivalries. The marriage market sets up rival sisters in *The Taming of the Shrew* where 'the preferment of the eldest sister' (*Shrew* 2.1.93) and the cultural preferment of the younger makes for an explosive mix. Bianca summarizes their animosity in the line 'Sister, content you in my discontent' (*Shrew* 1.1.80). There is something inherently comic in her appeals to Katherina's sisterly feelings 'Good sister, wrong me not, nor wrong yourself, / To make a **bondmaid** and a slave of me' when sisterly rivalries have led Katherina to tie Bianca up. Although they appear as binary opposites, the sisters are also doubles. Katherina fears having to dance barefoot on Bianca's wedding day while Bianca must 'dress your sister's chamber up' for her wedding day (*Shrew* 2.1.33 and 3.1.83) At the feast, Bianca must 'take her sister's room' (*Shrew* 3.2.250) as **bride**, a transition point at which they begin to swap positions in the cultural order. **Adriana** and **Luciana** represent another instance of doubling in the identity games of *The Comedy of Errors*. To deflect Antipholus's attention from herself onto a sister, Luciana urges

> Luciana: Why call you me love? Call my sister so.
> S. Antipholus: Thy sister's sister
> Luciana: That's my sister
> A. Antipholus: No.
>
> (*Err.* 3.2.59–60)

With traces of the story of incest in the myth of Tereus and **Philomel**, Antipholus of Syracuse compares the sister that his soul abhors with the 'fair sister' who 'hath almost made me traitor to myself' (*Err.* 3.2.162). Luciana's patronizing recommendations 'be patient, sister' (*Err.* 2.1.9) are irritating, yet she does adopt a protective attitude to her sister with critical remarks: 'Fie, brother . . . When were you wont to use my sister thus?' (*Err.* 2.2.152–3) and 'If you did wed my sister for her wealth, / Then for her wealth's sake use her with more kindness' (*Err.* 3.2.5–6).

The same pattern of doubling and opposition develops in *King Lear* where **Regan** models herself after **Goneril**, declaring, 'I am made of the self metal as my sister, / And prize me at her worth' (*KL* 1.1.69–70). The evil sisters are set in opposition to **Cordelia** who tells them, 'I know you what you are, / And like a sister am most loath to call / Your faults as they are named' (*KL* 1.1.269–71). Goneril and Regan function effectively as a sisterly team to deconstruct Lear's patriarchal power, as is shown when they take hands (*KL* 2.4.194–5). Cordelia, horrified by what they are doing, no longer recognised them as her sisters:

> Cried 'Sisters, sisters! Shame of ladies! Sisters!
> Kent! father! sisters! What, i' th' storm? i' th' night?
> Let pity not be believ'd!'
>
> (*KL* 4.3.27–9)

Sisterhood crumbles in the face of Goneril and Regan's desire for Edmund, which sets them fatally against each other as rivals (*KL* 5.3). The presence of a man renders sisterhood ultimately self-destructive.

Much more poignantly, Katherine in *Love's Labour's Lost* laments losing her sister. She will never be friends with the god Cupid who 'kill'd your sister' by making her 'melancholy, sad and heavy, / And so she died' (*LLL* 5.2.13–15). An imaginary sister is conjured again as trope of loss, an almost inevitable consequence of ideal female passivity, in **Viola**'s haunting account, 'My father had a daughter loved a man' who sat like 'Patience on a monument / Smiling at grief' (*TN* 2.4.107–1).

Female characters who are related by marriage rather than by blood use sisterly appellations to foster common sympathies with other women on stage. In *Richard III*, for example, **Queen Elizabeth** greets Richard's wife **Anne**, Duchess of Gloucester with the words 'good sister' and 'Kind sister' (*RIII* 4.1.7 and 11), for supporting her quest to see the Princes in the Tower. In *Twelfth Night*, recognizing sisters-in-law forms part of the resolution. **Olivia** prompts Orsino to 'think me as well as sister as a wife' (*TN* 5.1.317) and he responds by calling her 'sweet sister'. Olivia cannot retrieve her brother as Viola has recovered Sebastian, but the play signals clearly that she recognizes a new kind of relationship with Cesario: 'A sister! you are she' (*TN* 5.1.326).

Relationships between male and female siblings work differently because they are founded on difference rather than sameness. Male characters frequently respond emotionally to the welfare of their sisters. The Duke of York in *Richard II* is so shocked and preoccupied by the death of the **Duchess** 'my sister Gloucester' (his sister-in-law), that he accidentally calls Queen **Isabel** 'sister' (*RII* 2.2.90 and 105). A sister is a source of male pride for many male characters. Launce believes his sister is 'as white as a lily and as small as a wand' (*TGV* 2.4.20–1) while Laertes describes **Ophelia** as a sister

> Whose worth, if praises may go back again,
> Stood challenger on mount of all the age
> For her perfections.
>
> (*Ham.* 4.7.27–9)

Sebastian likewise boasts that Viola was 'of many accounted beautiful' and 'thus far will I boldly publish her: she bore a mind that envy could not but call fair' (*TN* 2.1.26–9). He weeps at the thought of her death. Male characters thus value their sisters with protective, even possessive force. Laertes alerts Ophelia to Hamlet's sexual interest in her by warning 'Fear it, Ophelia, fear it, my dear sister' (*Ham.* 1.3.133). Feste is also protective, wishing 'my sister had had no name' (*TN* 3.1.16–20) because the slipperiness of language would make her **wanton** by association if not in material terms. In *Titus*, Lucius apparently sympathizes with his mutilated sister's suffering, lamenting 'how my wretched sister sobs and weeps' (*Tit.* 3.1.137). The sister as victim is an inspiration to revenge. Hector is certain that his sister's divination should 'work / Some touches of remorse' amongst her brothers (*T&C* 2.2.114–15).

Claudio defines the ideal form of sibling love of 'a brother to his sister' as one of 'Bashful sincerity and comely love' (*MAdo* 4.1.53–4). Hamlet implicitly suggests that Laertes has transgressed those emotional boundaries when he upbraids Leartes for jumping into Ophelia's grave with the counter-claim, 'I loved Ophelia / Forty thousand brothers / Could not with all their quantity of love / Make up my sum' (*Ham.* 5.1.269–71). Octavius Caesar is more physically restrained, but perhaps no less emotionally charged in bidding farewell to **Octavia**, his feminine opposite and double. Caesar uncharacteristically weeps in giving away his sister to Antony: 'A sister I bequeath you, whom no brother / Did ever love so dearly' (*A&C* 2.2.149–50). He describes her as 'a great part of myself' and asks her to effectively become his creation: 'Sister, prove such a wife / As my thoughts make thee' (*A&C* 3.2.24–6). Because Octavia is by name and status Octavius's double, she is also, inevitably, a political figure. When she comes to Rome he reprimands her, 'You come not / Like Caesar's sister' (*A&C* 3.6.42–3). Sisters such as Octavia are presented as tools to make political matches or alliances. Even Poins has apparently sworn that Prince Hal is 'to marry his sister' (*2HIV* 2.2.128).

Mortimer's sister **Anne** is the root of Richard, Duke of York's claim to the throne (*1HVI* 2.5 and *2HVI* 2.2). Lady **Bona**, 'the French King's sister' (*3HVI* 3.1) would be a suitable alliance for Henry VI. Lewis seems concerned for her welfare, 'Tell me for truth the measure of his love / Unto our sister Bona', and then asks her opinion: 'Now, sister, let us hear your firm resolve'. She constructs herself as an echo of his wishes: 'Your grant, or your denial shall be mine' (*3HVI* 3.3.120–1 and 129–30). Half-sisters or sisters-in-law are vulnerable to dubious alliances in *Hamlet* and *Cymbeline*. **Gertrude** is 'our sometime sister, now our queen' (*Ham.* 1.2.8) while **Imogen** is the subject of Cloten's plots to secure the kingdom as his inheritance.

Same-sex sisterly bonds are shown dissolving in the interests of patriarchy and heterosexual desire. **Helena** pleads with **Hermia**

> Is all the counsel that we two have shar'd,
> The sisters' vows, the hours that we have spent,
> When we have chid the hasty-footed time
> For parting us – O, is all forgot?
> (*MND* 3.2.198–201)

Celia and **Rosalind**'s loves 'Are dearer than the natural bond of sisters' (*AYLI* 1.2.275–6). Their disguises permit a temporary continuation of this bond where Rosalind, cross-dressed as Ganymede, can live unremarkably 'with this shepherdess, my sister; here in the skirts of the forest, like fringe upon a **petticoat**' (*AYLI* 3.2.335). The appellation is especially convenient for Rosalind, allowing her to elicit Celia's help and support by frequent appellations of 'sister', as seen in the mock marriage ceremony: 'Come, sister, you shall be the priest, and marry us. Give me your hand, Orlando. What do you say, sister?' (*AYLI* 4.1.124–6).

More formal communities of sisters are represented in groups of nuns and witches, and in references to the **Fates**. Wilson's *Christian Dictionarie* explained that the Church of Christ was 'called his Sister' because it was born of God and became 'Flesh of his Flesh, and Bone of his Bone' (Wilson 1612: 199). The 'sisterhood of holy nuns' to which Friar Lawrence intends to take Juliet appears a very poor substitute for Romeo since she commits suicide (*R&J* 5.3.157). Theseus suggests to **Hermia** that to become 'a barren sister all your life / Chanting faint hymns to the cold fruitless moon' (*MND* 1.1.72–3) is not an attractive option. **Celia** assumes that vows of **chastity** make sisterly bonding cold: 'A nun of winter's sisterhood kisses not more religiously' (*AYLI* 3.2.16), although Traub (2002) and Jankowski (2000) both suggest that the possibilities of lesbian passion in sisterly relationships would have been visible to early modern audiences and readers. In *Measure for Measure*, **Isabella** is torn between her blood-ties as a sister and her wish to join a sisterhood. Although she is 'a very virtuous maid' she cannot be 'shortly of a sisterhood' and the saviour of her brother's life (*MM* 2.2.20–1). Her dilemma is encapsulated in the way her entrance is announced: 'One Isabel, a sister, desires access to you' (*MM* 2.4.18). It is not clear whether Isabella is speaking from the position of a 'sweet sister', a kindly sibling, a 'young sister' or novice, or both (*MM* 3.1.132 and 151) at any given point in the play.

A more threatening group of women is the trinity of 'weird sisters' who prophesy for Macbeth and Banquo (*Mac.* 1.3.32). 'The weird sisters, hand in hand' speak and move with ritual formality:

> Thrice to thine and thrice to mine
> And thrice again, to make up nine.
> Peace! the charm's wound up.
>
> (*Mac.* 1.3.35–7)

In a perversely protective fashion, the **weird sisters** determine 'cheer we up his sprites / And show the best of our delights' (*Mac.* 4.1.127–8). They are, ultimately, like the **Fates**, the most powerful trinity of sisters in Shakespeare. Macbeth vows, 'I will to the weird sisters: / More shall they speak; for now I am bent to know, / By the worst means, the worst' (*Mac.* 3.4.132–4). Pistol flamboyantly commands 'Untwine the Sisters Three!' (*2HIV* 2.4.199), but ultimately no character has power over this sororal trinity, whose hands may be 'as pale as milk' but who have power to stop the life of anyone by cutting 'With shears his thread of silk' (*MND* 5.1.338 and 341).

(c) Miller and Yavneh's collection *Sibling Relations and Gender in the Early Modern World* (2006) contains essays exploring the positions of sisters in family and religious communities in early modern Europe.

slut, (a) a person (usually female) of dirty, slovenly or untidy habits or appearance. Related to this, a woman of a low or loose character; a bold or impudent girl; a hussy, jade, connoting sexual profligacy.
(b) Like **stale**, this word frequently defines woman as food for male sexual appetites. The whores **Phrynia** and **Timandra** whose role is to satisfy male lust are invited to 'Hold up, you sluts, / Your **aprons** mountant' (*Tim.* 4.3.135–6). Speaking of appetite, Iachimo argues that 'Sluttery, to such neat excellence [as Imogen's] oppos'd, / Should make desire vomit emptiness, / Not so allur'd to feed' (*Cym.* 1.6.44–6). In each case, the term's associations with dirt make the commodity unwholesome. Lavatch comments that 'Fortune's displeasure is but sluttish, if it smell so strongly as thou speak'st of' (*AWW* 5.2.6–7). The pageant

of fairies cautions Falstaff that 'Our radiant Queen hates sluts and sluttery' and tortures him as 'corrupt, and tainted in desire' (*MWW* 5.5.46 and 90). When Touchstone tries to construct **Audrey** as a consumable but expendible commodity, she readily accepts the slovenly, dirty or untidy dimensions of the term but firmly rejects the sexual sense:

Touchstone: . . . to cast away honesty upon a foul slut were to put good
meat into an unclean dish.
Audrey: I am not a slut, though I thank the gods I am foul.
Touchstone: Well, prais'd be the gods for thy foulness! sluttishness may
come hereafter.

(*AYLI* 3.3.35–41)

Sexual profligacy is brought sharply into focus by Ulysses in *Troilus and Cressida* who comments that **Cressida**'s 'accosting welcome' with language in 'her eye, her cheek, her lip' and '**wanton** spirits' in 'every joint and motive of her body' sets her down as one of the 'sluttish spoils of opportunity / And daughters of the game' (*T&C* 4.5.55–63). **Venus**'s hungry desire for Adonis is implicitly slandered in the detail that her tears scorn 'to wash the foul face of the sluttish ground' (*V&A* 983).

(c) Mann (2008: 199) reads Iachimo's discussion with Imogen as a kind of sexual assault.

smock, (a) a woman's undergarment, loose, full length and made of cotton or linen, with either a high or square neck, sometimes decorated with embroidery. A smock or shift was often used as nightwear. The term is also used metaphorically to denote a woman, often with bawdy associations.

(b) Spring's song at the end of *Love's Labour's Lost* describes a scene where the flowers 'lady-smocks' in the meadows are matched by the **maid**ens who 'bleach their summer smocks' (*LLL* 5.2.906). Since smocks are the usual costumes for **nymph**s, most famously in Titan's *Flora* (Mellencamp 1969), the nymphs in the betrothal masque of *The Tempest* were probably dressed in smocks. 'Smock' is used to denote **Beatrice**'s nightwear, and implicitly, her vulnerability in love when Leonato reports that she will 'sit in her smock till she have writ a sheet of paper' or love letter to Benedick (*MAdo* 2.3.132–3). Smocks feature on stage in several plays. Presumably Beatrice enters wearing her smock on **Hero**'s wedding morning (*MAdo* 4.4.38) since she has just woken up. Smocks are probably worn by the actors playing **Cressida** (*T&C* 4.2) and **Juliet** (*R&J* 3.5) in the morning after scenes, telegraphing their sexuality and vulnerability. Macbeth and **Lady Macbeth** quickly undress before reappearing on stage with the summons of the bell to be told of Duncan's murder (*Mac.* 2.3.81) and Lady Macbeth wears the same shift and night-gown for the sleepwalking scene in which she replays the night of the murder (*Mac.* 5.1.5–8). As a symbol of her penance and vulnerability, Lady Macbeth's smock may recall the white sheet or garment of penance that **Eleanor**, Duchess of Gloucester must wear in *Henry VI Part II* (2.4.16 SD). **Desdemona** goes to bed in a smock and, after smothering her, Othello describes her white face as 'Pale as thy smock!' (*Oth.* 5.2.273), associating her with **chastity**. The smock as underwear takes on bawdier meaning when Alençon jokes that the Dauphin 'shrives this woman to her smock' (*1HVI* 1.2.119) since his interview with **Joan La Pucelle** is taking so long. Their suspicions are probably confirmed when the English surprise the 'unready' French from their beds at Orleans and Joan and the Dauphin enter together (*1HVI* 2.1.40–50).

Autolycus as salesman at the sheepshearing fair draws attention to the metaphorical use of 'smock' for 'woman' when he praises the embroidered garment: 'you would think a smock were a she-angel, he so chaunts to the sleeve-hand and the work about the square on't' (*WT* 4.4.208–210). Bertram uses the word disparagingly to refer to the **wife** he is yoked to in marriage, just as male and female horses are paired in a yoke: 'I shall stay here the forehorse to a smock' (*AWW* 2.1.30). Romeo and Mercutio mock the **Nurse** by referring to her and the page Peter as two sails 'a shirt and a smock' (*R&J* 2.4.103), and Enobarbus crudely refers to Antony's luck in the death of his wife **Fulvia** using the words 'your old smock brings forth a new petticoat', since he can now pursue an alliance with **Cleopatra** (*A&C* 1.2.175).

(c) Arnold (1988: 224–5) gives details of embroidered smocks in Queen Elizabeth's great wardrobe of garments. Emma H. Mellencamp (1969) discusses the use of smocks as appropriate dress for nymphs, arguing that Titian's *Flora* is costumed in this style.

spinster, (a) a woman who spins, especially one who spins as a regular occupation. Spinning, like other textile work such as sewing and weaving, was deemed a mark of virtue following the description of an ideal wife set out in the Bible. This and the model of **Penelope** as a spinner and weaver were much cited as models of female industry and loyalty in conduct books for women. 'Spinster' was in legal use to describe women by their occupation and, by the seventeenth century, less specifically to designate any woman still unmarried. The occupations of spinning and weaving were those assigned to the three **Fates** or **Destinies**.

(b) Orsino chooses an old song that 'spinsters and knitters in the sun' and **maids** who make lace 'do use to chaunt it' (*TN* 2.4.43–6). This depicts spinning as a communal female activity amongst the common people. In Fletcher and Shakespeare's *Henry VIII*, **Queen Katherine** and Norfolk speak up for the interests of such subjects whose livelihood is ruined by the King's new taxation. 'The spinsters, carders, fullers, weavers' whom the clothiers can no longer afford to employ, are at the bottom of the financial ladder, 'Unfit for other life, compell'd by hunger / And lack of other means', so likely to riot (*HVIII* 1.2.30–7). Although Katherine sews rather than spins in the play, her support of these fellow textile workers models the biblical ideal woman who spins and produces valuable textiles and 'stretcheth out her hands to the poor, yea, she reacheth her hands to the needy' (Prov. 31.18–20). A woman's ability to spin is seen as both a financial asset and a wifely virtue by Launce, whose girlfriend's virtues include:

Speed: '*Item:* She can spin.'
Launce: Then may I set the world on wheels, when she can spin for her
living.

(*TGV* 3.1.316)

Vives's *Instruction of a Christian Woman*, which was published in nine editions between 1529 and 1592, recommended that all women should spin, no matter what their class, since the purpose of spinning was not to produce material wealth but 'by the occasion of working, she should think on nothing by such as pertaineth unto the service of our Lord' (Jones and Stallybrass 2000: 107). Female spinning is defined as a domestic task in contrast with male activity abroad. Iago complains that Cassio knows nothing more about military matters 'than a spinster' (*Oth.* 1.1.24). When Collatine returns from fighting for Rome, he 'finds his wife, though it were late in the night, spinning amongst her maids' unlike the other ladies who are dancing and revelling (*Luc.* Argument. 16–19). **Lucrece** presents the biblical ideal wife whose price is above rubies, whose 'candle goeth not our by night' but who 'layeth her hands to the spindle and her hands hold the distaff' and 'eateth not the bread of idelness' (Prov. 31.18–19 and 27). Shakespeare's contemporary, Drayton, depicts an early modern noblewoman modelling herself as a rustic **Penelope** in a country cottage 'where to our Distaves as we sit and spin' she and her maid 'passe the Night, while Winter tales we tell', again suggesting female community as well as virtuous industry (Jones and Stallybrass 2000: 114).

Minsheu's 1617 dictionary gives an early definition of 'spinster' in the modern sense of 'unmarried woman' saying it is 'a terme, or an addition in our Common Law, onely added in Obligations, Euidences, and Writings, vnto maids vnmarried' (Minsheu 1617). A grotesque caricature of the spinster, weeping for the absence of a man, killing and eating their children, is given by the Amazon Queen **Hippolyta** in Fletcher and Shakespeare's *Two Noble Kinsmen* (1613). She jokes that if Pirithous 'stay to see of us such spinsters, we shall hold you here for ever' (*TNK* 1.1.18–24). As these lines show, the ideal image of the spinster was shadowed by a fear of women's threatening will, symbolized in the pride of Arachne, and their power, personified by the **Fates**. Ovid's *Metamorphoses* detailed the seductive power of the woman with the distaff in Arachne, who 'on the Rocke doth spinne the handwarpe woofe' with a dangerous 'grace', producing thread and then tapestries that shamed the gods with depictions of their lewd activities (Ovidius 2000: 137). Sir Toby Belch uses the lewd associations of spinning to invoke an image of oral sex, telling Sir Andrew Aguecheek that his hair 'hangs like flax on a distaff; and I hope to see a housewife take thee between her legs and spin it off' (*TN* 1.3.102–4). The fairies vainly trying to protect **Titania**, refer to Arachne's sinister power in their charm that bids 'Weaving spiders, come not here; / Hence, you long-legg'd spinners, hence!' (*MND* 2.1.20–1). For references to female textile production and the determining powers of destiny, *see* the entry on the **Fates**.

(c) Ovid's story of Arachne appears in Book VI, lines 7–181 of *Metamorphoses* (Ovidius 2000: 136–41). Jones and Stallybrass (2000) give many examples of spinning as ideology, includuing Drayton's *Heroical Epistles* (London, 1619) and Vives' *Instruction of a Christian Woman* (1529).

stale, (a) a derogatory term for a woman as a piece of sexual bait, deriving from a combination of the meanings of stale as a decoy, but also as urine and adjectivally, meaning 'no longer fresh'.

(b) The term's associations with food, bait and trickery are invoked in examples from the canon referring to women. When her husband 'feeds from home', **Adriana** feels 'poor I am but his stale' (*Err.* 2.1.100–1). The idea of public exposure to be 'common-hackney'd in the eyes of men, / So stale and cheap to vulgar company' (*1HIV* 3.2.40–1) takes on sexual dimensions in *The Taming of The Shrew* where **Katherina** complains that by leaving her amongst the men in the public street, her father abandons her as devalued, remaindered goods: 'Is it your will / To make a stale of me amongst these mates?' (*Shrew* 1.1.58). Here the sexual use of 'stale' takes on the more common meaning of being stale or contaminated by lack of use or overuse. Most insultingly, Mercutio refers to the **Nurse** as 'a lenten pie, that is something stale and hoar ere it be spent' (*R&J* 2.4.132–3). **Cleopatra**'s remarkable seductive power is evident since 'Age cannot wither her nor custom stale / Her infinite variety' (*A&C* 2.1.234–5). In *Cymbeline*'s conceit of garments as signifiers for identity, **Imogen** sees herself as cast-off clothes: 'Poor I am stale, a garment out of fashion, / And for I am richer than to hang by th' walls, / I must be ripp'd. To pieces with me!' (*Cym.* 3.4.51–3) Unusually, Shakespeare has one instance of the term applied to a male character. Hortensio vows that if **Bianca** is so indiscriminating or 'humble' to cast her 'wand'ring eyes on every stale', such as the schoolteacher (Lucentio in disguise), he will not bother to woo her further (*Shrew* 3.1.89–90).

Robert Greene's *Notable discovery of coosenage* (1592) described how prostitutes functioned 'as stales to drawe men into hell', or as bait. The stale walked in the streets or fields and unwary men 'letting slippe the libertie of their eies on their painted faces, feede upon their unchast beauties, till their hearts be set on fire: then come they to these minions, and court them with many faire words' but 'straight she carries him to some bad place, and there picks his pocket' (Greene 1592: sig. C3). Shakespeare does not make an explicit connection between stale and bait as part of a trick, as when **Celia** is accused of being Bonario's accomplice, 'The stale to his forg'd practise', in Jonson's *Volpone* (Jonson 1999: 4.5.84). However, these associations do colour the references to **Hero** as 'a contaminated stale' and 'a common stale' (*MAdo* 2.2.25 and 4.1.65), when she is doubly framed as part of a plot to deceive Claudio and Don Pedro.

(c) Greene's *Notable Discovery of coosenage* (London 1592), details the practices of stales. Gordon Williams (1994: 1303–5) lists instances of 'stale' as a sexual term in Shakespeare and other Stuart drama.

stepdame, *see* **stepmother**

stepmother, (a) a woman who is the second (or subsequent) wife of a father, after the death or divorce of the natural mother. In early modern English the term also referred to a mother-in-law.

(b) The caricature of the malicious stepmother, infamous from myth and folk tale and probably originating in the figure of **Juno**, was perpetuated in early modern writings. Henry Smith's sermon warned stepmothers that 'Their name dooth shewe them their duetie . . ., for a stepmother doth signifie a stedmother, that is, one mother dieth, and another commeth in her stead: therefore that your loue may settle to those little ones as it ought, you must remember that ye are their stedmother, that is in sted of their mother, and therefore to loue them, and tender them, and cherish them as their mother did' (Smith 1593: 67–8). Huarte set out the commonplace view of stepmothers' natural cruelty, observing that 'the earth is conditioned like a stepmother, who very carefully brings vp her owne children which shee breeds her selfe, but takes away the sustenance from those which appertaine to her husband, and so we see that her owne children are fat and fresh, and her stepchildren weake and ill coloured' (Huarte 1594: 14–15). The type appeared in literary texts such as Sidney's *Countess of Pembroke's Arcadia*, where Parthenia's mother attacks Argalus 'as euer the euil stepmother *Iuno*' tried to destroy 'the famous *Hercules*' (Sidney 1593: Book 1 Folio 9v) and the stepmother of Plangus plots against him. Phaedra is referred to as the 'cruell stepdame' of Hippolytus in Spenser's *Faerie Queene* (Spenser 1970: 1. v. 390) and Peele's play *The Troublesome Reign of King John*, which Shakespeare probably knew, contains the tag phrase 'A mother, though she were unnatural, / Is better than the kindest stepdame is' (Peele 2010: 2:2.140–1). The type finds its way into Shakespeare's texts. The step-dame, like the **dowager**, is blamed for 'Long withering out a young man's revenue' (*MND* 1.1.5–6) or depriving sons of their inheritance. **Cressida**'s examples of archetypal falsehood include the 'step-dame to her son' (*T&C* 3.3.195). The queen in *Cymbeline*, who is unnamed as if to emphasize her cardboard villainy, fulfils the stereotype perfectly. She protests:

> be assur'd you shall not find me, daughter,
> After the slander of most stepmothers,
> Evil-ey'd unto you.
>
> (*Cym.* 1.1.70–2)

but goes on to prove herself just that, 'hourly coining plots' against **Imogen** (*Cym.* 2.1.59). Her ambitions for her own son and hate of Imogen are accompanied by an interest in poisoning. The doctor recognizes that 'malice' makes her proposed experiments with 'poisonous compounds' that will bring 'languishing death', so are very dangerous (*Cym.* 1.5.8–10 and 33–6). Imogen immediately sees through the dissembling of the 'fine tyrant' (*Cym.* 1.1.84) and effectively sums her up with the label 'a step-dame false' (*Cym.* 1.6.1). Cymbeline, however, is blind to the scheming of this 'most delicate fiend', asking with bemusement 'Who is't can read a woman?' (*Cym.* 5.5.47–8).

(c) Early modern writings include Henry Smith's advice to stepmothers in *The Sermons of Maister Henrie Smith* (1593: 67–8), Juan Huarte's, *The examination of mens vvits . . . translated out of the Spanish tongue by M. Camillo Camili. Englished out of his Italian, by R.C. Esquire* (1594: 14–15). Book 1 Canto V, verses 37–9 of *The Faerie Queene* in Edmund Spenser's *Poetical Works* (1970), tell of Phaedra's lust for and fury towards her stepson and the prejudice against stepmothers is dramatized in *The Troublesome Reign of King John* (1589–90), almost certainly by Peele. Adelman's *Suffocating Mothers* (1992: 200–7) and Peggy Munoz Simonds (1991) include discussion of the nameless queen's role as a villain. Roger Warren (1998: 39–45) discusses her similarity to the wicked stepmother from folk tales, including *Snow White.*

stomacher, (a) a small decorative piece of material worn over the chest and abdomen to cover the front opening of a bodice or body.
(b) In the early modern theatre, it signalled a covering for the fastenings over **boy actors**' female costumes, sometimes with self-conscious innuendo, as when Autolycus advertises 'Golden coifs and stomachers / For my lads to give their dears' amongst his wares at the sheepshearing feast (*WT* 4.4.224–5).
(c) Arnold (1988: 148–9) gives details of stomachers made of lawn, satin and taffeta, and sometimes stiffened as part of the wardrobe of Queen Elizabeth and her ladies.

strumpet, (a) a debauched or unchaste woman, a **harlot**, prostitute.
(b) The term 'strumpet' commonly carries associations of pollution, evil, impudence and inconstancy in Shakespeare's texts. A strumpet infects not only those with whom she has sex, but also those married to them. **Adriana** tells her husband that, since they are one, she is polluted by his relationship with the **courtezan**: 'My blood is mingled with the crime of lust' and 'I do digest the poison of thy flesh, / Being strumpeted by thy contagion' (*Err.* 2.2.141–3). Both Posthumus and Imogen feel physically injured by the slander that Imogen has 'played the strumpet' (*Cym.* 3.4.21–2). His letter claims that Iachimo's testimonies 'lie bleeding in me' (*Cym.* 3.4.22–3) and Imogen says that, having heard 'I am a strumpet', her ears 'can take no greater wound' (*Cym.* 3.4.113–14). Moral as well as physical pollution is implied in the image of 'maiden virtue rudely strumpeted' (*Son.* 66.6). '[T]hat strumpet' Tamora is 'unhallowed' (*Tit.* 5.2.190). Richard III, following from Hall's *Chronicle*, demonized 'that **harlot** strumpet **Shore**' as a 'damned strumpet' (*RIII* 3.4.71–4). Unlike Dekker's *The Whore of Babylon* or Foxe's *Actes and Monuments* which cited the slander calling 'the Pope him selfe a strong strumpet, and a common baude vnto the world' (Foxe 1583: 799), Shakespeare's texts do not use 'strumpet' as part of allegorical religious propaganda. Strumpets are, however, a cause of decadence: on a personal level in *Antony and Cleopatra* where Antony, 'The triple pillar of the world', is 'transform'd / Into a strumpet's fool' (*A&C* 1.1.12–13), and on a national level in the case of **Helen** and the fall of Troy. **Lucrece** protests 'Show me the strumpet that began this stir, / That with my nails her beauty I may tear' even though it is Paris's lust which 'did incur / This load of wrath that burning Troy doth bear' (*Luc.* 1522).
'Strumpet' carries additional approbation because it is associated with female

outspokenness or assertiveness. Angelo is repelled by 'the strumpet, / With all her double vigour' (*MM* 2.2.182–3). Antipholus's automatic reaction to his **wife**'s clamorous distress is to call her 'O most unhappy strumpet' (*Err.* 5.4.121). **Helena** in *All's Well* says she is willing to risk 'Tax of impudence, / A strumpet's boldness' in order to be given the chance to cure the King (*AWW* 2.1.170–1). **Diana**'s boldness in addressing the King endangers her reputation too. Bertram argues 'She's impudent my lord' a camp-follower; her riddles make the King believe she is 'come common customer' and she must defend herself: 'Great king, I am no strumpet, by my life' (*AWW* 5.3.187 and 286–92). **Joan** La **Pucelle**'s pride infuriates Talbot who is determined to 'chastise this high-minded strumpet' (*1HVI* 1.5.12). There is some validity to York's anger when she claims she is a holy **virgin**, and then that she is pregnant in an attempt to save her own life: 'Strumpet, thy words condemn thy brat and thee: / Use no entreaty, for it is in vain' (*1HVI* 5.4.84–5). Othello calls **Desdemona** 'Impudent strumpet!' asks her outright 'Are not you a strumpet?' (*Oth.* 4.2.81 and 82) and, like Helena and Joan, she seeks to define herself against the default position of strumpet to which the misogynist prejudice that dominates these all-male military contexts has consigned her:

> No, as I am a Christian.
> If to preserve this vessel for my lord
> From any other would unlawful touch
> Be not to be a strumpet, I am none.
> (*Oth.* 4.2.82–6)

In these Shakespearean uses, 'strumpet' connotes a 'whore' (*Oth.* 4.2.86), a 'common gamester to the camp' or camp follower (*AWW* 5.3.188) and prostitution in military contexts. **Cleopatra** fears the attention of the Roman officers who 'will catch at us like strumpets' if she and **Charmian** are led in triumph (*A&C* 5.2.214–15).

The strumpet's supposed impudence, arising from self-assertion, carries further negative connotations of dishonesty which are applied figuratively as in Andrew Boorde's *Breviary of Health*: 'I do say that an uryne is a strumpet, or an harlot, for it wyl lye, and the best Doctour of Phisicke of them all maye be deceyved in an uryne' (Boorde 1547: lxxiii. 21(b)). The female personification of **Fortune** is defined as a strumpet for her unpredictable qualities; most famously in Hamlet's question 'In the secret parts of Fortune? O! most true! She is a strumpet', and the exclamation 'Out, out, thou strumpet Fortune!' (*Ham.* 2.2.235–6 and 493). The 'strumpet Fortune' tricks **Constance** and Arthur out of their supporters (*KJ* 3.1.61). Gratiano picks up on Fortune's associations with the sea to imagine ships putting out into 'the strumpet wind!' only to return 'Lean, rent and beggar'd' by the same 'strumpet wind!' (*Mer.* 2.6.16–19).

More sympathy for the strumpet's vulnerability and emotions are evident in *Othello*. The adage ''tis the strumpet's plague / To beguile many and be beguiled by one:' (*Oth.* 4.1.96–7) is amply demonstrated by **Bianca**. Bianca is devoted to Cassio in an uneasy parallel to the so-called strumpet **Desdemona**'s devotion to

Othello, and is derided as a 'notable strumpet' (*Oth.* 5.1.78). Bianca is a **courtezan** but she is not responsible for Cassio's injury as Iago implies. Her stout response to **Emilia**'s charge 'O fie upon thee strumpet!' raises pertinent questions about the loading of blame: 'I am no strumpet, but of life as honest / As you that thus abuse me' (*Oth.* 5.1.121–3).

(c) Hall's account of Edward IV's reign in *The vnion of the two noble and illustrate famelies of Lancastre and Yorke* (1548: sig. 21) and Foxe's *Actes and Monuments* (1583: 799/2) give early modern uses of 'strumpet' as a derogatory term. Jonathan Dollimore (1985: 84–6) discusses the surveillance of prostitution in *Measure for Measure* and in early modern London. Stanton (2000) considers the naming of women as whores. Muriel Schulz (1975) cites 'strumpet' as part of a much wider pattern of semantic derogation of women.

suckle, (a) feed a baby at the breast.

(b) The word only appears twice in the Shakespeare canon but 'suck' is used to mean 'suckle' more frequently. The most prestigious image of suckling was that of 'the *blessed Virgin*: as her womb bare our blessed saviour so her papps gave him sucke' (*Countesse of Lincolns Nurserie* 1622: 5). Iago's reductive view of woman's role 'to suckle fools and chronicle small beer' (*Oth.* 2.1.160) trivializes the importance of female nurturing. In *Coriolanus*, **Volumnia**'s striking view that

> The breasts of **Hecuba**
> When she did suckle Hector look'd not lovelier
> Than Hector's forehead when it spit forth blood
> (*Cor.* 1.3.40–2)

graphically demonstrates her obsession with military glory rather than conventionally maternal sympathies. Justifying her nurturing of Coriolanus as a military machine, she tells her son 'Thy valiantness was mine / Thou suck'st it from me' (*Cor.* 3.2.129). The idea that suckling and breastmilk formed the child informs Lavinia's belief about the cruelty of Tamora's sons: 'The milk thou suck'st from her did turn to marble, / Even at thy teat thou had'st thy tyranny' (*Tit.* 2.3.144–5). The absence of 'breast' here emphasizes the hard image of Tamora that Lavinia wants to create.

Suckling is regarded as something that connects humans to the wider natural environment. Aaron will send his son to 'feed on curds and whey and suck the goat' (*Tit.* 4.2.178). Friar Lawrence imagines all the diverse creatures of the earth feeding or 'sucking on her natural bosom' to find the various foods they need (*R&J* 2.3.12–13). The **goddess Venus** uses it to mark Adonis's humanity, calling him 'a son that suck'd an earthly mother' (*V&A* 863), though here it also hints at the dominant quasi-maternal passion she has for him. In *As You Like It*, the lioness's threat to Orlando is not malicious but part of her need: her 'udders all drawn dry' mean she is 'suck'd and hungry' (*AYLI* 4.3.114 and 126). Suckling is also associated with comfort for mother and child, most memorably in **Cleopatra**'s contentment 'Dost thou not see my baby at my breast / That sucks the nurse asleep' (*A&C* 5.2.213) but also in Suffolk's remarkable wish to remain in **Margaret**'s lap like a 'cradle-babe / Dying with mother's **dug** between its lips' (*2HVI* 3.2.392–3) rather than part from her. Suckling is a way to share grief for the death of Henry V, a means to provide comfort but also to perpetuate the mourning of the state that has lost a mighty father figure:

> Posterity, await for wretched years,
> When at their mothers' moist'ned eyes babes shall suck,
> Our isle shall be made a nourish of salt tears,
> And none but women left to wail the dead.
>
> (*1HVI* 1.1.48–51)

Separating the mother and suckling infant is a traumantic experience. Morocco's boast that he would 'Pluck the young sucking cubs from the she-bear' (*Mer.* 2.1.29) attributes it to a male initiative to show individual prowess. Infamously, Lady Macbeth cites it as an example of her own masculine determination:

> I have given suck, and know
> How tender 'tis to love the babe that milks me;
> I would, while it was smiling in my face,
> Have pluck'd my nipple from his boneless gums,
> And dash'd the brains out, had I so sworn as you
>
> (*Mac.* 1.7.54–8)

The violence of tearing the baby's sucking mouth away from the **breast** is, arguably, even more disturbing than the more explicitly brutal vision of murder since it marks the detachment of the Macbeths from natural cycles of nurturing and regeneration.

(c) *The Countesse of Lincolns Nurserie* (1622) is a full treatise on the advantages of breastfeeding. For further reading and further images of breastfeeding *see* entries on **breast**, **nurse** and **bosom**.

Susanna, (a) name of the eldest child of William and **Anne** Shakespeare, baptized on 26 May 1583. 'Susan', the English vernacular form, is the name of the child of **Juliet**'s **Nurse** and her husband, a daughter who died as a baby or child. The name comes from the biblical apocrypha (Chapter 13 of the Book of Daniel). Susanna is the wife of Joakim of Babylon. Two Jewish elders watch while she is bathing in her garden, and when she refuses their sexual advances they publicly accuse her of adultery. A young man called Daniel intervenes to reveal their perfidy and restore her innocence, after which they are executed.

(b) The story of Susanna and the elders was well known in early modern England and the name was popular amongst Puritans, although not in Stratford where only six Susannas appear in the baptismal records. Susanna Shakespeare may have been named after Susanna Tyler (née Woodward), whose father-in-law William Tyler had connections with the Shakespeare family, and may even have stood as godfather to William Shakespeare. Susanna Tyler had a sister called Judith and two daughters called Judith and Susanna. The Tylers were strong Protestants, as were the parents of the other two Susannas baptized in Stratford in the same year (Weis 2007: 62–4). Susanna Shakespeare wrote in secretary hand, probably taught by her father, and may have been to petty school in Stratford (ibid.: 217–18).

The name of the Nurse's daughter in *Romeo and Juliet* may contain an allusion to Susanna Shakespeare who would have been the same age as Juliet and to the fictional Susan, had she lived:

> Susan and she – God rest all Christian souls! –
> Were of an age. Well, Susan is with God,
> She was too good for me.
>
> (*R&J* 1.3.18–20)

Weis (2007: 203) suggests that Shakespeare played the Nurse, thus adding resonance to a covert reference to his daughter, and alluding obliquely to the lost Hamnet, who had just died. The biblical associations of the name suggest another connection between Susanna Shakespeare and Juliet. The story of the innocent baby Juliet falling in the garden to be picked up by Susan's father and teased about falling 'backward' to lose her virginity is a comic replay of the Susanna story. Perhaps this dramatized Shakespeare's reminiscences and protective attitude towards a daughter verging on adolescence. The name 'Susan' appears again as that of a servant admitted to the Capulet household for the ball, Susan Grindstone (*R&J* 1.5.9). If Susanna Shakespeare's mother was making malt at home, as seems likely (Greer 2007: 218–19), this detail may refer to one of the tasks Susanna was responsible for. The name does not occur anywhere else in Shakespeare's work.

Susanna Shakespeare was presented at the local church court for refusing to take the Eucharist in 1606, though we do not know whether this was on Catholic or strict puritan grounds (Greer 2007: 239–40). The following year, on 5 June 1607, she married the puritan doctor, John Hall and was given a **dowry** of 107 acres (Weis 2007: 308, 319–20). However, the prayer Susanna and her sister Judith Shakespeare inscribed on their mother Anne's tomb is remarkable for its openly Catholic style. Another, less comic version of the apocryphal Susanna story plagued Susanna Hall in 1613 when John Lane (like the Jewish elders) accused her of having 'been naught' or committing adultery (Greer 2007: 279–80). When Susanna died on 11 July 1649, she was praised as

> Witty above her sex but that's not all
> Wise to salvation was good Mistress Hall.
> Something of Shakespeare was in that, but this
> Wholly of him with whom she's now in bliss.
>
> (Greer 2007: 240)

The phrase 'wise to salvation' recalls Susanna's confidence that God will come to her aid when she is tried for adultery, and, in addition, the Nurse's confidence that Susan is with God, being 'too good' for an adult world of marriage.

(c) Weis (2007) considers Susanna's naming (pp. 62–4), her marriage (pp. 319–20), her recusancy, which he reads as mysteriously Catholic, a sign of rebellion against her father which is reflected in the broken father–daughter relationships of *King Lear*, (pp. 306–9). Greer (2007) describes malt making (pp. 166–7 and 217–19) and suggests Susanna's recusancy may have been a puritan objection to the way the sacrament was celebrated (pp. 239–40), but does not consider the Catholic tone of the elegy to Anne Hathaway. For further details, *see* **Hathaway, Anne**.

Sibyl, *see* **prophetess**

Sycorax, (a) mother of Caliban in *The Tempest*. Sycorax does not appear on stage and appears to have died long before the play begins. She is described by Prospero who, in turn, relies on Ariel's memory of her. Her name has not been adequately explained but may derive from the Greek word *corax*, for 'raven', a common symbol of witchcraft.

(b) According to Prospero, Sycorax was a blue-eyed **hag**, a 'damn'd **witch**' who was sentenced to death as a witch in Algiers, in North Africa, for 'mischiefs manifold and sorceries terrible' (1.2.264) but because of her pregnancy she was instead banished to the island on which the play is set. Sycorax is associated with the raven when Caliban refers to his mother's magic potions as 'wicked dew as e'er my mother brush'd / With raven's feather' (1.2.321–2). Ariel endorses Prospero's account of her spell imprisoning the spirit in a pine tree and, implicitly, her physical unattractiveness as the 'foul witch Sycorax, who with age and envy / Was grown into a hoop'; that is, bent double (1.2.228–9). The name 'hag' (1.2.269 and 283) implies both age and ugliness. Prospero's assumption that she has had sex with the devil himself draws on popular views that witches achieved this through intercourse with an incubus. It obscures an alternative view that Sycorax was a blue-eyed Petrarchan beauty, monstrously pregnant outside marriage, whose supernatural power is associated with the powerful figure of **Medea** (Marcus 1996: 16–17). Ovid's account of Medea, the raven of Scythia, in Book VII of *Metamorphoses* (Ovidius 1965: Book VII ll.1–509) is the strongest source for Sycorax's role and for Prospero's speech on magic (5.1.33–57), a parallel that allies the sorcery of the two characters in ways that disturb the legitimacy of colonial power and patriarchal control. Another source for Sycorax's name may be Corax of Syracuse, one of the founding fathers of rhetoric. Such associations would draw attention to the power of language as a means of control in the play.

(c) Ovid's *Metamorphoses*, translated by Golding 1567 (Ovidius 2000: 161–91). Hamilton, *Virgil and the Tempest* (1990: 115–16 and 127) discusses the similarities between Sycorax, Prospero and Elizabeth I. Orgel (1987: 19–23) likewise argues that from Caliban, Ariel and even Ferdinand's perspectives, Prospero 'looks very much like Sycorax' (p. 20) an idea discussed by Jonathan Bate (1993: 8–10 and 254–6). Leah Marcus, 'The Blue-Eyed Witch' (1996: 5–17) considers how editorial glosses of 'blue-eyed' to mean blue eyelids associated with pregnancy have obscured a reading of Sycorax as a more powerful, controlling figure like Prospero. Diane Purkiss (1996: 250–75) discusses Sycorax as one example of the witch as marginalized other. Rachana Sachdev's essay 'Sycorax in Algiers: Cultural Politics and Gynecology in Early Modern England' (2000) reads Sycorax through early modern writings on African culture, especially the practice of female circumcision as a mark of barbaric otherness and necessary containment of female or native transgression. Katherine Callen King (1990: 1–3) argues that the classical Greek exclamation '*Es korakas*' (go to hell) may be another source for Sycorax's name. Dan Harder, '*The Tempest* in the Trivium' sets out the more unusual argument for Corax of Syracuse, discussed also by Rhodes (2004: 144–5).

tail, (a) bawdy slang meaning the vulva when applied to women (and the penis when applied to men).

(b) Petruchio tries to shock **Katherina** with his reference to having 'my tongue in your tail' alluding obliquely, but fairly obviously, to oral sex:

> Petruchio: Who knows not where a wasp does wear his sting?
>   In his tail.
> Katherina: In his tongue.
> Petruchio: Whose tongue?
> Katherina: Yours, if you talk of tales, and so farewell.
> Petruchio: What, with my tongue in your tail? Nay, come again.
> (Shrew 2.1.213–18)

The shock tactic and her surprise is perhaps the one thing that stops her from exiting the stage on her line 'and so farewell', which threatens to break off the wooing process. The innuendo on 'tail' and 'tongue' derives from the proverb 'a likerous mouth most han a likerous tayl' (Tilley 1950: 395) used by Chaucer's Wife of Bath (Williams 1994: 1356). Stephano picks up on this when singing of the girl Kate who, although she scolded sailors with her 'tongue with a tang' and yet 'a tailor might scratch her where e'er she did itch' (*Temp.* 2.2.50–3).

If a tail is a woman's vulva then, by association, a tailor is one who serves a woman's sexual appetite. When the tailor is commanded to take back Katherina's gown to the shop for the use of his master (the head tailor) in *Taming of the Shrew*, Grumio emphasizes the 'deeper' bawdy meaning: 'Take up my mistress gown for his master's use! / O fie, fie, fie!' (*Shrew* 4.3.161–3). The same bawdy innuendo informs Falstaff's jokes about the woman's tailor whom he recruits in Gloucestershire. Whatever his military strength, as a tailor Feeble has the reputation of making 'many holes' in a 'woman's **petticoat**' (*2HIV* 3.2.153–5). Mistress

387

Tail-porter is an appropriate name for the **midwife** who helps women to bear or deliver babies from the **womb** and vulva, and who is alluded to by Autolycus (*WT* 4.4.269–70).

(c) On the bawdy uses of tail as applied to women and to men see Gordon Williams (1994: 1355–8). The proverb is listed in Tilley (1950: 395) and quoted by the Wife of Bath in line 466 of her Prologue in *The Canterbury Tales* (Chaucer 1968: 80).

Tamora, (a) a character in *Titus Andronicus* whose name appears to be a variant spelling of the Hebrew name *Tamar.*

(b) The stories of the two Old Testament characters named Tamar contain elements with similarities to *Titus*. In Genesis, the widowed daughter-in-law of Judah, who is passed over as a wife to Shelah his son, takes revenge by disguising herself with her **veil** like a prostitute to have sex with Judah and becomes pregnant, bearing twins (Gen. 38.11–30). Shakespeare's Tamora likewise shifts from the position of **widow**, prisoner to the Romans, to engage in a transgressive sexual relationship with Aaron the Moor. (In 2 Samuel 13 the rape of Tamar by her half-brother and revenge by her brother bears more resemblance to the fate of **Lavinia**.) Shakespeare may have conflated the biblical name with that of Tomyris, the Scythian Queen who killed the Persian Emperor Cyrus in revenge for her son's death in battle. Tomyris reputedly threw Cyrus's head into a bucket of human blood, inviting him to drink his fill. She appeared in Jonson's *Masque of Queens* (1609).

Shakespeare's Tamora occupies a swift succession of subject positions in the opening scene. She introduces herself as a **mother**, appealing for her eldest son's life with the claim that 'Sweet mercy is nobility's true badge' (*Tit.* 1.1.119). Titus's refusal produces a change to avenging **queen**: Demetrius hopes that **Hecuba**, Queen of Troy, will favour the revenge of 'Tamora, the Queen of Goths'. In the Peacham drawing illustrating an extract from the play, Tamora wears a crown and a dress which resemble those worn by Queen **Elizabeth** (Cerasano 1994: 47). However, Demetrius is immediately forced to qualify Tamora's title with the words 'When Goths were Goths and Tamora was queen' (1.1.136–40). Tamora is 'prisoner to an emperor' (1.1.258) rather than queen. Remarkably, within another 60 lines she rises to an even more powerful position as '**Empress** of Rome' (1.1.320), because of her dusky skin's exotic and erotic appeal to Saturninus (1.1.261–2). She is thus well placed to pursue her revenge on Titus and his family. Like Tomyris, she exacts it bloodily. **Lavinia** claims that Tamora is in a class of her own for cruelty: 'barbarous Tamora / No name fits thy nature but thy own!' (2.3.118). Tamora goes on to prove her name in conspiracy with Aaron: by murdering Titus's sons Quintus and Martius and son-in-law, and licensing the rape and mutilation of Lavinia. Lavinia's appeals to her as another **woman** are fruitless; Tamora bears 'a woman's face' (2.3.136) but, like Titus before her, is pitiless. Tamora's absence of conventionally gendered behaviour is perceived as much more monstrous:

> No grace? no womanhood? ah, beastly creature,
> The blot and enemy to our general name!
> Confusion fall –
>
>   (*Tit.* 2.3.182–4)

In addition to sharing Tomyris's brutal physicality, Tamora shares the biblical Tamar's skill in devious plotting. She triumphs 'thus it shall become / High-witted Tamora to gloze with all' (4.4.34–5), and she succeeds in duping Saturninus and Titus until Act 5 when she over-reaches herself in disguise as **Revenge**. Tamar's plot was that she 'put her widow's garments off from her and covered her with a vail and wrapped her self and set in an open place' (Gen. 38.14). Tamora's is to cover herself with 'strange and sad habiliments' and 'say I am Revenge, sent from below' (*Tit.* 5.2.1–3). While Judah does not see through Tamar's disguise, Titus forewarns Tamora, 'I know thee well / For our proud Empress, mighty Tamora' (*Tit.* 5.2.25–6) and usurps her role to plot his own counter-revenge. Lavinia's belief that Tamora has foresworn all womanhood is realized at the feast where conventions of hospitality and gender are grotesquely inverted. Titus plays the female roles of cook and of Procne the revenger while Tamora plays the part of Tereus in consuming her own sons' flesh. Titus confines the **Empress**'s supernatural ambitions to a self-consuming dinner-table jest. All her hopes for the future are, metaphorically, reduced and contained in the pie 'Whereof their mother daintily hath fed / Eating the flesh that she herself hath bred' (5.3.61–2).

On a grander scale, Tamora's eating of her sons' flesh is compared to the power of the feminized **earth** as **womb** and tomb (5.3.191). Her closeness to earthly fertility is dramatized in Act 2. Remarkable sensuality and sensitivity pulse through her lines describing to her lover the beauty of the forest grove and its secret cave (2.3.10–29). Aaron the Moor tells Tamora that **Venus** governs her desires (2.3.30). As with Tamar in Genesis, Tamora's pursuit of a taboo relationship sows confusion, manifested with the birth of a mixed-race baby: 'Our Empress' shame, and stately Rome's disgrace' (4.2.60). Tamora's command to have it killed before it betrays her adultery anticipates the ruthless pragmatism she pursues when leaving her sons with Titus.

(c) Ben Jonson's *The Masque of Queens* (1609) with the dramatization of Tomyris is in *Court Masques*, edited by David Lindley (1995: 35–53). Wynne-Davies (1991) and Tina Mohler (2006) discuss Tamora as part of the play's extended trope of the womb and tomb. S. P. Cerasano (1994) analyses the Peacham drawing and the queenly presentation of Tamora at its centre. Liz Oakley-Brown (2009) analyses the character with reference to an ongoing rhetorical and symbolic construction of queenship.

Tearsheet, (a) The surname of a character in *Henry IV Parts I* and *II*, a whore who is mistress to Sir John Falstaff.

(b) Her name means sheets made of hemp, not that she tears sheets (Greer 2007: 152–3). For further information, *see* **Dorothy**.

temperance, (a) one of the four cardinal virtues, the habit of restraining oneself in passion, desire, eating or drinking, though not specifically in relation to abstinence from alcohol in early modern English usage. Temperance connoted continence and sobriety in humans and moderation in non-human contexts such as temperature and climate.

(b) A single reference, 'Temperance was a delicate **wench**' (*Temp.* 2.1.44) by Antonio in his discussion of the island's climate, conflates woman and territory, a technique that will later be used of **Miranda** in the betrothal masque. Sebastian cynically picks up on the implications of 'wench', to mean 'prostitute' or 'serving maid', in noting that Temperance is 'a subtle' woman. She may thus be far from possessing the delicate, restrained and virtuous qualities implied by her name. Thomas Wilson's *Christian Dictionarie* defined temperance as 'a moderation of the minde in the vse of outward blessings, holding vs backe from excesse' (Wilson 1612: 480). Evidence that Shakespeare uses the term ironically is found where Mistress **Quickly** tells Doll Tearsheet 'you are now in an excellent good temperality' meaning she is in good health in spite of having 'drunk too much canaries, and that's a marvellous searching wine' (*2HIV* 2.4.22–9). As a prostitute and a heavy drinker of wine, Doll is the exact opposite of the chastity and self-denial commonly associated with the virtue in early modern England.

(c) Thomas Wilson, *A Christian Dictionarie* (1612: 480) defines the virtue as one of self-regulation.

Thaisa, (a) a character in *Pericles*, daughter of Simonides and wife to Pericles whose name is taken from one of Shakespeare's sources.

(b) In Gower's *Confessio Amantis* and Twine's *Patterne of Painefull Adventures* (in Bullough Vol. VI (1966)), it is the daughter figure (**Marina**) who is named Thaisa (Williams 2002: 605). However, *Pericles* creates parallels between the three mother-less daughters of the play: Antiochus's daughter and Thaisa, who have no mothers, and then Marina, whose mother is supposed dead and drowned at sea. Thaisa is structurally the mediatory figure between Antiochus's **daughter** and Marina: the pivot on which Pericles's story moves from the site of outlawed incestuous family bonds to the restoration of a nuclear family. She is 'beauty's child, whom nature gat / For men to see and seeing wonder at' (2.2.6–7), an introduction that glances back to the forbidden prize that is Antiochus's daughter. By choosing her own husband, Thaisa moves determinedly out of the incest narrative, demonstrating the kind of agency that her daughter inherits and uses to survive in Myteline. Thaisa's close kinship with Marina is clear in Lychorida's description of the baby as 'a piece of your dead queen' and then 'all that is left living of your queen' (3.1.17–18 and 20). Thaisa's supposed death dramatically lengthens the usual period of female confinement and absence from the community that occurred after childbirth. Her revival at the hands of Cerimon is an organic process that looks back to her identity as a '**beauty**'s **child** whom nature gat'. Cerimon points out '**Nature** awakes / A warmth breathes out of her' (3.2.92–3). Thaisa's retirement to **Diana**'s temple in a '**vestal** livery' (3.4.10) recreates the illusion of a **virgin**al daughter and the re-making of a legitimate family for Pericles when he recognises her:

> Thaisa: Did you not name a tempest,
>   A birth, and death?
> Pericles: The voice of dead Thaisa!
> Thaisa: That Thaisa am I, supposed dead
>   And drown'd.
>
> (*Per.* 5.3.33–6)

In these lines Thaisa adopts the chiastic structure that characterises the play as a whole. Her name and identity stand at the centre of the text on micro and macro levels, as the pivot to turn the play from tragedy to comedy.
(c) Twine's *Patterne of Painefull Adventures* which names Thaisa as the daughter figure is found in Bullough, Vol. VI (1966: 423–82). Deanne Williams' (2002) essay, primarily about Marina, pays attention to Thaisa's place in the play's shift from the dangers of incest and tragedy to comic family resolution. Gossett (2003) draws attention to events in Shakespeare's family, and the potential dangers surrounding the birth of Elizabeth Hall to his daughter Susanna in 1608, as an influence on the play.

Thetis, (a) a semi-divine figure from Greek mythology, the daughter of Nereus and Doris, one of the **Nereids** who was fated to bear a son mightier than his father. She was the mother of Achilles.
(b) Antony refers to **Cleopatra** as 'Thetis' (*A&C* 3.7.59), appropriately allying her with Thetis as a powerful sea figure in view of the imminent sea battle. In Golding's translation of Ovid's *Metamorphoses* (1567), Thetis is introduced as an openly erotic figure 'Starke naked, ryding bravely on a byrdled Dolphins backe' (Ovidius 2000: XI.271), perhaps recalling the mermaid described by Oberon (*MND* 2.1.150) and eroticizing this allusion to Queen **Elizabeth** I. 'Thetis' is certainly an apt name for the Cleopatra of 'infinite variety' (*A&C* 2.2.235) because the sea nymph is also a metamorphic creature who assumes the shape of bird, a log, and a tiger to evade Peleus in the love chase (Ovidius, 2000: XI.277–9). Nestor and **Dionyza** identify 'gentle Thetis' as **goddess** of the sea, whose '**patient** breast' bears boats. Her serenity here disguises strength and self-assertion; when provoked by Boreas the wind, she rouses the seas (*T&C* 1.3.38–41). Dionyza describes the sea-born **Marina** as 'Thetis' birth-child' (*Per.* 4.4.41) and recounts the sea-goddess's anger at her death. Thetis creates storms 'and swears she'll never stint, / Make raging battery upon shores of flint' (*Per.* 4.4.42–3). Less respectful references to Thetis occur in *Troilus and Cressida* as part of the bathos used to satirize the Greek and Trojan heroes. The proud and foolish Achilles is greeted as 'great Thetis' son!' (*T&C* 3.3.94) but Achilles' horse is said to be as valuable as 'many Thetis' sons', or many Achilleses (*T&C* 1.3.211–12).
(c) Details about Thetis's role in mythology can be round in the *Oxford Classical Dictionary* edited by Hammond and Scullard (1970: 1063–4). Thetis appears in Book XI of Ovid's *Metamorphoses*, lines 270–302 (Ovidius, 2000: 280–1). *See also* **nereids** and **nymphs**).

thing, (a) bawdy slang meaning the vagina in relation to women and the penis with reference to men; more generally, 'thing' is a degrading term for a woman.

(b) Bawdy allusions to a woman's 'thing' are always demeaning in Shakespeare's texts. When **Emilia** prepares to offer Iago the handkerchief to 'please his fantasy', he crudely asks 'You have a thing for me? It is a common thing?' (*Oth.* 3.3.299–302) implicitly aligning **Desdemona**'s potential sexual profligacy as well as Emilia's as the product of his biased, misogynist viewpoint. Launce is less disturbed by the thought that his **mistress** 'is too liberal', acknowledging that although he can control her tongue and her spending, 'of another thing she may, and that I cannot help' (*TGV* 3.1.348–52). Flute draws upon the innuendo of both 'thing' and '**nothing**' to observe that 'A paramour is / (God bless us!) a thing of naught' (*MND* 4.2 14). Hamlet's refusal to acknowledge Claudius as anything but his mother leads him to define the King in these typically feminine terms, too:

> Hamlet: The King as a thing –
> Guildenstern: A thing my lord?
> Hamlet: Of nothing.
>
> > (*Ham.* 4.2.28–30)

Degraded sexuality is often suggested by the term. Kent vows that he is neither too young 'to love any woman for singing nor so old to dote on her for any thing' (*KL* 1.4.37–8). The Dauphin derides the French Constable's sexual taste by saying 'Thou mak'st use of any thing' to which the latter responds, punning on horse/whores, 'Yet I do not use my horse for my mistress' (*HV* 3.7.65–7). Less immediately crude, but none the less offensive, are the voyeuristic observations of Edward IV's brothers as he tries to sexually bribe the **widow**ed Lady Elizabeth Grey: 'I see the lady hath a thing to grant, / Before the King will grant her humble suit' (*3HVI* 3.2.12–13). Compliments are rendered self-consciously distasteful by the euphemism 'thing'. When Lord Sands asks **Anne** Bullen to join in his toast, in Fletcher and Shakespeare's *Henry VIII*, she engages knowingly in the flirtatious game of innuendo:

> Sands: Here's to your ladyship, and pledge it, madam
>   For 'tis to such a thing –
> Anne: You cannot show me.
>
> > (*HVIII* 1.4.47–8)

Even Lucio's description of **Isabella** as 'a thing enskied and sainted' (*MM* 1.4.34) defines her reductively as an inviolable sexual **commodity**.

By its very nature, the term objectifies women's bodies. Petruchio insults **Katherina** by defining her as goods and chattels: 'My household stuff, my field, my barn, / My horse, my ox, my ass, my any thing' (*Shrew* 3.2.230–2), but perhaps the most degrading objectification of woman is Touchstone's introduction of **Audrey** as 'an ill-favor'd thing, sir, but mine own' (*AYLI* 5.4.57–8). No one has a clearer sense of the marketable nature of sexuality than **Cressida** who regards her virginity as a thing whose value can be increased or at least maintained by witholding it from the market rather than immediately pursuing her desire:

> Yet hold I off. Women are angels, wooing:
> Things won are done, joy's soul lies in the doing.
> She that belov'd knows nought that knows not this:
> Men prize the thing ungain'd more than it is.
> (*T&C* 1.2.286–9)

The value of **Helen**'s sexuality is debated by the Trojans; Hector arguing that she is 'a thing not ours, nor worth to us / (Had it our name) the value of one ten' of the soldiers they have lost (*T&C* 2.2.22–3). Even more blatantly, Iachimo tempts Posthumus into bargaining over **Imogen**'s sexuality by challenging his view that it is 'not a thing for sale' (*Cym.* 1.4.84). In *Pericles*, **Marina**'s virginity is offered for sale and described as 'no cheap thing, if men were as they have been' (*Per.* 4.2.61–2).

The term registers, often bitterly, that a woman is a disposable **commodity** since 'Love is like a child / That longs for every thing that he can come by' (*TGV* 3.1.124–5). Ladies can do nothing but accept that 'Men were deceivers ever . . . To one thing constant never' (*MAdo* 2.3.65–5). **Julia** pretends to talk about the musicians but thinks about Proteus's infidelity, when she would 'always have one play but one thing' (*TGV* 2.4.72). **Portia** scathingly adds to the sexual connotations of **ring** by describing it as 'A thing stuck on with oaths upon your finger' and tells Bassanio, 'I will become as liberal as you' and will not deny the doctor 'any thing I have / No not my body, nor my husband's bed' (*Mer.* 5.1.168 and 226–8). Gratiano picks up on the double entendre in vowing to 'fear no other thing / So sore as keeping safe Nerissa's ring' (*Mer.* 5.1.306–7).
(c) Patricia Parker (1987: 105–46 (esp.) 118–21), examines the representation and exposure or opening of female privacy and sexual organs, with some discussion of the term 'thing'.

Thisbe, (a) a character from mythology who is represented by Flute the bellows-mender in Peter Quince's 'Pyramus and Thisbe' the play-within-the-play in *A Midsummer Night's Dream*. Thisbe is a young woman of Babylon, beloved of Pyramus.
(b) The myth, which originated in Asia Minor as the tale of the river god Pyramus for the fountain Thisbe (Taylor 2007: 282), was popularized in early modern England by Ovid's *Metamorphoses*, especially the 1567 English translation (Ovidius 2000: IV.67–201). Ovid recounts how Pyramus and Thisbe's parents forbade their love so they talked through a chink in a wall, plotting to elope at night and meet beside a mulberry tree at Ninus's tomb outside the walls of the city of Babylon. Thisbe, who arrived first, was frightened off by a lioness, dropping her mantle or scarf which the lion tore to pieces with its bloody mouth. Pyramus, on discovering the bloodied mantle, committed suicide, dyeing the white fruit of mulberry tree with his blood. Thisbe returned to find her dead lover and killed herself with his

sword, appealing to their parents to bury them in one grave. As well as inspiring Peter Quince's dramatic adaptation '*The most lamentable comedy and most cruel death of Pyramus and Thisby*' (*MND* 1.2.11–12), Thisbe's tragedy informs that of **Juliet** and plays out the potentially tragic consequences of **Hermia**'s elopement with Lysander. Mercutio glances across to *Midsummer Night's Dream*, commenting that, to the besotted Romeo, even the beautiful Thisbe would only be rated as 'a grey eye or so, but not to the purpose' (*R&J* 2.4.45). Although Shakespeare knew Ovid's version well, his own references to Thisbe's fate seem to draw on additional sources in which the lion is male, in particular John Gower's account of 1390 in *Confessio Amantis* (Taylor 2007: 282), and possibly Thomson's *New Sonet of Pyramus and Thisbe* in *A Handful of Plesant Delites* (1584) which also has a male lion. In *Merchant of Venice*, Jessica refers to Thisbe's story as an archetype of daring love,

> In such a night
> Did Thisby fearfully o'ertrip the dew,
> And saw the lion's shadow ere himself,
> And ran dismayed away.
>
> (*Mer.* 5.1.6–9)

The dew on the grass here recalls Lysander's lines about eloping with **Hermia** (*MND* 1.1.211) rather than Ovid. The male lion remains in Peter Quince's dramatization of the tale in *A Midsummer Night's Dream*. Even in the mechanicals' mangled translation, Thisbe's lines echo details from the earlier retellings. She calls Pyramus 'most lily-white of hue' like the fruit of the mulberry tree at Ninus's tomb, which Flute comically reinvents as 'Ninny's tomb' (*MND* 3.1.93–7).

Thisbe's name and role strategically draw attention to the performance of women's roles by **boy actor**s. Flute the bellows-mender is told 'You must take Thisby on you', not a wandering knight of romance but 'the lady that Pyramus must love' (*MND* 1.2.44–6) The boy complains 'let me not play a woman, I have a beard coming' but is quickly told he can play it in a **mask**. As if to underline the accepted theatrical convention that women's parts were played by adolescent or child boy actors, not adult male actors, Bottom gives a grotesque performance of Thisby in a 'monstrous little voice', presumably falsetto: 'Ah, Pyramus my lover dear! thy Thisby dear, and lady dear!' (*MND* 1.2.47–54). The vocal strain may dramatize the literal breaking point for boy performers, after which they would no longer be able to perform leading roles like Rosalind or Cleopatra because their voices had changed. No more complaints are heard from Flute whose voice, as his name implies, is still a treble.

In the performance at Theseus's court, the interaction between the lovers via the third actor playing the wall gives ample opportunity for physical comedy. Thisbe's performance, in particular, may have inspired Thomas Moffett's rewriting of the tale as an encomium that verges on mock encomium in *The Silkwormes and their Flies* (London, 1599), written for the Countess of Pembroke and the ladies of her household. Thisbe's complaints to the wall whose stones she has often kissed are taken up by Moffett's lines that 'kisses staide on eithers side fast linckt, / Seal'd to the wal with lips and Louers glue' (Moffett 1599: 11). His focus on Thisbe leaving the house (not found in Ovid or dramatised by Peter Quince) seems closer to **Juliet**'s haste and Friar Lawrence's warning:

> Loue made her bold, loue gaue her swiftnesse more
> Then vsually is found in weaker sexe,
> But all in vaine: nay rather to her ill,
> For haste made waste, and speede did speeding kil.
>
> (Moffett 1599: 12)

The mock-tragic yet poignant tone that characterizes Moffett's retelling of the story was perhaps specifically designed to appeal to the Countess of Pembroke, a dozen years after the death of her brother, Philip Sidney.

In Shakespeare, Thisbe's mourning for Pyramus: 'These lily lips, / This cherry nose, / These yellow cowslip cheeks', is comically distracted, a muddled version of the usual blazon applied to women (*MND* 5.1.330–2). At the same time there is an opportunity for the boy actor playing Flute who is playing Thisbe to sound a note of raw emotion in his/her sense of loss; that these qualities 'Are gone, are gone!' (*MND* 5.1.333). Sam Rockwell's performance, a redeeming feature of the 1999 film version directed by Michael Hoffman, plays Thisbe's loss as tragic, demonstrating the potential of cross-dressed boy actors to perform major tragic roles. In a performance on the early modern public stage, Flute-as-Thisbe's grief at losing the lily lips and cherry nose would have been doubly inflected: it dramatizes every boy actor's imminent farewell to the woman's part that, as an adult, he would no longer play.

(c) Pyramus and Thisbe's story is in Book 4, lines 67–201 of Ovid's *Metamorphoses*, as translated by Golding in 1567 (Ovidius 2000: 88–91). J. Thomson's *A New Sonet of Pyramus and Thisbe* in *A Handful of Plesant Delites* (1584), is reprinted in Bullough, Vol. I (1964: 409–11). Thomas Moffett's poem *The Silkwormes and their Flies* (London, 1599), has been the cause of considerable critical debate with Kenneth Muir (1954) and A. S. T. Fisher (1949) arguing that it is a source, a view conclusively refuted by Katherine Duncan-Jones (1981). She further persuasively argues, in 'Frances Meres, Playgoer' (2009) that Francis Meres identified Thisbe with the tragic heroine Juliet, having seen *Dream* in performance before its publication. Taylor, 'John Gower and "Pyramus and Thisbe"' (2007: 282–3) draws attention to the Gower source. Stanley Wells (2009) summarizes the arguments for adolescent boys rather than adult male actors performing the roles of women. Sam Rockwell plays Thisbe as tragic by taking off his wig for the last part of the performance in *A Midsummer Night's Dream*, directed by Michael Hoffman (1999). Stephen Buhler, *Shakespeare in the Cinema: Ocular Proof* (2002: 185–7) comments very briefly on its moving quality.

Timandra, (a) a character in *Timon of Athens* who, like her friend **Phrynia**, is a **courtezan** to Alcibiades and just appears in one scene of the play.

(b) Timon takes an interest in this character as the 'Athenian minion' (*Tim.* 4.3.80) or darling of the city and addresses her specifically by name.

> Timon: Art thou Timandra?
> Timandra: Yes.
> Timon: Be a whore still. They love thee not that use thee.
>
> (*Tim.* 4.3.82–4)

Alcibiades then repeats her name 'sweet Timandra' in conjunction with the hero's 'brave Timon' (4.3.89–91) paralleling the two. The similarity in name sounds suggests that these two characters function allegorically as gender opposites; both are as former favourites of the city now scrabbling for a living. Woman continues to occupy an inferior role as dependant since Timon finds gold and pours it into Timandra and Phrynia's **aprons** (4.3.135–6), continuing to buy them as **whores** even after he is supposedly dispossessed of material concerns.

(c) Kahn (1997: 154–6) comments on these characters' contribution to the play's bitter satire. *See* **Phrynia**.

tire, (a) an elaborate fashionable headdress made of wire and worn by wealthier women. The headdresses could be twisted into a variety of elaborate shapes.

(b) Shakespeare probably had first-hand experience of the construction of tires and their popularity as luxury fashion accessories from his acquaintances in Silver Street and lodging with Marie **Mountjoy** and her husband from 1602. Christopher Mountjoy was a tire-maker who had at least one commission from Court (Schoenbaum 1987: 260–1). The accounts for Queen Elizabeth's wardrobe afford a glimpse of how expensively decorated tires could be. In 1603, for example, Dorothy Speckard was paid for making 'three dozen of devices made of blacke silke and wyer in the maner of leaves; twelve devces made of heare in the maner of Peramides; twenty fourse devices in maner of globes' (Arnold 1988: 226). The 12 pyramid-shaped devices incorporated prosthetic hair.

Falstaff flatters Mistress **Ford**, telling her that the beauty of her brow would look well in any of the fashionable head-dresses: 'the ship tire, the tire-valiant, or any tire of Venetian admittance' (*MWW* 3.3.56–7). The fashion for elaborate headdresses on stage is mocked in Marston's *Histrio-mastix* (1610), in which Post-haste asks 'My maisters, what tire wears your lady on her head?' and Belch answers, 'Foare Squirrels tails ti'de in a true loves knot' (sig. C2v). **Hero**'s wedding head-dress apparently includes prosthetic hair since **Margaret** observes, 'I like the tire within excellently, if the hair were a thought browner' (*MAdo* 3.4.13–14). **Julia**, disguised as a page, scrutinizes a picture of her rival and admires **Silvia's** 'tire' or head-dress. Having compared their hair colour, she vows to get an auburn periwig if that is what Proteus prefers (*TGV* 4.4.185–91). The tire is a clearly gendered piece of costume in *Antony and Cleopatra* where Cleopatra claims she has dressed the drunken Antony up in her '**tires**' and worn his sword (*A&C* 2.5.21–3).

(c) Arnold (1988: 28–30 and 226) contains illustrations of tires worn by the queen and nobility but little description of these. See also Georgine De Courtais (1973: 62).

Titania, (a) a character in *A Midsummer Night's Dream*, whose name Shakespeare appears to have taken from the Latin original of Ovid's *Metamorphoses*. The name derives from the Titans, the twelve elder gods (six male and six female) of the early Greeks. The female gods were Rhea, Themis, Mnemosyne, Theia, **Phoebe** and **Tethis**.

(b) Ovid refers to multiple goddesses – Diana, Latona, Circe, Pyrrha – as Titan's daughters (Bate 1993: 136). In Shakespeare, 'Titan' is used exclusively to mean the god of the sun, as in 'Titan's rays on earth' or 'Titan's face / Blushing to be encount'red with a cloud' (*Tit.* 1.1.226 and 2.4.31–2), so it seems probable that the name 'Titania' in *A Midsummer Night's Dream* is designed primarily to invoke the Titan **Phoebe**, goddess of the **moon**. The first time the name is heard or read is Oberon's angry line, 'Ill met by moonlight, proud Titania' (*MND* 2.1.60). In Titania's first speech she appears to identify herself with the moon, the 'governess of floods' (2.1.103), by recounting how 'the winds, piping to us in vain, / As in revenge, have suck'd up from the sea / Contagious fogs' (2.1.88–90). Titania's anger with Oberon is aligned with the moon's who 'Pale in her anger, washes all the air, / That rheumatic diseases do abound' (2.1.203–5). Titania aligns herself and her counterpart Oberon with elder gods or Titans, reminding him that their 'dissension' or disagreement makes them responsible for environmental disorders on earth: 'We are their parents and original' (2.1.115–17). As Thomas Baynes noted in 1880, by choosing 'Titania' as the name for the fairy queen, Shakespeare implicitly empowers her with the same status as the early Greek gods: the ultimate power of the universe (Kennedy and Kennedy 1999: 274–6). Raising the fairy queen's status by this means makes her coupling with Bottom appear all the more paradoxical and shameful. Puck gleefully juxtaposes the two: 'so it came to pass / Titania wak'd, and straightway lov'd an ass' (3.2.33–4).

Although Titania's name links her most directly with the moon, her behaviour does carry traces of other Titan goddessses whose shared powers overlap with the triple goddess (Phoebe-Diana-Hecate). Like the maternal figure Rhea, Titania refuses to surrender a child to her spouse. Like Theia (goddess of sight), she takes an overview of the world and its environment. As Phoebe, her power extends over the sea, like the goddess Thetis, and she watches over the 'embark'd traders on the flood' (2.1.127). Titania personifies Mnemosyne's character as goddess of memory in her determination to honour the memory of her **votaress** 'and for her sake do I rear up her boy / And for her sake I will not part with him' (2.1.136–7). Titania's determination to remember signals a continued commitment to the **Amazon**ian culture of female agency (linked to **Diana** and to Queen **Elizabeth** I) which challenges patriarchy in the play. The fairy queen's kinship with Themis (goddess of prophecy and divine law) is glimpsed in her belief that the lovers' dreams

> More witnesseth than fancy's images,
> And grows to something of great constancy;
> But howsoever, strange and admirable.
>
> (*MND* 5.1.25–7)

At the level of plot, the divine autonomy Titania represents is ultimately eclipsed, the moon appropriated as a male tool, the Amazonian past and the female characters silenced. Titania's awakening from her dream marks the beginning of this confinement. Oberon refers to her as 'my Titania' and 'my sweet **queen**' and it is on these terms that she dutifully takes hands to accept him as 'my Oberon' (4.1.75–6).

(c) Shakespeare's choice of 'Titania', derived from the Latin original of Ovid which uses the name Titania for Diana (III.173) and Titan's daughter for Diana, Latona (VI.346), **Circe** (XIV.382 and 438) and Pyrrha (I.395), was noted by Arthur Baynes in 1880 (reprinted in the *Critical Heritage* volume on the play, edited by Kennedy and Kennedy (1999: 274–6). Bate (1993: 136) also refers to this. Briggs (1962) and Buccola (2006) discuss Titania in the context of early modern beliefs in magic and fairies.

tongue, (a) the fleshy, muscular organ in the mouth used by humans for articulating speech in addition to tasting; also a particular language form. Because conduct books modelled the ideal woman as **chaste**, silent and obedient in early modern England, control of the tongue was a critical part of women's self-fashioning.

(b) A woman's tongue, along with her sexual and social status, is a defining feature. The most fearful punishment the men of Navarre can devise to enforce the decree that 'No woman shall come within a mile of my court' is not death but 'on pain of losing her tongue' (*LLL* 1.1.120–4). One of the first things **Cleopatra** wants of know about **Octavia** is whether she is 'Shrill-tongued or low'? (*A&C* 3.3.12). Injunctions for women's conduct placed limitations on their tongues, idealizing the soft voice as a symbolic mark of **chastity** and obedience as well as silence. Bartholomew the Page must speak 'with soft low tongue' (*Shrew* Ind. 1.114) to play the part of a desirable **lady**-wife and Lucrece's **maid** has a 'soft slow tongue, true mark of modesty' (*Luc.* 1220). To Iago, the ideal woman is one who 'hath tongue at will, and yet was never loud' (*Oth.* 2.1.149). Launce remembers that his mistress cannot be 'too liberal' 'of her tongue' since 'her chief virtue' in his view, is that 'she is slow in words', and 'to be slow in words is a woman's only virtue' (*TGV* 3.1.332–6 and 348–50). **Portia**, bound by the terms of her father's will, falls back on the cultural convention, 'a maiden hath no tongue but thought', in order to explain her silence and frustration at not being able to help Bassanio with the casket test (*Mer.* 3.2.8).

Such references to women's tongues make it clear that women are not naturally silent. Their tongues must be trained to serve the purposes of their masters; their action carefully self-policed by their owners. **Octavia**, who prefers to whisper rather than speak out in public, models the ideal of strategic female speech used gently in the service of men. Her tongue becomes a trope for her mediatory role between Antony and Octavius Caeasar.

> Her tongue will not obey her heart, nor can
> Her heart inform her tongue, – the swan's down feather,

> That stands upon the swell at full of tide,
> And neither way inclines.
>
> (*A&C* 3.2.47–50)

Volumnia's advice to speak 'such words that are but rooted in / Your tongue, though but bastards and syllables / Of no allowance to your bosom's truth' is based on years of schooling her own tongue (*Cor.* 3.2.55–7). **Hermione** manages her verbal dexterity much less successfully. She plays a dangerous game by pretending to perform verbal subordination. When Leontes questions her silence, 'Tongue-tied our queen?' she tells him, 'I had thought, sir, to have held my peace until / You had drawn oaths from him [Polixenes] not to stay' (*WT* 1.2.27–9). This flaunting of her superior persuasive rhetoric undermines Leontes's confidence in her sexual fidelity. **Goneril** and **Regan**'s flattering lies do fool Lear and silence **Cordelia** who is sure 'my love's / More ponderous than my tongue' (*KL* 1.1.77–8). Nevertheless, she fully appreciates that her lack of 'such a tongue / That I am glad I have not', and her failure to use hers strategically is disastrous and 'hath lost me in your liking' (*KL* 1.1.230–2).

Female characters who speak what they feel rather than what they ought to say to please their male superiors, are well aware of the risks. **Paulina** is referred to as 'lewd-tongu'd' (*WT* 2.3.172) for no logical reason and sexually libelled as 'a **callet** / Of boundless tongue' (*WT* 2.3.91–2) by Leontes, but nevertheless determines to speak out in Hermione's defence:

> If I prove honey-mouth'd, let my tongue blister;
> And never to my red-look'd anger be
> The trumpet any more.
>
> (*WT* 2.1.31–3)

She knows her real duty is to 'use that tongue I have' and is confident that 'if wit flow from't / As boldness from my **bosom**' (*WT* 2.1.50–2), she must do some good. This does not happen immediately but her words to Leontes, 'as bitter / Upon thy tongue as in my thought' (*WT* 5.1.18–19), are the harsh medicine that ultimately crafts the play's resolution. **Constance**, too, feels that male injustice justifies her tongue's power to speak out and curse John: 'since law itself is perfect wrong, / How can the law forbid my tongue to curse?' (*KJ* 3.1.189–90). She wishes 'that my tongue were in the thunder's mouth!' since criticisms from 'a lady's feeble voice' are seldom heeded (*KJ* 3.4.38–41).

For a lower-class woman to use her tongue is potentially even more transgressive. Acute sensitivity to class rather than gender constraints silences **Helena** in *All's Well*: 'only sin / And hellish obstinacy tie thy tongue, / That truth should be suspected. Speak, is't so?' observes the **Countess** (*AWW* 1.3.179–81). Being a **dower**less daughter whose royal title is suspect, Queen **Margaret** of Anjou should not 'let thy tongue detect thy base-born heart' (*3HVI* 2.2.142–3), according to Richard of Gloucester. He later admits that her 'sland'rous tongue' provoked him to murder Prince Edward (*RIII* 1.2.97).

Two references explicitly reverse the injunction on women to be chaste, silent and obedient. The fairy queen **Titania**, whose tongue carries the same exceptional authority as **Elizabeth** I, commands, 'Tie up my love's tongue, bring him silently' (*MND* 3.1.201). The garrulous Gratiano claims that 'silence is only commendable / In a neat's tongue dried and a maid not vendible' – that is, not attractive enough to marry on other virtues than the conventional silence of the **sex** (*Mer.* 1.1.111–12). More often, women's tongues in Shakespeare are presented negatively as the objects of male fear and mockery and women's self-mockery.

The tongue is, of course, the weapon of the **scold**, its phallic associations endowing her with a supposedly unseemly masculine power. **Katherina** is 'Renown'd in Padua for her scolding tongue' (*Shrew* 1.2.100) while **Bianca** must 'bear the penance of her tongue' and be enclosed within the house (*Shrew* 1.1.89). Petruchio's hyperbolic comparison of a woman's scolding to lions roaring, storms at sea, thunder, and the sounds of battle makes it patently obvious that the extraordinary noise associated with the scold's tongue is a cultural construct rather than a natural phenomenon:

> Have I not in a pitched battle heard
> Loud 'larums, neighing steeds, and trumpets' clang?
> And do you tell me of a woman's tongue,
> That gives not half so great a blow to hear
> As will a chestnut in a farmer's fire?
>
> (*Shrew* 1.2.205–9)

When Katherina insists that a wasp wears his sting 'in his tongue' (allying her scolding with a masculine defence), Petruchio appropriates the trope 'Whose tongue?' to declare his intentions of matching her outrageous speech. His bawdy vision of their engagement 'with my tongue in your **tail**' also reveals the subversive sexual excitement Katherina's scolding gives him (*Shrew* 2.1.215–18). Stephano's song in *The Tempest* features another scolding Kate who 'had a tongue with a tang / Would cry to a sailor "Go hang!"' (*Temp.* 2.2.50–1).

Cleopatra immediately slanders her rival **Fulvia**, remarking that Antony blushes with shame 'when shrill-tongu'd Fulvia scolds' (*A&C* 1.1.32). Although Cleopatra's jibe is motivated by jealousy, it may also draw on the common knowledge that Fulvia was not to be trifled with since she had cut out the tongue of the philosopher Cicero (Willet 1602: sig A3). The scold type is very obviously a misogynist construct in *Othello* where Iago jokes that if **Emilia** gives Cassio 'as much of her lips / As of her tongue she bestows on me, / You would have enough', a charge to which she responds, appropriately, with silence. Though **Desdemona** points out 'Alas! she has no speech', Iago protests 'too much', saying Emilia 'puts her tongue a little in her heart / And chides with thinking' (*Oth.* 2.1.100–7). The text silently persuades readers and spectators to authorise the female tongue and condemn the spirit of misogyny which forbids it when Emilia is commanded 'charm your tongue' and refuses: 'I will not charm my tongue; I am bound to speak' (*Oth.* 5.1.183–4). Emilia's outspoken tongue and the truth it carries is, like that of her smothered mistress, silenced by murder. The associations between scold, tongue and truth are maintained in *Measure for Measure*, when **Isabella** calls from outside the prison, and the Duke exclaims 'the tongue of Isabel' rather than the voice, as if anticipating a tirade once she hears Claudio is dead. In the following scenes Angelo also recognizes 'How might she tongue me!' (*MM* 4.3.107 and 4.4.25).

The sharpness of women's tongues, even those who are not labelled as scolds, is a cause of male anxiety. The **Princess** of France and her ladies have amazingly sharp wits and rhetorical skills which make their tongues threatening weapons:

> The tongues of mocking wenches are as keen
> As is the razor's edge invisible,
> Cutting a smaller hair than may be seen;
> Above the sense of sense, so sensible
> Seemeth their conference, their conceits have wings
> Fleeter than arrows, bullets, wind, thought, swifter things
> (*LLL* 5.2.256–61)

Benedick calls **Beatrice** 'Lady Tongue', claiming that 'she speaks poinards and every word stabs' (*MAdo* 2.1.275 and 247–8). Indeed, Leonato warns her, 'thou wilt never get a husband, if thou be so shrewd of thy tongue' (*MAdo* 2.1.18–19). Disparagingly compared to a parrot, Beatrice tells Benedick, 'A bird of my tongue is better than a beast of yours', who would not speak, to which he retorts, 'I would my horse had the speed of your tongue, and so good a continuer' (*MAdo* 1.1.139–42). **Margaret**, too, is challenged for volubility: 'What pace is this that thy tongue keeps?' (*MAdo* 3.4.93). As the confrontations between characters like Constance and Eleanor show, women's tongues can be used as weapons against each other. Mowbray describes 'a woman's war' as 'the bitter clamour of two eager tongues' (*RII* 1.1.49). The painful breakdown of same sex relations between women is half-consciously registered in **Helena**'s line to her former friend 'Will you tear / Impatient answers from my gentle tongue?' (*MND* 3.2.286–7).

Female tongues are credited with the power to poison, tempt and deceive. Alençon voices a common male opinion that 'these women are shrewd tempters with their tongues' (*1HVI* 1.2.123) and **Joan** La **Pucelle**, the 'enchantress', is commanded 'hold thy tongue!' as though her speech is dangerous (*1HVI* 5.3.52). Margaret of Anjou's tongue 'more poisons than the adder's tooth' (*3HVI* 1.4.112) and Lear accuses the false Goneril of striking him 'with her tongue / Most serpent-like, upon the very heart' (*KL* 2.4.160–1). The seductive power of women's tongues is often masked: through physical disguises like **Rosalind**'s Ganymede, or linguistic masks like Lady **Mortimer**'s Welsh. Mortimer tells his wife

> thy tongue
> Makes Welsh as sweet as ditties highly penn'd,
> Sung by a fair queen in a summer's bower,

> With ravishing division, to her lute
>
> (*1HIV* 3.1.205–8)

but only Welsh speakers can understand this secret language of seduction. **Helen**'s supposedly 'golden tongue' (*T&C* 1.2.105), shown in only one scene of *Troilus and Cressida*, is disappointingly trivial and conventional in its concerns. The idea of the powerfully seductive female tongue is exposed as a delusion in *A Midsummer Night's Dream* and *Titus Andronicus*. Helena's wish that 'My tongue should catch your sweet tongue's melody' (*MND* 1.1.189) is produced by desperate envy. Marcus's thought that **Lavinia** would charm her rapists by the 'heavenly harmony / Which that sweet tongue hath made' (*Tit.* 2.4.48–50) is hopelessly romantic and unrealistic.

Because women's tongues are culturally circumscribed, volubility is comically gendered as a female vice although the texts show that men's tongues wag as frantically as women's. Falstaff has a 'whole school of tongues in this belly of mine' (*2HIV* 4.3.18–22). Hotspur is reprimanded 'what a wasp-stung and impatient fool / Art thou to break into this woman's mood, / Tying thine ear to no tongue but thine own! (*1HIV* 1.3.236–8). The excited Rosalind is likewise reprimanded by **Celia** for leaving no room for interlocutors: 'Cry "holla" to thy tongue, I prithee; it curvets unreasonably' (*AYLI* 3.2.244–5). Perhaps this long part was designed to be spoken quickly; **Phoebe** comments 'faster than his tongue / Did make offence, his eye did heal it up' (*AYLI* 3.5.116–17).

However frequently the female tongue is a focus of mockery, anxiety or derision, it is clear that Shakespeare's texts regard it as essential to women's self-fashioning. **Rosalind** argues, 'You shall never take her without her answer, unless you take her without her tongue' (*AYLI* 4.1.172–3). Since mothers were responsible for teaching their children to speak, male characters regard rhetorical dexterity as a valuable maternal legacy. Prince Edward is told, 'Whoever got thee, there thy mother stands / For well I wot, thou hast thy mother's tongue' (*3HVI* 2.2.133–4) and Moth asks 'my father's wit and my mother's tongue assist me' (*LLL* 1.2.96). Longaville later jokes with **Katherine**, 'You have a double tongue within your mask / And would afford my speechless visage half' (*LLL* 5.2.245–6). Katherina expresses most eloquently women's need to speak, even if it is not what men wish to hear:

> My tongue will tell the anger of my heart
> Or else my heart concealing it will break,
> And rather than it shall, I will be free,
> Even to the uttermost, as I please, in words.
>
> (*Shrew* 4.3.77–80)

Her proposal that men should 'stop your ears' if they do not wish to hear, further validates the reasonable nature of her point.

Given the importance of the tongue, Lavinia's fate is especially horrific. Demetrius taunts her, 'So now go tell, and if thy tongue can speak / Who 'twas that cut thy tongue and ravish'd thee'. Reminding her that she cannot write either, he points out 'She hath no tongue to call, nor hands to wash, / And so let's leave her to her silent walks' (*Tit.* 2.4.1–2 and 7–8). Marcus attentively reads the 'bubbling fountain stirred with wind' that 'doth rise and fall between thy rosed lips' (*Tit.* 4.2.23–4) as a sign that Lavinia has been raped. Because the tongue connotes the clitoris, its loss signifies Lavinia's loss of ownership of her own sexuality. In comparing her to **Philomel**, Aaron and Marcus both fail to recognize the significance of Lavinia's tongue. The former reads her tragedy 'to lose her tongue to-day' simply as Bassanius's 'day of doom' (*Tit.* 2.3.41–2). Marcus comments that that 'Fair Philomela' 'but lost her tongue, / And in a tedious sampler sew'd her mind' (*Tit.* 2.4.38–9). His wish to rail at her rapists appears to be born out of a genuine concern for her suffering but, shockingly, his fear that 'Sorrow concealed, like an oven stopp'd / Doth burn the cinders where it is' is totally self-centred. He wants 'to ease my mind!' rather than hers (*Tit.* 2.4.35–7). Titus equates glossectomy with loss of life, saying that Chiron and Demetrius, who 'ravish'd her and cut away her tongue', effectively killed Lavinia (5.3.56–7). Nevertheless, as Hamlet observes, 'murther, though it have no tongue, will speak / With most miraculous organ' (*Ham.* 2.2.593–4). Following Marcus's example of writing with a stick, Lavinia '*takes the staff in her mouth*', wielding it like a grotesquely elongated tongue, to spell out '*Stuprum* – Chiron – Demetrius' (*Tit.* 4.1.77SD). The clumsy staff only allows Lavinia to express herself within the limits of the patriarchal script, but it does restore her a powerful tongue with which to participate in the revenge. She enters to confront her rapists at the moment Titus orders 'stop their mouths', (*Tit.* 5.2.161) the gags symbolically revenging Lavinia's glossectomy. Even if a female character is, as Rosalind fears, taken 'without her tongue',(*AYLI* 4.1.173) Shakespeare's texts do find ways to expose her unjust silencing.

(c) Thomas Thomkins, *Lingua or the Combat of the Tongue and the Five Senses for Superiority* (London: 1607) illustrates the range of foundational powers associated with the tongue in early modern English culture. Andrew Willet (1602) moralizes the lesson to be learned from Fulvia's attack on Cicero in the context of a battle between Protestants and Catholics: '*Are you sowell taught, that, whome you can not answer, you will take off his head, and cut out his tongue that will not hold his peace?* So did Fulvia to Cicero, and Herod to Iohn. And thus did the Papists deale with the learned Martyrs' (sig. A3). Juliet Fleming (1994) analyses women's use of rhetoric in early modern England. Oakley-Brown (2006: 26–31) gives a detailed account of Lavinia's experience with reference to Philomel's tale in Ovid's *Metamorphoses*. Douglas E. Green (1989) analyses how Lavinia communicates after her rape and dismemberment. Carla Mazzio, 'The Sins of the Tongue' (1997), and her book *Slips of the Tongue: Rhetoric, Print and Speech in Early Modern England* (1998) give a fuller survey of the tongue's symbolic power.

treasure, (a) used of women, and especially their sexuality, in a transfigurative sense to mean something valued and to be preserved as precious.

(b) In Shakespeare, 'treasure', as applied to women, is predominantly but not exclusively a term that connotes male ownership. In *The Taming of the Shrew* it is associated with material wealth and emotional investment. **Bianca**, co-heiress to Baptista, is 'my treasure' to her suitor Hortensio (*Shrew* 1.2.118). **Katherina** then accuses her father of favouritism, protesting 'Nay, now I see / She is your treasure' (*Shrew* 2.1.31–2). Leontes, realizing the true value of **Hermione**, uses the term in purely emotional terms wishing he might 'have taken treasure from her lips' again (*WT* 5.1.54).

The term refers transfiguratively to women's sexuality as something precious when **Isabella** is told she 'must lay down the treasures of your body' as a bribe to save her brother's life (*MM* 2.4.96). In *Hamlet* the term implies that the preservation or locking away of **Ophelia**'s virginity by her father and brother is sinister. Ophelia is told firmly she must not open 'your chaste treasure' or virginity, to Hamlet's desire (*Ham.* 1.3.31). Hamlet uses the figure ironically, jesting with Polonius:

> Hamlet: O Jephthah, judge of Israel, what a treasure had'st thou!
> Polonius: What a treasure had he, my lord?
> Hamlet: Why
>   "One fair daughter, and no more,
>   The which he loved passing well."
>
> (*Ham.* 2.2.404–8)

Since Jephthah was obliged to sacrifice his daughter as a burnt offering as part of a bargain with the Lord to win the supposedly bigger prize of victory over the Ammonites (Judg. 11.30–6) just how much Polonius treasures Ophelia is rendered questionable here. Whatever Hamlet or Polonius's feelings for Ophelia, he provocatively constructs her and her virginity as a pawn to Polonius's political ambitions in Denmark. Jephthah's daughter is released to bewail her virginity for two months on the mountains before being burned to death (Judg. 11.37–40), so the lament and sense of waste is also conjured up by Hamlet's biblical allusion.

For married women, the treasure trope signifies the property of another man. For Chiron and Demetrius to 'revel in Lavinia's treasury' (*Tit.* 2.1.131) is to raid Bassianus's goods, according to older definitions of **rape**. In *The Rape of Lucrece*, **Lucrece**'s sexuality is 'a treasure stol'n away' by Tarquin so she vows 'To burn the guiltless casket where it lay' (*Luc.* 1056–7). By emerging from a trunk supposedly filled with treasure, Iachimo pretends to have 'pick'd the lock and ta'en / The treasure of her [Imogen's] honor' (*Cym.* 2.2.41–2). The much earlier play *Henry VI Part II* juxtaposes affectionate and sexual uses of the term to offer a limited challenge to the conventional pattern of commodification. **Margaret** of Anjou asserts her emotional and royal ownership of Suffolk, calling him 'my soul's treasure' (*2HVI* 3.2.382), but the Lieutenant who captures him turns the trope back on her, suggesting that Suffolk's affair in kissing the **Queen**'s lips has been an act of pollution in consuming her or 'swallowing the treasure of the realm' (*2HVI* 4.1.74).

(c) See Traub (1992: 25–49 (esp.) 39–43), on the fetishization of female sexuality in *Othello* and *Winter's Tale*.

trull, (a) a lower-class prostitute or concubine, equating to **drab**, **strumpet** and trollop.

(b) 'Trull' connotes a low-born woman, one whom Robert Greene describes as a street prostitute: 'in summer euenings, and in the winter nightes, these trafickes, these common truls I meane, walke abroad either in the fields or streetes' (1592: sig. C3). The application of the term to high-status women is thus deliberately insulting. The Empress **Tamora** vaunts her social superiority to **Lavinia** by saying she will 'let my spleenfull sons the trull deflow'r' (*Tit.* 2.3.191). Richard of York compares the victorious Queen **Margaret** to 'an Amazonian trull' who triumphs unnaturally over her unfortunate victims, in an attempt to lower her status (*3HVI* 1.4.114–15). The term also insults **Joan** La **Pucelle**, the shepherd's **daughter** turned holy **maid**. Burgundy sarcastically notes, 'I scar'd the Dolphin and his trull / When arm in arm they both came swiftly running / Like to a pair of loving turtle-doves' (*1HVI* 2.2. 28–30).

(c) Robert Greene's *A notable discovery of coosenage* (London, 1592) and Williams (1994: 1428–9) offer early modern uses of the term. *See also* **drab** and **stale**.

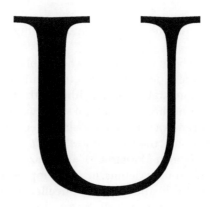

Ursula, (a) a waiting woman to Silvia in *Two Gentleman of Verona* and to Hero in *Much Ado*. 'Ursula' also appears to be a Christian name of Mistress Quickly. The name is a diminutive of 'she-bear' deriving from the Latin *ursa* and the name of a British saint.

(b) In *Two Gentlemen of Verona*, Ursula does not speak but simply brings the picture of **Silvia** which then prompts the disguised **Julia** to talk about a representation of herself. Ursula in *Much Ado* is a livelier figure. She jokes with Antonio about his failure to conceal his identity behind a **mask** in the ball, candidly telling him 'Here's his dry hand up and down. You are he, you are he' and then flattering him about his excellent wit (*MAdo* 2.1.112–24). Her self-assurance suggests that she is an older, mature character rather than a young serving **maid**. Falstaff's reference to Mistress Quickly as 'old Mistress Ursula' (*2HIV* 1.2.239) may imply that both these older female parts were written for the same actor. In early modern literature, the mother bear was thought to lick her young cubs into shape (see Donne 1990: 59) so Shakespeare's characterisation of Ursula may draw on the maternal associations of the name or perhaps on its connections with Saint Ursula. John Dodderidge's study of names glossed 'Ursula' as 'a little beare, heretofore a name of great reputacion in honour of vesula the brittaine virgin Saint martired' (Dodderidge c. 1626). **Hero** looks to Ursula for 'counsel' on what to wear at her **wedding** (*MAdo* 2.3.102–3). Ursula delights in the plot to trap Beatrice:

> The pleasant'st angling is to see the fish
> Cut with her golden oars the silver stream,
> And greedily devour the treacherous bait;
> So angle we for Beatrice.
>
> (*MAdo* 3.1.26–9)

True to her promise that she will not miss her 'part in the dialogue' (*MAdo*

406

3.1.31), Ursula carefully cues Hero's comments with questions guaranteed to whet Beatrice's appetite for news about Benedick, and re-shape Beatrice as a lover. As a maidservant to Hero, Ursula is asked to undertake various tasks (*MAdo* 3.4.1–2 and 95–9) and is listed along with Margaret as a servant rather than a cousin (*MAdo* 5.4.78). Shakespeare's first publisher and townsman Richard Field had a sister called Ursula (Greer 2007: 180) so Shakespeare may have known someone of this name.

(c) The mother bear is depicted as licking her new-born cub in lines 4–5 of John Donne's 'Elegy 13: Love's Progress' (Donne 1990: 59). Germaine Greer, *Shakespeare's Wife* (2007: 180) demonstrates how Ursula Field bought the apparel and bedding clothes of her widowed sister Margaret Young when the latter ran into financial difficulties.

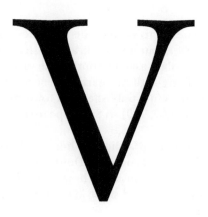

Valeria, (a) a Roman **matron** who appears alongside **Volumnia** and **Virgilia** in *Coriolanus* and is marked out for praise by the protagonist. Her name is the feminine form of Valerius, a common Roman name.

(b) Valeria's small role in *Coriolanus* derives largely from Plutarch's account of the life of Coriolanus, in which she persuades Volumnia and Virgilia to appeal to Coriolanus not to attack Rome (Bullough Vol. V 1964: 537–8). Coriolanus recognizes Valeria as 'The noble sister of Publicola'. Valerius Publicola, also included in Plutarch's *Lives*, was an eminent statesman in the Roman Republic, so Valeria's name immediately identifies her with her dead brother who did 'such notable service to the Romaines, both in peace and warres'. Plutarch notes that she was 'greatly honoured & reverenced amonge all the Romaines: and did so modestlie and wiselie behave her selfe, that she did not shame or dishonour the house she came of' (Bullough Vol. V 1964: 537). Shakespeare distils this praise and pre-empts any criticism of Valeria as an idle gossip with Coriolanus's lines that reverence her as 'The **moon** of Rome' a model of **chastity** (5.3.65–7). Plutarch's account explains Shakespeare's brief characterization of Valeria as a highly respected maternal figure in the Roman state, one who has heard the latest news about Roman foreign policy from 'a senator' (1.3.95–100) yet whose duty, she says, is to visit a woman in labour (1.4.57).

Act 1 Scene 3 adapts Plutarch's account of how Valeria went 'straight to the house of *Volumnia, Martius* mother: and coming in to her, founde her and *Martius* wife her daughter in lawe set together' with her children. In Plutarch, however, Valeria is a spokeswoman for the noblewomen of Rome: 'all the traine of these Ladies sittinge in a ringe rounde about her: *Valeria* first began to speake' (Bullough Vol. V 1964: 537). Instead, Shakespeare scripts a single strong female voice in Volumnia, although the physical presence of the actor playing Valeria on stage in Act 5 Scene 3 is important in visually recreating the narrative rule of three (seen again in the three **queens** of *The Two Noble Kinsmen*).

(c) Plutarch's Life of Coriolanus *Plutarch's Lives*, translated by Thomas North (1579) is reprinted in Bullough Vol. V (1964: 505–49) (see pp. 537–8 for Valeria). Martindale and Martindale (2004: 162), discuss Valeria.

veil, (a) a head covering worn by nuns as part of the habit of their order, or a fashion accessory worn by secular women consisting of a translucent piece of cloth made from net, fine lawn or tiffany (a lightweight silk material) designed to hang from the back of the head and, in some cases, to be pulled over the face. Some veils were wired to stand up behind the head across the shoulders and many were elaborately decorated. The veil was a social marker of modesty in the case of maids; of memory and withdrawal, as worn by those in mourning. It was also an accessory associated with eroticism, as worn by Venetian **courtezans**.
(b) Shakespeare's **nun** characters (**A**emilia in *Comedy of Errors*, **Francisca** and **Isabella** in *Measure for Measure*) would all have worn the veil as part of their costume. Francisca emphasizes the garment's function to signal withdrawal, reminding the novice Isabella that, after her profession of vows, 'if you speak, you must not show your face' (*MM* 1.4.12). In conjunction with Isabella's silence in response to the Duke's proposal of marriage, the veil may be a sartorial signifier of her intent to continue her profession of vows at the end of the play.

In secular culture, the practical reasons for wearing a veil are to protect the face from sun and wind (*V&A* 1081–2). Junius Brutus is amazed that the 'veil'd' Roman dames will commit their cheeks 'to th' wanton spoil / Of Phoebus' burning kisses' to look directly at Coriolanus (*Cor.* 2.1.215–18). Shakespeare's texts exploit the full range of cultural significations. Ford refers to the 'veil of modesty' (*MWW* 3.2.41) while **Elizabeth** vows to throw 'the veil of infamy' over her daughter to prevent a match with Richard III (*RIII* 4.4.209). The three **Queens** kneel before Theseus and **Hippolyta** '*in black with veils stain'd*' (*TNK* 1.1.24SD) to show their mourning. Linen and silk veils were stained with charcoal or dye (Arnold 1988: 77). Fynes Moryson, a traveller to Venice, commented on the **courtezans**' tendency to wear veils in imitation of modest maids, widows or wives: 'prostitutes who want to gain credit by means of feigned modesty wear widows' clothing, and that of married women, especially in the color worn by brides', he remarks. 'So as not to be completely enclosed and covered by their long veils and yet not allowed to be visible, they are forced to reveal themselves slightly, so they cannot fail to be recognized by this gesture' (Rosenthal 2006: 62).

Such cultural paradoxes make the veil a perfect piece of costume for **Mariana** at the end of *Measure for Measure*, concisely exemplifying her own ambiguous status as mourning daughter and sister, modest and yet sexually experienced fiancée. The veil – like the **mask** – conceals; other characters do not know how to read the veiled woman: as a **maid**, **widow** or '**punk**' (*MM* 5.1.179–80)? The Peacham drawing suggests that the ambiguous figure of **Tamora**, widowed Queen of the Goths, **bride** of Bassianus and lover of Aaron, also wears a veil. In *Measure for Measure*, Mariana's unveiling at her husband's command is a ritual marker of her status as respectable **wife** and begins the process of recognition and self-recognition for Angelo (*MM* 5.1.206). A similar ritual restores **Hero** at the end of *Much Ado* although her face-covering is probably a mask to echo the dance scene. Olivia takes the veil with semi-religious associations, vowing that 'Like a cloistress she will veiled walk', weeping 'to season / A brother's dead love' and keep his memory fresh for seven years (*TN* 1.1.25–31). Her determined withdrawal, even as she admits Orsino's messenger, is marked by the ritual of putting the veil over her face. If **Maria** veils as well, this provides a reason for Cesario's questions about which is the **lady** of the house (*TN* 1.5.167–85). The veil takes on potentially more erotic resonance when Cesario / **Viola** asks to see **Olivia**'s face and she self-consciously tells him 'we will draw the curtain and show you the picture' (*TN* 1.5.233–4).

(c) Arnold (1988) details the 94 mantles and veils listed in records of Queen Elizabeth's wardrobe, outlining examples of wired, decorated and starched veils. Ferber (1999: 222–3) gives an overview of the veil as a literary symbol. Paula Loscocco mentions the different early modern significations of the veil in 'Veiled Truths: Wives, Widows and Whores Early modern Europe' (2007). Margaret F. Rosenthal (2006) gives illustrations of courtezans wearing veils and quotes from Fynes Moryson's journal account of his visit to Venice. Zahira Veliz (2004) uses Velázquez's painting 'Lady With A Fan' as the starting point for a discussion of costume, including the veil, in the creation of identity.

Venus, (a) the Roman goddess of love (Aphrodite in Greek mythology), supposedly born from the foam of the sea on the shores of Cythera. She was married to Vulcan, god of the forge, but had numerous lovers including the god Mars. Cupid, the god of physical desire, was her son. Her symbols are the dove, the sparrow (proverbially regarded as lecherous) and the myrtle tree. She appears as a protagonist in Shakespeare's best-selling poem *Venus and Adonis*.

(b) According to Robert Albott, '*Venus* vvyfe of *Vulcan*, is faigned to bee borne of the froth of the Sea, the Goddesse of loue, beauty, and all sensuall delights, she was adored in Cyprus' (Albott 1599: 143). Shakespeare's texts make reference to these commonly agreed characteristics and may even hint at Cyprus being the Isle of Venus in *Othello* (Doloff 2000). At the end of *Venus and Adonis*, Venus 'yokes her silver doves' to carry her chariot through the skies 'to Paphos' (*V&A* 1190–3). In *The Tempest*, Shakespeare returns to the same image. **Iris** reports 'I met her Deity / Cutting the clouds towards Paphos; and her son / Dove-drawn with her' (*Temp.* 4.1.92–4). In between these early and late examples, however, and throughout *Venus and Adonis*, Venus is invoked in many different guises in Shakespeare's work. This is typical of early modern confusion about what Venus meant. Catari's *Fountaine of Ancient Fiction* (1599) observed it was necessary to examine the 'seueral natures & conditions vnderstood & signified by her' including wantonness, wedlock, beastly lust, natural affection and courage, 'as being a furtherance & light to conceiue the reasons why so many diuers statues & pictures were so diuersly fashioned & composed of her' (Catari 1599: sig Cc2).

'The **goddess** Venus' is petitioned at her altar by the lover Palamon in Fletcher and Shakespeare's *Two Noble Kinsmen*, as a heavenly being, a

> sovereign **queen** of secrets, who hast power
> To call the fiercest tyrant from his rage,
> And weep unto a **girl**; that hast the might,
> Even with an eye-glance, to choke Mars's drum
> And turn th' alarm to whispers;
>
> (*TNK* 5.1.77–81)

She can control mortal kings and subjects, sick and well, old and young (her magical influence recalling **Helena**'s miraculous cure of the King in *All's Well*). Furthermore, 'what godlike power / Hast thou not power upon?' (*TNK* 5.1.89–90) asks her knight, his eventual success in winning **Emilia** from Mars's knight Arcite, apparently proving his opinion. The Venus of Shakespeare's poem reminds Adonis that she 'overswayed' Mars, 'Leading him prisoner in a red rose chain' (*V&A* 109–10). Mysteriously, she has no power over Adonis's feelings but there are hints of her supernatural qualities existing elsewhere: 'Being judge in love, she cannot right her cause' (*V&A* 220). Somewhat comically, Venus swears by her own 'fair immortal hand' (*V&A* 80) and, perhaps unwittingly, she dooms Adonis to destruction: 'I prophesy thy death, my living sorrow, / If thou encounter with the boar to-morrow' (*V&A* 671–2). The goddess in this poem may be fleshy, but she is also magical, light enough not to crush the flowers beneath her body and able to fly from the earth when 'Two strengthless doves will draw me through the sky' (*V&A* 153).

Several references to Venus identify her as the evening star. The love-struck Demetrius claims that **Hermia** is 'as bright, as clear / As yonder Venus in her glimmering sphere' (*MND* 3.2.60–1) and when he is charmed by the love potion, **Helena**'s becomes the heavenly body that 'shine[s] as gloriously / As the Venus of the sky' (*MND* 3.2.106–7). The image is used satiricially to comment on **Doll Tearsheet**'s unheavenly body kissing Falstaff in Hal's joke that 'Saturn and Venus' the gods of age and love, are 'this year in conjunction', something that was astronomically impossible (*2HIV* 2.4.263). **Joan** La **Pucelle**'s identity as a Christian holy **maid** is rendered suspect by Charles's enamoured address to her, 'Bright star of Venus, fall'n down on the earth / How may I reverently worship thee enough?' (*1HVI* 1.2. 144–5).

The heavenly Venus is supremely beautiful, her **beauty** a manifestation of divine status. Catari, following Ovid, notes that she has 'the shape of a most beautiful and amorous yong woman, which seemed also to stand vpright in the midst of a huge shell of a fish'. **Rosaline** jokes that if Boyet is Cupid's grandfather, 'Then was Venus like her mother, for her father is but grim' (*LLL* 2.1.256). **Imogen**'s beauty makes images in 'the shrine of Venus' look lame in comparison (*Cym.* 5.5.63–4). Venus knows her 'beauty as the spring doth yearly grow' (*V&A* 141), but the 'sick-thoughted' **goddess** comically tells Adonis he is 'Thrice fairer than myself' (*V&A* 5–7).

Venus's power to inspire affection is symbolized in her doves, who are 'most abundantly inclined to procreation' and produce young who 'vpon their first association and coupling together, they do kisse one another, and as it were

411

embrace, and friendly intertain their acquaintance and friendship' like human young lovers (Catari 1599: sig. Ccii). Shakespeare adopts this when describing Venus and Adonis in 'beauteous combat, willing and unwilling / Showed like two silver doves that sit a billing' (*V&A* 365–6) and 'Her arms do lend his neck a sweet embrace; / Incorporate then they seem, face grows to face' (*V&A* 539–40). The chaste Hermia innocently swears 'By the simplicity of Venus' doves' (*MND* 1.1.171), and Salerio says that 'Venus' pigeons' supposedly fly ten times faster to 'seal love's bonds new made' (*Mer.* 2.6.5–6). The culmination of urgent amorous affection inspired by Venus is **marriage**: 'vnto hir they ascribe the care and charge of marriages and holie wedlockes' (Catari 1599: sigs. Ccii–Cciiv) and, perhaps surprisingly, associate her with **Juno**. It is this version of Venus to whom Paris refers when he tells Capulet he has not talked of love to **Juliet** yet 'For Venus smiles not in a house of tears' (*R&J* 4.1.7–8).

The goddess of love's wide influence over humans, animals and gods leads to a common understanding that 'Venus doth signifie that secret & hidden vertue by which all creatures whatsoeuer are drawne with association, effectuating thereby the art of generation' (Catari 1599: sig. Ccii). Even Titan, the sun, longs to draw near to Venus's side (*V&A* 180) Shakespeare's imagery of nature and natural settings that provide a *locus amoenus* (a garden or landscape for love) draws on this idea, most explicitly in *Venus and Adonis*. In deliberately erotic style, Venus describes her body as a park or landscape with mountains, dales and 'pleasant fountains' (*V&A* 230–8) through which Adonis, her deer, can roam. Her influence and kinship with mother **earth**, leads to her being titled 'the **mother** of loue, because that without a certaine loue & simpathie of affections, those desires are sildome accomplished' (Catari 1599: Ccii). The maternal nature of Venus's love for Adonis manifests itself in a deep desire to enfold and protect him, in details that project an image of her as much bigger than he is. As well as holding him safely in the fenced park of her body (*V&A* 229–40), she tells him 'I'll make a shadow for thee of my hairs' (*V&A* 191) to shield him from sunburn. When he leaves, she retires 'to a myrtle grove' (*V&A* 865), her symbolic tree, but cannot rest and so seeks him out 'Like a milch doe, whose swelling dugs do ache / Hasting to feed her fawn hid in some brake' (*V&A* 875–6). Venus's contradictory identities in the poem as threateningly overpowering and protectively maternal mean that readers are never sure 'whether surrender to Venus would be an initiation into manhood or a regression to infancy' (Mortimer 2000: 190).

The imagery of nature allows a slip from the heavenly love into the more common view, promoted by poets that 'Venus was taken to be the goddesse of wantonnes & amorous delights' who inspired 'libidinous desires, and lustfull appetites' and promoted men's 'lose concupiscence'. She also transformed women, purportedly assisting the Lacedemonian women to overthrow their enemies, which 'successe they supposed to haue proceeded from the power and assistance of Venus, as inspiring into those womans hearts manly courages, sto[u]tnesse, and resolutions' (Catari 1599: sigs. C2 and Cc4–Cc4v). Venus is associated with **Hero**'s supposedly ungoverned desire in *Much Ado*:

> [Y]ou are more intemperate in your blood
> Than Venus, or those pamp'red animals
> That rage in savage sensuality.
>
> (*MAdo* 4.1.59–61)

In *The Tempest* Venus and Cupid are excluded from **Miranda** and Ferdinand's **betrothal** masque because they had planned 'to have done / Some **wanton** charm upon this man and **maid**' (*Temp.* 4.1.94–5). Venus here is 'Mars's hot minion' while Cupid, sulking because they have been prevented, vows to 'play with sparrows' also sacred to Venus and proverbially lecherous (*Temp.* 4.1.92–5 and 98–100). Venus's promotion of illegitimate sexual activity is embodied by Cupid, 'that same wicked bastard of Venus' (*AYLI* 4.1.211). Shakespeare's depiction of Venus in his poem illustrates her as the embodiment and victim of her own influence to promote lustful appetites, manly courage and resolution in women's hearts.

When Adonis allows her to kiss him the growth of her sexual excitement is expressed in blatantly physical terms:

> . . . having felt the sweetness of the spoil,
> With blindfold fury she begins to forage;
> Her face doth reek and smoke, her blood doth boil,
> And careless lust stirs up a desperate courage,
> Planting oblivion, beating reason back,
> Forgetting shame's pure blush and honor's rack.
>
> (*V&A* 553–8)

Adonis, repelled by such sexually assertive behaviour, lectures her 'Call it not love, for Love to heaven is fled, / Since sweating Lust on earth usurp'd his name' (*V&A* 793–4). Her fall from heavenly to human, even animal passion invokes a series of other binary oppositions from Adonis to emphasize her decadence. 'Love is all truth, Lust full of forged lies' he insists (*V&A* 804). Shakespeare's Venus 'flatly falleth down' (*V&A* 463) to lust only to rise into the empty sky in her dove-drawn carriage as a heavenly body (Doebler 1983: 34). She functions simultaneously as the protective mother of love and the assertive bold woman. As such she is a paradox who captures the contradictory views about Venus held by the early moderns and by classical thinkers.

The idea of Venus as a multiple personality, both heavenly and mortal, was discussed by Pausanius in Plato's *Symposium*, who identified the higher, heavenly form as a male strain of love and the earthly or common love as female (Plato 1951: 45–7). Allusions to Venus in *Troilus and Cressida* are modelled on this gendered, divisive pattern. Aeneas swears 'By Venus' hand' that no man loves 'so excellently' as he does Diomedes, the man he will meet in battle and kill (*T&C* 4.1.23–5). Ulysses vows 'for Venus's sake' he will never claim a kiss of **Cressida**, invoking the goddess in terms of pure, exclusively masculine isolation (*T&C* 4.5.49–52). **Helen** of Troy is praised as 'the mortal Venus, the heart-blood of beauty, love's invisible soul' but the conflation of mortal and heavenly love is comically undercut by Pandarus's 'Who? my cousin Cressida?' (*T&C* 3.1.32–4). Hector swears 'By Mars his gauntlet!' to greet Menelaus, and then draws attention to Helen's debasement of vows to Venus: 'Mock not that I affect th' untraded oath, / Your quondam wife swears still by Venus' **glove**' (*T&C* 4.5.177–9). This is, again, the mortal Venus. The war effectively brings the gods Venus and Mars together, but in a debased way except for Troilus's own passion, expressed in his vow to shed Diomedes' blood 'In characters as red as Mars his heart / Inflam'd with Venus' (*T&C* 5.2.164–5). This famous coupling: 'what Venus did with Mars', is the subject of the eunuch Mardian's fantasies (*A&C* 1.5.18). Antony and **Cleopatra**, who have superhuman qualities, replicate it when Cleopatra appears in fantastic, seductive spectacle 'o'er picturing that Venus where we see / The fancy outwork nature' (*A&C* 2.2.200–1). In the Shakespeare canon, Venus is an intrinsic part of nature and yet transcends it as a creation of fancy or desire on the part of characters, readers and spectators.

(c) Vincenzo Catari's short essay on Venus in *The Fountaine of Ancient Fiction* (1599: sigs Cc2r–4v), translated into English by Richard Lynche, brings together a rich array of diverse opinions of Venus. John Doebler (1983) gives a fine account of the many faces of Venus in Shakespeare's poem. Pausanius's differentiation between the Heavenly Aphrodite (Venus) and the Common Aphrodite is in Plato's *Symposium* (1951: 45–7). Hulse (1978) identifies three Venuses: a comic, a sensual and a violent one, in *Venus and Adonis*. Mortimer's *Variable Passions* (2000), a book-length study of *Venus and Adonis*, is a subtle close reading. Belsey (1995) considers the operation of desire in the poem. Steven Doloff (2000) notes veiled allusions to the Isle of Venus in *Othello*, but not the hero's view that in meeting Desdemona here his 'soul hath her content so absolute' that to die would be 'most happy' (*Oth.* 2.1.189–93).

vestal, (a) originally one of the priestesses in charge of the sacred fires in the temple of Vesta (Hestia in Greek), goddess of the hearth, but more generally applied to any woman dedicated to chastity and serving in a religious community.

(b) Florio defined a vestal as 'of or pertayning to the Goddesse of Chastity' and the vestal virgins as those 'whose charge was to keepe and preserue fire in a certaine temple in Rome from going out or being quenched' (Florio 1611). No vestal virgins appear in Shakespeare's Roman plays, although North's translation of *Plutarch's Lives*, which Shakespeare knew, noted that Numa Pompilius 'hath the keeping of the holy virgines which they call Vestales' (Plutarch 1579: 68). Allusions to the vestal virgins do occur. In *Coriolanus* **Volumnia**, **Valeria** and **Virgilia** function like vestals as guardians of the Roman state: they are greeted back with 'triumphant fires' and Coriolanus tells them, 'Ladies you deserve / To have a temple built you' (*Cor.* 5.3.206–7 and 5.5.3). The penalty for vestals breaking vows of **chastity** was to be buried alive, yet Octavius Caesar arrogantly believes that, since women are not strong, 'want will perjure / The ne'er touch'd vestal' and that, just as easily, he can bend **Cleopatra** to his will (*A&C* 3.12.29–31). **Lucrece** draws on the idea that the vestal virgins' conduct directly influenced the life of Rome, listing them first in a catalogue of disasters caused by the evils of Opportunity:

Thou makest the vestal violate her oath;
Thou blow'st the fire when **temperance** is thaw'd;
Thou smother'st **honesty**, thou murder'st troth;
Thou foul abettor! thou notorious **bawd**!

(*Luc.* 883–6)

Diana's temples in Athens and Ephesus offer equivalent venues for vestals in Shakespeare and Fletcher's *Two Noble Kinsmen* and in *Pericles*. **Emilia** is presented as a vestal virgin in *Two Noble Kinsmen*. On the day before her **wedding** she prays to Diana as 'sweet, solitary, white as chaste and pure' like the 'order's robe' that Emilia and her followers wear (*TNK* 5.1.139–42). Having lit the equivalent to a sacred vestal fire, Emilia laments 'This is my last / Of vestal office' and includes in her petition the possibility 'I may / Continue in thy band' (*TNK* 5.1.149–50 and 161–2). After hoping that the single rose is a sign granting her wish, she sees it fall and interprets this as a dismissal from her vestal duties: 'O mistress / Thou here dischargest me. I shall be gather'd' (*TNK* 5.1.169–70). Having lost her husband, **Thaisa** vows 'a vestal livery will I take me to, / And never more have joy' (*Per.* 3.4.11–12). The final scenes of *Pericles* present Diana's Temple with 'THAISA *standing near the altar as high priestess; a number of* VIRGINS *on each side*' (5.2.0SD). **Marina**, too, wears Diana's 'silver livery' of chastity (*Per.* 5.3.7). Although she is not a vestal she produces a remarkable effect on the customers of the brothel, one of whom comically pronounces 'I am for no more bawdy-houses: / Shall's go hear the vestals sing?' (*Per.* 4.5.6–7). Thaisa's service as a chief priestess in Ephesus recalls the **Abbess** in *Comedy of Errors*, although the only reference to vestals in this play is to **Nell** 'the kitchen-vestal' who keeps the household hearth alight (4.4.76).

Romeo appropriates the trope of vestal virginity in a secular context to suggest **Juliet**'s absolute purity. Diana is envious of her beauty, and Juliet should leave worship of the virgin goddess, he argues, since 'Her vestal livery is but sick and green / And none but fools do wear it' (*R&J* 2.2.8–9). The references to colour and illness allude to **green sickness**, the virgins' disease. After their wedding night, Juliet still retains her purity in Romeo's eyes; her lips 'even in pure and vestal modesty, / Still blush, as thinking their own kisses sin' (*R&J* 3.3.38–9). Another secular reference to 'a fair vestal throned by the west' is an elegant compliment to **Elizabeth** I as virgin queen (*MND* 2.1.158). Unsurprisingly, **Venus** has a more negative view of 'fruitless chastity' describing its followers as

Love-lacking vestals and self-loving nuns,
That on the earth would breed a scarcity
And barren dearth of daughters and of sons,
Be prodigal: the lamp that burns by night
Dries up his oil to lend the world his light.

(*V&A* 751–6)

The vestals' service to keep the temple fires burning is aligned with a rewriting of the parable of the wise **virgins** (Matt. 25.1–13) to encourage fertility instead of chastity.

(c) Florio (1611) defines the Vestal Virgins as above. Paul Stapfer (1880) reprinted in George (2004: 201–13 (esp.) 211) notes the vestal allusions to Volumnia. Sir Roy Strong (1977: 153–4) discusses Elizabeth I's promotion of the cult of the Vestal Virgin. For more details on the temple of Vesta and the duties of the vestal virgins see Merriam-Webster's *Encyclopedia of World Religions*, edited by Wendy Doniger (1991: 1132).

Viola, (a) a character in *Twelfth Night*, whose name derives from the Latin for 'violet' and was a popular Italian name. It is also a feminized form of viol, a popular early modern stringed instrument.

The opening lines of the play introduce both aspects of Viola's name although, interestingly, the character is not named on stage until Act 5, before which she is known as Cesario, cross-dressed in imitation of her twin brother. Sebastian metaphorically resurrects his **sister** by vowing that, if she were dressed as a woman, he would say 'Thrice welcome drowned Viola' (5.1.240). Before this, Viola's name is hinted at. Orsino describes a falling cadence in music 'like the sweet sound / That breathes upon a bank of violets / Stealing and giving odour' (1.1.4–7). Many of Viola's qualities resemble those attributed to the flower in early modern culture. It was characterized by its diminutive stature, 'a little hearbe' which 'is better fresh and newe', growing in springtime, and prized for the beneficial effects of its perfume: 'the smell thereof abateth heate of the braine, & refresheth and comforteth the spirites of féeling, and maketh sléepe, for it cooleth & tempereth & moystneth the braine' (Batman 1582: fol. 331). Viola brings refreshment to Illyria in her encounters with Orsino and **Olivia**, the former stagnating in futile love-sickness and the latter fossilized in mourning. To Olivia, Viola brings new life to awaken 'the spirits of feeling', and her influence over Orsino gradually leads him to temper and modify his passion, redirecting it in more fruitful ways. To succeed as a pivotal figure in the love triangle requires remarkable diplomacy on Viola's part. Sebastian says that in addition to being 'accounted beautiful', she 'bore a mind that envy could not but call fair' (2.1.26, 29).

The violet's freshness and diminutive stature also makes it fragile, however. It is closely associated with melancholy, prescribed as a cure for this condition (Schleiner 1983) but also imbued with it. Laertes expects violets to spring from Ophelia's pure and unpolluted flesh, and Gertrude gives 'sweets to the sweet' as they mourn over her grave (*Ham.* 5.1.239–40, 243). Viola, too, draws attention to her own fragility, lamenting that women are destined to wither like **flowers** 'To die, even when they to perfection grow' (*TN* 2.4.41), and painting a self-portrait of reserve in which her imaginary sister never tells her love 'But let concealment like a worm i' th' bud / Feed on her damask cheek', pining 'with a green and yellow melancholy' (2.4.110–13). Here, Viola assumes the characteristic modesty of the **flower**, whose bent head was supposedly the source of its excellent qualities: 'the more vertuous the flowre therof is, the more it bendeth the head thereof downward' (Batman 1582: fol. 331). Viola confesses her own sensitivity, telling

Olivia and **Maria** 'I am very comptible even to the least sinister usage' (1.5.175–6). Her disguise as Cesario, in memory of her brother, serves as a very effective form of self-effacement throughout the play. Even her emphatic declaration that she loves Orsino 'more than my life' (5.1.135) is accompanied by a willingness to annihilate herself: 'To do you rest, a thousand deaths would die' (5.1.132–3). Her self-effacement continues even when she acknowledges her name. Her feminine identity is not fully present since Viola is still hidden behind her 'masculine usurped attire' and the boy actor. She tells Sebastian

> Do not embrace me till each circumstance
> Of place, time, fortune, do cohere and jump
> That I am Viola.
>
> (*TN* 5.1.251–3)

Viola's appearance as herself is thus modestly deferred beyond the public arena of the stage.

Viola draws attention to the musical dimension of her name in her first scene when she asks the captain to present her as 'an eunuch' at Duke Orsino's court 'for I can sing / And speak to him in many sorts of music' (*TN* 1.2.56–8). The analogy between Viola and a musical instrument has sexual resonances. A parallel instance when Pericles refers to Antiochus's daughter as a 'fair viol' creates her as a sexually charged instrument to be played upon and 'finger'd to make man his lawful music' (*Per.* 1.1.81–4). In *Twelfth Night* Olivia is excited by Viola / Cesario's determination to 'Write loyal cantons of contemned love / And sing them loud, even in the dead of night', echoing Olivia's name (1.5.270–1). Orsino's first waking thought is to share again with Viola / Cesario the song they heard last night because 'it did relieve my passion much' (2.4.4). Having been played on and with by both protagonists, Viola ends the play silently, pledged to Orsino as his 'mistress, and his fancy's queen' (5.1.387), as Feste's final song accompanies their exit.

(c) Stephen Batman, *Batman vppon Bartholome his booke De proprietatibus rerum, newly corrected, enlarged and amended* (1582), gives a description of the violet from the thirteenth-century writer Anglicus Bartholomaeus. Shleiner (1983) argues that Shakespeare's choice of name may have been influenced by Violetta in Emmanuel Forde's *Famous History of Parisnus* (1578) and describes the violet in relation to melancholy. Stevie Davies, *Idea of Woman* (1986) reads the hermaphrodite Viola / Cesario in mythic terms as a messenger (Hermes) of love (Aphrodite) who brings change to Illyria (pp. 109–17). Jameson's Victorian study considers her as a character of 'sentiment' or muted passion and imagination, very different from Rosalind (2005: 170–5). Greenblatt (1988) and Traub (1992) discuss Viola as a focus for homoerotic desires. Kier Elam, 'The Fertile Eunuch' (1996: 1–3) and Yu Jin Ko (2004) both give fine readings of the disguise and unfulfilled desire. Katalin Komolós (1999) prints and discusses Hayden's musical setting of Viola's self-restraint in her speech about her imaginary sister. Zoe Wanamaker (1988) describes an actor's approach, while interpretations of Viola in the play's stage history are outlined in Gay, *As She Likes It* (1994: 17–47). Catherine Thomas considers the queer politics of Nunn's film version (2008).

Virgilia, (a) a character in *Coriolanus*, wife to the eponymous hero and mother to his young son Martius.
(b) In her **sew**ing, her refusal to leave her house, her sobriety and her few words, Virgilia is effectively cast as a 'manifest housekeeper' (*Cor.* 1.3.51–2), a model of early modern **housewif**ely conduct. **Valeria**'s comment, 'you confine yourself most unreasonably' (1.3.76) captures the essence of this role; Virgilia's physical confinement in the household signals wider emotional and cultural confinements and ultimately her generic confinement within the text. Hers is a subordinate part: the tragedy of Coriolanus is not her story. Kahn notes that 'Virgilia's name connects her subordinate role as wife to the *pietas* or filial piety central to Rome's epic' (Kahn 1997: 156). Her adamant refusal to turn 'idle huswife' in her first scene shows that she can be just as firm as **Volumnia**, but has stronger self-restraint. When Coriolanus returns from Corioli, she is the last to be noticed; her greeting expressed through silent tears:

> Coriolanus: My gracious silence, hail!
> Would'st thou have laugh'd had I come coffin'd home,
> And weep'st to see me triumph?
> (*Cor.* 2.1.175–7)

Her silence is gracious as a mark of wifely virtue and it provides a space besides the highly charged rhetoric of Volumnia. Ironically, it has the power to open up a vein of sensitivity and sympathy for the suffering women in Corioli, for just a moment, in Coriolanus's martial consciousness (Stockholder 1970: 228–30). In Act 5 Scene 3, Virgilia leads the petition with a short greeting and sartorial appeal that make her husband 'forget my part' (5.3.37–41). Thereafter, she resumes a subordinate role to Volumnia, speaking little but weeping again. Even the weeping must be restrained. Ripley (1998: 88) describes how in Thomson's 1749 adaptation, the Virgilia figure wept freely all over Coriolanus's hand during the intercession scene, travestying the mute effect indicated in Shakespeare's text. Virgilia may be a deliberately 'vexing exemplar' of Shakespeare's 'adamant refusal to allow emotion free rein' at moments of heightened tension (ibid.: 341), alerting readers and spectators to the frustrations caused by the model of wifely virtue, not just for wives but for others in the family.
(c) Ripley's survey of the stage history of *Coriolanus* (1998: 88, 283 and 341), recognizes the limitations of the role as intrinsic to its design. Stockholder (1970) points out that Virgilia's silence and weeping threaten to open up an 'other' sensitive Coriolanus; Kahn (1997: 156) and Martindale and Martindale (1990) mention her only in passing.

virgin, (a) a woman, especially a young woman, who is, or remains, in a state of inviolate **chastity**; an absolutely pure maiden or **maid**. Sometimes the term was

418

applied to men in early modern England but not as a generic defining character-istic. In ecclesiastical terms, the 'Virgin' designated **Mary**, the mother of Christ. In the Christian church, virgins who chose a lifestyle distinguished by chastity, piety and steadfastness were revered for their holy life. **Elizabeth** I's identity as the Virgin **Queen** raised the profile of virginity in secular life.

(b) In Shakespeare, 'virgin' is a defining category of female identity, although references to 'Virgins and boys' (*T&C* 2.2.104) and to the 'virgin voice' (*Cor.* 3.2.114) bring together **boy actors** and the female creations they played. The King of Navarre's proclamation is careful to list 'virgin' as one of the groups of women excluded from his court (*LLL* 1.1.295). In *All's Well*, **Helena** refers to **Diana** reductively as 'this virgin' (*AWW* 3.5.100) since virginity is the crucial qualification for participating in Helena's plot. **Katherina** points up the absurdity of Petruchio's naming of the world around him by misrecognizing Vincentio with the generic form of address 'young budding virgin' (*Shrew* 4.5.37). The term is a more precise indicator of a woman's sexual status than '**maid**'. Ferdinand prom-ises to make **Miranda** Queen of Naples 'if a virgin' (*Temp.* 1.2.448), even though she has already told him she is maid. Touchstone pointedly describes the low-born **Audrey** as 'a poor virgin' rather than the ambigious 'maid' (*AYLI* 5.4.57), since she has made it clear that marriage must precede sex. When Costard is caught with **Jaquenetta**, he plays on the difference between the two, arguing 'I deny her virginity; I was taken with a maid' (*LLL* 1.1.296).

A male definition of the term is given by Parolles: 'Virginity is peevish, proud, idle, made of self-love, which is the most inhibited sin in the canon. Keep it not, you cannot choose but lose by it' (*AWW* 1.1.144–6). Such negative assessments are in tune with sixteenth-century humanism, a move away from the Catholic ascetic ideal of the monastery and the merits of single life (Dusinberre 1996: 40). Theseus adds his voice to humanist and more extreme Protestant arguments that virginity denied the fullness of life: he argues for married life rather than one 'withering on the virgin thorn' (*MND* 1.1.37). Quite how **Elizabeth** I would have responded to such arguments towards the end of her life is intriguing. To Parolles, virginity is 'too cold a companion' (*AWW* 1.1.132). He rehearses conventional arguments about its perversity: that 'by ever being kept, it is ever lost' (*AWW* 1.1.131). For men 'virginity murthers itself' (*AWW* 1.1.139) and for women 'to speak on the part of virginity is to accuse your **mothers**' (*AWW* 1.1.136–7). In contrast, the urge to procreate is natural: 'Loss of virginity is rational increase, and there was never virgin [got] till virginity was lost' (*AWW* 1.1.127–9).

In line with these negative perspectives, virginity is associated with feminine weakness. Troilus describes himself as 'less valiant than the virgin in the night' (*T&C* 1.1.11). Helena in *All's Well* is 'a poor unlearned virgin' (*AWW* 1.3.240) whose voice may not be listened to at Court. The appeal of such vulnerability to male appetites is recognized by **Portia** who, at the casket test, declares 'I stand for sacrifice' (*Mer.* 3.2.56–8) and compares herself to Hesione, the 'virgin tribute' paid to the sea monster by the Trojans. Unconquered virginity is not simply a sign of weakness; it offers a challenge to male sexuality. The 'spotless virgin's chastity' (*2HVI* 5.1.186) is exciting to male characters like Angelo because it simultaneously invites male reverence and defilement. Whatever their physical weakness, female characters believe in the power of their virginity. **Marina**'s constitutes resilience in *Pericles* in spite of her vulnerability. Boult is told to 'crack the glass of her virginity, and make the rest malleable' (*Per.* 4.6.142–3). Female definitions of virginity value the 'not' or denial that Parolles sees in such negative terms. Marina thinks it is worth sacrificing her life for: 'If fires be hot, knives sharp, or waters deep / Untied I still my virgin knot shall keep' (*Per.* 4.2.146–7). **Isabella** is prepared to sacrifice her brother to Angelo rather than 'yield him my virginity' (*MM* 3.1.97). **Joan** La **Pucelle** proudly declares herself a 'A virgin from her tender infancy / Chaste, and immaculate in every thought' (*1HVI* 5.4.50–1). The English men take delight in collapsing this strong image of a 'virgin pure' when she pleads pregnancy to save her life (*1HVI* 5.4.82–3). To be a 'holy virgin' (*Tim.* 5.1.173) like the **vestals** of Rome or in imitation of the Virgin Mary whose intact virginity mitigates the penalties of the Fall, grants a woman elevated spiritual and social status.

The esteem of holy virgins and the popular idea of the religious life of **nuns** (only available to English women on the Continent after the Reformation) fostered an illusion that virginity meant female agency. Queen Elizabeth I, the Virgin Queen, was a potent example of this in the secular context. One of the bridesmaids in Samuel Rowlands' poem *The Bride*, for example, declared:

> Virginity is life of chaste respect
> No worldly burden thereupon is laid
> Our single life all peace and quiet brings,
> And we are free from careful earthly things.
>
> We may do what we please, go where we list,
> Without *pray husband will you give me leave?*
> Our resolutions no man can resist,
> Our own's our own, to give or to receive,
> We live not under this same word: *obey*,
> *Till death depart us at our dying day.*
> (Quoted in Aughterson 1995: 85–6)

Virgin figures in Shakespeare's texts are frequently endowed with a strong sense of independence. Helena determines to 'stand for't a little, though therefore I die a virgin' (*AWW* 1.1.133–4) and Diana vows to remain a virgin rather than marry (*AWW* 4.2.74). **Emilia** too wishes to remain one of Diana's 'female knights' or vestal virgins (*TNK* 5.1.140). In spite of women's vulnerability, the patronage of Diana the huntress gives strength and honour to the idea of virginity. Helena is convinced Diana would be 'no queen of virgins' if she 'would suffer her poor knight surpris'd without rescue in the first assault or ransom afterwards' (*AWW* 1.3.114–16). The supposed virgin-martyr **Hero** is celebrated as Diana's 'virgin knight' (*MAdo* 5.3.13).

Because virginity is a key term for defining female identity, it is inevitably a **commodity** in a woman's quest to find a marriage partner or an alternative place in the world as a holy maid. Parolles brusquely points out "Tis a commodity that will lose the gloss with lying: the longer kept, the less worth. Off with't while it is vendible' (*AWW* 1.1.153–5). **Anne** Page 'is pretty virginity' and extremely 'vendible' (*MWW* 1.1.47). **Hermia** goes some way to claiming ownership of her own 'virgin patent' (*MND* 1.1.77). However, Helena in *All's Well* is the character who owns and manages her virginity most actively. Even at the beginning of the play, she is 'meditating on virginity', keen to 'lose it to her own liking' (*AWW* 1.1.110 and 151). It is both a commodity likely to depreciate in value in the marriage market and a weapon. She first defines it conventionally as vulnerable and passive, a territory waiting to be conquered, through her question 'Man is an enemy to virginity; how might we barricado it against him?' In a startling reversal of Parolles's view that virgins will inevitably capitulate to men to be 'blown up' or made pregnant by them, she counters, 'Is there no military policy how virgins might blow up men?' (*AWW* 1.1.112–22). The rest of the play dramatizes her pursuit of this goal, substituting her own virginity for Diana's in order to lose it to her liking and outwit Bertram's plot to disown her as a wife.

Virginity is signified by the colour white in the costumes prescribed for the vestal virgins in *Pericles* and *Two Noble Kinsmen*. The purity of 'white cold virgin snow' (*Temp.* 4.1.55) signals the purity of Ferdinand's thoughts and Miranda's body. Because silver is the metal of Diana, it is also regarded as a 'virgin hue' (*Mer.* 2.7.22).

The 'green virginity' referred to by Timon alludes to **green-sickness**, the disease commonly thought to affect virgins. Images of nature, especially **flowers** and springtime are also associated with 'fresh-fair virgins' (*HV* 3.3.14). **Princess** Elizabeth is celebrated as 'a virgin / A most unspotted lily' (*HVIII* 5.5.61). **Ophelia**'s 'virgin crants' (*Ham.* 5.1.232) are garlands, and Katherine of Aragon asks to be buried with flowers, like a virgin, to show her chastity (*HVIII* 4.2.168–70). The women at the sheepshearing feast 'wear upon your virgin branches yet / Your maidenheads growing' (*WT* 4.4.115–16). Much more pejoratively, Parolles says 'old virginity' is 'like one of our French wither'd pears, it looks ill, it eats drily' and concludes with the definition ''tis a wither'd pear' (*AWW* 1.1.161–3).

All the signs used to advertise virginity actually point to its invisiblity. Marina looks like a good asset for the brothel but nothing can adequately advertise 'warrant of her virginity' (*Per.* 4.2.58). Even the evidence of hymeneal blood was not trustworthy evidence of virginity according to many medical experts. This being so, virginity remained a mystery, 'the fetishised commodity that is and is not' (Carroll 2001: 28). Virginity is continually invoked in Shakespeare's texts but can only be represented obliquely. Lucio recognizes this, addressing **Isabella** 'Hail, virgin, if you be, as those cheek-roses / Proclaim you are' (*MM* 1.4.16). However pious her blush makes her appear, her virginity is ultimately inscrutable. The **maid**'s blush or 'virgin crimson of modesty' (*HV* 5.2.296) was not a reliable signifer. Posthumus's letter which 'look'st / So virgin-like without', but commands **Imogen**'s murder, effectively symbolizes his readiness to doubt her chastity and Iachimo's verbal slander of her (*Cym.* 3.2.21–2). **Jaquenetta** is certainly not the 'demoiselle virgin' of Don Armado's polite address (*LLL* 4.2.127). When

Shakespeare's texts invoke virginity, then, the term immediately conjures mystery, raises curiosity and invites scrutiny.

(c) An extract from Samuel Rowlands' poem *The Bride* (London, 1617) is reprinted in Aughterson (1995: 85–9). Elisja Schulte van Kessel (1993: 132–46) outlines the high-status position held by virgins, including semi-religious 'tertiaries' and virgin martyrs in early modern European culture. Ulrike Strasser's (2004) fine historical case study of Bavaria considers holy and human virginity in political terms as constitutive of the Catholic State, setting up a useful model for reading virginity and its relationship to community formation. Dusinberre (1996: 40–51 and 51–62) analyses virginity as a virtue and a commodity like property. Jankowski's *Pure Resistance* (2000) is a full-length, nuanced reading of virginity in early modern drama and religious culture, including analyses of *Measure for Measure, Merchant of Venice* and *Twelfth Night*. William Carroll, in 'Language and Sexuality in Shakespeare' (2001: 18–29) and his earlier essay 'The Virgin Not' (1994) discusses the representation of virginity in Shakespeare, examining its invisibility with reference to medical opinions on the hymen. Marie H. Loughlin's *Hymeneutics* (1997) is mainly about virginity in Fletcher's plays but conducts a useful survey of early modern medical opinions on the hymen, and has a section on hunting virginity in *Cymbeline*.

voice, *see* **breath** and **tongue**

Volumnia, (a) a character in *Coriolanus*, mother to the eponymous protagonist.
(b) Volumnia's name, taken from the source in Plutarch's *Lives*, is only spoken once in *Coriolanus* but that instance neatly captures her meaning within the Roman world of the play:

> This Volumnia
> Is worth of consuls, senators, patricians,
> A city full; of tribunes such as you,
> A sea and land full.
>
> (5.4.52–5)

Volumnia is a mother of the Roman state and of its champion Coriolanus. She is 'our patroness, the life of Rome!' (5.5.1). Her shrewd understanding of how the Senate and the Republic work lets Volumnia advise her son and produce the fine rhetoric of patriotism that will ultimately save Rome. What is missing from the list of citizens who give Rome its identity is its soldiers: an identity that Volumnia can only embody vicariously through her son.

Visually Volumnia appears to be a model Roman **matron** when she appears on stage sitting down to **sew** in a domestic setting, yet her admiration for bloody battles, fame and wounds already marks a discontinuity between her feminine performance and her desires (1.3). As a **widow**, Volumnia focuses her attention exclusively on Coriolanus to the extent that 'she can hardly be said to have any existence independent of him' (Latham, reprinted in George 2004: 216). She fashions herself as a powerful **mother** who, in turn, shapes her son according to Rome's military model of manhood. Volumnia imagines that **suck**ling Coriolanus has created him in her image: 'Thy valiantness was mine, thou suck'dst it from me', she tells him. She further boasts, 'I mock at death / With as big heart as thou', displacing her own frustrated masculine energies onto Coriolanus and living them through him (3.2.127–30). She wants to out-perform Hercules, undertaking six of the labours herself (4.1.15–19). Coriolanus reminds her 'My mother, you wot well / My hazards still have been your solace' (4.1.2–4 and 27–8). Volumnia's words 'Anger's my meat; I sup upon myself, / And so shall starve with feeding' (4.2.50–2) signal the destructive and self-destructive quality of this perverted form of maternal nurture.

Plutarch explains how Volumnia locks Martius into a suffocating symbiotic bond: 'the only thing that made him to love honour was the joye he sawe his mother dyd take of him' and 'thinking all due to his mother' he 'dyd not only content him selfe to rejoyce and honour her, but at her desire tooke a wife also . . . yet never left his mothers house therefore' (Bullough Vol. V 1964: 508). To escape, as Shakespeare's Volumnia points out, he must 'tread . . . on thy mother's **womb** / That brought thee into this world' (5.3.123–5). Martius's surrender as he *holds her by the **hand**, silent* proves her power to call him back to Rome and his destruction even when he seeks 'a world elsewhere', with Aufidius (3.3.135). Volumnia's role as protective civic mother to the Roman state follows in the path of the **vestal** virgins but is at odds with her role as a biological mother. The part accommodates opposed readings of her as a 'cannibalistic mother' who 'stands at the darkest center of the play' (Adelman 1992: 158) or as an inspiring example of maternal sacrifice who 'knew that when she begged mercy for her country she devoted her only son to death' (Latham, reprinted in George 2004: 228), yet struggles to repress her natural affection 'with an iron hand' and use her persuasive power to save Rome.

(c) Plutarch's Life of Caius Martius Coriolanus is in *Lives of the Noble Grecians and Romans*, trans. Sir Thomas North (1579: 505–49). Agnes Latham's nineteenth-century paper on Volumnia, presented to the New Shakespeare Society, is reprinted in George (2004: 214–29). While recognizing her as 'a failure' as far as her son was concerned, it praises her courage for grasping the 'opportunity to do well for her country' and compares her to examples of powerful women in early modern England (p. 218). Roberts (1992: 148–50) and Adelman (1992: 146–64), read Volumnia as a frightening example of the dominant mother or crone figure. Kahn (1997: 144–59) and Jankowski (1992: 102–21) discuss the complexities of being a public and private mother that are explored in the role. Ripley (1998) outlines the theatrical traditions, including Veturia (as she is called in Thomson's 1749 adaptation) drawing a dagger in the intercession scene as though to commit suicide (p. 88); Volumnia offering her hand to Coriolanus (at 5.3.182) in the Irving production (p. 192); performances by Sarah Siddons (pp. 140–1), Genevieve Ward (p. 245) and Sybil Thorndike (pp. 274–5); Fay Compton as a chillingly ruthless Volumnia (p. 289); Edith Evans (p. 295–6) and Irene Worth (pp. 325–6) as a mixture of attractive femininity and fearsome ambition. Samuel

Crowl, 'A World Elsewhere: Shakespeare's Roman Plays on Film and Television' (1994: 162) notes Irene Worth's performance on the BBC TV version.

votaress, (a) a female votary, a woman devoted to a religious life or to a special saint.

(b) The gendered term 'votaress' is used of women, as opposed to the male votary or votaries of love in *Love's Labour's Lost* (5.2.892 and 2.1.37), in all cases except Sonnet 154 where one of **Diana**'s nymphs is referred to as 'the fairest votary' (*Son.* 154.5). **Isabella** describes the **sister**hood of nuns as 'the votarists of Saint Clare' (*MM* 1.4.5) but all other votaresses dedicate themselves to pagan deities. **Titania**'s bond to the 'vot'ress of my order' is a strong one, lasting beyond death in Titania's promise to rear up the woman's child. Titania's all-female 'order' has links to the Amazon community in the daylight world of Athens. The two women appear to have been close companions: 'full often hath she **gossip**'d by my side / And sat with me on Neptune's yellow sands'. Nevertheless, a clear status difference exists between mistress and votaress. Titania remembers that the votaress 'did fetch me trifles' from across the land even when heavily pregnant (*MND* 2.1.123–34). The 'fair vestal' or 'imperial votaress' whom Oberon saw pass by 'in maiden meditation fancy free' is certainly not devoted to service of her deity in the same practical way (2.1.158–64). She is 'throned', suggesting a link to **Elizabeth** I, the **virgin** queen. The absent saint here is presumably Diana, patron of chastity. It is to Diana's Temple that **Thaisa** retires as a 'votaress' in *Pericles*, because she believes she has lost her husband forever (*Per.* 4. Gower. 4). Inside the temple, Thaisa stands near the altar as 'chief priestess' presumably because of her seniority to the other **vestal** votaresses who appear but do not speak (*Per.* 5.2.0SD).

waiting-gentlewoman, (a) a well-born servant attending on a noble **lady** or **queen**. An unnamed waiting-gentlewoman appears with the doctor to watch Lady Macbeth in the sleepwalking scene in *Macbeth*.

(b) Dramatically speaking, the role of waiting-gentlewoman serves to create an atmosphere of female companionship and loyalty. In spite of their obviously lower status, the characters of waiting-gentlewomen do chat intimately to their mistresses, as companions. Named characters such as **Lucetta**, **Nerissa**, **Charmian**, **Iras**, Imogen's **Helen**, Katherine of Aragon's **Patience**, Silvia's **Ursula** all serve as waiting-gentlewomen who also provide companionship and trust. So does the **Old Lady** who talks to Anne Bullen in *Henry VIII* and the unnamed ladies who attend on Queen **Hermione**, help to look after Mamillius (*WT* 2.1.1–20), and accompany Hermione to prison where she gives **birth**. In such all-female company, the waiting-gentlewoman contributes to **gossip** and speculation that, often, would not be risked in a public forum. Such parts were probably played by less experienced **boy actors** who would have learned by watching the senior boy actors who played their mistresses; they were literally gentlewomen in waiting. In-house jokes draw attention to the actors behind the roles. The actor playing **Beatrice** announces that if God sent her a man with no beard she would 'dress him in my apparel and make him my waiting-gentlewoman' (*MAdo* 2.1.33–5). The actor playing Hotspur may recall one of his own early performances or that of one of his peers when he complains about the tattling court messenger who talked 'so like a waiting-gentlewoman' yet fancied himself as a soldier on the exclusively male battlefield (*1HIV* 1.3.55).

The usual atmosphere of trust between waiting-gentlewomen and their mistresses makes betrayal, witting or unwitting, all the more painful. **Margaret**, the waiting-gentlewoman to **Hero** (*MAdo* 2.2.14) makes bawdy jokes, teases Beatrice about her affection for Benedick and gossips about Hero's wedding clothes on her **wedding** morning (*MAdo* 3.4). The audience knows, however, that a few hours earlier she participated in a plot to slander Hero by borrowing her mistress's clothes (probably her wedding dress), to meet her lover at the window of Hero's chamber. Margaret participated in the window assignation 'against her will' (*MAdo* 5.4.5), we are told, but the fact that she was persuaded to usurp her lady's place is potentially uncomfortable, particularly since she appears masked, alongside her mistress at the second wedding ceremony when 'another Hero' is revealed (*MAdo* 5.4.51SD and 62). Scandal surrounding waiting-gentlewomen, especially Elizabeth I's ladies, was the subject of much court gossip especially if it involved pregnancy or covert marriage. When the Old Shepherd finds baby **Perdita** he immediately reads 'waiting-gentlewoman in the scape' and assumes she is the result of 'some stair-work, some trunk-work, some behind-door-work' or secret assignation (*WT* 4.1.72–5).

Lady Macbeth's waiting-gentlewoman, not otherwise named in the text, tries to be loyal and supportive to her mistress but against impossible odds. In contrast to the intimate domestic exchanges between other mistresses and waiting-gentlewomen elsewhere in Shakespeare, here the two women are absolutely isolated from each other. What is even more disturbing is the curious parallels between them. The waiting-gentlewoman refuses to report what Lady Macbeth has said in her sleep, just as her mistress has had to conceal or repress her feelings about the crime. 'You see her eyes are open' notes the doctor and it is clear that the waiting-gentlewoman's eyes and ears have also been open to much that has been revealed by Lady Macbeth. 'Go to, go to; you have known what you should not', reprimands the Doctor. 'She has spoke what she should not, I am sure of that', retorts the waiting-gentlewoman (*Mac.* 5.1.46–9). Shadowing her mistress, she vows 'I would not have such a heart in my bosom for the dignity of the whole body', yet the 'cry of women' (*Mac.* 5.5.7–8) suggests Lady Macbeth's legacy is inescapable. Having watched for so long, the boy actor who played the waiting-gentleman anticipated both the 'dignity' of the royal persona and a share of the suffering that went into the performance of it.

(c) McEwin (1983) and Elizabeth Brown (1999) offer discussions of the intimacy and frustrations between mistresses and their attendants. Mahood (1998: 44–6) comments on the roles of female 'supporters' such as Lady Macbeth's gentlewoman.

wanton, (a) a flirt or sexually loose woman, though the term is also applied to young children, especially boys, to mean careless perhaps based on the popular image of Cupid as a careless boy.

(b) As an adjective or a noun denoting women, 'wanton' is an erotic term that usually carries at least a hint of disapproval. It is associated with flirtatious, artful carelessness in the phrase 'a wanton ambling nymph' (*RIII* 1.1.17). Most openly derogatory are the jealous Oberon's upbraiding of **Titania**, 'Tarry, rash wanton! Am not I thy lord?' (*MND* 2.1.63) and Claudio's slander of **Hero** as 'an approved wanton' (*MAdo* 4.1.44). **Cressida** is deemed a '**daughter** of the game' because, to lustful male eyes, 'her wanton spirits look out / At every joint and motive of her body' (*T&C* 4.5.56–63). The noun carries a sense of female deception when Iago inflames Othello's jealousy by suggesting that "'tis the spite of hell, the fiend's arch-mock, / To lip a wanton in a secure couch, / And to suppose her chaste!' (*Oth.* 4.1.70–2). According to Berowne (though with no supporting evidence), **Rosaline** is 'A witely wanton with a velvet brow', one 'that will do the deed / Though Argus were her eunuch and her guard' (*LLL* 3.1.196–8). Ford, who suffers from a similar insecurity, finally apologizes to his **wife** and promises he will rather 'suspect the sun with cold / Than thee with wantonness' (*Mer.* 4.4.7–8).

Venus's 'wanton talk' supposedly offends the modest ears of Adonis (*V&A* 831–2), though his prurient complaint serves to increase the titillating effect of her words for readers. Language is itself wanton, Feste reasons, because of its openness and common circulation. His **sister**'s name lays her open to wantonness because 'her name's a word; and to dally with that word might make my sister wanton' (*TN* 3.1.19–20). The signs of wantonness are themselves open, Shakespeare frequently demonstrating that wantonness is in the eye of the beholder rather than the female subject. While **Lucrece**'s visibly sharp sewing needle clearly warns Tarquin 'This glove to wanton tricks / Is not inured', under his gaze, her hair sends more equivocal messages 'O modest wantons! wanton modesty!' as it moves under her breath (*Luc.* 320 and 401). Wantonness is exposed by the operation of the wind, something invisible that suggests a woman's carelessness about her reputation rather than something intrinsically lascivious about her. In Sonnet 54, **flowers**, a common metaphor for female sexuality, 'Hang on such thorns and play as wantonly / When summer's breath their masked buds discloses' (*Son.* 54.7–8).

The movement of wind in rushes or hair is a common trope for female wantonness. In *Taming of the Shrew*, the Lord's 'wanton pictures' include one of

> Adonis painted by a running brook,
> And Cytherea all in sedges hid,
> Which seem to move and wanton with her breath,
> Even as the waving sedges play with wind.
>
> (*Shrew* Ind. 2.50–3)

Mortimer's wife invites him 'on the wanton rushes lay you down / And rest your gentle head upon her **lap**' (*1HIV* 3.1.211–12). Fear of being entangled and trapped in a wanton woman's hair is linked to Shakespeare's images of **mermaids** or **sirens**. Bassanio is suspicious of 'those crisped snaky golden locks / Which make such wanton gambols with the wind' comparing their deceptive power to 'the guiled shore / To a most dangerous sea; the beauteous scarf / **Veil**ing an Indian beauty' (*Mer.* 3.2.92–99).

More liberal images of female wantonness are found in Sonnet 97 where the naturally swollen womb shows its effects (*Son.* 97 6–8), and in Shakespeare and Fletcher's *Two Noble Kinsmen*. **Emilia**'s woman, who has described **flowers** opening in the wind, is reprimanded flirtatiously with the words 'Thou art a wanton' and the two women go off to negotiate how they will 'lie down' together (*TNK* 2.2.146–152). In *Romeo and Juliet*, **Juliet**, always candid about sexuality, compares herself to a lascivious and sexually mature woman for talking with Romeo at her balcony (implicitly like a prostitute). She does not wish to let him go

> further than a wanton's bird;
> Who lets it hop a little from her hand,
> Like a poor prisoner in his twisted gyves,
> And with a silk thread plucks it back again,
> So loving-jealous of his liberty.
>
> (*R&J* 2.2.177–81)

Even this more positive perception of the female wanton registers the threat of imprisonment or entanglement for a man. The conceit probably expresses Juliet's own sense of a need for self-restraint in giving voice to her desire. When she hears that Romeo will be waiting as a husband to make her a **wife**, the **Nurse** notes 'Now comes the wanton blood up in your cheeks' (*R&J* 2.5.70).

Youth is typically depicted as wanton, probably deriving from the figure of Cupid 'wanton as a child, skipping and vain' (*LLL* 5.2.771), so as an adjective or noun used to describe young boys in phrases like 'the wanton way of youth' (*AWW* 5.3.211) or Gloucester's 'As flies to wanton boys are we to th' gods' (*KL* 4.1.36–7), 'wanton' draws a connection between nubile female characters and the **boy actors** who played them. Lewis is 'a beardless boy, / A cocker'd silken wanton' (*KJ* 5.1.69–70) while Prince Hal is a 'young wanton and effeminate boy' (*RII* 5.3.10). Hamlet's critical remarks to **Ophelia** draw attention to the overlap between boy actor and young woman using make-up: 'God hath given you one face, and you make yourselves another. You jig, you amble, and you lisp, you nickname God's creatures and make your wantonness your ignorance' (*Ham.* 3.1.143–6). The cross-dressed **Imogen**'s protest that s/he is 'not so citizen a wanton as / To seem to die ere sick' (*Cym.* 4.2.8–9) associates wantonness with deception and common exposure, dangers that affect the woman and boy actor alike.

weaker-vessel, (a) an adjectival phrase to describe women, originating in the Bible.
(b) Peter's first Epistle exhorted husbands to give 'honour unto the wife, as unto the weaker vessel' (1 Pet. 3.7), and the phrase, replete with biblical authority, was used as shorthand to justify women's subordination on the grounds of natural difference. Don Armado's letter introduces '**Jaquenetta** (so is the weaker vessel called)' (*LLL* 1.1.272), its ostenatious style sounding a warning note about ironic or ridiculous uses of the epithet elsewhere in Shakespeare's canon. Gender-specific behaviour is exposed as performative by **Rosalind**, disguised as Ganymede. A **boy actor**, playing a female character who is then costumed as though in disguise as a boy, says s/he wants to 'cry like a woman' on arriving in Arden, but determinedly assumes a protective role to her supposed **sister**: 'I must comfort the weaker vessel, as doublet and hose ought to show itself courageous to **petticoat**' (*AYLI* 2.4.5–7).
Mistress Quickly amusingly betrays her own mental limitations in telling **Doll**

that she must give way to Falstaff since 'you are the weaker vessel, as they say, the emptier vessel', a view that **Doll** vociferously rejects anyway (*2HIV* 2.4.60–2). In their capacity to run a business in the tavern or provide comfort and sex for the customers, both these characters occupy subordinate roles in that they serve men. They also show determination, resilience, financial independence, and a limited sense of agency in the London world of the play, characteristics that do not readily evoke the designation 'weaker vessel'. The idea that 'women, being the weaker vessels are ever thrust to the wall' (*R&J* 1.1.20) may be true in the sense that women's experiences are marginalized in comparison with those of men in many of Shakespeare's texts. Female characters are not always, or easily, thrust to the wall, however – Adonis may try, but Venus still dominates the text.

(c) Antonia Fraser's book *The Weaker Vessel: Woman's Lot in Seventeenth-Century England* (1985) gives a lively introduction to the topic. Much feminist scholarship since the 1980s has been devoted to disproving the assumption that early modern women were simply victims of the dominant patriarchal culture of early modern England. For an overview, see Phyllis Rackin, *Shakespeare and Women* (2005: (esp.) 1–51).

wedding, (a) the ceremony or performance of the marriage-rite, with its attendant festivities and traditions, including wedding **ring**s, clothes, gifts such as **gloves**, a wedding feast and rituals for sending the couple to bed. The word comes from 'wed' to pledge or covenant. 'Wedding' is also used figuratively to mean a pledge between two parties.

(b) Since, for women, **marriage** was the 'greatest change in my life', as Alice Thornton put it (Cressy 1997: 291), the wedding to mark that transition was a highly significant occasion, arguably more so for women than men. When **Hero** is asked 'when are you married?' she replies 'every day tomorrow' as if the rest of her life is encapsulated in the anticipated wedding day (*MAdo* 3.1.100–1). Shakespeare's texts use a woman's perspective to highlight the highly charged nature of weddings. Hamlet refers to 'my mother's wedding' not simply because he wishes to excise Claudius from every waking thought (*Ham.* 1.2.178); **Desdemona** refers to 'my wedding sheets' as a precious material memory. The fact that every woman grew up in anticipation of this ritual is hinted at in *Much Ado*. Even **Beatrice**, who has vowed not to marry, has thought about what a wedding should be like:

> Wooing, wedding and repenting is as a Scotch jig, a measure and a cinquepace; the first suit if hot and hasty like a Scotch jig, and full as fantastical; the wedding, mannerly-modest, as a measure, full of state and ancientry; and then comes repentance and with his bad legs falls in the cinquepace faster and faster, till he sink into his grave.
>
> (*MAdo* 2.1.73–80)

Apart from the wedding arranged at Theseus's court (which we do not see), only one wedding ceremony in Shakespeare conforms to the orderly pattern imagined here and that is organized by a woman: **Rosalind** in *As You Like It*, although Orlando lays the initial preparations: 'Let your wedding-day be tomorrow; thither will I invite the Duke and all's contented followers' (*AYLI* 5.2.13–15). Having claimed that she can bring Rosalind by magic, Rosalind bids Orlando 'put you on your best array, bid your friends' (*AYLI* 5.1.71–2). She orchestrates pledges from Silvius, Orlando, **Phoebe** and herself in preparation for smooth running of the public pledges, and, implicitly by her own magic, enters with Hymen, the god of marriage, and her cousin **Celia** for the ceremonies. Rosalind gives herself to her father and husband-to-be before handing over control to Hymen. The wedding service is as unconventional as Rosalind's all-female orchestration of the event. It does not follow the official form set down in the English Book of Common Prayer or any variation from it. (Rosalind/Ganymede and Orlando's rehearsal (*AYLI* 4.1.124–41) comes closer to this). There is no reference to God, no giving of the bride, no exchange of rings or verbal pledges. Instead, Hymen directs the couples to take hands 'in Hymen's bands', blesses each in turn and then directs everyone to think over the confusions in communion 'Whiles a wedlock hymn we sing' (*AYLI* 5.4.128–38). Singing the wedlock hymn together is the ritual moment that bestows the community's approval of each of the four couplings:

> Wedding is great **Juno**'s crown
> O blessed bond of board and bed!
> 'Tis Hymen peoples every town,
> High wedlock then be honored.
> Honor, high honor, and renown
> To Hymen, god of every town.
>
> (*AYLI* 5.4.141–6)

All other weddings in Shakespeare's texts are disrupted or immediately followed by disruptions which cause pain to the **bride**. When Jaques advises Touchstone that he cannot be married by the hedge priest, Sir Oliver Martext, and the ceremony must be abandoned, **Audrey** is upset:

Touchstone: We shall find a time, Audrey, **patience**, gentle Audrey.
Audrey: Faith, the priest was good enough, for all the old
gentleman's saying.

(*AYLI* 5.1.1–4)

In *Merchant of Venice* the threat of Antonio's sacrifice makes **Portia** tell her husband 'you shall hence even on your wedding day' (*Mer.* 3.2.313). Shakespeare and Fletcher's *Two Noble Kinsmen*, stages a spectacular wedding procession, led by Hymen carrying a flaming torch, a boy attendant in white robe, a bride and female attendants with loose hair (as was traditional), wheaten wedding garlands, strewing of flowers, and a wedding song, all of which is interrupted by the petition of three **widow**ed **queens**. The moment of anticipation where 'All dear **Nature**'s children', springtime **flowers** and birds are directed to attend and bless the bridehouse and the couple (*TNK* 1.1.1–24) is not fulfilled in stage terms, where the ceremony is replaced by a funeral.

The same pattern of ritual replacement occurs in *Romeo and Juliet* and *Much Ado About Nothing*. The mutually agreed private wedding of Romeo and **Juliet** is followed by Capulet's hurried orchestration of a public wedding ceremony for Juliet and Paris. Ironically, Juliet's **mother** objects 'we shall be short in our provision', opening a potential space for the discovery of Friar Lawrence's lost letter and prevention of tragedy, but her husband overrules her (*R&J* 4.2.36–40). Juliet seems conscious of a conjunction between wedding and dying from the beginning the play. On first seeing Romeo, she uncannily predicts 'my grave is like to be my wedding bed' (*R&J* 1.5.137); after Tybalt's murder she vows, 'I'll to my wedding-bed / And death not Romeo take my **maid**enhead' (*R&J* 3.2.137–8). By taking the potion, she rehearses the wedding of marriage and death; Paris is told 'the night before thy wedding-day / Hath death lain with thy wife' (*R&J* 4.5.32SD and 36–7). Friar Lawrence redirects the traditional ceremonies of festival to those of funeral as though following Juliet's script:

> Our instruments to melancholy bells,
> Our wedding cheer to a sad burial feast;
> Our solemn hymns to sullen dirges change:
> Our bridal **flower**s serve for a buried corse;
> And all things change them to the contrary.
> (*R&J* 4.5.86–90)

Finally, Juliet rejects the offer of single life in a nunnery in favour of joining death and Romeo.

The disruption of **Hero** and Claudio's wedding (discussed more fully in the entry on **marriage**) is made all the more shocking by the careful preparation for it especially amongst the women. 'The wedding being there to-morrow there is a great coil tonight' (*MAdo* 3.3.92–4), which takes two forms. Don John brings Claudio to see his wife's supposed infidelity 'the very night before the intended wedding' (*MAdo* 2.2.46) while Hero asks **Ursula** to give her advice on 'some attires' for the wedding (*MAdo* 3.1.102). Act 3 Scene 4 shows the women discussing the wedding dress and accessories and exiting to help Hero to dress on the wedding morning. The male and female preparations come together in the wedding scene where Hero appears furnished with all the wedding garments, and, on the grounds of what he has seen 'even the night before her wedding day', Claudio vows 'in the congregation where I should wed, there will I shame her' (*MAdo* 3.3.113–14 and 124–5). Only **Beatrice** fully appreciates the horror of what Hero experiences as Claudio bears 'her in hand until they come to take hands, and then, with public accusation, uncover'd slander, unmitigated rancour –' destroys the wedding she has looked forward to ever since she could remember (*MAdo* 4.1.303–6). The Friar's words 'This wedding day / Perhaps is but prolong'd' would be of little comfort to Hero (*MAdo* 4.1.253–4).

Petruchio's mockery of wedding ceremonies in *Taming of the Shrew* is designed to shame **Katherina** with no less cruelty although the on-stage effects are more comic. Having built up her expectations for the appointed day with promises that he will 'buy apparel 'gainst the wedding day' so that 'my Katherine shall be fine' (*Shrew* 2.1.315 and 317), Petruchio fails to appear. She cries with shame:

> Now must the world point at poor Katherine,
> And say, "Lo there is mad Petruchio's wife,
> If it would please him come and marry her!"
> (*Shrew* 3.2.18–20)

indicating that he has driven her to distraction, and wishing that she had never seen him. Baptista 'cannot blame thee now to weep / For such an injury would vex a very saint' (*Shrew* 3.2.27–8). The temporary relief of the news that Petruchio is about to arrive is quickly superseded by his shocking appearance in 'unreverent robes' (*Shrew* 3.2.112):

> Why, sir, you know this is your wedding day.
> First we were sad, fearing you would not come,
> Now sadder, that you come so unprovided.
> Fie, doff this habit, shame to your estate,
> An eye-sore to our solemn festival!
> (*Shrew* 3.2.97–101)

We are given a full account of how Petruchio mocks the ceremony itself; making the priest drop the Bible in shock at Petruchio's reply 'Ay, by gogs-wouns' instead of 'I do'; stamping and swearing, and 'after many ceremonies done / He calls for wine' and toasts everyone as if in a public house. Even kissing the bride is disorderly 'with such a clamorous smack / That at the parting all the church did echo' (*Shrew* 3.2.179–80).

Baptista has 'prepar'd great store of wedding cheer' to dine after the ceremony (*Shrew* 3.2.186) but Petruchio refuses to attend and brutally snatches Katherina away as his goods and chattels, telling others to 'feast, revel and domineer' in their absence (*Shrew* 3.2.224). Katherina's prediction that she would 'dance barefoot on her [sister's] wedding day' (*Shrew* 2.1.33) is effectively borne out when **Bianca** takes her place as bride, while she has to greet Petruchio's servants, carefully dressed in their white stockings and 'wedding garments' and groomed, when she is 'be-moil'd' or covered in mire, having fallen off her horse into the dirt (*Shrew* 3.2.49 and 57–80). Instead of the customary feast, followed by traditional wedding-night ceremonies for bedding the couple, Katherina retires to bed without food to hear her husband rail, swear and complain, while preaching a sermon of continency to her. He then vows to throw the wedding sheets, pillows and covers about the room to prevent her getting any sleep (*Shrew* 4.1.182–5 and 199–204). However she accommodates herself (or not) to the role of tamed wife, Katherina never has the chance to repeat her wedding day and must be content to attend her sister's.

Blanch's politically arranged marriage to Lewis does takes place successfully off stage and is heralded as a 'blessed day', and a 'holy day' to be feasted perpetually for making peace between England and France (*KJ* 3.1.75–82). Immediately afterwards, however, it is cursed by **Constance**, the political alliance breaks and, to Blanch's horror, Lewis vows to raise arms:

> Blanch: Upon thy wedding-day?
> Against the blood that thou hast married?
> What, shall our feast be kept with slaughtered men?
> Shall braying trumpets and loud churlish drums,
> Clamors of hell, be measures to our pomp?
> (*KJ* 3.1.300–4)

When he refuses to back down, Blanch laments 'The sun's o'ercast with blood; fair day, adieu!' (*KJ* 3.1.326), imagining herself whirled round and torn in two by the rival armies since her loyalties are divided.

The material traces of weddings, in particular **rings**, hold strong symbolic resonance in Shakespeare's texts and are manipulated most effectively by women. The **Countess** of Salisbury makes skilful use of her wedding knives, symbolic gifts hung from the bride's girdle, in scenes probably composed by Shakespeare in *Edward III*. She presents them to the lascivious King Edward who is trying to seduce her, as an palpable reminder of her married status. They have an immediate, dramatic and a metaphorical function, allowing her to turn the course of events. She challenges him to stab his queen in his own heart with one while she commits suicide with the other in order to prevent them from betraying their vows to their spouses:

> [*Turning suddenly upon him and showing two daggers*]
> Here by my side, doth hang my wedding knives:
> Take thou the one, and with it kill thy Queen,
> And learn by me to find her where she lies;
> And with this other I'll despatch my love,
> Which now lies fast asleep within my heart.
> (*EIII* 2.2.171–6)

The Countess's gamble is successful: the knives and her threat of suicide convert Edward's lust into remorse. He bids her 'Arise, true English **Lady**', and determines to leave her castle and go forward with his soldiers. Presumably the knives are symbolically hung back at her girdle in anticipation of the feast at her husband's return.

Two figurative uses of 'wedding' occur in Shakespeare, one in *Richard II* (5.1.94), the other a more interesting gendered example in *Henry VI Part I* where **Joan** La **Pucelle** signals her military conquest of Rouen with the words 'Behold, this is the happy wedding torch / That joineth Roan unto her countrymen' (*1HVI* 3.2.26–7). Even though the holy maid insists she 'must to yield to any rites

433

of love' (*1HVI* 1.2.113), she still imagines her role as France's saviour in terms of a wedding.

(c) Cressy (1997: 285–97, 336–49 and 350–76) comprehensively details a fascinating range of religious and festive practices for weddings including the form of service, use of rings, clothes, accessories and celebrations. Dash (1981) remains an excellent reading of the dynamics of power in wooing and wedding in Shakespeare. Neely (1993) is the fullest analysis of broken nuptials in Shakespeare's plays. Page (1935b) looks at the significance of Hero's repudiation at the altar. Patricia A. Cahill reads the wedding knives in *Edward III* as specifically female, disciplinary weapons that function to defend Englishness in her article 'Nation Formation and the English History Plays', in Dutton and Howard (eds), Vol. II (2003: 79–81). For further reading on the state of wedlock rather than the wedding ceremony *see* under the entry on **marriage**.

weird sisters, (a) the three figures in *Macbeth* who greet the hero and Banquo with prophecies of their future, and behave as **witch**es. The adjective 'weyard' or 'weyward' means having the power to control the fate or destiny of human beings.

(b) Shakespeare took this term from Holinshed's history of Scotland, which describes the weird sisters in the same equivocal terms as the figures who appear in *Macbeth*. They are introduced as 'three women in strange and wild apparell, resembling creatures of elder world'. Holinshed continues, 'the common opinion was, that these women were either the weird sisters, that is (as ye would say) the goddesses of destinie, or else some **nymphs** or feiries, indued with knowledge of prophesie by their necromanticall science, bicause everie thing came to passe as they had spoken' (Bullough 1973: Vol. VII, pp. 494–5). Shakespeare's play retains the dual identity of the characters, presenting them as both witches, human women involved in spells and necromancy, and as supernatural figures like the **Fates**. 'Weird sisters' as a name for the Fates preceded both Shakespeare and Holinshed. It is found in the fifth book of Douglas's 1553 translation of Virgil's *Aeneid* where questions are asked about who is shaping the fate of Aeneas: is it one's own desires that are granted, or is it is it the fates 'the fatis' that guide, the 'weird sisteris' who give them the country? (Virgil 1553: sig. Cxvi verso).

In *Macbeth*, as in Holinshed's account, the weird **sisters** are first thought to be an illusion, perhaps because of their remarkable appearances, but on further reflection Banquo and Macbeth identify them with the Fates. Macbeth writes to **Lady Macbeth** 'These weïrd sisters saluted me, and referred me to the coming on of time' (*Mac.* 1.5.8). Banquo recognizes, 'Thou hast it now: king, Cawdor, Glamis, all, / As the weïrd women promised' (*Mac.* 3.1.2). Macbeth says he will

> to the weïrd sisters.
> More shall they speak; for now I am bent to know,
> By the worst means, the worst.
>
> (*Mac.* 3.5.132–4)

'By the worst means' implies witchcraft but, more forcefully, the lines suggest prophecy and the three sisters as keepers of destiny, like the Fates. Their likeness to the Fates is also conjured through the charm that they weave, which dramatizes metaphorically and possibly kinetically through movement or dance, the Fates' ability to spin and weave the **destinies** of humans:

> The weïrd sisters, hand in hand,
> Posters of the sea and land,
> Thus do go, about, about,
> Thrice to thine and thrice to mine,
> And thrice again to make up nine.
> Peace, the charm's wound up.
>
> (*Mac.* 1.3.32–7)

The verb 'wound up' especially, invokes images of the Fates as spinners.

The characters are always named as 'weïrd sisters' or 'weïrd women' and never as 'witches' in the spoken script of *Macbeth*. The Folio text uses 'weyard' and 'weayward' a term that appeared in contemporary dictionaries, associated with strangeness as well as irritating uncontrollability. Florio (1611) links 'wayward' with the terms 'strange', 'skittish', 'coye' and 'fantasticall' while Cotgrave (1611) gives 'forward, hard to rule, ill to intreat' and 'out of all order' as synonyms for 'wayward'.

Shakespeare's presentation of the characters suggests these qualities. Banquo asks, 'Are ye fantastical, or that indeed / Which outwardly ye show?' (*Mac.* 1.353–4). They speak, appear and disappear unpredictably, ignoring Macbeth's command 'Speak, I charge you' by vanishing. The men wonder

> Banquo: The earth has bubbles, as the waters has,
>   And these are of them. Whither are they vanish'd?
> Macbeth: Into the air, and what seem'd corporal melted
>   As breath into the wind.
>
> (*Mac.* 1.3.79–82)

Their wilful refusal to obey Macbeth's words and their uncontrollable agency makes them a manifestation of male fears about female insubordination. Their strange, hermaphroditic appearance as women with **beard**s (*Mac* 1.3.45–7) may visually demonstrate their usurpation of masculine authority. They are insubordinate towards their mistress **Hecate** who **scold**s the weird sisters as 'saucy and overbold' for acting without her authority (*Mac.* 3.5.3–9). Even the spirits they conjure are wayward and 'will not be commanded' (*Mac* 4.1.74). In spite of Macbeth's daring to 'do all that may become a man' (*Mac.* 1.5.46–7), the weird sisters personify his inability to control destiny.

(c) Holinshed's description of the weird sisters is found in Bullough, Vol VII (1973: 494–5). For analysis of the weird sisters in performance see Brown (2005, esp. pp. 11–18, 57–9, 61–7, 117). For further information *see* entries for **witch** and **Fates**.

wench, (a) a female child, girl, or young woman, often with a class inflection, meaning a girl of the rustic or working class. A pejorative sense of a wanton woman or prostitute dates from the end of the sixteenth century.

(b) 'Wench' invariably connotes youth in the Shakespeare canon; it is an early modern equivalent of our modern term 'girl', with an equally fascinating range of meanings. At its warmest, it carries with it positive nuances of affection, familiarity, companionship. In addition, however, it invariably endows speakers with a sense of superiority to the subject by virtue of seniority. In sympathetic uses this produces an impression of protective, parental caring. 'Wench' can also be a patronizing or disparaging term of reference for a woman. At its most pejorative it refers to a prostitute.

At its simplest, 'wench' distinguishes gender. **Charmian** asks the soothsayer 'how many boys and wenches must I have?' (*A&C* 1.1.36). Falstaff makes the same distinction in a sexist way as he argues that that men who drink no wine 'fall into a kind of male **green-sickness**; and then, when they marry, they get wenches' (*2HIV* 4.3.92–4), the second sex. 'Wench' in Shakespeare signifies a female child, adolescent or fairly young woman unless used as a companionate form of address between older characters. For example: Queen Guinevere 'was a little wench', (*LLL* 4.1.123–4); Philoten is 'a wench full grown' (*Per.* Gower. 4.16), and Falstaff affectionately refers to Mistress **Quickly** as 'a most sweet wench' (*1HIV* 1.2.40). One meaning of 'wench' in early modern England was a girl of rustic working class. The unmanly Parolles 'weeps like a wench that had shed her milk' (*AWW* 4.3.107). 'A wench' is the first term for 'woman' used to describe the dairy-woman **Jaquenetta** (*LLL* 1.1.262). A sense of disparagement colours Don Armado's admission that that being a base soldier, he is 'in love with a base wench' (*LLL* 1.2.58). More strongly, Bolingbroke's familiarity to the common people, and something of Richard's disgust, is captured in the gesture 'off goes his bonnet to an oyster-wench' (*RII* 1.4.31). Berowne's first attempt to woo 'in russet yeas and honest kersey noes' like Costard is to address **Rosaline** as 'wench' (*LLL* 5.2.414). 'Wench' marks class difference in Mercutio's mockery 'Laura to his lady was but a kitchen-wench' (*R&J* 2.4.39–40) and **Nell** is the 'kitchen wench' in *Comedy of Errors* (3.2.95).

As a term of address, 'wench' denotes affection and care for a younger woman, especially a daughter, sweetheart, or wife. Even though **Juliet** is her **mistress**, the **Nurse** familiarly addresses her as 'wench' a term – like 'lamb' and 'ladybird' – that recalls the warmth of the nursery (*R&J* 2.5.44). Titus expresses love and pity for his mutilated **daughter** by calling her 'sweet wench' (*Tit.* 3.1.283). The term connotes **Desdemona**'s absolute vulnerability and innocence when Othello exclaims over her dead body 'O ill-starred wench! / Pale as thy smock!' (*Oth.* 5.2.272–3). Mistresses often use wench to indicate a maternal affection and care for their female servants and, of course, they did stand *in loco parentis* for **maids** sent out to serve in another household and learn its practices. **Lucrece**'s maid who weeps in sympathy without knowing why is called 'gentle wench' (*Luc.* 1273). **Katherine** of Aragon calls **Patience**, a lady-in-waiting, 'gentle wench' and 'good wench' (*HVIII* 4.2.81 and 167). She is concerned, like a mother, for the welfare of her ladies after her death since they will be left in a hostile environment:

> Alas, poor wenches, where are now your fortunes!
> Shipwreck'd upon a kingdom, where no pity,
> No friend, no hope, nor kindred weep for me.
>
> (*HVIII* 3.1.148–50)

Petruchio uses the term cleverly to treat **Katherina** like a child, pretending not to notice her bad behaviour and offering a model to aspire to instead. Prospero adopts just such a teacherly attitude when he tells **Miranda**, 'Well demanded, wench' (*Temp.* 1.2.139). In *Taming of the Shrew*, Petruchio's reaction to **Katherina** breaking the lute over her teacher's head is to declare her 'a lusty wench!' – a spirited girl (*Shrew* 2.1.160). His assertion that she does not 'bite the lip, as angry wenches will' probably mocks the actor's facial gestures (*Shrew* 2.1.248). Petruchio's 'parenting' strategy demeans Katherina's anger and suffering, yet the role of immature 'wench' does open opportunities for her to re-learn, to change. Having utterly ruined her wedding day, Petruchio then offers to protect his vulnerable 'sweet wench' from the society of Padua (*Shrew* 3.2.238). When she publicly declares her subjection in the final scene, his exclamation, 'Why there's a wench! Come on and kiss me Kate', probably registers affection as well as domination (*Shrew* 5.2.180).

Male characters invariably use 'wench' in a patronizing way. The King of Navarre's lame response to the French ladies' high-status display of wit is to patronize them: 'Farewell mad wenches, you have simple wits' (*LLL* 5.2.264). Having murdered **Anne**'s next of kin, Richard III presumes the 'readiest way to make the wench amends / Is to become her husband and her father' (*RIII* 1.1.155–6). Casca feels that wenches are naive or of inferior mental capacity, as well as being socially inferior:

> Three or four wenches, where I stood, cried 'Alas, good soul!' and forgave him with all their hearts: but there's no heed to be taken of them; if Caesar had stabbed their mothers, they would have done no less.
>
> (*JC* 1.2.271–5)

Even as a term of affection, the word often carries a patronizing tone, as if speaking to a young girl, and can be used manipulatively by men. Falstaff flatters **Mistress Quickly** by telling her 'there's not a better wench in England' (*2HIV* 2.1.148–9) because he owes her money. He bids farewell to her and Doll 'my good wenches' (*2HIV* 2.4.374) as a man of military action, with his bill unpaid and his ego boosted. The only hint of warmth Iago ever shows to **Emilia** is when he asks for the handkerchief. A sinister sense of his domination lies behind his words: 'A good wench, give it me' (*Oth.* 3.3.313). Boyet, who is presumably older than the French ladies, pulls rank on them by indulgently calling them 'my mad wenches' (*LLL* 2.1.258).

The pejorative meaning of 'wench' as 'prostitute' quickly established itself in late sixteenth-century England (Williams 1994: 1512). Lucio is presented at the bawdy court 'for getting a wench with child' (*MM* 4.3.170) and those in the brothel at Mytilene complain, 'We lost too much money this mart by being too wenchless' (*Per.* 4.2.4–5). At the other end of the social scale, **Cleopatra** is referred to as 'Royal wench!' in her capacity as the mistress of Julius Caesar. Perhaps Agrippa's exclamation is also an attempt to make the exotic familiar (*A&C* 2.2.226). The **Courtezan** of Ephesus in *Comedy of Errors* is a rich but less prestigious sexual plaything. Antipholus boasts about her:

> I know a wench of excellent discourse,
> Pretty and witty; wild, and yet, too, gentle:
> There will we dine. This woman that I mean,
> My wife (but, I protest, without desert)
> Hath oftentimes upbraided me withal
>
> (*Err.* 3.1.109–13)

The gentleman doth protest too much, as the Courtezan's appearances on stage amply demonstrate. Dromio remarks that she is likely to bring damnation or at least painful sexual disease because she is the devil's **dam**

> in the habit of a light wench: and thereof comes that the wenches say 'God damn me;' that's as much to say 'God make me a light wench.' It is written, they appear to men like angels of light: light is an effect of fire, and fire will burn; ergo, light wenches will burn.
>
> (*Err.* 4.3.51–7)

The adjectives 'light' or 'hot' increase the erotic charge of the term. Hal refers to 'a fair hot wench in flame-coloured taffeta' (*1HIV* 1.210); Moth suspects that **Jaquenetta** is 'a light wench' (*LLL* 1.2.124); Berowne feels that the men may deserve no better than 'light wenches' (*LLL* 4.1.382), and **Katherine** teasingly calls **Rosaline** a 'light wench' in their match of wit (*LLL* 5.2.25). Many references to 'wench' in Shakespeare's texts invoke more than one meaning of the word, colouring innocent young women with bawdy potential or whores with the vulnerability of girls. Gonalzo's lines at the opening of *The Tempest* demonstrate the fluidity of the term. He says the potentially sinking ship is 'as leaky as an unstaunch'd wench' (*Temp.* 1.1.47–8) referring literally to the female body as dangerously open, permeable: able to menstruate and give birth. Because woman is a leaky vessel that cannot be contained, the word 'wench' also suggests sexual openness, a prostitute. This is the problem posed by Prospero's 'wench', the nubile **Miranda**.

whore, (a) a derogatory term, meaning a woman who prostitutes herself for hire; a prostitute or **harlot**. More generally, 'whore' denotes an unchaste or lewd woman; a fornicatress or **adulteress**. It could also denote a male prostitute; any promiscuous or unprincipled person.
(b) The word 'whore' is the subject of a joke based on **Mistress Quickly**'s

misunderstanding of William's Latin lesson, where he inflects the genitive case plural of a Latin pronoun:

William: *Genitivo, horum, harum, horum.*
Quickly: Vengeance of Jenny's case! Fie on her! never name her, child, if she be a whore.

(MWW 4.1.61–4)

Whether or not William is a dramatic cameo of William Shakespeare's schooldays, the exchange presents a sketch of how the canon represents whores. To the boy, the implications of his words are negligible; they are a set lesson, taught by an older man in time-honoured tradition. To Quickly, the words are shocking, and have immediate, dramatic consequences for the imaginary Jenny. Like Mistress Quickly and Jenny, women in Shakespeare are deeply affected by the word. Hearing Iachimo's lies about **Imogen**'s infidelity Posthumus says 'She hath bought the name of whore thus dearly' (*Cym.* 2.1.128). He surrenders his **ring** and with it her position as his wife. To call a woman whore 'not only casts aspersions on her morals but takes away her position in society' (Dusinberre 1996: 52) so it is much more damaging than to accuse a man of sexual infidelity. In *Troilus and Cressida* Patroclus suffers no great loss of status or position by being called Achilles's 'masculine whore' (*T&C* 5.1.17) but **Cressida** is utterly transformed by pledging herself to Diomedes and admitting her turpitude. 'A proof of strength she could not publish more, / Unless she said "My mind is now turn'd whore."' says Thersites and that is how she is then viewed (*T&C* 5.2.112–14). Her new classification as 'whore' rather than 'Cressida' is published in Thersites's repetition of the word 'this whore' (*T&C* 5.2.197), 'the whore there' (*T&C* 5.4.5–9), 'Hold thy whore, Grecian! – now for thy whore, Trojan!' (*T&C* 5.4.24–5). Thersites is an appropriate commentator because he is illegitimate. He points out 'If the son of a whore fight for a whore, he tempts judgment' (*T&C* 5.7.21–2) and so remains as an advertiser and celebrator of the whore's infidelity.

Othello explores the tragic aspect of a woman's defamation as a whore, Cressida's side of the story. Othello recognizes the seriousness of the charge, insisting 'be sure thou prove my love a whore, / Be sure of it' (*Oth.* 3.3.359–60) and warns Iago

> If thou dost slander her and torture me,
> Never pray more; abandon all remorse;
> On horror's head horrors accumulate;
> Do deeds to make heaven weep, all earth amaz'd;
> For nothing can'st thou to damnation add
> Greater than that.

(Oth. 3.3.368–73)

The horrors of being called a whore are played out in Act 4 Scene 2. Othello's words hit **Desdemona** with something like physical force; 'hath so bewhored her . . . As true hearts cannot bear' (*Oth.* 4.2.115–7) **Emilia** says. To have 'call'd her whore', showed both the baseness of a beggar and the savagery of a drunkard (*Oth.* 4.2.120–1). Since Desdemona has sacrificed all her other social contacts to marry Othello, the slander is all the more devastating and unfair:

> Hath she forsook so many noble matches?
> Her father? and her country? and her friends?
> To be call'd whore? Would it not make one weep?
>
> (*Oth.* 4.2.125–7)

Desdemona's sense of revulsion is such that she 'cannot say "whore":/ It does abhor me now I speak the word', she protests. Her difficulty in speaking the word shows what force it has, as well as emphasizing her innocence (*Oth.* 4.2.161–2). As Kay Stanton observes (2000: 88–9), the only female character to bewhore herself is Doll Tearsheet, who does so in order to present herself as a victim of unfair exploitation (*2HIV* 2.4.144–5). Once labelled as a whore, a woman cannot escape the term. Bellafront in Dekker's *The Honest Whore* curses 'that minute (for it was no more / So soon a maid is chang'd into a whore!) / Wherein I first fell' and was condemned to a life of prostitution (Dekker 2010: 2.1.443–4). Timon of Athens also recognizes that prostitution is a self-perpetuating trade: even when he gives gold 'Enough to make a whore forswear her trade' she will go on 'to make more whores' as a bawd (*Tim.* 4.3.134–5).

In fact, it is men who make whores, as Shakespeare's texts amply show. Edmund mocks any 'whore-master man' who attempts to blame his 'goatish disposition' on astronomical influence (*KL* 1.2.126–8). Mercutio lists the whore as a male accessory; 'By Jesu, a very good blade! a very tall man! a very good whore!' (*R&J* 2.4.29–30). The Fool's counsel 'Leave thy drink and thy whore, / And keep in-a-door' likewise identifies male desire as the starting point for prostitution (*KL* 1.4.124–5), an idea taken up by King Lear:

> Thou rascal beadle, hold thy bloody hand!
> Why dost thou lash that whore? Strip thine own back.
> Thou hotly lusts to use her in that kind
> For which thou whip'st her.
>
> (*KL* 4.6.160–3)

This is the situation dramatized in *Measure for Measure*. Here and in *Henry IV Part II*, we are afforded glimpses of the whore as part of a social and business community based on prostitution. (*Pericles* also features a brothel but its whores are referred to as **wenches** and do not appear on stage.) Pompey refers casually to 'ever your fresh whore and your powdered **bawd**' (*MM* 3.2.58) as an insider to the trade and reveals a 'mystery' of the trade:

> Painting, sir, I have heard say, is a mystery; and
> your whores, sir, being members of my occupation,
> using painting, do prove my occupation a mystery;
>
> (*MM* 4.2.36–8)

Hal imagines a wench in 'flame-color'd taffeta', showing familiarity with the colour (red) characteristically worn by whores even in the early modern period (*1HIV* 1.2.10). Mistress Quickly, in the role of bawd, prepares and encourages the whore Doll Tearsheet in preparation for her customer, Falstaff's, arrival. Quickly checks her pulse and her colour, ensuring that she is fit to work in spite of a bad hangover (*2HIV* 2.4.22–32).

Hal calls Doll Falstaff's 'whore' to Poins, but in public 'this honest, virtuous, civil gentlewoman' (*2HIV* 2.4.302), presumably a description drawn from another profession of needlewoman suggested by her name **Tearsheet**. Mistress Quickly refers to the 'dozen or fourteen gentlewomen that live honestly by the prick of their **needles**' in her house, which is nevertheless known as 'a bawdy-house' (*HV* 2.1.33–5). **Bianca,** the real whore in *Othello,* **sews** too; it is to copy Desdemona's handkerchief that Cassio hands it to her, though Iago quickly reinterprets this as the handing over of a token: 'She gave it him, and he hath giv'n it his whore' (*Oth.* 4.1.176–7). Sewing together would have given opportunities for female companionship in the brothel, and we get a hint of this in the nickname devised by the whores for Shallow, who was 'lecherous as a monkey'. Because he is so thin that he looks 'like a fork'd radish', the 'whores call'd him mandrake' (*2HIV* 3.2.310–15).

For all their commodification as the servants and objects of male desire, whores have an autonomous power that is threatening; not just to individuals but to social and civic structures. Timon tells Alcibiades, 'This fell whore of thine / Hath in her more destruction than thy sword, / For all her cherubim look' (*Tim.* 4.3.62–4). The most immediate example of the whore's subversive power is her spreading of disease. Timon tells **Timandra**

> Be a whore still. They love thee not that use thee;
> Give them diseases, leaving with thee their lust.
> Make use of thy salt hours, season the slaves
> For tubs and baths; bring down rose-cheek'd **youth**
> To the tub-fast and the diet.
>
> (*Tim.* 4.3.84–8)

The whore's destructive potential is much greater than the spreading of physical disease. She is a female invasion of the male arena of commerce and a trope for the common circulation of value, promoting at the very heart of male desire, an individualist, commercial ideology that utterly disregards the interests of family and community. This is graphically represented on stage where Timon pours gold, 'the common whore of mankind' (*Tim.* 4.3.43–4), into the aprons of the two whores **Phrynia** and Timandra. Just as the whore's trade is infinitely self-perpetuating, man's greed (like his sexual appetite) is insatiable, quickly extinguishing any moral alternative:

> Spare your oaths;
> I'll trust to your conditions, be whores still.

441

And he whose pious breath seeks to convert you,
Be strong in whore, allure him, burn him up.

(*Tim.* 4.3.139–42)

The misanthropic Timon urges them to 'whore still' and 'consumption sow / In the hollow bones of men' (4.3.151). By promoting a culture of consumption, Phrynia and Timandra will destroy the legal and religious institutions which underpin Athenian society: 'crack the lawyer's voice' and 'hoar the flamen [the priest]'. The Fool in *King Lear* repeats this idea in his vision of a time 'when usurers tell their gold i' th' field, / And bawds and whores do churches build' (*KL* 3.2.92–3). As a result of their corrosion of legal and church institutions, the whores will remove the vital connection between the individual with 'his particular' concerns and the 'general weal', or interests of the commonwealth (*Tim.* 4.3.153–9). Having directed them, Timon commands 'more whore, more mischief' from them in exchange for more gold (*Tim.* 4.3.168).

Outside the professional sphere, **adulteress**es or women who are suspected of adultery are referred to as 'whore', buying the name dearly as **Imogen** does (2.4). Posthumus implicitly prostitutes her by wagering the **ring** for the **bracelet**. **Helen** of Troy's real adultery costs very heavily in terms of lives. Thersites reduces the epic Trojan war to its apparently trivial roots: 'all the argument is a cuckold and a whore; a good quarrel to draw emulous factions and bleed to death upon' (*T&C* 2.3.72). Diomedes compares Menelaus and Paris's relationships to 'whorish' Helen and ultimately finds no difference between them; both are 'the heavier for a whore' having endured losses during the Trojan war (*T&C* 4.1.67). *Othello*, with its domestic focus, traces the emotional cost of finding, or being found a whore. The whore within the house is frighteningly deceptive: 'This is a subtle whore, / A closet lock and key of villainous secrets' who will nevertheless 'kneel and pray' (*Oth.* 4.2.21–3). She confounds platonic reason which assumes that external beauty is a sign of internal spiritual beauty. Othello asks in bemusement: 'Was this fair paper, this most goodly book, / Made to write "whore" upon?' (*Oth.* 4.2.71–2). Even her speech cannot be trusted:

Othello:	What not a whore?
Desdemona:	No, as I shall be saved.
Othello:	Is't possible?
Desdemona:	O, heaven forgive us!
Othello:	I cry your mercy then.
	I took you for that cunning whore of Venice
	That married with Othello.

(*Oth.* 4.2.86–9)

Desdemona's identity has been taken over by that of the whore, the creation of Iago's plots and Othello's insecurities. Although innocent, she dies 'a whore's death', being suffocated in her bed in a state of undress (Jardine 1996: 29).

The whore is a caricature of woman's supposedly voracious appetite and inconstancy, and references of this type related to both married and unmarried women. The Fool in *King Lear* counsels that one should never trust 'a whore's oath' (*KL* 3.6.19). Antony has 'given his kingdom / Up to a whore' (*A&C* 3.6.66–7) in Roman eyes because Cleopatra's reputation as the lover of Pompey and Julius Caesar (following the death of her husband Ptolemy) precedes her. Antony includes himself in this history when accusing her of betraying him for Octavius Caesar: 'Triple-turn'd whore! 'tis thou / Hast sold me to this novice' (*A&C* 4.12.13–14). Rather than '**trull**' and '**wench**', which are also used of Cleopatra, the term 'whore' constructs her as a prostitute, trading her body in exchange for her kingdom's independence from Roman rule. Cleopatra's dear-bought political independence makes the thought of being paraded in Rome to watch 'Some squeaking Cleopatra boy my greatness / I' the posture of a whore' (*A&C* 5.2.220–1) particularly abhorrent. The whore's inconstancy, her ability to 'triple turn' or 'turn and turn; and yet go on / And turn again' (*Oth.* 4.1.253–4) likens her to the untrustworthy goddess 'Fortune, that arrant whore' (*KL* 2.4.52). In war-torn Scotland, Fortune perversely smiled on the revolting faction and 'Show'd like a rebel's whore' (*Mac.* 1.2.14–15).

In some cases, 'whore' has nothing to do with the passing of money for sex, or a woman's illegitimate sexual activity. Instead the 'culturally constructed figure of the whore or harlot' functions as a means of degrading an assertive woman (Jardine 1996: 23). **Emilia** pointedly asks

> Why should he call her whore? who keeps her company?
> What place? what time? what form? what likelihood?
> (*Oth.* 4.2.137–8)

One answer to Emilia's question may be that Desdemona's assertive behaviour in eloping from her father's house and insisting on Cassio's re-appointment gives Othello grounds to suspect her of being a whore, or at least grounds to call her one. Aaron calls the **nurse** who brings his baby 'ye whore' because of her outspoken, racist condemnation of the child (*Tit.* 4.2.71). In fact, Emilia's own fate provides an answer to her question. She is called 'Villainous whore' (*Oth.* 5.2.229) for speaking out and telling the truth:

> I will speak as liberal as the north:
> Let heaven and men and devils, let them all,
> All, all, cry shame against me, yet I'll speak.
> (*Oth.* 5.2.220–2)

Iago cannot tolerate Emilia's speech either for pragmatic reasons, or because it constitutes a non-sexual betrayal of him, demonstrating his failure to manage her as a husband should. The self-destructive effect of women's assertive behaviour is shown in the example of **Charmian** and **Iras**'s mischievous determination to cuckold Alexas. They would do so at any cost, even if they had to 'make themselves whores' (*A&C* 1.2.77).

(c) Dekker's *The Honest Whore Parts I and II* (1604), edited by Joost Daalder (forthcoming 2010), is a city comedy with a detailed dramatic representation of bawdy houses and prostitution. Lisa Jardine, *Reading Shakespeare Historically* (1996: 18–34) reads the slander of Desdemona as an example of the verbal prostitution of women in early modern drama. Kay Stanton (2000) works through the representations of 'whore' in Shakespeare's texts and questions how women readers should align themselves with these. Laura Gowing (1994) discusses the word 'whore' as a shorthand for a range of grievances brought to the courts. R. S. White (1992: (esp.) 98–100) examines Shakespeare's critique of capitalism as the 'common whore of mankind' in *Timon of Athens*.

widow, a woman whose husband is dead and who has not remarried, the name deriving from the root 'separate', 'without one's spouse', In early modern culture the widow occupies a liminal position associated with incompleteness, proximity with the reality of death and with a realm beyond. Unusually, the feminine 'widow' is the primary form of the term, in contrast to the masculine 'widower'. In ideological terms, the separation of widowhood represented a third phase of life of relative independence for many women (following the subordinate roles of wife and daughter). For all these reasons, the widow is a culturally threatening figure to early modern society. The majority of widows were relatively poor and powerless; **dowager** was the name used of wealthier women who inherited part of their husbands' estates or title.

(b) The **Countess** of Rossillion occupies the typically liminal position of the widow, caught between this life and the next. The Clown jokes she is well but for two things: 'One, that she is not in heaven, whither God send her quickly! the other, that she's in earth, from whence God send her quickly!' (*AWW* 2.4.11–13). **Paulina** in *The Winter's Tale* embodies the widow as primary figure, offering guidance to her supposed male counterpart, Leontes. Once certain of Antigonus's death, she promises to 'wing me to some wither'd bough' and lament her mate 'like an old turtle' until her own death (*WT* 5.3.132–5). Leontes's command for her to marry Camillo merely modifies an idealized patriarchal harmony of female fidelity and obedience. The weeping widow is a figure representing loss and incompleteness in Sonnet 9, and is used to criticize the young man for his refusal to marry. More than making a widow cry, he will bereave the whole world:

> The world will be thy widow and still weep,
> That thou no form of thee hast left behind,
> When every private widow well may keep,
> By children's eyes her husband's shape in mind.
>
> (*Son.* 9.5–8)

The striking, **veil**ed figures of the three widowed **Queen**s in *Two Noble Kinsmen* likewise present 'such heart-pierc'd demonstrations' of grief that **Hippolyta**, **Emilia** and eventually Theseus are moved to help them (*TNK* 1.1.124). The third Queen's 'hot grief' renders her unable to articulate her petition (*TNK* 1.1.106–9).

Katherine, Lady Percy, defines herself as incomplete, dedicating her tears and words to an always-inadequate remembrance of her husband. As a widow she will never have a life long enough 'To rain upon remembrance with mine eyes, / That it may grow and sprout as high as heaven, / For recordation to my noble husband' (*2HIV* 2.3.57–61).

In contrast to these examples, the Player Queen in 'The Mousetrap' presents the stereotype of inconstancy described in Thomas Overbury's 'Character' of 'An Ordinary Widow': 'The end of her Husband begins in teares; and the end of her tears beginnes in a Husband' (Overbury: 1616: sig. L4). Shakespeare's texts appear to comment ironically on the remarrying stereotype. Lady Macduff's son teases her that if her husband were dead 'you'ld weep for him; if you would not, it were a good sign that I should quickly have a new father' (*Mac.* 4.2.61–3). In *Richard III* Lady **Anne**, widow of Prince Edward of Lancaster, embodies Overbury's stereotype when Richard successfully woos her. She prophetically inflicts a curse of illimitable grief on herself by wishing that Richard's future wife (herself) will suffer even more pain than she does now in widowhood (*RIII* 1.2.27–9). With grim irony, it is wedding – not mourning – that brings Anne such grief. In *Hamlet* the Player Queen likewise believes she should be 'accurs'd' for marrying again (*Ham.* 3.2.178) but protests too much in her declaration, 'Both here and hence pursue me lasting strife / If once a widow, ever I be wife' (*Ham.* 3.2.222–3). As a theatrical synecdoche for **Gertrude**'s behaviour, the Player **Queen** as widow represents the proverbial frailty of **woman**, her inability to function properly as the keeper of her husband's memory, the guardian of his earthly immortality (*Ham.* 3.2.130–5).

Benedick echoes Hamlet's fears in his view that 'if a man do not erect in this age his own tomb ere he dies, he shall live no longer in monument than the bell rings and the widow weeps' (*MAdo* 5.2.77–80). Hamlet's disgust with Gertrude's sexuality is at least partly motivated by the stereotype of the lusty widow whose corporeal desire figured as a monstrous betrayal of her role as guardian of her husband's disembodied identity on earth. It is perhaps no accident that Hamlet introduces the story of the grieving **Hecuba** with reference to the ambiguous figure of **Dido**. *The Tempest* plays on her identity as widow, queen and lusty lover of Aeneas in the series of uneasy jokes about 'widow Dido'. Antonio, Sebastian and Adrian all reject that definition: 'Widow? a pox o' that! How came that widow in? Widow Dido!', perhaps betraying their fear of the type in the prospect of a widowed Queen **Claribel** who might return to make a claim to the kingdom of Naples (*Temp.* 2.1.76–86).

Mistress **Overdone** who has had nine husbands – 'Overdone by the last' (*MM* 2.1.202) – is a deliberate exaggeration of the lusty widow stereotype. In *The Taming of the Shrew*, Tranio proclaims confidently that Hortensio will 'have a lusty widow now / That shall be wooed and wedded in a day' (*Shrew* 4.2.50–1). Hortensio's view that he can easily win the 'wealthy widow' (*Shrew* 4.2.37) points to important economic and cultural dimensions in Shakespearean representations of widowhood. Widowhood could grant a character considerable property: Petruchio promises Katherina control of his lands and leases after his death and Lysander refers to his 'widow aunt, a **dowager**, / Of great revenue' (*MND* 1.1.157–8) as a source of help. Even Mistress **Quickly** who claims that she is 'a poor widow of Eastcheap', is owner of a thriving business and obviously something of a prize since Pistol and Nym are rivals for her hand (*2HIV* 2.1.70; *HV* 2.1.3–25). Male characters in Shakespeare's texts regard widows as rich prizes to be won. Timon of Athens comments satirically that gold makes the 'wappen'd' or worn-out widow an attractive marriage prospect:

> She, whom the spital-house and ulcerous sores
> Would cast the gorge at, this embalms and spices
> To the April day again.
>
> (*Tim.* 4.3.39–42)

Duke Vincentio believes that he has empowered **Mariana** by granting Angelo's estate to 'widow you withal, / To buy you a better husband' (*MM* 5.1.424–5). Listed among the debutantes invited to the Capulet ball is 'the lady widow of Vitruvio' (*R&J* 1.2.66), perhaps a prize for a young suitor. Even Edmund's liaison with **Regan** in *King Lear* can be read in terms of a widow hunt.

Widowhood is seen as advantageous in financial and social terms by female characters too. **Charmian** expresses her desire for autonomous power as a wish to 'marry three kings in a forenoon, and widow them all' (*A&C* 1.2.26–30), as if to compete with her **mistress**, Queen **Cleopatra**, who is 'Egypt's widow' (*A&C* 2.1.37) having been married to Ptolemy XIII and her own younger brother Ptolemy XIV. Widows in Shakespeare's texts enjoy access to public speech, action and influence normally denied to wives and daughters. Indeed, the young Oxford scholar William Page saw 'no reason why a woman should not be content to be a widow seeing in this estate she cometh nearest to the preeminence and prerogative of a man' (Page c. 1620: 233). Hortensio's widow plays out this truth; when sent for, she makes no excuse for her refusal to obey, but counters his order: 'she bids you come to her' (*Shrew* 5.2.92). The two widowed matriarchs in *All's Well That Ends Well*, the **Countess** of Rossillion and **Diana**'s mother (simply named as 'Widow of Florence') both enjoy some benevolent agency in the play. The Widow of Florence offers lodgings to pilgrims as a means of living and is not only able to shelter **Helena** (*AWW* 3.5.30–44) but to help her with a 'shrewd turn' in the form of the bed-trick, which seems originally to be the widow's idea (*AWW* 3.2.68). In contrast, Cymbeline's **Queen** demonstrates how the widow's malevolent power can operate in a family.

The widow's intimacy with the reality of death is staged in *Richard III* where the widowed Anne appears with the corpse of her father-in-law, and in *Two Noble Kinsmen* where the three Queens enter '*with the hearses of their Knights*'. They part on their different ways with the lines, 'The world's a city full of straying streets / And death's the market place, where each one meets' (*TNK* 1.5.15–16). Such intimacy with death often makes the widow a threatening figure even if she is not villainous. Sandra Gilbert argues that 'It is the power – not the emptiness – of the widow that unnerves the world, not just her rage and grief but the sudden, mysteriously privileged access to the otherworld that such rage and grief bestows' (Gilbert 2001: 569). **Constance** in *King John* eloquently voices the widow's grotesquely unnerving closeness to death:

> Death, death. O amiable, lovely death!
> Thou odoriferous stench! sound rottenness!
> Arise forth from the couch of lasting night,
> Thou hate and terror to prosperity,
> And I will kiss thy detestable bones,
> And put my eyeballs in the vaulty brows,
> And ring these fingers with thy household worms,
> And stop this gap of breath with fulsome dust,
> And be a carrion monster like thyself.
> Come, grin on me, and I will think thou smil'st,
> And buss thee as thy wife.
>
> (*KJ* 3.4.25–35)

Constance's love for rather than fear of death, gives her a strength that transcends all her material and physical weaknesses. Even though she is deserted by the 'perjur'd' kings of France and England who have created a mutually beneficial alliance to disinherit her son, her voice carries strong moral authority in criticizing their actions. When Constance's appeals to heaven to 'be husband to me' (*KJ* 3.1.107–8) also appear to be ignored in the person of Cardinal Pandulph, her widow's intimacy with death gives her a power to dwarf the authority of the holy fathers. **Katherine** of Aragon 'widow to Prince Arthur' (*KJ* 3.2. 69–70) in *Henry VIII*, gains spiritual authority as she loses worldly power, and remains a troubling figure to Henry throughout the play.

Alongside Constance, the most powerfully vocal widows are the chorus of women in Act 4 of *Richard III*. Queen **Margaret**, widow of Henry VI, makes her peace with the Yorkist women, the Duchess of York (mother of Richard), and Queen **Elizabeth**, widow of Edward IV, and the three join forces to curse the 'bottled spider'. Queen Elizabeth's experience of widowhood, which dates back to her first appearance in *Henry VI Part III*, makes her a strong match for Richard. Elizabeth speaks with confidence and determination through her first interview with King Edward IV. Edward recognizes in her an agency that can 'challenge sovereignty' (*3HVI* 3.2.86). Elizabeth brings that experience of shrewd, independent negotiation she has learned as a widow to her interview with Richard III, who wants to marry her daughter for political reasons. She deceives Richard and, taking advantage of her autonomous position as a widow, arranges a match between her daughter and Richmond. Richmond is the hero who physically destroys Richard in battle, but Elizabeth the widow has the power to displace his future: firstly by forcing him to recognize his own mortality and what lies beyond; secondly, by reconciling the white rose and the red in the marriage she arranges.

(c) Contemporary impressions of widowhood can be found in Thomas Overbury's character of 'An Ordinarie Widow' in *Sir Thomas Overbury his wife* (1616: sig. L4) and Wye Saltonstall's *Picturae Loquentes* (1635: B3v–C1v). Its advantages for women are summarized in the female-authored 'Memorandum of Martha Moulsworth, Widow' (1632), reprinted in Booy (2002: 60–4). The only English treatise on widowhood is William Page's manuscript 'The Widdowe Indeed', Bodleian Library, Oxford, MS Bodl. 115 (c. 1620), discussed in Barbara J. Todd (1999). On early modern widowhood and finance see Amy Louise Erickson (1993). Allison Levy's collection (2003) which includes essays on Englishwomen's experiences and Bess of Hardwick offers a fine introduction to the ways in which early modern widows were spiritually, artistically and culturally framed in Europe. Barbara J. Todd (1985) reconsiders the stereotype of the remarrying widow. Ira Clark (2001) analyses the widow as a prize in non-Shakespearean drama and popular literature. Jennifer Panek (2007) offers a detailed historicist reading of widows and suitors in comedies. Dorothea Kehler (1995) discusses Gertrude's remarriage, while Sandra M. Gilbert (2001) gives a feminist account of the widow's power.

wife, (a) a woman joined to a man by marriage; a married woman. In early modern England the term distinguished a woman legally and culturally from the categories of **maid** and **widow**. In religious contexts wife could signify the Church as being married to Christ. The term was also adapted in more specialized uses to denote a woman engaged in the sale of some commodity, usually in connection with her husband's business, such as fish wife, or tinker's wife.

(b) 'Wife' is a secular term in the Shakespeare canon referring to a married woman as distinguished from a maid or widow, although definitions of 'wife' are strongly influenced by biblical authority. Paul's Letter to the Ephesians commanded, 'Wives submit yourselves unto your own husbands, as unto the Lord' because 'the husband is the head of the wife' and directed husbands to 'love your wives' as Christ loved the church 'so ought men to love their wives as their own bodies. He that loveth his wife loveth himself. For no man ever yet hated his own flesh; but nourisheth and cherisheth it' (Eph. 5.22–5). These dictates formed the basis of the marriage ceremony and the pledges taken by the couple. The title of 'wife' was thus replete with significance as is evident from its use in Shakespeare. The fact that Coriolanus never addresses **Virgilia** by name, but chooses to call her 'my wife' (*Cor.* 4.1.20 and 5.3.22), 'my sweet wife' (*Cor.* 4.1.48) and directs 'Commend me to my wife' (*Cor.* 3.2.135) does not indicate lack of intimacy. Rather, the term defines Virgilia as one who has his love, shares his sense of selfhood and responsibilities, and owes him her obedience. The same principle applies to Lady **Northumberland**, who is not named other than as 'Loving wife' and 'sweet wife' (*2HIV* 2.3.1 and 7) by Northumberland. 'Wife' expresses his love alongside his expectation that she will sympathize with his need to uphold his honour and will accept his decision.

The title 'wife' marks a major change in female identity. **Juliet**'s **nurse** promises her that at the church 'there stays a husband to make you a wife' (*R&J* 2.5.69). More tentatively, Dumaine asks his beloved, 'Shall I say thank you, gentle wife?' (*LLL* 5.2.836) and **Katherine** refuses the title, for 12 months at least. Paris tells Juliet, 'Happily met, my lady and my wife!' to which she replies, 'That may be, sir, when I may be a wife' (*R&J* 4.1.18–19). She disguises the fact she is already Romeo's wife with the appearance of visiting Friar Lawrence to prepare herself for marriage. Florizel admits that **Perdita** will be a **princess** 'when once she is my wife' (*WT* 5.1.298), revealing that she does not yet have the right to either title. **Portia** sees the name of wife as an important first step in securing Bassanio as her husband, telling him 'First go with me to church and call me wife, / And then away to Venice to your friend' (*Mer.* 3.2.303–4). The name is not enough on its own, as Portia discovers: Bassanio vows that though he is 'married to a wife, / Which is as dear to me as life itself', he would be willing to sacrifice them all for Antonio's life. Portia remarks, 'Your wife would give you little thanks for that' (*Mer.* 4.1.282–8). Gratiano copies Bassanio and the women's quest is, at one level, to win back the wife's primary position in her husband's life.

The transformation from daughter, to woman, to wife is rhetorically enacted in the false etymology of the riddle in *Cymbeline*. **Imogen**, 'The piece of tender air' ('*mollis aer*') who is Cymbeline's 'virtuous daughter' becomes the Latin '*mulier*' for 'woman' and then 'this most constant wife' (*Cym.* 5.5.446–9). **Widows** also become wives. **Octavia** who 'was the wife of Caius Marcellus' 'is now the wife of Marcus Antonius' (*A&C* 2.6.111–12). The transition is not always as easy as these lines imply, however, especially in cases where questions of consanguinity put the legality of the marriage in doubt. Claudius, apprehensive about disapproval for marrying his brother's widow, cleverly interposes six parenthetical clauses between the words 'sometime sister' and the word 'wife' in his announcement to the Court (*Ham.* 1.2.8–14). Hamlet shows his disgust at the marriage by calling **Gertrude** 'your husband's brother's wife' (*Ham.* 3.4.15). Henry VIII is troubled on this account too; his 'marriage with his brother's wife' has 'crept too near his conscience' (*HVIII* 2.2.16). Consanguineous marriages parody and so offend the divine model in which a man is 'ioyned unto his wyfe, and they two shalbe one fleshe' (Boke of Common Praier 1583: sig. P2v). Hamlet's excuse for calling Claudius his **mother** is that 'man and wife is one flesh' (*Ham.* 4.3.52).

Lavatch uses the idea of man and wife as one flesh for a cuckoldry joke, arguing that 'he that comforts my wife is the cherisher of my flesh and blood; he that cherishes my flesh and blood loves my flesh and blood; he that loves my flesh and blood is my friend: *ergo*, he that kisses my wife is my friend' (*AWW* 1.3.46–50). **Adriana** calls on the idea of absolute unity between husband and wife in her appeal to the wrong Antipholus, fearing that 'I am not Adriana, nor thy wife' (*Err.* 2.2.112) because of his estrangement from her:

> How comes it now, my husband, O, how comes it,
> That thou art thus estranged from thyself?
> Thyself I call it, being strange to me,
> That, undividable, incorporate,
> Am better than thy dear self's better part.
> Ah, do not tear away thyself from me;
>
> (*Err.* 2.2.119–24)

The name 'wife', which signalled a woman's identification with her husband, gave her a fixed position in the social order. **Anne** presents herself by Henry VI's coffin as 'Wife to thy Edward', curses Richard of Gloucester's future wife, and then, ironically, becomes that figure (*RIII* 1.2.10 and 26–8). Her ghost proclaims itself as 'Richard, thy wife, that wretched Anne thy wife, / That never slept a quiet hour with thee' (*RIII* 5.3.159–60). Wifely forms of address demonstrate the different Yorkist and Lancastrian allegiances of the women in *Richard III* alongside their common sympathies as victims to Richard III's tyranny (*RIII* 4.4.59 and 114). In a gendered inversion of the patriarchal form of self-identification, Christopher Sly seeks to reorient himself in relation to his wife using the lower-class form 'goodman' for husband.

> Sly: Where is my wife?
> Page: Here, noble lord, what is thy will with her?
> Sly: Are you my wife and will not call me husband?
>   My men should call me 'lord'; I am your goodman.
> Page: My husband and my lord, my lord and husband.
>   I am your wife in all obedience.
>
> (*Shrew* Ind. 2.102–7)

While Bartholomew the page plays wifely deference, Sly follows the teaching of marriage guides which pointed out that wives were not the same as servants, but helpers (*see* section (c) of this entry – Smith 1591: 11). **Goneril**'s subversive desires to call herself Edmund's wife (*KL* 4.6.270) lead to what Albany sees as a perversion of matrimony which was supposed to unite couples until death parted them. He bars **Regan**'s claim to Edmund 'in the interest of my wife' in a mockery of a **wedding**. ''Tis she is sub-contracted to this lord, / And I, her husband, contradict your banes' (*KL* 5.3.85–7).

Whatever its demands on women to submit themselves to a man, wife is a role longed for by female characters of all classes. **Nell** the kitchen maid is 'she that would be your wife' in *Comedy of Errors* (4.4.148); the gentlewoman **Viola** is already certain that 'Whoe'er I woo, myself would be his wife' (*TN* 1.4.42); and the Empress **Cleopatra** is jealous of Antony's wife **Octavia**, 'with her modest eyes / And still conclusion' (*A&C* 4.15.27). The name brings respectability to **Mistress Quickly** who claims 'I am an honest man's wife' (*1HIV* 3.3.119) as though her status can cover the fact that she is probably not **honest** in the sexual sense. **Constance** can imagine no role for herself beyond that of wife and **mother** and when she loses those, re-constructs herself as the loving wife of a personified Death (*KJ* 3.4.35–6).

Becoming a wife gave women a secure cultural position. **Rosalind** warns Orlando that it also gave licence for a whole series of changes in mood:

> **Maid**s are May when they are maids, but the sky changes when they are wives. I will be more jealous of thee than a Barbary cock-pigeon over his hen, more clamorous than a parrot against rain, more new-fangled than an ape, more

giddy in my desires than a monkey. I will weep for nothing, like **Diana** in the fountain, and I will do that when you are dispos'd to be merry; I will laugh like a hyen, and that when thou are inclin'd to sleep.

(*AYLI* 3.2.148–56)

Rosalind's misogynistic view that wives are illogically emotional is not borne out by their depiction in Shakespeare's texts. **Adriana,** who is of 'sober virtue, years and modesty' (*Err.* 3.1.90) may be jealous, but with just cause; wives like **Virgilia** who weep do so for good reason. Mistresses **Page** and **Ford** are far from being giddy in their desires, as they enjoy teaching Falstaff: 'Now, good Sir John, how like you Windsor wives?' (*MWW* 5.5.106). Only **Cleopatra**, who is unmarried, is so perverse as to pretend to laugh when Antony is sad, and weep if he is merry (*A&C* 1.3.3–5).

Idealizations of marriage as an estate made in Paradise promoted the view that a wife was man's perfect helper, precisely suited to him because she had been made from his own rib. 'No man nor Angell brought the Wife to the Husband but GOD himselfe', Henry Smith pointed out in his *Preparative to Marriage* (Smith 1591: 3). Ferdinand regards his marriage to **Miranda** under the protection of Prospero as a return to pre-lapsarian perfection: 'So rare a wonder'd father and a wife / Makes this place Paradise' (*Temp.* 4.1.122–3). The *Riverside Shakespeare* prints 'wise', an adjective for Prospero that completely eclipses Miranda from Ferdinand's thoughts, but 'wife' is also a possible reading following the discovery by Jeanne Addison Roberts that some copies of the Folio print an 'f', and the long 'S' in some is an 'f' printed with a letter block where the cross-bar had broken (Roberts 1978). **Katherine** of Aragon in Shakespeare and Fletcher's *Henry VIII* defines herself as the ideal wife to Henry, an obedient mirror of his wishes and desires:

> Heaven witness,
> I have been to you a true and humble wife,
> At all times to your will conformable;
> Ever in fear to kindle your dislike,
> Yea, subject to your countenance – glad or sorry,
> As I saw it inclin'd. When was the hour
> I ever contradicted your desire?
> Or made it not mine too? Or which of your friends
> Have I not strove to love, although I knew
> He were mine enemy?
>
> (*HVIII* 2.4.22–31)

Having acted thus in an obedient hope for over 20 years, having produced offspring, and having remained faithful to her 'bond to wedlock' with love and duty, Katherine justifiably cannot see why Henry can, 'in God's name', turn her away (*HVIII* 2.4.32–42) She later reiterates the qualities of a 'true' wife (*HVIII* 3.1.126–35). Lady Grace Mildmay's testament that she always carried 'reverent respect' towards her husband for 'the good parts which I knew to be in him' and that she did not 'challenge him for the worst word or deed which ever he offered me' but 'in silence passed over all such matters between us' (Mildmay 1993: 41–2) suggests that Katherine's behaviour may not be as removed from reality as it appears. Nevertheless, her saintly death, without ever criticizing Henry's behaviour, perhaps suggests that the ideal wife is fitter for heaven than earth. **Juliet** realizes she has immediately fallen short of the ideal by criticizing Romeo's actions: 'Ah, poor my lord, what tongue shall smooth thy name, / When I, thy three-hours wife, have mangled it? (*R&J* 3.2.98–9). Mistress **Quickly** inadvertently mocks the model of wifely behaviour in her praise of Mistress **Page** as a 'fartuous' rather than virtuous 'civil modest wife' who 'will not miss you morning nor evening prayer' (*MWW* 2.2.97–9).

The theory that wives should be subject to their husbands, who were the natural head, came from St Paul: 'Wives, submit yourselves unto your own husbands, as unto the Lord' (Eph. 5.22). Lady Grace Mildmay (1993: 38–9 and 44–5) and Lady Elizabeth Cavendish (Egerton 1999: 190) both reproduce ideas on wifely obedience without irony, suggesting that they were at least nominally accepted by women of the upper classes as part of their godly duties. Henry Smith pointed out 'the Wife is much despised for taking rule over her Husband, as he for yeelding it unto her. It becomes not the Mistress to be Master, no more than it beseemeth the Master to be Mistris' (Smith 1591: 78). The Duke of Gloucester is mocked for being in awe of his wife: 'Thy wife is proud; she holdeth thee in awe, / More than God or religious churchmen may' (*1HVI* 1.1.39–40). Richard of Gloucester explains that 'when men are ruled by women' injustice follows:

> 'Tis not the king that sends you to the Tower:
> My Lady Grey his wife, Clarence, 'tis she
> That tempers him to this extremity.
>
> (*RIII* 1.1.63–5)

Boyet goes so far as to suggest 'curst wives' seek to dominate their husbands and 'strive to be / Lords o'er their lords' as a mark of pride (*LLL* 4.1.36–8). The overbearing wife also threatens to endanger her husband since husbands were deemed legally responsible for their wives' conduct. Male characters, such as the Earl of Derby, are commonly advised to look to their wives: 'Stanley, look to your wife; if she convey / Letters to Richmond, you shall answer it' (*RIII* 4.2.92–3).

Petruchio's policy to tame the curst and shrewish **Katherina** purports to combine the biblical commands to love one's wife and to dominate her so that she will obey. 'This is a way to kill a wife with kindness, / And thus I'll curb her mad and headstrong humour.' (*Shrew* 4.1.208), he declares. The performance of ideal wifehood is framed in *The Taming of the Shrew* by the Lord's instructions to the Page Bartholomew who is to play Sly's lady wife. Bartholomew must say

> 'What is't your honor will command,
> Wherein your lady, and your humble wife,
> May show her duty and make known her love?'
> And then with kind embracements, tempting kisses,
> And with declining head into his bosom,
> Bid him shed tears, as being overjoyed
> To see her noble lord restor'd to health,
>
> (*Shrew*. Ind. 1.115–21)

Petruchio imposes this model on to Katherina, 'this most patient, sweet, and virtuous wife' (*Shrew* 3.1.193–5), after their wedding. Her re-education at the taming school makes him confident enough to bet on her in the competition to see 'whose wife is most obedient' (*Shrew* 5.2.67). Katherina's appearance when commanded bodes 'peace and love, and quiet life, / And aweful rule, and right supremacy' (*Shrew* 5.2.108–9). Katherina's long speech on women's proper subordination to the men they call 'thy lord, thy king, thy governor' (*Shrew* 5.2.137) features well-known prescriptions from the ceremony of matrimony and from domestic conduct books. The blessing following the marriage vows asked that the woman may be loving, wise, obedient 'and in al quietnesse, sobrietie, and peace, be a folower of holy and godly matrones' (*Boke of Common Praier*, 1583: sig P2r). Smith's printed sermon explained:

> *Paule* calleth the husbande the wives head: nor of the foote, for he must not set her at his foote: the servant is appoynted to serve, the wife to helpe. If she must not match with the head, nor stoope at the foote, where shall he set her then? He must set her at his heart, and therefore she should like in his bosome, was made in his bosome, and should bee as close to him as his ribb of which she was fashioned.
>
> (Smith 1591: 11)

Katherina refers to the husband as 'Thy head, thy sovereign, one that cares for thee' and outlines the labours for which women owe obedience (*Shrew* 5.2.147). She goes on to offer state models for domestic obedience, again following the style of marriage manuals that saw the family as a microcosm for the state:

> Such duty as the subject owes the prince
> Even such a woman oweth to her husband;
> And when she is froward, peevish, sullen, sour,
> And not obedient to his honest will,
> What is she but a foul contending rebel,
> And graceless traitor to her loving lord?
>
> (*Shrew* 5.2.155–60)

She concludes by outdoing Smith's model of obeisance and offering to put his hand beneath her husband's foot (*Shrew* 5.2.177–9). Remarkably, throughout the speech Katherina never uses the word 'wife'. Neither does Petruchio; he congratulates her with 'there's a **wench**!' (*Shrew* 5.2.180). Has the 'wife' of companionate marriage been killed with so-called kindness and is Katherina wearily rehearsing what she ought to say? Is the word's absence from the speech designed to insulate it from the conventional prescriptions of marital duty, and to suggest Katherina's identity as wife happens outside those boundaries? The script, however conventional, is open to interpretation, as were prescribed ideas about wifely conduct.

Sex is a key part of marriage since procreation was cited as one of the divine reasons for it. **Diana** tells Bertram that her mother did her duty in yielding her virginity to her husband 'such, my lord / As you owe to your wife' (*AWW* 4.2.13). Wifely status allows women a more open expression of sexuality. Leontes is shocked that **Hermione** 'arms her with the boldness of a wife / To her allowing husband!' in conversing with Polixenes (*WT* 1.2.183–5). Flirting with other men contravened the ideal of wifely sobriety: 'a light wife doth make a heavy husband' (*Mer.* 5.1.130), though, with a wry critique of the double sexual standard, **Iras** suggests that while it is 'heartbreaking to see a handsome man loose-wiv'd, so it is a deadly sorrow to behold a foul knave uncuckolded' (*A&C* 1.2.71–2). Admiration of a wife should not be a cause for jealousy according to Othello

> 'Tis not to make me jealous
> To say my wife is fair, feeds well, loves company,
> Is free of speech, sings, plays and dances well;
> Where virtue is, these are more virtuous:
>> (*Oth.* 3.3.183–6)

Shakespeare's wives are acutely conscious of the fact that sexual infidelity contravened the marriage vows of 'forsakyng al other . . . so long as you both shal live' (*Boke of Common Praier* 1583: O3v–O4). Juliet is desperate to 'live an unstain'd wife to my sweet love' (*R&J* 4.1.98). **Lucrece** believes that violation of her soul and body 'kept for heaven and for Collatine' (*Luc.* 1166) is loss of her identity as Collatine's wife. Her thoughts raise the question of a distinction between mental and corporeal chastity as she ponders

> when I fear'd I was a loyal wife:
> So am I now – O no, that cannot be,
> Of that true type hath Tarquin rifled me.
>> (*Luc.* 1048–50)

Only her suicide can restore that identity in the eyes of the men who vow to avenge the death of 'this true wife' (*Luc.* 1841).

Shakespeare's plays do not dramatize Cominius's view that 'the fittest time to corrupt a man's wife is when she's fallen out with her husband' (*Cor.* 4.3.31–2). Instead, male anxiety about wifely adultery is examined and usually discredited. Ford, taking the idea of the wife as the 'weaker vessel' to an extreme, will not trust 'my wife with herself' (*MWW* 2.2.304). Ford's language of determined correction is extreme. He believes 'our revolted wives share damnation together' and vows to 'torture my wife' and 'pluck the borrowed **veil** of modesty from the so seeming Mistress Page' (*MWW* 3.2.39–42). King John has a more pragmatic viewpoint, arguing that if Lady Falconbridge 'did play false, the fault was hers; / Which fault lies on the hazards of all husbands / That marry wives' (*KJ* 1.1.118–20). *Othello* defends all wives' reputations since, if Desdemona is false, 'There's no man happy; the purest of their wives / Is foul as slander' (*Oth.* 4.2.18–19). Leontes seeks to include husbands in the audience in his own paranoia:

> many a man there is (even at this present,
> Now, while I speak this) holds his wife by th' arm,
> That little thinks she has been sluic'd in's absence,
> And his pond fish'd by his next neighbor – by
> Sir Smile, his neighbor.
>
> (*WT* 1.2.192–6)

He takes comfort in the companionship of other cuckolds, believing that 'Should all despair / That have revolted wives, the tenth of mankind / Would hang themselves' (*WT* 1.2.198–200). By putting such beliefs into the mind of someone who is proved to be wildly deluded, Shakespeare discredits them. Posthumus warns other married men to learn from his own mistake: 'if each of you should take this course, how many / Must murder wives much better than themselves / For wrying but a little!' (*Cym.* 5.1.2–5).

Mutual liking was the fundamental basis of successful relationship between husband and wife. William Gouge's popular guide *Domesticall Duties*, which drew on previous marriage manuals, argued:

> If at first there be a good liking mutually and thoroughly settled in both their hearts of one another, love is like to continue in them for ever, as things which are well glued, and settled before they be shaken up and down, will never be severed asunder; but if they be joined together without glue, or shaken while the glue is moist, they cannot remain firm.
> Mutual love and good liking of each other is as glue.
>
> (Keeble 1994: 127)

The most important qualification of a wife, then, was to love her husband. **Jessica** promises she will 'Become a Christian and thy loving wife' (*Mer.* 2.3.21). **Cordelia** escapes a marriage not founded on mutual liking with Burgundy 'Since that respects of fortune are his love, / I shall not be his wife' (*KL* 1.1.248–9). **Isabel**, the French **Queen** asks God to bless Henry V and **Katherine**'s marriage and 'Combine your hearts in one, your realms in one!' so that the personal glue of love will make national identity indistinguishable just as the 'man and wife, being two, are one in love' (*HV* 5.2.360–1).

Where there is no such mutual liking, the results are disastrous in Shakespeare's work. Smith argued that 'He which loveth not his Wife, loveth his shame, because she is his glorie' (Smith 1591: 64). Bertram, who believes that 'war is no strife / To the dark house and the detested wife' (*AWW* 2.3.309) is shamed for leaving **Helena** and supposedly causing her death. **Diana** sympathizes with her: ''tis a hard bondage to become the wife / Of a detesting lord' (*AWW* 3.4.64–5). Shakespeare makes it clear that Antipholus of Syracuse could not be a substitute husband for **Adriana** whom his soul 'Doth for a wife abhor' (*Err.* 3.2.159). Elbow's difficulties with language create an amusing inversion to the ideal of marital sympathy

> Elbow: My wife, sir, whom I detest before heaven and your honour –
> Escalus: How? thy wife?
>
> (*MM* 2.1.70–1)

More disturbingly, Cymbeline learns that his **queen** 'confess'd she never loved you', and married him out of ambition: 'was wife to your place; / Abhorr'd your person' (*Cym.* 5.5.37–40). Cymbeline's response, that he wouldn't have believed it if she had told him herself, demonstrates a lack of true companionship and a wife's self-betrayal in having to live this lie. The lack of sympathy between Antony and his new wife **Octavia** is less extreme but still unpromising, for all Octavia's wifely virtue:

> Enobarbus: Octavia is of a holy, cold and still conversation.
> Menas: Who would not have his wife so?
> Enobarbus: Not he that himself is not so; which is Mark Antony.
>
> (*A&C* 2.6.123–5)

Only brief examples of companionate marriage in the canon, such as the relationship between Mistress Page and her husband (*MWW* 1.1.194–5 and 2.1.148–9), support the view expressed by Elizabeth Cavendish Egerton, writing later in the seventeenth century, that marriage is 'a friendshipp never to be broke' (Egerton 1999: 191), with the wife cast as friend. Prince Hal imagines a breakfast-time conversation between Hotspur and his wife as they talk over those he has killed (*1HIV* 2.4.101–8). In *Julius Caesar*, Portia argues that failure to share confidences makes her Brutus's **harlot** rather than his wife. He assures her 'You are my true and honourable wife' and, asking the gods to 'Render me worthy of this noble wife' (*JC* 2.1.287–303), promises to confide in her. The negative side of sharing such confidences is seen in the Macbeths' marriage where Macbeth's letter to his 'dear wife' (*Mac.* 3.2.36) creates a fatal, murderous chemistry between them. Once this intimacy is lost, Lady **Macbeth** mourns the loss of wifely identity, which appears to have been killed along with Lady **Macduff**: 'The thane of Fife had a wife: where is she now?' (*Mac.* 5.1.41–2).

The canon registers awareness that abandoning a wife contravenes the biblical injunction 'Let not the wife depart from her husband; let not the husband put away his wife' (I Cor. 7:10), and critiques such behaviour. Touchstone's wish that 'not being well married will be a good excuse for me hereafter to leave my wife'

(*AYLI* 3.3.92–4) is overridden. Troilus argues that having chosen a wife by free will and individual judgement

> how may I avoid,
> (Although my will distaste what it elected),
> The wife I chose? There can be no evasion
> To blench from this and to stand firm by honor:
>
> (*T&C* 2.2.65–8)

Bertram does not have a choice of wife, but *All's Well* fosters the view that 'He has much worthy blame laid upon him for shaking off so good a wife and so sweet a **lady**' (*AWW* 4.3.8) as Helena. **Diana** bluntly observes, 'You, that have turn'd off a first so noble wife, / May justly diet me' (*AWW* 5.3.220–3). The text dramatizes **Helena**'s pain: the chiasmus in '"Till I have no wife, I have nothing in France." / Nothing in France, until he has no wife!' (*AWW* 3.2.99–100) suggests the finality of her exclusion. Her quest to win the place of a wife in name and substance depends on a female conspiracy, where Diana mysteriously tells Bertram 'You have won / A wife of me' (*AWW* 4.2.64–5). Helena falls back on male validation of her role in order to give it substance, presenting herself with the words ''Tis but the shadow of a wife you see, / The name and not the thing' (*AWW* 5.3.306–7). Smith's marriage sermon pointed out that a man's second wife 'doth signifie a shadowe, because she was not a wife, but the shadowe of a wife: for this cause the Scripture never biddeth man to love his wives but to love his Wife' (Smith 1591: 17). By echoing this idea, Helena challenges Bertram to forsake all others and dedicate himself to her alone.

Many of Shakespeare's texts explore the pain of estrangement between husband and wife. Glendower rightly predicts that 'there will be a world of water shed / Upon the parting of your wives and you' (*1HIV* 3.1.92–3) as the men leave for battle. Hotspur and his wife **Katherine** do not appear to say goodbye before he goes off to his death, so her tears are postponed until Act 2 Scene 3 of *Henry IV Part II*. Richard II complains that his enemies have violated 'A twofold marriage, 'twixt my crown and me, / And then betwixt me and my married wife' (*RII* 5.1.73–4). The Duke of Gloucester and his wife **Eleanor** are parted psychologically and physically by her ambition; he promises to 'banish her my bed and company' (*2HVI* 2.1.188), leaving Eleanor with no social identity as she is led along the streets in penance:

> teach me to forget myself
> For whilst I think I am the married wife
> And thou a prince, Protector of the land,
> Methinks I should not thus be led along.
>
> (*2HVI* 2.4.27–30)

Eleanor is disturbingly like Cymbeline's queen, in that her grief seems to be more for her loss of position than estrangement from a man she loves (*2HVI* 2.4.42).

The ultimate estrangement by death is stunningly realized in *Romeo and Juliet* and in *Othello*. Having nervously joked about Tybalt's death and the prospect of his own as 'a lightning before death', Romeo abruptly realizes the finality of losing Juliet: 'O, how may I / Call this a lightning? O my love! my wife!' (*R&J* 5.3.91). Romeo's loss is followed by that of his father who bleakly announces the loss of Lady **Montague**: 'My wife is dead tonight' (*R&J* 5.3.210). It is in *Othello* that the loss of a wife is most deeply felt, by both wife and husband.

> Othello: what art thou?
> Desdemona: Your wife, my lord; your true
>   And loyal wife.
>
> (*Oth.* 4.2.33–4)

Desdemona loses the name of loyal wife and, reconfigured as **whore**, she is completely at Othello's mercy. By murdering her, he destroys the thing as well as the name of wife, and is heartbroken at what he has done even before he knows of her innocence:

> My wife, my wife! what wife? I have no wife.
> O insupportable! O heavy hour!
> Methinks it should be now a huge eclipse
> Of sun and moon, and that th' affrighted globe
> Did yawn at alteration.
>
> (*Oth.* 5.2.97–101)

The comic resolutions of *The Comedy of Errors*, *The Winter's Tale*, and *Pericles* rely for their emotional effect on the parting and reunion of husbands and wives. **Adriana** firmly tells the **Abbess**

> I will not hence and leave my husband here;
> And ill it doth beseem your holiness
> To separate the husband and the wife.
>
> (*Err.* 5.1.109–11)

Her lines prepare for **Aemilia**'s story of long estrangement from Egeon (*Err.* 1.3.83), which she resolves by asking him if he is the man 'That hadst a wife once call'd **Aemilia** / That bore thee at a burden two fair sons' (*Err.* 5.3.342–4). *Much Ado* has another version of this comic restoration. Anticipating the imminent completion of their wedding vows, **Hero** tells Claudio, 'And when I lived, I was your other wife / And when you loved, you were my other husband' (*MAdo* 5.1.60–1). Memory is powerful factor in the restoration of Pericles and **Thaisa**'s marriage. He wonders that 'My dearest wife was like this **maid**' his **daughter**, and recalls Thaisa's stature, her 'square brows', her eyes and voice (*Per.* 5.1.108–13). There is emotional and ritual power in Helicanus's simple announcement, 'If you have told **Diana**'s altar true, / This is your wife' (*Per.* 5.3.17). **Paulina** works hard to convince Leontes that there are 'No more such wives, therefore no wife' (*WT* 5.1.56–7) following the death of **Hermione**, in preparation for her restoration in the statue scene. Leontes attempts to compensate for Paulina's loss of her husband according to their agreement that 'Thou shouldst a husband take by my consent, / As I by thine a wife' (*WT* 5.3.136). Leontes may feel that Paulina, a powerfully autonomous **widow**, needs to be reconfigured as a wife, though the play does suggest that Camillo will help to fill the emotional gap left by Antigonus's death.

In contrast to all the foregoing examples, some lines in the canon construct wives in very material terms. The most obvious are references to wives as trades-women, defined by their husbands' jobs. We hear of a 'comfit-maker's wife' (*1HIV* 3.1.248), a 'haberdasher's wife' (*HVIII* 5.3.47), a 'tinker's wife' (*WT* 4.3.97); 'goldsmiths' wives', (*AYLI* 3.2.271) and 'bakers' wives' (*1HIV* 3.3.70), for instance. Ford's confidence that 'Money buys lands, and wives are sold by fate' (*MWW* 5.5.233) is not altogether borne out by Shakespeare's texts. Petruchio says he is looking for 'one rich enough to be Petruchio's wife' and comes 'to wive it wealthily in Padua; / If wealthily, then happily in Padua' (*Shrew* 1.2.67 and 75–6). After wooing, he insists 'I must and will have Katherine to my wife' (*Shrew* 2.1.180). The same determination fires Bassianus who seizes **Lavinia** and claims it cannot be rape 'to seize my own, / My truth-betrothed love and now my wife', insisting 'I am possess'd of that is mine' (*Tit.* 1.1.405–8). Bassianus's words may be fired by emotional passion but other instances expose the very callous treat-ment of wives as chattels or objects. Falstaff's ambition 'An I could get me but a wife in the stews, I were mann'd, hors'd, and wiv'd' (*2HIV* 1.2.53–4) lists 'wife' as an acquisition, particularly through the verb 'get' used commonly in the canon in the phrases 'get thee a wife' (*Cor.* 2.3.33; *MAdo* 5.14.122), 'if thou can'st get a wife' (*Mer.* 3.2.197).

Bertram boasts that he has 'buried a wife' amongst a list of other chores he has completed (*AWW* 4.3.87–91). Having argued that wives cannot be abandoned, Troilus goes on to make some very unsavoury comparisons, likening them to soiled silks or 'remainder viands' that are no longer wanted (*T&C* 2.2.69–2). Enobarbus, who is not married, fails to appreciate the significance of **Fulvia**'s death and compares her to old clothing that can be easily replaced (*A&C* 1.2.162–5). By contrast, Antony's simple repetition of her name (*A&C* 1.2.155–60) effectively conveys the dumbing sense of loss and the admiration that informs his later lines to Octavius Caesar:

> As for my wife,
> I would you had her spirit in such another:
> The third o' th' world is yours, which with a snaffle
> You may pace easy, but not such a wife.
>
> (*A&C* 2.2.61–4)

Given Shakespeare's own experience of marriage – his physical distance from Anne **Hathaway** and probable sexual infidelities – these curiously exaggerated lines perhaps acknowledge the worth of a neglected wife at a personal as well as a dramatic level. By pointing out that Octavius Caesar could encompass a third of the world more easily than the value of 'such a wife', the text acknowledges the complexity and emotional value of wives from a male perspective, a mystery that the rest of the canon amply explores.

(c) The marriage service Shakespeare would have used is found in *The Boke of Common Praier* (London, 1583), sigs. O3r-P3r. Henrie Smith's *A Preparative to Marriage* (1591) demonstrates how scriptural comments on marriage were translated into practical advice for couples. Useful extracts from this and other marriage conduct books defining the role of wife, including William Gouge's *Of Domesticall Dueties* (1622) are reprinted in Keeble (1994: 125–30 and 143–68). David Booy's anthology *Personal Disclosures* (2002: 41–90) includes male and female personal writings on marriage. Mendelsohn and Crawford (1998: 126–48) offer a good overview of early modern women's experience of marriage, including quotations from women's own viewpoints. Fuller examples of women's attitudes to marriage are found in Lady Grace Mildmay's autobiography, meditation on the corpse of her husband and rehearsal of the virtuous principles of married life (1993: 31–47) and Elizabeth Cavendish Egerton's meditations on marriage (Egerton 1999: 190–2). Greer's *Shakespeare's Wife* (2007) uses Anne Hathaway as a focus for a study of the experiences of wives in early modern England, with reference to their representations in Shakespeare's work. Lisa Hopkins's *The Shakespearean Marriage* (1998) is a full-length study of the topic in Shakespeare with useful chapters on the position of wives in the history plays, Roman plays and tragedies as well as on daughters' entry to marriage in the last plays and its function of comic closure in the comedies. Hennings (1986) reads Adriana as a spokeswoman for affectionate marriage in *Comedy of Errors*. For further information and reading *see* entries on **betrothal** and **marriage**.

witch, (a) a person who practises magic or sorcery, who is in congress with the devil or evil spirits and able by their co-operation to perform supernatural acts. In early modern England the term was usually applied to women. Unlike the term 'wise-woman', also used of those who made charms, 'witch' was a pejorative label associated with ugliness and age as well as evil. Allegations of witchcraft were serious because those accused could be tried at law and executed.

(b) Witchcraft is implicitly or explicitly feminine in Shakespeare's texts, used to designate a power beyond male control. Witches' ability to enchant by means of spells or charms is employed metaphorically to explain the subversive, sexual power of women. Temptation and betrayal are characteristic features. **Perdita** is described as a 'fresh piece / Of excellent witchcraft' (*WT* 4.1.422–3) for charming the heart of Prince Florizel. Pompey exhorts **Cleopatra** to 'Let witchcraft join with beauty' to enchant Antony (*A&C* 2.1.22) and when she is suspected of plotting with Octavius Caesar, Antony determines 'The witch shall die' (*A&C* 4.12.47), following the command in the Bible, 'Thou shalt not suffer a witch to live' (Exod. 22.18). The same sense of betrayal enrages Claudio who argues 'beauty is a witch / Against whose charms faith melteth into blood (*MAdo* 2.1.179).

Joan La **Pucelle** in *Henry VI Part I* and **Margery** Jordan in *Henry VI Part II* are both condemned as witches. In Joan's case, the evidence presented on stage in Act 5 Scene 3 gives strong support to the English characters' views that she is an 'enchantress' like **Circe** (*1HVI* 5.3.34–42). Joan appears alone on stage to appeal to her 'speedy helpers, that are substitutes / Under the lordly Monarch of the North' (*1HVI* 5.3.5–6); that is, the devil's substitutes. Fiends appear on stage and she admits that she has been accustomed to feeding these 'familiar spirits' with her blood. She offers to amputate a limb, to surrender her whole body and her soul in exchange for their help (*1HVI* 5.3.10–17). The staging of popular beliefs in witches suckling familiars and trading their souls in order to gain earthly power encourages spectators to share York's view of Joan as an 'ugly witch', a '**hag**' (*1HVI* 5.1.34, 42). The stage appearance of the fiends tends to confirm the English view that Joan is 'devil or devil's dam' who makes Talbot's mind whirl and beats the army by sorcery: 'A witch by fear, not force, like Hannibal, / Drives back our troops and conquers as she lists' (*1HVI* 1.5.5 and 19–22). England's defeat when Joan's trickery recaptures the city of Rouen is again explained as the supernatural power of 'that witch, that damned sorceress' (*1HVI* 3.2.38) who does not fight by proper military means. Rather than admitting that a woman might be a military equal, the English condemn the Dauphin for 'despairing of his own arm's fortitude / To join with witches and the help of hell' (*1HVI* 2.1.17–18).

The same suspicion of feminine skill or craft in military situations is found in allegations of witchcraft made against Coriolanus for seducing Aufidius's soldiers (*Cor.* 4.7.2), Prince Hal for dazzling the soldiers on the battlefield (*1HIV* 4.1.110) and the French courtier LaMord's astonishing horsemanship (*Ham.* 4.7.85). Likewise, Burgundy's first thought is to attribute his dishonourable desertion of the English to Joan's sorcery: 'she hath bewitch'd me with her words' (*2HVI* 3.3.58).

The alternative, French view that Joan is divinely inspired by the **Virgin Mary** collapses when the fiends appear. Joan is 'condemn'd to burn', (*1HVI* 5.4.1) denies her parentage and then claims she is pregnant in a last bid to save her life. She exits with a curse (which proves prophetic in terms of civil war in England). York's fear of her enduring power is shown in his reaction 'Break thou in pieces and consume to ashes / Thou foul accursed minister of hell' (*1HVI* 5.4.92–3). Immediately after Joan's arrest, she is followed on stage by **Margaret**, who will become another threatening presence to masculine power throughout *Henry VI Parts II* and *III* and *Richard III*. When she appears in *Richard III*, Gloucester calls her 'Foul wrinkled witch' (*RIII* 1.3.163). **Margery** Jordan, a 'cunning witch' (*2HVI* 1.2.75), who is summoned by **Eleanor**, Duchess of Gloucester, confirms the association of witchcraft with female ambition in Shakespeare's histories. Eleanor is exiled but 'the witch in Smithfield shall be burnt to ashes' (*2HVI* 2.3.7), a scapegoat for Eleanor's transgression. Margery's subjection is physically enacted in the conjuring scene where she is commanded 'be you prostrate / And grovel on the earth', and then conjures the fiend with the somewhat surprising words 'By the eternal God, whose name and power / Thou tremblest at' (*2HVI* 1.4.10–11 and 25–7).

Caliban's mother, **Sycorax**, does not appear in *The Tempest* but is described as 'a witch, and one so strong / That could control the **moon**, make flows and ebbs, / And deal in her command without her power' (*Temp.* 5.1.269–71), a power that she shares with the enchantress **Circe**. Like Joan and Margery Jordan, Sycorax was condemned to death for 'mischiefs manifold and sorceries terrible' (*Temp.* 1.2.264), though her genuine pregnancy commuted her sentence to one of exile to the island. Here 'the foul witch Sycorax, who with age and envy / Was grown into a hoop' (bent double), imprisoned Ariel within a pine tree (*Temp.* 1.2.258– and 274–7). Her black magic haunts the present of the play, blurring disturbingly with that of Prospero.

Witchcraft is a comic trope for exotic otherness and confusion in *Comedy of Errors*. Antipholus of Syracuse is convinced that the exotic city of Ephesus is full of 'Dark-working sorcerers that change the mind, / Soul-killing witches that deform the body' (*Err.* 1.2.99–100), and the confusion of identities reinforces his view that 'There's none but witches do inhabit here' (*Err.* 3.2.156), including the **Courtezan** whom he calls 'a sorceress' (*Err.* 4.3.66). Dromio of Syracuse says he's nearly persuaded to 'turn witch' to stay amongst the friendly Ephesians. A broader swipe at the demonic stereotyping of old women, especially village wise-women, and the paranoia of witch-hunters is seen in Ford's reaction to the wise woman of **Brainford**:

A witch, a **quean**, an old cozening quean! Have I not forbid her my house? She comes of errands, does she? We are simple men; we do not know what's brought to pass under the profession of fortune-telling. She works by charms, by spells, by the figure, and such daub'ry as this is, beyond our element; we know nothing. Come down, you witch, you **hag**, you; come down, I say!

(*MWW* 4.2.172–9)

Ford's paranoid association of female sexuality and witchcraft is shared by Leontes whose determination to put **Paulina** out of doors as 'A mankind witch!' and 'A most intelligencing **bawd**!' is potentially comic in its absurdity (*WT* 2.3.68–9). Nevertheless, Richard III's ridiculously exaggerated claims that Queen **Elizabeth** 'that monstrous witch' has conspired with 'that **harlot** strumpet Shore' to wither his arm 'by their witchcraft' reminds spectators that accusations of witchcraft always carried the threat of execution, and were thus always dangerous (*RIII* 3.4.68–72). **Charmian** reassures the Soothsayer 'I forgive thee for a witch' (*A&C* 1.2.40), in one of the rare cases in Shakespeare where a man is called a witch (the other is Posthumus by the false Iachimo *Cym.* 1.6.166).

In *Merry Wives* when the disguised Falstaff appears, Ford's fear makes him physically beat the wise woman: 'Out of my door, you witch, you hag, you baggage, you polecat, you runyon! out, out!' and demand 'Hang her, witch!' (*MWW* 4.2.184–91). His lines are a comic version of Edgar's performance of terrified demonic possession 'Aroint thee, witch, aroint thee!' (*KL* 3.4.124) and the opening scene of *Macbeth* where the first **weird sister** recalls the reaction of the sailor's wife: '"Aroint thee, witch!" the rump-fed ronyon cries' (*Mac.* 1.3.6). Sir Hugh

Evans's opinion that the Old Woman of Brainford 'is a witch indeed: I like it not when a woman has a great **beard**' (*MWW* 4.2.193–4) again looks forward to the appearance of the weird sisters and Banquo's remark, 'You should be women, / And yet your beards forbid me to interpret / That you are so' (*Mac.* 1.3.45–7).

Witchcraft is felt most powerfully in *Macbeth*: in the roles of the **weird sisters**, the additional exchanges featuring **Hecate** which are probably by Thomas Middleton, and in Lady **Macbeth**'s imitation of their demonic practices by summoning spirits to 'come to my woman's breasts / And take my milk for gall' like familiars (*Mac.* 1.5.47–8). Tradition has it that the witch scenes were written specifically to cater to the tastes of James I who had written his own account of witchcraft: *Daemonologie* (Edinburgh 1597; London 1603), following a treacherous journey across the North Sea during which he feared his boats had been attacked by witches. The weird sisters, as they call themselves, are more supernatural **Fates** than village wise-women. Their unholy trinity of voices speak in short rhyming verse lines and paradoxes. They address their invisible familiar spirits, Graymalkin, Paddock and Harpier. They create a harmful charm in Act 1 Scene 3, have the ability to prophesy (*Mac.* 1.3.48–69), to hover through the air (*Mac.* 1.1.12) and vanish at will (*Mac.* 1.3.77–82). In Act 4 they are seen at a witches' sabbat with Hecate and a further three witches, preparing a charm in a cauldron by adding a range of grotesque ingredients and chanting the lines 'Double, double, toil and trouble / Fire burn and cauldron bubble' (*Mac.* 4.1.10–11). They sing about the cauldron (the songs are also found in Middleton's *The Witch*) and then have the power to conjure apparitions. The three apparitions' messages are riddles that Macbeth is unable to understand. However, he despairs at the line of Banquo's sons as kings stretching 'out to th' crack of doom' this final 'horrible sight' confirming the witches' ability to see into the future like the Fates (*Mac.* 4.1.111–23).

The influence of the weird sisters pervades the play. On his way to assassinate Duncan, after midnight, Macbeth comments, 'Nature seems dead and wicked dreams abuse / The curtain'd sleep; witchcraft celebrates / Pale Hecate's offerings' (*Mac.* 1.7.50–2). Hamlet, too, sees midnight as 'the very witching time of night' (*Ham.* 3.2.388). **Night** is personified as a witch by the Chorus in *Henry V* but here, the opposite image of an aged village outcast is conjured up to suggest the frustration of the over-confident French who

> chide the cripple tardy-gaited night
> Who, like a foul and ugly witch, doth limp
> So tediously away.
>
> (*HV* 4. Chorus. 20–2)

By contrast, Troilus curses Night with the words 'Beshrew the witch!' since 'with venemous wights she stays / As tediously as hell, but flies the grasp of love / With wings more momentary-swift than thought' (*T&C* 4.2.12–14). This quotation aptly illustrates the slipperiness of the term 'witch' in Shakespeare's work. The witch is a supernatural, dangerous power threatening all mankind but also the wretched, village wise-woman. The changes between these opposites are more 'momentary-swift than thought', making allusions to a witch a source of ambiguity and dangerous fascination.

(c) Briggs (1962) and Keith Thomas (1971) are foundational studies of magic in early modern literature and cultural history. Christina Larner (1984) looks at witchcraft beliefs in a Scottish context, Sharpe (1996) at English beliefs and Stuart Clark (1997) at beliefs in the European context. Diane Purkiss (1996) compares early modern and twentieth-century interpretations of women as witches. Stephen Orgel (1999) and Kathleen McLuskie (2003) give very good readings of witchcraft in *Macbeth*.

woman, (a) an adult, female human being. Early modern English frequently makes a play on the word as meaning '"woe" to man'. It invariably carries an implicit class distinction from **lady**, and is often used to mean a servant or **maid**. Generically, the term means the whole female sex and in the plural it can mean illicit sexual intercourse with women (e.g. 'let him keep himself from women'). It can also be used to refer to the characteristic qualities of a woman or qualities in a man that are usually attributed to the female sex – such as proneness to tears or emotions, capriciousness – or to the traditional subjection of woman (e.g. to 'make a woman' of someone is to bring them into submission). In contrast, to be one's own woman is to be **mistress** of oneself.

(b) 'Woman' is used to mark middle- or lower-class status in Shakespeare's work, and to indicate a female servant. In *All's Well That Ends Well*, the Clown's girlfriend is simply called 'Isbel the woman' in contrast to 'your ladyship' the **Countess** of Rosillion (*AWW* 1.3.337). The snapshot of a haberdasher's wife who calls on the apprentices to help her when she loses her cap (*Henry VIII* 5.3.46–53) locates 'woman' within the citizenry of London rather than the court. *Cymbeline* conflates 'woman' as servant and as female of middle social standing when **Imogen** refers to '**Dorothy** my woman' and 'my woman **Helen**' (*Cym.* 2.3.138 and 1.2.1), and goes on to reveal more about the social status of one of these in her plans to escape from the court disguised:

> Go, bid my woman feign a sickness, say
> She'll home to her father; and provide me presently
> A riding-suit, no costlier than would fit
> A franklin's huswife.
>
> (*Cym.* 3.2.74–7)

Female companions are called 'women' in several plays. **Lychorida** is **Thaisa**'s 'woman', **Emilia** is addressed as 'woman' by Othello, and **Miranda** recalls 'Had I not / Four or five women once that tended me?' (*Temp.* 1.2.47), for example. The stage direction for Act 3 Scene 2 of *Henry VIII*, one of the scenes ascribed to Shakespeare, reads '*Enter QUEEN KATHARINE and her Women, as at work*'. The servants here are individuated with the names, **Patience** and **Dorothy**, appropriate for companions of the abused English queen who describes herself, fallen from favour, as 'a wretched lady, / A woman lost amongst ye / laugh'd at, scorn'd'

(*HVIII* 3.1.106–7). The term is adopted very deliberately by the Empress and Egyptian Queen **Cleopatra** in order to ally herself with her servants. Echoing Queen Elizabeth's wish to be a common milkmaid 'with a pail on mine arm' rather than the 'greatest monarch' (Elizabeth I 2000: 170), Cleopatra defines herself as:

> No more, but e'en a woman and commanded
> By such poor passion as the maid that milks
> And does the meanest chares.
> (*A&C* 4.15.73–5)

She goes on to group herself with **Charmian** and **Iras** in the common task of mourning for Antony whose death appears to have struck out all sense of social identity with its reminders of common mortality: 'Ah, women, women, look, / Our lamp is spent, it's out!' (*A&C* 4.15.84–5).

Generic uses of 'woman' to indicate a series of concepts are much more complex, as Cymbeline recognizes in the words, 'Who is 't can read a woman? Is there more?' (*Cym.* 5.5.48), referring in this case to the deceptive and evil plots of his **Queen**. His words register the ways in which Shakespeare's female characters often surprise others by altering the qualities traditionally associated with the term 'woman'. Berowne uses a more mechanistic metaphor to convey his own apprehension in engaging with the opposite sex:

> A woman, that is like a German clock,
> Still a-repairing, ever out of frame,
> And never going aright, being a watch,
> But being watch'd that it may still go right!
> (*LLL* 3.1.190–3)

Already, the arrogance and futility of male attempts to control women like machines through constant surveillance is obvious to spectators, although this is something Berowne and his friends learn through *Love's Labour's Lost*.

Touchstone's pragmatic dictionary gloss of the term simply redefines 'female' as 'woman' in 'the common' tongue, alluding to **Audrey** (and William's) lower-class status (*AYLI* 5.1.49–50). Shakespeare uses the word as a generic term for the sex to show how a female character can be reduced to the object of male desire. In *Titus*, Demetrius says of Lavinia, 'She is a woman, therefore may be woo'd; / She is a woman, therefore may be won' (*Tit.* 2.1.82–3), his words prefiguring the brothers' physical brutality in raping her. Suffolk's use of the same phrase in *Henry VI* indicates his physical attraction to Margaret's **beauty** (*1HVI* 5.3.79). A more comic effect is achieved when Romeo muses, 'in sadness, cousin, I do love a woman' and Benevolio replies, 'I aim'd so near when I suppos'd you lov'd' (*R&J* 1.2.204–5). Behind the laughter, the exchange demonstrates the vagueness of Romeo's passion before he meets Juliet.

The word's associations with corporeal identity appear in the Gravedigger's jest that the grave is for 'one that was a woman, sir, but, rest her soul, she's dead' (*Ham.* 5.1.135). The ability to give **birth** is woman's most fundamental defining physical characteristic, seen in the repeated totemic phrases 'born of woman' (*Mac.* 5.5.11) and 'of woman born' (*Mac.* 4.1.80) in *Macbeth*. The idea of woman as creator is what Berowne uses to legitimate abandoning the all-male academy in *Love's Labour's Lost*, swearing by 'women's sake, by whom we men are men' and determining that to foreswear women would be 'to lose ourselves' (*LLL* 4.3.357–9). Posthumus, believing women are inconstant, is revolted by the part they play in reproduction and longs for an alternative: 'Is there no way for men to be but women / Must be half-workers?' (*Cym.* 2.5.1–2). 'Woman' is a term indicating sexual knowledge in cases like Malcolm's profession of virginity 'I am yet / Unknown to woman' (*Mac.* 4.3.125–6) or in Hamlet's 'man delights not me, no, nor women neither, though by your smiling you seem to say so' (*Ham.* 2.2.309–10). In contrast to **maid**, it advertises female sexual experience in *Measure for Measure* where Pompey equivocates that **Juliet** is not 'a maid with child by' Claudio but 'a woman with maid by him' (*MM* 1.2.91–2). Juliet registers the sin surrounding carnal knowledge by describing herself like **Eve** as 'the woman that wrong'd him' (*MM* 3.2.25). The Clowns in *Antony and Cleopatra* and *All's Well* make an elaborate jest out of the association between woman and sin (*A&C* 5.1.272–7 and *AWW* 1.3.82–9).

'Woman' signifies the distinctiveness of female identity in **Beatrice**'s lament, 'I cannot be a man with wishing, therefore I will die a woman with grieving' (*MAdo* 4.1.322–3). **Nerissa**'s jest that Gratiano will only be telling the truth in insisting he gave the **ring** to a man 'if a woman live to be a man' also implies absolute gender difference (*Mer.* 5.1.160). However, the distinction is less absolute when we consider that the **boy actor** speaking these words *should* 'live to be a man' (*Mer.* 5.1.159).

'Woman' is used much more provisionally of cross-dressed heroines and boy actors in *Twelfth Night* and *As You Like It*: 'Were you a woman, as the rest goes even' (*TN* 5.1.239); 'were I a woman' (*TN* 2.4.108) and the boy actor playing **Rosalind** telling spectators, 'If I were a woman' (*AYLI* Epilogue. 18). Here, where attention is drawn to the male body of the actor, female identity seems to reside in articles of clothing or 'woman's weeds' (*TN* 5.1.256). Womanhood is exposed as artificial in *Henry IV Part II* where Mistress **Quickly** swears 'there's neither faith, truth or womanhood in me else' but Falstaff retorts that she has no more faith than a stewed prune, no more truth than in a crafty fox and 'as for womanhood, Maid **Marian** may be the deputy's wife of the ward to thee' (*1HIV* 3.3.110–15). The superficial meaning is that she is no more reputable than the dubious figure of Maid Marian in the Robin Hood plays. Since the character was always played by a man, the implication, with reference to the boy actor playing Quickly, is that there is no more authentic basis of womanhood in Quickly than there would be in the figure of Maid Marian performed by a boy.

The physiological and cultural constructions of 'woman' from a male perspective are advertised as artificial, as when Sampson, the somewhat ironically named Capulet servant, proclaims that 'women being the weaker vessels, are ever thrust to the wall' (*R&J* 1.1.15–16) or when Richard, Duke of York, tells Queen Margaret 'Women are soft, mild, pitiful and flexible; / Thou stern, obdurate, flinty, rough, remorseless' (*3HVI* 1.4.141–2). The narrator of **Lucrece**'s fate and **Isabella** in *Measure for Measure* both have a more heightened awareness of how the label 'woman' is an empty vessel into which men pour their own desires and, more often, prejudices: 'O let it not be held / Poor women's faults that they are so full-filled / With men's abuses' (*Luc.* 1258–60). Isabella complains 'Women! Help Heaven! men their creation mar / In profiting by them.' She does place some of the blame on women, anticipating feminist arguments by defining women's frailty as being passively 'credulous to false prints' or false impressions (*MM* 2.4.127–30). The workings of patriarchal ideology are elaborated in *Lucrece* using the metaphor of marble for the wills of men who shape the waxen minds of women:

> For men have marble, women waxen, minds,
> And therefore are they form'd as marble will;
> The weak oppress'd, th' impression of strange kinds
> Is form'd in them by force, by fraud, or skill:
> Then call them not the authors of their ill,
> No more than wax shall be accounted evil
> Wherein is stamp'd the semblance of a devil.
>
> (*Luc.* 1240–6)

One of the most skilful manipulators of such ideology is Iago. When **Desdemona** asks him to define 'a deserving woman' whose merit could elicit nothing but praise from a man, Iago gives the following catalogue of attributes:

> She that was ever fair, and never proud,
> Had tongue at will, and yet was never loud,
> Never lack'd gold, and yet went never gay,
> Fled from her wish, and yet said 'Now I may';
> She that being ang'red, her revenge being nigh,
> Bade her wrong stay, and her displeasure fly;
> She that in wisdom never was so frail
> To change the cod's head for the salmon's tail,
> She that could think, and ne'er disclose her mind,
> See suitors following and not look behind,
> She was a wight (if ever such wight were) . . .
>
> (*Oth.* 2.1.148–58)

In *The Winter's Tale*, **Paulina** proclaims **Hermione** a living embodiment of female perfection, better than any amalgamation of good qualities in others 'To make a perfect woman' (*WT* 5.1.15), but, significantly, the misogynist Iago cannot complete his sentence, being unable to contemplate the possibility that a deserving woman does exist. His catalogue draws on a conventional list of womanly vices: pride in good looks, a tendency to vanity in fine clothes and the delight of being admired by suitors; verbal volubility, loudness, and an inability to keep secrets; impulsive behaviour, including the pursuit of **revenge**; weakness of wit or wisdom, linked closely to sexual infidelity (changing the superior 'salmon's tail' or husband for the lover's 'cod's head' or penis). The same characteristics are set forth even less sympathetically, as a catalogue of vices which Posthumus is certain constitutes the 'woman's part':

> It is the woman's part: be it lying, note it,
> The woman's; flattering, hers; deceiving, hers;
> Lust and rank thoughts, hers, hers; revenges, hers;
> Ambitions, covetings, change of prides, disdain,
> Nice longing, slanders, mutability,
> All faults that name, nay, that hell knows,
> Why, hers, in part or all; but rather, all.
>
> (*Cym.* 2.5.22–9)

Female characters work around the conventional list of characteristics, and its misogyny, often quite deliberately. **Rosalind** protests (too much), 'I thank God I am not a woman, to be touch'd with so many giddy offences' as her wise uncle 'hath generally tax'd their whole sex withal' and when Orlando asks for a list of the 'principal evils' laid to the charge of women she strategically deflects his request (*AYLI* 3.2.348–52).

Vanity and social ambition are knowingly cited as female traits by the Old **Lady** of Henry VIII's court, who plays on her greater experience to unmask **Anne** Bullen's aspirations, telling her that her physical 'fair parts of woman' are matched by 'a woman's heart; which ever yet / Affected eminence, wealth, sovereignty' (*HVIII* 2.3.29–30). Affectation of social eminence through wearing the clothes of the social élite is typical of proud city-women according to the satirical Jacques (*AYLI* 2.7.75–8), and even the humble **Audrey** in *As You Like It* desires to be 'a woman of the world'. The Fool in *King Lear* notices vanity in every 'fair woman' who makes 'mouths in a glass' (*KL* 3.2.35).

Women's softness, seen in the images of wax, gives them an advantage of flexibility over their male counterparts. Brutus refers to 'the melting spirits of women' (*JC* 2.1.122) and **Julia** bitterly recognizes that it is more appropriate for 'women to change their shapes than men their minds' (*TGV* 5.4.109). This is seen to advantage in *Henry V* where **Isabel** the French Queen says she will join the council for peacemaking since 'Haply a woman's voice may do some good, / When articles too nicely urged be stood on' (*HV* 5.2.93–4). When **Paulina** presents baby Perdita to the angry Leontes as an 'office / Becomes a woman best' she is thinking not just of the practical matter of childcare, but diplomatic skill in emotive situations (*WT* 2.2.29–30).

The negative side to woman's flexibility is her supposed inconstancy. Rosalind says that women are 'for every passion something and for no passion truly anything' (*AYLI* 3.2.413–15). Other references suggest that this vice is inaccurately attributed to the sex. 'Relenting fool, and shallow, changing woman!' exclaims

Richard III on **Elizabeth** of York (*RIII* 4.34.431), congratulating himself on repeating his earlier success in wooing Lady **Anne**, but Elizabeth's subsequent secret betrothal of her daughter to Richmond shows this is far from the truth. Queen **Katherine** cleverly defines herself as a typically 'constant woman' who also has patience, virtues in which King Henry is signally lacking (*HVIII* 3.1.134–7). The more high-status queen, **Cleopatra** defines herself against her sex in committing herself to suicide:

> I have nothing
> Of woman in me: now from head to foot
> I am marble-constant; now the fleeting moon
> No planet is of mine.
>
> (*A&C* 5.2.238–41)

Nevertheless, the suicide she stages, with an asp as the baby at her **breast**, redefines marble-constant resolution (implicitly male, Roman stoicism), as a female, Egyptian quality. The particular weakness of female inconstancy in love is blazoned in deliberately exaggerated ways, most famously in Hamlet's 'Frailty thy name is woman!' (*Ham.* 1.2.146), his view that the dumbshow is 'As brief / as woman's love' (*Ham.* 3.2.153) or Sonnet 20's belief that 'shifting change', is typical of 'false women's fashion' (*Son.* 20.4), though this is something the young man is also apparently guilty of.

Iachimo's slanderous suggestion that inconstancy is 'What woman is, yea, what she cannot choose / But must be' (*Cym* 1.6.71–2) is, of course, proved wrong in the play although the view that it is a generic fault rather than an individual vice is shared by Orsino. He patronisingly explains inconstancy as the result of woman's inherent physiological inferiority. His opinion that 'no woman's heart' can compare to his own since they are smaller and 'lack retention' and so 'suffer surfeit, cloyment, and revolt' (*TN* 2.4.93–7) comically reverses what he has just said 60 lines earlier about men's fancies being more giddy and infirm 'than women's are' (*TN* 2.4.32–4). **Viola**, disguised as Cesario, offers a strong counter-argument (*TN* 2.4.105). In *Othello* **Emilia** admits that there are women who do abuse their husbands, but only in response to the men's example, and **Luciana** reverses the stereotype in declaring 'poor women' the victims rather than the offenders in cases of infidelity (*Err.* 3.2.21). In exposing the double sexual standard, each reveals how the stereotype of woman's inconstancy is bred by male anxieties about **adultery** and legitimacy. The only legitimate male protest is that of Troilus, and even his response contains a warning not to move from the particular to the general as Hamlet does: 'Let it not be believed for womanhood', exclaims Troilus, anxious not to 'square the general sex / By Cressid's rule' (*T&C* 5.2.129–33).

Emotion rather than reason dominates the sex. **Lucetta** explains her opinion of Proteus as 'A woman's reason; I think him so because I think him so' (*TGV* 1.2.23). Troilus condemns his own behaviour in staying away from the battle and giving no good reason with reference to the female stereotypes of whimsical expression and fear: 'This woman's answer sorts / For 'tis womanish to be hence' (*T&C*

1.1.106–7). In extreme cases, woman's lack of reason is associated with Dionysian madness or abandonment to the emotions as in the Amazons' mad dance at Timon's masque or Launce imagining his **mother** mad with grief 'like a wood woman' at his departure (*TGV* 2.3.31). Male abandonment to extreme emotions and lack of reason is referred to as womanish. Romeo's ungoverned passions result in womanish tears and wild acts that are beastly, making him appear 'Unseemly woman in a seeming man' or a monstrous hermaphrodite (*R&J* 3.3.112).

Emotional sensitivity and intuition makes woman especially vulnerable to fears, a convention to which both male and female characters refer. Hamlet's suspicions about the duel are such 'as would perhaps trouble a woman' (*Ham.* 5.2.216). **Constance** defines herself as 'a woman, naturally born to fears (*KJ* 3.1.15) while, in contrast, the Bastard receives ill news with the words 'I am no woman, I'll not swoon at it' (*KJ* 5.6.22). Women's proneness to fear reaches cataclysmic proportions during the stormy night in *Julius Caesar* where Casca saw 'a heap a hundred ghastly women, / Transformed with their fear' (*JC* 1.3.22–3). In a much more local reference, Slender points out that women 'cannot abide' bearbaiting and 'cried and shrieked', though of course this may have been revulsion at blood sports rather than fear of the bear Sackerson (*MWW* 1.1. 296–7). Fear is one of the female characteristics Princess **Imogen** will have to alter in cross-dressing. Pisanio tells her:

> You must forget to be a woman; change
> Command into obedience: fear and niceness –
> (The handmaids of all women, or, more truly,
> Woman its pretty self) into a waggish courage.
> (*Cym.* 3.4.154–7)

In the more extreme gender inversion of *Henry VI Part I*, **Margaret**'s 'undaunted spirit, / More than in women commonly is seen' (*1HVI* 5.5.71) makes her chastise Suffolk as a 'coward woman and faint-hearted wretch' for lacking the spirit to curse his enemies (*2HVI* 3.2.307).

Uncontrolled speech is frequently associated with the sex in Shakespeare's work, often in the form of jokes. 'Do you not know I am a woman? When I think, I must speak' (*AYLI* 3.2.249–50), declares **Rosalind**. Northumberland makes fun of Hotspur's voluble anger with the king by chastising his 'woman's mood / Tying thine ear to no tongue but thine own!' (*1HIV* 1.3.237). **Paulina** plays on the assumption that women speak spontaneously to create a space in which she can criticise Leontes's foolish behaviour in *Winter's Tale*, telling him 'Alas! I have show'd too much / The rashness of a woman', whereas in fact her criticisms are wise and apt (*WT* 3.2.220–1). Closely linked is the belief that women cannot keep secrets. Both Hotspur (*1HIV* 2.4.99–103) and Brutus refuse to tell their wives details of the conspiracies in which they are involved but the jokes about 'How hard it is for women to keep counsel!' (*JC* 2.4.9) probably disguise the men's intense desires to protect their wives from interrogation. The inability to keep secrets and proneness to fear are assumptions **Portia** protests against:

> I grant I am a woman; but withal
> A woman that Lord Brutus took to wife:
> I grant I am a woman; but withal
> A woman well-reputed, Cato's **daughter**.
> Think you I am no stronger than my sex,
> Being so father'd and so husbanded?
>
> (*JC* 2.1.292–7)

Although, verbally, she claims superiority with reference to her male relations, her own deed, in giving herself a 'voluntary wound' in the thigh and bearing this silently, prove that a woman can have both courage and secrecy.

The supposed verbosity of women's speech carries negative associations with the **shrew** and the **scold**. Mowbray scorns 'the bitter clamour of two eager tongues' as 'a woman's war' (*RII* 1.1.49). Even the expression of grief is seen in negative terms as excessive: 'Grief hath two tongues, and never woman yet / Could rule them both without ten women's wit' (*V&A* 1007–8). In line with Posthumus's view that women lie, female verbal dexterity denotes a capacity to deceive. **Rosalind** says that a wife will never be 'without her answer, unless you take her without her tongue' and will be quick to shift the blame to her husband (*AYLI* 4.1.147–51). Richard III delegitimizes the women's voices that delegitimize his claim to the throne, calling them 'tell-tale women' (*RIII* 4.4.150), a view shared by Leontes who suspects a conspiracy between **gossip**ing women to proclaim children are like their fathers to cover up female **adultery**: 'women say so, / That will say anything' (*WT* 1.2.130–1). Cordelia who says 'nothing' and whose voice is 'ever soft, / Gentle, and low – an excellent thing in woman' (*KL* 1.1.87 and 5.3.273–4) is the ideal contrast to the stereotype. The sound of a woman's voice as 'small' (*MWW* 1.1.44), refers to a key characteristic of the **boy actor**, and is seized upon by Bottom, eager to play **Thisbe** (*MND* 2.2.51).

Proneness to weeping is the mark of a woman, and 'woman's gift / To rain a shower of commanded tears' is one that the page Bartholomew in *Shrew*, like the boy actor in the theatre, is encouraged to adopt, with an onion to assist if necessary (*Shrew* Ind. 1.124–5). The thought that women's tears might be command performances informs Othello's view that Desdemona sheds crocodile tears (*Oth.* 4.1.245–6). In a futile attempt to bluff his way out of an excruciatingly poignant moment, Enobarbus the soldier protests he is 'onion-ey'd', or feigning, and bids Antony 'for shame, / Transform us not to women' (*A&C* 4.2.35–6). Tears of pity (*KJ* 4.1.36) or cowardice (*RIII* 1.4.261) in the face of torture or murder, subservience (*JC* 1.3.83–4) and even fear of death (*HVIII* 2.1.38) are all scornfully regarded as 'womanish', though in each case the scenes makes clear that they represent a more humane or reasonable response to the situation. Timon of Athens has a more healthy attitude, telling the weeping Flavius

> I love thee,
> Because thou art a woman and disclaimst
> Flinty mankind, whose eyes do never give

>   But thorough lust and laughter
>
>   (*Tim.* 4.3.482–5)

The naïvety of Henry VI shows when he expects **Margaret** to inspire pity because of her typically feminine quality of weeping. He imagines that with the French king 'Her tears will pierce into a marble heart; / The tiger will be mild whiles she doth mourn' (*3HVI* 3.1.36–41). Of course it is Margaret herself who is a 'tiger's heart wrapp'd in a woman's hide' (*3HVI* 1.4.137), showing no touch of pity and utterly confounding the male characters' understanding of the word 'woman'. Lack of the womanly virtues of compassion, gentleness and pity is seen as monstrous. Albany declares of **Goneril**: 'Proper deformity seems not in the fiend / So horrid as in woman' (*KL* 4.2.60–1). Lavinia is horrified when **Tamora** hands her over to be raped: 'No grace? no womanhood? ah, beastly creature / The blot and enemy to our general name' (*Tit.* 2.3.182). But female aberration from the conventions of womanhood is not as offensive as male adoption of them. Whatever the sexual orientation of the man, he should not adopt feminine behaviour in battle since 'A woman impudent and mannish grown / Is not more loathed than an effeminate man / In time of action' (*T&C* 3.3.217–8).

In addition to advertising women's emotional and physical weakness, the Shakespeare canon pays lip service to the idea that women are mentally weaker, usually with the effect of suggesting the contrary. Queen Margaret describes herself as 'a silly woman' (*3HVI* 1.1.243–5), but it is her husband whose political folly has just been demonstrated in surrendering Edward's right to the crown. In *Henry VIII* Henry acknowledges that in addition to holding the typical feminine quality of gentle disposition, **Katherine** has displayed 'wisdom / O'ertopping woman's power' (*HVIII* 2.4.87–8). It is with considerable irony, then, that **Katherine** tells the devious Cardinals Wosley and Campeius 'You know I am a woman, lacking wit / To make a seemly answer to such persons' (*HVIII* 3.1.177–8), implicitly setting her innocence against their cunning.

All the generic characteristics of woman outlined thus far are corralled together as reasons to justify female subjection, particularly in marriage, as seen most famously in **Katherina**'s speech designed to correct 'headstrong women' in *The Taming of the Shrew*.

>   I am asham'd that women are so simple
>   To offer war where they should kneel for peace,
>   Or seek for rule, supremacy, and sway,
>   When they are bound to serve, love, and obey.
>   Why are our bodies soft, and weak, and smooth,
>   Unapt to toil and trouble in the world,
>   But that our soft conditions, and our hearts
>   Should well agree with our external parts?
>
>   (*Shrew* 5.2.161–8)

The opinion that every woman rightly owes absolute duty to her husband, like a subject to a monarch, is not shared by other female characters, however. **Beatrice** objects to the doctrine in Genesis setting out the gender hierarchy: 'Would it not grieve a woman to be overmastered with a pierce of valiant dust? to make an account of her life to a clod of wayward marl?' (*MAdo* 2.1.60–3). From the opposite, male, perspective, the Clown in *All's Well* pretends to be shocked 'That a man should be at woman's command and yet no hurt done!' (*AWW* 1.3.92–3). Cassius too believes that it is unbecoming for men to be governed in an autocracy since 'Our yoke and sufferance show us womanish' (*JC* 1.3.84). The exclusion of women from systems of government and inheritance is neatly summed up in Pharamond's law 'No woman shall succeed in Salique land' although, as appropriate for a play written and performed in the reign of **Elizabeth** I, the Archbishop of Canterbury is at pains to discredit the application of the 'female bar' to land beyond Germany (*HV* 1.2.38–41). *King Lear* offers a nightmare vision of the 'indistinguish'd space of woman's will' when the patriarchal model of subjection is abandoned by **Goneril** and **Regan** (*KL* 4.6.271).

More positive impressions of female autonomy appear in epilogues where Shakespeare's texts register the importance of women as a distinctive group of spectators for his plays. At the end of *As You Like It*, women are addressed as a group and invited to enjoy 'as much of this play as please you' (*AYLI* Epilogue. 13), acknowledging their status as fee-paying customers. The Chorus in *Henry VIII* says the play's only likely success is in 'The merciful construction of good women' (*HVIII* Epilogue. 10), falling back on their traditional qualities of kindness, indulgence and flexibility while, simultaneously, recognizing their power as playgoers.

(c) Anna Murphy Jameson's 1858 study *Shakespeare's Heroines* (2005) set an important marker for the serious study of the roles and their relationship to social and moral conventions. In the second wave of feminism, Juliet Dusinberre, *Shakespeare and the Nature of Women* (1996) and Lisa Jardine, *Still Harping on Daughters* (1983) are the two pioneering full-length studies of Shakespeare's female characters. Lenz, Greene and Neely's collection of essays, *The Woman's Part* (1983), offers a range of very useful starting points for studies of individual roles and issues while Linda Woodbridge's *Women and the English Renaissance* (1984) gives essential information about the formal controversy over the nature of women in early modern England. Carol Thomas Neely's 'Shakespeare's Women' (1989) and Phyllis Rackin's more recent *Shakespeare and Women* (2005) give concise accounts of the issues raised by Shakespearean representations and our responses. David Mann's *Shakespeare's Women* (2008) takes performance as a starting point for reading Shakespearean and non-Shakespearean types.

womb, (a) in early modern English a general term for the abdomen and internal organs (stomach and bowels), and cavity or ventricle; more specifically, the uterus. Metaphorically, the female womb denotes a place or medium of conception and development; a place of origin and growth.
(b) In a few instances, references to 'womb' in Shakespeare are ungendered. Falstaff uses womb to mean 'belly', attributing the 'whole school of **tongues**' there

to 'My womb, my womb, my womb' (*2HIV* 4.3.18–22). In the Bastard's warning that 'the smallest thread / That ever spider twisted from her womb / Will serve to strangle thee' (*KJ* 4.3.128), the spider's internal organs merge with her womb as she is female, and a spinner, like the **Fates**.

More often, 'womb' indicates the uterus, sometimes with a vivid sense of the mystery of gestation as a woman grows 'round-womb'd' (*KL* 1.1.14), seen in the cases of **Hermione**, **Juliet**, and possibly **Helena** at the end of *All's Well*. In *Measure for Measure*, Lucio sees Juliet's womb like a field of 'teeming foison' sown by Claudio, or a cornucopia rich with bounty: 'her plenteous womb / Expresseth his full tilth and husbandry' (*MM* 1.4.43–4). The same male-centred view of the womb as fertile territory for husbandry is found in **Ceres**'s blessing to **Miranda** and Ferdinand (*Temp.* 4.1.110–17), in the Sonnets (*Son.* 3.5–6 and 16.6–7) and in *Edward III*. The muddled line of French succession means that because the English king Edward is the son of **Isabel**, born 'from the fragrant garden of her womb', he can make a claim to French territory (*EIII* 1.1.14). Even in the case of false pregnancies, **Joan** La **Pucelle** and **Doll Tearsheet** draw on the appeal of the womb as a fertile place; pleading for 'fruit within my womb' (*1HVI* 5.4.63 and *2HIV* 5.4.12–13) as a form of self-defence.

A more surprising image of female fertility is found in Sonnet 97 where the year is feminized as 'The teeming autumn, big with rich increase, / Bearing the wanton burthen of the prime, / Like **widow**ed wombs after their lords' decease' (*Son.* 97.6–8). For a husband, the womb of his wife (guaranteed by her honour or chastity), is the site of self-perpetuation and earthly immortality. Cominius in *Coriolanus* protests that his love for Rome is worth more 'than mine own life, / My dear wive's estimate, her womb's increase, / And treasure of my loins' (*Cor.* 3.3.113–15). Henry VIII believes he is punished by heaven through his 'lady's womb' which, 'if it conceiv'd a male-child by me, should / Do no more offices of life to't than / The grave does to th' dead' (*HVIII* 2.4.189–92).

Male speakers use 'womb' figuratively to describe their creative processes. Holofernes explains that his ideas are 'begot in the ventricle of memory, nourish'd in the womb of pia mater, and delivered upon the mellowing of occasion' (*LLL* 4.2.68–70). Iago's evil plotting, promising that 'there are many events in the womb of time which will be delivered' (*Oth.* 1.3.370), is a perverse appropriation of female gestation. Men's imitations are comparatively barren, however. The speaker of Sonnet 86 says his verse miscarries in the light of a rival poet whose efforts 'did my ripe thoughts in my brain inhearse, / Making their tomb the womb wherein they grew' (*Son.* 86.3–4). **Titania** recalls how she and her votaress mocked the poor imitations of pregnancy in the trading ships whose sails swelled with nothing but wind, while she

> with pretty and with swimming gait
> Following (her womb then rich with my young squire)
> Would imitate, and sail upon the land.
>
> (*MND* 2.1.130–2)

The rich merchandise (*MND* 2.1.134) of the votaress's womb is far more valuable than anything the merchants can gather, this passage romantically suggests. **Lady Macbeth** and Macbeth's abuse of Scotland's fertility through processes of perverse un**sex**ing and murder appropriately meet their nemesis in Macduff who 'was from his mother's womb / Untimely ripp'd' (*Mac.* 5.8.15–16).

Because the production of children was regarded as a woman's primary function, from an early modern perspective Lear's curse of **Goneril** is terrible, striking at the centre of her social identity:

> Into her womb convey sterility,
> Dry up in her the organs of increase,
> And from her derogate body never spring
> A babe to honor her!
>
> (*KL* 1.4.278–81)

More sadly, conceiving and bearing a child in the womb will be an unfulfilled dream for **Charmian**. When she wonders how many boys and girls she will have, the Soothsayer enigmatically tells her 'If every of your wishes had a womb / And fertile every wish, a million' (*A&C* 1.2.38–9). **Cleopatra** calls her children 'the memory of my womb' (*A&C* 3.13.163) and the **Countess** of Rossillion tells Helena of her wish to become her mother 'And put you in the catalogue of those / That were enwombed mine' (*AWW* 1.3.143–4). The plural indicates that there were more children than Bertram, so perhaps the Countess's wish to adopt Helena is an attempt to replace a **daughter** who died in infancy. Women's wish to mark such a sad event is expressed in the writing of upper-class women such as Frances Matthew who recorded 'The birthe of all my children' and the deaths of four of them between 1575 and 1601 (Ostovich and Sauer 2004: 248–9) or Elizabeth Cavendish Egerton who recorded 'never was there so Fond a Child of a mother, but now she is not in this world, which greeves my heart; even my Soule, but I must submitt, & give God my thanks, yt he once was pleased to bestow so great a blessing as yt sweet Child upon me' (Egerton 1999: 199).

Volumnia, who fully appreciates the political value of the womb, chooses to sacrifice her biological maternity to her role as guardian or mother of Rome, arguably at great personal, emotional cost. Having depicted Coriolanus as a husband, father and son 'tearing / His country's bowels out' she accuses him with attacking the womb itself and is joined by Virgilia:

> Volumnia: thou shalt no sooner
> March to assault thy country than to tread
> (Trust to't, thou shalt not) on thy mother's womb,
> That brought thee to this world
> Virgilia: Ay, and mine,
> That brought you forth this boy, to keep your name
> Living to time.
>
> (*Cor.* 5.3.122–7)

Volumnia's strategy relies on the idea that 'all love the womb that their first being bred' (*Per.* 1.1.107). The womb is a place of security and nurturance. The baby of Aaron has, he reminds Chiron and Demetrius, been 'sensibly fed / Of that self-blood that first gave life to you' (*Tit.* 4.2.122–3). The womb provides fleshy clothing for the soul as Sebastian remembers when he introduces himself as a spirit 'But am in that dimension grossly clad / Which from the womb I did participate' (*TN* 5.1.237–8). Medical books described the membranes of the womb in terms of protective fabric. Helkiah Crooke, for example, compared it to a 'coate' which was 'fleshy or very thick that it might have heat to cherish the infant' (Crooke 1615: 229) while Raynalde's *Birth of Mankind* compared the outer of the three coats to 'a broade gyrth or swadlyng bande' (Raynalde 1565: sig. G1r). **Marina**'s emergence from this comfort zone is a traumatic introduction to a harsh environment 'As fire, air, water, earth, and heaven can make, / To herald thee from the womb' (*Per.* 3.1.32–4). The Duchess of Gloucester invokes the womb as a place of origin to raise York's revenge for the murder of his brother, crediting the womb with the power to fashion offspring.

> Ah, Gaunt, his blood was thine! That bed, that womb,
> That metal, that self mould, that fashioned thee
> Made him a man; and though thou livest and breathest,
> Yet art thou slain in him.
>
> (*RII* 1.2.22–5)

As in these lines, Shakespeare's texts often suggest an emotional and cultural umbilical cord attaching male characters to their mothers' wombs. Sons are anxious not to 'shame my mother's womb' (*1HVI* 4.5.35) through behaviour such as cowardice or villainy which suggests they are not their fathers' sons. Mothers are likewise anxious to see that their offspring do credit to the wombs that fashioned them. Physical as well as moral and social imperfection is regarded negatively. A child 'full of unpleasing blots and sightless stains, / Lame, foolish, crooked, swart, prodigious' or 'Patch'd with foul moles and eye-offending marks' is regarded as 'Ugly and slanderous to thy mother's womb' (*KJ* 3.1.282). Slander to the mother's womb carries allegations of her sexual misconduct because monstrosity or deformity was believed to be a sign of virtual or real adultery on the woman's part, her thoughts producing an imperfect baby or one that looks like a man not her husband. Richard of Gloucester, who believes that 'love forswore me in my mother's womb' (*3HVI* 3.2.153), is deemed a 'slander of thy mother's heavy womb!' (*RIII* 1.3.231) by reason of his moral and physical deformities.

In such cases, female characters are obliged to prove that 'Good wombs have borne bad sons' (*Temp.* 1.2.120) by separating themselves from their children and their own bodies. Richard's mother, the **Duchess** of York, exclaims, 'O my accursed womb, the bed of death! / A cockatrice hast thou hatch'd to the world / Whose unavoided eye is murderous (*RIII* 4.1.54–7). **Margaret** of Anjou berates her even more vehemently, saying that 'From forth the kennel of thy womb hath crept / A hell-hound that doth hunt us all to death'. The natural process of birth is reconfigured as irresponsible gatekeeping whereby the Duchess's 'womb let loose' a monster 'to chase us to our graves' (*RIII* 4.4.47–8 and 54).

Wombs are a link to the future. After Edward IV's death, his **widow** Queen Elizabeth's future safety lies in her womb. It redeems her from 'despair / For love of Edward's offspring in my womb' and teaches her patience, moderation and care of her own body, 'Lest with my sighs or tears I blast or drown / King Edward's fruit, true heir to the English crown' (*3HVI* 4.4.18–24). Given Elizabeth's care of her womb as a place to carry the past into the future, Richard III's attempted appropriation of her daughter's womb takes on the quality of **rape**. He regards Princess Elizabeth's womb as place to rewrite a history of wrongs he has done to Queen Elizabeth and her family:

> If I have kill'd the issue of your womb,
> To quicken your increase, I will beget
> Mine issue of your blood upon your daughter.
> (*RIII* 4.4.296–8)

When she objects he has killed her sons, he promises 'in your daughter's womb I bury them / Where in that nest of spicery they shall breed / Selves of themselves, to your recomforture' (*RIII* 4.4.423–5).

In spite of its positive associations with comfort and security, the womb also appears as a biological tiring room or prison, especially for male children. Posthumus's father 'died whilst in the womb he [Posthumus] stay'd / Attending nature's law' (*Cym.* 5.4.37–8). Aaron tells Chiron and Demetrius that they share the same liberation from the womb as their black half-brother: 'from that womb where you imprison'd were / He is enfranchised and come to light' (*Tit.* 4.2.122–5). **Paulina** plays on the differences between physical, cultural and legal confinement to assure **Hermione**'s jaoler

> This child was prisoner to the womb, and is
> By law and process of great **Nature** thence
> Freed and enfranchised.
> (*WT* 2.2.57–9)

More extreme references associate the womb with the tomb, aligning the female body metaphorically with the earth and the grave. Gaunt calls the grave 'a hollow womb' which 'inherits nought but bones' (*RII* 2.1.83). Quintus in *Titus Andronicus* regards the pit in which Bassianus is buried as a 'swallowing womb' that will consume three of Titus's remaining sons (*Tit.* 2.3.239). It is the rural equivalent of the Andronicus tomb in Rome which swallows the sons who have died defending Rome and Mutius, whom Titus casually slaughters, apparently indifferent to the female cost of carrying, bearing and nurturing children. Other sinister alignments between the creative power of the womb and the annihilation of life occur in *Romeo and Juliet*. A death-dealing shot 'Doth hurry from the fatal cannon's womb' and Romeo addresses the entrance to the Capulet tomb as 'thou womb of death' (*R&J* 5.1.65 and 5.3.45). These references contrast with Friar Lawrence's much more optimistic, eloquent description of a natural process of mortality:

> The earth that's nature's **mother** is her tomb;
> What is her burying grave that is her womb,
> And from her womb children of divers kind
> We sucking on her natural **bosom** find.
>
> (*R&J* 2.3.9–12)

Metaphoric uses of 'womb' to describe the earth are common in Shakespeare. Timon of Athens sees earth as a womb and mother impregnated by the 'blessed breeding sun' and bringing forth vermin and infection, 'Twinn'd brothers of one womb' (*Tim.* 4.3.1–5). The earth is a common mother 'Whose womb unmeasurable and infinite breast / Teems and feeds all' indifferently (*Tim.* 4.3.178–9). The earth's womb is a secretive place in *Lucrece* (549), *Hamlet* (1.1.137) and *Winter's Tale* (4.4.490). It is constructed in negative terms in the phrase 'foul womb of night' as a result of male anxiety before the battle in *Henry V* (Chorus 4.4).

The emotional umbilical cord linking children to the mother's womb makes it a useful metaphor to invoke loyalty to the nation or mother-country. John of Gaunt romantically refers to England as 'this blessed plot, this earth, this realm, . . . This nurse, this teeming womb of royal kings' (*RII* 2.1.50–1) in a speech that has been reproduced for propaganda purposes on many occasions in Britain. Even though, or perhaps because, no women are on stage, Henry IV confidently predicts

> Forthwith a power of English shall we levy;
> Whose arms were moulded in their mother's womb
> To chase these pagans in those holy fields
>
> (*1HIV* 1.1.22–4)

Rebellion against the mother country is an attack on the womb, as Volumnia's words, discussed above, recognize. The rebel lords in *King John* are like 'bloody Neroes, ripping up the womb / Of your dear mother **England**' (*KJ* 5.2.152).
(c) Thomas Raynalde's popular medical book, *The Birth of Mankynde, otherwyse named the womans booke* (London, 1565) which was reprinted in 1572, 1585, 1598, 1604 and 1613 gives very detailed descriptions of the womb and its operation in the processes of reproduction. Adelman (1992: (esp.) 1–10) discusses the swallowing womb as a threat to masculine identity, beginning with consideration of Richard of Gloucester. Wynne-Davies (1991) gives a fine account of the womb as tomb in *Titus Andronicus*. Garber (1981: 148–52) notes Shakespeare's dramatic interest in the fruits of marriage and Bicks (2003) the popular idea of female forces shaping the foetus inside the womb.

Xantippe, (a) the wife of Socrates, an infamous shrew and **scold** who was frequently cited as part of the formal controversy about the nature of women as part of the misogynist attack on the sex.

(b) Petruchio names Xantippe in a list that sounds as if it has come form his reading of the early modern genre of antifeminist writing on women. He says he is determined to woo **Katherina**

> Be she as foul as Florentinus' love,
> As old as **Sybil**, and as curst and shrowd
> As Socrates' Xantippe, or a worse,
> She moves not me.
>
> (*Shrew* 1.2.69–72)

Petruchio enters the encounter with Katherina with knowledge about the formal debate and ready to enact this. He immediately finds she is not ugly or old, so it is with the Xantippe model of the scold that he models his wooing strategy. Diogenes Laertius's biography of Socrates recounted that the philosopher explained to friends that he had got used to being scolded, or even having water thrown over him by Xantippe and liked her as a horseman appreciates a spirited horse (Davis and Frankforter 2004: 517). Petruchio adopts this strategy when he hears she has broken the lute over Hortensio's head: 'Now by the world it is a lusty **wench**! / I love her ten times more than e'er I did' (*Shrew* 2.1.160–1). One witty defence of women argued that '*Socrates* so confest that *Zantippe* his wife did him as much good at home by chiding, to learne him patience; as he did in Schoole to learne his schollars Phylosophy' (Lloyd 1607: sig F3v). At one level, Petruchio constructs the taming school on just these terms. Grumio warns the servants that they will find him 'more shrew that she' when he comes home, which they do. His own angry scolding leads Katherina to recommend 'Patience, I pray you' to stop him

479

scolding the servant who accidentally poured water on him and bid him 'be not so disquiet' (*Shrew* 4.1.156 and 168). He concludes by acknowledging a mutual fault, telling her that he cannot eat the burnt meat because it engenders choler 'And I expressly am forbid to touch it' and so they should both be patient and fast for company 'Since of ourselves, ourselves are choleric' (*Shrew* 4.1.170–8).

(c) Lodowick Lloyd's *The Choyce of Iewels* (London, 1607), follows the formal pattern of exempla to defend women. It is quoted in Woodbridge (1984: 71). Woodbridge (1984) is the best account of the formal controversy over women's nature, mentioning Xantippe on pp. 69, 71, 104 and 127.

youth, (a) the state or quality of being young, associated in early modern England with vigour, freshness, immaturity and rashness. It is also the name for a young man. Female characters who cross-dress are called 'youth' in their adopted masculine personae.

(b) Youth, as a state of being, indicates dangers of vulnerability, inexperience and potential lack of self-restraint when applied to women in Shakespeare. **Bianca** will have schoolmasters 'Fit to instruct her youth' (*Shrew* 1.1.95). **Hero** is deemed vulnerable to Claudio's seduction because 'the resistance of her youth' (*MAdo* 4.1.47) is not strong. The **Countess** of Rossillion is likewise able to sympathize with the strong sense of desire **Helena** feels for Bertram. Her lines validate the passions of young women as natural through the image of the rose (the **flower** being a typical symbol of female sexuality):

> This thorn
> Doth to our rose of youth rightly belong;
> Our blood to us, this to our blood is born.
> It is the show and seal of nature's truth,
> Where love's strong passion is impress'd in youth.
> (*AWW* 1.3.129–33)

Evidence suggests that young people in early modern England were 'more promiscuous' than married adults and that young women 'sometimes displayed independence, openness and even initiative in their relationship with young males' (Ben-Amos 1994: 201) so the Countess's portrait and **Helena**'s pursuit of her desire and Bertram may have been sympathetically received by some early modern spectators and readers.

As a concrete noun, the word means a specific type of young man in Shakespeare's texts. Although Hamlet and Laertes, amongst others, are called

481

'youth', the defining characteristic of the type appears to be a lack of facial hair. 'He that hath a **beard** is more than a youth' (*MAdo* 2.1.36) according to **Beatrice**, while Lennox reports 'many unrough [beardless] youths that even now / Protest their first of manhood' have joined the army (*Mac.* 5.2.10). Flute argues that he cannot play Thisbe since he has a beard coming (*MND* 1.2.47). This suggests that the noun 'youth' alludes obliquely to any one of the team of beardless **boy actors** who could and did play women's roles. In *All's Well That Ends Well*, for example, Bertram's address to **Diana**, 'If the quick fire of youth light not your mind / You are no maiden but a monument' (*AWW* 4.2.5–6) contains a covert joke about the boy performer. The quick fire of youth is the life-blood of the actor that animates the role.

Shakespeare's use of the term becomes especially interesting in plays with cross-dressed female characters such as **Julia**, **Portia**, **Rosalind** and **Viola** whose freedom of movement in the plays may reflect the period of relative autonomy young women had as they moved out of the family home in a range of formal and informal apprenticeships in town and country (Ben-Amos 1994: 134). In Shakespeare's plays, youth becomes a marker for gender sameness and a metatheatrical marker for the boy actor whose presence destabilizes the heterosexual romance in the plays. The young male characters are first established: for example Frederick tells Orlando, 'thou art a gallant youth' (*AYLI* 1.2.229) and Bassanio looks back to his (presumably recent) childhood to describe himself as 'like a wilful youth' (*Mer.* 1.1.146). When a cross-dressed heroine appears 'like a wilful youth' and is signified by the same term, synergies of sameness rather than difference are signalled. When **Portia** asks 'show my youth old Shylock's house' (*Mer.* 4.2.11), 'youth' refers to the cross-dressed **Nerissa** and sets up an opposition between the youth who plays her and the mature actor who plays 'old Shylock'. Allusions to the boy actor behind the female role are again highlighted by Gratiano's protest that he gave the ring 'to a youth, / A kind of boy, a little scrubbed boy' (*Mer.* 5.1.161), suggesting an alternative same-sex bond between boy-actor and master behind the marriage of Nerissa and Gratiano. In the case of the twins in *Twelfth Night*, the identities of the two youths overlap even more closely. Antonio says he rescued, restored and worships Sebastian: 'This youth that you see here' (*TN* 3.4.359), though in fact he is speaking to Viola disguised as Cesario.

Julia, **Rosalind** and **Viola** are referred to as 'youth' more often than by name when they are cross-dressed as Sebastian, Ganymede or Cesario. To early modern audiences, the qualifying adjectives in 'gentle youth' (*TGV* 4.4.178), 'pretty youth' or 'Fair youth' (*AYLI* 3.2.252 and 404) refer just as readily to the attractiveness of the boy actor as to the character's costume or her absent female body. The term marks the presence of the boy actor playing the female character as cattle of one colour, a point made explicit in the voice of the boy actor playing Rosalind disguised as Ganymede, who explains how he

being but a moonish youth [would] grieve, be effeminate, changeable, longing and liking, proud, fantastical, apish, shallow, inconstant, full of tears, full of smiles; for every passion something, and for no passion truly any such thing, as boys and women are for the most cattle of this colour.

(*AYLI* 3.2.409–15)

These are the qualities of youth, qualities that one would not associate with a mature woman, but are shared by young women and the boy actors or youths who performed their roles. Youth in *Twelfth Night* offers a more mature perspective on the boy actor as immanent but not lasting, erotically seductive but ultimately untouchable. **Olivia** addresses Cesario in a dramatic equivalent of Sonnet 20 where the master mistress has 'one thing to my purpose nothing' (*Son.* 20:12):

> Be not afraid, good youth, I will not have you,
> And yet when wit and youth is come to harvest,
> Your wife is like to reap a proper man.

(*TN* 3.1.131–3)

A distinctly homoerotic subtext is visible when Cesario swears by his innocence 'and by my youth' that his single heart, bosom and truth will never be owned by a woman (*TN* 3.1.157–60). The rest of the play knows that youth is transient, however, and with reference to the mature boy actor on the cusp of manhood, this was especially obvious. The master-mistress of Feste's song can 'sing both high and low' so his voice is about to break. He is told:

> In delay there lies no plenty,
> Then come and kiss me sweet and twenty;
> Youth's a stuff will not endure.

(*TN* 2.3.50–2)

In the festive world of *Twelfth Night* and the theatre, queer sexuality (one which recognizes no borders between different sexual orientations but sees them as points on a continuum) can flourish as boy actors, female characters and the assumed personae of 'gentle youth' create an elaborate web of possible routes for the expression of desire. Like youth, this is temporary, but like youth it is vibrant and fantastical, 'for every passion something, and for no passion truly any such thing' (*AYLI* 3.2.413).

(c) Ben-Amos's *Adolescence and Youth in Early Modern England* (1994) is a detailed examination of male and female experiences including assumptions about youth, apprenticeship spirituality and sexuality and rites of passage to adulthood. For the similarities and dynamics between boy actors and young women see Jardine (1983: 9–36), Orgel (1996b), Shapiro (1996) and Dusinberre (2000). On the age of boy actors see Kathman (2005), McMillin (2004) and Wells (2009).

Zenelophon, (a) the beggar maid with whom a legendary African King, Cophetua, fell in love when he saw her from his window. She is more often known as Penelophon. She agreed to marry him and they lived happily until their deaths and were buried in the same tomb.

(b) This story was probably known to Shakespeare from a popular ballad. Mercutio mocks the idea of love at first sight 'When King Cophetua lov'd the beggar maid' (*R&J* 2.1.14) and Henry IV is embarrassed at the spectacle of his aunt the **Duchess** of York kneeling to him to beg for her son's life, saying the serious scene of treachery is 'now chang'd to "The Beggar and the King"' (*RII* 5.3.79–80). A version of the ballad is found in Richard Johnson's anthology *A crowne garland of goulden roses* (1612, sig. D4r-D6r). Don Armado immediately thinks of 'the King and the Beggar' (*LLL* 1.2.109–10) and identifies with the King from his own position of loving **Jaquenetta** the 'country girl that I took in the park' (*LLL* 1.2.110–19). In a letter to Jaquenetta he refers to himself as King Cophetua and Jaquenetta as the beggar maid to explain the difference in their social status and the curious way in which wooing appears to reverse the dominant positions based on gender and class. 'The magnanimous and most illustrate King Cophetua set eye upon the pernicious and indubitate beggar Zenelophon . . .' he begins, and goes on to aggrandize the King's actions in the heroic style of *veni, vidi, vici*, arguing that he overcame the beggar, but then 'enrich'd' the 'captive' beggar by marrying her. He then adopts a subservient mode to Jaquenetta: 'Shall I entreat thy love? I will' (*LLL* 4.1.64–82).

(c) 'A Song of A Beggar and A King' is found in Richard Johnson's *A crowne garland of goulden roses* (1612), sigs. D4r-D6r. Eric Brown (2003) discusses the reversals in Don Armado's letter as typical of the comic reversal of gender norms in the play.

Bibliography

Abate, Corinne S. (ed.), *Privacy, Domesticity and Women in Early Modern England* (Aldershot: Ashgate, 2003).

Abbott, Robert, *England's Parnassus* (London: 1600).

Acheson, Arthur, *Mistress Davenant: The Dark Lady of Shakespeare's Sonnets* (London: Quaritch, 1913).

Adelman, Janet, 'Her Father's Blood: Race, Conversion and the Nation in *The Merchant of Venice*'. *Representations*, 81 (2003): 4–31.

——'Making Defect Perfection: Shakespeare and the One-Sex Model' in Viviana Comensoli and Anne Russell (eds), *Enacting Gender on the English Renaissance Stage* (Urbana and Chicago, IL: University of Illinois Press, 1999), pp. 23–52.

——*Suffocating Mothers: Fantasies of Maternal Origin in Shakespeare's Plays: Hamlet to The Tempest* (London: Routledge, 1992).

Aebischer, Pascale, *Violated Bodies: Stage and Screen Performance* (Cambridge: Cambridge University Press, 2003).

Aguirre, Manuel, 'Life, Crown and Queen: Gertrude and the Theme of Sovereignty'. *RES*, 47(186) (1996): 163–74.

Ainsworth, Henry, *An animadversion to Mr Richard Clyftons advertisement* (London: 1613).

Ake, Jami, 'Glimpsing a "Lesbian" Poetics in *Twelfth Night*'. *SEL*, 43(2) (2003): 375–94.

Albott, Robert, *Wits Theater of the Little World* (London: 1599).

Alexander, Catherine M. S. and Stanley Wells (eds), *Shakespeare and Sexuality* (Cambridge: Cambridge University Press, 2001).

Alexander, Hélène, *Fans* (London: Batsford, 1984).

Alfar, Christina Leon, *Fantasies of Female Evil* (London: Associated University Presses, 2003).

——'Looking for Goneril and Regan in *King Lear*' in Corinne S. Abate (ed.), *Privacy, Domesticity and Women in Early Modern England* (Aldershot: Ashgate, 2003), pp. 167–98.

Amtower, Laurel and Dorothea Kehler (eds), *The Single Woman in Medieval and Early Modern England* (Medieval and Renaissance Texts and Studies) (Tempe, AZ: 2003).

Amussen, Susan, *An Ordered Society: Gender and Class in Early Modern England* (Oxford: Basil Blackwell, 1988).

Anderson, Linda, *A Place in the Story: Servants and Service in Shakespeare's Plays* (Newark, DE: University of Delaware Press, 2005).

Archer, Jayne, Elizabeth Goldring and Sarah Knight (eds), *The Progresses, Pageants and Entertainments of Elizabeth I* (Oxford: Oxford University Press, 2007).

Ariosto, Lodovico, *Orlando Furioso in English heroical verse, by Sir Iohn Haringto[n]* (London: 1607).

Armin, Robert, *The history of the two maids of More-clacke* (London: 1609).

Arnold, Aerol, 'The Hector-Andromache scene in Shakespeare's *Troilus and Cressida'. MLQ* 14(4) (1953): 335–9.

Arnold, Janet, *Patterns of Fashion: The Cut and Construction of Clothes for Men and Women c. 1560–1620* (London: Macmillan, 1985).

——*Queen Elizabeth's Wardrobe Unlock'd* (Leeds: Maney, 1988).

Ashelford, Jane, *A Visual History of Costume* (London: Batsford, 1983).

Aughterson, Kate (ed.), *Renaissance Woman: Constructions of Femininity in England* (London: Routledge, 1995).

St Augustine, *Of the Citie of God vvith the learned comments of Io. Lod. Viues. Englished by I.H.* (London: 1610).

Awdelay, John, *The Fraternity of Vacabondes* (London: 1575).

Aylmer, John, *An Harborowe for faithfull and trewe subiectes* (London: 1559).

Bacon, Francis, *Sylva Sylvarum or A Naturall Historie* (London: 1627).

Baines, Barbara, 'Assaying the power of chastity in *Measure for Measure'. SEL*, 30(2) (1990), 283–301.

Bale, John, *The first two partes of the actes or vnchast examples of the Englysh votaryes* (London: 1551).

——*The Pageant of Popes* (London: 1574).

Bamber, Linda, *Comic Women Tragic Men: A Study of Gender and Genre in Shakespeare* (Palo Alto, CA: Stanford University Press, 1982).

Barber, Frances, 'Ophelia' in Russell Jackson and Robert Smallwood (eds), *Players of Shakespeare 2* (Cambridge: Cambridge University Press, 2001), pp. 137–50.

Barnes, Barnaby, *The Devil's Charter* (London: 1607).

Barroll, Leeds, 'The Allusive Tissue of *Antony and Cleopatra'* in Sara Munson Deats (ed.), *Antony and Cleopatra: New Critical Essays* (London: Routledge, 2005), pp. 275–90.

——*Anna of Denmark, Queen of England: A Cultural Biography* (Philadelphia, PA: University of Pennsylvania Press, 2001).

Bartels, Emily C., 'Strategies of Submission: Desdemona, the Duchess, and the Assertion of Desire'. *SEL*, 36(2) (1996), 417–33.

Bate, Jonathan, *Shakespeare and Ovid* (Oxford: Oxford University Press, 1993).

Bate, Jonathan, Jill L. Levenson and Dieter Mehl (eds), *Shakespeare and the Twentieth Century* (Newark, DE: University of Delaware Press, 1998).

Batman, Stephen, *Batman vppon Bartholome his booke De proprietatibus rerum, newly corrected, enlarged and amended* (London: 1582).

Battenhouse, Roy, 'Theme and Structure in *The Winter's Tale'. ShS*, 33 (1980): 123–38.

Bean, John C., 'Comic Structure and the Humanizing of Kate in *The Taming of the Shrew'* in Carolyn Ruth Swift Lenz, Gayle Greene and Carol Thomas Neely (eds), *The Woman's Part* (Champaign, IL: University of Illinois Press, 1983), pp. 65–78.

Beard, Thomas, *The Theatre of Gods Judgement* (London 1597).

Beauregard, David N., '"Inspired Merit": Shakespeare's Theology of Grace in *All's Well That Ends Well'*. *Renascence*, 51(4) (1999): 218–30.

Beckman, Margaret Boerner, 'The Figure of Rosalind in *As You Like It'*. *SQ*, 29(1) (1978): 44–51.

Becon, Thomas, *A new postil conteinyng most godly and learned sermons vpon all the Sonday Gospelles* (London: 1566).

Beilin, Elaine V., *Redeeming Eve: Women Writers of the English Renaissance* (Princeton, NJ: Princeton University Press, 1987).

Bell, Fiona, 'Joan of Arc in Part I of *Henry VI* and Margaret in Parts 1, 2, and 3 of *Henry VI* and *Richard III'* in Robert Smallwood (ed.), *Players of Shakespeare 6* (Cambridge: Cambridge University Press, 2004), pp. 163–83.

Bell, Ilona, *Elizabethan Women and the Poetry of Courtship* (Cambridge: Cambridge University Press, 1998).

Bell, Thomas, *The Woeful Crie of Rome* (London: 1605).

Belsey, Catherine, 'Cleopatra's Seduction' in Terence Hawkes (ed.), *Alternative Shakespeares 2* (London: Routledge, 1996), pp. 38–62.

——'Disrupting sexual difference: meaning and gender in the comedies', in John Drakakis (ed.), *Alternative Shakespeares* (London: Routledge, 1988), pp. 166–90.

——'Love as *trompe-l'œil*: Taxonomies of desire in *Venus and Adonis'*. *SQ*, 46(3) (1995), 257–77.

——*The Subject of Tragedy* (London: Routledge, 1985).

——'Tarquin Dispossessed: Expropriation and Conceit in *The Rape of Lucrece'*. *SQ*, 52(3) (2001): 315–36.

Ben-Amos, Ilana Krausman, *Adolescence & Youth in Early Modern England* (New Haven, CT: Yale University Press, 1994).

Bennett, Judith M., *Ale, Beer and Brewsters in England: Women's Work in A Changing World 1300–1600* (Oxford: Oxford University Press, 1996).

Benson, George, *A sermon preached at Paules Crosse the seauenth of May, M.DC.IX* (London: 1609).

Bentley, Greg, 'Carousing Gertrude'. *Hamlet Studies*, 25 (2003): 81–122.

Bentley, Thomas, *The Fift Lampe of Virginitie* (London: 1582).

Bergeron, David M. (ed.), *Reading and Writing in Shakespeare* (Newark, DE: University of Delaware Press, 1996).

Berry, Edward I, *Shakespeare and the Hunt* (Cambridge: Cambridge University Press, 2001).

Berry, Philippa, 'Between Idolatry and astrology: modes of temporal repetition in *Romeo and Juliet'* in Richard Dutton, Alison Findlay and Richard Wilson (eds), *Religion, Region and Patronage: Lancastrian Shakespeare* (Manchester, Manchester University Press, 2003), pp. 68–83.

Berry, Ralph, *Shakespeare and Social Class* (Atlantic Highlands: Humanities Press International, 1988).

Bicks, Caroline, *Midwiving Subjects in Shakespeare's England* (Aldershot: Ashgate, 2003).

——'Midwiving Virility in Early Modern England' in Naomi J. Miller and Naomi

Yavneh (eds), *Maternal Measures: Figuring Caregiving in Early Modern England* (Altershot: Ashgate, 2000), pp. 49–64.

Black, James, 'The Unfolding of *Measure for Measure*'. *ShS*, 26 (1973): 119–28.

Bloom, Harold, *Joan of Arc* (London: Chelsea House, 1992).

Blount, Thomas, *Glossographia or A Dictionary* (London: 1656), searchable as part of the *Lexicons of Early Modern English* database (ed. Ian Lancashire) (University of Toronto, 2009). Available online at: http://leme.library.utoronto.ca/ (accessed 6 January 2010).

Blundell, Sue, *Women in Ancient Greece* (Cambridge, MA: Harvard University Press, 1995).

Boehrer, Thomas, 'Bestial Buggery in *A Midsummer Night's Dream*' in David Lee Miller, Sharon O'Dair and Harold Weber (eds), *The Production of English Renaissance Culture* (Ithaca, NY: Cornell University Press, 1994), pp. 123–50.

——*Shakespeare Among the Animals: Nature and Society in the Drama of Early Modern England* (Houndmills, Baskingstoke: Palgrave, 2002).

Boethius, *Consolation of Philosophy*, translated by Patrick Gerard Walsh (Oxford: Oxford University Press, 1999).

Boitani, Piero, *The European Tragedy of Troilus* (Oxford: Oxford University Press, 1989).

The Boke of Common Praier (London: 1583).

Bond, Ronald B., '"Dark Deeds Darkly Answered": Thomas Becon's *Homily against Whoredome and Adultery*, Its Contexts and Its Affiliations with Three Shakespeare Plays'. *Sixteenth Century Journal*, 16(2) (1985): 191–205.

Bonfield, L., R. M. Smith and K. Wrightson (eds), *The World We Have Gained: Histories of Population and Social Structure* (Oxford: Blackwell, 1986).

Bono, Barbara, *Literary Transvaluation: From Vergilian Epic to Shakespearean Tragicomedy* (Berkeley, CA: University of California Press, 1984).

Boorde, Andrew, *A Breviary of Health* (London: 1547).

Boose, Lynda E. 'The Father and the Bride in Shakespeare'. *PMLA*, 97(3) (1982): 325–47.

——'The father's house and the daughter in it' in Lynda Boose and Betty S. Flowers (eds), *Daughters and Fathers* (Baltimore, MD: Johns Hopkins University Press, 1989), pp. 19–74.

——'Scolding Brides and Bridling Scolds: Taming the Woman's Unruly Member'. *SQ*, 42 (1991): 179–213.

——'*The Taming of the Shrew*, Good Husbandry, and Enclosure' in *Shakespeare Reread: The Texts in New Contexts* (Ithaca, NY: Cornell University Press, 1994), pp. 193–225.

Boose, Lynda and Betty S. Flowers (eds), *Daughters and Fathers* (Baltimore, MD: Johns Hopkins University Press, 1989).

Booth, Stephen, *An Essay on Shakespeare's Sonnets* (New Haven, CT: Yale University Press, 1969).

——*Shakespeare's Sonnets Edited with Analytic Commentary* (New Haven, CT: Yale University Press, 1977).

Booy, David (ed.), *Personal Disclosures: An Anthology of Self-Writings from the Seventeenth Century* (Aldershot: Ashgate, 2002).

Bowerbank, Sylvia Lorraine, *Speaking for Nature: Women and Ecologies of Early Modern England* (Baltimore, MD: Johns Hopkins University Press, 2004).

Bowling, Laurence E., 'Duality in the Minor Characters in *Antony and Cleopatra*'. *College English*, 18(5) (1957): 251–5.

Braginton, Mary V., 'Two Notes on Senecan Tragedy'. *MLN*, 41(7) (1926): 468–9.

Brandon, Samuel, *The Vertuous Octavia* (London: 1598).

Briggs, Katherine M., *Pale Hecate's Team: An Examination of the Beliefs on Witchcraft and Magic among Shakespeare's Contemporaries and his Immediate Successors* (London: Routledge & Kegan Paul, 1962).

Bristol, Michael D., '*Charivari* and the Comedy of Abjection in *Othello*'. *Renaissance Drama*, 21 (1990): 3–22.

Brockbank, Philip (ed.), *Players of Shakespeare I* (Cambridge: Cambridge University Press, 1985).

Brome, Richard and Thomas Heywood, *The Late Lancashire Witches* [1634], ed. Laird H. Barber, Garland Renaissance Drama (New York: Garland Publishing, 1979).

Brooks, Charles, 'Shakespeare's Romantic Shrews'. *SQ*, 11 (1960): 351–6.

Brooks, Harold F. (ed.), *A Midsummer Night's Dream*, Arden Shakespeare (London: Routledge, 1979).

Brown, Carolyn E., 'Juliet's Taming of Romeo'. *SEL*, 36(2) (1996): 333–55.

Brown, Elizabeth A., '"Companion Me with My Mistress": Cleopatra, Elizabeth I and their Waiting Women' in Susan Frye and Karen Robertson (eds), *Maids and Mistresses, Cousins and Queens: Women's Alliances in Early Modern England* (Oxford: Oxford University Press, 1999), pp. 131–45.

Brown, Eric, 'Shakespeare's Anxious Epistomology: Shakespeare's *Love's Labour's Lost* and Marlowe's *Doctor Faustus*'. *Texas Studies in Literature and Language*, 45 (2003): 20–41.

Brown, John Russell, *Macbeth: A Guide to the Text and its Theatrical Life* (Houndmills, Basingstoke: Palgrave Macmillan, 2005).

Brown, Pamela Allen, '"Fie, What a foolish duty call you this?": *The Taming of the Shrew*, Women's Jest and the Divided Audience' in Richard Dutton and Jean E. Howard (eds), *Blackwell Companion to Shakespeare*, Vol. 3, *The Comedies* (Oxford: Basil Blackwell, 2003), pp. 289–306.

Brown, Susan, 'Queen Elizabeth in *Richard III*' in Robert Smallwood (ed.), *Players of Shakespeare 4* (Cambridge: Cambridge University Press, 2000), pp. 101–13.

Brown, Sylvia (ed.), *Women's Writing in Stuart England: The Mothers' Legacies of Dorothy Leigh, Elizabeth Joscelin and Elizabeth Richardson* (Stroud: Sutton, 1999).

Bruster, Douglas, 'The Jailer's Daughter and The Politics of Madwomen's Language'. *SQ*, 46 (1995): 277–300.

Bry, Theodore de, *Emblemata Nobilitatis* (Frankfurt: 1592).

Buccola, Regina, *Fairies, Fractious Women and the Old Faith: Fairy Lore in Early Modern British Drama and Culture* (Selingsgrove, PA: Susquehanna University Press, 2006).

Buccola, Regina and Lisa Hopkins (eds), *Marian Moments in Early Modern Drama* (Aldershot: Ashgate, 2007).

Buhler, Stephen, *Shakespeare in the Cinema: Ocular Proof* (Albany, NY: State University of New York Press, 2002).

Bullough, Geoffrey, *Narrative and Dramatic Sources of Shakespeare.*
——Vol. I Early Comedies, Poems, *Romeo and Juliet* (London, Routledge & Kegan Paul, 1964).
——Vol. II The Comedies (1597–1603) (London: Routledge & Kegan Paul, 1958).
——Vol. III Earlier English History Plays: *Henry VI, Richard III, Richard II* (London: Routledge & Kegan Paul, 1966).
——Vol. IV Later English History Plays: *King John, Henry IV, Henry V, Henry VIII* (London: Routledge & Kegan Paul, 1968).
——Vol. V The Roman Plays: *Julius Casar, Antony and Cleopatra, Coriolanus* (London, Routledge and Kegan Paul, 1964).
——Vol. VI 'Classical' Plays: *Titus, Troilus, Timon, Pericles* (London: Routledge and Kegan Paul, 1966).
——Vol. VII Major Tragedies: *Hamlet, Othello, King Lear, Macbeth* (London: Routledge and Kegan Paul, 1973).
——Vol. VIII Romances: *Cymbeline, Winter's Tale, Tempest* (London: Routledge and Kegan Paul, 1975).
Burden, Michael (ed.), *A Woman Scorn'd: Responses to the Dido Myth* (London: Faber and Faber, 1998).
Burnett, Mark Thornton, *Masters and Servants in English Renaissance Drama and Culture: Authority and Obedience* (Houndmills, Bastingstoke: Macmillan, 1997).
Burns, Edward (ed.), *King Henry VI Part I* (London: Methuen, 2000).
Cahill, Patricia A., 'Nation Formation and the English History Plays' in Richard Dutton and Jean E. Howard (eds), *A Companion to Shakespeare*, Vol. 2 (Oxford: Basil Blackwell, 2003), pp. 70–93.
Callaghan, Dympna (ed.), *A Feminist Companion to Shakespeare* (Oxford: Blackwell, 2000).
——'Looking well to linens: women and cultural production in *Othello* and Shakespeare's England' in Jean E. Howard and Scott Cutler Shershow (eds), *Marxist Shakespeares* (London: Routledge, 2001), pp. 53–81.
——*Women and Gender in Renaissance Tragedy: A Study of King Lear, Othello, the Duchess of Malfi and The White Devil* (Brighton: Harvester Wheatsheaf, 1989).
Calvin, John, *The Sermons of M John Calvin upon the Epistle of S. Paul to the Ephesians*, translated by Arthur Golding (London: 1577).
Calvo, Clara, 'Pronouns of address and social negotiation in *As You Like It*'. *Language and Literature*, 1 (1992): 5–27.
Camino, Mercedes Maroto, *"The Stage Am I": Raping Lucrece in Early Modern England* (Mellen Press, 1995).
Campbell, Lily B. (ed.), *The Mirror for Magistrates* (Cambridge: Cambridge University Press, 1938).
Campbell, Julie D., '"Merry, Nimble Stirring Spirits": Academic, Salon and Commedia dell'arte Influence in *Love's Labour's Lost*' in Peter Parolin and Pamela Allen Brown (eds), *Women Players in England: Beyond the All-Male Stage* (Aldershot: Ashgate, 2008), pp. 145–70.
Candido, Joseph, 'Dining out in Ephesus: Food in *The Comedy of Errors*'. *SEL*, 30(2), Elizabethan and Jacobean Drama (1990): 217–41.

Capp, Bernard, *When Gossips Meet: Women, Family and Neighbourhood in Early Modern England* (Oxford: Oxford University Press, 2003).

Carew, Robert, *Survey of Cornwall* (London: 1602).

Carlisle, Carol J., 'Helen Faucit's Lady Macbeth'. *ShSt*, 16 (1983): 205–21.

Carroll, Nancy, 'Lady Percy in Parts I and II of *Henry IV* in Robert Smallwood (ed.), *Players of Shakespeare 6* (Cambridge: Cambridge University Press, 2004), pp. 117–27.

Carroll, William C. 'Language and Sexuality in Shakespeare' in Catherine M. S. Alexander and Stanley Wells (eds), *Shakespeare and Sexuality* (Cambridge: Cambridge University Press, 2001), pp. 14–34.

——(ed.), *The Two Gentlemen of Verona* (London: Thomson, 2004).

——'The Virgin Not: Language and Sexuality in Shakespeare'. *ShS*, 46 (1994).

Cary, Elizabeth, *The Tragedy of Mariam*, ed. Stephanie Hodgson-Wright (Peterborough, ON: Broadview, 2000).

Catari, Vincenzo, *The Fountaine of Ancient Fiction* translated into English by Richard Lynche (London: 1599).

Catty, Jocelyn, *Writing Rape, Writing Women in Early Modern England* (Houndmills, Basingstoke: Macmillan, 1999).

Cavallo, Sandra and Lyndan Warner (eds), *Widowhood in Medieval and Early Modern Europe* (Harlow: Pearson, 1999).

Cavanagh, Dermott, Stuart Hampton-Reeves and Stephen Longstaffe (eds), *Shakespeare's Histories and Counter-Histories* (Manchester: Manchester University Press, 2006).

Cavendish, Margaret, *Poems and Fancies written by the Right Honourable, the Lady Margaret Newcastle* (London: 1653).

Cawdry, Robert, *A table alphabeticall conteyning and teaching the true writing, and vnderstanding of hard vsuall English wordes* (London: 1604), currently searchable as part of the *Lexicons of Early Modern English* database (ed. Ian Lancashire) (University of Toronto, 2009). Available online at: http://leme.library.utoronto. ca/ (accessed 6 January 2010).

Cerasano, S. P., '"Borrowed Robes", costume prices and the drawing of *Titus Andronicus*'. *ShSt*, 22 (1994): 45–57.

Chamberlain, Stephanie, 'Capitalizing on the Body: *Measure for Measure* and the Economics of Patrilineal Worth'. *Journal of the Wooden O Symposium* 3 (2003): 12–22.

——'Fantasizing Infanticide: Lady Macbeth and the Murdering Mother in Early Modern England', *College Literature*, 32(3) (2005): 72–91.

Charlton, Kenneth, *Women, Religion and Education in Early Modern England* (London: Routledge, 1999).

Charney, Maurice, and Hannah Charney, 'The Drama of Madwomen in Shakespeare and His Fellow Dramatists'. *Signs*, 3 (1977): 451–60.

Chaucer, Geoffrey, *The Complete Works of Geoffrey Chaucer*, 2nd ed., ed. F. N. Robinson (Oxford: Oxford University Press, 1968).

Chegdzoy, Kate (ed.), *Shakespeare, Feminism and Gender: Contemporary Critical Essays*, New Casebooks (Houndmills, Basingstoke: Palgrave, 2001).

Chettle, Henry, *Englands Mourning Garment* (London: 1603).

Christensen, Ann, '"Because their business still lies out a' door": Resisting the Separation of the Spheres in Shakespeare's *The Comedy of Errors*'. *Literature and History*, 5(1) (1996): 19–37.

Churchyard, Thomas, *The firste parte of Churchyardes chippes* (London: 1575).

——'Howe Shores Wife, Edward the fowerthes concubine, was by king Richarde despoyled of all her goodes, and forced to do open penance' in Lily B. Campbell (ed.), *The Mirror for Magistrates* (Cambridge: Cambridge University Press, 1938), pp. 373–86.

Clare, Janet, *Revenge Tragedies of the Renaissance* (London: Northcote, British Council, 2006).

Clark, Ira, 'The Widow Hunt on the Tudor Stuart Stage'. *SEL*, 41(2) (2001): 399–416.

Clark, Sandra, '"Wives may be merry and yet honest too": Women and Wit in *The Merry Wives of Windsor* and Some Other Plays' in J. W. Mahon and T. A. Pendleton (eds), *"Fanned and Winnowed Opinions": Shakespeare Essays Presented to Harold Jenkins* (London: Methuen, 1987), pp. 249–67.

Clark, Stuart, *Thinking with Demons: The Idea of Witchcraft in Early Modern Europe* (Oxford: Oxford University Press, 1997).

Clifford, Lady Anne, *The Diaries of Lady Anne Clifford*, ed. D. J. H. Clifford (Stroud: Alan Sutton, 1990).

Cohen, Walter, 'The undiscovered country: Shakespeare and mercantile geography' in Jean E. Howard and Scott Cutler Shershow (eds), *Marxist Shakespeares* (London: Routledge, 2001), pp. 128–58.

Coles, Elisha, *An English Dictionary* (London: 1676).

Collington, Philip D., '"I would Thy Husband Were Dead": *The Merry Wives of Windsor* as Mock Domestic Tragedy'. *ELH* 30(2) (2000): 184–212.

Collins, A. J., *Jewels and Plate of Queen Elizabeth I* (London: British Museum, 1955).

Collinson, Patrick, 'Elizabeth I (1533–1603)', *Oxford Dictionary of National Biography* (Oxford: Oxford University Press, 2004; online edition, May 2008). Available online at: http://www.oxforddnb.com/view/article/8636 (accessed 26 March 2009).

Combe, Thomas, *The theater of fine deuices containing an hundred morall emblemes. First penned in French by Guillaume de la Perriere, and translated into English by Thomas Combe* (London: 1614).

Comensoli, Viviana and Anne Russell (eds), *Enacting Gender on the English Renaissance Stage* (Urbana and Chicago, IL: University of Illinois Press, 1999).

Connolly, Anneliese and Lisa Hopkins (eds), *Goddesses and Queens: The Iconography of Elizabeth I* (Manchester: Manchester University Press, 2007).

Cook, Ann Jennalie, *Making a Match: Courtship in Shakespeare and His Society* (Princeton, NJ: Princeton University Press, 1991).

Cook, Carol, '"The sign and semblance of her honour": Reading Gender Difference in *Much Ado*'. *PMLA*, 101 (1986): 186–202.

Cook, Judith, *Women in Shakespeare* (London: Harrap, 1980).

Copland, Robert, *Iyl of braintfords testament* (London: 1567).

Coryat, Thomas, *Coryat's Crudites reprinted from the edition of 1611 To which are now added his letters from India*, 3 Vols (Salisbury: W. Carter, Samuel Hayes, J. Wilkie and E. Easton, 1776).

Cotgrave, Randle, *A dictionarie of the French and English tongues* (London: 1611).

Cotton, Nancy, 'Castrating Witches: Impotence and Magic in *The Merry Wives of Windsor*'. *SQ*, 38(3) (1987): 320–6.

Council, Norman, *When Honour's At the Stake: Ideas of Honour in Shakespeare's Plays* (London: Allen and Unwin, 1973).

The Countess of Lincolns Nurserie (London: 1622). A full text is available from the Brown Women Writers' Project's 'Renaissance Women Online'. Available online at http://www.wwp.brown.edu/texts/rwoentry.html (accessed 6 January 2010).

Cox, Catherine S., '"An excellent thing in woman": virgos and viragos in *King Lear*'. *MP*, 96(2) (1998): 143–57.

Cox, John D., 'Local References in *3 Henry VI*'. *SQ*, 51(3) (2000): 340–52.

Crane, Mary Thomas, '"Players in your huswifery and huswives in your beds": Conflicting identities of Early Modern English Women' in Naomi Miller and Naomi Yavneh (eds), *Maternal Measures: Figuring Caregiving in the Early Modern Period* (Aldershot: Ashgate, 2000), pp. 212–23.

Crawford, Patricia, '"The only ornament in a woman": needlework in Early Modern England' in *All Her Labour. 2: Embroidering the Framework* (Sydney: Hale and Ironmonger, 1984), pp. 7–20.

Cressy, David, *Birth, Marriage and Death: Ritual, Religion, and the Life Cycle in Tudor and Stuart England* (Oxford: Oxford University Press, 1997).

——*Bonfires and Bells: National Memory and the Protestant Calendar in Elizabethan and Stuart England* (London: Weidenfeld and Nicholson, 1989).

Crocker, Holly A., 'Affective Resistance: Performing Passivity and Playing a-part in *The Taming of the Shrew*'. *SQ*, 54(2) (2003): 142–59.

Crooke, Helkiah, *Mikrokosmographia a description of the body of man. Together vvith the controuersies thereto belonging* (London: 1615).

Crowl, Samuel, 'A World Elsewhere: Shakespeare's Roman Plays on Film and Television' in Anthony Davies and Stanley Wells (eds), *Shakespeare and the Moving Image* (Cambridge: Cambridge University Press: 1994), pp. 146–63.

Danby, John F., *Shakespeare's Doctrine of Nature: A Study of King Lear* (London: Faber and Faber, 1948).

Dane, Gabrielle, 'Reading Ophelia's Madness'. *Exemplaria*, 10 (1998): 405–23.

Daniel, Samuel, *Certaine small poems lately printed with the tragedie of Philotas* (London: printed by G Eld for Simon Waterson and Edward Blount, 1605).

——*Tethys Festival* (1610) in *Court Masques*, ed. David Lindley (Oxford: Oxford University Press, 1998), pp. 54–65.

Dash, Irene, 'A Penchant for Perdita on the Eighteenth Century Stage' in Carolyn Ruth Swift Lenz, Gayle Greene and Carol Thomas Neely (eds), *The Woman's Part: Feminist Criticism of Shakespeare* (Urbana, IL: University of Illinois Press, 1983), pp. 271–84.

——*Wooing, Wedding and Power: Women in Shakespeare's Plays* (New York: Columbia University Press, 1981).

Davey, James Joseph, *The Function of the Dark Lady in Shakespeare's Sonnets* (Trieste: University of Trieste, 1986).

Davis, Natalie Zemon and Arlette Farge (eds), *A History of Women in the West: Renaissance and Enlightenment Paradoxes* (Cambridge, MA: Belknap, 1993).

Davies, Stevie, *The Idea of Woman in Renaissance Literature: The Feminine Reclaimed* (Brighton: Harvester, 1986).

Davis, J. Madison and A. Daniel Frankforter, *The Shakespeare Name Dictonary* (New York and London: Routledge, 2004).

Dekker, Thomas, *Blurt Master Constable* (London: 1602).

——*Satiro-mastix. Or The vntrussing of the humorous poet* (London: 1602).

——*The Whore of Babylon* (London: 1607).

D'Estienne, Henri, *A world of vvonders: or An introduction to a treatise touching the conformitie of ancient and moderne wonders* (London: 1607).

De Courtais, Georgine, *Women's Headdress and Hairstyles in England from AD 600 to the Present Day* (London: Batsford, 1973).

De La Tour, Frances, 'Cleopatra in *Antony and Cleopatra*' in Robert Smallwood (ed.), *Players of Shakespeare 5* (Cambridge: Cambridge University Press, 2005), pp. 212–30.

Dean, Paul, 'Dramatical Mode and Historical Vision in *Henry VIII*'. *SQ*, 37(2) (1988): 175–89.

Dekker, Thomas, *The Belman of London* (London: 1608).

——*Satiro-mastix* (London: 1602).

——*The Honest Whore Parts I and II* (1604), Joost Daalder (ed.), *Revels Plays* (Manchester: Manchester University Press, forthcoming 2010).

——*The seuen deadly sinnes of London drawne in seuen seuerall coaches, through the seuen seuerall gates of the citie bringing the plague with them* (London: 1606).

——*The Shoemaker's Holiday* (London: 1600).

Delaney, John J., *Dictionary of Saints: Abridged Edition* (New York: Doubleday, 1983).

Deloney, Thomas, *The pleasant historie of John Winchcomb in his yonguer yeares called Jack of Newbery* (London: 1626).

Desens, Marliss C., *The Bed-Trick In English Renaissance Drama: Explorations in Gender, Sexuality and Power* (London: Associated University Presses, 1994).

Diehl, Huston, '"Does Not the Stone Rebuke Me?" The Pauline Rebuke and Paulina's Lawful Magic in *The Winter's Tale*' in Paul Yachnin and Patricia Badir (eds), *Shakespeare and the Cultures of Performance* (Aldershot: Ashgate, 2008), pp. 69–82.

——'Horrid Image, Sorry Sight, Fatal Vision: The Visual Rhetoric of *Macbeth*'. *ShSt*, 16 (1983): 191–204.

DiGangi, Mario, 'Pleasure and Danger: Measuring Female Sexuality in *Measure for Measure*'. *ELH*, 60 (1993): 589–609.

——'The Social Relations of Shakespeare's Comic Households' in Richard Dutton and Jean E. Howard (eds), *A Companion to Shakespeare*, Vol. 3 (Oxford: Basil Blackwell, 2003), pp. 90–113.

Dillon, Janette, *Theatre, Court and City 1595–1610: Drama and Social Space in London* (Cambridge: Cambridge University Press, 2000).

Dod, John, and Robert Cleaver, *A Godly Forme of Householde Government* (London: 1598).

Dodderidge, John, *Glossary of Proper First Names* (c. 1626–8) (British Library Sloane MS 3479). Currently searchable as part of the *Lexicons of Early Modern English* database (ed. Ian Lancashire) (University of Toronto, 2009). Available online at: http://leme.library.utoronto.ca/ (accessed 6 January 2010).

Doebler, Bettie Ann, 'Othello's Angels: The *Ars Moriendi*'. *ELH*, 34(2) (1967): 156–72.

Doebler, John, 'The Many Faces of Love: Shakespeare's *Venus and Adonis*'. *ShSt*, 16 (1983): 33–44.

Dolan, Frances E., *Dangerous Familiars: Representations of Domestic Crime in England 1550–1700* (Ithaca, NY: Cornell University Press, 1994).

——*The Taming of the Shrew: Texts and Contexts* (New York: St Martin's Press, 1996).

Dollimore, Jonathan, *Sexual Dissidence: Augustine to Wilde, Freud to Foucault* (Oxford: Oxford University Press, 1991).

——'Shakespeare Understudies: The Sodomite, the Prostitute, the Transvestite and Their Critics' in *Political Shakespeare: Essays in Cultural Materialism*, 2nd ed. (Manchester: Manchester University Press, 1994), pp. 129–52.

——'Transgression and Surveillance in *Measure for Measure*' in Jonathan Dollimore and Alan Sinfield (eds), *Political Shakespeare* (Manchester: Manchester University Press, 1985), pp. 72–87.

Doloff, Steven, '"Well Desir'd in Cyprus": Othello on the Isle of Venus'. *NQ*, 47 (2000): 81–3.

Donaldson, Ian, *The Rapes of Lucretia: A Myth and Its Transformations* (Oxford: Clarendon Press, 1982).

Doniger, Wendy (consulting ed.) *Merriam-Webster's Encyclopedia of World Religions* (Springfield, MA: Merriam-Webster, 1991).

Donne, John, *John Donne*, ed. John Carey (Oxford: Oxford University Press, 1990).

Doran, Madeleine, 'The Idea of Excellence in Shakespeare'. *SQ*, 27(2) (1976): 133–49.

Doran, Susan and Thomas S. Freeman (eds), *The Myth of Elizabeth* (Basingstoke: Palgrave Macmillan, 2003).

Drayton, Michael, *Poems: by Michael Drayton Esquire Viz. The barons warres, Englands heroicall epistles, Idea, Odes* (London: 1619).

——*Poly-Olbion* (London: 1612).

Dreher, Diane, *Domination and Defiance: Fathers and Daughters in Shakespeare* (Lexington, KY: University of Kentucky Press, 1986).

Dubrow, Heather, '"I fear there will come a worse in his place": Surrogate Parents and Shakespeare's *Richard III*' in Naomi J. Miller and Naomi Yavneh (eds), *Maternal Measures: Figuring Caregiving in the Early Modern Period* (Ashgate, 2000), pp. 348–62.

Duffy, Eamon, *The Stripping of the Altars: Traditional Religion in England 1400–1580* (New Haven, CT: Yale University Press, 1992).

Duncan-Jones, Katherine, 'Frances Meres, Playgoer'. *NQ* (2009): 56: 579.

——'Pyramus and Thisbe: Shakespeare's Debt to Moffett Cancelled', *RES* 32(127) (1981), 296–301.

Dusinberre, Juliet (ed.), *As You Like It* (Arden Shakespeare) (London: Thompson, 2006).

——'*As You Like It*' in Richard Dutton and Jean E. Howard (eds), *A Companion to Shakespeare's Works. Vol 3: The Comedies* (Oxford: Basil Blackwell, 2003a), pp. 411–28.

——'*King John* and Embarrassing Women'. *ShS*, 42 (1989): 37–52.

——'Pancakes and a date for *As You Like It*'. *SQ*, 54 (2003b): 371–405.

——*Shakespeare and the Nature of Women*, 2nd ed. (Houndmills, Basingstoke: Macmillan, 1996).

——'Women and Boys Playing Shakespeare' in Dympna Callaghan, ed., *A Feminist Companion to Shakespeare* (Oxford: Blackwell, 2000), pp. 251–62.

Dutton, Richard, '*The Comedy or Errors* and *The Calumny of Apelles*: An Exercise in Source Study' in Richard Dutton and Jean E. Howard (eds), *A Companion to Shakespeare's Works. Vol 3: The Comedies* (Oxford: Basil Blackwell, 2003a), pp. 307–19.

——'Shakespeare and Lancaster' in Dutton, A. Richard, Alison Findlay, and Richard Wilson (eds), *Religion, Region and Patronage: Lancastrian Shakespeare* (Manchester: Manchester University Press, 2003b), pp. 143–68.

Dutton, Richard (ed.), *New Casebooks: A Midsummer Night's Dream* (Basingstoke: Macmillan, 1996).

Dutton, Richard and Jean E. Howard (eds), *Blackwell Companion to Shakespeare. Vol. 1: The Tragedies* (Oxford: Basil Blackwell, 2003a).

——*A Companion to Shakespeare's Works. Vol. 2: The Histories* (Oxford: Basil Blackwell, 2003b).

——*A Companion to Shakespeare's Works. Vol. 3: The Comedies* (Oxford: Basil Blackwell, 2003c).

——*A Companion to Shakespeare's Works. Vol. 4: The Poems, Problem Comedies, Late Plays* (Oxford: Basil Blackwell, 2003d).

Dutton, Richard, Alison Findlay, and Richard Wilson (eds), *Religion, Region and Patronage: Lancastrian Shakespeare* (Manchester: Manchester University Press, 2003).

—— (eds), *Theatre and Religion: Lancastrian Shakespeare* (Manchester: Manchester University Press, 2003).

Dyer, Christopher, 'Mary Arden and Mary Arden's House, based on material provided by Professor Christopher Dyer, Centre for English Local History, University of Leicester' (Stratford: Shakespeare Birthplace Trust, 2003). Available online at: http://www.shakespeare.org.uk/content/view/51/51 (accessed 6 January 2010).

Dyson, J. P., 'The Structural Function of the Banquet Scene in *Macbeth*'. *SQ*, 14(4) (1963), pp. 369–78.

Eagleton, Terry, *Myths of Power: A Marxist study of the Brontës* (London: Macmillan, 1975).

——*William Shakespeare* (Oxford: Basil Blackwell, 1987).

Earle, John, *Microcosmographie* (London: 1628, reprinted London: Dent, 1934).

Earnshaw, Steven, *The Pub in Literature, England's Altered State* (Manchester: Manchester University Press, 2000).

Easson, Angus, 'Marina's Maidenhead', *SQ*, 24(3) (1973): 328–9.

Edgcombe, Rodney, 'Shakespeare's *A Midsummer Night's Dream*'. *Explicator*, 58(4) (2000): 181–4.

——'"Singing it out" in *The Two Gentlemen of Verona*'. *American Notes and Queries*, 17 (2004): 12–14.

Egan, Gabriel, *Green Shakespeare: From Ecopolitics to Ecocriticism* (London: Routledge, 2006).

Egerton, Elizabeth Cavendish, *Subordination and Authorship in Early Modern England: The Case of Elizabeth Cavendish Egerton and her "Loose Papers"*, ed. Betty Travitsky (Tempe, AZ: Arizona Center for Medieval and Renaissance Studies, 1999).

Eggert, Katherine, *Showing Like a Queen: Literary Experiment in Spenser, Shakespeare and Milton* (Philadelphia, PA: University of Pennsylvania Press, 1999).

Elam, Kier, 'The Fertile Eunuch: *Twelfth Night*, Early Modern Intercourse and the Fruits of Castration'. *SQ*, 47 (1996): 1–36.

Elizabeth I, *Collected Works*, eds Leah S. Marcus, Janel Mueller, Mary Beth Rose. (Chicago, IL: University of Chicago Press, 2000).

Ellinghausen, Laurie, *Labour and Writing in Early Modern England 1567–1667* (Aldershot: Ashgate, 2008).

Empson, William, *The Strengths of Shakespeare's Shrew: Essays, Memoirs and Reviews*, ed. John Haffenden (Sheffield: Sheffield Academic Press, 1996).

Enterline, Lynn, *The Rhetoric of the Body From Ovid to Shakespeare* (Cambridge: Cambridge University Press, 2002).

Ephraim, Michelle, *Reading the Jewish Woman on the Elizabethan Stage* (Aldershot: Ashgate, 2008).

Erasmus, Desiderius, *Apophthegmes*, translated by N. Udall (London: 1542).

——*The Colloquies* (1519), trans H. M. (1671), pp. 301–2.

Erickson, Amy Louise, *Women and Property in Early Modern England* (London: Routledge, 1993).

Erickson, Peter, 'The failure of relationship between men and women in *Love's Labor's Lost*'. *Women's Studies*, 9 (1981), 65–81.

——The Order of the Garter, The Cult of Elizabeth and Class-Gender Tension in *The Merry Wives of Windsor*' in Jean Howard and Marion F. O'Connor (eds), *Shakespeare Reproduced: The Text in History and Ideology* (New York, Methuen: 1987), pp. 116–40.

Estrin, Barbara L., *Laura: Uncovering Gender and Genre in Wyatt, Donne, Marvell* (Durham, NC: Duke University Press, 1994).

Evangelisti, Silvia, *Nuns: A History of Convent Life 1450–1700* (Oxford: Oxford University Press, 2007).

Evans, Joan, *A History of Jewellery 1100–1870*, 2nd ed. (London: Faber and Faber, 1970).

Evenden, Doreen, *The Midwives of Seventeenth-Century London* (Cambridge: Cambridge University Press, 2000).

——'Mothers and their Midwives in Seventeenth Century London' in Hilary Marland (ed.), *The Art of Midwifery: Early Modern Midwives in Europe* (London, Routledge, 1993), pp. 9–26.

Ewbank, Inga-Stina, '"My name is Marina": the language of recognition', in Philip Edwards, Inga-Stina Ewbank and G. K. Hunter (eds), *Shakespeare's Styles: Essays in Honour of Kenneth Muir* (Cambridge: Cambridge University Press, 1980), pp. 111–30.

—— 'The Fiend-Like Queen: A Note on *Macbeth* and Seneca's *Medea*'. *ShS*, 19 (1966): 82–94.

Feldman, Martha and Bonnie Gordon, *The Courtesan's Arts: Cross-Cultural Perspectives* (Oxford: Oxford University Press, 2006).

Felperin, Howard, '"Tongue tied our queen?": the deconstruction of presence in *The Winter's Tale*' in P. Parker and G. Hartman (eds), *Shakespeare and the Question of Theory* (London: Methuen, 1986), pp. 3–18.

Ferber, Michael, *A Dictionary of Literary Symbols* (Cambridge: Cambridge University Press, 1999).

Ferguson, Margaret, Maureen Quilligan and Nancy J. Vickers (eds), *Rewriting the Renaissance* (Chicago, IL: University of Chicago Press, 1986).

Field, Nathan, *Amends for Ladies* (London: 1618).

Fildes, Valerie, *Breasts, Bottles and Babies: A History of Infant Feeding* (Edinburgh: Edinburgh University Press, 1986).

——*Wet Nursing: A history from antiquary to the present* (Oxford: Blackwell, 1988).

Fildes, Valerie (ed.), *Women as Mothers in Pre-Industrial England* (London: Routledge, 1990).

Finch, Sir Henry, *The sacred doctrine of diuinitie gathered out of the worde of God* (Middelberg, 1589).

Findlay, Alison, '"Adam's Sons are My Bretheren": Reading Beatrice's Feminism, Past and Present' in Helen Wilcox and Douglas A. Brooks (eds), *The Shakespeare Yearbook 2003, 14: New Studies in the Shakespearian Heroine* (Lewiston, NY: Edwin Mellen, 2004), pp. 1–18.

—— *A Feminist Perspective on Renaissance Drama* (Oxford: Basil Blackwell, 1998).

——'*Hamlet*: A Document in Madness' in Mark Thornton Burnett and John Manning (eds), *New Essays on Hamlet* (New York: AMS, 1994a), pp. 189–205.

——*Illegitimate Power: Bastards in Renaissance Drama* (Manchester: Manchester University Press, 1994b).

——'*Much Ado About Nothing*' in Richard Dutton and Jean E. Howard (eds), *A Companion to Shakespeare's Works*, Vol. 3 (Oxford: Basil Blackwell, 2003), pp. 393–410.

——'"One that's dead is quick: Virgin re-birth in *All's Well That Ends Well*' in Regina Buccola and Lisa Hopkins (eds), *Marian Moments in Early Modern British Drama* (Aldershot: Ashgate, 2007), pp. 35–45.

——*Playing Spaces in Early Women's Drama* (Cambridge: Cambridge University Press, 2006).

Findlay, Deborah, 'Portia in *The Merchant of Venice*' in Russell Jackson and Robert

Smallwood (eds), *Players of Shakespeare 3* (Cambridge: Cambridge University Press, 1993), pp. 52–67.

Fineman, Joel, *Shakespeare's Perjured Eye* (Berkeley, CA: University of California Press, 1986).

——'The Turn of the Shrew' in Patricia Parker and Geoffrey Hartmann (eds), *Shakespeare and the Question of Theory* (New York: Routledge, 1985), pp. 138–59.

Finkelstein, Richard, 'Differentiating *Hamlet*: Ophelia and the Problems of Subjectivity'. *Renaissance and Reformation*, 21(2) (Spring 1997): 5–22.

Fisch, Harold, '"Antony and Cleopatra": The Limits of Mythology'. *ShS*, 23 (1970): 59–67.

Fisher, A. S. T., 'The Source of Shakespeare's Interlude of Pyramus and Thisbe: A Neglected Poem', *NQ* CXCIV (1949), 376–9, 400–2.

Fisher, Will, 'The Renaissance Beard: Masculinity in Early Modern England'. *RQ*, 54(1) (2001): 155–87.

Fissell, Mary E. 'The Politics of Reproduction in the English Reformation'. *Representations*, 87 (2004): 43–81.

Fleissner, Robert F., *A Rose by Another Name: A Study of Literary Flora from Shakespeare to Eco* (West Cornwall, CT: Locust Hill, 1989).

Fleming, Juliet, 'Dictionary English and the Female Tongue', in Richard Burt and John Michael Arthur (eds), *Enclosure Acts: Sexuality, Property and Culture in Early Modern England* (Ithaca, NY: Cornell University Press, 1994), pp. 290–325.

Fletcher, Anthony, and John Stevenson (eds), *Order and Disorder in Early Modern England* (Cambridge: Cambridge University Press, 1987).

Fletcher, John, *Cupid's Revenge* (London: 1615).

Florio, John, *Queen Anna's New World of Words* (London: 1611).

Fludd, Robert, *Utriusque Cosmi majoris scilicet et minoris metaphysica atque technica historia in duo volumina secundin cosmic differentiam divisa* (Oppenheim, 1617).

Fly, Richard D., 'Cassandra and the Language of Prophecy in *Troilus and Cressida*'. *SQ*, 26(2) (1975): 157–71.

Forker, Charles, 'Royal Carnality and Illicit Desire in the English History Plays of the 1590s'. *Medieval and Renaissance Drama in England*, 17 (2005): 99–131.

Forse, Hames H., *Art Imitates Business: Commercial and Political Influences in Elizabethan Theatre* (London: Popular, 2004).

Foxe, John, *Actes and Monuments* (London: 1583).

Fraser, Antonia, *The Weaker Vessel: Woman's Lot in Seventeenth-Century England* (London: Methuen, 1985).

Freedman, Barbara, 'Shakespearean Chronology, Ideological Complicity and Floating Texts: Something is Rotten in Windsor'. *SQ*, 45 (1994): 190–210.

Freeman, Jane, 'Life-Long Learning in *All's Well That Ends Well*'. *Renascence*, 56(2) (2004): 67–85.

Friedman, Michael D., *The World Must Be Peopled: Shakespeare's Comedies of Forgiveness* (Madison, NJ: Fairleigh Dickinson University Press, 2002).

Frye, Susan and Karen Robertson (eds), *Maids and Mistresses, Cousins and Queens: Women's Alliances in Early Modern England* (Oxford: Oxford University Press, 1999).

Fulton, Robert C., 'Shakespeare, Timon and the Amazons'. *ShSt*, 9 (1976): 283–99.

Garber, Marjorie, *Coming of Age in Shakespeare* (London: Methuen, 1981).

——*Vested Interests: Cross-Dressing and Cultural Anxiety* (London, Routledge, 1992).

Gardiner, Judith, 'Shakespeare's *The Tempest* IV.1.76–82 (Iris and Hymen)'. *Explicator*, 35(1) (1976): 25–7.

Gaudet, Paul, 'Lorenzo's "Infidel": The Staging of Difference in *The Merchant of Venice*'. *Theatre Journal*, 38(3) (1986): 275–90.

Gay, Penny, *As She Likes It: Shakespeare's Unruly Women* (London: Routledge, 1994).

Geckle, George L., 'Shakespeare's Isabella', *SQ* 22 (1971): 163–8.

George, David (ed.), *The Critical Tradition: Coriolanus* (London: Continuum, 2004).

Gibbons, Brian, *Jacobean City Comedy* (London: Methuen, 1980).

Gibson, Joan, 'The Logic of Chastity: Women, Sex and the History of Philosophy in the Early Modern Period'. *Hypatia*, 21(4) (2006): 1–19.

Gibson, Marion, *Witchcraft and Society in England and America 1550–1750* (London: Continuum, 2003).

Gilbert, Sandra M., 'Widow'. *Critical Inquiry* 27(4) (2001): 559–79.

Gilbreath, Alexandra, 'Hermione in *The Winter's Tale*' in Robert Smallwood (ed.), *Players of Shakespeare 5* (Cambridge: Cambridge University Press, 2003), pp. 74–90.

Gillespie, Stuart, *Shakespeare's Books* (London: Continuum, 2001).

Gless, Daryl, *Measure for Measure, the Law and the Convent* (Princeton: Princeton University Press, 1979).

Golding, Arthur (Sir), *The xv Bookes of p. Ovidius Naso, entytled Metamorphosis, translated oute of Latin into English meeter, by Arthur Golding, Gentleman* (London: 1567).

Goldstein, Neal L., '*Love's Labour's Lost* and the Renaissance Vision of Love'. *SQ*, 25(3) (1974): 335–50.

Gossett, Suzanne, '"You not your child well loving": Text and Family Structure in *Pericles*' in Richard Dutton and Jean E. Howard (eds), *Blackwell Companion to Shakespeare*, Vol. 4 (Oxford: Basil Blackwell, 2003), pp. 348–64.

Gouge, William, *Of Domesticall Duties* (London: 1622).

Gough, Melinda J., '"Her Filthy Feature Open Showne" in Ariosto, Spenser and *Much Ado About Nothing*'. *SEL*, 39(1) (1999): 41–67.

Gowing, Laura, 'Language, power and the law: women's slander litigation in early modern London' in Jennifer Kermode and Garthine Walker (eds), *Women, Crime and the Courts in Early Modern England* (Chapel Hill, NC: University of North Carolina Press, 1994), pp. 26–47.

Goy-Blanquet, Dominique, 'Shakespeare and Voltaire Set Fire to History' in *Joan of Arc: A Saint for All Seasons: Studies in Myth and Politics*, ed. Dominique Goy-Blanquet (Aldershot: Ashgate, 2003), pp. 1–38.

Green, Douglas E., 'Interpreting "Her Martyr'd Signs": Gender and Tragedy in *Titus Andronicus*'. *SQ*, 40(3) (1989): 317–26.

Green, Martin, 'Emilia Lanier *IS* the Dark Lady of the Sonnets'. *English Studies*, 87(5) (2006): 544–76.

Green, Susan, '"A Mad Woman! We are Made, Boys!" The Jailer's Daughter in *The Two Noble Kinsmen*' in Charles H. Frey (ed.), *Shakespeare, Fletcher and The Two Noble Kinsmen* (Columbia, MO: University of Missouri Press, 1989), pp. 121–32.

Greenblatt, Stephen, *Renaissance Self-Fashioning* (Chicago, IL: University of Chicago Press, 1980).

——*Shakespearean Negotiations: the circulation of social energy in Renaissance England* (Berkeley, CA: University of California Press, 1988).

Greene, Gayle, 'Shakespeare's Cressida: "A kind of self"' in Carolyn Ruth Swift Lenz, Gayle Greene and Carol Thomas Neely (eds), *The Woman's Part: Feminist Criticism of Shakespeare* (Urbana, IL: University of Illinois Press, 1983), pp. 133–49.

Greene, Robert, *Greenes carde of fancie* (London: 1608).

——*Mamillia, a mirrour or looking glasse for the ladies of Englande* (London: 1583).

——*A notable discouery of coosenage Now daily practised by sundry lewd persons, called connie-catchers, and crosse-byters* (London: 1592).

——*Philomela* (London: 1592).

Greenfield, Thomas A., '"Excellent Things in Women": The Emergence of Cordelia'. *South Atlantic Bulletin*, 42(1) (1977): 42–52.

Greer, Germaine, *Shakespeare's Wife* (London: Bloomsbury, 2007).

Greer, Germaine, Jeslyn Medoff, Melinda Sansone and Susan Hastings (eds), *Kissing The Rod: An Anthology of Seventeenth Century Women's Verse* (London: Virago, 1988).

Grieco, Sara F. Matthews, 'The Body, Appearance and Sexuality', in Natalie Zemon Davis and Arlette Farge (eds), *A History of Women in the West: Renaissance and Enlightenment Paradoxes* (Cambridge, MA: Belknap, 1993), pp. 46–84.

Gurr, Andrew, *The Shakespeare Company 1594–1642* (Cambridge: Cambridge University Press, 2004).

Guyol, Hazel Sample, 'A Temperance of Language: Goneril's Grammar and Rhetoric'. *English Journal*, 55(3) (1966): 316–19.

Gyer, Nicholas, *The English phlebotomy: or, Method and way of healing by letting of blood Very profitable in this spring time for the preseruatiue intention, and most needful al the whole yeare beside* (London: 1592).

Hackenbroch, Yvonne, *Renaissance Jewellery* (London: Southeby Part Bernet, 1979).

Hackett, Helen, '*A Midsummer Night's Dream*' in Richard Dutton and Jean E. Howard (eds), *A Companion to Shakespeare*, Vol. 3 (Oxford: Basil Blackwell, 2003), pp. 338–57.

——*Shakespeare and Elizabeth: the meeting of two myths* (Princeton, NJ: Princeton University Press, 2009).

——*Virgin Mother, Maiden Queen: Elizabeth I and the Cult of the Virgin Mary* (Basingstoke: Macmillan: 1995).

Hales, Nancy K., 'Sexual Disguise in *Cymbeline*'. *MLQ*, 41(3) (1980): 231–48.

Hall, Edward, *The vnion of the two noble and illustrate famelies of Lancastre [and] Yorke* (London: 1548).

Hamilton, Donna B., *Virgil and the Tempest* (Columbus, OH: Ohio State University Press, 1990).

——*The Winter's Tale* and the Language of Union, 1604–1610, *ShSt*, 21 (1993): 228–51.

Hamilton, Sharon, *Shakespeare's Daughters* (Jefferson, NC and London: McFarland, 2003).

Hammond, N. G. L. and H. H. Scullard, *The Oxford Classical Dictionary*, 2nd ed. (Oxford: Clarendon, 1970).

Hampton-Reeves, Stuart and Carol Rutter, *The Henry VI Plays: Shakespeare In Performance* (Manchester: Manchester University Press, 2006).

Happé, Peter (ed.), *English Mystery Plays* (Harmondsworth: Penguin, 1975).

Harder, Dan, '*The Tempest* in the Trivium'. Available online at: http://sycoraxcorax.com/_wsn/page4.html (accessed 6 January 2010).

Harmon, A. G., 'Shakespeare's Carved Saints', *SEL*, 45(2) (2005): 315–31.

Harris, Barbara, J., 'Women and Politics in Early Tudor England'. *The Historical Journal*, 33(2) (1990): 259–81.

Harris, Frank, *The Women of Shakespeare* (New York: Mitchell Kennerley, 1912).

Harris, Jonathan Gil, *Sick Economies: Drama, Mercantilism and Disease in Shakespeare's England* (Philadelphia, PA: University of Pennsylvania Press, 2003).

Hart, Elizabeth F., '"Great is Diana" of Shakespeare's Ephesus'. *SEL*, 43(2) (2003): 347–75.

Hartley, T. E. (ed.), *Proceedings in the Parliaments of Elizabeth I. Vol 1: 1558–1581* (Leicester: Leicester University Press, 1981).

Hartman, Joan E. and Adele Seeff (eds), *Structures and Subjectivities: Attending to Early Modern Women* (Newark, DE: University of Delaware Press, 2007).

Haslam, Lori Schroeder, '"O Me, the word Choose!": Female voice and catechical ritual in *The Two Gentlemen of Verona* and *The Merchant of Venice*'. *ShSt*, 22 (1994): 122–41.

Hattaway, Michael, '"Fleshing His Will in the Spoil of Her Honour": Desire, Misogyny and the perils of chivalry'. *ShS*, 46 (1994), pp. 121–36.

——(ed.), *The Cambridge Companion to Shakespeare's History Plays* (Cambridge: Cambridge University Press, 2002).

Hawkes, Terence (ed.), *Alternative Shakespeares 2* (London: Routledge, 1996).

Hayes, Elizabeth T. (ed.), *Images of Persephone: Feminist Readings in Western Literature* (Gainesville, FL: University of Florida Press, 1994).

Hayes, Janice, 'Those "soft and delicate desires": *Much Ado* and the Distrust of Women' in Carolyn Ruth Swift Lenz, Gayle Greene and Carol Thomas Neely (eds), *The Woman's Part: Feminist Criticism of Shakespeare* (Urbana, IL: University of Illinois Press, 1983), pp. 79–99.

Heal, Felicity 'Giving and Receiving on Royal Progress' in Jayne Elisabeth Archer, Elizabeth Goldring, Sarah Knight (eds), *The Progresses, Pageants & Entertainments of Queen Elizabeth I* (Oxford: Oxford University Press, 2007), pp. 46–62.

——*Hospitality in Early Modern England* (Oxford: Clarendon, 1990).

Hedley, Jane, *Power in Verse: Metaphor and Metonymy in the Renaissance Lyric* (University Park, PA: Penn State University Press, 2008).

Helgerson, Richard, *Adulterous Alliances: Home, State and History in Early Modern Drama and Painting* (Chicago, IL: University of Chicago Press, 2000).

Henderson, Diana E., 'The disappearing Queen: Looking for Isabel in *Henry V*' in Edward J. Esche (ed.), *Shakespeare and His Contemporaries in Performance* (Aldershot: Ashgate, 2000), pp. 339–55.

Hendricks, Margo, '"A word, sweet Lucrece": Confession, Feminism, and The Rape of Lucrece' in Callaghan (ed.), *A Feminist Companion to Shakespeare* (Oxford: Blackwell, 2000), pp. 103–18.

Henning, Standish, 'Branding harlots on the brow'. *SQ*, 51 (2000): 86–9.

Hennings, Thomas P., 'The Anglican Doctrine of Affectionate Marriage in *Comedy of Errors*'. *MLQ*, 47(2) (1986): 91–107.

Henryson, Robert, *The testament of Cresseid, compylit be M. Robert Henrysone, sculemaister in Dunfermeling* (Edinburgh, 1593).

Henslowe, Philip, *Henslowe's Diary*, 2nd ed., ed. R. A. Foakes (Cambridge: Cambridge University Press, 2002).

Herbert, Mary Sidney, Countess of Pembroke, *Antonius* (1592), in Margaret P. Hannay, Noel J. Kinnamon and Michael G. Brennan (eds), *Collected Works*, Vol. 2 (Oxford: Clarendon Press, 1998), pp. 152–206.

Heywood, Thomas, *The Brazen Age* (London: 1613).

——*The First and Second Parts of Edward the Fourth*, ed. Richard Rowland, Revels Plays (Manchester: Manchester University Press, 2009).

——*The General History of Women* (London: 1657).

——*The Golden Age* (London: 1611).

——*Gyneikon* (London: 1624).

—— *The Silver Age* (London: 1613).

Higgins, John, *The first part of the Mirour for Magistrates . . . The last parte of the Mirour for Magistrates . . . newly corrected and amended* (London: 1574).

Hill, James L., '"What, are they Children?" Shakespeare's Tragic Women and the Boy Actors'. *SEL*, 26(2) (1986): 235–58.

Hillman, David and Carla Mazzio (eds), *The Body in Parts: Fantasies of Corporeality in Early Modern Europe* (London: Routledge, 1997).

Hinds, Hilary, *Gods Englishwoman: Seventeenth-Century Radical Sectarian Writing and Feminist Criticism* (Manchester: Manchester University Press, 1996).

Hobby, Elaine (ed.), Jane Sharp, *The Midwives Book* (Oxford: Oxford University Press, 1999).

Hodgdon, Barbara, *The End Crowns All: Closure and Contradiction in Shakespeare's History* (Princeton, NJ: Princeton University Press, 1991).

Holbrook, David, *Images of Women in Literature* (New York: New York University Press, 1989).

Holland, Norman F., 'Hermia's Dream'. *Annual of Psychoanalysis* 7 (1979) 369–89, reprinted in Richard Dutton (ed.), *A Midsummer Night's Dream: Contemporary Critical Essays* (New Casebooks) (Houndmills, Basingstoke: Macmillan, 1996), pp. 61–84.

Holland, Peter, 'Theseus' Shadows in *A Midsummer Night's Dream*'. *ShS*, 47 (1994): 139–52.

Holland, Peter and Stephen Orgel (eds), *From Script to Stage in Early Modern England* (Basingstoke: Palgrave Macmillan, 2004).

Holmes, Clive, 'Women: Witnesses and Witches'. *Past and Present*, 140 (1993): 45–78.

Hopkins, Lisa, *The Shakespearean Marriage: Light Wives and Heavy Husbands* (Houndmills: Palgrave Macmillan, 1998).

Horrox, Rosemary, 'Elizabeth (1466–1503)', *Oxford Dictionary of National Biography* (Oxford: Oxford University Press, 2004). Available online at: http://www. oxforddnb.com/view/article/8635 (accessed 6 January 2010).

Hosley, Richard, 'How Many Children Had Lady Capulet?'. *SQ*, 18:1 (1967): 3–6.

Howard, Jean E., *The Stage and Social Struggle in Early Modern England* (London & New York, Routledge, 1994).

——*Theater of a City: The Places of London Comedy 1598–1642* (Philadelphia, PA: University of Pennsylvania Press, 2007).

Howard, Jean E. and Phyllis Rackin, *Engendering A Nation: A Feminist Account of Shakespeare's English Histories* (London: Routledge, 1997).

Howard, Jean E. and Scott Cutler Shershow (eds), *Marxist Shakespeares* (London: Routledge, 2001).

Huarte, Juan, *The examination of mens vvits . . . translated out of the Spanish tongue by M. Camillo Camili. Englished out of his Italian, by R.C. Esquire* (London: 1594).

Hughes-Hallett, Lucy, *Cleopatra: Queen, Lover and Legend* (London: Pimlico 1990).

Hull, Suzanne, *Chaste, Silent and Obedient: English Books for Women 1475–1640* (San Marino, CA: Huntingdon Library, 1982).

Hulse, S. Clark, 'Shakespeare's Myth of Venus and Adonis' *PMLA*, 93 (1978): 95–105.

Hunt, Maurice, 'The Double Figure of Elizabeth in *Love's Labour's Lost*'. *Essays in Literature*, 19(2) (1992): 173–92.

Hunter, Kelly, 'Constance in *King John*' in Robert Smallwood (ed.), *Players of Shakespeare 6* (Cambridge: Cambridge University Press, 2004), pp. 37–49.

Irigaray, Luce, 'Women in the Market' in Alan D. Schrift (ed.), *The Logic of the Gift* (London: Routledge, 1997): 174–89.

Jackson, Russell and Robert Smallwood (eds), *Players of Shakespeare 2* (Cambridge: Cambridge University Press, 1988).

——*Players of Shakespeare 3* (Cambridge: Cambridge University Press, 1993).

James VI of Scotland, I of England, *Daemonologie* (Edinburgh 1597; London 1603).

James, Heather, 'Cultural Disintegration in *Titus Andronicus*: Mutilating Titus, Vergil and Rome' in, Philip C Kolin (ed.), *Titus Andronicus: Critical Essays* (New York: Garland Publishing, 1995), pp. 285–304.

——'Dido's Ear: Tragedy and the Politics of Response'. *SQ*, 52(3) (2001): 360–82.

Jameson, Anna Murphy, *Shakespeare's Heroines: Characteristics of Women Moral, Poetical, and Historical*, ed. Chari L. Larsen Hoeckley (Peterborough, ON: Broadview, 2005).

Jankowski, Theodora A., 'Hymeneal Blood, Interchangeable Women and the Early Modern Marriage Economy in *Measure For Measure* and *All's Well That Ends Well*' in Richard Dutton and Jean E. Howard (eds), *A Companion to Shakespeare*, Vol. 4 (Oxford: Basil Blackwell, 2003), pp. 89–105.

——*Pure Resistance: Queer Virginity in Early Modern English Drama* (Philadelphia, PA: University of Pennsylvania Press, 2000).

——'"Where there can be no cause of affection": redefining virgins, their desires, and their pleasures in John Lyly's *Gallathea*' in Valerie Traub, M. Lindsay Kaplan and Dympna Callaghan (eds), *Feminist Readings of Early Modern Culture: Emerging Subjects* (Cambridge: Cambridge University Press, 1996), pp. 253–74.

——*Women in Power in the Early Modern Drama* (Urbana, IL: University of Illinois Press, 1992).

Jardine, Lisa, *Reading Shakespeare Historically* (London: Routledge, 1996).

——*Still Harping on Daughters: Women and Drama in the Age of Shakespeare*, 2nd ed. (London: Harvester Wheatsheaf, 1983).

Jed, Stephanie, *Chaste Thinking: The Rape of Lucrece and the Birth of Humanism* (Bloomington, IN: Indiana University Press, 1989).

Jenstad, Janelle, '"Smock-secrets": Birth and Women's Mysteries on the Early Modern Stage' in Kathryn M. Moncrief and Kathryn R. McPherson (eds), *Performing Maternity in Early Modern England* (Aldershot: Ashgate, 2007), pp. 87–100.

Jewel, John, *The second tome of homilees of such matters as were promised, and intituled in the former part of homilees. Set out by the aucthoritie of the Queenes Maiestie: and to be read in euery parishe church agreeably* (London: 1571).

Johnson, Richard, *A crowne garland of goulden roses Gathered out of Englands royall garden* (London: 1612).

Jones, Ann Rosalind, 'Maidservants of London: Sisterhoods of Kinship and Labor' in Susan Frye and Karen Robertson (eds), *Maids and Mistresses, Cousins and Queens* (Oxford: Oxford University Press, 1999), pp. 21–32.

Jones, Ann Rosalind and Peter Stallybrass, *Renaissance Clothing and the Materials of Memory* (Cambridge: Cambridge University Press, 2000).

Jones, Gemma, 'Hermione in *The Winter's Tale*' in Philip Brockbank (ed.), *Players of Shakespeare 1* (Cambridge: Cambridge University Press, 1985), pp. 153–66.

Jones, John, *The arte and science of preseruing bodie and soule in al health, wisedome, and catholike religion phisically, philosophically, and diuinely deuised* (London: 1579).

Jones, Norman, 'Shakespeare's England', in *A Companion to Shakespeare*, ed. David Scott Kastan (1999), pp. 25–42.

Jones, William M., 'William Shakespeare as William in *As You Like It*'. *SQ,* 11(2) (1960): 228–31.

Jones Davies, Margaret, '*Cymbeline* and the Sleep of Faith' in Richard Dutton, Alison Findlay and Richard Wilson (eds), *Theatre and Religion: Lancastrian Shakespeare* (Manchester: Manchester University Press, 2003), pp. 197–217.

Jonson, Ben, *The Alchemist*, ed. Richard Dutton (Revels Plays) (Manchester, Manchester University Press, forthcoming 2011).

——'The Masque of Queens' (1609), in David Lindley (ed.), *Court Masques* (Oxford: Oxford University Press, 1995), pp. 35–53.

—— *Volpone*, ed. Brian Parker (Revels Plays) (Manchester: Manchester University Press, 1999).

Johnston, Alexandra F., 'The Robin Hood of the Records', in Lois Potter (ed.),

Playing Robin Hood: The Legend as Performance over Five Centuries (London: Associated University Presses, 1998), pp. 27–44.

Kahan, Jeffrey, 'A Further Note on Semiramis'. *ANQ*, 18(2) (2005), pp. 27–8.

Kahane, Henry and Renée Kahane, 'Desdemona: A Star-Crossed Name'. *Names*, 35 (1987): 232–5.

Kahn, Coppélia, 'The Absent Mother in *King Lear*' in Margaret Ferguson, Maureen Quilligan and Nancy J. Vickers (eds), *Rewriting the Renaissance* (Chicago, IL: University of Chicago Press, 1986), pp. 33–49.

——'Magic and Bounty in *Timon of Athens*: Jacobean Patronage and Maternal Power' in Shirley Nelson Garner and Madelon Sprengnether (eds), *Shakespearean Tragedy and Gender* (Bloomington, IN: Indiana University Press, 1996), pp. 135–71.

——*Roman Shakespeare: Wounds, Warriors and Women* (London: Routledge, 1997).

Kastan, David Scott (ed.), *A Companion to Shakespeare* (Oxford: Blackwell, 1999).

Kathman, D., 'Grocers, Goldsmiths and Drapers: Freemen and Apprentices in the Elizabethan Theatre'. *SQ*, 55:1 (2004): 1–49.

——'How Old Were Shakespeare's Boy Actors?'. *ShS*, 59 (2005): 220–46.

Kaula, David, 'Autolycus's Trumpery'. *SEL*, 16 (1976): 287–303.

Keeble, N. H. (ed.), *The Cultural Identity of Seventeenth Century Woman* (London: Routledge, 1994).

Kegl, Rosemary, *The Rhetoric of Concealment: Figuring Gender and Class in Renaissance Literature* (Ithaca, NY: Cornell University Press, 1994).

Kehler, Dorothea, '"The Comedy of Errors" as Problem Comedy', *RMRLL*, 41(4) (1987): 229–40.

——'The First Quarto of *Hamlet*: Reforming Widow Gertred'. *SQ*, 46 (1995): 398–413.

——'Jacquenetta's Baby's Father: Recovering Paternity in *Love's Labour's Lost*' in Felicia Hardison Londré (ed.) *'Love's Labour's Lost': Critical Essays* (Shakespeare Criticism, 13) (New York, NY: Garland, 1997), pp. 305–12.

——'Shakespeare's *Cymbeline*'. *Explicator*, 54 (1996), pp. 70–3.

——'Shakespeare's Emilias and the Politics of Celibacy' in Dorothea Kehler and Susan Baker (eds), *In Another Country: Feminist Perspectives on Renaissance Drama* (Metuchen, NJ and London: Scarecrow Press, 1991), pp. 157–80.

Kehler, Dorothea and Susan Baker (eds), *In Another Country: Feminist Perspectives on Renaissance Drama* (Metuchen, NJ and London: Scarecrow Press, 1991).

Kelly, Philippa, 'Finding *King Lear*'s Female Parts' in Helen Wilcox and Douglas A Brooks (eds), *New Studies in the Shakespearean Heroine, Shakespeare Yearbook* 14 (2004), pp. 19–44.

Kelso, Ruth, *Doctrine for the Lady of the Renaissance* (Urbana, IL: University of Illinois Press, 1956).

Kennedy, Judith, and Richard F. Kennedy (eds), *Shakespeare, The Critical Tradition: A Midsummer Night's Dream* (London: Athlone, 1999).

Kiefer, Frederick, *Fortune and Elizabethan Tragedy* (San Marino, CA: Huntington Library, 1982).

——'Fortune and Providence in the *Mirror for Magistrates*'. *SP*, 74(2) (1977): 146–65.

——'"Written Troubles of the Brain": Lady Macbeth's Conscience' in David M. Bergeron (ed.), *Reading and Writing in Shakespeare* (Newark, NJ: University of Delaware Press, 1996), pp. 64–81.

Kietzman, Mary Jo, '"What is Hecuba to Him or [S]he to Hecuba?"'. *MP*, 91(1) (1999): 21–45.

King, Helen, *The Disease of Virgins: Green Sickness, Chlorosis and the Problem of Puberty* (London: Routledge, 2003).

King, Katherine Callen, 'Go to Hell Sycorax', *ELN*, 27(4) (1990): 1–3.

King, John, *Lectures vpon Ionas deliuered at Yorke in the yeare of our Lorde 1594*, newlie corrected and amended (London: 1594).

Kinney, Arthur, *Lies Like Truth: Shakespeare, Macbeth and the Cultural Moment* (Detroit, MI: Wayne State University Press, 2001).

Kinney, Clare R., 'Feigning Female Faining: Spenser, Lodge, Shakespeare and Rosalind', *MP*, 95 (1998): 291–315.

Klein, Joan Larsen, 'Lady Macbeth: "Infirm of Purpose"' in Carolyn Ruth Swift Lenz, Gayle Greene and Carol Thomas Neely (eds), *The Woman's Part: Feminist Criticism of Shakespeare* (Urbana, IL: University of Illinois Press, 1983), pp. 240–55.

Klein, Lisa M., '"Your Humble Handmaid": Elizabethan Gifts of Needlework'. *RQ*, 50 (1997): 459–93.

Kleiner, Diana E. E., *Cleopatra and Rome* (Cambridge, MA: Belknap, 2005).

Knowles, James, '"To Enlight the Darksome Night, Pale Cynthia Doth Arise": Anna of Denmark, Elizabeth I and the Images of Royalty' in Clare McManus (ed.), *Women and Culture at the Courts of the Stuart Queens* (Aldershot: Palgrave, 2003), pp. 21–48.

Knowles, Richard, 'Cordelia's Return'. *SQ*, 50 (1999): 33–51.

Ko, Yu Jin, 'The Comic Close of *Twelfth Night* and Viola's *Noli Me Tangere*'. *SQ*, 48(2) (2004): 391–405.

Kökeritz, Helge, 'Punning Names in Shakespeare'. *Modern Language Notes*, 65(4) (1950): 240–3.

Kolin, Philip C. (ed.), *Titus Andronicus: Critical Essays* (New York: Garland Publishing, 1995).

Komolós, Katalin, 'Viola's Willow Song: She Never Told Her Love'. *Musical Times*, 140(1868) (1999): 36–41.

Korda, Natasha, *Shakespeare's Domestic Economies: Gender and Property in Early Modern England* (Philadelphia, PA: University of Pennsylvania Press, 2002).

Krier, Theresa M., *Birth Passages: Maternity and Nostalgia, Antiquity to Shakespeare* (Ithaca, NY: Cornell University Press, 2001).

Kurtz, Martha A., 'Rethinking gender and genre in the history play'. *SEL*, 36(2) (1996): 267–88.

Kusunoki, Akiko, '"Oh most pernicious woman": Gertrude in the Light of Ideas on Remarriage in Early Seventeenth-Century England' in Uéno Yoshiko (ed.), *Hamlet and Japan* (New York: AMS Press, 1995), pp. 169–84.

Lambarde, William, *A perambulation of Kent; conteining the description, hystorie, and customes of that shyre* (London: 1596; reprinted London: Baldwin, Cradock and Joy, 1826).

The Lamentable Tragedy of Locrine (anon.) (London: 1595).

Lander, Bonnie, 'Interpreting the Person: Tradition, Conflict and *Cymbeline's* Imogen'. *SQ,* 59(2) (2008): 156–84.

Lanyer, Aemilia, *The Poems of Aemelia Lanyer,* ed. Susanne Woods (Oxford: Oxford University Press, 1993).

Laoutaris, Chris, *Shakespearean Maternities: Crises of Conception in Early Modern England* (Edinburgh: Edinburgh University Press, 2008).

Larner, Christina, *Witchcraft and Religion: The Politics of Popular Belief* (Oxford: Blackwell, 1984).

Larson, Jennifer, *Greek Nymphs: Myth, Cult, Lore* (Oxford: Oxford University Press, 2001).

Lasocki, David, with Roger Prior, *The Bassanoes: Venetian Musicians and Instrument Makers in London 1531–1665* (Aldershot: Ashgate, 2005).

Laurence, Anne, *Women in England 1500–1760* (London: Weidenfeld and Nicolson, 1994).

The Lawes Resolutions of Womens Rights [T[homas] E[dwards]] (London: 1632).

Lawner, Lynn, *Lives of the Courtesans: Portraits of the Renaissance* (Rizzoli, 1987).

Lecercle, Anne, 'Country House, Catholicity and the crypt(ic) in *Twelfth Night*' in Richard Dutton, Alison Findlay, and Richard Wilson (eds), *Religion, Region and Patronage: Lancastrian Shakespeare* (Manchester: Manchester University Press, 2003), pp. 84–100.

Lee, Patricia-Ann, 'Reflections of Power: Margaret of Anjou and the Dark Side of Queenship'. *RQ,* 39(2) (1986): 183–217.

Leggatt, Alexander, *Shakespeare's Political Drama: The History Plays and The Roman Plays* (London: Routledge, 1988).

Leigh, Dorothy, 'A Mother's Legacie 1616' in Sylvia Brown (ed.), *Women's Writing in Stuart England* (Stroud: Sutton, 1999).

Leininger, Lorie Jerrell, 'The Miranda Trap: Sexism and Racism in Shakespeare's *Tempest*' in Carolyn Ruth Swift Lenz, Gayle Greene and Carol Thomas Neely (eds), *The Woman's Part: Feminist Criticism of Shakespeare* (Urbana IL: University of Illinois Press, 1983): 285–94.

Lenton, Francis, *Characterisms: or Lentons Leasures* (London: 1631).

Lenz, Carolyn Ruth Swift, Gayle Greene and Carol Thomas Neely (eds), *The Woman's Part: Feminist Criticism of Shakespeare* (Urbana, IL and Chicago, IL: University of Illinois Press, 1983).

Leslie, Thomas 'The Theatrical Rhetoric of *Edward III*'. *Medieval and Renaissance Drama in English,* 15 (2002): 43–56.

Leverenz, David, *The Language of Puritan Feeling* (New Brunswick, NJ: Rutgers University Press, 1980).

Levin, Carole, *The Heart and Stomach of a King: Elizabeth I and the Politics of Sex and Power* (Philadelphia, PA: University of Pennsylvania Press, 1994).

Levin, Carole and Robert Bucholz (eds), *Queens and Power in Medieval and Early Modern England* (Lincoln, NE: University of Nebraska Press, 2009).

Levin, Carole, Jo Eldridge-Carney and Debra Barrett-Graves (eds), *Elizabeth I: Always Her Own Free Woman* (Aldershot: Ashgate 2003).

Levin, Richard, 'Did Helen Have a Renaissance?' *English Studies*, 87(1) (2006): 23–34.

——*Love and Society in Shakespearean Comedy: A Study of Dramatic Form and Content* (Newark, DE: University of Delaware Press, 1985).

Levine, Laura, *Men in Women's Clothing: Anti-theatricality and Effeminization 1579–1642* (Cambridge: Cambridge University Press, 1994).

Levine, Nina S., 'The case of Eleanor Cobham: Authorizing History in *2HVI*'. *ShS*, 22 (1994): 104–22.

Levy, Allison Mary (ed.), *Widowhood and Visual Culture in Early Modern Europe* (Aldershot: Ashgate, 2003).

Lewis, Cynthia, '"We know what we know": Reckoning in *Love's Labor's Lost*'. *SP*, 105 (2008): 245–64.

——'"With Simular Proof Enough": Modes of Misperception in *Cymbeline*'. *SEL*, 31(2) (1991): 343–64.

Lindheim, Nancy, 'Rethinking Sexuality and Class in *Twelfth Night*'. *University of Toronto Quarterly*, 76(2) (2007): 679–713.

Lindley, David (ed.), *Court Masques: Jacobean and Caroline Entertainments 1605–1640* (Oxford: Oxford University Press, 1995).

—— 'Music, masque and meaning in *The Tempest*' in *The Court Masque*, ed. David Lindley (Manchester: Manchester University Press, 1984), pp. 47–59.

——(ed.), *The Court Masque* (Manchester: Manchester University Press, 1984).

——*The Trials of Frances Howard: Fact and Fiction in the Court of King James* (London: Routledge, 1993).

Little Moreton Hall, Cheshire (National Trust Guidebook) (London: The National Trust, 1998).

Lloyd, Michael, 'Cleopatra as Isis'. *ShS*, 12 (1959): 88–94.

Lodge, Thomas, *Prosopopeia containing the teares of the holy, blessed, and sanctified Marie, the Mother of God* (London: 1596).

——*Rosalynde*, ed. Brian Nellist (Keele: Keele University Press, 1995).

The London prodigall As it was plaide by the Kings Maiesties seruants. By VVilliam Shakespeare (anon.) (London: 1605).

Loehlin, James N., *Henry V: Shakespeare in Performance* (Manchester: Manchester University Press, 1996).

Londré, Felicia Hardison (ed.), *"Love's Labour's Lost": Critical Essays* (Shakespeare Criticism, 13) (New York: Garland, 1997).

Lording, Barry, *Ram-Alley or Merry Tricks* (London: 1611).

Loscocco, Paula, 'Veiled Truths: Wives, Widows and Whores Early Modern Europe' in Joan E. Hartman and Adele Seeff (eds), *Structures and Subjectivities: Attending to Early Modern Women* (Newark, DE: University of Delaware Press, 2007), pp. 217–18.

Lloyd, Lodowick, *The Choyce of Iewels* (London: 1607).

Loughlin, Marie H., *Hymeneutics: Interpreting Virginity on the Early Modern Stage* (Lewisburg, PA: Bucknell University Press, 1997).

Lugo, Jessica, 'Blood, Barbarism and belly laughs: Shakespeare's *Titus* and Ovid's Philomela'. *English Studies*, 88(4) (2007): 410–17.

509

Lyly, John, *Endymion or the Man in the Moon* [1591], ed. David Bevington (Revels Plays) (Manchester: Manchester University Press, 1996).

——*Loue's metamorphosis* (1601), ed. Leah Scragg (Revels Plays) (Manchester: Manchester University Press, 2008).

—— *Midas* (1592), in *Galatea*, ed. George K. Hunter; *Midas*, ed. David Bevington (Revels Plays) (Manchester: Manchester University Press, 2008).

——*The Woman in the Moon* (c. 1595), ed. Leah Scragg (Revels Plays) (Manchester: Manchester University Press, 2006).

Maassen, Irmgard, 'Canonized by Love: Religious Rhetoric and Gender Fashioning in the Sonnet' in Suzanne Rupp and Tobias Doring (eds), *Performances of the Sacred in Late Medieval and Early Modern England* (Amsterdam: Rodopi, 2005), pp. 169–88.

MacDonald, Michael, *Mystical Bedlam: Madness, Anxiety and Healing in Seventeenth Century England* (Cambridge: Cambridge University Press, 1981).

MacKenzie, Clayton G., 'Fortuna in Shakespeare's Plays'. *Orbis Litterarum*, 56(5) (2001): 355–67.

Maguire, Laurie, *Shakespeare's Names* (Oxford: Oxford University Press, 2007).

Magnusson, A. L. and C. E. McGee (eds), *Elizabethan Theatre XIII* (Toronto, ON: Meany, 1994).

Mahood, M. M., *Playing Bit Parts in Shakespeare* (London: Routledge, 1998).

Mann, David, *Shakespeare's Women: Performance and Conception* (Cambridge: Cambridge University Press, 2008).

Marcus, Leah, 'The Shakespearean Editor as Shrew-Tamer'. *ELR*, 22 (1992): 177–200.

—— *Unediting the Renaissance: Shakespeare, Marlowe, Milton* (London: Routledge, 1996).

Markham, Gervase, *The English Housewife* (London: 1622).

——*Country Contentments* (London: 1615).

Marland, Hilary (ed.), *The Art of Midwifery: Early Modern Midwives in Europe* (London: Routledge, 1993).

Marlowe, Christopher, *Dido, Queen of Carthage* (London: 1594).

Marshall, Peter and Alexandra Walsham (eds), *Angels in the Early Modern World* (Cambridge: Cambridge University Press, 2006).

Marston, John, *The metamorphosis of pigmalion's image and other satires* (London: 1598).

—— *Antonio and Mellida* (London: 1602).

——*Antonio's Revenge*, ed. W. Reavley-Gair (Revels Plays) (Manchester: Manchester University Press, 1978).

——*Histrio-mastix* (London: 1610).

Martindale, Charles and Michelle, *Shakespeare and the Uses of Antiquity* (London: Routledge, 1990).

Mason, Pamela, '*Henry V*: 'the quick forge and working house of thought' in *The Cambridge Companion to Shakespeare's History Plays*, ed. Michael Hattaway (Cambridge: Cambridge University Press, 2002), pp. 177–92.

Masten, Jeffrey, '*Two Gentlemen of Verona*' in Richard Dutton and Jean E. Howard (eds), *A Companion to Shakespeare*, Vol. 3 (Oxford: Basil Blackwell, 2003), pp. 266–88.

Mauss, Marcel, *The Gift: The Form and Reason for Exchange in Archaic Societies*, translated by Ian Cunnison (London: Cohen and West, 1954).

Maxwell Baldwin, 'Hamlet's Mother'. *SQ*, 15 (1964): 235–46.

Mazzio, Carla Jane, 'The Sins of the Tongue', in David Hillman and Carla Mazzio (eds), *The Body in Parts: Fantasies of Corporeality in Early Modern Europe* (London: Routledge, 1997), pp. 53–79.

——*Slips of the Tongue: Rhetoric, Print and Speech in Early Modern England* (Cambridge, MA: Harvard University Press, 1998).

McEwin, Carole, 'Counsels of Gall and Grace: Intimate Conversations between women in Shakespeare's Plays' in Carolyn Ruth Swift Lenz, Gayle Greene and Carol Thomas Neely (eds), *The Woman's Part: Feminist Criticism of Shakespeare* (Urbana, IL: University of Illinois Press, 1983), pp. 117–32.

McGrady, Donald, 'The Topos of "Inversion of Values" in Hero's Description of Beatrice'. *SQ*, 44(4) (1993): 472–6.

McLuskie, Kathleen E., *Dekker and Heywood* (New York: St Martin's Press, 1994).

——'*Macbeth*, the Present and the Past' in Richard Dutton and Jean E. Howard (eds), *A Companion to Shakespeare*, Vol. 1 (Oxford: Basil Blackwell, 2003), pp. 393–410.

——*Renaissance Dramatists* (Brighton: Harvester Wheatsheaf, 1989).

McManus, Clare, 'Memorialising Anna of Denmark's Court: *Cupid's Banishment* at Greenwich Palace' in Clare McManus (ed.), *Women and Culture at the Courts of the Stuart Queens* (Houndmills, Basingstoke: Palgrave, 2003), pp. 81–99.

——*Women and Culture at the Courts of the Stuart Queens* (Houndmills, Basingstoke: Palgrave, 2003).

——*Women on the Renaissance Stage: Anna of Denmark and Female Masquing at the Stuart Court* (Manchester: Manchester University Press, 2002).

McMillin, Scott, 'The Sharer and His Boy: Rehearsing Shakespeare's Women' in Peter Holland and Stephen Orgel (eds), *From Script to Stage in Early Modern England* (Basingstoke: Palgrave Macmillan, 2004): 231–45.

McMullan, Gordon (ed.), *Henry VIII* (Arden Shakespeare) (London: Thomson, 2000).

McNamara, Kevin, 'Golden Worlds at Court: *The Tempest* and Its Masque'. *ShS*, 19 (1987): 183–203.

McNeill, Fiona, *Poor Women in Shakespeare* (Cambridge, Cambridge University Press, 2007).

McNeir, Waldo F., 'Comedy in Shakespeare's Yorkist Tetralogy', *Pacific Coast Philology* 9 (1974): 48–55.

——'The Role of Edmund in *King Lear*'. *SEL*, 8(2) (1968): 187–216.

Meakin, H. L., *John Donne's Articulations of the Feminine* (Oxford: Clarendon, 1998).

Meakin, Heather, *The Painted Closet of Lady Anne Bacon Drury* (Aldershot: Ashgate, 2008).

Melchiori, Giorgio (ed.), *King Edward III* (Cambridge: Cambridge University Press, 1998).

Mellencamp, Emma H., 'A Note on the Costume of Titian's *Flora*'. *The Art Bulletin*, 51(2) (1969): 174–7.

Mendelson, Sara and Patricia Crawford, *Women in Early Modern England* (Oxford: Clarendon, 1998).

Merriam, Thomas, 'The Old Lady or All is Not True'. *ShS*, 54 (2001): 234–46.

Metzger, Mary Janell, '"Now by my hood, a Gentle and no Jew": Jessica, *The Merchant of Venice* and the discourse of Early Modern English Identity'. *PMLA*, 113(1) (1998): 52–64.

Meyer, Rosalind S., '"The Serpent Under't": Additional Reflections on *Macbeth*'. *NQ*, 47(1) (2000): 86–91.

Micheli, Linda, '"Sit By Us": Visual Imagery and the Two Queens in *Henry VIII*'. *SQ*, 38(4) (1987): 452–66.

Middleton, Thomas, *The Collected Works*, ed. Gary Taylor and John Lavagnino (Oxford: Clarendon, 2007).

Mildmay, Grace (Lady), *With Faith and Physic: The Diary of a Tudor Gentlewoman 1552–1620*, ed. Linda Pollock (London: Collins and Brown, 1993).

Millard, Barbara C., 'Virago with a Soft Voice: Cordelia's Tragic Rebellion in *King Lear*'. *PQ*, 68(2) 2 (1989): 143–65.

Miller, Naomi and Naomi Yavneh (eds), *Maternal Measures: Figuring Caregiving in the Early Modern Period* (Aldershot: Ashgate, 2000).

——*Sibling Relations and Gender in the Early Modern World: Sisters, Brothers and Others* (Aldershot: Ashgate, 2006).

Miller, Patricia Cox, 'Is there a Harlot in this Text?: Early Modern Hagiography and the Grotesque'. *Journal of Medieval and Early Modern Studies*, 33(3) (2003): 419–36.

Millett, Kate, *Sexual Politics* (New York: Doubleday, 1970).

Minsheu, John, *Hegemon eis tas glossas, id est, Ductor in lingua; The guide into tongues* (London: 1617).

Moffett, Thomas, *The Silkwormes and their Flies* (London: 1599).

Mohler, Tina, '"What is thy body but a swallowing Grave": Desiring Underground in *Titus Andronicus*'. *SQ*, 57(1) (2006): 23–44.

Moncrief, Kathryn and Kanthryn R. McPherson (eds), *Performing Maternity in Early Modern England* (Aldershot: Ashgate, 2007).

Montrose, Louis Adrian, 'Elizabeth Through the Looking Glass: Picturing The Queen's Two Bodies' in Regina Schulte (ed.), *The Body of the Queen: Gender and Rule in the Courtly World* (Oxford: Berghahn, 2006), pp. 61–87.

——'The Place of a Brother in *As You Like It*: Social Process and Comic Form'. *SQ*, 32 (1981): 28–54.

——'"Shaping Fantasies": Figurations of Gender and Power in Elizabethan Culture' in Richard Dutton (ed.), *New Casebooks: A Midsummer Night's Dream* (Basingstoke: Macmillan, 1996), pp. 101–38.

Moore, Jeanie Grant, 'Queen of Sorrow, King Of Grief: Reflections and Perspectives in *Richard II*' in Dorothea Kehler and Susan Baker (eds), *In Another Country: Feminist Perspectives on Renaissance Drama* (1991) pp. 19–35.

——'Riddled Romance: Kingship and Kinship in *Pericles*'. *RMRLL* 57(1) (2003): 33–48.

Moore, Mary B., 'Wonder, Imagination and the Matter of Theatre in *The Tempest*'. *Philosophy and Literature*, 30 (2006): 496–511.

Morris, Harry, 'Some Uses of Angel Iconography in English Literature'. *Comparative Literature*, 10(1) (1958): 36–44.

Mortimer, Anthony, *Variable Passions: A Reading of Shakespeare's Venus and Adonis* (New York: AMS Press, 2000).

Moryson, Fynes, *An Itinerary of London* (London: 1617).

Mueller, Martin, *Children of Oedipus* (Toronto, ON: University of Toronto Press, 1980).

Muir, Kenneth, 'Pyramus and Thisbe: A Study in Shakespeare's Method', *SQ* 5 (1954): 141–53.

Mulcaster, Richard, *The Queen's Majesty's Passage through the City of London to Westminster the Day before Her Coronation* (1558), in *Renaissance Drama: An Anthology of Plays and Entertainments* ed. Arthur F. Kinney (Oxford: Blackwell Publishers, 1999), pp. 17–34.

Nahoum-Grappe, Veronique, 'The Beautiful Woman', translated by Arthur Goldhammer, in Natalie Zemon Davis and Arlette Farge (eds), *A History of Women in the West: Renaissance and Enlightenment Paradoxes* (Cambridge, MA: Belknap, 1993): 85–100.

Nashe, Thomas, *Have With You to Saffron Walden* (London: 1596).

——*Pierce Penilesse* (London: 1592).

Neely, Carol Thomas, *Broken Nuptials in Shakespeare's Plays* (Urbana, IL: University of Illinois Press, 1993).

——*Distracted Subjects: Madness and Gender in Shakespeare and Early Modern Cultures* (Ithaca, NY: Cornell University Press, 2004).

——'Documents in Madness: Reading Madness and Gender in Shakespeare's Tragedies and Early Modern Culture'. *SQ*, 42 (1991): 315–38.

——'Shakespeare's Women: Historical Facts and Dramatic Representations' in Norman H. Holland, Sidney Homan and Bernard J. Paris (eds), *Shakespeare's Personality* (Berkeley, CA: University of California Press, 1989), pp. 116–34.

Nelson, Jonathan Katz, *Leonardo et la reinvenzione de la figure femminile: Leda, Lisa e Maria* (Firenze: Commun di Vinci, 2007).

Nevo, Ruth, *Comic Transformations in Shakespeare* (London: Methuen, 1980).

Newcomb, Lori Humphrey, 'Unfolding the Shepherdess: A Revision of Pastoral' in Constance Caroline Relihan and Goran V. Stanivukovic (eds), *Prose Fiction and Early Modern Sexualities 1570–1640* (Basingstoke: Macmillan, 2004), pp. 235–55.

Newman, Jane O., '"And Let Mild Women to Him Lose Their Mildness": Philomela, Female Violence and Shakespeare's *The Rape of Lucrece*'. *SQ* 45(3) (1994): 304–26.

Newman, Karen, *Fashioning Femininity and English Renaissance Drama* (Chicago, IL: University of Chicago Press, 1991).

——'Portia's Ring: Unruly Women and the Structure of Exchange in *The Merchant of Venice*'. *SQ*, 38 (1987): 19–33.

Noling, Kim H., 'Grubbing Up The Stock: Dramatizing Queens in *Henry VIII*'. *SQ*, 39 (1988): 291–306.

Norberg, Kathryn, 'Prostitutes' in Natalie Zemon Davis and Arlette Farge (eds),

A History of Women: Renaissance and Enlightenment Paradoxes (Cambridge, MA: Belknap, 1993), pp. 458–74.

Oakley-Brown, Liz, '"My Lord Be Ruled by Me: Shakespeare's Tamora and the failure of queenship' in *The Ritual and Rhetoric of Queenship: Medieval to Early Modern* (Dublin: Four Courts, 2009), pp. 222–37.

——*Ovid and the Cultural Politics of Translation in Early Modern England* (Aldershot: Ashgate, 2006).

Oakley-Brown, Liz, and Louise Wilkinson (eds), *The Ritual and Rhetoric of Queenship: Medieval to Early Modern* (Dublin: Four Courts, 2009).

Oldfather, C. H. (trans.), *Diodorus of Sicily, Vol. II* (Cambridge, MA: Harvard University Press, 1935).

Orgel, Stephen, 'Gendering the Crown' in Margreta de Grazia, Maureen Quilligan and Peter Stallybrass (eds), *Subject and Object in Renaissance Culture* (Cambridge: Cambridge University Press, 1996a), pp. 133–65.

——*Impersonations: The Performance of Gender in Shakespeare's England* (Cambridge: Cambridge University Press, 1996b).

——'*Macbeth* and the Antic Round'. *ShS*, 26 (1999): 143–53.

——'Prospero's Wife' in Stephen Greenblatt (ed.), *Representing the English Renaissance* (Berkeley, CA: University of California Press, 1988), pp. 217–30.

—— (ed.), *The Tempest* (Oxford Shakespeare) (Oxford: Oxford University Press, 1987).

Ostovich, Helen, '"Here in this garden": The Iconography of the Virgin Queen' in Regina Buccola and Lisa Hopkins (eds), *Marian Moments in Early Modern Dram* (Aldershot: Ashgate, 2007), pp. 21–34.

Ostovich, Helen and Elizabeth Sauer, *Reading Early Modern Women: An Anthology of Texts in Manuscript and Print 1550–1700* (London: Routledge, 2004).

Overbury, Thomas, *Sir Thomas Overbury his wife . . . whereunto are annexed new newes and characters* (London: 1616).

Ovidius, Publius Naso, *Ovid's Metamorphoses, The Arthur Golding Translation*, ed. John Frederick Nims (Philadelphia, PA: Paul Dry, 2000).

——*Ouid's elegies three bookes, by C.M. Epigrames by I.D.* (London: 1603).

Pafford, J. H., 'Music and the Songs in *The Winter's Tale*'. *SQ*, 10(2) (1959): 161–75.

Page, Nadine, 'Beatrice: "My Lady Disdain"'. *MLN*, 50(8) (1935a): 494–9.

——'The Public Repudiation of Hero'. *PMLA*, 50(3) (1935b): 739–44.

Page, William, 'The Widdowe Indeed' Bodleian Library, Oxford, MS Bodl. 115 (c. 1620).

Palfrey, Simon, *Late Shakespeare: A New World of Words* (Oxford: Oxford University Press, 1997).

Palfrey, Simon and Tiffany Stern, *Shakespeare in Parts* (Oxford: Oxford University Press, 2007).

Palmer, D. J., '*Twelfth Night* and the Myth of Echo and Narcissus'. *ShS* 32 (1979): 73–98.

Palmer, Daryl W., *Hospitable Performances: Dramatic Genre and Cultural Practices in Early Modern England* (West Lafayette, IN: Purdue University Press, 1992).

Panek, Jennifer, *Widows and Suitors in Early Modern English Comedy* (Cambridge: Cambridge University Press, 2007).

Paris, Bernard J., *Bargains with Fate: Psychological Crises and Conflicts in Shakespeare and His Plays* (New York: Plenum, 1991).

Parker, Douglas H., 'Shakespeare's Female Twins in *Twelfth Night*: In defence of Olivia'. *English Studies in Canada*, 13 (1987): 23–34.

Parker, Patricia, *Literary Fat Ladies: Rhetoric, Gender, Property* (London: Methuen, 1987).

——'Proposterous Reversals: *Love's Labor's Lost*'. *MLQ*, 54 (1993): 435–83.

Parker, Patricia and Geoffrey Hartman (eds), *Shakespeare and the Question of Theory* (New York: Routledge, 1985).

Parker, Roszika, *The Subversive Stitch: Embroidery and the Making of the Feminine* (London: The Women's Press, 1984).

Paster, Gail Kern, *The Body Embarrassed: Drama and the Disciplines of Shame in Early Modern England* (Ithaca, NY: Cornell University Press, 1993).

Paster, Gail Kern, Mary Floyd-Wilson and Katherine Rowe (eds), *Reading the Early Modern Passions: Essays in the Cultural History of Emotion* (Philadelphia, PA: University of Pennsylvania Press, 2004).

Pearson, Jacqueline, 'Shakespeare and *Caesar's Revenge*'. *SQ*, 32(1) (1981): 101–4.

Pechter, Edward, 'Why Should We Call Her Whore? Bianca in *Othello*' in Jonathan Bate, Jill L. Levenson and Dieter Mehl (eds), *Shakespeare and the Twentieth Century* (Newark, DE: University of Delaware Press, 1998), pp. 364–77.

Peele, George, *The Arraignment of Paris* (London: 1584).

——*The Troublesome Reign of King John*, ed. Charles Forker (Revels Plays) (Manchester: Manchester University Press, forthcoming 2010).

Philip, Ranjini, 'The Shattered Glass: The Story of (O)phelia'. *Hamlet Studies*, 13 (1991): 73–84.

Phillips, Roderick, *Putting Asunder: A History of Divorce in Western Society* (Cambridge: Cambridge University Press, 1988).

Pisan, Christine de, *The Boke of the Cyte of Ladyes*, translated by Bryan Ansley (London: 1521).

Plato, *The Symposium*, trans. Walter Hamilton (Harmondsworth: Penguin Books, 1951).

Pliny the Elder, *Pliny's Historie of the world, commonly called the Natural historie* tr. p. Holland (London: 1601).

Prayers appointed to be used in the Church at Morning and Evening Prayer by Every Minister for the Queenes Safe Deliverance (London: 1605).

Prior, Mary (ed.), *Women in English Society 1500–1800* (London: Routledge, 1985).

The Problemes of Aristotle (London: 1595).

Plutarch, *Lives of the Noble Grecians and Romans Englished by Sir Thomas North* (London: 1579).

——*The Philosophie, commonlie called the Morals*, translated by Philemon Holland (London: 1603).

Pollock, Linda, *Forgotten Children: Parent Child Relations from 1500–1900* (Cambridge: Cambridge University Press, 1983).

515

Poole, Kristen, '"The Fittest Closet for All Goodness": Authorial Strategies of Jacobean Mothers' Manuals'. *SEL* 35(1) (1995): 69–88.

Potter, Lois (ed.), *Playing Robin Hood: The Legend as Performance in Five Centuries* (London, Associated University Presses, 1998).

——(ed.) *The Two Noble Kinsmen* (London: Thomson, 1997).

Purkiss, Diane, *The Witch in History: Early Modern and Twentieth Century Interpretations* (London: Routledge, 1996).

Raber, Karen, *Dramatic Difference: Gender, Class and Genre in the Early Modern Closet Drama* (Newark, DE: University of Delaware Press, 2001).

Rackin, Phyllis, *Shakespeare and Women* (Oxford: Oxford University Press, 2005).

——*Stages of History: Shakespeare's English Chronicles* (London: Routledge, 1990).

——'Women's roles in the Elizabethan history plays' in Michael Hattaway (ed.), *The Cambridge Companion to Shakespeare's History Plays* (Cambridge: Cambridge University Press, 2002), pp. 71–85.

Ralegh, Sir Walter, *The Discoverie of the Large, Rich and Bewtiful Empyre of Guiana* (1596), ed. Neil. L. Whitehead (Manchester: Manchester University Press, 1997).

Ranald, Margaret Loftus, '"As Marriage Binds, and Blood Breaks": English Marriage and Shakespeare'. *SQ,* 30(1) (1979): 68–81.

Ray, Sid, *Holy Estates: Marriage and Monarchy in Shakespeare and his Contemporaries* (Selinsgrove, PA: Susquehanna University Press, 2004).

Raynalde, Thomas, *The Birth of Mankynde, otherwyse named the womans booke* (London: 1565).

Record, Robert, *The Castle of Knowledge* (London: 1556).

Reeves, W. P., 'Shakespeare's Queen Mab' *MLN*, 17 (1) (1902), 10–14.

Reid, Robert Lanier, *Shakespeare's Tragic Form: Spirit in the Wheel* (Newark, DE: University of Delaware Press, 2000).

Relihan, Constance Caroline, and Goran V. Stanivukovic (eds), *Prose Fiction and Early Modern Sexualities 1570–1640* (Basingstoke: Macmillan, 2004).

Reiter, Rayna, R. (ed.), *Toward an Anthropology of Women* (New York: Monthly Review Press, 1975).

Rhodes, Neil, *Shakespeare and the Origins of English* (Oxford: Oxford University Press, 2004).

Richmond, Hugh, 'The Dark Lady as Reformation Mistress'. *Kenyon Review,* 8 (1986) 91–105.

Riddell, James A., 'Talbot and the Countess of Auvergne'. *SQ,* 28(1) (1977): 51–7.

Ripley, John, *Coriolanus on Stage in England and America 1609–1994* (Madison, NJ: Fairleigh Dickinson University Press, 1998).

Roberts, Jeanne Addison, *Shakespeare's English Comedy: 'The Merry Wives of Windsor' in Context* (Princeton, NJ: Princeton University Press, 1962).

——*The Shakespearean Wild: Geography, Genus and Gender* (Lincoln, NB: University of Nebraska Press, 1991).

——'"Wife" or "Wise" – *The Tempest* l. 1786'. *University of Virginia Studies in Bibliography,* 31 (1978): 203–8.

Robertson, Elizabeth and Christine M. Rose (eds), *Representing Rape in Medieval and Early Modern Literature* (Basingstoke: Palgrave Macmillan, 2001).

Robertson, Karen, 'A Feminine Revenging Hand in *Twelfth Night*' in David M. Bergeron (ed.), *Reading and Writing in Shakespeare* (Newark, DE: University of Delaware Press, 1996), pp. 116–30.

Robinson, Richard, *A Moral Method of Civil Policie* (London: 1576).

Rogers, Thomas, *Celestial Elegies of the Goddesses and the Muses* (London: 1598).

Romanska, Magda, 'Ontology and Eroticism: The Two Bodies of Ophelia'. *Women's Studies*, 34(6) (2005): 485–513.

Rose, Mary Beth, '"Where Are the Mothers in Shakespeare?" Options for Gender Representation in the English Renaissance'. *SQ*, 42(3) (1991): 291–314.

Rosen, Barbara (ed.), *Witchcraft in England 1558–1618* (Amherst, MA: University of Massachusetts Press, 1991).

Rosenberg, Marvin, *The Masks of Macbeth* (Berkeley, CA: University of California Press, 1978).

Rosenthal, Margaret F., 'Cutting a good figure: The fashions of Venetian courtesans in the illustrated albums of early modern travelers', in Martha Feldman and Bonnie Gordon (eds), *The Courtesan's Arts: Cross-Cultural Perspectives* (Oxford: Oxford University Press, 2006), pp. 52–74.

——*The Honest Courtesan: Veronica Franco, citizen and writer in sixteenth century Venice* (Chicago, IL: University of Chicago Press, 1992).

Rowe, Katherine, 'Dismembering and Forgetting in *Titus Andronicus*'. *SQ*, 45(3) (Autumn, 1994), 279–303.

——'Humoural Knowledge and Liberal Cognition in Davenant's *Macbeth*' in Gail Kern Paster, Mary Floyd Wilson and Katherine Rowe (eds), *Reading the Early Modern Passions: Essays in the Cultural History of Emotion* (Philadelphia, PA: University of Pennsylvania Press, 2004), pp. 169–91.

Rowlands, Samuel, *The Bride* (London: 1617).

Rowse, A. L., *The Poems of Shakespeare's Dark Lady* (London: Cape, 1978).

Rubin, Gayle, 'The Traffic in Women: Notes on the "Political Economy" of Sex' in Rayna R. Reiter (ed.), *Toward an Anthropology of Women* (New York: Monthly Review Press, 1975): 157–210.

Rutter, Carol, *Clamorous Voices: Shakespeare's Women Today*, ed. Faith Evans (London: Women's Press, 1988).

——*Enter the Body: Women and Representation on Shakespeare's Stage* (London: Routledge, 2001).

——'Of tygers' hearts and players' hides', in Dermot Cavanagh, Stuart Hampton-Reeves and Stephen Longstaffe (eds), *Shakespeare's Histories and Counter-Histories* (Manchester: Manchester University Press, 2006), pp. 182–97.

Sachdev, Rachana, 'Sycorax in Algiers: Cultural Politics and Gynecology in Early Modern England' in Callaghan (ed.), *A Feminist Companion to Shakespeare* (Oxford: Blackwell, 2000), pp. 208–25.

Sales, Roger (ed.), *Shakespeare In Perspective*, Vol. 2 (London: British Broadcasting Association and Ariel Books, 1985).

Saltonstall, Wye, *Picturae Loquentes or pictures drawne forth in characters* (London: 1635).

Sanchez, Melissa E., 'Seduction and Service in *The Tempest*'. *SP*, 105(1) (2008) 50–82.

Santore, Cathy, 'Julia Lombardo, "Somtusoa Meretrize": A Portrait by Property'. *RQ*, 41(1) (Spring, 1988): 44–83.

Sardona, Mark 'Patience and the Agents of Renaissance Drama, unpublished dissertation (Harvard University Press, 1989); extracted essay 'Patientia Regina: Patience as Character from the Morality Play to Jacobean Tragedy' is available online at the Centre for Medieval and Renaissance Studies (Los Angeles, University of California), http://repositories.cdlib.org/cgi/viewcontent.cgi?article=1129&context=cmrs/comitatus

Savage, Roger, 'Dido Dies Again' in Michael Burden (ed.), *A Woman Scorn'd: Responses to the Dido Myth* (London: Faber and Faber, 1998), pp. 3–38.

Sawday, Jonathan, *The Body Emblazoned* (London: Routledge, 1995).

Scarisbrick, Diana, *Jewellery in Britain 1066–1837* (Wilby: Michael Russell, 1994).

Schafer, Elizabeth, *Ms-Directing Shakespeare* (London: The Women's Press, 1998).

Schnell, Lisa, 'Breaking the "rule of Cortezia": Aemilia Lanier's Dedications to *Salve Deus Rex Judaeorum*'. *Journal of Medieval and Early Modern Studies*, 27(1) (1997): 77–101.

Schoenbaum, Samuel, *William Shakespeare: A Compact Documentary Life*, revised ed. (Oxford: Oxford University Press, 1987).

Schofield, R., 'Did the Mothers Really Die? Three Centuries of Maternal Mortality in "The World We Have Lost"' in L. Bonfield, R. M. Smith and K. Wrightson (eds), *The World We Have Gained: Histories of Population and Social Structure* (Oxford: Blackwell, 1986).

Schrift, Alan D. (ed.), *The Logic of the Gift* (London: Routledge, 1997).

Regina Schulte (ed.), *The Body of the Queen: Gender and Rule in the Courtly World* (Oxford: Berghahn, 2006).

Schulz, M., 'The Semantic Derogation of Women' in Barrie Thorne and Nancy Henley (eds), *Language and Sex Difference and Dominance* (Rowley, MA: Newberry House, 1975), pp. 64–73.

Schwartz, Kathryn, *Tough Love: Amazon Encounters in the English Renaissance* (Durham and London: Duke University Press, 2000).

Scot, Thomas, *The second part of Philomythie, or Philomythologie* (London: 1616).

Scott, Maria Margaret, *Representing 'Jane Shore': Harlot and Heroine* (Aldershot: Ashgate, 2005).

Sedinger, Tracy, 'Working Girls: Status and Sexual Difference' in Laurel Amtower and Dorothea Kehler (eds), *The Single Woman in Medieval and Early Modern England* (Medieval and Renaissance Texts and Studies) (Tempe, AZ: Center for Medieval and Renaissance Studies, 2003), pp. 167–91.

Semenza, Gregory M. Colon, 'Sport, War and Contest in Shakespeare's *Henry VI*'. *RQ*, 54(4) (2001): 1251–72.

Seneca, *Seneca His Tenne Tragedies*, translated by John Studley (London: 1581).

Sengupta, Debjani, 'Playing the Canon: Shakespeare and the Bengali Actress in Nineteenth-Century Calcutta' in Poonam Trivedi and Dennis Bartholomeusz (eds), *India's Shakespeare: Translation, Interpretation and Performance* (Dehli: Pearson Education and Dorling Kindserley, 2006), pp. 216–31.

Shalivi, Alice, *The Relationship of Renaissance Concepts of Honour to Shakespeare's Problem Plays* (Salzberg: University of Salzberg, 1972).

Shand, G. B., 'Realising Gertrude: The Suicide Option' in A. L. Magnusson and C. E. McGee (eds), *Elizabethan Theatre XIII* (Toronto, ON: Meany, 1994), pp. 95–118.

Shannon, Laurie J., *Sovereign Amity: Figures of Friendship in Shakespearean Contexts* (Chicago, IL: University of Chicago Press, 2002).

Shapiro, Michael, *Gender in Play on the Shakespearean Stage: Boy Heroines and Female Pages* (Ann Arbor, MI: University of Michigan Press, 1996).

Sharp, Jane, *The Midwives Book*, ed. Elaine Hobby (Oxford: Oxford University Press, 1999).

Sharpe, James, *Instruments of Darkness: Witchcraft in England 1550–1750* (London: Hamish Hamilton, 1996).

Sharpham, Edward, *The Fleire* (London: 1607).

Shaw, Fiona and Juliet Stevenson, 'Celia and Rosalind in *As You Like It*', in Russell Jackson and Robert Smallwood (eds), *Players of Shakespeare 2* (Cambridge: Cambridge University Press, 1988), pp. 55–71.

Shephard, Amanda, *Gender and Authority in Sixteenth Century England: The Knox Debate* (Keele: Ryburn and Keele University Press, 1994).

Shepherd, Simon, *Amazons and Warrior Women: Varieties of Feminism in Seventeenth Century Drama* (Brighton: Harvester, 1981).

Shleiner, Winifred, 'Orsino and Viola: Are the Names of Serious Characters in *Twelfth Night* Meaningful?'. *ShSt*, 16 (1983): 135–42.

Showalter, Elaine, 'Representing Ophelia: women, madness and the responsibilities of feminist criticism' in Patricia Parker and Geoffrey Hartman (eds), *Shakespeare and the Question of Theory* (New York: Routledge, 1985), pp. 77–94.

Sidney, Philip, *The Countesse of Pembrokes Arcadia* (London: 1593).

Simard, Rodney (1986), 'Source and *Antony and Cleopatra*: Shakespeare's Adaptation of Plutarch's Octavia'. *Shakespeare Jahrbuch* 122 (1986): 65–74.

Simonds, Peggy Munoz, *Myth, Emblem and Music in Shakespeare's 'Cymbeline': An Iconographic Reconstruction* (Newark, DE: Delaware University Press, 1991).

——'"To the very heart of loss": Renaissance Iconography in *Antony and Cleopatra*'. *SQ*, 22 (1994): 220–76.

Singh, Jyotsna G., 'Gendered "Gifts" in Shakespeare's Belmont: The Economics of Exchange in Early Modern England' in Dympna Callaghan (ed.), *A Feminist Companion to Shakespeare* (Oxford: Blackwell, 2000), pp. 144–59.

——'A Politics of Empathy in *Antony and Cleopatra*: A View From Below' in Richard Dutton and Jean E. Howard (eds), *A Companion to Shakespeare's Works*, Vol. 1 (Oxford: Basil Blackwell, 2003), pp. 411–29.

——'Race and gender conflict in postcolonial readings of *The Tempest*' in Valerie Traub, M. Lindsay Kaplan and Dympna Callaghan (eds) *Feminist Readings of Early*

Modern Culture: Emerging Subjects (Cambridge: Cambridge University Press, 1996), pp. 191–209.

Slights, Camille, 'In Defence of Jessica: The Runaway Daughter in *The Merchant of Venice*'. *SQ,* 31 (1980): 357–68.

Slights, Jessica, 'Rape and the Romanticisation of Shakespeare's Miranda'. *SEL,* 41(2) (2001): 357–70.

Slights, Jessica and Michael Morgan Holmes, 'Isabella's Order: Religious acts and personal desires in *Measure for Measure*'. *SP,* 95(3) (1995): 263–93.

Smallwood, Robert (ed.), *Players of Shakespeare 5* (Cambridge: Cambridge University Press, 2005).

——*Players of Shakespeare 6* (Cambridge: Cambridge University Press, 2004).

Smith, Henry, *A Preparative to marriage* (London: 1591).

——*The Sermons of Maister Henrie Smith* (London: 1593).

Smith, Rebecca, '"A Heart Cleft in Twain": The Dilemma of Shakespeare's Gertrude' in Carolyn Ruth Swift Lenz, Gayle Greene and Carol Thomas Neely (eds), *The Woman's Part* (Urbana and Chicago, IL: University of Illinois Press, 1983), pp. 194–210.

Snyder, Susan, '*All's Well that Ends Well* and Shakespeare's Helens: Text and Subtext, Subject and Object'. *ELR,* 18 (1988) 66–77.

——'Naming Names in *All's Well That Ends Well*'. *SQ,* 43 (1992): 265–79.

Sokol, B. J. and Mary Sokol, *Shakespeare, Law and Marriage* (Cambridge University Press, 2003).

Spacks, Patricia M., *Gossip* (Chicago, IL: University of Chicago Press, 1985).

Spaeth, Barbette Stanley, *The Roman Goddess Ceres* (Austin, TX: University of Texas Press, 1996).

Spence, Richard T., *Lady Anne Clifford* (Stroud: Sutton, 1997).

Spenser, Edmund, *Poetical Works*, ed. J. C. Smith and E. De Selincourt (Oxford: Oxford University Press, 1970).

Spurgeon, Caroline, *Shakespeare's Imagery and What it Tells Us* (Cambridge: Cambridge University Press, 1935).

Stallybrass, Peter (1992), 'Transvestism and the "body beneath": speculating on the boy actor' in Susan Zimmerman (ed.), *Erotic Politics: Desire on the Renaissance Stage* (London: Routledge, 1992), pp. 64–83.

Stanton, Kay, '"Made to write 'whore' upon?": Male and Female Use of the Word "Whore" in Shakespeare's Canon' in Dympna Callaghan (ed.), *A Feminist Companion to Shakespeare* (Oxford: Blackwell, 2000), pp. 80–102.

Stapleton, M. L., '"My False Eyes": The Dark Lady and Self Knowledge'. *SP,* 90 (1993): 213–30.

——'"Shine like a comet of revenge": Seneca, John Studley and Shakespeare's Joan La Pucelle'. *CLS,* 31(3) (1994) 229–51.

Staub, Susan C., 'Early Modern Medea: Representations of Child Murder in Street Literature of Seventeenth Century England' in Naomi Miller and Naomi Yavneh (eds), *Maternal Measures: Figuring Caregiving in the Early Modern Period* (Aldershot: Ashgate, 2000), pp. 333–47.

Steible, Mary, 'Jane Shore and the Politics of Cursing'. *SEL,* 43(1) (2003), pp. 1–17.

Stephens, John, *Essayes and Characters* (London: 1615).

Stockholder, Katherine, 'The Other Coriolanus'. *PMLA*, 85(2) (1970), 228–36.

Stone, Lawrence *The Road to Divorce: England 1530–1987* (Oxford: Oxford University Press, 1990).

Stopes, C. C., *Shakespeare's Environment*, 2nd ed. (London: Bell, 1918).

Strasser, Ulrike, *State of Virginity: Gender, Religion and Politics in an Early Modern Catholic State* (Ann Arbor, MI: University of Michigan Press, 2004).

Strong, Sir Roy, *The Cult of Elizabeth: Elizabethan Portraiture and Pageantry* (Berkeley and Los Angeles, CA: University of California Press, 1977).

Stubbes, Philip, *The Anatomie of Abuses* (London: 1595).

Suzuki, Mihoko, 'Gender, Class and the Ideology of Comic Form: *Much Ado About Nothing* and *Twelfth Night*' in Dympna Callaghan (ed.), *A Feminist Companion to Shakespeare* (Oxford: Blackwell, 2000), pp. 121–43.

Symons, Julian, '*Macbeth*' in *Shakespeare in Perspective*, Vol. 2, ed. Roger Sales (London: Ariel Books, British Broadcasting Coroporation, 1985), pp. 167–73.

Synnott, Anthony, 'Truth and Goodness, Mirrors and Masks – Part I: A Sociology of Beauty and the Face'. *British Journal of Sociology*, 40(4) (1989): 607–36.

Taylor, A. B., 'Golding and the Myth Underlying Hermia's Dream'. *NQ*, 50(1) (2003): 31–2.

——'John Gower and "Pyramus and Thisbe"'. *NQ*, 54 (2007, September): 282–3.

——(ed.) *Ovid's Metamorphoses* (Cambridge: Cambridge University Press, 2000).

Thomas, Catherine, 'Nunn's Sweet Transvestite: Desiring Viola in *Twelfth Night*'. *Journal of Popular Culture* 41(2) (2008): 306–20.

Thomas, Keith, *Religion and the Decline of Magic: Studies in Popular Beliefs in Sixteenth and Seventeenth Century England* (London: 1971).

Thomkins, Thomas, *Lingua or the Combat of the Tongue and the Five Senses for Superiority* (London: 1607).

Thompson, Ann, 'Feminist Theory and the Editing of Shakespeare: *The Taming of the Shrew* Revisited' in Kate Chegdzoy (ed.), *Shakespeare, Feminism and Gender: Contemporary Critical Essays* (New Casebooks) (Houndmills, Basingstoke: Palgrave, 2001), pp. 49–69.

——'Person and Office: The Case of Imogen, Princess of Britain' in Vincent Newey and Ann Thompson (eds), *Literature and Nationalism* (Liverpool University Press, 1990), pp. 79–86.

——'Philomel in *Titus Andronicus* and *Cymbeline*'. *ShS*, 31 (1978): 23–32.

Thompson, Ann, and Sasha Roberts (eds), *Women Reading Shakespeare 1660–1900: An Anthology of Criticism* (Manchester: Manchester University Press, 1997).

Thomson, Peter, *Shakespeare's Theatre*, 2nd ed. (London: Routledge, 1983).

Tigner, Amy L., '*The Winter's Tale*: Gardens and the Marvels of Transformation', *ELR*, 36 (1) (2006): 113–34.

Tilley, Morris P., *A Dictionary of the Proverbs in England in the Sixteenth and Seventeenth Centuries* (Ann Arbor, MI: University of Michigan Press, 1950).

Tobin, J. J. M., 'The Irony of Hermia and Helena'. *ANQ*, 17(10) (1979): 154–6.

Todd, Barbara J., 'The remarrying Widow: a stereotype reconsidered' in Mary Prior (ed.), *Women in English Society 1500–1800* (London: Routledge, 1985), pp. 54–92.

——'The Virtuous Widow in Protestant England' in Sandra Cavallo and Lyndan Warner (eds), *Widowhood in Medieval and Early Modern Europe* (Harlow: Pearson, 1999), pp. 66–83.

Topsell, Edward, *Historie of Serpents* (London: 1608).

Tracy, Robert, 'The Owl and the Baker's Daughter: A Note on *Hamlet* 4.5.42–3'. *SQ,* 17(1) (1966): 83–6.

The Tragedy of Caesar and Pompey, or Caesar's Revenge (London, c. 1592).

Traub, Valerie, *Desire and Anxiety: Circulations of Sexuality in Shakespeaean Drama* (London: Routlege, 1992).

——*The Renaissance of Lesbianism in Early Modern England* (Cambridge: Cambridge University Press, 2002).

Travitsky, Betty, ed., *Subordination and Authorship in Early Modern England: The Case of Elizabeth Cavendish Egerton and Her "Loose Papers"* (Tempe, Arizona: Arizona Center for Medieval and Renaissance Studies, 1999).

——*The Paradise of Women: Writings by Englishwomen of the Renaissance* (New York: Columbia University Press, 1989).

Trivedi, Poonam and Dennis Bartholomeusz (eds), *India's Shakespeare: Translation, Interpretation and Performance* (Dehli: Pearson Education, Dorling Kindserley, 2006).

The True Ophelia: And Other studies of Shakespeare's Women by An Actress (anon) (London and Toronto, ON: Sidgwick and Jackson, 1913).

Truebowitz, Rachel, '"But Blood Whitened": Nursing Mothers and Others in Early Modern Britain' in Naomi Miller and Naomi Yavneh (eds), *Maternal Measures: Figuring Caregiving in the Early Modern Period* (Aldershot: Ashgate, 2000), pp. 82–101.

Trusser, Thomas, *Five hundreth pointes of good husbandrie* (1573).

Tvordi, Jessica, 'Female Alliance and the Construction of Homoeroticism in *As You Like It* and *Twelfth Night*' in Susan Frye and Karen Robertson (eds), *Maids and Mistresses, Cousins and Queens: Women's Alliances in Early Modern England* (Oxford: Oxford University Press, 1999), pp. 114–30.

Twine, Thomas, *The Patterne of Paineful Adventures* (London: 1594).

Twycross, Meg and Sarah Carpenter, *Masks and Masking in Medieval and Early Tudor England* (Aldershot: Ashgate, 2002).

Underdown, D. E., 'The Taming of the Scold: The Enforcement of Patriarchal Authority in Early Modern England' in Anthony Fletcher and John Stevenson (eds), *Order and Disorder in Early Modern England* (Cambridge: Cambridge University Press, 1987), pp. 116–36.

Valbuena, Olga L., *Subjects to the King's Divorce: Equivocation, Infidelity and Resistance in Early Modern England* (Bloomington, IN: Indiana University Press, 2003).

Van Kessel, Elisja Schulte, 'Virgins and Mothers between Heaven and Earth', translated by Clarissa Botsford, in Natalie Zemon Davis and Arlette Farge (eds), *A*

History of Women in the West: Renaissance and Enlightenment Paradoxes (Cambridge, MA: Belknap Press of Harvard University Press, 1993), pp. 132–66.

Van Wyhe, Cordula (ed.), *Female Monasticism in Early Modern Europe: An Interdisciplinary View* (Aldershot: Ashgate, 2008).

Vanita, Ruth, 'Mariological Memory in *The Winter's Tale* and *Henry VIII*'. *SEL*, 40(2) (2000): 311–37.

Vaughan, Virginia Mason, '*King John*' in Richard Dutton and Jean E. Howard (eds), *A Companion to Shakespeare*, Vol. 2 (Oxford: Basil Blackwell, 2003), pp. 379–94.

Veliz, Zahira, 'Signs of Identity in "Lady With A Fan" by Diego Velázquez: Costume and Likeness Reconsidered'. *The Art Bulletin*, 8691 (2004), pp. 75–95.

Velz, John, 'The Ovidian Soliloquy in Shakespeare'. *ShSt*, 18 (1986): 1–24.

Vendler, Helen, *The Art of Shakespeare's Sonnets* (Boston, MA: Harvard University Press, 1999).

Vickers, Diana, '"The blazon of sweet beauty's best": Shakespeare's *Lucrece*' in P. Parker and G. Hartman (eds), *Shakespeare and the Question of Theory* (1985), pp. 95–115.

Virgil, *Aeneid*, translated by Thomas Phaer and Thomas Twyne (London: 1584).
——*The xiii. bukes of Eneados of the famose poete Virgill translatet out of Latyne verses into Scottish metir, bi the Reuerend Father in God, Mayster Gawin Douglas* (1553).

Vives, Jean Luis, *The Instruction of A Christian Woman*, translated by Richard Hyrde (London: 1529).

Vredeveld, Harry, 'Deaf as Ulysses to the Sirens' Song: The Story of A Forgotten Topos'. *RQ*, 54(3) (2001): 846–82.

Wade, Mara R., 'The Queen's Courts: Anna of Denmark and her Royal Sisters – Cultural Agency at Four Northern European Courts in the Sixteenth and Seventeenth Centuries' in Clare McManus (ed.), *Women and Culture at the Courts of the Stuart Queens* (Houndmills, Basingstoke: Palgrave, 2003), pp. 49–80.

Waites, Zoe, and Matilda Ziegler, 'Viola and Olivia in *Twelfth Night*' in Robert Smallwood (ed.), *Players of Shakespeare 5* (Cambridge: Cambridge University Press, 2003), pp. 60–73.

Waith, Eugene M., 'The Metamorphosis of Violence in *Titus Andronicus*'. *ShS*, 20 (1957): 39–49.

Walker, Claire, *Gender and Politics in Early Modern Europe: English Convents in France and the Low Countries* (Houndmills, Basingstoke: Palgrave McMillan, 2003).

Wall, Wendy, '*The Merry Wives of Windsor*: Unhusbanding Desires in Windsor' in Richard Dutton and Jean E. Howard (eds), *A Companion to Shakespeare*, Vol. 3 (Oxford: Basil Blackwell 2003), pp. 376–92.

Walter, Harriet, 'Imogen in *Cymbeline*' in Russell Jackson and Robert Smallwood (eds), *Players of Shakespeare 3* (Cambridge: Cambridge University Press, 1993), pp. 201–19.

Walthaus, Rina and Marguérite Corporaal (eds), *Heroines of the Golden StAge: Women and Drama in Spain and England 1500–1700* (Kassel: Edition Reichenberger, 2008).

Wanamaker, Zoe, 'Viola in *Twelfth Night*' in Russell Jackson and Robert Smallwood (eds), *Players of Shakespeare 2* (Cambridge: Cambridge University Press, 1988), pp. 81–92.

Warner, Marina, *Monuments and Maidens: The Allegory of the Female Form* (London: Picador, 1985).

Warren, Roger (ed.), *Cymbeline* (Oxford Shakespeare) (Oxford: Clarendon Press, 1988).

Watson, Curtis Brown, *Shakespeare and the Renaissance Concept of Honor* (Princeton, NJ: Princeton University Press, 1960).

Watson, Robert and Stephen Dickey, 'Wherefore art thou Tereus? Juliet and the Legacy of Rape'. *RQ*, 58(1) (2005): 127–56.

Watt, Diane, *Secretaries of God: Women Prophets in Lady Medieval and Early Modern England* (Woodbridge, Suffolk: Boydell and Brewer, 2001).

Wayne, Valerie, 'Historical Differences: Misogyny and *Othello*' in Valerie Wayne (ed.), *The Matter of Difference: Materialist Feminist Criticism of Shakespeare* (New York: Harvester Wheatsheaf, 1991), pp. 153–80.

Wayne, Valerie (ed.), *The Matter of Difference: Materialist Feminist Criticism of Shakespeare* (New York: Harvester Wheatsheaf, 1991).

Weaver, Elissa B., *Convent Theater in Early Modern Italy: Spiritual Fun and Learning for Womem* (Cambridge: Cambridge University Press, 2002).

Weimann, Robert, 'Mingling Vice and "Worthiness" in *King John*'. *ShSt*, 27 (1999): 109–34.

Weis, René, *Shakespeare Revealed: A Biography* (London: John Murray, 2007).

Wells, Stanley, 'Boys Should be Girls: Shakespeare's Female Roles and the Boy Players'. *New Theatre Quarterly*, 25(2) (2009): 172–7.

——'Juliet's Nurse: the uses of inconsequentiality', in Philip Edwards, Inga-Stina Ewbank and G. K. Hunter (eds) *Shakespeare's Styles: Essays in Honour of Kenneth Muir* (Cambridge: Cambridge University Press, 1980), pp. 51–66.

Whateley, William, *A Bride Bush* (London: 1617).

White, R. S., *Innocent Victims: Poetic Injustice in Shakespearean Tragedy* (London: Athlone, 1986).

——'Marx and Shakespeare'. *ShS*, 45 (1992): 89–100.

Whitney, Geffrey, *A Choice of Emblems* (London: 1586).

Wickham, Glynne, 'Masque and Anti-Masque in *The Tempest*'. *Essays and Studies*, 28 (1975): 1–14.

Wilbern, David, 'Rape and Revenge in *Titus Andronicus*'. *ELR*, 8 (1978): 159–82.

Wilcox, Helen and Rina Walthaus 'Cleopatras in English and Spanish Golden Age Drama' in Rina Walthaus and Marguérite Corporaal (eds), *Heroines of the Golden Stage: Women and Drama in Spain and England 1500–1700* (Kassel: Edition Reichenberger, 2008), pp. 32–49.

——'Shakespeare's Miracle Play? Religion in *All's Well, That Ends Well*' in Gary Waller (ed.), *All's Well, That Ends Well: New Critical Essays* (Routledge, 2007), pp. 140–54.

Wilcox, Helen and Douglas A Brooks (eds), *The Shakespeare Yearbook 2003: New Studies in the Shakespearian Heroine*, Shakespeare Yearbook 14 (Lewiston, NY: Edwin Mellen, 2004).

Wilders, John, ed., *Shakespeare in Production: Macbeth* (Cambridge: Cambridge University Press, 2004).

Wilkinson, Richard H., *The Complete Gods and Goddesses of Ancient Egypt* (Cairo: American University in Cairo Press, 2003).

Willet, Andrew, *A catholicon, that is, A generall preservative or remedie against the pseudocatholike religion gathered out of the catholike epistle of S. Jude* (London, 1602).

Williams, Deanne, 'Dido, Queen of England'. *ELH*, 73(1) (2006): 31–59.

——'Elizabeth I: size matters' in Anneliese Connolly and Lisa Hopkins (eds), *Goddesses and Queens: The Iconography of Elizabeth I* (Manchester: Manchester University Press, 2007), pp. 69–82.

——'Papa Don't Preach. The Power of Prolixity in *Pericles*'. *University of Toronto Quarterly*, 71(2) (2002): 595–622.

Williams, Edward, *Virginia, more especially the south part thereof, richly and truly valued* (London: 1650).

Williams, Gordon, *A Dictionary of Sexual Language and Imagery in Shakespearean and Stuart Literature*, 3 vols (London: Athlone, 1994).

Williamson, Marilyn L., *The Patriarchy of Shakespeare's Comedies* (Detroit, MI: Wayne State University Press, 1986).

——'The Ring Episode in *The Merchant of Venice*'. *South Atlantic Quarterly*, 71 (1972): 587–94.

Willis, Deborah, *Malevolent Nurture: Witch-hunting and maternal power in Early Modern England* (Ithaca, NY: Cornell University Press, 1995).

Wilson, Adrian, 'The Ceremony of Childbirth and Its Interpretation', in Valerie Fildes (ed.), *Women as Mothers in Pre-Industrial England: Essays in Memory of Dorothy McLaren* (London: Routledge, 1990), pp. 68–107.

Wilson, Richard, *Will Power: Essays on Shakespearean Authority* (Brighton: Harvester Wheatsheaf, 1993).

Wilson, Thomas, *A Christian Dictionarie, Opening the signification of the chiefe wordes dispersed generally through Holie Scriptures of the Old and New Testament, tending to increase Christian knowledge. Whereunto is annexed: A perticular Dictionary For the Reuelation of S. Iohn. For the Canticles, or Song of Salomon. For the Epistle to the Hebrues* (London: 1612).

Wolf, Janet S., '"Like an old tale still": Paulina, "Triple Hecate" and the Persephone Myth in *The Winter's Tale*' in Elizabeth T. Hayes (ed.), *Images of Persephone: Feminist Readings in Western Literature* (Gainesville, FL: University of Florida Press, 1994), pp. 32–44.

Woodbridge, Linda, *Women and the English Renaissance: Literature and the Nature of Womankind 1540–1620* (Brighton: Harvester, 1984).

Woods, Suzanne, *The Poems of Aemilia Lanyer: Salve Deus Rex Judaeorum* (Oxford: Oxford University Press, 1993).

Wynne-Davies, Marion, '"The Swallowing Womb": Consumed and Consuming Women in *Titus Andronicus*' in Valerie Wayne (ed.), *The Matter of Difference: Materialist Feminist Criticism of Shakespeare* (New York: Harvester Wheatsheaf, 1991), pp. 129–51.

Yachnin, Paul, '"The Perfection of Ten": Populuxe Art and Artisanal Value in *Troilus and Cressida'. SQ,* 56(3) (2005): 306–27.

Yachnin, Paul and Patricia Badir (eds), *Shakespeare and the Cultures of Performance* (Aldershot: Ashgate, 2008).

Yarnall, Judith, *Transformations of Circe: the history of an enchantress* (Urbana, IL: University of Illinois Press, 1994).

Yates, Francis A., *Astraea: The Imperial Theme in the Sixteenth Century* (London, Routledge and Kegan Paul, 1975).

Zimmerman, Susan (ed.), *Erotic Politics: Desire on the Renaissance Stage* (London: Routledge, 1992).

Index